Aging,
the Individual,
& Society

SIXTH EDITION

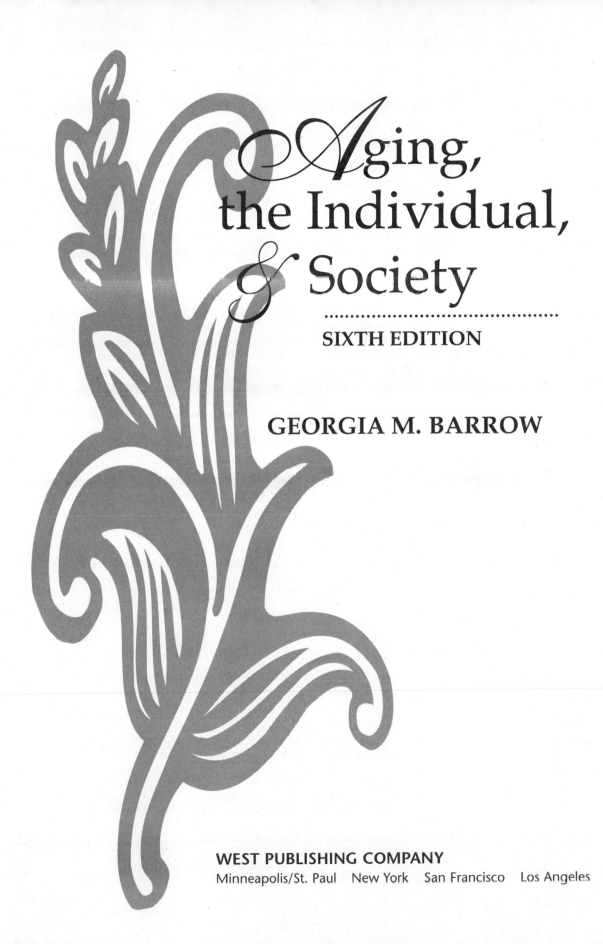

Aging, the Individual, & Society

SIXTH EDITION

GEORGIA M. BARROW

WEST PUBLISHING COMPANY

Minneapolis/St. Paul   New York   San Francisco   Los Angeles

Production Credits
....

Cover Image   Ethan Hubbard; Craftsbury Common Books

Interior Design   Roslyn M. Stendahl, Dapper Design

Copyediting   Kathleen R. Pruno

Art   Alice Thiede and Will Thiede, Carto-Graphics

Composition   Parkwood Composition

Cartoons   Bülbül

Chapter Opening Photo Illustrations   Roslyn M. Stendahl, Dapper Design

Photo credits follow index

WEST'S COMMITMENT TO THE ENVIRONMENT

In 1906, West Publishing Company began recycling materials left over from the production of books. This began a tradition of efficient and responsible use of resources. Today, up to 95 percent of our legal books and 70 percent of our college and school texts are printed on recycled, acid-free stock. West also recycles nearly 22 million pounds of scrap paper annually—the equivalent of 181,717 trees. Since the 1960s, West has devised ways to capture and recycle waste inks, solvents, oils, and vapors created in the printing process. We also recycle plastics of all kinds, wood, glass, corrugated cardboard, and batteries, and have eliminated the use of Styrofoam book packaging. We at West are proud of the longevity and the scope of our commitment to the environment.

Production, Prepress, Printing and Binding by West Publishing Company.

British Library Cataloguing-in-Publication Data. A catalogue record for this book is available from the British Library.

Photo Credits
....

1 Chapter One Opening collage, vintage farm scene, *America Remembered* (c) 1993 Boraventures Publishing, used with permission; **2** Patricia McCormack, UPI/Bettmann; **15** James Shaffer; **18** David Frazier Photolibrary, Inc.; **23** Ed Kennedy, *The Palm Beach Post;* **28** A/P Wide World; **41** James Shaffer; **46** Shizuo Kambayashi, A/P Wide World; **50, 55** James Shaffer; **67** Joe Marquette, A/P Wide World; **72** James Shaffer; **79** David Frazier Photolibrary, Inc.; **84** James Shaffer; **94** Doug
Continued after Index

COPYRIGHT © 1979, 1983, 1986, 1989, 1992   By WEST PUBLISHING COMPANY

COPYRIGHT © 1996   By WEST PUBLISHING COMPANY
610 Opperman Drive
P. O. Box 64526
St. Paul, MN 55164-0526

Library of Congress Cataloguing-in-Publication Data
Barrow, Georgia M.
    Aging, the individual, and society / Georgia M. Barrow, -- 6th ed.
        p.   cm.
    Includes bibliographical references and index.
    ISBN 0-314-04444-2 (soft : alk. paper)
    1. Gerontology. 2. Aged. 3. Aged—United States. I. Title.
    HQ1061.B37   1996
305.26'0973--dc20

95-30482
CIP

To three of my Kansas kin
with love: My Mom Edna Coleman;
her sister, my Aunt Georgine Coleman;
and my Dad's sister, Aunt Georgia Sales.

················

ontents

CHAPTER *7*

Work and Leisure   150

CHAPTER *12*

Preface

I am very pleased to have written a text that is now in its sixth edition. It is my belief that its success can be attributed to the heartfelt concern about aging expressed throughout the book in the words, the photos, and the cartoons.

The first edition of this text appear 16 years ago. The text has aged, the author has aged, and society has aged over these 16 years! I recall speaking to one who was hesitant about the possibility of writing a textbook when I was in my early 30's. She asked me, "What can you possibly know about aging when you are so young?" Now I have passed the 50-year mark and am receiving invitations to join aging groups such as the AARP. She would be happy to know that I have arrived at the threshold of old age, and that my knowledge of aging from a personal standpoint has grown considerably.

In comparing all of the editions, the tone and the message about aging have become increasingly positive. Students of gerontology are arriving at an exciting time in the history of the field. There has been a remarkable increase in the amount of information and attention given to aging issues. As research has broadened, so has the vision of what older people can experience, enjoy and accomplish.

Previous editions of this text have been well-received by students and professors. The general format of this edition remains the same but includes new studies and discoveries. References to major ground-breaking studies of the past are retained to give the student a perspective on current directions of research. The original goals of the first edition of this text still stand. A major goal is to bring a social problems approach to the study of gerontology and, secondly, to capture a sense of urgency regarding these problems. Another goal is to combine academic research with the daily life experiences of older persons in order to involve students emotionally as well as intellectually. A final aim is to encourage students to actively seek solutions to the social problems confronting elders in U.S. society.

At the beginning of each chapter is an Old Is News section. A current article is presented that draws attention to an older person in the news. These articles underscore the human drama of aging and the unique aspects of aging on an individual basis. New cartoons enhance the text and contribute an activist perspective. The cartoonist, Bülbül (her pen name), has provided cartoons for all six editions, stating that her cartoons reflect the "struggle for wholeness" we all seek. She offers her cartoon characters as "zany role models to encourage people to take control of their lives, to live fully and democratically." Further, throughout the text are boxed insets on aging issues as well as poems written by older individuals. These features are meant to involve the student in a more personal way.

Questions for Discussion and Fieldwork Suggestions at the end of each chapter draw students closer to topics by encouraging their direct participation. Not only are References given, but the Further Readings provoke thinking and provide detailed sources of information that will prove useful in the student's own research.

Credit goes to Professor Guy Shuttlesworth, University of Texas at Austin, for his contributions in revising Chapter Nine, and Karen Altergott, Purdue University, for helping with Chapter Five. Acknowledgment must also go to these reviewers for their valuable contributions in the preparation of this edition:

Roger C. Barnes
Incarnate Word College

David L. Petty
Stephen F. Austin State University

Brenda Forster
Elmhurst College

George F. Stine
Millersville University

Deborah M. Merrill
Clark University

Patricia A. Tripple
University of Nevada, Reno

The author thanks Carol Idler, head of the Interlibrary Loan Program at the Santa Rosa Junior College Library. Her patience must have been tried by the volume of books I ordered for months on end (and my occasional late returns), yet she was always smiling and eager to help. My thanks also goes to Reta Kyle for the typing of the manuscript. She is an accurate and speedy typist and so much more. Her organization and efficiency, her interest and enthusiasms for the topic, along with her moral support is truly remarkable and greatly valued. My appreciation extends also to the poets who shared their work, especially Don Emblen, retired English instructor from Santa Rosa Junior College, who contributed three poems and directed me to other poems; to Papier Mache Press for their cooperation in printing poems from *When I Am An Old Woman I Shall Wear Purple,* and to Oryx Press for their willingness to have me reprint so many tables appearing in their *Statistical Handbook on Aging Americans.*

Thanks is given to West Publishing personnel Steve Schonebaum, acquisitions editor; and Peggy Brewington, assistant production editor, for their hard work and expertise throughout this endeavor. Finally, a special word of gratitude to all contributors included in the text, without which this book, and the field of gerontology, could not be successful.

Georgia M. Barrow

1

Aging in America

CHAPTER OUTLINE

- An Interdisciplinary Topic
- Ageism as a Social Problem
- A Social Problems Approach
- The Graying of America

Friedan's New Crusade

■ PATTI DOTEN

SAG HARBOR, N.Y.—The voice on the phone is gruff. Impatient. Off-putting.

"What day are you coming?" she barks. "What time?. . . No come later. Come at noon."

That done, there's no goodbye.

Only a click. A dial tone.

But Betty Friedan is an American icon. And perhaps at age 72, she can be forgiven a prickly and mercurial personality. After all, it was her 1963 book, "The Feminine Mystique," that ignited the contemporary women's movement that freed American housewives from their full-time aprons and encouraged them to enter the workplace.

Several days later, in person, the diminutive Friedan is on her best behavior. A veritable declawed pussycat compared to the brusque barracuda on the phone. Obviously a woman who suffers no fools, she is no fool herself. She's got a new book to sell, "The Fountain of Age," (Simon & Schuster) and knows the press can help her sell it.

Although it takes an hour for this fragile-looking woman, who lost 25 pounds after open-heart surgery in 1992, to finally settle down for a chat with her visitor, you forgive her. It's the Friday of Labor Day weekend, and this woman who once told a reporter, "I'm nasty, I'm bitchy, I get mad but, by God, I'm absorbed in what I'm doing," is very busy.

There's a dinner party to give that evening.

House guests are coming for the weekend.

The air conditioning on the second floor is spouting hot air.

And so many other things to tend to. . . .

"I give wonderful parties," she says. "I use paper plates and don't make a fuss."

She's ordering Chinese takeout for tonight's party of 18.

"I'll get three containers of five different things," she tells the young woman who is cleaning her house.

The house is very modest, and it's furnished like a college student's apartment—eclectic attic clutter, perfect for visits by her three children and eight beloved grandchildren.

Betty Friedan has written an important new book, "The Fountain of Age."

The catalyst that set her on her decade-long research into the aging process was her 60th birthday. Her friends and children threw a surprise birthday party, but Friedan was not amused. She found the toasts hostile and the attendees publicly "pushing me out of life, out of the race." She was depressed for months.

Then she accepted a fellowship at Harvard, in 1982, and began her research on aging. The work allowed her to resolve her own feelings about getting older and to understand that growth was indeed possible in the third stage of life. The end result is a dense, heavily researched 671-page book.

"People today have a third or half more years of life than they've ever had before," says Friedan, who crisscrossed the country interviewing scores of men and women in their 60s and 70s who were living vital and pleasurable lives. "People should draw on their strengths and not forfeit these years with a preoccupation with death or a loss of youth."

"I can't predict whether my book will have the same electric effect as 'The Feminine Mystique,'" says Friedan, who is a visiting professor during the winter months at the University of Southern California and during the fall at New York University.

"But I believe the times are such that we are on the verge of profound change. And it must not be polarized—us against them or age vs. youth. And I certainly don't want older people to be the scapegoats during the present economic and health-care crisis."

Friedan said many of her thoughts about aging were tested when she underwent open-heart surgery, twice. The first new valve she received, a pig's, didn't work. A human valve did.

"When I was going through the surgeries, I had worked through dying, but I didn't want to die right then," says Friedan. "I'd worked so hard and long on this book, I wanted to see it in bookstores. My friends and family were very supportive and I made an amazing recovery."

Ed. Note: The final triumphant line of her book is "I have never felt so free." ☼

SOURCE: *Boston Globe,*16 September 1993, p. D1. Reprinted courtesy of *The Boston Globe.*

Who is growing old! We all are! In many people's minds, growing old, like dying, is something that happens only to others and only to individuals older than themselves. If you have not yet reached your sixties, can you imagine yourself to be 65, 75, or 90? With reasonable care and a bit of good luck, you will live to be 75 or more. With advances in medical science and technology, we all can anticipate long lives.

But what will be the quality of our lives? As we advance through life, aging may bring either despair or enhanced vitality and meaning. To insure the latter, Betty Friedan, feminist turned gerontologist, advocates a search, not for the fountain of youth, but for the fountain of age. She found in her search that aging did not have to bring fear and dread; it could bring the joy of a life fulfilled. We can better control the changes aging brings if we are aware of its certainty. Furthermore, knowing more about ourselves and our environment can make aging more successful and rewarding.

☼ An Interdisciplinary Topic

The topics of aging and the aged are reflected in almost any discipline one studies and can be examined from many perspectives, including biological, psychological, and sociological. First, and perhaps most basic, is the perspective of biology. Without the biological aging process, we could all theoretically live forever. But the body gradually loses ability as various functions diminish. The vital senses become less acute, and the immune system is not as effective in warding off disease. Biologists study decline but they also look for ways to slow down the aging process. One of the most promising studies of increasing longevity comes from developmental biologists' studies of fruit flies, such as those by Michael Rose at the University of California at Irvine. His evolutionary theory of aging predicts that the earlier an animal reaches maturity, the earlier the onset of aging. He studied fruit flies because they mature in 5 days and have a very short life span (about 25 days). By selectively breeding fruit flies that matured late in life, Rose succeeded in expanding their life spans by 100 percent. He predicts achieving a 200 percent increase with more research.

> It's not just an increase in life span, but an actual postponement of aging. Their ability to reproduce and to fly are enhanced at older ages. It would be like being 120 years old and still capable of playing a good game of tennis. (Science, 1990, p. 622).

CHAPTER 1 *Aging in America*

The biological approach to aging includes studies of all kinds of animals, including detailed analyses of the human body. The effects of diet and exercise on longevity are an important focus of study.

Second, psychologists are interested in the aging mind—how perception, motor skills, memory, emotions, and other mental capacities change over time. Motivation, adaptability, self-concept, and morale have an important influence on how we age. Most psychologists believe these variables powerfully affect "successful" aging.

Third, the sociological perspective examines the structure of society—its norms and values—and their influence on how a person perceives and reacts to the aging process. A society that gives the aging person high status can expect more positive outcomes for its aging population, whereas a society that accords the aged a low or marginal status can expect more negative outcome. Within the sociological circle are anthropologists, who, in documenting the aging process around the world, find that cultures offer elders enormously varied roles. Also in the circle are political scientists, social policy experts, and historians, who have an interest in the aged. Demographic and population experts provide information on the numbers and distribution of older persons in countries around the world. Finally, studies of older people cannot be complete without considering philosophy, spirituality, and death and dying. The position of elderly on the far end of the life-death continuum automatically brings questions: What was this life all about? What does it mean? How should I view my eventual death?

To consider aging in its entirety we must bring many approaches into play; therefore aging is a prime topic for interdisciplinary studies. The word **gerontology** means "study of the older person." Scholars studying older adults in any of the above-mentioned fields are considered *gerontologists*, and those who emphasize social components of aging, as opposed to the biological components, are called **social gerontologists.** Gerontologists can apply their specialty in many fields—nursing, medicine, dentistry, economics, social work, mental health, and physical education. Aging is a broad and complex topic with numerous branches of inquiry reaching into virtually every discipline.

☀ A Social Problems Approach

This text considers aging from a social problems approach, relying heavily on information from social gerontologists. A social problems approach targets widespread patterns of behavior that lower the quality of life. The causes and solutions do not remain solely at the individual level but must ultimately be found at a higher level. The problems lie with large numbers of people; the causes and solutions may be at a group, societal, or global level. Although it is people who create social problems, it is people who can also find solutions.

In this text we emphasize social situations that are problematic or undesirable for a large proportion of older adults. We need to raise the status of those aged 65 and over, expand their social roles, and address their needs. Thus, given the unnecessarily low status of elders in the United States, we have the makings of a broad social problem with many subcategories. Chapter by chapter, this text addresses problems that older people face— problems with status, roles, income, transportation, housing, health care (both physical and mental), work, leisure, and sexuality. The text not only describes problems, but also suggests solutions.

Old age has not always been viewed as a social problem (Brown, 1990). Until 1900 or so, only the debilitating illnesses related to old age, not growing old in itself, were defined as problems. With the industrialization that began in the late 1800s, the problems associated with growing old were reconceptualized, not just on a physical level but on social, economic, and psychological levels as well. By the 1930s and 1940s this new conceptualization of the aged had made them an identifiable group with problems that called for collective action. For example, their "right" to a decent income at retirement was at issue. Applying the phrases of sociologist C. Wright Mills, a family's "private troubles" had become "public issues" (Mills, 1959). Responsibility for aging individuals now fell not only to family members but also to society. Older people got more public attention paid to their needs, but in the process they began to be viewed as helpless and dependent. These negative images were universally applied for many years in spite of improvements in the health of the "young-old" aged 65 to 74, and in spite of the countless people aged 75 and over who stayed active and involved in society. This view of the aged as a social problem has been tempered, but it still continues today. Most social problems textbooks, for example, include a chapter on the status of older persons. The caution to be exercised in using the social problems approach is not to "blame the victim" when the blame may lie in the way our society is structured.

We have to be careful not to view older people as more dependent and helpless than they are. We must identify and give positive support for institutions and social structures that foster independence and self-reliance.

The critical perspective in sociology is an excellent example of a social problems approach. It draws sharp attention to inequities in U.S. society, attacking broad and fundamental structures of U.S. society such as the class system, capitalism, sex roles (sexism), and age roles (ageism). It is the most radical sociological approach in the strength of its attack, and in its suggestions for completely new structures to replace failing ones. Gerontologists have recently been making use of the critical perspective to understand the problems of aging in a broad political, social, and economic content (Minkler and Estes, 1991). Reference will be made to this perspective in the chapters on finances, women and minorities, and senior power.

Any social problems approach, including the critical perspective, considers ageism in our society as a major problem. Aversion, hatred, and prejudice toward elders, and the manifestation of these emotions in the form of discrimination on the basis of age, is **ageism,** a term coined by Robert Butler (1975). The critical perspective looks to the class system and capitalism for root causes of ageism.

However, before we can consider ageism we must define and describe the older population and its tremendous growth.

☼ The Graying of America

Both the number and the proportion of older people in the United States continue to rapidly increase, thus, the "graying of America." More than one out of every ten Americans, or 13 percent of the population, is now over 65. This percentage represents a dramatic increase from the turn of the century. In 1900, 3 million persons, or 4 percent of the population, were age 65 or older; by 1995 that number reached more than 33 million. Since 1900 the percentage of Americans aged 65 and over has tripled; and their number increased more than 10 times (from 3.1 million to 33 million). Current U.S. Census Bureau projections indicate that the older population will continue to grow rapidly into the twenty-first century, yielding more than one person in five (22 percent) by the year 2040 (see Figure 1.1).

The median age of the population—the number at which half the people are older and half are younger—was 22.9 years in 1900; in 1994 it was close to 34; by the year 2030, the median age will be 37.5 years. This dramatic shift is a transformation that will surely affect our values and our way of life.

The 1990 Census Bureau findings also indicated the strong growth of the older population from 1980 to 1990. Table 1.1 reflects these changes. Notice in Table 1.1 that the fastest-growing age groups are the oldest ones. The population aged 95 to 99 nearly doubled in 10 short years. And the centenarian group grew 77 percent in the same time period. That means that 57,000 Americans reached the 100-year milestone in 1990.

Figure 1.1

....

Percentage of Population Age 65 and Over

SOURCE: U.S. Census Bureau, *Current Population Reports,* Series P-25 (Washington, D.C.: U.S. Government Printing Office, 1990).

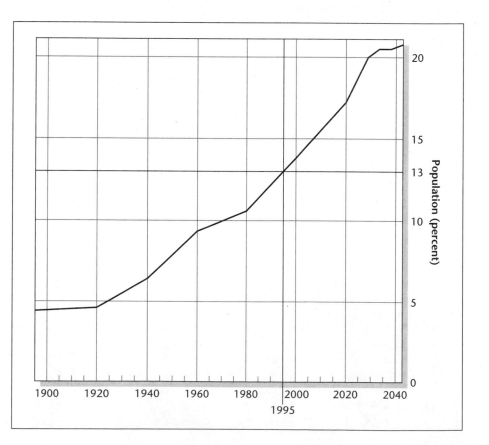

Table 1.1
....

Population by Age
Group

| | **1992** | | **1980** | | |
Age Group	Population (thousands)	Distri-bution	Population (thousands)	Distri-bution	% Change
55 to 59	10,487	4.3	11,615	5.1	–9.7
60 to 64	10,441	4.3	10,088	4.8	3.4
65 to 69	9,997	4.1	8,783	3.9	13.8
70 to 74	8,483	3.2	6,799	3.0	24.8
75 to 79	6,415	2.4	4,794	2.1	33.8
80 to 84	4,150	1.5	2,935	1.3	41.4
85 to 89	2,162	0.8	1,520	0.7	42.2
90 to 94	834	0.3	557	0.2	49.7
95 to 99	217	0.1	131	0.1	65.6
100 or older	45	*	32	*	40.6

*less than 0.1%

SOURCE: U.S. Bureau of the Census, Statistical Abstract of the United States, 114th ed., Washington, D.C.: U.S. Government Printing Office, 1994, Table 15, p. 15.

All older age groups starting at age 65 show large increases. Generally speaking the higher the age interval, the greater the increase. In other words, the old as a group are becoming much older.

The numbers of the very old will continue to mushroom. By the year 2000, half of those over 65 will be the "oldest old" (those 75 and over). Fully one in three seniors will be over 80 years old. By 2030, there will be about 66 million older persons, more than double their number in 1990. By the same year, there will be as many people over 85 as there are over 65 today. And by the year 2050, one-fourth of all Americans will be over 65.

Two major reasons for the increasing proportion of older people are increased life expectancy and a declining birth rate. We will consider each topic separately.

INCREASED LIFE EXPECTANCY

Life expectancy in the United States has consistently increased throughout the nineteenth and twentieth centuries. A dramatic increase in life expectancy occurred in the 1920s as a result of reduced infant mortality, health-care advances, and improved nutrition. White males born in 1920 could expect to live to 54; white females, to 56. The life expectancy at birth in 1991 for white males was 73; for white females, 80. However, white males live more than six years longer than African-American males, whose life expectancy in 1992 was 66. The life expectancy for African-American females in 1991 was 74. We will examine this gap in Chapter 13, which discusses minority elders.

We can compute life expectancies for any age. The longer a person has lived, the greater is that person's statistical life expectancy. In 1991, a 60-year-old person could expect to live to age 81, and an 85-year-old person could expect to live past 91. Table 1.2 shows life expectancies for persons of various ages 60 and beyond. Notice that African Americans have a shorter life expectancy at all ages. But at the ages of 80 and 85 the differences between whites and African Americans become negligible. Women at every age, both African American & white, have longer life expectancies than men.

Over the years there have been dramatic reductions in the death rates for diseases of the heart, cerebrovascular disease, and pneumonia. Even though life expectancy for males is not as high as for females, both genders' expectan-

Table 1.2
....

Life Expectancies
in 1991

Age	Average of Total	White Male	White Female	African American Male	African American Female
				Years Expected to Live	
60	20.8	18.7	23.0	15.9	20.5
61	20.1	18.0	22.2	15.4	19.8
62	19.4	17.3	21.4	14.8	19.1
63	18.6	16.6	20.6	14.3	18.5
65	17.2	15.9	19.1	13.2	17.2
70	13.9	12.1	15.4	10.7	14.1
75	10.9	9.4	12.0	8.6	11.2
80	8.3	7.1	9.0	6.7	8.6
85 and over	6.1	5.2	6.4	5.0	6.3

SOURCE: U.S. Census Bureau, *Statistical Abstract of the United States,* (Washington, D.C.: U.S. Government Printing Office, 1994), p. 88, table 116.

cies have increased considerably over the last several decades. Male or female, the following factors are associated with longevity: long-living relatives, being near an ideal weight for one's stature, low blood pressure, low cholesterol, not smoking, not drinking alcohol, vigorous exercise four to five times a week, healthy diet, relaxed and unstressed life style, and safe driving (Silberner, 1991).

Medical control of disease has greatly increased life expectancy. For example, we have seen a reduction in the death rates from heart attacks. Doctors are recommending that heart patients change their destructive patterns of diet, smoking, and nonexercise. As a result, the death rate from heart disease has been declining considerably in adult age groups. However, *heart disease remains the leading cause of death for persons aged 65 and over and for those 85 and over as well.* One-half of those 85 and over die from this cause. Cancer is second and stroke is a close third for those 85 and over (see Figure 1.2).

Although some scientists believe the genetic code programs men for a shorter **life span** than women, lifestyle differences between men and women are another factor in life expectancy figures. Males tend to drink more alcohol, take more chances, and be more stressed than women (Poinsett, 1991). Males also have a higher incidence of heart disease, due partially to more cigarette smoking and poor diet choices such as too much fat or salt intake. Stress expends the body's resources, placing undue strain on the heart and circulatory system. This in turn increases the individual's chances of suffering heart attack, heart failure, or high blood pressure. By age 65, many more females than males are still alive.

Studies comparing the longevity of men and women show that the top causes of death kill more men than women. Heart disease, lung cancer, homicide, suicide, accidents, and cirrhosis of the liver all kill men at more than twice the rate as they do women (Dolnick, 1991). Each of these causes of death is linked to behaviors that our culture either encourages or finds more acceptable in males than in females: using guns, drinking alcohol, smoking, working at hazardous jobs, or appearing fearless. Such cultural expectations seem to contribute to males' elevated mortality. Men suffer three times as many homicides as women and have twice as many fatal car accidents (per mile driven) as women. Men are more likely to drive through an intersection when they should stop, are less likely to signal a turn, and are more likely to drive after drinking alcohol. But behavior doesn't entirely explain the longevity gap. Women seem to have a genetic makeup that "programs" them to live

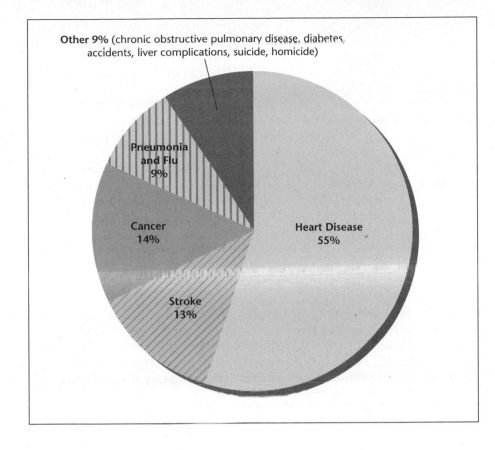

Other 9% (chronic obstructive pulmonary disease, diabetes, accidents, liver complications, suicide, homicide)

Pneumonia and Flu 9%

Cancer 14%

Heart Disease 55%

Stroke 13%

Figure 1.2

Causes of Death for Persons Aged 85 and Over

SOURCE: Based on U.S. Census Bureau, *Statistical Abstract of the United States, 1990* (Washington, D.C.: U.S. Government Printing Office, 1993), p. 92, table 127.

longer. Some scientists think that the longevity gaps may be due to chromosomal or hormonal differences, but they are not sure (Dolnick, 1991).

The leading causes of death for men and women over age 65, ranked in order from most to least common, are (1) diseases of the heart; (2) malignant neoplasms (tumor); (3) cerebrovascular disease (stroke); (4) chronic obstructive pulmonary disease; (5) pneumonia and flu; (6) chronic liver disease; (7) accidents; (8) diabetes; and (9) suicide. Men have higher death rates in all the categories, except diabetes. Lung cancer, for example, kills four times as many men as women.

DECREASING BIRTH RATE

When the birth rate declines, the number of young people decreases in proportion to the number of old people. The birth rate has gradually declined since public record-keeping began in the eighteenth century. A baby boom in the 1940s and 1950s increased the birth rate temporarily but did no reverse its long-term trend. In 1972, we witnessed a near zero population birth rate (2.1 children born for every couple): the number of live births nearly equaled the number of deaths, stabilizing the population. The birth rate then dipped lower until it rose slightly in the early and mid-1980s. According to the Population Reference Bureau in Washington, D.C., the 1991 birth rate had evened out at 2.1 children. If the United States maintains a lower birth rate, the proportion of older people will further increase. With no increase in the total population, the relative proportion of older persons will grow each year.

The post–World War II baby boomers of 1946–1950 are one of our largest age groups, as are baby boomers of the 1950s. Now in midlife, these persons will begin to reach age 65 in 2011, massively increasing the over-65 population. If we assume continued low birth rates and further declines in death rates, the older populations will jump tremendously by the year 2030. As we saw earlier, their numbers will double and their percentage of the population will rocket to over 20 percent.

A controversy rages as to whether medical science can do anything further to extend life expectancy at birth to more than 85 years. In the past 125 years, the life expectancy of Americans has almost doubled: from 40 to nearly 80 years. But these gains in life expectancy, most of which have come through a combination of reducing deaths of the young (particularly infants) and mothers in childbirth, may have been the "easy" ones. Some medical experts and laboratory scientists say that the period of *rapid* increases in life expectancy has come to an end. They argue that advances in life-extending technologies or the alteration of aging at the molecular level, the only ways to extend life expectancy, will be either improbable or long, slow processes. And, though they do agree that eliminating cancer, heart disease, and other major killers would increase life expectancy at birth by about 15 years, cures for these diseases are not in sight.

Other scientists are more positive about extending life expectancy. Findings of a study by Ken Monton at Duke University, reported in 1990, predict that Americans could very well live to age 99 if they quit smoking, drinking alcohol, and eating high-cholesterol foods. Populations with low-risk lifestyles, such as Mormons in the United States or the Japanese, already have achieved life spans exceeding 80 years (Krieger, 1990).

AGING AMERICA AND THE AGING WORLD

Table 1.3 shows states of the United States with high percentages of older people. These states are the wave of the future. In several states, 15 percent or more of the population is 65 or older. Notice that Florida, a retirement haven, far outpaces all other states with a percentage of 18.4 aged. Many of the other states are farm belt states where younger people are leaving farms for jobs in cities. The increasing percentage of older people means that more and more families will be made up of four generations instead of two or three though they do not typically live in one household. The implications of this are: more

Table 1.3

States in the United States with the Highest Percent 65 Years of Age and Over: 1993

	Percent 65 Years and Over
United States	*12.7*
1 Florida	18.6
2 Iowa	15.5
3 Rhode Island	15.5
4 West Virginia	15.3
5 Arkansas	15.0
6 North Dakota	14.8
7 South Dakota	14.7
8 Missouri	14.2
9 Nebraska	14.2
10 Massachusetts	14.0
11 Kansas	13.9

SOURCE: Adapted from Table 33. State Population Age Groups, U.S. Bureau of the Census, *Statistical Abstract of the United States: 1994* (114th edition) Washington, D.C., 1994, p.32.

children will grow up with the support of older relatives, and more people in their 60s will be called on to care for 80- and 90-year-old parents.

Age-sex pyramids illustrate the effects of population composition on the structure of a nation's population. In Figure 1.3, Kenya's pyramid has a large base, indicating high birth rates, and a small top, indicating a high death rate and few surviving older people. This pyramid was typical of the United States as a developing nation in the early 1800s, and it is typical of most developing nations. Countries with this pyramid form have trouble caring for all their young.

Countries like the United States, with a more boxlike structure, have lower (constricted) birth rates and lower death rates, meaning that there are fewer young people and more older people. And countries like Denmark have an even higher percentage of the elderly than the United States. They have achieved virtual zero population growth, thus a "stationary" pyramid. The implications are that the needs of a society change with a changing age structure. Housing, health care, and other services for elders must be expanded as their population increases.

☼ Ageism As A Social Problem

We have defined a social problem as a widespread negative social condition that people both create and solve. Ageism is such a problem. We know that the number of older persons is large and growing larger, and ageism directly affects the older population.

Ageism, discrimination on the basis of age, has been called the third "ism," after racism and sexism. Whereas racism and sexism prevent racial minorities and women—and, in what is called "reverse sexism," men—from developing their full potential as people, ageism limits the potential development of individuals on the basis of age. Ageism can oppress any age group, young or old. If you are young, you may have been told that you are too inexperienced, too immature, too untested. If you are elderly, you may have been told you are out-of-date, old-fashioned, behind the times, of no value or importance. At both ends of the scale, young and old, you may be the victim of ageism. Although ageism may affect the young as well as the old, our concern here is with the senior members of society.

Ageism is a complex phenomenon affected by technology, industrialization, changing family patterns, increased mobility, demographic changes, increased life expectancy, and generational differences. A discrimination leveled by one group against another, ageism is not an inequality associated with biological aging alone. It is created and institutionalized by many forces—historical, social, cultural, and psychological.

AGEISM TODAY

Our Western cultural heritage decrees that work and financial success establish individual worth. Industrialization has reinforced the high value of productivity and added further problems for the aging worker. The speed of industrial, technological, and social change tends to make skills and knowledge rapidly obsolete. Most people must struggle to keep abreast of new discoveries or skills in their fields. The media have used the term *Detroit Syndrome* to describe older people in terms of the obsolescence that exists for cars. When younger, stronger, faster workers with newly acquired knowledge are available, employers tend to replace, rather than retrain, the elderly.

Figure 1.3
....

Age-Sex Population
Pyramids

SOURCE: Arthur Haupt and
Thomas T. Kane,
Population Handbook, 3d
ed. (Washington, D.C.:
Population Reference
Bureau, 1991), p. 10.

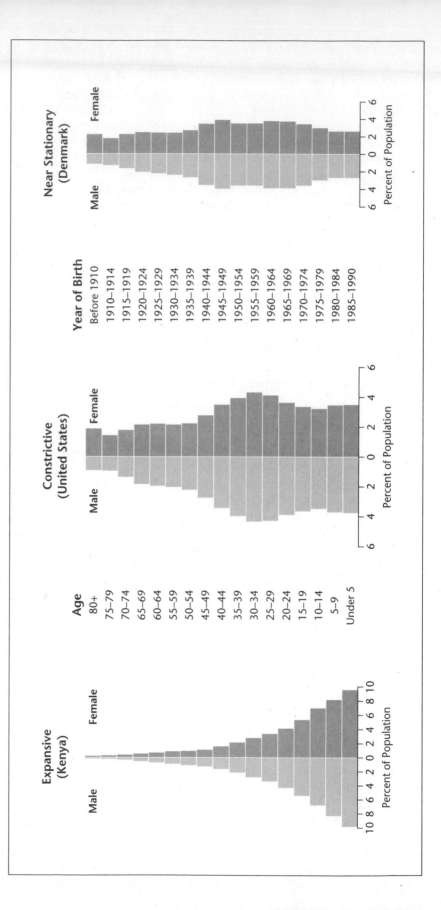

Thinking about Aging

Generation Gap at Seniors' Mecca

■ KENNETH GARCIA

A curious thing happened to Leisure World, the nation's largest seniors-only community. It got old.

Leisure World, it seems was not particularly well-suited for the aging. It was supposed to be the model for active seniors, a veritable theme park for recreation-oriented retirees. But the years have opened cracks in the community's carefree facade, exposing divisions among residents along clearly defined age lines.

Who would have expected that so many of the once-active seniors would age to a point where an on-site assisted living center would seem more attractive than the 27-hole golf course? Or that a 67-year-old would be considered part of the younger generation—10 years younger than the average Leisure World resident?

How it happened is as much a story about the nation's elderly as it is about Leisure World itself, but few places provide such stark examples of the country's gradual graying.

"The newer communities should learn from the lessons of Leisure World," said John Pynoos, a professor of gerontology at the University of Southern California. "These communities weren't designed with the aging process in mind. It was designed on a suburban model, as a large-scale subdivision."

The demographic shift at the Orange County facility has created a need for more health-related services, a change that has been resisted by some of the younger members who do not want to be reminded of their mortality. Some residents older than 70 have been shut out of the younger singles scene and denied entrance to one of the more active community clubs. . . .

Many of the people who thought Leisure World would be their last stop discovered that a commu-

nity for active retirees was not equipped for the increasingly less active among them. As their health declined, they found themselves needing nursing and nutrition services—not another square-dancing or sculpture class.

Leisure World's environment is particularly bad for hundreds of aging residents who suffer from arthritis and Alzheimer's disease. . . .

Leisure World has its own bus system to ferry residents around town, but none of the vehicles is wheelchair accessible. The community's sprawl has made it increasingly difficult for some older people to get around. And many of the sickest residents cannot afford private, in-home care.

Lobbying by some of the younger residents has blocked attempts to construct an assisted-living facility, where frail residents could get help with dressing, eating, and transportation.

The age dispute has also been raised over recent real estate troubles. About 700 of Leisure World's beige stucco homes are for sale, more than at any other time in the community's history. And many of the younger residents believe that the rising age of residents is deterring younger and wealthier retirees from relocating to Leisure World.

Professor Anabel Pelham, director of gerontology programs at San Francisco State University, said that communities like Leisure World still provide valuable services for seniors. She said she expects that large-scale retirement havens will integrate more health-related services in the future to meet the growing demand.

SOURCE: *San Francisco Chronicle,* 15 February 1993, p. A1. Reprinted by permission.

Within the workforce, older persons have often been considered a surplus population. As such, they suffer the potential for being managed much like surplus commodities: devalued and discounted.

Social change can create a generation gap that contributes to ageism. Rapid social change can cause our values to be somewhat different from our parents' and significantly different from those of our grandparents. Those who grew up in a given time period may have interpretations of and orientations toward social issues that differ from those who grew up earlier or later. For example, the now-older person who matured in the 1940s and experienced the patriotism of World War II may be unable to understand the behavior and attitudes of those who matured in the 1960s and protested the wars in Vietnam or the Persian Gulf. Further, young people maturing in the 1990s may not understand the historical rationale for the United States intervening in small countries like Panama or El Salvador. For another example, these young people, many of whom are postponing marriage and childbearing, may be unable to grasp the reasons for early marriage and large families held by the now-elderly generations. The study of intergenerational relations, which provides insights into similarities and differences in values across generations, reveals that communicating and understanding across generations are difficult when values are different.

Ageism also appears in the many euphemisms for old age and in the desire to hide one's age. The elderly themselves do not want to use the term *old*, as the names of their local clubs show: Fun After 50, Golden Age, 55 Plus, and Senior Citizens Club. Some forgo their "senior citizen discounts" because they do not want to make their age public. Fear of aging shows when men and women want to keep their age a secret. They hope that their appearance denies their age and that they project a youthful image. Many people suffer a crisis of sorts upon reaching age 30 and repeat it to some extent when entering each new decade. Some even experience an identity crisis as early as their late twenties, because they are entering an age that the youth culture considers "old." Many counselors recognize the "over 39" syndrome as a time when young adults come to terms with the fact that youth does not last forever but blends gradually with the responsibilities of maturity. Then again, some people who are age 39 stay that age forever!

Greeting-card counters are filled with birthday cards that joke about adding another year. Despite their humor, they draw attention to the fear of aging that birthdays bring. Some birthday cards express the sentiment that to be older is to be better, but then add a note that says, in effect, that no one would want to be better at the price of aging. Though birthday cards often joke about physical or sexual decline, the fear in the minds of many is no joke at all. Fear of aging can damage psychological well-being and lead us to shun older people. Ageism is a destructive force for both society and the individual.

Ageism as a concept in gerontological literature has been described in a general sense, but it also has been measured in more specific ways. Alex Comfort (1976) used the term *sociogenic* to imply ageism in a broad sense. He described two kinds of aging: *physical*, which is a natural biological process; and *sociogenic*, which has no physical basis. Sociogenic aging is imposed on the elders by the folklore, prejudices, and stereotypes about age that prevail in our society. Thus, age prejudice, as it exists in our minds, has become institutionalized in many sectors of our society.

We can find more specific evidence of ageism in our laws, particularly those dealing with employment, financial matters, and legal definitions relating to "competency" as an adult. Income differences, occupation differences, and education differences vary by age. One aspect of ageism is age inequality in education and occupation, caused by the fact that newer generations receive an education attuned to a highly technical and computerized society and are therefore better qualified for jobs. Elders are easily left behind on the "information highway" as the "high tech" knowledge of younger age groups rises. Income inequality based on age is caused not only by younger age groups having more extensive formal or technical education, but also by age discrimination in employment. Gerontologists believe that ageism in employment dates back to the early 1800s. In the work and leisure chapter, this age prejudice will be covered in more detail.

AGEISM YESTERDAY: THE EARLY AMERICAN EXAMPLE

A look at older people in earlier times, when age relationships were different, provides us with a clearer view of ageism now and in the future. Generalizing about ageism in the past is not easy. Some historians believe the status of older people was elevated in the colonial period—the time during which early settlers, especially the Puritans, founded America and formed the thirteen colonies. In contrast, other historians point to ageism and neglect of older persons in the colonial days.

Early Colonial Days

According to David Fischer, author of *Growing Old in America* (1977), the power and privilege of old age were deeply rooted in colonial times, when age, not youth, was exalted. To be old was to be venerated by society and to be eligible for selection to the most important positions in the community. Meetinghouse seats were assigned primarily by age, and the elderly sat in positions of highest status. According to Fischer, the national heroes were "gray champions." Community leaders and political officeholders tended to be older men, and the elderly were honored during ceremonial occasions.

Older adults were believed to be in favor with God. Their long life was thought of as an outward sign they would be "called" or "elected" to heaven.

With training older people can keep pace on the "information highway" and help young people do the same.

Biblical interpretation suggested that good persons would be rewarded with long life: "Keep my commandments, for length of days and long life shall they add unto thee." The Puritans pictured Jesus as an old man with white hair, even though, according to most theologians, Jesus died in his early thirties. Respect for age was also evident in manner of dress. Increase Mather, the president of Harvard College from 1685 to 1701, wrote that old men whose attire was gay and youthful, or old women who dressed like young girls, exposed themselves to reproach and contempt. Male fashions during the 1600s, and even more in the 1700s, flattered age. The styles made men appear older than they were. Clothing was cut specifically to narrow the shoulders, to broaden the waist and hips, and to make the spine appear bent. Women covered their bodies in long dresses. Both sexes wore white, powdered wigs over their hair. Not until the 1800s did clothing styles begin to flatter the younger man or woman.

Fischer studied other historical data that indicate **age status.** American literature, for example, emphasized respect for old age from the 1600s until after the American Revolution. A careful examination of census data shows that in the 1700s individuals tended to report themselves as older than they actually were, in order to enhance their status. (In the mid-1800s this tendency reversed itself.)

The tradition of respect for the elderly was rooted not only in religious and political ideology, but also in legal and financial reality. The elders owned and controlled their own land, which did not pass to their sons until they died. The sons, therefore, had financial reason to show respect for and deference to their fathers. In these conservative times, the young had little choice other than to honor, obey, and follow the ways of the old.

A word of caution must guide our consideration of the older person's status in colonial times. "Status" is a multidimensional concept, measurable in many ways, that indicates one's social ranking in society. Deference, respect, health, economic resources, material possessions, occupation, education, and political power are all possible indicators of social status. By some measures, the colonial elders had high status. They were shown deference and respect, and they had political power and financial control of their land. But not all elderly colonial citizens had financial and political power. Colonial legal records show that widows who had no means of support wandered from one town to another trying to find food and shelter. Older African Americans had an especially difficult time because of their low economic status; many were indentured servants or slaves. Also, most old people suffered from health problems that medical science was unable to cure or alleviate. Benjamin Franklin, for example, was wracked with pain in his later years because of gout and "the stone" (gallstone). Yet the old, in spite of their infirmities, were expected to be models of service and virtue to their communities. The very veneration that brought older persons respect kept them from enjoying close, intimate relationships with younger people. Youth/elder relationships were distant and formal, causing the old to suffer loneliness in their elevated position.

A number of historians take exception to Fischer's rosey picture of colonial days. Haber (1983) described old age in colonial times as more dire than Fischer's work indicates. Haber believes that although select, well-to-do elderly had high status in the Puritan days, they did not live in a golden era of aging. Too many not so well-to-do fared badly; they were viewed with scorn and contempt. Haber advises that a careful sociologist or historian must try not to idealize the past, but to recapture reality by examining all of its facets: political, historical, economic, and social. Quadagno (1982) and Cole

(1992) make the same point as Haber, emphasizing that multiple forces, some positive and some negative, shaped life in colonial times.

Changing Age Status

According to Fischer, change throughout the 1800s altered the **system of age relationships** in a negative way, leading to social problems for the aged. The most fundamental change took place in political ideology. The principles formulated in the Declaration of Independence became stronger: equality for all in legal, social, and political matters. This trend affected older persons because "lovely equality," in Jefferson's words, eradicated the hierarchy of age, and hence the respect automatically accorded the old. A study of word origins shows that most of the negative terms for old men first appeared in the late 1700s and early 1800s. *Gaffer*, which originally expressed respect, changed from a word of praise to one of contempt. Before 1780, *fogy* meant a wounded soldier; by 1830 it had become a term of disrespect for an older per- son. *Codger, geezer, galoot, old goat,* and *fuddy duddy* came into general usage in the early 1800s.

The preeminence of the religious elders began to wane as doctors and other technologists replaced preachers as the custodians of virtue and learning. The United States became more industrialized. In the 1800s, the city became a means of escape from both farming and parental control. Instead of waiting for his father to provide him with land, a young man could move to the city and find work in a factory. As long as America had remained a traditional agricultural society, in which parents controlled property until their advanced years, older adults had exercised considerable power. Urban and industrial growth led to diminished parental control over family, wealth, and possessions (Haber, 1983). By the late 1800s, the young pioneer and the young cowboy had become popular heroes; Teddy Roosevelt was young, rough, and ready. The youth cult began to replace the age cult.

The older population grew rapidly during the 1800s and 1900s. Retirement gradually became more and more common. However, many of the older people who retired had no source of income and were increasingly neglected. Old age became a burden to those who lived it and a social problem to those who analyzed it.

Fischer divided U.S. history into two general periods:

1. 1600 to 1800: an era of growing **gerontophilia.** Old age was exalted and venerated, sometimes hated and feared, but more often honored and obeyed.

2. 1800 to present: an era of growing **gerontophobia.** Americans increasingly glorified youth instead of age, and the elderly often became victims (self-victims as well as social victims) of prevailing attitudes and social arrangements (Fischer, 1977).

Fischer states that we may eventually enter another period of age relations, one that will create better conditions for older adults. The goal, stages Fischer, should be to make a new model, a fraternity of age and youth, and a world in which "the deep eternal differences between age and youth are recognized and respected without being organized into a system of inequality" (Fischer, 1977, p. 199). The example of colonial America shows that the position of elders in our society can be something other than what it is now. We can be aware of various age relationships and possibilities more positive than the situations we have created.

AGEISM TOMORROW: RIDING THE AGE WAVE

For many years our society has suffered from gerontophobia. In fact, to conceive of any status for elders other than that to which we are accustomed is difficult. We have accepted tension between youth and age. Respect by the young for the old in our society is not a given. It is not deeply imbedded in the fabric of our society.

Some people view the increasing number of older adults as a burden on society, referring to the economic burden of providing care for the unemployed elders who depend on society for financial aid. The number of old persons relative to the working population is called the **old age–dependency ratio.** If the population age 65 and older grows faster than the working population (age 21 to 64), the cost to the taxpayer of providing for the elderly population rises. The percentage of elders to the working population was 10.6 percent in 1940, 17 percent in 1965, and 30 percent in 1994. Put another way, in 1940 there were about 11 persons 65 and over for every 100 persons of working age; in 1965, about 17; in 1994, about 30. It is projected to rise to 39 elders for every 100 working adults in the future. Obviously, there are increasingly fewer workers in relation to the retired, a trend that will continue for a long time to come. A larger proportion of seniors requires more Social Security and Medicare payments and, consequently, higher taxes. You may be aware that the Social Security deduction from your earnings has increased over the years. The reason for the continual increase is that the employed are supporting the system of Social Security payments to the retired. The prospect for the future rests on one simple fact: if you go to work at a young age, you will have to live a very long time to receive in benefits what you will have paid into Social Security. People younger than you, who will maintain the benefit system for you when you retire, are decreasing in number. If we view elders only as an economic burden, ageism may increase as the number of retired, sick, or frail elderly increases.

Some gerontologists believe that we have become an age-segregated society, with separate schools for the young and separate retirement communities for the old. Undeniably, segregation creates misunderstandings and conflict.

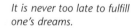

It is never too late to fulfill one's dreams.

Others, however, maintain that ageism is declining. They point to the improved health of seniors and to retirement communities composed of increasingly younger retirees who seem happy and content. In such contexts the image of older persons is improving. The increasing numbers of elders may be leading to a psychological shift away from a youth-oriented culture.

Gerontologist and marketing consultant Ken Dychtwald (1989) believes that the increasingly large number of older persons is eroding the youth cult. He explains that the baby boomers of the 1940s, 1950s, and 1960s had a major impact on the economics and consumerism of the 1980s. Young adults of the 1980s, many of them "yuppies," prospered from relatively inexpensive college educations and the economic expansion of the times. These same baby boomers will age in unprecedented numbers and continue to influence our lifestyle and our economy. The main thrust of Dychtwald's book is that older people need not be a burden, either to themselves or to the nation. According to him, the senior boom "is not a chance to be old longer but a chance to live longer" (Boynton 1990). His prediction is that we will modify our culture to accommodate an older population—from changing how long it takes a traffic light to turn from green to red, to clothing styles, to increased services at airports.

Dychtwald believes that businesses will stop discriminating on the basis of age when they realize that there are not enough young people to go around and when they realize that older workers are good, solid employees, who, if treated well, will not choose to retire. Indeed, employers in the future may well pay to update the education of older employees, rather than contend with applicants from an increasingly illiterate younger workforce (Steinberg, 1991). Old age should be an exciting time of contributing to others and of self-fulfillment. All in all, Dychtwald predicts less ageism, not more: "It's inevitable there will be a shifting in power to the second half of life."

Chapter Summary

The topic of aging is interdisciplinary; the fields of biology, sociology, psychology, religion, philosophy, history, demography, and others contribute to gerontology. This text views aging from a social problems approach, where the causes of ageism and solutions to this problem may be found at a group, societal, or global level.

The proportion of older people in the United States has been increasing, and this trend will continue. The United States is aging and for several reasons. Life expectancy has increased, with more people living to old age. The question can be posed as to how far the life span of humans can be extended. No one theory is conclusive on this subject. The birth rate has also declined, contributing to a greater proportion of older people.

Ageism, or age prejudice, is present in our society today. No one wants to be labeled old, elderly, or aged, or suffer discrimination on the basis of age. The injustices of ageism are similar to those of racism and sexism in that discrimination and low status are the consequences. Gerontologists are hopeful that ageism will decline as the numbers of elders, and thus their influence, grows.

Key Terms

ageism

age-sex pyramid

age status

gerontology

social gerontologist
gerontophilia
gerontophobia
life expectancy

life span
old age–dependency ratio
system of age relationships

Questions For Discussion

1. Explore ageist attitudes within yourself, using some specific topics to focus on (such as your reaction to older drivers or your own fears of aging).

2. What are some implications of the "graying of America" not covered in this chapter? How will they affect advertising, fashion, or music?

3. How long do you expect to live, and how long do you want to live? Why?

4. How old are you in your mental outlook on life? How old are your parents? Your grandparents? What basis did you use for assigning the ages?

Fieldwork Suggestions

1. See how many people know the meaning of the word *ageism*.

2. Study ageism after first devising your own measures of ageism. Is society ageist?

3. Survey others to see how many people come in contact with an elderly person daily. Determine how age-segregated we are as a society.

4. Describe a chronologically young person who meets your criteria of being old.

5. Describe a chronologically old person who meets your criteria of being young.

References

Boynton, S. Aging Boomers! The Graying of a Generation. *Santa Rosa Press Democrat*, March 22, 1993, p. B1.

Brown, A. *Social Processes of Aging and Old Age.* Englewood Cliffs, NJ: Prentice Hall, 1990.

Butler, R. Why Survive? New York: Harper & Row, 1975.

Cole, T. The Journey of Life: A Cultural History of Aging in America. New York: Cambridge University Press, 1992.

Comfort, Alex. "Age Prejudice in America." *Sociology Policy* 17 (November/December 1976): 3–8.

Dolnick, Edward. "The Mystery of Superwoman." *San Francisco Chronicle* (16 July 1991): D3.

Dychtwald, Ken. *Age Wave.* Los Angeles, CA: Tarcher, 1989.

Fischer, David Hackett. *Growing Old in America.* New York: Oxford University Press, 1977.

Friedan, B. *The Fountain of Age.* New York: Simon & Shuster, 1993.

"Gerontology Research Comes of Age." *Science* Magazine 250 (November 1990): 622.

Haber, Carole. *Beyond Sixty-Five: The Dilemma of Old Age in America's Past.* New York: Cambridge University Press, 1983.

Kleiman, C. Generation Xers Don't Fit the Stereotype, Santa Rosa Press Democrat, April 17, 1995, p. D1.

Krieger, Lisa. "New Report Caps Life Expectancy: 85." *San Francisco Examiner* (2 November 1990): A1, A24.

Mills, C. Wright. *The Sociological Imagination.* New York: Oxford University Press, 1959.

Minkler, M., and C. Estes, eds. *Critical Perspectives on Aging.* Amityville, NY: Baywood Publishing, 1991.

National Safety Council. *Accident Facts.* Chicago, IL: National Safety Council, 1991.

Poinsett, A. "Why Women Live Longer than Men." *Ebony* (February 1991): 46, 112–115.

Quadagno, Jill S. *Aging in Early Industrial Society.* New York: Academic Press, 1982.

Silberner, J. "The Longevity Test." *U.S. News and World Report* (28 January 1991): 62–63.

Steinberg, Jon Robert. "Living and Working in the Year 2000." *New Choices for the Best Years* (January 1991): 52–56.

Waldrop, J., and T. Exter. "What the 1990 Census Will Show." *American Demographics* (January 1990): 20–25.

Further Readings

Barer, B. "Men and Women Aging Differently." *International Journal of Aging and Human Development* 38:1, (January 1994), p. 29–40.

Cole, T. and Winkler, eds. The Oxford Book of Aging: Reflections on the Journey of Life. New York: Oxford Univ. Press, 1994.

Friedan, B. *The Fountain of Age*. New York: Simon and Schuster, 1993.

Henderson, Z. P. "Toward a Rewarding Life in Old Age." *Human Ecological Forum* 21 (Winter 1993): 15–19.

Olson, L. K., ed. The Graying of the World: Who Will Care for the Frail Elderly? Binghamton, NY: The Haworth Press, 1994.

Schaie, K. W. "Ageist Language in Psychological Research." *American Psychologist* 48 (January 1993): 49–51

2 *Stereotypes and Images*

CHAPTER OUTLINE

■ Stereotypes of Aging   ■ Explaining Stereotypes   ■ Breaking Negative Stereotypes

"Good Times" For Rolle

"I spent a long time being a prop," Esther Rolle is mulling over her career. "I am not going to be a prop any more."

Rolle, former star of the TV comedy series *Good Times,* visited her hometown of Pompano Beach for her 50-year high school class reunion. Any observer would underestimate that by at least 15 years. Her hair is touched with gray, but she is as vital and forthright as the characters she plays.

In 1990, the National Association for the Advancement of Colored People gave Rolle its Civil Rights Award in Los Angeles.

The award is given "for commitment, service and deeds that lead to a contribution to the furtherance of civil rights.

"That's important," Rolle said. "Oscars and Emmys are nice, but being able to help my people see themselves with dignity is what really matters."

Rolle's insistence on that dignity gave shape to the popular sitcom *Good Times,* a spin-off from the show *Maude,* in which she played Maude's maid, Florida Evans. . .

It was her idea to cast John Amos as the hardworking father in *Good Times,* and break the stereotype of fatherless black households. Thanks to *Good Times,* "We now have black fathers on the little screen," she says.

In 1994 Rolle performed a one-person stage play on the life of Mary McLeod Bethune, the well known educator who founded Florida's Bethune-Cookman College and went on to advise President Franklin Roosevelt. She worked for 10 years to develop the show.

I wanted to see what I could do to make her more real to young people," Rolle says of a story ripe with dramatic potential. "I'd like to see her more recognized for the wonderful work she did and the powerful woman she was." Youngsters in particular are "being cheated not to know about her. She worked so hard for the children."

Rolle's parents were sharecroppers, and saw to it that all of their 18 children got the education they wanted.

"When I was a child here, blacks could only go to school through sixth grade," Rolle recalled. "My parents, all of us, worked so the older children could go to boarding schools in the northern part of the state. I picked beans, we all did."

She went to high school in Miami, won an acting scholarship, and was the first black student at New York City's New School. . .

That craving for knowledge is what she tries to pass along to young people today. "Black actors get so little chance to do anything besides the obvious. That's why I did *Raisin (in the Sun).* They deserve a chance to say those fine words."

After her theatrical and film experiences since *Good Times,* the adjustment back into television's more restrictive attitudes is not an easy one.

"I won't be a prop, be a mammy, not again. I don't need a Rolls-Royce. I don't need a hit series. I *had* one. I just need to do my work and be proud of it.

"There's a street here in town named after me. I think of it as a tribute to my parents, who wouldn't let me be kept down. If they hadn't given me the strength and desire to stand up for myself, none of this would have happened." ☀

SOURCE: Peter Smith, *Palm Beach Post* (30 June 1990) and Mike Weatherford, *Las Vegas Review Journal* (February 11, 1994). Used with permission.

*H*ave you ever heard the following statements or made them yourself? "Old people are narrow-minded." "They are set in their ways." "Old people make terrible drivers!" These statements are stereotypes. This chapter explores stereotypes based on age and provides information to explain why they exist.

☼ Stereotypes of Aging

Stereotypes are generalized beliefs or opinions based on individual experience, often produced by irrational thinking. Stereotyping and labeling seem to fulfill a human need to structure and organize situations in order to minimize ambiguity and to clarify where we stand in relation to others.

Yet stereotyping, whether direct or subtle, is usually inaccurate. When we generalize by putting people into categories, we tend to oversimplify reality. We ignore inconsistent information, and we emphasize only a few characteristics. Stereotyping does not consider individual variations. Thus, the statement "old people sit around all day" is a generalization that does not apply to the many active older individuals who still work, write, paint, sculpt, or involve themselves in community or international affairs. Although some stereotypes can be positive, most are negative; whether positive or negative, they are impressions and are not based on objective information. Stereotypes can arouse strong and often negative emotions, such as hatred. Hating any person or groups of people for any reason, but especially on the basis of a single trait such as age, is both ignorant and unfair.

POSITIVE AND NEGATIVE STEREOTYPES

Stereotypes of older people hide the reality that "older people" form an incredibly diverse group. No one can even say for sure when old age begins or if a person is "old."

The media perpetuate many **negative stereotypes** about aging. The music industry usually favors young audiences. The song "Old Folks," recorded by Jacques Brel, although poignant, conveys several negative stereotypes about old people, their homes, and their lifestyles. The old folks' home is dusty and its rooms are filled with faded photographs; although their home is near others, no one visits them; their voices crack and tears drop as they talk of the past; they watch the clock slowly tick away their remaining days. A song like this reinforces an image of the elderly broken in spirit and waiting for death. It screens out the reality that many are intensely involved in living. Advertising on television is especially guilty of stereotyping elders as helpless or sedentary. Comic books and children's stories commonly portray them as menacing; such threats to society are rarely found in reality. Birthday cards and jokes that refer to aging typically imply negative stereotypes.

Tuckman and Lorge (1953) were among the first gerontologists to study stereotypes. Using a list of statements with which subjects were asked to agree or disagree, they found that old people were perceived as being set in their ways, unproductive, a burden to their children, stubborn, grouchy, lonely, "rocking-chair types," and in their second childhood. Since the Tuckman and Lorge study, gerontologists have continued to find that society stereotypes older persons.

Palmore (1990) summarized the negative stereotypes of aging as including (1) illness, (2) impotency, (3) ugliness, (4) mental decline, (5) mental illness, (6) uselessness, (7) isolation, (8) poverty, and (9) depression (grouchy, touchy, cranky). He countered all these stereotypes with factual information disproving these stereotypes for the majority of older persons. Stereotypes, however, are no longer as negative as they were in the 1950s (Palmore, 1990). Palmore and others have cited studies showing increasingly positive attitudes toward elders over the last several decades.

A positive stereotype is a generalized belief that categorizes all older people in a favorable light. The most common positive stereotype is "wise." Other positive stereotypes are "well-to-do," "kind," "patient," "generous," "loving," and "friendly." As the poem, "Maybe at Eighty" indicates, not all older people believe that aging has made them wise, and in fact the stereotype of the wise elder does not apply to all, or even a majority, of older people. Social scientists are not even sure how to measure wisdom.

Despite this positive shift in social attitude, two kinds of negativism have become common in recent times. One is a new ageism that focuses only on the least capable, less healthy, least alert aged. Such a focus on the sick "biomedicalizes" gerontology and takes attention away from the healthy aged who defy the stereotypes (Estes and Binney, 1989; Estes, 1993). **Biomedicalization** has happened, in part, because of the rapid population increase of the very old.

The second kind of negativism is called **compassionate stereotyping.** Binstock (1983) coined this term to describe images that portray elders as disadvantaged on some level (economic, social, psychological), in need of help, and deserving help by others. This may sound harmless. But consider the reaction of disabled activists to posters of the Easter Seal Child—a poster designed to invoke pity for those with disabilities. Activists, including the elderly, do not want pity; rather, they want the tools for being independent and self-reliant. Compassionate stereotypes perpetuate dependency and low self-esteem, and unnecessarily lower expectations of what older people can achieve.

Maybe at Eighty?

■ **S. Minanel**

They say wisdom comes as you age—
Now I'm in a real jam—
at sixty I should be a sage—
look what a fool I am!

SOURCE: S. Minanel in *When I Am Old I Shall Wear Purple* (Papier-Mache Press, 1987).

WHO IS OLD?

When is a person old? Do the words *old, elderly, senior, mature adult, senior citizen,* mean the same thing? Or do they mean different things to different people? No definition of an older person has been universally agreed upon. Using age 65 to define the point at which an individual enters old age is arbitrary. Age 65 is used as a demarcation within U.S. society, but we must realize that one does not suddenly wake up "old" on one's sixty-fifth birthday. A multitude of factors color how a person ages. Broad references to "the elderly" as, say, poor or frail or needy implies that older people are all the same,

and thus stereotypes them. Aging is a gradual process with many influences. The reality is that people age differently.

A whole host of words now indicate categories of older people. Those who are relatively young, say 65 to 75, have been called the "young-old." Older people who are vigorous, fit, and healthy have been labeled as the "able elderly." Those 75 and older are variously called the "old-old," while those 80 and over have been labeled the "frail elderly," or the "extreme aged," depending on their health and the thrust of the gerontologist's work.

Some social scientists divide the elderly into three categories: the young-old (60 to 69), the middle-aged old (70 to 79), and the old-old (80 and older). All these terms bring our attention to the great diversity in both age and the ability to function. The multiplying numbers of words to describe older people underscore their differences and frustrate any attempts to narrowly categorize them.

Tradition

In the United States, as a result of the Social Security Act passed in 1935 under President Franklin D. Roosevelt, 65 is regarded as the onset of old age. Today, most companies, as well as state and local governments, have standard pension programs for retiring workers beginning at age 65. However, since the 1930s, medical science has extended longevity and improved general health. Many are wondering if 75, 80, or 85 might more accurately mark the beginning of old age. Whatever the age, any chronological criterion for determining old age is too narrow and rigid, for it assumes everyone ages in the same ways and at the same time.

Body Functioning

Some authorities say aging begins at the moment of conception. Others reserve the term *aging* to describe the process of decline following the peak in the biological characteristics of muscle strength, skin elasticity, blood circulation, and sensory acuity. Peak functioning in most capabilities occurs at relatively early ages. After the mid-twenties, for example, hearing progressively declines, and muscle strength reaches its maximum between 25 and 30 years of age.

We spend approximately one-fourth of our lives growing up and three-fourths growing old. Biological decline, a gradual process beginning in young adulthood and continuing gradually throughout the life span, varies among individuals in its speed and extent. One person may be biologically old at age 45, another may be physically fit at 80. All organs do not decline at the same rate, either. Someone may have a 30-year-old heart, a 60-year-old response rate, 80-year-old eyes—and be only 20 years old! That everyone ages in the same way and at the same pace is a myth.

Mental Functioning

Mental functioning includes the capacities to create, think, remember, and learn. Although we often assume that mental functioning declines with age, studies are now showing that this assumption is not necessarily true. Though older students enrolling in college after raising families or retiring are often concerned that they cannot keep up with younger students, most professors know that older, non-traditionally-aged students as a group prove to be outstanding in their classroom work. For most individuals, mental functioning remains constant throughout the life span; and for some it may even increase.

Most of us have known some men or women in their eighties or nineties whose minds are clear and alert and others who have memory lapses or confuse facts. The wide variations in the mental functioning of older people may be caused by disease, genetic makeup, or the effects of stress; and we are only beginning to realize how the aging process affects people psychologically. But, like body functioning, mental functions do not automatically decline with age.

Self-Concept

Self-concept significantly affects an individual's psychology. Its dimensions, which include a sensory of identity, body image, and self-esteem, play a large role in the aging process. Those who see themselves as old and accept as true all the negative characteristics attributed to old age may, indeed, *be* old. As sociologist W. I. Thomas (1923) stated, "If people define situations as real, they are real in their consequences" (p. 42). Those over age 65 adjust more readily to their advancing years if they have a self-conception of being "young" rather than of being "old." However, although one should not deny one's age, society does not permit good feelings and a positive self-concept in those who describe themselves as old. The dimensions of the self-concept that deal with self-esteem and a sense of social worth are the ones that our society is most likely to treat harshly.

Studies of identity indicate that many older persons do not see themselves as old. One researcher used the term *ageless self* to describe the phenomenon (Kaufman, 1987). She documented examples from interviews. The first was a woman of 70.

> SK (the interviewer and author): Do you feel 70?
> Martha: I don't feel 70. I feel about 30. I wear my hair the way I did then.
> . . . I just saw some slides of myself and was quite taken aback. That couldn't
> be me . . . (Kaufman, 1987, p. 8).

Another woman, Ethel, commented in a similar vein, "The only way I know I'm getting old is to look in the mirror . . . but I've only felt old a few times—when I'm really sick (Kaufman, 1987, p. 12).

Older people participating in a quality-of-life study in Toronto echoed the theme of an "ageless self":

> "It's our bodies getting old, not us."
> "You don't feel any different, but other people see you as older."
> "I'm always telling my children I'm still the same inside. I just have to walk for the bus now instead of run."
> "I never thought of myself as old until I looked in the mirror and thought, oh, don't fool yourself." (Tandemar Research, 1988, p. 23)

Those over 65 vary in how they view themselves. One may say, "I am old and useless and a bother to my family. I might as well be dead." Another may say, "Life begins at 80 and I have just begun to live." In this sense, we are as young as we believe ourselves to be. Therefore, self-concept may be the most important variable in determining who is old.

OCCUPATION

The age at which a person becomes old depends to some extent on the nature of his or her job. In his classic work, *Age and Achievement* (1953), Harvey Lehman studied the age at which superior productivity tends to occur in dif-

Occupation is one of many factors that determine when one is old. Tina Turner looks good and is going strong, but at 56 she is "old" in the world of rock 'n' roll.

ferent occupations. He found that in most fields, the productivity of adults peaked in their thirties. Only for a few fields did it peak in those in their forties or older. Researchers have been challenging and refining his work ever since. More recent studies show the forties and beyond to be highly productive for a number of professions. Novelists peak in their fifties and sixties; botanists and inventors, in their sixties; and scholars such as historians, humanists, and philosophers, in their sixties and seventies. If we can truly define old age as a time of reflection, we can understand why scholars are able to make major contributions in later life (Kramer, 1987).

Prime occupational performance may occur in the twenties or at any age after that. The following list gives some trends:

PROFESSION	PEAK PERFORMANCE AGE
Football or baseball players	Twenties
Female models	Twenties/thirties
Movie actors	Thirties/forties
Presidents of colleges	Forties/fifties
U.S. senators	Sixties
Outstanding commercial/industrial leaders	Sixties
Philosophers	Seventies
Millionaires	Eighties

Although many people who give peak performances in early adulthood continue top-notch performances throughout their lives, productivity rates do depend on the type of work an individual performs. Studies of blue-collar workers indicate that they reach their highest productivity at an earlier age than white-collar workers, because their work often requires physical skills that peak in early adulthood. In contrast, other studies show that executives see themselves as maturing slowly and believe that old age comes later for them.

COPING WITH STRESS AND ILLNESS

People who are chronologically young can be "old before their time" if they exhibit the physical and mental traits characteristic of more advanced age. Stress undoubtedly ages people and is a well-documented cause of anxiety, depression, migraine headaches, and peptic ulcers. Recent research implicates stress as a cause of coronary heart disease and stroke. Holmes and Rahe (1967) developed a rating scale for measuring stress over a year's time using 43 "life events." A rating of 100 points indicates the highest stress; a rating of 1 indicates the lowest stress. Some of the most stressful life events occur most frequently in one's later years:

LIFE EVENT	RATING
Death of spouse	100
Death of close family member	63
Personal injury or illness	53
Retirement	45
Change in family member's health	44
Change in financial status	38

How does stress affect the individual? According to Holmes and Rahe, scoring less than 150 points on the scale indicates only a 37 percent chance of illness during the next 2 years. On the other hand, a 300-plus score forecasts an 80 percent chance of becoming seriously ill. Not uncommonly, those under stress cannot eat or sleep well, neglect their self-care habits, find it impossible to make simple decisions, and become preoccupied with foreboding thoughts.

Aging often brings multiple life events. If the individual lacks the resources to cope with the consequent stress, illness may result or the aging process may speed up. An individual's "age," then, may depend on the number of severely stressful events he or she experiences and the ability to cope with them. Throughout life, adjustment requires adapting to change. Some people resist change, and stress hits them particularly hard. Others, who are more flexible, compromise and adapt to whatever life brings. Psychologically, the ability to accept change reflects how one will age.

STUDIES OF CHILDREN'S ATTITUDES

Research on the studies of young people, whether adolescents or children, has produced varied and contradictory results. Studies today are revealing more neutral or positive attitudes than 10 years ago and views still more positive than 20 or 30 years earlier.

Children formulate attitudes about elders and the aging process at an early age. Children as young as 3 can differentiate between young and old persons. Studies show that even fairy tales instill ageist feelings in the very young. The evil, ugly, always-old witches or the old stepmothers endanger the children in the stories. Some contemporary books are changing this theme. They emphasize the grandparent-grandchild connection (Steinberg, 1993). A classic study showing pencil sketches of adults to children revealed largely negative stereotypes (Seefeldt et al., 1977). Children of nursery-school age through grade six tended to stereotype the picture of an old man as helpless, incapable of self-care, and generally passive.

However, some studies find that school-age children do not subscribe to negative attitudes toward old age. *Overall, children's attitudes toward the elderly are mixed.* One study of elementary school children asked these questions as they looked at the pencil sketches:

Does s/he get into fights?

Is s/he mean?

Is s/he gentle?

Does s/he say bad words?

Is s/he good?

Is s/he fun to be with?

Does s/he make you feel happy?

Does s/he feel sorry when a kitten is hurt?

Is s/he weak?

Is s/he strong?

Does s/he look good?

Is s/he tired a lot?

Is s/he lazy?

They found that the children perceived the elderly as having more positive personality traits than younger persons, but more negative physical capabilities (Mitchell et al., 1985).

In a study of 30 four- and five-year-old children who visited infirm elders in a nursing home, the preschool children developed more negative attitudes toward elders. Though the trip seemed to be rewarding to the residents and a good learning experience for the children, the visits seemed to confirm to children that elders are passive and sick. The study concluded that such visits should have been balanced with contact with older adults who are competent, active, and able (Seefeldt, 1987).

Teachers can improve children's attitudes toward old age by telling about the physical and mental capabilities of old people. Teachers themselves can avoid being ashamed or shy about telling their age. They can use books and other materials that provide positive role models of old age. They can present accurate information about old age, and they can bring active, creative elders into the classroom.

STUDIES OF COLLEGE STUDENTS' ATTITUDES

Unlike the Tuckman and Lorge study, which asks participants to either agree or disagree with statements, another method of studying stereotypes calls for participants to respond in their own words. One such study (Barrow, 1994) used the word-association technique to survey views of the aged held by college students in sociology classes. Forty-two students age 18 to 35 were asked to list the first three words that came to mind upon seeing the word *aged*. Next, they were asked an open-ended question, "What are your general thoughts or views about the aged?" Because the students were free to respond in their own words, any stereotypes emerged directly from the students' minds, not from any potentially suggestive wording in preformulated phrases. For analysis the study divided the responses into three categories: physical, social, and psychological. Words similar in meaning were grouped together, and the responses (listed below) were ordered from most to least in frequency.

The word *aged* evoked both negative and positive responses. The most frequent association, mentioned 19 times, was "old" and its synonyms ("older," "prehistoric," "long living," etc.).

A salient point of the study was that students paid the most attention to the changing physical appearance and capabilities of older persons. Many students responded to the word *aged* with a description of physical decline. The following words describing physical condition account for the largest proportion of responses:

PHYSICAL WORD RESPONSES TO THE WORD "AGED"	FREQUENCY
Wrinkled	18
Gray hair	9
Slow, less energy	9
Helpless, dependent, weak	7
Deterioration, body broken down, over the hill, washed up	5
Death, dying	4
Walkers, canes, handicapped, arthritis, bad back	4
Hospitals, sick	4
Fragile, brittle	2
Stooped, shrinking	2
Ugly	2
Beautiful	1
65 or older	1
Over 50	1
Glasses	1
No teeth	1
Long life	1
Total physical word responses	72

Although large numbers of students responded to the word *aged* with a physical description, typically one of decline, some students responded with a word indicating a social position or role:

SOCIAL WORD RESPONSES TO THE WORD "AGED"	FREQUENCY
Bad drivers (slow, unskilled, in big cars)	4
Information, history, interesting life stories	3
Ragged, poor	2
Family, grandchildren	2
Bingo	1

Calm life	1
Priority seats in the bus	1
Degraded	1
Rich	1
Overworked	1
Workers	1
Old fashioned	1
Caretakers	1
Retirement	<u>1</u>
Total social word responses	21

The psychological category below contains words primarily used to describe personality characteristics.

PSYCHOLOGICAL WORD RESPONSES TO THE WORD "AGED"	FREQUENCY
Wise, wiser, wisdom	7
Lonely/loneliness	7
Experienced, seasoned, well-versed	2
Shrieking	1
Fear of death	1
Racist	1
Better	1
Inner conflicts	1
No spirit	1
Enraged	1
Smart	1
Gullible	1
Alzheimer's	1
Set in ways	1
Close minded	1
Opinionated	1
Giving	1
Genius	<u>1</u>
Total psychological word responses	31

Here we find a good mix of both positive and negative stereotypes of age. Notice the strong showing of the negative stereotype "lonely" and the positive stereotype "wise."

The second part of the questionnaire asked, "What are your general thoughts or views about the aged?" This question brought a variety of responses. Most of the answers were general and expressed stereotypes—some negative, some positive, and some the compassionate stereotypes defined earlier in the chapter.

On the negative side are these examples:

Old people are dim-witted, out-of-touch, plain, paranoid.

Their late years may be years of dependency on physicians, drugs, institutions and ambulatory medicine. The aged sometimes do not live their last few years of life with great happiness; it is a time of stress and unhappiness, pain, sorrow, weeping, and reversals in memory.

On the positive side, a student said:

I generally tend to respect the aged because they have done and seen so much. I view old people sort of as old cars, with some parts broken, but others running as smooth as ever. I feel it is always worth it to stop and talk to an elderly person. You never know when they could teach you a valuable lesson.

The open-ended question brought a host of responses that could be described as compassionate stereotypes; indeed, these dominated the replies. Students expressed both indignation and pity at the low status and suffering of the aged in this country. These quotes illustrate a problem inherent in compassionate stereotyping:

I think we must take care of our aged and provide good care for them. We must not treat them as a burden to society.

They have a lot to teach yet don't have a fair role in society. Some people, what I think, are just waiting to die because they're lonely. A lot of people put them aside. Cause—the amount of attention the elderly need seems to be a burden to a lot of families.

They are the only true wise ones. Their wisdom and life experience should not go unnoticed as they presently do. It's a crying shame. They have so much tenderness, forgiving heart filled with love of life and empathy towards everybody and everything that they should not be simply put into homes and forgotten.

This student put herself in a double bind. By perceiving the aged as "needing care," she is describing them as dependent and yet she wants them to have a "fair role" in society. She could avoid this bind if she perceived elders as able-bodied and independent.

☼ Explaining Stereotypes

We can explain the existence of stereotypes on a number of levels. On one level, the historical/cultural explanation requires the gerontologist to look at the roots and cultural context of our concepts about old age. On another level, current social explanations look at elements such as social class and the influence of the media. On a different level, psychologists ask why some individuals, either young or old, accept the negative stereotypes of old age whereas others accept the positive ones.

HISTORICAL/CULTURAL EXPLANATIONS

Understanding the relationships between generations and exploring views about growing old in a previous era are the jobs of a historian. For example, a historian in Chapter 1 described how, throughout American history, society's view of elders shifted from one of veneration and favor to one of scorn.

The exact time of the change and the extent of both the veneration and the scorn, however, remain disputed. Historians are making a major effort to unravel the threads that explain stereotypes based on age.

The words we use to describe older people provide a basis for the formation of stereotypes. This process is hardly unique to the twentieth century. Studying the **language of aging** used in the 1800s and several years prior, Covey (1988) found widely used terminology that augmented negative stereotypes about the elderly (see Table 2.1).

Present-day researchers observe few age-specific terms that refer positively to older people. Several of the rare examples are *mature, sage, venerable,* and *veteran.* A study of the language of aging found that even the terms *aged person* and *elderly* were considered less than positive (Barbato and Freezel, 1987). For example, presidents of companies or anyone in a position of power typically do not want to be called "aged" or "elderly." The core of the problem is that as long as there are negative attitudes about aging, even initially positive terms may develop into negative stereotypes.

Historians examine magazines, newspapers, poetry, sermons, and other written materials for information about aging in prior times. For example, sheet music of the 1800s and 1900s reflects the then popular sentiments about age (Cohen and Kruschwitz, 1990). With few exceptions, writers of tunes popular in the late nineteenth and early twentieth centuries saw old age as a time of failing capacities, clearly preferring youth and dreading growing old. In these songs, elders fear that their children will abandon them; they worry about spousal death, loneliness, disability, and their own deaths. "Silver Threads Among the Gold" (1873), a classic of the period, is a touching song that emphasizes the declines in old age. Another example is the song "Old Joe Has Had His Day" (1912).

A whole series of songs, such as "Will You Love Me When My Face Is Worn and Old?" (1914), echoes the fear of loss of attractiveness. Perhaps the most poignant of all is "Over the Hill to the Poor House" (1874). It ends with the four lines to the left.

In contrast, only a few songs during this time period celebrated positive aging—growing old together and being young at heart, for example.

Songs of recent decades continue the themes of the past. A well-known song, the Beatles' "When I'm 64," carries ambiguities about aging: although

The marks of time are creeping on
My hair is turning gray
The springtime of life has faded
With the flowers that grow by the way
We like the roses must wither and fade
There's nothing comes to stay
The allotted time is drawing near
Old Joe has had his day.

For I'm old and helpless and feeble
The days of my youth have gone by
Then over the hill to the poor house
I wander alone there to die.

Table 2.1	Terms for Old Women	Terms for Old Men	Either Sex
Historical Terminology Used to Describe Older People	Old bird	Old buzzard	Old bean
	Old trout	Old goat	Mouldy
	Old crow	Old coot	Crone
	Old hag	Old crock	Gummer
	Little old lady	Old fogey	Has-been
	Witch	Dirty old man	Fossil
	Tabby or cat		Dodo
	Old hen		Fuddy duddy
	Old bag		Gink
	Old biddy		
	Quail		

SOURCE: Adapted from Herbert Covey, "Historical Terminology Used to Represent Older People," *Gerontologist* 28 (May 1988): 291–297.

anticipating the joys of growing old together with his wife, the singer has doubts: "Will you still need me, will you still feed me, when I'm 64?" The Alan Parsons Project sees aging as a time to simply bid life farewell in "Old & Wise" (1982): "As far as my eyes can see/There are shadows approaching me." Bette Midler's "Hello in There" evokes the compassionate stereotypes with ". . . but old people they just grow lonely, waiting for someone to say 'Hello in there; hello'." One of the biggest country songs of 1990, "Where've You Been?" by Kathy Mattea, finds an elderly woman lying helplessly in a hospital, waiting for death and a last visit from her husband. We do not find all the answers to the status of elders in popular music, but we do see some historical roots of both acceptance and fear. We see various stereotypes, many of which are negative.

The fears of aging expressed in the songs at the turn of the century, such as going to the poor house to die, were more valid then than now. Life expectancy was lower and so was overall health status. Resignation and sadness were more appropriate to them. Older people are now leading healthier, more active lives. The negative stereotypes still present in popular songs are an example of the "cultural lag" that makes our attitudes slower to change than the technology that has improved our lives.

SOCIAL FORCES: THE MEDIA

Sociologists study present-day situations to find explanations for negative stereotyping. The media, which can both reflect and create society's views, have a strong impact on our views of life. Redbook magazine (April 1994) had a bold-face title on its cover which read: "When It's Smart to Lie about Your Age." The article inside cited sexual attractiveness and career pressures as reasons to lie. The author said, "We all want to be young. Despite feminist assertions, 20 implies desirable, attractive, sexy, and 40 doesn't." (Peters, 1994) This article creates a fear of aging in its readers. The obvious message is that by the age of 40, aging has taken an insurmountable toll on women.

Television

The Gray Panthers, a group organized to fight for the rights and interests of older persons, has vigorously protested television portrayals of the elderly. The **Media Watch Task Force,** supported by the Gray Panthers, zeroes in on programs that present stereotypical and unrealistic portrayals of elderly people.

"It's disgraceful the way some sponsors and program makers have depicted the aging," says Lydia Bragger, spokesperson for the Gray Panthers. "Look at how rarely we see older couples on TV sharing affection or, heaven forbid, making love" (Hickey, 1990).

Studies concur that television underrepresents older women (Mundorf and Brownell, 1990). Older female news anchors are a rare species. In a widely publicized, successful lawsuit, Christine Craft sued a Kansas City broadcasting station for sex discrimination, claiming she was demoted for being "too old, unattractive, and not deferential enough to men." The "elderly" Ms. Craft was 38.

Television typically pairs older women romantically with men who are older, thereby avoiding role models for same-age, or older woman/younger man relationships. Singer/actress Cher, at 45, said she worries about her looks as she gets older. "The roughest thing in the world," she said, "is to be an older woman." She was referring both to the entertainment world and to her personal life (DeVries, 1991). Sally Field, age 48, reports that only 8% of all theatrical roles go to women over 40, and in television, 9 percent. According to her, the Hollywood stigma attached to aging actresses has been around "since the beginning of time" (Bash, 1995).

Television is better in the 1990s than it used to be. Many older actors are portraying older characters; in the 1970s and before, the roles usually would have been played by younger performers made to look older. Elizabeth Taylor has achieved a star appeal that was once reserved for much younger women. Through her best-selling exercise books, audiotapes, and videocassettes, Jane Fonda, now in her fifties, offers women of all ages a role model with whom to stay in shape. Television has offered more programming with older stars: "The Golden Girls," a weekly sitcom about four older, single women sharing a house in Miami; "Murder She Wrote," starring Angela Lansbury as a writer and solver of murder mysteries; "Matlock"; and "Jake and the Fatman." The three generations of feisty women on "Who's the Boss?" were popular for many years. News reporters Mike Wallace and Morley Safer, talk show host Hugh Downs, and game show host Bob Barker remain television celebrities into their sixties and seventies.

Despite the increased exposure older performers now enjoy, television still has problems with its portrayal of older Americans. Television programming commonly and unfortunately uses a comedy gimmick—a **reversed stereotype of aging.** A reversed stereotype refers to older characters driving race cars, break-dancing with great abandon, or referring to their amazing sex life. Such images are, of course, intended to be comical, because they are in stark contrast with the held stereotypes of a low energy, sedentary lifestyle.

Reversed stereotypes used for comedy do more harm than good. The public tends to believe what stereotypes, reversed or not, present. Laughing at a reversed stereotype is showing unconscious, uncritical acceptance of the underlying negative image. Older respondents are even less critical than the young. In other words, older people as a general segment of the viewing public do not complain about their television image.

Aging experts believe that the television industry needs to revise its unrealistic portrayal of older Americans to become a medium that reflects the aging experience of the 1990s (Deets, 1993). The challenge of television is to offer a true portrait of the elderly. A sensitive, realistic portrayal is the goal. On the one hand, older adults must not be demeaned; yet on the other hand, television must not gloss over the real problems of aging. Portrayals should attempt to balance strengths and satisfactions with the real problems of aging.

Television viewing time increases with age. Nielsen Media Research estimates that women over age 55 watch more television (40 hours per week) than any other age group (Hickey, 1990; Mundorf and Brownell, 1990). Other sources list the 55-plus female viewing time as close to 30 hours per week. To isolated persons, television commonly acts as a companion. The widowed and lonely often prefer programs that emphasize family solidarity and a sense of belonging.

Media Advertising

Television advertising that urges the public to cover up the signs of aging can be particularly damaging. Advertising tells us that aging is primarily ugly, lonely, and bothersome. Advertisers create markets by instilling a fear of aging or by capitalizing on already existing fears. Commercials imply that the elderly are sluggish and preoccupied with irregularity and constipation. As a group, they suffer from headaches, nagging backaches, and loose dentures. Men are offered alternatives to baldness; both sexes are urged to buy products that will "wash away the gray"; women are urged to soften facial wrinkles and smooth "old-looking" hands with creams and lotions.

Whether or not this product "erases" wrinkles, advertisements such as the following promote youth-culture ideals that intensify an already unfavorable view of aging:

WOMEN WORLDWIDE HATE WRINKLES

And *Love* This Pharmacist!

Women all over the world who are worried about wrinkles just love this famous Pharmacist _____. His _____ cream helps smooth facial lines and has helped millions of women look younger . . . " People tell me I look 10–15 years younger" . . . "With the first application I looked in the mirror and loved my new younger look."

(Parade Magazine ad, 1993, p. 24).

Some advertisers, however, are beginning to present a more positive view of aging. Some active, happy older people are appearing in commercials on television and in magazines. Manufacturers increasingly recognize that older people are consumers; correspondingly, advertisers are devoting more commercial time and space to elders as their numbers and buying power increase.

But advertisers have to be careful not to alienate their target audience. One study showed that consumers in their fifties and sixties respond best to an actor around age 40. If the actors are older, advertisers may inadvertently be targeting the elderly parents of the 50-plus group (Lipman, 1991). Thus ageism rears its head among those who are theoretically opposed to it—the young-old who are turned off by ads if the actors are too old.

Critics of ads using older people complain that they sometimes look like "doddering old fools" (Goldman, 1993). In a Doritos chips ad a gray-haired woman shuffles along munching on chips oblivious to a steamroller behind her. Chevy Chase comes to the rescue to save the chips, and the woman is plowed into wet cement. In another spot for Denny's restaurants, an oldster stumbles over the name, repeatedly calling it Lenny's. Carol Morgan, president of the marketing group Strategic Directions, sees a "huge lack of sophistication" among people advertising to the mature market (Goldman, 1993).

Movies

For most makers of feature-length commercial films, a major aim is to reach young people, particularly males of ages 16 to 24. Studies conclude that most moviegoers are teenagers and young adults; studios market their products accordingly. Many commercially successfully movies seem to be rather mindless entertainment with a focus on high-speed chases and violence. Exceptions to the standard movie formula are rare. In the typical movie, youth holds much more promise than age. It is the exceptional movie that stars older persons and promotes understanding of the challenges and joys of aging.

The Chicago philanthropic group that gives annual "Owl" awards for film and television shows that treat older people with respect skipped feature films in 1992 because it did not find one that had enough merit. In 1989 and 1991 the Jessica Tandy films *Driving Miss Daisy* and *Fried Green Tomatoes* won

Thinking about Aging

Ads for Elderly May Give Wrong Message

■ JOANNE LIPMAN

Ms. Cadwell's agency, Cadwell Davis Partners, which specializes in marketing to older consumers, has just finished research that may call a lot of marketing campaigns into doubt. Every two years since 1985, the agency has queried 1,100 older Americans about old age—and has found that in their view, what constitutes old age is getting older all the time.

For consumers age 50 and older, the idea of when "old age" really begins was set at age 71 in 1985. They now believe it starts at the ripe age of 79, and they feel younger than ever before—15 years younger than their actual age, on average. Six years ago they felt just 11 years younger.

As a result, advertisers trying to reach older Americans may be delivering the wrong message, using ads that are "too old" for their audience, and appealing to far older consumers than they intended to reach.

Instead of appealing to the 50-plus crowd, advertisers may inadvertently be targeting that crowd's elderly parents. That is a costly mistake. Vigorous consumers in their 50s and 60s have enormous spending power, yet commercials using actors that age often conjure up images of people who are much older and infirm.

Ms. Cadwell and others have been preaching the virtues of 50-plus consumers for years. For years, the message has been ignored. But now that baby boomers are creeping toward retirement, the message is all the more critical. Considering that pop icons such as rock stars Mick Jagger and Paul McCartney are dancing around the half-century mark, Ms. Cadwell notes, "50-plus isn't that old anymore." ☀

SOURCE: *Wall Street Journal,* 31 December 1991, p. B4. Reprinted by permission of *Wall Street Journal,* Dow Jones & Company, Inc. All rights reserved worldwide.

awards (Newman, 1993). More recent movies that have also been recommended by experts on aging are:

Complaints of a Dutiful Daughter (1994) Oscar-nominated documentary about a daughter caring for her mother with Alzheimer's Disease.

The Cemetery Club (1993) Three widowed women who are best friends adjust to their new status in conflicting ways.

Enchanted April (1992, British) A snippy aristocratic widow joins three younger women in renting a vacation home on the Italian coast.

Strangers in Good Company (1991) Seven elderly women, stranded when their bus breaks down, share their stories, fears, and dreams.

Thank You and Goodnight! (1990) A documentary of a grandmother dying of cancer—her fear, pain, and humor.

Age Old Friends (1990) Two buddies living in a retirement home cope with frailty. Their minds remain sharp as their bodies decline.

Movies that describe aging, care of the ill, spousal relationships, friendships over the years, and intergenerational relationships are trying to portray older people as complex characters, not caricatures. For example, the 1993 movie *Shadowlands* portrayed writer C. S. Lewis (played by Anthony Hopkins) as someone willing to risk a new relationship, and as having depth to his person. Paul Newman, at age 70, brought insights into the possibilities for healing family relationships in his role as Sully in the 1994 movie *Nobody's Fool.*

The *Entertainment Tonight* documentary "Power and Fear" (July 26, 1990) showed that ageism remains a powerful force in the movie industry, which clearly still favors youth over age. Film and other popular media continue to glorify youth and play on fears of aging, thus enhancing negative stereotypes of age.

THE PSYCHOLOGY OF PREJUDICE

Those who hold negative stereotypes of aging are prejudiced against older persons. The two variables go hand in hand. To explain why an individual would subscribe to negative stereotyping is to explain why a person is prejudiced. The **psychology of prejudice** draws attention to the psychological causes of prejudice as opposed to social causes previously discussed, such as T.V. and magazine advertising.

One psychological explanation is self-concept. Someone having a positive self-concept may be less prone to believe the negative stereotypes of other groups. And when that person ages, he or she may well choose to accept only positive stereotypes of age. Psychologists use the term *projection* here. If we feel negative about ourselves, we project it on to others. This might explain why prejudice against elders correlates with one's personal degree of anxiety about death (Palmore, 1988).

Three well-known theories that explain racism may also be used to explain ageism (Palmore, 1990): (1) the **authoritarian personality,** in which less-educated, rigid, untrusting, insecure persons are the ones who hold prejudices; (2) the **frustration-aggression hypothesis,** in which those who are frustrated, perhaps by poverty and low status, take it out in aggression toward others; and (3) **selective perception,** in which we see what we expect to see and selectively ignore what we do not expect to see. Our perceptions then confirm our stereotypes. For example, we "see" only old drivers driving badly. We do not "see" young drivers mishandling a vehicle. Nor do we "see" all the old drivers who do well.

In fact, we may perceive as "old" only those who are stooped, feeble, or ill. For example, viewers perceive Angela Lansbury, heroine of "Murder She Wrote," as middle-aged, because she is so healthy, vigorous, and clever. Actually, she celebrated her 70th birthday in 1995. If viewers understood this, perhaps some of the negative stereotypes of old age would disappear.

☼ Breaking Negative Stereotypes

The negative stereotypes of age must be disproved if we are to have a true picture of older people. One way to do this is to draw attention to people who have made significant contributions in their old age. Michelangelo, Leo Tolstoy, Sigmund Freud, Georgia O'Keefe, Pablo Picasso, and Bertrand Russell, for example, continued to produce recognized classics until the ends of long lives. Other prominent men and women are still working productively at relatively advanced ages: writer Norman Mailer, the nation's first female poet laureate, Mona Van Duyn, pianist Alicia de Larrocha, stage actress Julie Harris, vocalist Lena Horne, jazz musician B. B. King, Dr. Jonas Salk, and scientist/lecturer Jane Goodall. Numerous Nobel prize winners in the sciences every year are 65 or over.

EMPHASIZING THE POSITIVE

Negative stereotypes must be countered with accurate information. For example, the myth that elders as a group suffer mental impairment still persists. More specifically, stereotyped beliefs are (1) that the mental faculties of older people decline, and (2) that old people are senile. However, longitudinal studies of the same persons over many years have found little overall decline in intelligence scores. Studies show that older individuals are just as capable of learning as younger people—although the learning process may take a little more time. One longitudinal study of intelligence in subjects ranging in age from 21 to 70 shows that on two out of four measures intelligence *increases* with age and concludes that "general intellectual decline in old age is largely a myth" (Baltes and Schaie, 1974).

The stereotype that all old people are senile simply is not true. Proportionately few ever show overt signs of senility. Those who do can often be helped by treatment. Although mental health is a problem for some, only a small percentage of the elderly have Alzheimer's disease or any other severe mental disorder.

Physical stereotypes are as common as mental ones and are just as false. More positive images are replacing the "rocking chair" stereotype of old age as older Americans stay more physically active and fit. The physical fitness craze has not been lost on the over-65 generation. Aerobics classes, jogging, walking, and bicycling have become very popular among this group.

Many sports now have competition in senior divisions. Tennis is one example. It's never too late for a shot at Wimbleton—"Senior Wimbleton West," that is, held annually in the western part of the United States. Divisions of this tournament, for both men and women, exist for those in their fifties, sixties, seventies, and eighties. Golf, swimming, cycling, bowling, softball, and even basketball have senior events. Sports and physical fitness can extend throughout one's life.

The key ingredient to a long, full life, according to psychologist Lee Hurwich, who happens to be in her seventies, is not physical health, but attitude (Opatrny, 1991). With the right attitude—one of passion about life, whether this passion is found in career, friendships, or interests—a person can enjoy some of the best and most rewarding years in later life. Hurwich, who interviewed active, committed women discovered that her subjects live in the present, squeezing from daily life all its enjoyment. They had relationships with people of all ages. Many had suffered physical afflictions that would send most people into despair, but they had optimistic attitudes and a trust in people. One woman was studying Spanish at age 87. Why? "I want to keep the cobwebs out of my head," she told Hurwich. As they reached their eighties and nineties, Hurwich's subjects still felt life has meaning, and they were satisfied with their lives. Four well-known women she studied in 1991 who were still vital at 70 and beyond are Elizabeth Terwilliger, naturalist; Betty Friedan, feminist leader; Julia Child, chef; and Jessica Mitford, author (Opatrny, 1991).

CONSEQUENCES AND IMPLICATIONS OF STEREOTYPING

Negative stereotyping of old people has detrimental effects on both society in general and old people in particular. First, negative stereotyping perpetuates ageism in our society. Ageism increases when society views all old people as senile, decrepit, and rigid. These and other negative stereotypes, which do not apply to the majority of elders, reinforce prejudice and lead to discrimi-

nation. Perpetuating ageism often results in polarization (a feeling of "us" against "them") and segregation. One student in an unpublished study by the author had this to say:

> I can't stand old people and I don't get along with them at all. To me they seem useless and without a purpose. I try to avoid the aged.

This opinion serves as a good example of the negative stereotyping and ageist attitudes that result in the avoidance of old people. When we avoid old people, society becomes age segregated. Real communication cannot take place in a segregated society, and the cycle of stereotyping, ageism, and polarization continues.

Ageism even affects professional objectivity. In a study of psychologists, ageism was evident. When presented with clinical vignettes in which the ages of the clients varied, clinical psychologists considered older, depressed clients to be significantly less ideal than younger clients with identical symptoms and histories; and older clients were given poorer prognoses than younger ones. However, older psychologists were more favorable toward older clients than were young psychologists (Ray et al., 1987). An experimental program was introduced in a medical school to improve the medical students' attitudes and skills in working with elders. In another study, an experimental group participated in four 10-minute group sessions that emphasized psychological and biological knowledge as well as communication skills. The experimental group developed more positive attitudes and more socially skilled behavior in their work with older adults than did members of a control group (Intrieri et al., 1993).

Employees could relate better to older clients if they rid themselves of negative stereotypes, especially the stereotype that older people are in their second childhood, which is a very poor way to elicit the highest potential from a resident. Even if the older person has a mental disorder and is physically dependent, the "second childhood" stereotype glosses over the ways in which he or she is not childlike.

Negative stereotyping fosters fear of aging in both old and young. Who wants to be "hunched over," "grouchy," "useless," "rejected," and "alone"? One study, which used agree-disagree statements to measure fear of aging, showed a clear and strong relationship between low fear of aging and subjective well-being (Klemmack and Roff, 1984). The study measured fear of aging with statements such as these:

I feel that people will ignore me when I'm old.

I am afraid that I will be lonely when I'm old.

I am afraid that I will be poor when I'm old.

Subjective well-being was measured by agree-disagree statements such as these:

I have made plans for things I'll be doing a month or year from now.

Compared to other people I get down in the dumps less often.

The things I do now are as interesting to me as they were when I was younger.

Those who did not fear aging felt good about themselves and their lives. On the other hand, those who feared aging did not have a good personal sense of well-being.

A question asked of the aged participants in the Berkeley Older Generation Study was "Looking back, what period of your life brought you the most satisfaction?" This question was asked when the respondents were, on the average, 69 years old, and 14 years later when the average age was 83. The findings remained consistent over time. Adolescence was considered the most unsatisfactory time. The decade of the thirties was named as most satisfying time period by 16 percent of the sample. The period of the fifties was second most popular named by 15% of the sample. Old age was seen as more satisfying than childhood. Twelve percent said their 60's brought them the most satisfaction; 13 percent named their 70's and 5 percent described their 80's as the most satisfying period of their lives. The common stereotypes that old persons are fixated on childhood memories, that youth is best, and that old age contains few satisfactions were, thus, dispelled (Field, 1993).

Negative stereotyping stifles the potential of older people and draws attention away from the happy, sociable, successful, active oldsters. A self-fulfilling prophecy is created: older people do not do anything because they assume they are not able. Their lives, therefore, are neither as satisfying nor as fulfilling as they might be.

We have hardly begun to explore the potential of elders in this society. Too often, larger companies try to remove the older persons from the labor market to make room for the young. Too often, we provide no alternative ways for them to make contributions. Too often, society works against elders instead of for them. We need to put more thought and effort into conserving a valuable natural resource: older Americans.

Chapter Summary

Many stereotypes of old age exist, and a large portion are negative. Sources of negative stereotyping are the language we use to describe elders, songs, speeches, television, advertising, movies, and so on. The psychology of prejudice is needed to examine and understand the roots of ageism. Historical and economic bases must also be studied to fully understand age prejudice.

The negative stereotypes must be disproved if we are to have a true understanding of the potential of elders. Emphasizing the accomplishments of older scholars, scientists, and artists is helpful. Senior sports events draw attention to the physical fitness potential of elders and their ability to enjoy competition. If we emphasize positive stereotypes of aging, young people will not fear aging and will be inspired to fulfill their potential in their later years.

Key Terms

authoritarian personality
biomedicalization
compassionate stereotypes
frustration-aggression hypothesis
Media Watch Task Force
negative stereotypes

positive stereotypes
psychology of prejudice
reversed stereotype of aging
selective perception
stereotypes
the language of aging

Questions for Discussion

1. Everyone bring one birthday card with an "age message." Is the message about aging positive or negative?

2. How does advertising contribute to negative or positive attitudes toward aging? Bring an advertisement with an "age message" to class.

3. Try to recall some children's literature that contains stories about or references to old people. What images are portrayed? Who were your aging "models" as a child? Have these models affected you in a positive or negative way?

4. Describe yourself at age 85: what you will look like, what you will be doing, where you will live, who your friends will be.

Fieldwork Suggestions

1. List the first ten words that come into your mind upon seeing the words *aged, middle aged, adult, adolescent.* Analyze your words. Do they reveal your personal biases and judgments about these age groups?

2. Design a study (word association, for example) to uncover stereotypes of aging.

3. Observe television programs and commercials. How is the topic of aging handled? Are old people visible? How are they characterized?

4. Study magazine ads of the 1960s, 1970s, 1980s, and 1990's in regard to aging. Do you observe any changes? Write a "good" ad for an antiaging skin cream.

References

Baltes, P., and W. Schaie. "Aging and I.Q.—The Myth of the Twilight Years." *Psychology Today* (March 1974): 35–40.

Barbato, Carole A., and Jerry D. Freezel. "The Language of Aging in Different Age Groups." *Gerontologist* 27 (August 1987): 527–531.

Barrow, Georgia. "Study of Stereotypes of Old Age." Unpublished. Santa Rosa, CA: Santa Rosa Junior College, 1994.

Bash, A. "Field Wields Clout within 'Means,'" *USA Today* February 17, 1995, p. 24.

Binstock, Robert. "The Aged as Scapegoats." *Gerontologist* 23 (February 1983): 136–143.

Cohen, E., and A. Kruschwitz. "Old Age in America Represented in Nineteenth and Twentieth Century

Popular Sheet Music." *Gerontologist* 30:3 (June 1990): 345–354.

Covey, Herbert. "Historical Terminology Used to Represent Older People." *Gerontologist* 28 (May 1988): 291–297.

Deets, H. B. "The Media and the Marketplace: A New Vision of Aging." *Vital Speeches* 50:5 (15 December 1993): 134 (3).

DeVries, H. "An Interview with Cher," Datebook Section of *San Francisco Chronicle* Dec. 8, 1991, p. 37.

Estes, C. "The Aging Enterprise Revisited." *Gerontologist* 33:3 (June 1993): 292–298.

Estes, C., and E. Binney. "The Biomedicalization of Aging," *Gerontologist* 29 (1989): 586–589.

Field, D. "Looking Back, What Period of Your Life Brought You the Most Satisfaction?" Paper presented to the Annual Gerontological Society Meeting, New Orleans, LA, November 1993.

Goldman, K. "Seniors Get Little Respect on Madison Avenue," *Wall Street Journal,* Sept. 20, 1993, p. B8.

Hickey, Neil. "Its Audience Is Aging . . . So Why Is TV Still Chasing the Kids?" *T.V. Guide* (20 October 1990): 22–24.

Holmes, T., and R. Rahe. "The Social Readjustment Rating Scale." *Journal of Psychosomatic Research* (1967): 213–218.

Intrieri, R. C., et al. "Improving Students' Attitudes Toward and Skills with the Elderly." *Gerontologist* 33:3 (June 1993): 373–378.

Kaufman, S. *The Ageless Self.* Madison: University of Wisconsin Press, 1987.

Klemmack, D., and L. L. Roff. "Fear of Personal Aging and Subjective Well-Being in Later Life." *Journal of Gerontology* 39 (November 1984): 756–758.

Kramer, D. A. "Cognition and Aging: The Emergence of a New Tradition." In *The Elderly as Modern Pioneers,* edited by P. Silverman, 45–58. Bloomington: Indiana University Press, 1987.

Lehman, Harvey. *Age and Achievement.* Princeton, NJ: Princeton University Press, 1953.

Lipman, J. "Ads for Elderly May Give Wrong Message." *Wall Street Journal* (31 December 1991): B4.

Mitchell, J., et al. "Children's Perceptions of Aging: A Multidimensional Approach to Differences by Age, Sex, and Race." *Gerontologist* 25 (April 1985): 182–187.

Mundorf, N., and W. Brownell. "Media Preferences of Older and Younger Adults." *Gerontologist* 30 (October 1990): 685–691.

Newman, R. J. "Older Folks Are Real People, Too." *U.S. News and World Report* (14 June 1993): 103.

Opatrny, S. "Women Who Stay Vital Past Seventy." *San Francisco Examiner* (3 March 1991): A1–A13.

Palmore, E. *The Facts of Aging* Quiz. New York: Springer, 1988.

———. *Ageism: Negative and Positive.* New York: Springer Publishing, 1990.

Parade Magazine, "Women Worldwide Hate Wrinkles" (Advertisement). (21 February 1993): 24.

Ray, Diane C., et al. "Differences in Psychologists' Ratings of Older and Younger Clients." *Gerontologist* 27 (February 1987): 82–86.

Ringle, Ken. "The Man Who Makes Bach Swing." *Washington Post* (9 January 1994): A6.

Seefeldt, Carole. "The Effects of Preschoolers' Visits to a Nursing Home." *Gerontologist* 27 (April 1987): 228–232.

Seefeldt, Carole, et al. "Using Pictures to Explore Children's Attitudes Toward the Elderly." *Gerontologist* 17 (December 1977): 506–512.

Steinberg, D. "Seniorities: How Fairy Tales Help Perpetuate Ageist Mythology." *San Francisco Examiner* (13 March 1993): C7.

Tandemar Research. *Quality of Life Among Seniors.* Toronto, Ontario: Tandemar Research, October 1988.

Thomas, W. I. *The Unadjusted Girl.* Boston: Little, Brown, 1923.

Tuckman, J., and I. Lorge. "Attitudes Toward Old People." *Journal of Gerontology* 32 (1953): 227–232.

Wolfe, W. "Labeling Folks as Senior Citizens Isn't as Easy as It Used to Be." *Minneapolis (Minnesota) Star and Tribune* (18 March 1991), p. B1.

Further Readings

Corelli, R. "Over What Hill?" *Maclean's,* January 10, 1994, p. 30–33.

Loelterle, B. Ageless Prose: A Study of the Media Projected Images of Aging. New York: Garland Pub., Inc. 1993.

Nemeth, M. "Amazing Greys," *Maclean's,* January 10, 1994, p. 26–29.

3 *A*dult Development

CHAPTER OUTLINE

The Stones Age

■ RICHARD HARRINGTON

Venerable archetypes in rock's longest-running soap opera, Keith Richards, Mick Jagger, Charlie Watts and Ron Wood (no longer the new boy after 19 years) have finished dinner and are waiting for their just desserts.

Just as Jagger mumbles to his wife that this last rehearsal seems to be ending with no nod to his birthday—surprise!—a gigantic and calorically daunting chocolate cake (sporting the "Voodoo Lounge" cover, of course) is wheeled out from the kitchen, adorned with a single candle. Jagger's birthday, his 51st, is actually a few days away, but it's the last time this whole group will be together until opening night.

This private moment is a decided contrast to last year, when Jagger's 50th birthday provoked ridiculous media coverage. After dinner, Jagger expresses relief not just at the single candle, but the absent fuss.

"God, yes!" he sighs.

Jagger's never been particularly fond of looking backward, which becomes a problem as the Stones mythology stretches into each new decade. Experientially, the distance between "It's All Over Now" and the new "Voodoo Lounge" album seems greater than 30 years. After all, rock-and-roll is central to a pop culture, and the music industry within it, where planned obsolescence is the norm and where longevity is traditionally suspect.

> "The Stones gave it everything they had; these old pros, crippled by age and dissipation, but still holding the flag high . . ."
>
> —Chet Flippo writing in *Rolling Stone*—back in 1978.
>
> "The Famous heads are going gray now, the faces beginning to sage like trail-weathered saddlebags . . ."
>
> —Same band, same magazine, Kurt Loder—in 1981.
>
> "The Stones are not anachronisms. They are still able, at will, to tap the unruly, anarchic essence of what their music has always been about . . ."
>
> —Ditto, ditto, Anthony DeCurtis—in 1989.

In the process of transforming themselves from rock's original menace to society into music industry

figureheads, the group that once sang "what a drag it is getting old" is finding what an interesting thing it is getting older.

"It is," insists Keith Richards, 50. "It's fresh because no one has taken a band this far down the road before. For that very reason you expect that 'Ah, they're still hackin' it out,' but that stuff is a really peripheral thing for us. Hey, you come up with something better, we'll get out of the way."

When the Stones were indicted—er, inducted—into the Rock and Roll Hall of Fame five years ago, The Who's Pete Townsend counseled: "Don't try to grow old gracefully, it wouldn't suit you!" That same year, the group released "Steel Wheels" and won both the readers and critics polls in *Rolling Stone* for artist of the year and tour of the year.

At times, a Rolling Stones group photo can look like a classic tintype. It would be easy to mistake them for a band of outlaws in a West still wild, or for Welsh miners not long out of the mines. They may sport elegant tailored clothes (the perennial prole Richards excepted) but the faces are all weathered (okay, Richard's is weather-beaten). The wear and tear of 30 years in the trenches is not absent even in the perpetually vigorous Jagger, whose impossibly thin waist and taut physique seem as time-defiant as his rooster strut. . . .

"We can maybe shed an old lady here and there, if necessary, but Mick and I, we cannot divorce each other," says Richards. "Even if we never wanted to see each other again, we'd have to! Even if it was just to deal with what we'd done already and never learn anything else.

"I suppose it's something to be pleased about, that a band can last that long," says Jagger, he of the perpetually mixed emotions. "Of course it has its down and up moments and there's bound to be periods where it's not much fun, and it doesn't have a lot of definition after a while. I think the beginning was all right but then you're just redoing it. . . . It's kind of hard to keep it all together, hard to make long-term plans because that monster looms on the horizon."

Author's Note: According to journalist Kurt Loder (1993), Mick Jagger and group have weathered some legendary wild times and are still up for occasional parties. Jagger, who owns a New York apartment, a retreat on a Caribbean Island, and a chateau in the Loire Valley of France, has every intention of continuing to perform his music. In the Voodoo album the subject of aging is touched on in a wistful way "I can still paint the town/All the colors of your evening gown/While I'm waiting/For your blond hair to turn gray." On another album Jagger sings "Hang on to me tonight . . . While there's youth upon your face." Jagger has 3 children (ages 9, 8, 2 in 1994) with Texas model Jerry Hall, a daughter Jade by ex-wife Bianca Jagger and daughter Karis (both girls in their early '20s) by Marsha Hunt. He became a grandfather in 1992 with the birth of Jade's daughter. ☼

SOURCE: © 1994 The Washington Post. Reprinted with permission.

*T*his chapter considers the human life cycle from the psychological perspective of adult development. In it, we see how developmental perspectives are useful in understanding the fear of aging and age transitions. The personality variables that affect aging and are in turn affected in the aging process are studied.

☼ Early Developmental Models

According to early developmentalists, distinct stages form the **life cycle** through which humans pass. We proceed from infancy to childhood, through adolescence to adulthood, and then into parenthood and grandparenthood, and the cycle begins anew for each newborn baby. The life cycle is the course of aging: Individuals adapt throughout their lives to their own biological, psychological, and social role changes.

The experiences common to all people in their passage through the life cycle give life some consistency; on the other hand, individual variations supply a measure of uniqueness to each person. We are all different, but we are not different in all ways. Yet we are like *all* others in that we are conceived and born in a given time period, we age, and we die.

Among the first theorists who studied human development, Sigmund Freud is probably the best known, especially for his descriptions of the developmental phases of childhood and adolescence. A contemporary of Freud's, Carl Jung, argued with the Freudian thinking that personality development ends in adolescence. A part of Jung's theory is that of personality balance. For example, **extroversion** and **introversion** in one person should be balanced for the optimal personality. His age-related theory is that young people are more extroverted. They are concerned with the external world of friends, mate selection, and jobs or careers. With age individuals become more introverted as they look within themselves to explore feelings about aging and mortality. The theory that individuals become more introverted with age (interiority) has become one of the most well-documented findings in personality research on aging (Cavanaugh, 1993, p. 259).

Erik Erikson is another well-known theorist. **Erikson's concept of stages** of human development extend beyond childhood and adolescence to include middle and old age (Erikson, 1963). Erikson recognized that personality development continues throughout the life cycle, and he believed that throughout eight psychosocial stages the individual continues to establish new orientations to self and the social world (see Table 3.1). Each of Erikson's stages may reach either a positive or a negative resolution. The first five psychosocial stages are similar to Freud's stages of psychosexual development. Identity development takes place during each stage: the completion of one stage lays the foundation for the successful completion of the next.

Erikson's last three stages deal with early, middle, and later adulthood. In early adulthood, intimacy versus isolation is the focus of psychosocial development. Relationships in friendship, sex, competition, and cooperation are emphasized. Mature, stable relationships tend to form in the late teens and twenties. According to Erikson, one's task in early adulthood is to first lose

Table 3.1	**Psychosocial Crisis**	**Age**	**Goal**
Erikson's Eight Stages	**1.** Basic trust vs. mistrust	0–1	Establish trust in parent/caretaker to meet basic needs vs. mistrust.
	2. Autonomy vs. shame and doubt	1–2	Develop will, independence, and self-control in such areas as toilet training vs. shame and doubt.
	3. Initiative vs. guilt	3–5	Learn to initiate interaction within family, develop language and conscience, gain sense of direction and purpose vs. guilt for being independent.
	4. Industry vs. inferiority	6–puberty	Develop interaction with teachers and peers, learn to accomplish tasks vs. feeling inferior and not trying to learn.
	5. Ego identity vs. role confusion	Adolescence	Interact primarily with peers. Develop heterosexual friendship. Integrate previous stages into unique sense of self vs. unresolved identity crisis.
	6. Intimacy vs. isolation	Early Adulthood	Develop intimate relationships with others, especially a member of opposite sex and begin to accept adult roles vs. remain isolated.
	7. Generativity vs. stagnation	Middle Adulthood	Have and care for children. Guide the future generation. Be productive and creative. Contribute to the world vs. being self-centered and unproductive.
	8. Ego integrity vs. despair	Late Adulthood	Reflect on one's place in the life cycle. Become assured that one's life had meaning. Face death with dignity and without fear vs. despair that life was useless.

and then find oneself in another, so that affiliation and love behaviors may be expressed. In middle adulthood the developmental task is generativity versus stagnation. *Generativity* involves a concern for the welfare of society rather than contentment with self-absorption. To create, to take care of, and to share are the positive outcomes of middle adulthood. Parenthood is a manifestation of generativity. With later adulthood, the psychosocial emphasis shifts to the considerations of being nearly finished with life and facing the reality of not being. The crisis of later adulthood is **integrity versus despair**. Erikson (1966) writes:

> It is acceptance of one's one and only life cycle as something that had to be and that, by necessity, permitted no substitutions. The lack or loss of this (accumulated) ego integration is signified by fear of death: the one and only life cycle is not accepted as the ultimate of life. Despair expresses the feeling that the time is now short, too short for the attempt to start another life and to try out alternate roads to integrity. Disgust hides this despair. Healthy children will not fear life if their elders have the **integrity** not to fear death.

We are fortunate if, in old age, our passage through the first seven stages has left us feeling fulfilled. On the positive side, one recognizes in this 8th stage that children provide continuity to life and that they, in turn, will perpetuate humankind. The negative resolution of this stage is one of meaninglessness and despair, the feeling that one's life has been useless. The final stage is one of reflection on major life efforts that are nearly complete. One observer said that this stage implies that the elderly are passive, that old age is a time for reflection, not action. Although Erikson does not deny that other activities are present, he does focus primarily on reflection at this stage of development (Erikson, 1982, 1985).

Nevertheless, Erikson does not exclude the possibility that reflection may also occur in earlier stages. Actually, one may take stock of one's life at any age. Resultant feelings, either despair or satisfaction, constitute the final stage. Further studies may better reveal how identity formations that begin in childhood continue or change throughout the life cycle. Such studies may also reveal at what point later-life orientations actually begin to develop.

Both Jung's and Erikson's theories are hard to test. However, their formulations give rise to many hypotheses concerning development of the basic personality orientations in childhood and in middle and old age. The works of Jung and Erikson represent theory. Ideally, the theories should be tested, corroborated, and refined using large samples of individuals over their lifetimes.

Loevinger (1976) extended the groundwork of Erikson. She proposed eight stages of **ego development**. The last level, the integrated stage, is achieved by very few people. They have a consolidated sense of identity and are at peace with themselves. They have resolved any inner conflicts. (This self-acceptance is rarely attained by people who are not old.) In the final stage they possess a greater understanding of their own dynamics and they mentally let go of the unattainable. Furthermore, they go beyond toleration of differences in others to cherish those differences. Being comfortable and secure with their individuality, they can reach outward to help others in a humanitarian way. Loevinger spent decades developing the Sentence Completion Test, which measures ego development. The measure consists of a sentence fragment (similar to "When I Think of Myself I _____") that respondents complete (Cavanaugh, 1993). Respondents are then scored for their level of ego development.

"Adult development" studies aging over the life course.

☼ Transitions in Adult Life: Developmental Patterns

Psychologists have drawn attention of the need for a **psychology of the life course**, a field of study called developmental psychology. This area of study concerns itself with continuity and discontinuity over time or, in other words, with stability versus change in personality and other psychological variables with age. Charting these changes brings a **developmental perspective** to the aging process. Prior developmental studies failed to sufficiently emphasize the fact that changes continue to occur in the last half of life. Psychologists are now concerned with middle and old age, in addition to childhood and adolescence.

The study of personality in middle and later life is sometimes referred to as *adult development*, an area of study receiving more and more attention. The word *transitions* is used to describe movement through the stages of the adult **life course**. (The concept of "life course" is preferred over "life cycle" as a way of deemphasizing the certainty of stages.) The developmental perspective focuses on the unfolding developmental process of the individual. As one matures, attitudes and behavior change in an orderly—or not-so-orderly—fashion.

At different **stages of adulthood**, we appear to have different levels of awareness of aging. Immediate concerns—careers, personal relationships, and leisure pursuits—tend to take up more of our time when we are younger. The most extensive preparation we may undergo for old age may come in our middle years, when we sense what is yet to happen to us, mentally and physically. As we grow older, we may experience an undercurrent of fear at the thought of aging. However, we may also experience awe, excitement, satisfaction, and anticipation. In any society, ageism encourages fear and dread while subordinating joy and excitement.

Disagreement also persists concerning the number of stages in the adult life course and the points at which they begin. Some people think that adulthood consists of four or more different life periods: young adulthood, maturity, middle age, and late adulthood (which can be divided into young-old and old-old). Others see only three categories: youth, middle age, and old age. Many young people connote middle age with being age 35 or thereabouts, whereas older people more often think of age 40, 45, or 50 as middle age; in other words, one's own age colors one's perceptions of the stage boundaries. We will now consider three broad stages of the life cycle: young adulthood, middle-age, and late adulthood. First, the point must be made that the developmental tasks in each stage are becoming less defined.

THE BLURRING OF LIFE PERIODS IN THE LIFE COURSE

The distinctions between life periods are becoming blurred. Some young people are postponing marriage and childbearing, and some may also experience a pattern of remarriage and divorce throughout their life courses. No longer is marriage necessarily reserved for young adulthood. Parenthood may happen at age 19 or age 38 or never. Consequently, one may be a grandparent for the first time before age 40, or after age 75, or not at all. People are also more flexible in entering and exiting jobs and careers. Some retire at age 50, whereas others start new careers at age 70 or beyond. Launching a new career is no longer the prerogative of the young, nor is education. Increasingly, people of all ages are attending school (Neugarten and Neugarten, 1986).

Events throughout the life course are becoming less predictable. Some teenagers face adulthood early by running away from home or by becoming emancipated minors. Others live at home for long periods, getting an education and saving money for a home. Teenage pregnancy forces some girls and boys into adulthood, whereas others delay taking on heavy family responsibilities until they are near age 40 or perhaps older. In some ways, even the line between childhood and adulthood is disappearing. Young girls rush into wearing makeup and adult clothing. Soap operas cater to young adolescents, and children know more about once-taboo topics, such as sex, drugs, suicide, and nuclear war. And divorce, no longer taboo for the older generation, is a common occurrence for married couples of all ages. Many older persons are changing their marital status—lifestyle—to "single" and making social adjustments once reserved for young adults. Our society is becoming more complex, and the developmental tasks that once seemed to be clearly in a set time frame no longer are.

YOUNG ADULTHOOD

Young adulthood comprises the years between 18 and 35 or so. A variety of challenging tasks present themselves at this time. Late adolescence in America often involves physical separation from one's family. College or military service can be the separating factor, or the young person may leave home to share an apartment or house with friends. Young people tend to have more friends than any other age group. This is perhaps to help them with the real task, which is one of psychological separation, of becoming an independent, autonomous person. Many adolescents find the passage stormy; identities are difficult to create when many options exist. "Who am I?" can bring much inner turmoil before an answer is formed.

Family and society have traditionally placed many "shoulds" on young

Family and society have traditionally placed many "shoulds" on young adults. After establishing an identity and an occupational goal, the young man or woman may be expected to finish his or her education, begin a job or career, get married, set up housekeeping, and have children. In the 1990s, however, the "shoulds" for getting married are not as strong as they once were. Young people are postponing the age at which they marry and the age at which they have a first child; they may even opt out of these activities altogether. Still, the average age for marriage in the United States is the mid-twenties, and for the birth of a first child, in the mid- to late-twenties.

When children do not follow the path expected by parents, generational clashes can ensue. Imelda H. from Houston, Texas, a 15-year-old girl, was told by her Mexican parents that she could not date until after her fifteenth birthday, an occasion to be celebrated by the quinceanera (a coming-of-age ritual for girls). On that day she wore a frilly dress and danced her first dance with her father. The day after, she told her parents she was pregnant and moving in with her boyfriend's father. The parents were devastated. Urban sociologists cite Imelda's example as one of the new generation of Mexican Americans shunning the old-country customs. The young generation is having more trouble assimilating than the older generation, because of the poor state of the American economy (Suro, 1992). Minority status can compound the difficulties in early adulthood.

Young adults, depending on their ethnicity, family resources, place of birth, and so on, have a relatively easy or difficult time maturing and finding a place in the world. Most are so busy coming to terms with life they are not consciously thinking about growing old. But when asked, they do express attitudes and opinions about aging.

Attitudes and opinions toward aging vary, as the responses of young sociology students show (Barrow, 1994). Students who were asked, "What is your personal reaction to growing old?" offered the following responses:

- As you get older, you become wise, less caring of time, and are not in a big rush as much as when you are younger.

- I can only hope that I find someone to marry that will love me in my old age. It's hard enough to grow old, but to do it alone would be just too unbearable.

- Growing old will be a lot easier to face if I feel that I've completed enough fulfilling things along the way. Right now I'm doing my best to make sure that happens.

- I look forward to growing old, simply to have the luxury of getting to live. I work as an AIDS hospice worker and watch young people die year after year.

- My first reaction will be can I take care of myself? Will I be a burden to someone? The fear of dying is not as great as growing old and having no one or being a burden.

- I personally hate the fact that I have to grow old. I look at elderly people and dread getting old. My biggest fear is looking old, being ugly and sick. I'm sure that sounds shallow but that's how I feel.

- Growing old scares me because I am scared to be alone. Being alone is the scariest thing that could happen to someone.

- How wrinkled will I get? Will I still want sex? Will I become a bitter old lady? How or when will I die? I just get so scared to even think of these things.

- One the one hand I look forward to being old and wise like my grandfather. But I don't want to die or become dependent on others. Or worse yet lose my memory and forget everything I learned from life.

- I enjoy growing older. The longer I am around, the more I know I don't know, and how much I can still learn. The older I get the more I see that there aren't any big deals. It's all just a movie, it's the journey, not the destination.

Although some responses show a degree of acceptance and anticipation of aging, others show fear. How and why do people come to fear aging? We can assume that fear and worry about aging does not make the coming stages of the life course easier. Apprehension makes every life stage more worrisome and less enjoyable. The two persons quoted above who were worried about getting wrinkled and ugly were female. Women seem to have the most fears, because their aging is judged more harshly by society. In other words, they, indeed, have more to fear.

A MIDLIFE CRISIS?

Gail Sheehy, in her book *Passages* (1976), terms the time between ages 35 and 45 the "deadline decade." Not much thought is given to aging during the teens and twenties, writes Sheehy; but in the thirties we realize we have reached a halfway mark; "yet even as we are reaching our prime, we begin to see there is a place where it finishes. Time starts to squeeze" (p. 244). She continues.

> The loss of youth, the faltering of physical powers we have always taken for granted, the fading purpose of sterotyped roles in which we have thus far identified ourselves, the spiritual dilemma of having no answers—any or all of these shocks can give this passage the character of crisis.

Sheehy observes that the years spanning the ages of 37 and 42 are a time of **midlife crisis**, the "peak years of anxiety for almost everyone." Although she does not claim that everyone experiences a midlife crisis, she has observed that many, if not most, people find it difficult to face their own aging during these years. She further states that somewhere between the ages of 35 and 45, if we permit ourselves to do so, most of us will have a full-out authenticity crisis, during which we may, as we did in adolescence, find ourselves desperately seeking to define our identity and purpose:

> I have reached some sort of meridian in my life. I had better take a survey, reexamine where I have been, and reevaluate how I am going to spend my resources from now on. Why am I doing all this? What do I really believe in? Underneath this vague feeling is the fact, as yet unacknowledged, that there is a down side to life, a back of the mountain, and that I have only so much time before the dark to find my own truth. (Sheehy, 1976, p. 242)

However, few corresponding scientific studies state unequivocally that age crises are to be expected within given time intervals for every individual. Soon after the publication of *Passages*, controversy ensued over whether the midlife crisis occurs or not.

Most studies have found the midlife crisis to exist for a minority of individuals and to take place, not just between ages 35 and 45, but anytime between, 30 and 60. Even before 30 some individuals refer to an "early midlife crisis," and others after 60 to a "late midlife crisis," thus rendering midlife as a factor predicting an age crisis virtually meaningless.

The words *transition* or *shift*, rather than *crisis*, more aptly describe the midlife experiences of most individuals. Everyone agrees that we all make many transitions in life, and young adulthood to middle age is one of them. The new perspective views **midlife transitions** as normal situations likely to confront anyone. Such times, which are marked by feelings of uncertainty and instability, eventually result in some kind of adaptation. Whether a midlife age transition becomes a crisis may depend, in part, on the attitudes toward aging that formed early in life. Some people reflect on aging and its consequences early. Others have their heads in the sand. They ignore aging and the passing of time until forced to consider them. Many people are reluctant to think of themselves as aging or old until something penetrates the defenses: a new wrinkle; not knowing any Top Forty tunes; having a doctor who looks too young to have graduated from medical school; being older than coworkers' parents; or the death of a close friend. Body changes or external events may bring such a shocked awareness of aging that it becomes a genuine crisis. For others, the awareness of aging may be gradual and continuous. For one author, midlife was not a crisis, but became rather, a "quest." He was so busy denying his age and avoiding a midlife crisis that he almost risked missing a new venture—starting over at midlife and experiencing new opportunities and transformations (Gerzon, 1990).

MIDDLE AGE

Middle age is an interesting period: the *transition* between young adulthood and old age. Yet it is often stereotyped as being dull, boring, routine. On the contrary, many exciting changes are possible at this time. Furthermore, our reactions and adjustments to changes in middle age surely affect our reactions and adjustments to old age, just as our response to aging at any point surely affects the points that follow.

Those in their middle years frequently accomplish or conclude certain developmental tasks. Most people typically spend their twenties settling down and become further established in their thirties, forties, and fifties. This frequently becomes a time to buy a house and settle into a job or career. In middle age, individuals may find their occupations rewarding but more demanding. Those who are married may feel satisfaction or discontent, and those who have not married and settled may feel a stronger push to do so. Age norms constrain those who do not fill the appropriate social role at the appropriate time, and those not following the socially approved course may suffer various negative labels. Those with alternative lifestyles, histories of unemployment, or no or many marriages are looked on as outside the norm by some and frowned on by others. In this case, these middle-aged persons have to defend their lifestyles.

New role changes and events generally occur in the forties and fifties. Our parents are likely to be in their old age, and this is our time to cope with their old age and eventual death. They, in turn, have to confront the reality of their children's middle age. Many new books attempt to act as guides for middle-aged children who are helping and coping with older parents. The death of contemporaries brings additional evidence that one cannot live forever.

Grown children launch out on their own. This event can be sad and depressing, a relief, or a mixture of both. Though the postparental period has often been described negatively, for many this new freedom is cause for a celebration rather than a crisis, depending on their outlook and, perhaps, on their ability to redefine their goals and purpose in life.

For those who have jobs or careers, the forties and fifties are generally also a time of experiencing peaks, or at least of evaluating a present occupation's potential for status, money, or power. This is a time to come to terms with what is not possible. We may acknowledge, at this point, the impossibility of becoming president of the company or of fulfilling any one of a host of goals. Those who are unemployed or in low-paying jobs may have more trouble squaring their dreams with reality. Aligning our dreams with the facts can be a large task or a small one, depending on the dreams and the degree of success we expect. Some individuals have both the inner strengths (self-confidence and motivation) and outer resources (monetary savings) to find new jobs or careers in their forties and fifties. However, those seeking new lines of work sometimes must forfeit seniority and retirement benefits from their original-career companies. Changing jobs may require risk taking and sacrifice and, for many, can literally be a time for starting over.

Middle age brings biological changes, as well as changes in career and family. For women, menopause is a biological reminder of aging. Menopause means that the childbearing years are over. At this time, women may experience physical symptoms that result from changes in hormone levels. Hormone replacement therapy helps many of those who have problems, but may have some risks. The matter is still under study. The possible discomfort (hot and cold flashes, etc.), along with the infertility that accompanies menopause is biological evidence of transition. It is a time of reflection and coming to terms with the ending of one stage of life and the beginning of another. Women in their forties and fifties may mourn the loss of their fertility, but at the same time be relieved. Women, and sometimes their partners, need reassurance that menopause does not, in itself, diminish sexuality. Rather, it can free partners from concern about pregnancy; and many couples report improved love lives after menopause.

Karp (1988) provides a symbolic interactionist perspective from which to view the middle-aged years from age 50 to 60. He describes these years as a

Each decade of adult life brings new opportunities and challenges. Lifelong dreams can be fulfilled.

decade of reminders that bring age consciousness to new heights. These reminders come from the reflections of self that come from the appraisals of other people, a "looking-glass self" who gives rise to self-appraisals about aging. Those in their fifties who were studied by Karp were surprised by their own aging. In their minds, they were young; but either their bodies or people around them were giving them different messages. A man who played on a basketball team was referred to as "sir" by a younger team member. Others were also treated deferentially because of their age.

One category of reminders was generational—fiftieth birthday bashes that seemed to center on the fact that the birthday "boy" or "girl" had made it to the "big 5-0"; the realization that children had grown up and were independent; having grandchildren; or losing parents and consequently becoming the oldest family member. A contextual category of reminders included such situations as being the oldest member of various groups and clubs; concern about going to places such as singles dances or bars where most people were young (for fear of standing out in the crowd); or being old enough to be the parent or grandparent of students, clients, or patients. Finally, mortality reminders came from friends and peers who died, emphasizing the point that life is finite, not infinite.

The age consciousness in Karp's study was not necessarily a negative commentary on aging. For many in their fifties, middle age was a time of personal liberation. Several respondents described a feeling of wisdom, of seeing their lives in a larger, more holistic way. Many were enjoying their "empty nests" and leading personally rewarding lives. Some researchers find the 50's to be the happiest time of life. Responsibilities may ease, and there may be more freedom to do as one pleases without such strong expectations from others (Gallagher, 1993).

LATE ADULTHOOD

Late adulthood is the developmentalist's phrase for the stage of the life course following one's sixty-fifth birthday. Some gerontologists divide late adulthood into "later maturity," which begins in the sixties, and "old age," which typically occurs in the late seventies. Early gerontological studies described late adulthood in rather negative terms calling for adjustment to role losses: loss of job, death of friends, death of spouse, and loss of health status. More recent studies document a remarkable ability of aging persons to adjust to role changes. Losses tend to be counterbalanced with gains: the death of spouse, for example, commonly leads to remarriage. Retirement from a full-time career may lead to part-time work at the same place or another job elsewhere, or to the expansion of a hobby. Loss of friends calls for the making of new friends. Women in the Wellesley Senior Citizen poetry writing group each wrote one line to finish the sentence "Aging is _____." Here are some lines from their poem.

Aging is:

sometimes a slide, sometimes a climb

coming to the last lines of the melody of life

a pain in every joint

another blessed open door

the small mysteries

enjoying a wonderful life

what happens to my body while my inner child stays young and beautiful
(*Jacobs, 1993, p. 199–200*)

These lines reflect more transitions than losses. Certainly, becoming a grandparent is a role addition, not a role loss. The roles of parent and grandparent vary widely in the amount of time and emotional energy they consume. Some grandparents are primary caretakers of grandchildren whose parents are on drugs, have AIDS, or are otherwise disabled. A 65-year-old child of 85-year-old parents may be involved in full-time care of his or her mother, father, or both. Therefore, we cannot assume that family roles are lost in late adulthood. Sometimes it does happen that way, however. For example, a move to a retirement community out of state or a move to Mexico, where living costs are lower, puts distance between older adults and their children or parents.

Extreme old age is a very special time. In his nineties, Erikson wrote from personal experience about the final stage of the life cycle model that he presented with the help of his wife, Joan, forty years earlier. He expanded on his late life stage, "integrity versus despair," by describing the wisdom that comes with age if one completes the developmental tasks that began earlier in the life cycle. For example, the basic trust learned in infancy evolves into the knowledge, in old age, of how interdependent we are, that is, of how much we need each other. In early childhood, the life cycle's second phase, learning physical autonomy and control of one's bodily functions, versus shame and doubt in not learning them, paves the way for coping with deterioration of the body in old age. Old age is basically the second phase in reverse. One must "grow" in order to avoid the shame and doubt that often accompany deterioration, just as one "learned" bodily development without having shame and doubt. Every stage offers lessons that can apply in old age.

In old age, we develop humility by comparing our early hopes and dreams with the life we actually lived. Humility is a realistic appreciation of our limits and competencies. On the individual level, in old age, one often achieves a sense of integrity, a sense of completeness, of personal wholeness strong enough to offset the downward psychological pull of inevitable physical disintegration (Goleman, 1988).

On the social level, however, Erikson sees a widespread failing in modern life: lack of regard for future generations. The only thing that can save the species is "generativity"—the promotion of positive values in the next generation. Unfortunately, greed and the depletion of the earth's resources are accomplishing the opposite.

Other social scientists have expanded on Erikson's model and have developed ways of testing it. For example, one retirement study that applied Erikson's concepts (Anatovsky and Sagy, 1990) set four developmental tasks for the retiring person: (1) deciding what to do with one's time (active involvement); (2) reevaluating one's life (reevaluation of life satisfaction); (3) developing a sense of coherence and wholeness about one's place in the world (reevaluation of a world outlook); and (4) developing a sense of the importance of good health (sense of health maintenance). These four tasks are a more detailed analysis of Erikson's final stage, integrity versus despair.

Becoming Sixty
■ *Ruth Harriet Jacobs*

There were terror and anger
at coming into sixty,
Would I give birth
only to my old age?

Now near sixty-one
I count the gifts
that sixty gave.

A book flowed from my life
to those who needed it
and love flowed back to me.

In a yard that had seemed full
space for another garden appeared.
I took my aloneness to Quaker meeting
and my outstretched palms were filled.

I walked further along the beach
swam longer in more sacred places
danced the spiral dance
reclaimed daisies for women
in my ritual for a precious friend
and received poet's wine
from a new friend who came
in the evening of my need.

From *Be an Outrageous Older Woman: A R.A.S.P. Remarkable Aging Smart Person.* K.I.T. Press, Manchester, Conn. 1993.

As a result of the longer life expectancy in the late twentieth century, most Americans can expect to pass through these age-linked events: long-term survival, empty nest, retirement, and an extended term of widowhood characterized by solitary living. Actually, a transition can be movement either from one age to another or from one age-linked event to another (e.g., children leave home or a spouse dies).

People in their seventies, as Erikson said, may be thoughtful and reflective about their lives, making transitions, in a sense, in their minds. Those who turn age 80 often feel pride in their longevity and newfound freedom. Every decade has its share of tasks and challenges. In later life, illness, death of a spouse, or increased frailty may take its toll; but personal growth and joy in living is still possible and probable. While Socrates awaited death in prison, at the age of 71, he was learning to play the lyre. Transitions do not end at age 65; we continue making them until the final transition. We can begin early in life to teach ourselves and our children that growing older is a natural event, one not to be feared, but rather one to be anticipated for new roles, new avenues of expressions, and new opportunities.

☼ Continuity Theory

Continuity theory is broad enough to be considered a sociological theory as well as a psychological one. Continuity theorists propose that a person's adaptations to young adulthood and middle age predict that person's general pattern of adaptation to old age. According to continuity theory, the personality formed early in life continues throughout the life span with no basic changes. This theory implies that neither activity nor disengagement theory explains adjustment to aging: adjustment depends on personality patterns of one's former years. This approach is consistent with the core of personality theory. Some therapists believe that significant personality change after about the age of 30 is unlikely. And, although some researchers continue to debate the degree to which the personality remains stable throughout the life course, continuity theory maintains that the individual achieves a core personality by adulthood. By adulthood people have adopted coping mechanisms, established stress and frustration tolerance levels, and defined ego defenses.

Researchers McCrae and Costa (1987) have said that lives change, but personality does not. They found, for example, that agreeability and conscientiousness are two personality characteristics that seem to remain stable over time. In fact, most psycho- and socio-biologists believe many aspects of personality and temperament to be inborn. Characteristics such as fearfulness, hostility, or being moody, critical, shy, introverted, or brooding can be evidenced in early childhood and seem to persist over the life course. The same is true for opposite characteristics, such as bravery.

Those who argue with the continuity theorists point to individuals who have made seemingly dramatic personality changes later in life. Consider this quote by Elia Kazan (at age 78), a noted Hollywood film director, when interviewed about his biography:

> I don't know any other biography that is so candid as mine. It was a hard journey getting to this point. For a lot of my youth, I didn't like myself. I thought, "I'm not as good as other filmmakers." But now I think I don't have to compare myself with anybody. I'm not afraid of anything and don't feel hostile to a soul in the world, which is new for me. (Kazan in conversation with reporter Alvin Sanoff about his biography, *Elia Kazan: A Life*, 1988)

It would appear that Kazan has become more open, more self-accepting, less hostile, and less fearful. Continuity theorists might respond to this quote by saying that we can at least make minor modifications to our personalities. Studies show that personality shortcomings can be addressed and, to some extent, overcome. With effort, tempers can be controlled, fears lessened, organization learned, and social skills practiced; thus, personalities can improve with age.

☼ Personality and Coping

THE MAAS-KUYPERS STUDY

The Maas-Kuypers study, which observed personality change in women and men over a 40-year period, found personality to be stable throughout adulthood. Evidence in the research suggested that "qualities of life in old age are, indeed, highly associated, in complex ways, to qualities of life 40 years earlier" (Maas and Kuypers, 1977). Those who had negative attributes in young adulthood had various negative personality characteristics in old age; fearful oldsters were rigid, apathetic, and melancholy as young mothers; anxious mothers were restless and dissatisfied in old age; the defensive elderly were withdrawn in early adulthood. The personality types that seemed most firmly connected to early adult-life behaviors were those with the most "negative" features. On the positive side, cheerfulness, lack of worries, and self-assurance in young adulthood seemed to match high self-esteem and self-satisfaction in old age.

THE ELDER-LIKER STUDY

Another 40-year longitudinal study assessed the **coping** mechanisms and consequences for women who lived through the Great Depression of the 1930s (Elder and Liker, 1982). During the Depression, financial losses were more severe for working-class women than for middle-class women; and many working-class women, lacking the educational, financial, or emotional resources to master their circumstances, were too hard hit to make a comeback. The researchers suggest that the hardship of the Depression offered these women a trial run through the inevitable losses of old age. Economic hardships meant new challenges for women: coping with unemployed husbands, taking in boarders for pay, looking for work, borrowing money from relatives, and getting along on less by reducing purchases to a bare minimum. In short, women had to become more self-reliant.

The women under study experienced the Depression as young married adults in their early childbearing years. On the whole, the Depression diminished the emotional health of the lower-status women but increased that of the middle-class women. The middle-class women who struggled through hard times turned out to be more self-assured and cheerful than a "control" group of women who had not been deprived. They were also less fretful, less worrisome, and less bothered by the limitations and demands of living. Hard times left them more resourceful, with more vitality and self-confidence. In contrast, Depression losses added to the psychological disadvantage of working-class women, lowering their self-esteem and increasing their feelings of insecurity and dissatisfaction with life.

The conclusion was that a life history of mastery enables women to manage traumatic experiences throughout their lives. Women like the middle-class women in the study are lucky if they have the resources for such mastery—economic resources do matter significantly. Coping skills are acquired in hard times, not in tranquil ones. One who experiences no hard times until old age, may not have developed coping skills. "Neither a privileged life nor one of unrelenting deprivation assures the inner resources for successful aging" (Elder and Liker, 1982).

A review of personality research revealing dramatic support for the resiliency of personality throughout life offered two conclusions: (1) we should get help for undesirable characteristics because bad traits are unlikely to change by themselves, and (2) the adjusted and cheerful will generally remain so for life in spite of any adverse circumstances brought about by time or aging (Costa and McCrae, 1987).

THE BALTIMORE STUDY

The Baltimore Longitudinal Study of Aging, spanning 30 years, confirmed that personality remains remarkably stable with aging. A cheerful, optimistic young person usually remains so throughout life. And, conversely, a negative person maintains pessimism (Shock et al., 1989).

Similarly, a study of 216 lower middle class individuals over a 12-year period suggested that continuity is the norm in personal functioning. Stress, however, altered this pattern. With high exposure to stress, morale and self-concept deteriorated. For example, severe health or personal problems inclined a person's outlook on life toward anxiety and lower self-confidence (Fiske and Chiriboga, 1990).

ADAPTING TO LOSS

A study monitoring the stress patterns experienced when relocated to different nursing homes found the very old to be unique. Continuity theory did not apply. Their roles had changed, their bodies had declined, important people in their lives had died. Issues of finitude and death were close to their hearts. Thus, the psychology of the very old assumes new dimensions. Discontinuity with earlier periods of life is the rule as the very old adapt to stresses such as relocation. Their coping patterns have changed, and their psychological survival seems to hinge on preserving a sense of self. For those in the study, survival strategies involved adopting myths of control and turning to their past to maintain self-identity. In other words, imagining themselves to be in control of their health and surroudings, and "living in the past" were successful coping strategies (Lieberman and Tobin, 1983).

Emotional problems are not physical in origin, but they may be related to physical losses. The older one is, the more likely one is to face physical disability and imminent death. Loss of hearing, loss of vision, and loss of the use of limbs have a strong psychological impact at any age. So does being told you have only five years, six months, or two weeks to live. Denial, depression, anger—even rage—are common responses.

Other age-related losses are the death of a spouse, the deaths of siblings, and the deaths of friends. Retirement, the loss of one's driver's license, the sale of the home, or a move to an institution are the types of losses that scare people about aging. They do not happen to every older person, but the longer a person lives, the more likely they are to happen. There is a considerable difference between the young-old (65 to 74) and the old-old (75 and over) as to the losses they can expect. In fact, by comparison, the young-old experience very few losses.

Numerous studies have shown that older persons, on the whole, adapt well to loss. Most elderly persons adapt to the loss of their spouse without severe psychiatric repercussions. However, the initial period of widowhood can be especially difficult. During the first year of widowhood, there are high incidences of psychological and physical symptoms, an increase in the use of psychiatric services, and an increased risk of suicide.

Those who experience emotional problems, with widowhood and with other losses, should reach out for help. A therapist, for example, may counsel an older woman who has undergone a mastectomy. She may feel a loss of femininity as a result of her surgery; she may be depressed, angry, or anxious. If family members are supportive and her attitude is positive, her loss can be minimized. However, if her husband, for example, is negative or rejecting, then she will have greater problems recovering emotionally.

Those in counseling and related fields should not regard elders as untreatable; nor should they have expectations for recovery that are too high or too low. Older persons can—and do—rebound after grieving over loss.

PERSONALITY THEORY

There are certain stereotypes of personality change in old age, none of which are supported conclusively by research findings. Old people were once thought to become more rigid or set in their ways, stubborn, grouchy, and crotchety. Studies lend little or no support to such changes as a natural consequence of the aging process.

With regard to learning, personality is an influential variable. Interest, motivation, self-esteem, rigidity, flexibility, cautiousness, fearfulness, and anxiety all affect one's ability to learn. Old people vary in personality characteristics just as young people do.

Personality theory focuses on the many traits of individual personality, such as friendliness, shyness, humor, and aggressiveness. The study of personality has been a major focus of developmentalists who analyze personality and personality change over the life course. Theorists have used personality variables to explain why some older individuals withdraw from society whereas others do not, and why some individuals are satisfied with an active lifestyle whereas others prefer noninvolvement. Personality theorists generally use personality characteristics to explain why some people readily adapt to and cope with aging and why others have problems.

Personality studies show that many older individuals are mature, focused types, happy and satisfied with life. But others are striving, defensive about aging, and discontent. Some are very passive types who depend on others. They may be apathetic and bored much of the time. They may see the

WHAT STAGE OF LIFE ARE YOU IN, AUNT LIZ

MY PRESENT STAGE OF LIFE IS...

EVALUATION CONTINUING GROWTH AND IMMENSE GRATITUDE...

FOR BEING ALIVE!

world as collapsing and become preoccupied with holding on to what they have. The most disorganized personalities suffer major impairments to their mental health and cannot function outside a mental hospital.

A constricted or rigid personality type has a difficult time dealing with change. In contrast, a flexible personality type adapts to change, whether it be positive or negative (such as widowhood, ailing health, or shrinking finances). An extensive longitudinal study of personalities grouped them into five categories:

1. Neurotic—characterized by feelings of anxiety, worry, hostility, and depression.

2. Extroverted—characterized by tendencies to be outgoing, active, and assertive.

3. Open—characterized by receptiveness to new experiences, new ideas, and change.

4. Agreeable–Antagonistic—Antagonistic types tend to set themselves against the grain and be opposed to others, whereas agreeable types are pleasers. Antagonists may be skeptical, mistrustful, stubborn, and rude.

5. Conscientious–Undirected—The conscientious are hardworking and responsible. They have a drive to achieve. The undirected have no focus and tend to be lackadaisical and aimless (Costa and McCrae, 1987).

The personality traits in the many studies reviewed by Costa and McCrae show astonishing stability. The traits remained consistent over time, and individuals who were extroverted and open experienced less stress as they aged.

LOCUS OF CONTROL

The personality characteristic, **locus of control**, is a concept that came under heavy scrutiny in the 1980s and continues to be examined in the 1990s. Locus, or center, of control may be perceived as internal if the person sees that his or her own actions bring about a reward or positive change. If, however, the person sees rewards as due to fate, luck, change, or powerful others, the locus of control is external. Research has found locus of control to be a long-standing personality component developed over years of positive and negative reinforcement. A person with an internal locus of control feels more control over the environment and is more likely to attempt to improve his or her condition.

Studies show that older people experience higher life satisfaction if they possess an internal locus of control. Thus, both psychologists and sociologists have reason to study locus of control. Changes in the social environment can facilitate the development of internal control. By allowing older individuals more self-determination and administration on policies that affect them and by increasing their involvement, control, and power in all aspects of their social and political lives, we can help them to develop greater satisfaction with their lives.

An older person who has received positive support from a cohesive family tends to have a strong internal locus of control. Social support, such as tangible assistance and emotional help, also tends to increase feelings of control, but only to a point. Beyond this point, additional support can decrease feelings of personal control. We need a word of caution concerning beliefs about both extreme internal and external loci of control: both extremes may hinder older adults' abilities to cope with stressful life events.

☼ Researching Developmental Models of Aging

The developmental model emphasizes the psychology of the individual. The developmentalists, who look at how individuals change throughout the life course, focus on the individual by studying variables such as personality, motivation, cognition, and morale. Social and cultural factors are examined for their role in personality changes. Maturation, or some inherent biological mechanism, may also be a strong force in creating change in persons as they progress through life. As theoretical models of aging are set forth, empirical studies test and refine them; such studies have yet to uncover which attitudes and behaviors throughout the aging process are intrinsic, or biologically based, and which are formed extrinsically by changes in social structures and social roles.

One example is research testing the hypothesis that men and women become more androgynous (having both male and female traits) as they age. It is thought that, starting in adolescence, males suppress feminine aspects and females suppress their maleness. As one ages, one may become more self-accepting and more comfortable exploring all sides to one's personality. Both sexes move psychologically closer to middle ground (Gutmann, 1987). The reasons may be intrinsic, that is, related to the biological aging process; or they may be due to lessened social constraints. Older men may be freer to give love and tenderness to their grandchildren than they were to their own children; and women may become more assertive and confident, not because of the aging process, but because they have ended parenting roles and entered the job market. Gutmann's research based on cross-cultural data shows that social structural events, not age per se, affect adult development and personality.

Chapter Summary

This chapter considers the human life course from the developmental point of view. From the developmental view, every individual passes through stages in his or her own life course. Internal or biological changes occur as we age, which affect the way we behave. Expected behavior patterns exist at every level of adulthood, whether young adulthood or advanced middle age. Ageism in a society leads to a fear of aging, which some individuals experience to a greater degree than others. Some individuals experience a midlife crisis when they try to come to grips with aging.

From psychologists comes personality theory, which draws attention to how personality changes as a function of age and how individual variations in personality may affect one's own aging process. Also from psychology is the continuity theory, which suggests that personality remains stable throughout life. Personality and the struggle to cope with the world interact to shape the aging process. Studies of locus of control determine the degree to which older people feel in control of their lives. Research on developmental models continues.

Key Terms

coping
developmental perspective
ego development
Erikson's concept of stages
extroversion
integrity versus despair
introversion
life course

life cycle
locus of control
midlife crises
midlife transitions
personality theory
psychology of the life course
stages of adulthood

Questions for Discussion

1. Why do some individuals have difficulty making the transition from early adulthood to middle age? From middle age to old age?

2. How do you, did you, or will you feel about reaching age 30? 40? 65? Do you know of anyone who went through a midlife crisis? Explain. What are, or were, your parents' and grandparents' reactions to their own aging?

3. What is your personal reaction to someone who tries to appear younger than he or she is?

4. What personality variables would you choose to examine in a longitudinal study of students throughout their lives? Why?

Fieldwork Suggestions

1. Interview someone who is age 65 or older. Ask what tasks and challenges that person faces. Is he or she in transition? From what and to what?

2. Interview a woman who has gone through menopause. Compare her expectations with the realities.

3. Ask ten middle-aged or older women their ages. Did you violate a norm? Did they answer you? What was their reaction?

4. Interview or survey people who have gray hair. What was their reaction to getting their first gray hairs?

References

Antonovsky, A., and S. Sagy. "Confronting Developmental Tasks in the Retirement Transition." *Gerontologist* 30:3 (June 1990): 362–368.

Barrow, Georgia. *Personal Reactions to Growing Old.* Unpublished. Santa Rosa, CA: Santa Rosa Junior College, 1994.

Cavanaugh, J. *Adult Development.* Pacific Grove, CA: Brooks/Cole, 1993.

Costa, P., and R. McCrae. "The Case for Personality Stability." In *Aging, the Universal Human Experience*, edited by G. Maddox and E. Busse, New York: Springer, 1987.

Elder, G., and J. Liker. "Hard Times in Women's Lives: Historical Influences Across Forty Years." *American Journal of Sociology* (1982): 241–267.

Erikson, Erik H. *Childhood and Society.* 2d ed. New York: Norton, 1963.

———. "Eight Ages of Man." *International Journal of Psychiatry* 2 (1966): 281–297.

———. *The Life Cycle Completed: A Review.* New York: Norton, 1982, 1985 (Parts 1 and 2).

Fiske, M., and D. Chriboga. *Change and Continuity in Adult Life.* San Francisco, CA: Jossey-Bass, 1990.

Gallagher, W. "Midlife Myths." *The Atlantic* 271:5 (May 1993): 51–63.

Gerzon, M. "Starting Over at Midlife: Why There's More Satisfaction to Life After 40." *Utne Reader* (January/ February 1990).

Goleman, D. "Erikson, in His Own Old Age, Expands His View of Life." *The New York Times* (14 June 1988).

Gutmann, D. *Reclaimed Powers: Toward a New Psychology of Men and Women in Later Life.* New York: Harper & Row, 1987.

Jacobs, R. Be An Outrageous Older Woman. Manchester, CT: Knowledge, Ideas, and Trends, 1993.

Karp, D. A. "A Decade of Reminders: Changing Age Consciousness Between Fifty and Sixty Years Old." *Gerontologist* 28:6 (1988): 727–738.

Kazan, Elia. Quoted in interview with Alvin P. Sanoff. "Famed Director Reflects on Hollywood Life." *San Francisco Chronicle* (19 June 1988): 11.

Lieberman, M., and S. Tobin. *The Experience of Old Age: Stress, Coping, and Survival.* New York: Basic Books, 1983.

Loevinger, J. *Ego Development.* San Francisco: Jossey-Bass, 1976.

Maas, H. S., and J. A. Kuypers. *From Thirty to Seventy.* San Francisco: Jossey-Bass, 1977.

Maslow, Abraham H. *Motivation and Personality.* New York: Harper and Row, 1954.

Neugarten, Bernice L., and Dail A. Neugarten. "Age in the Aging Society." *Daedalus Issue: The Aging Society* 115 (Winter 1986): 31–50.

Sheehy, Gail. *Passages: Predictable Crises from Adult Life.* New York: E. P. Dutton, 1976.

Shock, Nathan, et al. *Older and Wiser: The Baltimore Longitudinal Study.* Washington, DC: U.S. Department of Health and Human Services, 1989, HIN pub. no. 89-1797.

Suro, Roberto. "Generational Chasm Leads to Cultural Turmoil." *New York Times* (20 January 1992): A16(L).

Further Readings

··········

Aldwin, C. *Stress, Coping, and Development.* New York: Guilford Publications, Inc., 1994.

Callahan, J. *Menopause: A Midlife Passage.* Bloomington: Indiana University Press, 1993.

Cohen, S. and Reese, J. eds. *Life Span Developmental Psychology: Methodological Contributions.* Hillsdale, NJ: Lawrence Erlbaum, 1994.

Davis, N. *Faces of Women and Aging.* New York: Haworth Press, 1993.

Hockey, J., and A. James. *Growing Up and Growing Old.* Newbury Park, CA: Sage 1993.

$\mathcal{T}$heoretical Frameworks

CHAPTER OUTLINE
■ Activity versus Disengagement ■ Psychological Well-Being ■ Structural-Functional Frameworks ■ Age Groupings ■ Exchange Theory ■ Meaning in Everyday Life ■ Critical Gerontology ■ Pure versus Applied Research ■ The Future of Social Gerontology

A Generation Gap Is Widening in Israel as Ages React Differently to Violence

■ AMY DOCKSER MARCUS

JERUSALEM—When a lone Palestinian stabbed five teenagers and their principal at a high school in Jerusalem, Prime Minister Yitzhak Rabin criticized the students for running away instead of attempting to stop the knife-wielding attacker.

The prime minister urged students to get hand-to-hand combat training. Israelis, he said, must return to being a "fighting nation." In one speech, the 70-year-old Mr. Rabin said, "I belong to the generation of 1948," referring to the generation of young people who fought underground for the establishment of Israel in the country's War of Independence.

"If we were of (today's) kind, I'm not sure the country would have been established. Where is the Israeli public?"

Israeli Prime Minister Yitzhak Rabin listens to questions at a news conference.

Markedly Different Values

Answers to Mr. Rabin's question can be found in part at the Canion Jerusalem, the Middle East's largest shopping mall, which opened only a few days before the late March terrorist attack at the high school. The $80 million Canion contains 196 shops, an eight-screen movie theater, and a fast-food section with a good view of the Judean Hills. The mall also offers a glimpse of the Israel of Mr. Rabin's grandchildren, a generation whose self-image and values differ markedly from his own.

"What does Rabin want from us?" asked one 16-year-old boy working the costume jewelry counter and sporting two silver hoops dangling from his ear and blond bangs falling over his eyes. "You can't compare the two generations. Today, kids in Israel are like kids in America, or anywhere else in the world. We like discos, playing basketball and going to the mall. We're not interested in learning hand-to-hand combat."

Fifteen Israelis have been killed in attacks in recent weeks, one of the highest death tolls since the outbreak of the Palestinian intifada, or uprising, five years ago; 26 Palestinians also have been killed.

Public Anger, Despair

The Rabin government has to cope with public anger and despair over the almost daily shootings and stabbings.

In addition to the closure of the West Bank and the Gaza Strip, soldiers and other security personnel are now authorized to shoot armed Palestinians, even if they don't actually threaten to open fire, and more army units are being deployed in the occupied territories.

In speeches attempting to rally public morale, Mr. Rabin frequently harkens back to the Zionist ethos of an earlier era, when Israel still was shaped by spartan pioneering values, rather than those of the modern Western consumer. Paramilitary training programs for high school students, which had been severely cut back in the past, will be reintroduced after Passover. "Youths aged 16, 17, and 18 must take part when it is a case of defending the school, even with sticks if necessary. We've done so in the past. There's no reason not to do so now," said Mr. Rabin.

—Continued

Affluence vs. Zionism

The prime minister's apparent surprise at the reaction of Israeli youth to the current wave of terror illustrates the tensions marking a society whose new level of affluence has apparently come at the expense of some of the more traditional Zionist notions. "I think the prime minister was slightly disappointed with the fact that teenagers aged 16 to 18 made comments which could be interpreted as if they expect that everything will be done for them, as if they aren't part of the general effort (against terrorism)," said Gad Ben-Ari, Mr. Rabin's media adviser, reflecting on the prime minister's criticism after the stabbings at the high school.

"Yitzhak Rabin and his generation preach self-sacrifice but live in the best neighborhoods in Israel and drive posh cars with cellular telephones," says Yossi Melman, 42, whose book "The New Israelis" chronicles the new generation. "The teenagers see this and their values reflect it."

Sitting in a coffee house in Ramat Aviv, Mr. Melman says this affluent bedroom community outside Tel Aviv is representative of what he calls the "Subaru Syndrome," the Japanese car that has become the symbol for the average Israeli's suburban dream of a house, a garden, and a car in the garage. "Israeli's have gotten used to the good life and now Rabin is saying that all citizens need to be on alert and fully mobilized. It's hard to reverse directions," says Mr. Melman.

Articulating Values

Novelist Meir Shalev wrote that the current situation results from the government's failure to articulate Israeli society's values and future direction. "Rabin and his generation can't expect Israeli youth to have a will to fight and the endurance and stamina that come from an inner belief unless they are shown a direction and something to believe in," said Mr. Shalev, 45, in an interview.

"Maybe what's happening now will shake up society," he said. "The fact is that there are young people with values and stamina and the will to fight—but they're Arabs. It's the Palestinians now who feel they have something worth fighting for." ☀

SOURCE: *Wall Street Journal*, 8 April 1993, p. A10.

*W*hat happens to people as they grow old? What methods can we use to study old people—their bodies, their perceptions, their motivations, their relationship to society? These topics are the subject matter of gerontology. By omitting the physiology and biology of aging, we narrow the field to social aspects of aging. **Social gerontology,** the study of aging from a social science perspective, has been recognized as a distinct area of study for less than 60 years. Aging and related subjects have received limited attention since the mid-1940s, but now the sharp rise in the number of older persons, along with their increased visibility, has increased interest in the development of theory and in research. Social gerontology will continue to grow in importance as it becomes increasingly able to explain the phenomenon of aging.

In an effort to explain aging, social gerontologists have developed numerous theories to examine how people respond to the aging process. Strictly speaking, a **theory** is a set of statements, logically interconnected and interrelated propositions that explain why an event, or a set of events, occurs. A scientific theory differs from ideas or guesses in that it (1) must begin with generalized propositions about the concepts being studied (the propositions, in turn, must be capable of being rejected); (2) must answer how and why relationships occur among the concepts; and (3) must be testable through empirical research.

Scientists never entirely prove or disprove a theory. They merely develop greater confidence in the theory or move closer to rejecting it by proving that parts of it are untrue. Traditionally a theory does not rest on a single proposition but on a series of propositions, any one of which may be partially in error. Any single proposition contained in a theory, a hypothesis, can be subjected to testing by empirical research, which collects evidence that may or may not support the hypothesis. Through this testing, scientists formulate new questions that require further research. Also, social theories can be used to predict what will happen if society maintains its present course and to suggest ways the social world could be altered to achieve specific results. The **theoretical frameworks** we examine in this chapter attempt to identify the important factors in aging and offer guidelines for further inquiry.

☼ Activity Versus Disengagement

Controversy over two contradictory theories of aging shaped the field of social gerontology in the 1960s. Both activity theory and disengagement theory attempt to predict how one might respond to old age. Activity theory was the first social theory of aging, but only after the development of disengagement theory did it receive both its name and recognition as a distinct theory.

ACTIVITY THEORY

Because it continues to be widely accepted by social scientists, as well as by many people working with the elderly, we can say that activity theory is still a dominant theoretical perspective. **Activity theory** implies that social activity is the essence of life for all people of all ages. Early studies found that positive personal adjustment correlates highly with activity: the more active people are—mentally, physically, socially—the better adjusted they are. Early proponents of this theory believed that normal aging involves maintaining the activities and attitudes of middle age as long as possible. Any activities and roles that the individual has been forced to give up should be replaced with new activities. Activity theory predicts that those who are able to remain socially active will be more likely to achieve a positive self-image, social integration, and satisfaction with life, and that, therefore, they will probably age successfully.

The principles of activity theory are evident in the work of most gerontologists. The writings of Ernest Burgess from the 1940s show an orientation toward activity theory. Burgess, one of the founders of social gerontology, saw the elderly being left out of social activity and described them as having a "roleless role" (Burgess, 1960). Burgess felt that the old did not have to be excluded from socially meaningful activity. Instead, he felt that a new role for elders should include responsibilities and obligations that could lead to a productive existence. This stance clearly implies support for the activity theory.

The roleless role, which, according to Burgess, indicates a lack of social functions, is similar to Durkheim's concept of "anomie," a condition whereby some individuals in a society are in a normless state. These individuals lack a consensus on rules to guide their behavior and, therefore, receive no support or guidance from society. The result is that they are excluded from participation in social activities. If this exclusion were prevented, old age would be a satisfying period.

Most studies show that activity is related to well-being. Generally speaking, the last 50 years of research have found a positive correlation between

HANDLING TRANSITIONS IN LIFE CAN BE TOUGH

SOMETIMES IT'S LIKE GOING THROUGH A FOG BANK

IT'S HARD TO SEE ANYTHING.

BUT PERSEVERE: EVEN THE THICKEST FOG

.... WILL BURN OFF!

being active and aging successfully. But recent studies find it unnecessary for elders to maintain the same high degree of activity they had in middle age in order to have a high degree of life satisfaction in old age. Many older people want a somewhat more relaxed lifestyle and are quite happy when they achieve it. For example, a 65-year-old woman may long for the time when she can work half-time instead of full-time, sleep in, and devote more time to her aerobics classes and to reading the newspaper at a local coffeehouse.

DISENGAGEMENT THEORY

Disengagement theory is an explicit theory developed through research and explained in the book *Growing Old* (1961) by Elaine Cumming and William E. Henry. This book, one of the best known in the history of social gerontology, contends that it is both normal and inevitable for people to decrease their activity and seek more passive roles as they age. Disengagement is a mutual withdrawal of the elderly from society and society from the elderly in order to insure society's optimal functioning. Aging individuals, wishing to escape the stress resulting from recognition of their own diminishing capacity, collaborate in the withdrawal. The exact time and form of disengagement varies from individual to individual. The process involves loosening social ties through lessened social interaction. Knowing that the time preceding death is now short, feeling that the life experience is narrowing, and sensing a loss of self-esteem all signal the onset of disengagement. Ultimately, society's need for persons with new energy and skills, rather than the wishes of the older individual, dictates when disengagement occurs. In other words, as people approach their seventies, they become gradually disengaged from society, due to their declining energy and their desire for role loss. After an initial period of anxiety and depression, they accept their new status as disengaged and regain a sense of tranquility and self-worth.

The disengagement theory has generated much criticism (Achenbaum and Bengtson, 1994). Some say the theory is ethnocentric, in that it reflects the bias of an industrial society. Others have suggested that it discourages intervention to help old people. Still others have questioned why some elderly choose to disengage and others do not, contending that society pressures people into disengagement against their will. Disengagement theory continues to be attacked for both its methods and content. Indeed, although some of the research generated by the controversy supports disengagement theory, most of it does not.

Not all studies exploring disengagement theory have been negative. Many have expressed conditional support and suggested modifications. Researchers have found that disengagement occurs at differing rates and in different aspects of behavior. Others have found that the increased physical and social stress that often accompanies aging, rather than age per se, produces disengagement. One researcher observed that the elderly tend to disengage from contacts that are not totally satisfying and that they tend to maintain those that are. Another study suggested that older retired adults who spend a great deal of time alone enjoy their solitude and thus find disengagement a pleasant experience (Larson et al., 1985). In fact, these researchers state that the respondents were still highly engaged personally; they had only disengaged from interpersonal contact.

Despite these more positive findings, the controversy over disengagement theory continues. Unanswered questions remain about each of its major aspects: the role of the individual, the role of society, and satisfaction versus dissatisfaction with disengagement.

The Role of the Individual

Studies have demonstrated that disengagement is not inevitable with old age. Some elders disengage; others do not. Yet, according to the theory, the individual's inner processes lead to a loosening of social ties, which is a relatively natural process. This process is "primarily intrinsic, and secondarily responsive" (Cumming and Henry, 1961). Research should perhaps concentrate on the very old. If disengagement is a process preparing both the individual and society for the ultimate release of the elderly member, why should it begin at the relatively early age of 65? If disengagement is in fact a developmental task of old age, perhaps it actually begins in the eighties or nineties, when one is nearer death. We do not universally enter stages of life at a given age.

The Role of Society

According to disengagement theory, society must withdraw from its older members to insure the smooth operation and survival of the social system. Yet one can question this assumption. That disengaging older people from employment or other active roles is in society's best interest remains to be demonstrated. One might easily argue that the disengagement of older people is wasteful or dysfunctional because it removes many experienced, knowledgeable, and capable members. One might just as well speak of society excluding its older members as disengaging them; perhaps the older people who withdraw are merely reacting to a society that would exclude them anyway.

Satisfaction or Dissatisfaction with Disengagement

Neither activity theory nor disengagement theory fully explains successful or well-adjusted aging. More variables must be examined to explain why some people are happy in an active old age whereas others are content to narrow their activities and involvement in life.

☼ Psychological Well-Being

Well-being itself is a complex variable. It is one of the most popular, most persistently investigated issues in the social scientific study of aging. A major thrust in gerontology has attempted over the last 50 years to define and measure well-being and to identify factors that will increase it in the older population. Generally speaking, well-being means feeling good, or having good mental health. Oftentimes, researchers use the phrase *subjective well-being.*

The word *subjective* indicates a personal evaluation based on how the respondent feels, not an evaluation based on external criteria, such as visits to mental hospitals or psychologists' evaluations.

Psychological well-being is a broad term that has different meanings for different social scientists. Linda George offered a definition that differentiated among three concepts that measure well-being—morale, happiness, and **life satisfaction.** She made the following distinctions:

Morale—mental condition with respect to courage, discipline, confidence, enthusiasm, and willingness to endure hardship.

Happiness—transitory mood of gaiety or euphoria regarding one's current state of affairs.

Life satisfaction—an assessment of one's overall conditions of existence and/or one's progress toward desired goals. It refers to life in general over a long-range time period.

Although the three concepts may correlate, they are separate and distinct, stated George (1981). Well-being is an all-inclusive concept that can refer to one or more of these concepts.

The Life Satisfaction Index A (LSIA), the most frequently used scale in social gerontology, offers another method of defining well-being. One of the best-known instruments for measuring well-being, the LSIA, as originally developed by Neugarten, Havighurst, and Tobin (1961), consisted of 20 items representing five components: zest for life versus apathy; resolution and fortitude versus merely accepting that which life has given; congruence between desired and achieved goals; self-concept; and mood tone of optimism versus pessimism.

Researchers continue to refine the LSIA. They still debate whether the scale is valid (whether it measures what it is supposed to measure) and reliable (whether its results are consistent). They also continue to question whether the scale is unidimensional (measuring only the concept of life satis-

Social gerontologists struggle to define and measure "happiness." This woman has no problem with the concept.

faction) or is multidimensional (measuring more than one concept). Liang (1984) called for more conceptual clarity and more precise measurement of terms in the study of subjective well-being. Table 4.1 shows how Liang used the items in the Life Satisfaction Index A to measure three separate concepts.

The items in the LSIA provide us with a general overview of a person's psychological well-being. Horley (1984) believes that assessment of well-being should occur on three levels:

1. Overall life satisfaction; satisfaction with life as a whole: Have I gratified an appropriate proportion of the major desires of life?

2. The concern level; the more specific domains of life: Am I satisfied with my marriage, my employment, my friends?

3. The elemental level; the day-to-day specific action level: Do I want to take care of the grandchildren on Saturday? Is the weather good enough for a picnic? Am I having fun playing cards?

There have been attempts to consider these three levels, but more research is needed in this area.

A study by Krause (1991) tested the relationship between general evaluations of life satisfaction and evaluations of specific domains. Krause presented two hypotheses. The "top-down" hypothesis suggested that a person's ongoing sense of satisfaction with life as a whole predisposes him or her to develop similar feelings about specific domains such as health and employment. The "bottom-up" hypothesis maintained that satisfaction with the specific areas of one's life synthesize to form an overall sense of satisfaction with life as a whole. Krause, whose findings supported this latter theory,

---

Agree or Disagree with Each Item	**Table 4.1**
Mood Tone	A Proposed Use of the Twenty LSIA Items

Mood Tone
This is the dreariest time of my life.
I am just as happy now as when I was younger.
My life could be happier than it is now.
These are the best years of my life.
Compared to other people, I get down in the dumps too often.

Zest for Life
As I grow older, things seems better than I thought they would be.
I expect some interesting and pleasant things to happen to me in the future.
The things I do now are as interesting to me as they ever were.
I feel old and sometimes tired.
Compared to other people my age, I make a good appearance.
I have made plans for things I'll be doing a month or a year from now.
Most of the things I do are boring or monotonous.

Congruence
As I look back on my life, I am fairly well satisfied.
I would not change my past life even if I could.
I have gotten pretty much what I expected out of my life.
I have gotten more breaks in life than most of the people I know.
When I think back over my life, I didn't get most of the important things I wanted.

Other Items (Originated by Neugarten)
In spite of what people say, the lot of the average person is getting worse.
I feel my age but it does not bother me.
Compared to other people my age, I've made a lot of foolish decisions in my life.

SOURCE: Based on J. Liang, "Dimensions of the Life Satisfaction Index A: A Structural Formulation," *Journal of Gerontology* 39 (1984): 617.

expresses concern that survey self-assessment scales are the major tools used to study subjective well-being. Clinical observations might be another approach, or open-ended questions rather than agree-disagree items.

Obviously, no consensus exists on how to conceptualize and measure the many aspects of well-being. The contribution of the LSIA scale has been far-reaching, and many scholars continue to use and refine it. Other scales, such as the Philadelphia Geriatric Center Morale Scale (Liang and Bollen, 1985) and the Perceived Well-Being Scale (Reker et al., 1987), are also commonly employed.

In many cases, the researcher's goal is to understand how the older person achieves well-being and what factors adversely affect this well-being. If we had the key to well-being, we could use it to create more happiness for everyone.

A study of widows in retirement communities used Liang's version of the LSIA. For example, the item "These are the best years of my life" was scored 2 for "agree," 1 for "not sure," and 0 for "disagree." Widows with the highest scores of life satisfaction were more socially active and were the majority in the community. The ratio of marrieds to widows led to different levels of social interaction, which, in turn, influenced their life satisfaction (Hong and Duff, 1994).

In a study of the oldest-old (age 85 and over) in London, emotional well-being, as measured by the Life Satisfaction Index A, was most positively related to health status and moderately related to high levels of social support and informal help (Bowling and Browne, 1991). Another study found life satisfaction to be high if formal support (hospitals, organizations, etc.) rather than informal support (family and friends) were available for health problems (Krause, 1990). This study suggested that older people are embarrassed and ashamed to be too dependent on family and are happier to independently seek help from outside. Well-being, or life satisfaction, some studies assert is positively related to *quality* contact, such as having a close friend or confidant on whom to rely in time of need, not on the *number* of interpersonal contacts.

☼ Structural-Functional Frameworks

Sociologists study society—social factors such as values, norms, roles, social structures, institutions, stratification, and subcultures. Social gerontologists study these social factors as they affect elders. The studies that fall under this broad category delve into every social group in an older person's life. Studies have included economic structure, the family, race, and demography. Studies on the historical context of aging, the media, work, friendship, and communication networks provide data on the social context of aging.

Sociological theories of aging use the same concepts as those used in contemporary general sociological theory. One dominant framework in sociological theory is the structural-functional framework, which views societies as systems and subsystems of social rules and roles. Members become socialized by internalizing the social system's norms and values, and the entire system functions in a reasonably orderly fashion if its structures are organized and intact. The activity theory of aging and the disengagement theory are structural-functional in that they deal with systems of rules and roles for the aged in society. Three more structural-functional concepts for understanding aging are here: considered age stratification, role theory, and age grading.

Thinking about Aging

George Burns Philosophizes about Life

■ ROBERT MACY

Burns's philosophies of life are reflected in his humor. "In 1981, I played God," he said, referring to the first of three movies in which he played the deity. "I was a nervous wreck. We're both the same age, but we grew up in different neighborhoods."

"Why shouldn't I play God? Anything I do at my age is a miracle."

His formula for acting? "If the director wants me to cry, I think of my sex life. If the director wants me to laugh, I think of my sex life." About that sex life? "I'd go out with women my age, but there are no women my age."

Burns smokes 15 to 20 cigars and drinks several martinis a day. What do his doctors think of that?

"They're all dead."

Burns admits he was devastated—personally and professionally—by the death of Gracie Allen, his wife for 38 years.

But Burns, now single for nearly 30 years, has his own definitions of happiness:

1. Having a large, loving, caring, close-knit family; especially if they live in another city.

2. Hearing your proctologist say, "You can straighten up now."

3. Hearing your teenage kid say, "Dad, you're right." My son Ronnie is 49 and I'm still waiting.

4. A good martini, a good meal, a good cigar, and a good woman . . . or a bad woman, depending on how much happiness you can stand. ☀

SOURCES: Macy, Robert. "Burns Alive and Well at 95," *Boston Herald* (19 January 1991); and Burns, George. *Dr. Burns' Prescription for Happiness [Buy Two Books and Call Me in the Morning].* New York: Putnam, 1984; used with permission.

AGE STRATIFICATION

The **age stratification** theory studies older persons in relation to all other age groups, or age strata, in a society, examining the differences between the age strata and studying the way in which society allocates opportunities, social roles, rights, privileges, status, power, and entitlements on the basis of age. The persons in an age strata have similar characteristics because they are at the same stage in the life course and share a common history. Changing social environments produce different patterns of adaptation in successive age groups. And cultures vary in the extent to and manner in which they are stratified by age (Matras, 1990). Age stratification theory has been used to explain power and status inequities between young and old in given societies. For example, sociologists have used the theory to analyze the power—and lack of power—in younger generations in China.

ROLES, GENDER, AND ETHNICITY

Role is one of the most basic concepts in all of sociology, one that you will find used in almost every sociological framework. Sociologists are quick to point out that the word *role* is a concept, not a theory. A role is a status or position, which carries known attributes, accorded to an individual in a given social system. "Doctor," "mommy," "sports fan," and "churchgoer" are all roles.

In studies of aging we find analysis of age roles, role transitions, role acquisitions, role relinquishment, and socialization to and from roles. Roles are modified, redefined, and transformed as people age. Roles in marriage, families, careers, and community change throughout the life course. People have informal roles in friendship and neighboring. They have formal roles in institutional settings such as schools and hospitals and more informal roles in less structured settings. Role exit was once a major focus of aging studies, but role transition now seems a more appropriate term.

Gender roles have to do with the cultural aspects of being male or female. Male and female in every culture is linked to specific roles, attitudes, and behaviors. Because aging men and women are looked upon differently in our society and in cultures around the world, the study of gender is very important. Being old is a different experience for men than for women.

Ethnic diversity has become a major focus of gerontology. **Ethnicity** refers to one's identification with a sub-group in society having a unique set of values, traditions, or language, often originating in another country. The role of ethnicity as it affects aging and the aged was too often overlooked in the early studies of gerontology. Generalizations were made on the basis of white, middle-class respondents, but these generalizations did not apply to all racial and ethnic groups. Looking at elders in diverse groups has added to the richness and complexity of the research of aging.

AGE GRADING

We live in an age-graded society. **Age grading** means that age is a prime criterion in determining the opportunities people may enjoy. Our age partially establishes the roles we may play. Both children and old people are welcomed to or barred from various opportunities because of the often-stereotyped images society forms for the young and the old. Such beliefs often prevent the young and the old from expressing individual differences and, thereby, lead to injustices. In other words, older people may be less active not because of their biology or the aging process, but because they are expected to present an image of idleness; indeed, social roles sometimes do not permit elders to be active and involved. Role expectations at various age levels are called **age norms**. Society pressures individuals to engage in activities such as marriage, schooling, and child rearing at a socially approved age. One way to determine the presence of age norms would be to ask questions such as the following:

■ Would you approve of a woman who decided to have a child at age 42? age 60?

■ Would you approve of a couple who moved across the country to live near their married children when they were 50? 65? 80?

Answers to these and similar questions would reveal age norms for child-rearing and other activities. Age norms affecting the older population can be studied by asking a sample group whether situations such as the following are appropriate or inappropriate:

■ A very old man buys and drives a flashy new sports car.

■ An older woman dresses in "new age" fashion, including a nose ring.

■ A retired couple frequents heavy metal rock concerts and festivals.

We can view age norms as a form of social control. If one follows the age norms, one receives approval; if not, disapproval and possibly negative sanctions result. The author of the poem "In Love at 50 (with a younger man)" appears to have violated an age norm and is suffering some disapproval.

Studies show a continuing shift toward a loosening of age grading and age norms in the United States. Lives are becoming more fluid. There is no longer a definite age at which one marries, enters the labor market, goes to school, or has children. It no longer surprises us to hear of a 23-year-old computer company owner, a 34-year-old governor, a 36-year-old grandmother, or a retiree of 52. No one is shocked at a 60-year-old college student, a 50-year-old man who becomes a father for the first time, or an 80-year-old who launches a new business. Our ever-advancing technologies continue to test and stretch the limits of what people find acceptable. Recent medical developments permit the implantation of a fertilized donated egg in postmenopausal women. In 1993 a 59-year-old London woman gave birth to twins, and in 1994 a 62-year-old Italian woman had a baby boy. She decided to try for a pregnancy with the implantation after her only child was killed in an accident ("Giving Birth," 1994).

☼ Age Groupings

STUDYING COHORTS AND GENERATIONS

Studies of cohorts and generations are conducted by demographers, sociologists who study social change, and social psychologists studying the life course. A major problem in understanding age differences is determining whether change is due to "age" or "period" effects. A change due to an age effect is caused by maturation, that is, biological change from the physical aging process. Period effects are changes in different age groups resulting from historical events that have affected one age group differently than another.

Age Cohort

For our purposes, an **age cohort** is a group of individuals exposed to a similar set of life experiences and historical events. Demographers often use cohort analysis to compare groups of people born during specific time periods, usually separated by 5- or 10-year intervals. We expect that age cohorts will show similarities to one another. Cohort analysis permits the sociologist to study the effects that events or demographics may have on a broad group of individuals, all of whom have experienced the same events at a similar state of biological and physical development. For example, in the 1990s young adult cohorts in their twenties have been referred to by the media as Generation X (Giles, 1994). The "twenty somethings" who represent Generation X are described as whiners and slackers, complaining about the national debt they have inherited and totally unappreciative of "how good they have it." Generation X is the smallest cohort since the early 1950s and are thus labeled a "baby bust" group rather than baby boomers. For this reason, their chances in the job market are increased. And if the higher productivity of American business continues throughout the 1990s and homes stay affordable, Generation X should do well compared with the cohorts before them

....

In Love at 50 (with a younger man)
■ *Gloria Barron*

I'm wet. I'm dry.
I'm hot, then cold.
You're young.
I'm old.

"They" say your course has just begun.
That I could be your mother.
At thirty you can run full steam
That I should seek another.

Estrogen, Progesterone,
Menopause be damned!
If I'm half-way through the race
Why should I be slammed?

Never mind the wrinkles,
They're only on my chin.
Sing the national anthem.
Let the games begin.

I see your eyes glow brighter.
I watch your lip-line part.
Our flesh touches, trembling
You press against my heart.

The sport becomes poetic.
The poem transcends to art.
Heat pulses from the canvas.
Its vision to impart.

Now I'm the Mona Lisa,
Soft and coy and wise,
Knowing you will paint a smile
And mystify my eyes.

Behind the glaze, emotions churn.
Perhaps this shouldn't be so.
But I'll keep on loving,
Thinking inside,
"What do 'they' know?"

SOURCE: Unpublished poem by Gloria Barron written on Valentine's Day 1995 for T.R.S.
....

(Quinn, 1994). Thus, this cohort is set apart by its "ungrateful attitude" and its small size. We should point out that social scientists have not confirmed the attitude described by journalists in the media.

Despite the many similarities in individuals as members of cohorts, a word of caution must be entered about overgeneralizing. Subgroups within a cohort may experience the world in different ways based on such variables as class, gender, ethnic background, or region of residence. Not every young adult in the 1960s was a "hippie," and not every adult in the 1990s is a "yuppie."

Generations and Events

The concept of **generation** is more complex than the concept of a cohort. The journalistic and electronic media have used the term widely (and loosely) to indicate the differences in values between parents and children (the so-called generation gap). Others have used the term to identify the values of those who are older or younger than some arbitrary age—the "over-thirty generation" or the "under-thirty generation," for instance. Historians and sociologists have applied the term in additional ways. For them, *generation* may mean distinctive life patterns and values as they emerge by age; or it may connote not only distinctive life patterns but also a collective mentality that sets one age group apart from another.

Karl Mannheim (1952) formulated the latter definition. According to Mannheim, generations are not an arbitrarily defined number of years imposed by researchers; instead, they represent a reflection of historical events and social change. For example, the invention of the automobile may have led to the formation of two generations—those who grew up with access to cars and those who did not. And children's use of computers may lead nonusing parents to feel a generation apart from their kids.

An age group that has lived through a major social event, such as the Great Depression, may exhibit characteristics that are not due to internal or biological aging and that are not found in other age groups. The impact of widespread social events on their survivors has not received enough systematic investigation; indeed, events that your parents or you have experienced may well continue to influence your lives. What, for example, are the effects of having lived through the Vietnam or Watergate era? The war in the Persian Gulf? If you were a young adult during the Iran-Contra affair or the Savings and Loan crisis, will you be more skeptical of politicians than your children, assuming no comparable incidents occur in their early adulthood? Would a young adult of the Vietnam era be less patriotic than you, if you were a young adult during the 1990 war in Iraq? If so, one might conclude that events, rather than the aging process, made you more skeptical or more patriotic. Events of our younger years play an especially important role in shaping feelings and attitudes that persist throughout our lives.

According to Mannheim, broad social movements, including somewhat trivial changes in fads and fashions, are concrete manifestations of a generation's social reality. Consequently, if social change is rapid, then different generations could theoretically appear every few years. Conversely, if social change is slow, then the same generation might exist for several decades. Mannheim's definition of *generation* is quite specific: birth cohorts do not form "true generations" unless they develop not only a distinctive life pattern but also a collective identity and a political consciousness of themselves as a unique group.

Some social scientists speak of the post–World War II "generation," as opposed to the World War II "generation," in the sense Mannheim describes.

Those who remember the patriotism that World War II generated are not the same as those who were born too late to have experienced it. The post–World War II generation is described as less patriotic, less traditional, more alienated, and more skeptical of war. Collectively, in contrast, those who experienced World War II are more optimistic about the U.S. role in world politics and political leadership and show more support and respect for the president. During the 1991 war in the Persian Gulf, this patriotic mentality seemed to assert itself once again: perhaps a new "generation" has been born. Social commentators also define as a "new" generation those who use high-tech equipment—computers, video games, and VCRs—with ease. New technologies can indeed make one feel a generation removed, hopelessly dated and at odds with changing times. With motivation and training, however, one can join the new generation.

Lineage

Sociologists use the concept **lineage** to discuss generations within families. Parents transmit values to children, and continuity or discontinuity may distinguish the transmission of specific values within a particular family or families. Social, political, or technological events may intervene in this transmission and thereby alter roles and values within the family context. Consequently, the authority of older family members may be strengthened, weakened, or changed in a way that also alters parent-child relationships.

Given the increase in life expectancy in the United States today, four- and even five-generation families are quite common. Although this interaction of family members can be a source of great personal enrichment, differences in values can produce tension and conflict among the family's generations. These value differences may be a source of age prejudice, or ageism, within the family. We may reduce these age prejudices in our own families by understanding the social and historical development of another family member's generation.

Three generations in a Navajo family.

Explaining the Generation Gap

When a **generation gap** exists between young adults of, say, 20, and adults aged 50 and over, the cause may be biological maturation, historical or social events, or personal change such as education.

Biology   A 50-year-old mother may have acted like her 20-year-old daughter or son when she was the same age. That 20-year-old child may, in the process of aging, take on traits the same as the mother's. Thus, this generation gap between mother and child may be the result of differences in biological maturation or the biological aging process.

For example, a woman in her twenties may be extremely lively and active, wanting to constantly experience new adventures and excitement. But with age, she becomes more and more settled and more content to be relaxed and mellow. Her mother, who followed the same pattern, may have little tolerance for her lively lifestyle, constantly nagging her to settle down, even though she had a similar life experience as her daughter.

Historical/Social Events   Or, suppose a mother grew up in a conservative time period when say, early marriage was expected for women. We would probably label her values as traditional. We would consider her child, who grew up in a later time period that might be called more liberal, as having modern values such as living together. In this case, history or social events cause the generation gap. Sociologists are interested in knowing how "the times, they are a-changin'," as the song goes, affects relationships between generations.

Social change may be a major cause of age prejudice, principally because the more rapid the social change, the greater the possibility of value clashes. Social observers may sometimes overestimate the rapidity of social change. Studies have shown that *basic* value orientations remain fairly constant across several generations. For example, analysis of the generation gap in the late 1960s, a time of considerable social unrest, showed that politically liberal students tended to have politically liberal parents. Thus, measured in terms of differences between a specific parent and child, the generation gap of the 1960s was not as extreme as it appeared overall. The generation gap in such countries, as Israel, Russia, and Korea is greater than the gap in the United States because value systems for the young and the old show greater extremes in these countries and because many of these countries are undergoing rapid social change.

Personal Change   A generation gap caused by personal change is an individual matter that does not necessarily reflect widespread cultural changes. (Mannheim would not use the word *generation* in this context.) If one child, for example, moves from a cattle ranch to the city to get an education and, upon returning to visit her parents announces that she is now a vegetarian and that killing animals is morally wrong, the cattle-growing father may comment with exasperation about the "generation gap" between himself and his daughter. But this single occurrence does not *necessarily* imply that large numbers of young people are becoming vegetarians upon leaving home.

Although a number of studies have examined generational differences, most have focused on middle-aged parents and children. Few have focused on the very old. A generation gap can exist between middle-aged offspring and their parents, or between elders and their grandchildren or great-grandchildren. We generally think of young people when we hear the "generation gap." But differences between the beliefs and values of the middle-aged and oldsters can be as real as the differences between the beliefs and values of the old and the young.

CROSS-SECTIONAL VERSUS LONGITUDINAL STUDIES

Two helpful methods of studying different cohorts or generations have been cross-sectional and longitudinal studies. A **cross-sectional study** samples, at a given point in time, persons belonging to different cohorts or generations and observes the differences. **Longitudinal studies,** in contrast, sample individuals or cohorts and follow them over a long period of time. In general, longitudinal studies have been more fruitful than cross-sectional studies in analyzing change over the life course, because social scientists have drawn many erroneous conclusions by using cross-sectional studies of different age groups at a single point in time.

In general, longitudinal research is more accurate than cross sectional research. Although cross-sectional research offers the social scientist the unique opportunity of simultaneously studying the young, the middle-aged, and the old, it cannot account for the *process* of change. Differences in attitude or behavior may be due to the aging process or to other factors, but cause and effect are quite difficult to determine in a cross-sectional study. For example, if old persons attend church more often than younger people, can we assume that individuals become more religious with age? Not really. The older people have possibly always been faithful in attending church, even as youngsters; and the young who do not now attend church also may not do so in old age. Longitudinal studies are superior to studies conducted at any given point in time because they can follow the change (or lack of change) in individuals.

Generalizing about cause and effect may become more reliable with longitudinal study. Several years ago, an assumption that IQ decreased with age was based on cross-sectional studies that showed older people to have lower IQs than younger adults. However, these older individuals had left school earlier at a time when many children did not have an opportunity to attend high school, such as people usually have today. Differences in education (a cohort effect) explained much of the presumed decline found in the cross-sectional studies. In fact, longitudinal studies show that IQ does not decrease with age, but remains stable into the seventies. Many of our misconceptions about aging may be blamed on cross-sectional research.

Separating the effects of age (maturation that comes with the aging process), period (history and events), and cohort (differences in social class, education, and occupation) can be difficult. To separate these effects, one must first consider cross-sectional differences. Second, one must consider longitudinal differences. Let us use Figure 4.1 as an example. The top row of 20-year-olds, 40-year-olds, and 60-year-olds represents one cross-sectional study, which could compare all three age groups at once in 1990. The downward arrows, in contrast, represent longitudinal studies. A study using the model in Figure 4.1 would provide a basis for many interesting comparisons and would produce findings about the effects of the aging process, "the times" (external social forces), and cohort differences. If such a model were used to study voting behavior, fear of aging, personal contentment with life, or political alienation, what do you think the results would show? In the final analysis, one would have

One cohort of 20-year-olds;
Two cohorts of 40-year-olds;
Two cohorts of 60-year-olds;
One cohort of 80-year-olds.

Comparisons could be made within and between all these groups. If, for example, the two groups of 40-year-olds scored dramatically differently on a political alienation scale, one could assume that the time period during which they were raised, not biological aging, was a key factor. These massive studies incorporating both cross-sectional and longitudinal approaches may allow us to unravel the complicated effects of age, period and cohort differences.

☼ Exchange Theory

Exchange theory rests on the basic premises that

1. Individuals and groups act to maximize rewards and minimize costs;

2. An individual will maintain an interaction if it continues to be more rewarding than costly; and

3. When one individual is dependent on another, that individual loses power.

Power is thus derived from imbalances in social exchange. Social exchanges are more than economic transactions. They involve psychological satisfaction and need gratification. Though it may sound rather cold and calculating, social life, according to exchange theory, is a series of exchanges that add to or subtract from one's store of power and prestige.

The first gerontologist to apply exchange theory was J. David Martin (1971), who used the theory to aid in understanding visiting patterns among family members. Some older individuals have little power. Families feel an obligation to visit but may not really want to. The older person's persistent complaints that relatives do not visit may motivate some visiting behavior, but the complaints may also decrease any pleasure and satisfaction felt by those who visit. Those elders who have other sources of power, such as financial resources or having interesting stories to tell, are in a better position. In fact, they could hold "power" positions over "dependent" relatives. Similar equity considerations have been applied to the study of peer friendships among elders (Roberto and Scott, 1986).

Another way of discussing change is to use a concept popular among anthropologists: reciprocity. The **norm of reciprocity** involves maintaining balance in relationships by paying for goods or deeds with equivalent goods or deeds. It can be applied in business or in relationships with family and

Figure 4.1

··

Longitudinal Study
Method

Year of Study: 1990	20-year-old cohort ↓	40-year-old cohort ↓	60-year-old cohort ↓
Year of Study: 2010 (20 years later)	20-year-old cohort 20 years later at age 40	40-year-old cohort 20 years later at age 60	60-year-old cohort 20 years later at age 80

··

friends (McCulloch, 1990). For example, I'll trade you this radio and five cassettes for that stereo: the goods' values are equal; we're "balanced."

Some groups in society are unable to repay what they receive—children and the mentally handicapped are two examples. In these cases, beneficence becomes the norm. The person giving then does not expect a material reward, but does expect love or gratitude. The **norm of beneficence** calls into play such nonrational sentiments as loyalty, gratitude, and faithfulness. Dowd (1984) asserts that the very old—but not the young-old—in our society benefit from the norm of beneficence. (They receive gifts and have only their thanks to return.) He directs his attention not to personal relationships but to societal ones, noting that benefits from the government, such as Medicaid, Meals on Wheels and other social services, are being increasingly delayed and becoming increasingly unavailable to the young-old.

Exchange theory and the norms of reciprocity and beneficence remain valuable concepts with which to view the position of elders. We can apply exchange theory at a small-group level, between one older individual and ɑnother person, or at a societal level.

☼ Meaning in Everyday Life

Studies of the **meaning in everyday life** comes to us from philosophy, phenomenology, symbolic interaction, and social psychology. Needless to say, these studies are diverse. What they share is an interest in determining, from person to person, the meaning we attach to living our lives and to the communications we have with others. **Symbolic interaction,** for example, studies the way in which people attach meaning to their own behavior. This meaning may be based on their perceptions of others with whom they interact.

Some gerontologists are becoming increasingly concerned with what aging means to the individual experiencing it. To one researcher, the findings of old age are a paradox: although old age is often negatively described as a marginal status, this seems to have little effect on the everyday lives and feelings of older people (Ward, 1984). Old age may be derogated, yet old people are often happy with themselves and their circumstances. For example, attitudes toward, and satisfaction with, retirement are generally favorable.

Ward explains this paradox with the term *salience,* the degree to which something is central, important, or meaningful. If age is not salient to older people, they may not think about their age or feel the marginal status they supposedly hold. Older individuals may not feel that their age is a prominent trait, even though gerontologists and others think it is. They may not feel that their age changes their circumstances or their personal "worlds." We need to (1) clarify the conditions under which age is relevant (salient) to the aging individual, (2) determine the consequences to the individual when age becomes salient, and (3) examine how informal peer friendship networks can socialize people for old age and possibly insulate them from stigma (Ward, 1984).

Many studies of meaning in everyday life derive their basic approach from the school of sociological theory known as phenomenology. The phenomenological theory of aging is primarily concerned with the meaning that life and growing old have for aging people. Rather than constructing a theory about aging, phenomenologists attempt to define growing old through close association with those who are actively participating in the process. A major methodology of the phenomenological approach is to observe older people. Rather than, say, give the elders statements with which to agree or disagree, this approach would let their words or actions speak for themselves.

Meaning in life comes from many sources.

Sociologists have lived in the settings they studied. Gubrium (1975) constructed the meaning of living in the nursing home by documenting the lives of the participants, who included patients, residents, staff, administrators, and visitors. Jacobs (1975) followed a similar strategy in studying two other housing arrangements for elders—a middle-class retirement community and a high-rise apartment building in an urban environment. His more recent studies have focused on aspects of everyday life of which people have little conscious awareness—the small routine aspects of life. His studies direct attention to the "nontrivial nature of trivia"—the everyday, taken-for-granted knowledge, skills, and interactions of which most social life is composed (Jacobs, 1994).

Whether the study takes a phenomenological approach or not, researchers who study meaning in everyday life typically try to use techniques that do not allow the researcher's perspective or presence to influence the subjects' words and actions. The goal is to encourage respondents to articulate a life perspective free of any bias the researcher's theoretical framework might cause.

For example, in the study entitled *The Ageless Self: Sources of Meaning in Late Life* (1986), Kaufman used open-ended questions, rather than formulaic statements, while conducting in-depth interviews with 60 aged persons in their own homes. In studying the 60 people, Kaufman looked for themes that, for them, gave life its meaning. For 80-year-old Millie, life gained its meaning from close, emotional ties:

"My mother cherished me ... I adored my father and he clung to me ... I adored my principal ... I was attached to the other children in the neighborhood. I took care of all of them ... I loved my piano teacher ..." (Kaufman, 1986, p. 34)

Her meaning in life came from the positive feelings she got from relationships with others. For others, meaning in life came from a variety of sources: making money, overcoming alcoholism, or achieving status. Dorfman's study of Franklin Village is, in her words,

> a personal odyssey into the inner experience of aging. The journey began with my immersion into a community of elders and the honing of my observational skills. It ends with a clearer understanding of the phenomenology of aging— one that is divested of ageist myths and stereotypes and that highlights the significance of aspirations and values in late life. (Dorfman, 1994, p. xiii)

Franklin Village is a continuing-care retirement community in which the researcher lived and took part in the daily life of the community. What resulted is an ethnography (field research study) encompassing in-depth interviews, case studies, and participant observation. Eighty-one residents shared their aspirations with her in both prearranged interviews and informal chats. When she left she had 352 typewritten pages of narrative to analyze. She spent 1,000 hours talking to residents—who ultimately became her friends in addition to providing her with a look into the inner experience of aging. Examples of residents' aspirations were: (1) to be independent, (2) to have new experiences, (3) to have intimate contact, (4) to recreate past experiences, and (5) to have a quick, easy death when the time came (Dorfman, 1994).

Symbolic interaction, another theoretical framework, also studies meaning in everyday life. Symbolic interaction examines interactions that individuals have with each other: how verbal and nonverbal messages are communicated by one party to another and how these messages are understood by another party. Such interaction modifies one's self-concept and one's view of the other interactant, and on a larger scale, of the social order. Symbolic interaction offers a dynamic rather than a static view of social life. Individuals are ever-changing their self-concepts and views of others based on continuing interactions.

Meaning in life can also be gleaned from poems, diaries, journals, and other sources of life history narratives. Older persons who are not able to write may give their life history orally. Two sisters, Sarah and A. Elizabeth Delany, each over 100 years old, gave their life history of being born into slavery and eventually being freed, getting educations, and becoming educators themselves. Their account has become a book and movie (Heath, 1993).

Life narratives have wide appeal, because they promote the ideal of freeing people to reflect on their life and share personal meanings. Constructing a life story is thought to be therapeutic for older people, but gerontologists caution that the telling of life stories does not always enhance well-being for the aged person. It can bring distress if the memories are negative or painful. Another problem in this area of research is that very rarely is the entire text of the tale printed. Instead it is glimpsed in fragments selected by authors, despite its being upheld as a means to empower individual voices (Luborsky, 1993).

According to another expert on qualitative research, experience and voice should be represented from those studied—whether it be caregivers, care receivers, family members, or significant others:

> This requires—indeed—demands—keeping subjects and their worlds on center stage, never (not even late in the research process) in the background ...

Qualitative research is science. It tries to generate theoretically informed findings and is empirically based. (Gubrium, 1992)

Another problem is that the particulars of any story may or may not have ever occurred. This does not mean that the storyteller is lying. He or she may believe the story, but memory and circumstances may have altered the actual facts. However, if the teller and hearer of the story believe it is true, they act toward each other as if it were true. As the classic sociologist W. I. Thomas said, "Things perceived as real are real in their consequences."

☼ Critical Gerontology

Critical gerontology has evolved from critical sociology, which uses a neo-Marxian theory to critique the social fabric. Marxian theory looks to economic structures as the root cause of social manifestations. Members of society form an individual or group consciousness of their struggle against powerful economic forces. Only then can they unite to fight against these forces. (The focus on individual and group consciousness borrows from symbolic interaction theory). The "political economy of aging" draws attention to the political side of economics with regard to the aged—how political power affects the amount of money given to fund social services for elders. For example, critical theorists find that capitalism and the profit motive shortchange elders. It criticizes the class structure for perpetuating poverty among older women and minorities. "Liberal remedies" of more money thrown at the problem are criticized, because they treat only the symptoms, not the fundamental causes (Olson, 1982). The causes are rooted in market and class structures—in other words, American capitalist institutions.

Olson was one of the first gerontologists to apply the critical perspective to gerontology. He believes gerontologists have described a multitude of urgent issues facing elders, but have failed to identify the roots of the social ailments; and they have failed to see the limits to reform imposed by the present system. Moody (1988) continued this vein of thinking and described the challenges and promises that critical theory poses for gerontology.

Along the same lines Estes (1983) and Minkler and Estes (1991) have looked at American values that undermine true reform: the ethic of individual responsibility, the negative view of centralized government by so many citizens, and the individualistic view of social problems. These perceptions "obscure an understanding of aging as a socially generated problem and status" (Estes, 1983, p. 171). Laws (1995) argues that ageism is rooted in values that devalue the aged body. She wants to use critical theory to understand the way morality and values place their stamp upon our conceptions of the aging body.

The critical approach focuses on the negative experiences of aging, with the premise that the problems of aging are social and, thus can be corrected with political and social action. Structural explanation is, therefore, tied to activism. Many critical theorists advocate dismantling capitalism in favor of democratic socialism to free elders from the traps of poverty, poor housing, inadequate health care, and welfare-type dependency (Green, 1993).

Other branches of critical gerontology are working to identify wide social influences that shape what gets defined as a problem, how the problem gets looked at, and the consequences of different patterns of research. The worldviews of gerontologists should come under study as well as the people they are studying (Luborsky and Sankar, 1993.) These studies can overlap with philosophy. They are important in directing our attention to biases that affect our choice of what to study, how to study, and even our choice of concepts and the wording of hypotheses.

☼ Pure Versus Applied Research

Pure research is the search for knowledge in the most unbiased fashion possible. The natural, physical, and social sciences use the scientific method to test hypotheses objectively and to accept or reject hypotheses using clearly defined criteria. The pure researcher first formulates a theory; then he or she generates hypotheses and devises a plan for testing them. The researcher must find ways of empirically measuring theoretical concepts or variables.

Let us consider an example from the activity/disengagement controversy. A researcher might want to test the following hypothesis: the morale of the older person increases with the number of activities in which he or she is involved. To test this hypothesis, at least two variables must be measured—morale and number of activities. This task may seem easy, but it is not. Morale is a complex variable, hard to define and hard to scale in a meaningful way. The number-of-activities variable is somewhat easier to deal with, but it can present problems. The researcher must decide, for example, if watching television or reading should be regarded as activities. Once variables are defined and scaled, the pure researcher must then identify the sample group.

A study of all elderly persons is impossible, so some smaller group, or sample, must be identified and selected. The sample should be chosen on a random basis so that no particular selective factor confuses the issue. Next, methods of collecting the data from this sample must be devised. Typical methods for collecting data are the interview and the questionnaire. After the social scientist has collected all the data, he or she uses methods of analysis, which often involve statistical techniques, to tabulate the results of the study.

The objective of all this work is to produce a study that is valid (accurate) and replicable (capable of yielding the same results when repeated). The data analysis will usually determine whether the initial hypothesis should be accepted or rejected, but the study's validity and replicability are just as important in determining the authority and persuasiveness of the conclusions about the hypothesis made in the study.

Using scales and tabulating totals is known as **quantitative research.** Survey research is typically quantitative. Another kind of research widely used in the study of people is called **qualitative research.** Making observations in a retirement setting or nursing home, conducting lengthy oral interviews to get oral histories, or asking open-ended questions that explore the meaning of life may not yield results that can be scaled or analyzed statistically; yet these observations and interviews are scientific studies. They represent qualitative studies rather than quantitative ones. One qualitative study consisted of taped interviews, an approach the researcher called "retrospective life span analysis" (Job, 1983). Very old persons answered open-ended questions and told of important and meaningful life events.

Gerontologists do not agree on the best approach to study, or even that there is a best approach. In a sense, each one has a camera standing in a different position, getting a different angle on the subject.

The applied branch of any science is concerned with using the findings of pure research to improve the quality of life. **Applied research,** to state it simply, yields practical solutions to a particular problem and is not concerned with theoretical speculation as to why the problem exists. Are most elderly poorly nourished, poorly housed, victims of high crime rates, and living below the poverty line? If they are, what is the best way to solve these problems? Just as physicians apply findings from biological science to help people get well and engineers apply findings from the physical and natural sciences to build better dams, bridges, and buildings, the applied social scientist might analyze the delivery of services or devise ways to improve the social environment in which people live. Of course, individuals may have differing ideas of what constitutes an improvement. Applied gerontology should be used to evaluate housing, transportation, pensions, employment programs, and Older Americans Act services. Scholarly consideration should also be given to how government regulations affect older people (Kane, 1992).

One might think that the pure and applied approaches are separate and distinct, yet in gerontological study the pure and applied have often been mixed together. Some theories present obvious value judgments and imply how the research can be applied. The "everyday life" approach may or may not imply intervention. It can be pure research in the sense of its goal: to study the meaning that life has for old people. Yet some of the findings from this theoretical approach also imply ways for improving the lot of older people. Thus, the distinction between pure and applied research is often arbitrary. Applied research can identify and suggest ways to solve existing problems. Pure research can question why the problems exist. If solutions are implemented, applied research can then investigate the effectiveness of the solutions. All in all, pure and applied research stimulate each other.

☀ The Future of Social Gerontology

The social theories of aging come from two principal viewpoints—the psychological and the sociological—or from some combination of the two. Gerontology has been more interdisciplinary than many fields of study. Subjective well-being adds a psychological dimension to studies of aging, for example, whereas age stratification emphasizes the sociological dimension.

Sometimes the distinction between the psychological and sociological can be quite arbitrary, and this can be confusing to students just beginning their study of gerontology. If one can imagine gerontologists as photographers taking pictures of aging from many different angles, one can go on to conceptualize theorists looking at the lives of older people from many different angles. The pictures have a great deal in common, but the angles offer shades of difference and meaning. Theories overlap, but each has its unique emphasis.

Because older people face so many practical problems that demand immediate solutions, research in the field of gerontology has often been applied rather than purely theoretical. Researchers have invested much of their time in seeking effective social solutions, often ignoring the broader theoretical questions.

The 1960s brought forth a flurry of research instigated by the activity/disengagement controversy, whereas the 1970s and 1980s saw a greater diversity of theoretical frameworks. So far, the 1990s have brought an even wider and richer array of theories and concepts to the study of gerontology. As the percentage of older persons continues to climb, society needs more workers in fields such as education, outreach, and long-term care. We have many more research questions to answer before our society can fulfill the physical, psychological, and social needs of our older population.

Chapter Summary

Social gerontology studies social aspects of aging. Various theoretical frameworks have been used to study aging from a social science perspective. Controversy over the activity versus disengagement theory of aging shaped the field of social gerontology in the 1960s. The controversy has never been resolved, though the activity theory seems to be favored. The most often studied variable in all of gerontology is psychological well-being. The implications of this concept are deep and numerous. From sociology comes studies of how societies are stratified by age and how roles are differentiated by age. Society imposes age norms or age constraints, which also shape the way we behave at any given age. Every level of adulthood, whether young adulthood or advanced middle age, has expected behavior patterns. Exchange theory has been developed by sociologists and social psychologists and has been used to show that elders in society suffer from an imbalance of power. Balancing operations could bring more power and, thus, equality to the aged in the United States. From the school of sociological theory known as phenomenological sociology comes studies of the meaning that elders find in life—in everyday events and in their relationships with others. And from critical sociology comes the perspective that basic capitalist institutions interfere with the status and power of elders.

Key Terms

activity theory
age cohort
age grading
age norms
age stratification
applied research
critical gerontology
cross-sectional study
disengagement theory
ethnicity
exchange theory
gender
generation
generation gap
life satisfaction

lineage
longitudinal study
meaning in everyday life
norm of beneficence
norm of reciprocity
pure research
qualitative research
quantitative research
role
social gerontology
subjective well-being
symbolic interaction
theoretical framework
theory

Questions for Discussion

1. If you were to study aging from a sociological perspective, which theoretical framework would you choose and why?

2. How do our value systems affect the theoretical frameworks we design?

3. Do you personally expect to remain active or to disengage at age 65? At age 95? Explain.

4. Would you prefer to work in pure or applied social gerontology? Why?

Fieldwork Suggestions

1. Develop some measures of life satisfaction. Interview elderly people to determine their degree of life satisfaction. What are some of their sources of satisfaction or dissatisfaction?

2. Following a "meaning in everyday life" framework, observe several nursing homes. How would you describe the feelings and reactions of the elderly people there? Are they finding meaning in life? If so, how?

References

Achenbaum, W. A. and Bengtson, V. L. Re-engaging the Disengagement Theory of Aging *Gerontologist* 34:6 December, 1994, p. 756–763.

Bowling, A. and P. D. Browne. "Social Networks, Health, and Emotional Well-Being Among the Oldest Old in London." *Journal of Gerontology* 46:1 (1991): S20–32.

Burgess, Ernest W. *Aging in Western Societies*. Chicago: University of Chicago Press, 1960.

Cumming, Elaine, and W. E. Henry. *Growing Old: The Process of Disengagement*. New York: Basic Books, 1961.

Dorfman, R. *Aging Into the 21st Century: The Exploration of Aspirations and Values*. New York: Brunner/Mazel, 1994.

Dowd, J. "Beneficence and the Aged." *Journal of Gerontology* 39 (1984): 102–108.

Estes, C. "Austerity and Aging in the U.S.: 1980 and Beyond." In *Old Age and the Welfare State*, edited by A. Guillemard, 169–186. Beverly Hills: Sage, 1983.

George, Linda. "Subjective Well-Being: Conceptual and Methodological Issues." In *Annual Review of Gerontology and Geriatrics*, edited by C. Eisdorfer, (Spring 1981).

Giles, J. "The Myth of Generation X." *Newsweek*, (6 June 1994): 62–68.

"Giving Birth: How Old Is Too Old?" *Glamour* Magazine. (May 1994): 174.

Green, B. *Gerontology and the Construction of Old Age*. New York: Aldine de Gruyter, 1993.

Gubrium, Jaber. *Living and Dying at Murray Manor*. New York: St. Martin's Press, 1975.

Gubrium, J. "Qualitative Research Comes of Age in Gerontology." *Gerontologist* 32:5 (October 1992): 581.

Heath, Amy Hill, ed. *Having Our Say: The Delany Sisters' First 100 Years; Sarah and A. Elizabeth Delany*. New York: Kochanska International, 1993.

Hong, L., and R. Duff. "Widows in Retirement Communities: The Social Context of Subjective Well-Being." *Gerontologist* 34:3 (June 1994): 347–352.

Horley, J. "Life Satisfaction, Happiness, and Morale: Two Problems with the Use of Subjective Well-Being Indicators." *Gerontologist* 24 (April 1984): 124–127.

Jacobs, Jerry. *Older Persons and Retirement Communities: Case Studies in Social Gerontology*. Springfield, IL: Charles C. Thomas, 1975.

Jacobs, Jerry. *Professional Women at Work*. Westport, CT: Bergin and Garvey, 1994.

Job, E. "Retrospective Life Span Analysis: A Method for Studying Extreme Old Age." *Journal of Gerontology* 38 (1983): 367–374.

Kane, R. "The Literature Lives: Generations of Applied Gerontological Research." *Gerontologist* 32:6 (December 1992): 724–725.

Kaufman, S. R. *The Ageless Self*. Madison: University of Wisconsin Press, 1986.

Krause, Neal. "Perceived Health Problems, Formal/Informal Support and Life Satisfaction Among Older Adults." *Journal of Gerontology* 45:5 (1990): S193–205.

Krause, N. "Stressful Events and Life Satisfaction Among Elderly Men and Women." *Journal of Gerontology* 46:2 (1991): S84–92.

Larson, Reed, et al. "Being Alone versus Being with People: Disengagement in the Daily Experience of Older Adults." *Journal of Gerontology* 40 (May 1985): 381.

Laws, G. Understanding Ageism: Lessons from Feminism and Postmodernism, *Gerontologist* 35:1, February, 1995, p. 112–118.

Liang, Jersey. "Dimensions of the Life Satisfaction Index A: A Structural Formulation." *Journal of Gerontology* 39 (1984): 613–622.

Liang, Jersey, and Kenneth A. Bollen. "Sex Differences in the Structure of the Philadelphia Geriatric Center Morale Scale." *Journal of Gerontology* 40 (July 1985): 468–477.

Luborsky, M. "The Romance with Personal Meaning in Gerontology: Cultural Aspects of Life Themes." *Gerontologist* 33:4 (August 1993): 445–452.

Luborsky, M., and A. Sankar. "Extending the Critical Gerontology Perspective: Cultural Dimensions." *Gerontologist* 33:4 (August 1993): 440–454.

Mannheim, Karl. "The Problem of Generations." In *Essays on the Sociology of Knowledge*, 2d ed., edited by D. Kecskemeti, 276–322. London: Oxford University Press, 1952.

Martin, J. David. "Power, Dependence, and the Complaints of the Elderly: A Social Exchange Perspective." *Aging and Human Development* 2 (May 1971): 108–112.

Matras, Judah. *Dependency, Obligations, and Entitlements*. Englewood Cliffs, NJ: Prentice Hall, 1990.

McCulloch, B. J. "The Relationship of Intergenerational Reciprocity of Aid to the Morale of Older Parents: Equity and Exchange Theory Comparisons." *Journal of Gerontology* 45:4 (1990): S150–155.

Minkler, M., and C. Estes. *Critical Perspectives on Aging*. New York: Baywood, 1991.

Moody, J. "Toward a Critical Gerontology." In *Emergent Theories of Aging*, edited by J. Birren and V. Bengtson. New York: Springer, 1988.

Neugarten, B., R. J. Havighurst, and S. Tobin. "The Measurement of Life Satisfaction." *Gerontology* 16 (1961): 134–143.

Olson, L. *The Political Economy of Aging*. New York: Columbia University Press, 1982.

Quinn, J. "The Luck of the Xers," *Newsweek* June 6, 1994, p. 66–67.

Reker, Gary T., et al. "Meaning and Purpose in Life and Well-Being: A Life Span Perspective." *Journal of Gerontology* 42 (January 1987): 44–49.

Roberto, Karen A., and Jean P. Scott. "Equity Considerations in the Friendships of Older Adults." *Journal of Gerontology* 41 (March 1986): 241–247.

Ward, R. A. "The Marginality and Salience of Being Old." *Gerontologist* 24 (1984): 227–232.

Further Readings

Bengtson, V., and A. Achenbaum, *The Changing Contact Across Generations.* New York: Aldine De Gruyter, 1993.

Berman, H. *Interpreting the Aging Self: Personal Journals of Later Life.* New York: Springer, 1994.

Fried, S. et al. *Older Adulthood: Learning Activities for Understanding Aging.* Baltimore, MD: Health Professionals Press, 1993.

Kastenbaum, R. *Defining Acts: Aging as Drama.* Amityville, New York: Baywood Pub. Co., 1994.

Shenk, D. and W. Achenbaum eds. *Changing Perceptions of Aging and the Aged.* NY, NY: Springer Pub. Co., 1994.

5 Social Bonds

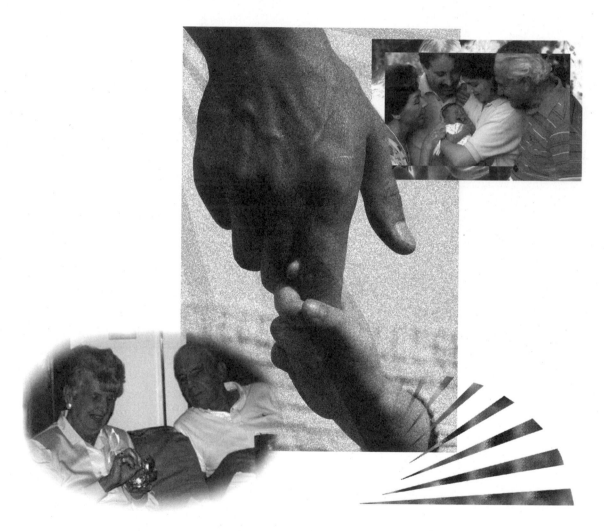

CHAPTER OUTLINE

President, Peacemaker, Poet

■ BETTIJANE LEVINE

The President-turned-peacemaker-and-poet looks happier, more fit and arguably more handsome now, at 70, than he did 14 years ago when Ronald Reagan's victory forced him out of the Oval Office—a one-term President dejected by defeat.

In Los Angeles for a few hours to promote his new book of verse, "Always a Reckoning," Carter looked every inch a man who has faced his demons and conquered them.

He answers to a Higher Authority, his beatific demeanor implies.

When he left the White House, he admits, "We were discouraged and we were broke." There was no more peanut business back home in tiny Plains, Ga. "I had to sell all the businesses I'd accumulated for 20 years in order to pay off debts that accumulated while I was President that I had no idea were accumulating.

"We didn't really know what we were going to do with the rest of our lives. I was quite young compared to other former Presidents. I was 54."

Back in Plains, Jimmy and Rosalynn Carter re-evaluated their lives and their goals. The songbirds still sang. In the small house where their four children were born—and where the Carters still sleep in a four-poster bed built by Jimmy with wood cut from 2,000 acres owned by the Carter family for generations—the world turned right-side-up again.

He says he realized his goals hadn't changed at all. He was still "the exact same man" as before he went to the White House. Someone who wanted to be good, and to do good. A man who wanted to help others purely "for the joy and pleasure we get out of helping."

And there were so many opportunities.

What he chose was to write prose and poetry (nine books so far), to teach at Emory University in Atlanta, to volunteer time each year building homes for the poor through Habitat for Humanity—and, most important, to create the Carter Center in Atlanta, through which he and Rosalynn work to help alleviate disease, homelessness and conflict in the world.

These are no small goals. Carter is perhaps the only ex-President likely to accomplish as much (or more) after leaving office as he did when he was in it.

In December, he waded into war-ravaged Bosnia and patched together a truce that got Muslims and Serbs to begin talking to each other.

In September, he negotiated in Haiti to remove Lt. Gen. Raoul Cedras from power, thereby winning for Haitians a last-minute reprieve from a military invasion already under way. (Carter then invited Cedras to address his Sunday school class in Plains.)

In June, Carter persuaded North Korea to modify its nuclear program. In May, he helped cement Panama's first democratic election. In February, 1990, he persuaded Nicaragua's Sandinistas to submit to their country's election results.

No other former President has intervened in so many international disputes and met with such immediate success. It's remarkable and unprecedented, historians say.

Carter smiles and shrugs. "We do what makes us happy."

The former peanut farmer uses the plural because he rarely talks about just himself. His wife is almost always included in his remarks.

"Rosalynn and I are full partners in absolutely everything—we just select the project that we find to be exciting and challenging and adventurous and unpredictable. And then we do it."

Stopping civil wars and building houses for the poor, while high-profile endeavors, account for only 10% of the Carters' time, he says.

"Most of our work is in the alleviation of suffering. We coordinate the immunization of the world's children from the Carter Center."

The center lists among its achievements the dramatic reduction of river blindness among 11 million citizens in the Third World and the near-eradication of Guinea worm disease, which once infected 2 million people a year in parts of India and Africa.

—Continued

"We do what makes us happy."

"We have 150,000 small-farm families in Africa whom we're teaching how to grow better grain to prevent starvation. We deal with human rights cases, too."

Carter comes up for air, considers his remarks, and worries that he might sound "too preachy"—something he has also been accused of in the press.

"I don't mean to sound that way," he says. "We really have fun doing what we do. Some people think we are making sacrifices. But we're not. It's very gratifying. It adds enjoyment to our lives. It brings me and Rosalynn closer together. We meet interesting people. We take off plenty of time to be with our (nine) grandchildren. We also climb mountains, go fly fishing and skiing . . . and, you know, we just have a good time."

Jimmy and Rosalynn, married in 1946, have three sons and a daughter. The oldest, John, was born in 1947. Their youngest, Amy was born almost exactly 20 years later. She is now a painter and art student in New Orleans, and hopes to become a museum curator.

Despite Carter's much publicized remark to a writer during his presidency that he had "lusted in his heart" for other women, his actions and poetry indicate a 50-year love affair with his wife. Of Rosalynn, he writes, "her smile still makes the birds forget to sing/and me to hear their song." ☀

SOURCE: *Los Angeles Times,* 10 February 1995, Section E, Life & Style. *Authors Note:* The poetic lines about Rosalynn are from a poem to Rosalynn on their 50th wedding anniversary, which is included in his book of poems *Always a Reckoning* (Random House, 1995).

his chapter examines social roles available to elders—the roles of family member, friend, and social participant—and assesses their meaning. Many elders lack the opportunity, but not the capacity, for intimate relationships. How society can offset reduced opportunities for social interaction is one of the topics we will consider in this chapter.

✸ The Need for Intimacy

Intimacy is the need to be close to, to be part of, and to feel familiar with another person. Old or young, we all need intimacy and social bonds with others. We may find our ability to maintain close relationships as strictly a personal problem. However, from a sociological viewpoint, the social environment does affect the maintenance of close or primary relationships. The norms, values, and social structure of a society may either foster or retard the development of social bonds.

Although most older people have strong social bonds, certain events are more likely to put constraints on their relationships. Disability and illness limit visiting, as does lack of transportation. Death takes friends and neighbors and, quite possibly a spouse. At the stage in life when retirement brings free time for social interaction, the opportunities for it may be reduced. Malcka R. Stern has experienced various losses, including her husband; she has moved to a nursing home; and is hearing impaired, but continues to reach out to others and respond to a warm social environment. Stern (1987) described her intimate group of friends in an article she wrote for the *Washington Post:*

> When I count the many blessings accrued to me in my long life of 93 years, high up on the list is the fact that I am a resident in the Attic Angle Tower, a senior citizens' apartment complex in Madison, Wisconsin. There are about 70 of us, average age 85, mostly widows.
>
> We have a beautiful dining area, and when we all sit together at dinner— the one meal we take together—four of us to a table, we really present a picture of a group of elegantly coiffed and attired older women.
>
> True, at the tables lucky enough to have among them one of our few men, there always seems to be much more animated conversation and much more gaiety. We do indeed miss our men.
>
> Our group is impressive. We have among us professional women, all retired, of course, from all walks of life. Teachers, social workers, scientists. Many are widows of renowned professors, doctors, judges, lawyers and businessmen. In our midst we have talented artists, knitting and weaving experts, even a poet in residence.
>
> But lest we become too smug and too satisfied with our way of life, we all remember that attached to our apartment complex is the nursing home to which sooner or later we will all have to enter at the last stop. We don't talk about it very much. . . .
>
> Our friendships are warm and close. We have all experienced the same troubles, lived through losses of loved ones. Our own health fails. You complain to your neighbor about your arthritis and she doesn't say a word, but holds out her own gnarled and twisted hands. And we both smile and pat each other on the shoulder and go on about our business.
>
> I am very hard of hearing and often fear that I must seem pixilated when I respond inappropriately to someone's question. One does get tired of saying "What? What?" all the time. . . .
>
> Some of us go to a discussion group every week, and last week it was about grieving. We read James Agee's "A Death in the Family," and then our group leader asked each of us to recall our first experience with grief.

When it came my turn I talked about the death of my first child, my Barbara, a baby of 2 who died of diphtheria. I began to tell them and I couldn't finish the story. To my embarrassment, I burst into tears. It was 60 years ago. It was yesterday.

☼ Family Development in Later Life

Later life is not a static, stagnant time for the older family member. Transition events such as widowhood, retirement, remarriage, or a child's departure punctuate the life course. Transitions lead to changed perceptions, ways of behaving, and interdependence with kin and community. The older person's life is also influenced by family development events in the past, such as whether he or she was childless or a parent.

All of these events add to the ever-changing character of the older person's role as a family member. Older persons may face adjustments equal to or more difficult than those younger family members face. For the newly married couple, the birth of a first child may require a difficult adjustment; but for the middle-aged or elderly couple, learning to relate to an independent adult offspring who was once "my baby" may be equally traumatic. Adjusting to the death of a spouse can be the most challenging of all changes in the life cycle. Each event in the life cycle calls for relating to others in new ways and facing the problems inherent in every transition.

Because of increased survival through childhood, adulthood, and into old age, Americans have experienced predictably longer lives in this century. Marriages are more likely to last 50 or 60 years, parents are more likely to survive to see their children become adults and to see their grandchildren grow up. Whole stages of life that were brief and rare in the past, such as the postparental stage, are now long lasting. Many kin relationships last much longer now than they did in past generations.

☼ Marital Status

The marital status of older people tells a great deal about their roles, patterns of interaction, and social bonds. This section considers older couples and three categories of older singles: the widowed, divorced, and never-married. An unknown percentage of older people live together without being married. Remarriage as a result of divorce or death of a spouse is becoming more common and is also discussed in this chapter.

ELDERLY COUPLES

Being married is a reality for many older women (42 percent of those 65 and older) and most older men (77 percent) (U.S. Bureau of the Census, 1990). This means less than half of women are married, but more than three-fourths of the men are married. When men and women are combined, 53 percent of those 65 and older living in the community were married (over 16.5 million) (U.S. Bureau of the Census, 1994).

In many respects, the older couple can be considered lucky. Most couples hope they can grow old together, but one or the other may die before old age. Studies show that the elderly couple is happier, less lonely, and financially more stable than older single persons. Together, they can usually live out their lives in a satisfying way and be a source of great comfort and support to one another. If one's social ties have decreased because of retirement or dis-

YOU WILL MEET A TALL DISTINGUISHED
STRANGER... WHO DOES HIS SHARE
OF THE HOUSEWORK

ability, the role of spouse takes on even greater importance. The relationship can become the focal point of the couple's everyday life.

Prior to retirement or disability, one or both partners may have been very active outside the home; consequently, the number of hours each week they actually spent together may have been limited. Retirement or disability can substantially increase this number of hours, allowing a couple to make more joint decisions and to participate together in most meals and activities. The outcome may be that individual activities and outside relationships become more peripheral compared to their new and enjoyable mutual intimacy. But this increasing togetherness can also produce tension—neither partner being accustomed to having the other around so much of the time. Both partners may view their increased time together as a considerable loss of freedom or independence, rather than an opportunity for greater intimacy. If the wife has been a homemaker and the husband retires, she may resent the continuous presence and the too-great attention of a restless spouse who may have no interests of his own or who may not have planned for his own retirement. Conversely, the newly retired wife may upset the routine of the home. For example, a 75-year-old man who has been retired for 10 years may suddenly find his "castle" invaded by his newly retired wife of age 65, who disrupts the order and quiet he has established at home.

Marital satisfaction frequently decreases for wives who continue to work outside the home after their husbands retire. The wives feel they are working outside the home while still doing the major domestic labor at home. Their resentment seems to be grounded in fact: retirement-age husbands spend less time, on the average, on domestic labor whereas wives spend many hours per week on housework.

In a national study of families, married people age 50 to 95 were selected for an analysis of work, housework, and marital satisfaction (Ward, 1993).

High levels of marital satisfaction were reported by husbands and wives, and retirement neither enhanced or reduced marital satisfaction in this study. Although women were found to do more household work, it was the perception of unfairness rather than the division of labor that led some wives to express dissatisfaction. It would seem that traditional sex roles die hard. If these roles become more equal for young couples, we may see a more equitable division of household labor between couples in their retirement years.

One primary marital stereotype is that, after the early stages of romantic love, the relationship begins to deteriorate. Recent studies find the opposite, namely, an increasing enchantment with each other in the later years. Marital satisfaction appears to follow an inverted bell-shaped trend: declining satisfaction after the initial years, leveling off in the middle years, and increasing again during the postretirement years. Satisfaction may, in fact, return to its initial high level of the early marriage years.

An inverted bell-shaped pattern also charts a husband and wife's opportunity to share time and common interests and to develop greater mutual respect and understanding. The time before the birth of their first child offers husband and wife maximum opportunity for mutual involvement and marital cohesion. The increasing time demands of careers combined with the new demands of parenting substantially reduce the amount of time husband and wife can spend together in their middle years. The last child's leaving home and the retirement of the husband and wife once again allow time for greater involvement, shared activity, and marital cohesion.

Not all studies show that marital relationships become rosier with advanced old age. The deteriorating health of both husband and wife can bring problems to a relationship. Outside intervention can help troubled couples in advanced old age. Too much stress, whether financial or health-related, is hard on a marriage at any age.

ELDER SINGLES: THE WIDOWED

Older singles may be divorced, never-married, or widowed. Only 5.3 percent of the aged are divorced and not remarried, and only 4.5 percent have never been married. The widowed make up the bulk of elderly singles. Thirty-four percent of all men and women age 65 and over are widowed (U.S. Bureau of the Census, 1993, p. 45).

Fully 10.4 million women over 60 are currently widowed, whereas only about 2 million men are widowed and not remarried (U.S. Bureau of the Census, 1994).

Table 5.1 compares the marital status of three age groups and compares males with females. In the United States, the differences between men and women have always been pronounced. Most white males at all age levels are married: 83 percent of those 65 to 74, 74 percent of those aged 75 to 84, and 53 percent of those 85 and over. Notice the very large percentages of women 85 and over who are widowed.

Widowhood is the predominant lifestyle for women who comprise the "old-old" (age 75 and above) and the "oldest-old" (age 85 and over). The proportion of widows is expected to increase in the years ahead. We can expect that, in the future, three out of four women will ultimately become widows. Only if a man lives to be 85 is there an even chance of his being widowed.

Several factors are responsible for widows outnumbering widowers by a ratio of more than four to one. Women outlive men and are, therefore, more

	65–74		75–84		85+	
	Men	Women	Men	Women	Men	Women
White (N = 26,000,000)						
Never-Married	5	5	4	6	3	6
Married	83	55	74	30	53	9
Widowed	8	36	19	61	42	83
Divorced	4	5	2	3	2	2
Black (N = 2,436,000)						
Never Married	4	4	6	5	—*	6
Married	67	39	60	27	—	16
Widowed	18	47	25	67	—	76
Divorced	11	9	9	2	—	2
Hispanic Origin (any race) (N = 1,005,000)						
Never Married	6	7	6	11		
Married	78	60	69	26	—	—
Widowed	9	34	21	58	—	—
Divorced	6	10	3	5	—	—

*Base less than 75,000

SOURCE: U.S. Bureau of the Census, "Marital Status and Living Arrangements: March 1989," *Current Population Reports,* Series P–20, No. 445, (Washington, D.C.: U.S. Government Printing Office, 1990).

woman younger than himself, thus adding to her chances of living longer than he will. The high proportion of older women decreases their likelihood of remarriage.

The transition from married to widowed status brings both personal and familial problems. The transition is not always successful. Statistics indicate that the widowed suffer higher rates of mortality, mental disorders, and suicide. Childless widows especially lack support. The feelings of loss after the death of a spouse are enormous, especially if the couple had been married 30, 50, or even 70 or more years. The empty chair and the empty place in bed reinforce memories of sharing family rituals. What does one do with the memories? How does one manage the grief? Many turn to other family members for emotional support; others simply suffer alone.

Loss of a spouse may cause the most difficult role change that a person must cope with in a lifetime. The widow has lost the support and services of an intimate person in her life. If she doesn't find substitute supports, she is on her own. Her social life may be altered. She, as a single person, may be either uninvited to, or feel uncomfortable, in social settings where she had once been welcome. She may lose contact with her husband's friends and relatives. She, then, must form new relationships and make new friends.

Lopata (1973) described the **stages of widowhood** as follows:

1. Official recognition of the event
2. Temporary disengagement or withdrawal from established lines of communication
3. Limbo
4. Reengagement

Official recognition of the event typically begins with the funeral and the initial mourning period. The term **grief work** (coined by Lopata) describes healthy confrontation and acknowledgment of the emotions brought about by death. The widow must accept the finality of her loss in order to get on with living. Grief work for the widow takes time and may bring a temporary withdrawal from past social activities and responsibilities as she reassesses her life. Once she answers the question "Where do I go from here?" she can become reengaged in society.

Studies of widowhood typically characterize the period beginning about 6 months after the spouse's death as a reorganization stage different from the phase of intense grief that comprises the first few months after the event. Research on the later phases of coping with widowhood has zeroed in on the importance of friends and family as sources of social support.

Some older widow–adult children relationships seem to have a negative side. Older widows sometimes feel unappreciated, that they're making too many sacrifices for their children when their children should be offering comfort (Talbot, 1990). Even friends' attempts at support are occasionally misguided.

> This business of people saying "You're doing so well." I hated that. Or "You're so strong" . . . Because I was really feeling terrible, and I needed someone to say, "Gee, it's really rough for you right now." (Morgan, 1989)

The most valued lifestyle is interdependence: asking for help and giving help to others.

Friends can offer more useful support by not trying to speed recovery, emphasizing strength, and not forcing a new identity. They can just listen, not argue, and provide unconditional love.

Interviews with 300 recently widowed women in an urban community showed them to be self-sufficient in managing their daily lives. They did not lean heavily on anyone for help with the basic tasks of daily living unless they were in advanced age and/or experiencing poor health. The research suggested that too much independence and self-sufficiency can lead to social isolation. Asking for help and giving help to others results in *interdependence,* which is the most valued lifestyle (O'Bryant, 1991).

Different women react differently to the loss of a spouse (Levy, 1994). Women in traditional marriages, who see their role of wife as central and who invested their identity, time, and energy primarily in this role, suffer immensely. If the marriage was close, the loss cuts especially deep into all aspects of the survivor's life. Reactions of widows may also vary by social class. Wives of blue-collar workers typically are not as emotionally close to their husbands. However, their generally low income levels as widows promote isolation and loneliness. Many widows, have lower morale and fewer social ties because they are poorer than their married counterparts. Generally speaking, the higher the widow's personal resources, such as income and education, and the higher her social and community participation, the better she can cope with her status.

Silverman's studies of widowhood indicate that grief never ends. Grief continually resurfaces, and the loss of a spouse irrevocably changes the individual (Silverman, 1988). Indeed, all the developmental phases of widowhood are more complex than previously thought. People may move back and forth between stages or be in several stages simultaneously. Those with previously happy marriages are more likely to consider remarriage or to make a successful life for themselves alone; in contrast, women whose marriages were poor are less likely to consider remarriage and seem to lack the emotional, social, and economic resources for entering new roles and relationships.

A number of organizations offer outreach services to widows and widowers. They may be religious, social service, or mental health groups. The American Association of Retired Persons (AARP) has a program, Widowed Persons Service (WPS), in which volunteers who have been widowed 18 months or more are trained to reach out and offer support to the newly widowed. This program is offered in 220 communities nationwide. WPS conducts special outreach to minorities and other groups who are typically less active in such programs (*Widowed Persons Service Fact Sheet,* 1990). Participation in outreach programs can be a lifesaver for elders willing to seek help.

WIDOWS AND WIDOWERS COMPARED

Family sociologists disagree whether husbands or wives experience greater difficulty in coping with the death of a spouse. A husband as the surviving partner of a traditional relationship may have the greater difficulty. He may have to learn the new role of housekeeper, learn to cook, to assume cleaning chores. Further, the widower is less likely than the widow to move in with his children, less likely to have a high degree of interaction with relatives, and less likely to have close friends. If the wife was the initiator of family contacts, her death typically lessens the widow's interaction with other family members. Statistics paint a grim picture for the husband who survives his wife.

Widowers die four times as often from suicide, three times as often from accidents, ten times as often from strokes, and six times as often from heart disease as do married men of the same age (*Widowed Persons Service Fact Sheet*, 1990).

On the other hand, the widow's situation may be equally difficult, both socially and psychologically. Lopata (1979) points out that about half of the widows she studied spent a significant period of time providing care to ill husbands before becoming widowed. They may have depleted social and emotional resources. Widows have fewer chances for remarriage than do widowers, and the financial resources of the widow are typically less than those of the widower. Data from a national sample of widows show that widowhood decreases income by 18 percent and pushes below the poverty line the incomes of 10 percent of women whose pre-widowhood incomes were above the poverty line. However, surprisingly, two-thirds of those widows who entered poverty left it within five years (Bound et al., 1991).

Silverman's comparison of **widows** and **widowers,** mentioned above, indicated that men and women change in different directions. The men are more "in search of others." They become more aware and appreciative of friends and relationships. Women, by contrast, are more "in search of themselves." They develop confidence, assertiveness, and independence. Widows had been more wrapped up in the role of wife than the widowers in the role of husband. New relationships developed by each seemed to allow more flexible roles and less dependency. Both sexes found new excitement about the changes in their lives.

ELDERLY SINGLES: THE DIVORCED

Divorce among the 65 and older population, once uncommon, is increasing. The 1970 U.S. Census reported that 10.2 percent of those over 65 had experienced a divorce at some point in their adult life. By 1990, that percentage had more than doubled. By 2025, no more than 37 percent of women aged 65 to 69 will be in first marriages. When one considers both widowhood and divorce, only half of all women entering old age in 2025 will be in a marriage. This figure could be less than half if divorce rates continue to increase in middle and old age and if remarriage rates continue to decline (Uhlenberg et al., 1990). Though divorce has gained acceptance as a solution to an unpleasant or difficult marriage, the impact of the increasing divorce rate in old age spells trouble if divorce impairs financial status or disrupts kinship networks.

A study of 310 recently separated men and women, which compared the experience of separation for younger and older persons, found that older individuals tend to suffer more disruption than younger divorcees and that older divorcees were more unhappy, reporting fewer positive emotional experiences (Chiriboga, 1982). Their dealings with the social world were more tortured, and they suffered more negative psychological symptoms, such as greater pessimism and dissatisfaction. Some, however, felt they should have divorced years ago and were glad that it finally happened.

The reasons older people suffer more in time of separation and divorce are not clear. Possibly, the greater number of years married may mean greater difficulty in letting go. And older people, especially women, may face a more limited range of options than younger persons. There may be greater uncertainty and a greater sense of failure. Certainly, the socioeconomic well-being of divorcees (of any age) is significantly below that of widowed or married women. Divorced men fare better economically and have the highest likelihood of remarriage of all elderly singles. Separation and divorce is a time of crisis. Not as much social support exists for the divorced as for widowed elders. More research is needed to find ways to alleviate emotional pain and to examine long-term adaptation to divorce.

ELDERLY SINGLES: THE NEVER-MARRIED

The never-married constituted 4.5 percent of the aged population in 1992. Few never-marrieds marry in old age: first marriages constitute less than 10 percent of all marriages of elders. One might expect elderly singles who have never married to be unhappy and lonely. But the never-married have typically adjusted to being single in their younger years and are well practiced in those skills of self-reliance and independence that make living alone a desirable and workable lifestyle. They do, however, report slightly more loneliness than married persons. But, because the never-married will never experience the death of a spouse, they are spared the grief and loneliness that follows such an event.

However, the never-married do suffer from losses. They tend to have highly valued friends and relatives. When these important people in their lives die, they suffer greatly. The never-married are a diverse group—some are isolated; others have many friends. Some wish they were married; some are glad they are not married.

The measurement of social connections allows gerontologists to compare the single and the married. To measure friendship, Rubenstein asked older persons to write "the one person or persons who are the very closest" in the innermost of three circles on a piece of paper, people not quite as close but who are still important in the middle circle, and those who are less close but still important in the outer circle. The results indicated that married people have more connections in the inner and middle circles (their spouse being the most intimate), whereas singles had more outer-circle relationships (Rubenstein, 1987).

REMARRIAGE

Today we hear a great deal more about the occurrence of late-life marriages. Remarriage in old age is becoming more common for two reasons: (1) more older people are divorcing, which places them in the remarriage market; and (2) remarriage has become more acceptable for the widowed. Although remarriage of widowed and divorced women over age 65 currently constitutes only 4 percent of all marriages (U.S. Bureau of the Census, 1993), remarriage seems to work well for most older people. Many have had long, reasonably happy second (or third) marriages and are glad to have found another compatible partner. They do not take relationships or marriage for granted. Older singles in search of relationships try to meet partners at church functions, local clubs and organizations, parties, and dances. The extroverted might try video dating, computerized dating, or advertise in the personal columns of newspapers. Here is a sampling:

- All I want is a kind, spiritual NS/ND/ND gentleman who has a house with a garden to grow vegetables. I am 5'7", 67 and into holistic health and metaphysics. I love nature and people, too.
- SINGLE WOMAN 60ish enjoys everything from opera to country, dining out, picnics, playing pool, horseback riding, swimming, reading and more! Would love to meet male with similar interests.
- Cuddly, down to earth, emotionally and financially stable WM, 55, to share dance, movies, ocean walks, tennis, his heart and more w/very loving N/S slim SWF w/good values.

Thinking about Aging

Never Too Late

■ MARSHA KING

His summer shirt is open partway down his chest, and the skirt of her flowered dress is flying as he whirls her laughing around the dance floor at the Greenwood Senior Center.

They act like a couple of love-struck kids. Giggling. Touching. His hand squeezes her arm. She shyly glances at him. He plants a warm, surprise kiss on her lips. Her cheeks flush. He breaks into a small, pleased smile.

Claire Ridinger and Dorothy Kreitle, in their "70's," say it's never too late to fall in love. And you'd better believe it's just as exciting, if not better, than when they were young.

"It isn't over just because you've hit another birthday," insists Kreitle, a widow for 21 years. ". . . You should enjoy every day, 'cause no one knows when your time's gonna be up."

The pair met last year at a Seattle Center dance for seniors. She was light on her feet and a lot of fun. He bought her coffee and gave her a ride home, then won a date for Saturday night. In the early weeks, he called four times a day. She didn't spurn his attention.

Now the couple dances five times per week, travel together, eat dinner out, double-date with friends, share holidays with each other's children. And here and there they spend a night or two together. But it's a bittersweet affair. Ridinger still is married to his first wife of 48 years, who has Alzheimer's disease and has lived in a nursing home the past two-and-a-half years.

"My first love is my wife. I see her every other day, and Dorothy doesn't mind that," he says. . . . He supports his wife financially, even does her washing.

"It's not a deserting proposition. I'm not leaving her," he says. "We had a marriage, but I just got lonely and needed company. . . ."

One happy fact is clear: Romance may be touted for the firm, smooth and young, but age is no foe of love. Seniors want and need physical and emotional contact with the opposite sex as much as younger people. . . .

"So many younger people have the misconception that we're dead, with one foot in the grave and the other on a banana peel," says Carl Kossen, 77, from Ballard.

The heart still beats faster. The palms still get sweaty. The head spins. And a kiss is still a kiss. "Oh, hell yes. I enjoy kissing as much now as I did when I was 18, if she's a good kisser," Kossen says.

Initially, there may be some awkward feelings over a face or body that's seen a few years. But as Kossen puts it from a man's point of view: Senior ladies may not look like those gals in sexy TV ads, "but to older eyes they're still beautiful. When you have a few wrinkles yourself, you can't hardly condemn them that have a few also." ☀

SOURCE: King, Marsha. "Never Too Late," *Seattle (Washington) Times* (July 26, 1987): A1–A2. Reprinted with permission of *The Seattle Times*.

■ An early 70's N/S DWM seeks the companionship of a woman who manifests spirituality and intelligence. A few of my interests are theatre, Dixieland jazz, and strenuous hiking. In 1994 I traveled to Europe and China. Please respond to . . .

■ TIRED OF ROAD KILL? Desire an energized rabbit? Tall, fit, SWM, 69. Keeps going . . . and going . . . and going.

—*(Santa Rosa Press Democrat,*
"The Meeting Place," 28
February 1995, p. F3.)

Such ads indicate that the desire for courtship and meaningful relationships lasts a lifetime. Beginning in the 1980s, researchers called for more attempt to understand dating and mate selection in later life. However, we know little about the process of courtship in later life. Although we know that intimate relationships are important and that older people seek intimacy and meaningful relationships, we have not yet examined the process leading to remarriage.

A positive aspect of remarriage in old age is that children are grown and out of the house; the couple does not typically experience great daily strain being stepparents. Of course, problems can arise over financial matters, such as inheritances. Jealousies may surface between the new spouse and the children from the remarried partner's previous marriage. But studies show that older persons on the whole are happier and more satisfied if they remarry.

☼ Elders in the Kin Structure

The family has a vital part of the elders person's life. Elderly persons give a great deal to their families, and they receive a great deal in return. Family members tend to exchange emotional and financial support throughout their lives. A person's confidant in life is typically a close family member—spouse, child, or sibling. Only when a closely related family member is unavailable does a friend rather than a relative act as confidant (Kendig et al., 1988). In this section, we will discuss siblings and grandparenthood. Parent-child ties are discussed in the next chapter.

THE ELDER SIBLING

Although **elderly siblings** may cause problems for one another, they can also extend support to one another in a social environment that does not always foster the development of social bonds (Connidis, 1994). Studies show that bonds between siblings typically extend throughout life and are second only to mother-child ties.

Most elders have a living sibling. The parents of today's elderly produced more children than did the elders themselves; any given married adult probably has more siblings than offspring. If the birthrate is now at the replacement level of two children per couple, we can expect there will be fewer children, and thus fewer siblings, in the future. The family support system will be smaller in the years ahead.

The sister/sister tie is closer than other sibling ties, followed by sister/brother, and brother/brother. The number and sex of siblings influences the older person: a large number of female siblings typically means increased emotional support; and sisters, particularly older sisters, sometimes assume a maternal role to hold a family together after the mother's death. Sibling ties can sometimes be closer than the tie to a spouse, and the sibling relationship can have the longest duration of any kin relationship. Siblings are often emotionally supportive, sharing feelings and concerns as they face common problems of their age group.

People in lower socioeconomic classes tend to rely more greatly on their siblings for support and closeness. They are more likely to remain geographically stable and to interact more frequently than siblings with higher educational and financial attainment, who move more and are exposed to a wider variety of people, thus reducing their need for sibling closeness. Those from families with more than two children (especially those with four or more) seem to be more intimate with their siblings in late life (Gold et al., 1990).

Elders are affected by their place in the birth order. The youngest member of a large family may experience enormous loss throughout his or her life as other family members die. Many residents of rest homes have no living family members. The individual's reaction to and method of coping with this total loss of family represents an important area of study (Moss and Moss, 1989). The death of a brother or sister may shock an older person more than the death of any other kin, because a sibling's death brings a sense of one's own mortality. Contact with surviving siblings allows one to renew good memories about a deceased brother or sister and to maintain warm feelings toward remaining siblings.

VARIATIONS IN KIN RELATIONS

The demography of the kin system varies widely also. Some older people have large and extensive kinship systems, with many relatives nearby, whereas other older people have managed to outlive siblings, children, spouse, and other kin. The relationships among kin members vary by sex, social class, and locale (urban/rural).

Females maintain closer relationships with other family members than do males. Beginning in infancy, the female child is closer to the mother than to the father. The mother is typically the primary child caregiver and primary source of emotional closeness for the family. Couples are more likely to live near the wife's parents, and they are likely to visit them more often. In old age, the mother tends to keep closer, more meaningful ties with children.

Blue-collar families tend to have close family ties, which members maintain by living near each other. Visits from kin often constitute the major, if not the only, form of social activity for such families. White-collar family ties are also fairly strong: such families are geographically scattered by career opportunities, yet they often maintain contact in spite of distance.

Gerontological literature inconsistently reports differences between rural and urban families. On the one hand, rural areas are shown to be bastions of traditional values, one being family responsibility and respect for elders. We can picture rural family reunions at which the aged are celebrities looking with pride at the family line of children, grandchildren, and great-grandchildren. In this picture, kinship ties are strong and meaningful. Small-town newspapers often reflect the apparent importance of family and neighborly ties by featuring articles on who has visited whom, who is in the hospital, or who went out of town to visit relatives.

Another picture of rural areas is one of poverty, isolation, and despair. In spite of the assumed traditional values, rural elders interact less with their children than do their urban counterparts. Studies have shown that, compared with urban older people, rural elders have substantially smaller incomes, are more restricted in terms of mobility, experience poorer physical health, and have a more negative outlook on life. Kin ties should be promoted and supported in a society where they are so threatened by social and demographic change.

GRANDPARENTHOOD

The three-generation family is becoming common, and even four- and five-generation families are on the increase. Rossi and Rossi (1990) found, though, that two- and three-generational lineages are most common. About 80 percent of those over 65 have living children, and 80 percent of those, or 60 percent of all older people, have at least one grandchild. If one becomes a parent at age 25, one may well be a grandparent at age 50. If parenthood at age 25 continues for the next generation, the individual would be a great-grandparent at age 75, thus creating a four-generation family.

Note that middle age, not old age, is the typical time for becoming a grandparent. Most grandparents do not fit the image of jolly, white-haired, bespectacled old people with shawls and canes: many are in their forties and fifties.

Researchers are becoming more concerned with the meaning of grandparenthood for grandparents and grandchildren and for society. The recent findings on the meaning of this role for older people appear inconsistent. The word *grandparent* evokes positive feelings and images for most of us. Yet studies show that grandparents seldom develop close intimate relationships with their grandchildren. However, the majority of grandparents seem to gain considerable pride and pleasure from interaction with their grandchildren.

Studies of the meaning of grandparenthood show great variation. For some it is a time to have childish fun or to indulge grandchildren—perhaps even a chance to reexperience one's youth. At the opposite end of the spectrum would be the more formal, distant grandparent—perhaps one who tries to be a role model or the repository of family wisdom—the grandparent children go to for the best cookie recipe or for stories about their parents, aunts, and uncles. For some, grandparenthood is personally meaningful because it represents the continuation of the family line. Certainly, one grandparent might find great joy in many aspects of grandparenting. For a small percentage, though, the role of grandparent is meaningless because, for a variety of reasons, they have very little contact with their grandchildren. Probably the most common would be a troubled relationship with an adult child, which could estrange both children and grandchildren.

A study (Miller and Cavanaugh, 1990) showed that being retired affected the meaning of grandparenthood. So did one's number of grandchildren. Retirement allows more time for interaction and meaningful relationships. And, of course, having more grandchildren increases the opportunity for interaction.

Grandfather, on the Front Steps at Midnight, New Year's Eve, Thinks About his Newborn Twin Grandsons

(The Salton Arm Poem)

■ *D. L. Emblem*

Through naked branches of the sycamores,
two bright planets twinkle—
whole, emerging worlds embedded
in the black, protective velvet
of the mother-father womb of night,
so full of light of love itself,
a million other glimmerings shine through.

I was like that once, a something far far off
on the other side of a sphere of time.
Now everything seems so close at hand
I cannot sever wax from wane,
so deeply am I caught in both.
I remember now how easily one confuses dusk and dawn
for lack of knowing each to be the edge of each.

When these bare trees leaf out
(it seems only now I've raked the last of them),
those two will creep toward walking,
and I toward crawling once again,
but I will hold their hands
and feel once more the seamless round
of growth into one thing, growth into another.

For some grandparents, their role is essentially that of substitute parent. Because their adult child is unable or unavailable to parent—because of drug abuse, death, divorce, AIDS, a mental health problem, career choice, or a host of other modern-day complications—grandparents sometimes end up with full-time care of their grandchildren. The number of support groups, such as GAP (Grandparents as Parents), indicates the size of this modern-day problem. A grandparent undertaking the stressful job of parenting is probably not doing so by choice. But most struggle to do the best they can, and a weekly support group can offer hope and help (Larsen, 1990/1991).

For other grandparents, the role is a marginal one. Lopata, in her study of widowhood, found that only slightly more than half of widowed grandmothers feel close to even one of their grandchildren. Another study found that only 10 percent of married young adults see their grandparents as often as weekly.

Women are much more likely than men to look forward to the role of grandparent. Women often visualize themselves as grandparents well ahead of the birth of the first grandchild, and the grandmother role is positive and desirable to most women, even though it can make young grandmothers feel old. Men typically become grandfathers when their primary identity is still with the work role. Consequently, they may postpone involvement with their grandchildren until retirement.

Anthropologist Dorothy Dorian Apple (1956) explored grandparent/grandchildren relationships in 75 societies. She found that in societies where grandparents retain considerable household authority, the relationship between grandparents and grandchildren tended to be stiff and formal. In societies such as the United States, where grandparents retain little control or authority over grandchildren, the relationship is friendly and informal. Others have likewise observed that American grandparents, more than grandparents in other societies, engage in companionable and indulgent relationships with their grandchildren and usually do not assume any direct responsibility for their behavior.

One of the most representative samples of grandparents of teenagers affirmed many of these results. Grandparents often played a background, supportive role, helping most during times of crisis (Cherlin and Furstenberg, 1992). On the other hand, in the late 1980s, 5 percent of all children lived in the household of their grandparents (U.S. Bureau of the Census, 1990). For some of these children, no parent is present and the grandparent is a parental surrogate. For others, the grandparent is assisting a single parent by providing housing and perhaps other services. Even if they do not live with their grandparents, millions of American children receive childcare from their grandparents each day (U.S. Bureau of the Census, 1990).

Many grandparents enjoy companionable and indulgent relationships with their grandchildren.

CHAPTER 5 Social Bonds

One can conclude that grandparenthood carries meaning for some elders, but not for others. This meaning may be biological, social, or personal. The degree of involvement with grandchildren varies. Current evidence seems to indicate that in the United States, grandparenthood, for many, is not a primary role, although it is enjoyed by most. It may be a primary role, however, for grandparents who provide the majority of care for their families' children. Becoming a grandparent is not going to fill voids left by shortcomings in marriage, work, or friendships.

THE IMPACT OF DIVORCE ON GRANDPARENTHOOD

The consequences grandparents experience when their children divorce is now under study by sociologists and under legal scrutiny in the courtroom. If a couple divorces and the in-law gets custody of the offspring, grandparents often cannot enjoy the relationship they desire with their grandchildren.

In one study, grandparents were emotionally distant enough from their adult children's lives to maintain cordial relations with former in-law adult children. Half of the grandparents were "friendly" with their child's former spouse. They tended to be friendly if the ex-spouse was a female, but they tended to lose contact if the ex-spouse was male, even if he had custody of the grandchildren. Matilda White Riley writes about the "matrix of voluntary kin relationships." Given the emphasis on individualism and social ties based on mutual interest, kinship can be complex in U.S. society. These social norms make the negotiation of kin relationships a necessary task. Good relationships with former daughters-in-law, for example, may determine whether grandparents can remain close to grandchildren. If informal negotiation fails, more and more people may be arguing in court for the right to spend time with a given child.

Maternal grandparents are in the best position to maintain a relationship with grandchildren in the event of divorce. The reasons are twofold: a daughter is more likely than a son to get custody, and she is more likely than a son to keep in close contact. After divorce, custodial grandparents were more likely to have seen their grandchild about once a week or more often (39 percent) than were noncustodial grandparents (16 percent) (Cherlin and Furstenberg, 1992).

Let us say that the adult son divorces his wife, and that the wife, who gets the children, is angry at her husband. She may not want any of his relatives to have a relationship with the children, even the grandparents. Some grandparents have succeeded in gaining visitation rights through the courts. However, strong laws that support the rights of grandparents do not exist.

Grandparents have traditionally had no standing in cases involving visitation and adoption of grandchildren, and the courts have upheld the supremacy of the parent-child relationship. Traditionally, a legal relationship between grandparent and grandchild existed only when both parents were incapable or dead, meaning that the courts had to judge the child's parents unfit before the grandparents had any rights.

Today, at least one legal precedent has been set: if provisions for visiting grandparents had been made prior to divorce, visitation is generally permitted after divorce. Thus, grandparents can, under limited circumstances, get visitation rights. (They have no rights, however, if parents choose to give their children up for adoption.) More and more grandparents are pressing for rights with regard to their grandchildren. The changes are slow, but as each grandparent takes a case to a local courtroom, momentum builds for developing guidelines for grandparents' rights.

We should also note that elders add new relatives to their kinship system when their adult children remarry. Remarriage, which may take place more than once, brings not only new sons- and daughters-in-law but may bring stepgrandchildren. When older parents can maintain ties with their childrens' former spouse(s), grandchildren lead more stable lives. Grandparents who can remain flexible and friendly have the benefit of enjoying an expanded kinship system. This "new extended family" (Cherlin and Furstenberg, 1992) created by stepgrandparenthood may lead to close kin ties. Some grandparents report that there is no difference between stepgrandchildren and biological grandchildren. Often, younger grandchildren and those who live close will develop more involved relationships.

☼ Social Networks

One stereotypical picture of old age is of a solitary person, in a tiny hotel room, staring silently into space. Another is of oldsters in a rest home, propped up in adjacent armchairs but worlds apart. Either way, the picture is one of isolation and loneliness. Do the elderly have friends—really good friends—they can count on? Simply stated, most do, but some do not. Numerous factors affect the likelihood of close friendships in old age.

ELDERS AS FRIENDS AND NEIGHBORS

Friendship, now a legitimate area of study, is extremely important in the lives of elderly people (Adams and Bliezner, 1989). Let us contradict one stereotype about friendships among the elderly by saying that most older people maintain active social lives. In a study of widows, respondents were asked how many times in the past year friends had helped them with transportation, household repairs, housekeeping, shopping, yard work, illness, car care, important decisions, legal assistance, and financial aid. They also were asked how many times they had given help. Only 8.2 percent of the respondents indicated that they did not have a close friend. For the first close friend, 84.4 percent of the respondents named a woman. The average length of acquaintance with the friend was over 20 years; 81.3 percent keep in touch at least weekly (Roberto and Scott, 1984/85).

The researchers used equity theory to formulate hypotheses and analyze results. According to equity theory, which says that an equitable relationship exists if all participants are receiving gains, participants will be distressed if they contribute too much to, or receive too little from, a friendship. Equity is related to high morale, and, as expected, the equitably benefited women had the highest morale. An unexpected finding was that the overbenefited (those who received more help than they gave) had the lowest morale: receiving goods and services that one cannot repay may leave one feeling uncomfortable or inferior, resulting lower morale. Also unexpected was the high morale that existed among the underbenefited, the ones giving more than they received. Perhaps the underbenefited woman feels good that she does not need help and enjoys giving without receiving. The single women who lived alone compensated for lack of a marriage companion through extensive and meaningful friendship networks with other women.

Researchers differentiate between a confidant and a companion. A **confidant** is someone to confide in and share personal problems with, whereas a

companion is one who regularly shares in activities and pastimes. A companion may be a confidant, but not necessarily. One study revealed that adult children were apt to be confidants for the elderly and that spouses and friends were apt to be companions. Single women particularly had siblings in their companion network (Connidis and Davies, 1990).

SOCIAL ORGANIZATIONS

Are elders "joiners"? To what rates do they participate socially in voluntary organizations? Many, in fact the majority, join and are actively involved in voluntary organizations (nonprofit groups that elders join only if they choose to do so).

Lodges and fraternal organizations such as the Moose Lodge, Elks, Eastern Star, and the like are the most commonly joined volunteer associations. Membership in them tends to increase with age, and leadership positions are concentrated among older persons, perhaps because these organizations have a respect for elders that other organizations lack. The second most frequently reported form of participation is in the church. Church-related activities involve more than attending services; they include participation in church-sponsored groups such as missionary societies and Bible-study classes. Except for lodges and church, other voluntary associations generally decline in participation with age. When social class is controlled, however, no decline is evident. This means that being a "joiner" is related to a middle- or upper-class lifestyle, and aging by itself does not necessarily change this lifestyle.

Senior centers, as opposed to clubs, offer services and activities in addition to recreation; they may offer libraries, music rooms, health services, counseling, physical exercise, and education. Many senior centers operate under the auspices of churches, unions, or fraternal organizations. Often, individuals who began senior centers in their own communities now find them successful and popular years later.

The demand for senior clubs and centers continues to rise. Someday every community may have a senior center, and it will be as natural for older people to use their senior center as it is for children to go to school.

NETWORK ANALYSIS

We can conceive of the combination of social ties—organization memberships, friends, neighbors, and family—as a **social network.** Each person has some kind of social network. The process of analyzing the strengths and weaknesses of an older person's social network, called **network analysis,** enables caretakers to tell whether social or health intervention might be necessary. An overall picture of the aged's social networks could assist in forming an integrated social policy responsive to the needs of the older population.

In recent years, a great deal of research has focused on social networks of elders. A study using the **convoy model** provides us with detailed information showing that older individuals are in frequent contact with both family and friends. The term *convoy* is used to evoke the image of a protective layer of family and friends who surround a person and offer support. Convoys are thought to be dynamic and lifelong in nature. A national study of 718 older adults asked respondents who their intimates were, how many of them there were, and what services and supports they exchanged. The average older person's support network consists of about nine members, who offer themselves as confidants, give reassurance and respect, provide care when ill, talk when upset, and discuss health (Antonucci and Akiyama, 1987).

☼ Religion

The religious dimension of aging encompasses the spiritual, social, and developmental aspects of a person's life. The last few years have seen a growing awareness of the importance of religion in the field of aging. In the past, the studies have been too few and too narrow in range. Most of the past research centered on easily quantified questions such as "Do you believe in God?" "How often do you go to church?" A decline in church attendance may mean either health problems or a decline in religiosity; thus more open-ended questions are needed. What is missing in many studies is the place that religious beliefs and practices hold in the lives of the aging individual. Some argue that a more phenomenological approach (see Chapter 4 for a definition) would correct this shortcoming.

The religious dimension can be conceptualized and measured in a variety of ways. One can have religious ideas, religious beliefs, religious faith, and religious practices. All these concepts are important in determining the role of religion in a person's life. Thomas (1994) conceptualized an intrinsic-extrinsic pole of religiousness for the individual in which the intrinsically religious find within themselves their ultimate meaning in life from religion. For these types, religion is the fundamental motive for living. The extrinsically religious use religion for more superficial social purposes or to justify their politics and prejudices. Their religion is extrinsic to their fundamental reason for being.

Church and synagogue attendance for older people exceeds that of other age groups. Further, those 65 and over are the most likely of any age group to belong to clubs, fraternal associations, and other church-affiliated organizations, such as widows and widowers groups, Bible-study groups, and volunteer groups serving the sick and needy. Older people are more likely than younger ones to believe in God and immortality, and say that God is influential in their lives (Cox and Hammonds, 1988). Older people are more likely than younger ones to be more orthodox or conservative in their beliefs—that is, to adhere to traditional, literal interpretations of their scripture. Also, elders tend to have positions of leadership in their respective churches.

Overall, religion has great importance for elders in U.S. society. This is especially true for African Americans for whom religion has intrinsic meaning and provides a means of integration into the larger community. Other ethnic groups, such as Mexican Americans, Puerto Ricans, and Native Americans, attach great meaning to religion or spirituality. Questions do remain, however. This question has not been fully answered: Do people become more religious with age or have elders today been more religious all their lives than younger people today? More longitudinal studies are necessary to fully explore this issue. Another matter involves the relationship between life satisfaction (or happiness or well-being) with religiosity. More often than not, a correlation is found. Such a correlation may be due to having a greater sense of meaning in life, lessened fear of death, more positive self-concept, greater sense of belonging and usefulness, closer friendships, greater participation in community affairs, greater sense of security, and more power to make change. According to Cox and Hammonds (1988), the church becomes a focal point of social integration and activity, providing older members with a sense of community and well-being. For example, a study of widows' church participation in a small town in rural Ohio showed church activity to bring great emotional closeness among the women (Stuckey, 1993).

Overall, studies tend to document religion as a positive in the lives of elders who describe themselves as religious. Many people consider themselves spiritual without being religious. Spirituality means a belief that there is some unseen order to which a person adjusts by developing characteristics that are loving and respectful, both to people and to the surrounding environment. But it does not necessarily indicate participation in traditional Western organized religion. Many Eastern and New Age religions (one example is the Church of Religious Science) promote spirituality without literal interpretations of scripture or heavy reliance on formal church attendance. In the Church of Religious Science, for example, the emphasis is on love and forgiveness of self and others. Some seekers of spiritual development have metaphysical concerns such as "connecting with the universe." Or religion may have a political thrust such as that emphasized by Gandhi or Havel (1990). The role of elders in all spiritual pursuits is of interest to gerontologists.

Elders benefit from the services of religious groups that minister to the needs of the sick, frail, disabled, and homebound. Church attendance declines after age 70, but this finding is attributed to transportation and health limitations in getting to the church, synagogue, or religious institution rather than decreased religious fervor. Carl Jung said:

> Among all my patients in the second half of life—that is to say, over 35—there has not been one whose problem in the last resort was not that of finding a religious outlook on life. (Jung, 1955)

This quote brings to mind questions about why and how and who enters a "spiritual journey" in the second half of life. The awesome challenges of facing loss, suffering, pain, and death: of finding ultimate meaning and purpose; of setting priorities and integrating the threads of one's life are possible reasons for such a quest. These are developmental tasks of aging, and religion may be useful in handling them. Jung's quote also brings to mind Erik Erickson's developmental concept of "integrity versus despair" discussed in Chapter 3: If a person can come to terms with life they have integrity; if not, they experience despair.

In contrast to increased religiosity with age are the observations of a minister to elders in Cambridge, Massachusetts. He reports being distressed that so many people in old age lack "self-knowledge and spiritual discernment." He states that they lack "the peace of soul which would make old age much more satisfying." He believes one of the most neglected aspects of old age in America is the need for spiritual development. With spiritual development one can experience a growing benevolence and a deeper empathy with fellow human beings (Griffin, 1994). It is not a given, then, that individuals become more religious with age. More studies are needed to document the circumstances under which this occurs. Such studies are now being conducted by means of participant observation (Eisenhandler, 1994) and interview and survey research (Rubenstein, 1994).

☼ Strengthening Social Bonds

Although elders are not as lonely and isolated as stereotypes would have us believe, many live out their last years without the close emotional or social bonds that they need and desire. For some, such isolation may result from their inability to establish and maintain intimate relationships with others. For many, however, isolation results from the new social situation that old age brings. Changing family patterns means less need for the services of older members within the family. The trend toward smaller families means fewer siblings and children with whom to interact. Very old age may bring the loss of a driver's license and car, physically curtailing social opportunities. Physical disability and illness also can hinder one's social life, and if these events do not happen to one aged individual, they may happen to his or her friends. For other aged, social organizations may not be available to provide friends and companionship.

We need more commitment to strengthening the social bonds of elders and providing them with the resources to develop the intimate ties and friendships they need to enjoy a meaningful life. The formation of supportive groups among people with common experiences could produce age-integrated as well as age-segregated groups. Fostering connections across age groups is vital, along with encouraging alliances among older people.

We need to explore other solutions—from nightclubs and centers to communes that cater to seniors. The suggestion of nightclubs is valid, not because older people need to drink, but because they have few places to interact socially. Perhaps expanding senior clubs and centers would be more to the point. The motivating factor is the same: to increase the older person's opportunities to find sociable companions. The provision of transportation is critical to those who are homebound.

The communal concept is being emphasized in some retirement housing, designed with rooms clustered around a communal kitchen and dining facility. The elderly share meals together but find privacy in their own rooms. With some imagination, communal concepts could find further approval in the aged community and, in turn, enhance social relationships of the elderly who want to participate.

Social, legal, and financial pressures on older people discourage remarriage. Many retirement programs pay the surviving spouse a monthly income

Intimate ties and friendships are necessary to enjoy a meaningful life.

that remarriage voids or reduces. A second factor is pressure from children, who may discourage an aging mother or father from remarrying for fear that, upon the parent's death, his or her assets will be in the hands of the second marital partner. Reluctance to marry out of respect for the deceased spouse poses another barrier to remarriage. Finally, old people may fear ridicule or condemnation if they choose to marry in old age. The barriers to marriage or remarriage are also barriers to the formation of intimate relationships. But, as living together without legal marriage becomes a more acceptable lifestyle for young people, it also becomes more acceptable for the old.

Widow-to-widow programs exist in many communities. These programs, which locate widows and help them to get together to share experiences, also provide legal assistance, social activities, and employment counseling. Churches are another source of counseling and other services for widows. We can strengthen social bonds and friendships through a genuine effort to provide these and other services and interaction that elders need.

Chapter Summary

Old or young, we all need intimacy and social bonds with others. Sadly, our social structure and values are such that old age often reduces opportunities for social interaction. Elders are at the latter stages of the family life cycle. Adjustments must be made to children leaving home, retirement, job changes, death or divorce of spouse, and remarriage. More women than men must cope with death of spouse and widowhood. Aged siblings often provide support and companionship. Grandparenthood is a role that most elders experience. However, it is not a central role for many. The aged are happier if they form intimate friendships with others. Neighbors and social organizations such as lodges, church, and senior centers are important sources of social interaction. And religion is a source of spiritual and soul support. More attention should be directed to strengthening the social bonds of elders.

Key Terms

companion
confidant
convoy model
elderly sibling
grief work
intimacy
marital satisfaction

network analysis
senior centers
social networks
stages of widowhood
widowers
widows

Questions for Discussion

1. What are the advantages and disadvantages of being married in later life? To being single?

2. Who offers the elderly the best chance of an intimate relationship, a family member or a friend?

3. What are the ages of those with whom you are most intimate? How much time do you share with your parents or grandparents, and they with you? How close to your parents do you expect to be in 10 or 20 years?

4. Would you want either or both parents to live with you in their old age? Would they want to?

5. As an older person yourself, how close will you want to be to your children or relatives? Who would you like to live with in old age if you were married? If you were single?

Fieldwork Suggestions

1. Attend a social function for older people, such as a club, senior center, ballroom, or folk dancing. Or attend a National Association of Retired Persons (NARP) or American Association of Retired Persons (AARP) meeting. What were the informal topics of conversation? What kind of interaction took place? What norms and values did you observe?

2. Interview two grandmothers and two grandfathers about the closeness of their relationships with their children and grandchildren. Include questions that explore how the relationships developed. How much interaction is there across the generations for these individuals? Why is the amount of involvement higher for some and lower for others?

References

Adams, R., and R. Bliezner. *Older Adult Friendship: Structure and Process.* Beverly Hills, CA: Sage, 1989.

Antonucci, Toni C., and H. Akiyama. "Social Networks in Adult Life and a Preliminary Examination of the Convoy Model." *Journal of Gerontology* 42 (October 1987): 519–527.

Apple, Dorothy Dorian. "The Social Structure of Grandparenthood." *American Anthropologist* 58 (August 1956): 656–663.

Bound, J., et al. "Poverty Dynamics in Widowhood." *Journal of Gerontology* 46:3 (May 1991): S115–S124.

Cherlin, Andrew, and Frank F. Furstenberg. *The New American Grandparent: A Place in the Family, A Life Apart.* Cambridge, MA: Harvard University Press, 1992.

Chiriboga, D. A. "Adaptation to Marital Separation in Later and Earlier Life." *Journal of Gerontology* 37 (1982): 109–114.

Connidis, I. "Sibling Support in Older Age," *Journal of Gerontology* vol. 49, November 1994, pp. 5309–5317.

Connidis, I., and L. Davies. "Confidants and Companions in Later Life: The Place of Family and Friends." *Journal of Gerontology* 45:4 (July 1990): 141–149.

Cox, H., and A. Hammonds. "Religiosity, Aging, and Life Satisfaction." *Journal of Religion and Aging* 5:1 (1988): 1–21.

Eisenhandler, S. "A Social Milieu for Spirituality in the Lives of Older Adults." In *Aging and the Religious Dimension,* edited by L. Thomas and S. Eisenhandler, 140–168, Westport, CT: Auburn House, 1994.

Gold, D., et al. "Relationship Classification: A Typology of Sibling Relationships in Later Life." *Journal of Gerontology* 45:2 (March 1990): S43–S51.

Griffin, R. "From Sacred to Secular." in *Aging and the Religious Dimension,* edited by L. Thomas and S. Eisenhandler, 90–112, Westport, CT: Auburn House, 1994.

Havel, V. *Disturbing the Peace.* New York: Vintage Books, 1990.

Jung, C. *Modern Man in Search of a Soul.* San Diego, CA: Harcourt-Brace, 1955.

Kendig, Hal L., et al. "Confidants and Family Structure in Old Age." *Journal of Gerontology* 43 (April 1988): 531–540.

Larsen, D. "Unplanned Parenthood." *Modern Maturity* (December 1990/January 1991): 33–36.

Levy, L. et al. "Differences in Patterns of Adaptation in Conjugal Bereavement." *Omega,* 29:1 (January, 1994): 71–87.

Lopata, Helena. *Widowhood in an American City.* Cambridge, MA: Schenkman, 1973.

Lopata, Helena Z. *Women as Widows: Support Systems.* New York: Elsevier, 1979.

Miller, S., and J. Cavanaugh. "The Meaning of Grandparenthood." *Journal of Gerontology* 45:6 (November 1990): 244–246.

Morgan, D. "Adjusting to Widowhood: Do Social Networks Make it Easier?" *Gerontologist* 29:1 (February 1989): 101–107.

Moss, Sidney, and Miriam S. Moss. "The Impact of the Death of an Elderly Sibling: Some Considerations of a Normative Loss." *American Behavioral Scientist* 33:1 (1989): 94–106.

O'Bryant, S. "Older Widows and Independent Lifestyles." *International Journal of Aging and Human Development* 32:1 (January 1991): 41–51.

Roberto, K., and J. Scott. "Friendship Patterns Among Older Women." *International Journal of Aging and Human Development* 19 (1984/85): 1–9.

Rossi, Alice, and Peter Rossi. *Of Human Bonding: Parent-Child Relations Across the Life Course.* New York: Aldine de Gruyter, 1990.

Rubenstein, R. "Generativity as Pragmatic Spirituality." In *Aging and the Religious Dimension,* edited by L. Thomas and S. Eisenhandler, 205–218, Westport, CT: Auburn House, 1994.

_____. "Never-Married Elderly as a Social Tie: Reevaluating Some Images." *Gerontologist* 27 (February 1987): 108–113.

Santa Rosa Press Democrat, Classified Ads, (28 February 1995): F 3.

Silverman, Phyllis. "Research as a Process: Exploring the Meaning of Widowhood." In *Qualitative Gerontology*, edited by S. Reinharz and G. Rowles, 217–240. New York, NY: Springer, 1988.

Stern, Malcka R. "At 93, Blessings and Memories." *Washington Post* (April 1987): 23.

Stuckey, J. "The Sunday School Class: The Meaning of Older Women's Participation in Church." Paper read at 1993 Annual Meeting of the Gerontological Society, New Orleans, LA, 1993.

Talbot, M. "The Negative Side of the Relationship Between Older Widows and Their Children." *Gerontologist* 30:5 (October 1990): 595–603.

Thomas, L. *Introduction, Aging and the Religious Dimension*, edited by L. Thomas and S. Eisenhandler, 1–20, Westport, CT: Auburn House, 1994.

Uhlenberg, P., et al. "Divorce for Women Afte. *Journal of Gerontology* 45:1 (January 1990): S3–S

U.S. Bureau of the Census. *Marital Status ana Arrangement*. Current Population Reports (Series No. 455). Washington, D.C.: U.S. Government Prin Office, 1990.

U.S. Bureau of the Census. *Statistical Abstract of the Unite States*, 113th edition. Washington, D.C.: U.S. Government Printing Office, 1993.

U.S. Bureau of the Census. *1990 Census of Population and Housing: Special Tabulation on Aging* (CD90-AoA-USA). Washington, D.C.: U.S. Department of Commerce, 1994.

Ward, Russell. "Marital Happiness and Household Equity in Later Life." *Journal of Marriage and the Family* 55:2 (1993): 427–438.

Widowed Persons Service Fact Sheet. Washington, D.C.: American Association of Retired Persons (October 1990).

Further Readings

Altergott, Karen. *Daily Life in Later Life: Comparative Perspective*. Newbury Park, CA: Sage, 1988.

Blieszner, R., and V. Bedford (Eds.). *Handbook on Aging and the Family*. Westport, CT: Greenwood Press, 1995.

Norris, J., and J. Tindale. *Among Generations: The Cycle of Adult Relationships*. New York: W. H. Freeman, 1994.

$\mathcal{P}$hysical Health and Sexuality

CHAPTER OUTLINE

- The Aging Body
- Major Health Problems
- Biological Theories of Aging
- Longevity
- Wellness
- Sexual Visibility or Invisibility
- Findings on Sexuality
- Improving Attitudes about Aging and Sexuality

Secrets of the Seniors: Older Athletes Change the Image of Aging

■ CAROL KRUCOFF

When 60-year-old Phil Mulkey jumps, pole vaults, and hoists the shot put at this year's Senior Olympics, he'll be battling a far tougher opponent than merely the other mortals in his age group. "I'm fighting against nature and trying to hold my own," says Mulkey, a former decathlete on the 1960 U.S. Olympic team. Now a retired businessman living in Marietta, Ga. Mulkey has been training three to four hours a day, three days a week, to vie for Senior Olympic gold when the seven-day U.S. National Senior Sports Classic IV begins on Saturday in Baton Rouge.

"I view each workout as a kind of test to see if my strength is ebbing," says Mulkey, who can run 50 yards in 5.32 seconds and bench press 250 pounds, just 50 pounds less than he could lift in his twenties. "I find that my body doesn't recover as quickly from a tough workout as it did. But once I'm warmed up, I can still do well, maybe even break some records."

Mulkey is one of 7,000 athletes 55 and over, including five women and 15 men in the nineties, who will compete in the fourth Senior Sports Classic. Begun in 1987 with 2,600 participants, the biennial event is sponsored by the U.S. National Senior Sports Organization, a nonprofit group designated by the U.S. Olympic Committee to run the games and to promote excellence in fitness and health for mature adults.

"Some of these senior athletes have reaction times comparable to people in their twenties," says Daniel S. Rooks, an exercise physiologist at Beth Israel Hospital/Harvard Medical School. "They blow a hole through the notion of what aging should be."

Rooks will study 500 to 600 of this year's competitors to evaluate the effects of long-term athletic training on older adults. "For years, people thought certain physical characteristics decline with age," he says. "But some of this decline may actually be from inactivity. The Senior Olympics present a great opportunity to evaluate older people who've exercised regularly for a major part of their life. We can

Runners take off at the start of the 10,000 meter race at the U.S. National Senior Olympics.

then compare them to their age-related sedentary peers to see how exercise helps maintain specific body functions with age."

Current research suggests that "older people who exercise regularly have faster reaction times, better balance and more strength than those who don't," Rooks notes. These are three key risk factors for falling, which is the leading cause of accidental death for people over 65.

Most Senior Olympians are not former world class athletes but people who enjoy both their sport and the idea of changing the way society views aging.

"I feel the same as I did at 40," says runner Dottie Gray of St. Louis, who will turn 68 during the Senior Games. The mother of six, Gray says she didn't have time for sports when her children were younger. She took up tennis at 45 and running at 54 and now runs five miles a day and plays tennis two or three days a week. It makes me feel so good to get out and be active," says Gray, who set an American record in her age group for the 1,500

—Continued

'91 Senior Games. "It gives me ener-
weight down and is lots of fun."

nurse Lois Scofield credits walking seven
day and playing tennis 15 hours a week with
her from getting arthritis like her sedentary
ster. "I've always been an optimist," says Scofield
of Stamford, Conn., who started playing tennis in
her thirties after having four children. Now 61, she
takes particular pride in beating opponents 15 years
her junior.

"At 75, I'm having the time of my life, and I'm
in the best shape of my life," says cyclist Gordy
Shields of San Diego, who bikes 30 miles a day
when he's in training and "just" 20 to 25 miles a day
when he's not. A retired guidance counselor, Shields
starting cycling at age 50 when bursitis in his shoul-
der interfered with his tennis game. He won four
gold medals at the '91 games and says he loves
"how competition gets the old adrenaline flowing."

A major goal of the Senior Olympics, these athletes stress, is to inspire other older adults to get
active. "It's never too late to find a sport you like and
go for it," Shields says. "Because 55 is no limit at
all." ☀

SOURCE: *Washington Post*, 8 June 1993, vol. 116, p. WH16.

*U*nderscoring a fundamental truth about biological functioning,
the phrase "Use it or lose it" is often used to refer to sexual
capacity in particular and to physical abilities in general.
We are all sexual beings from the time we are born until the time we die.
Masters and Johnson have said repeatedly that sexuality does not decline as
long as there is an "interesting and interested partner available." Surely there
are peaks in sexual drive, but sexual interest and expression can last throughout the life span.

The best way to achieve lasting sexual expression is to have a continuing,
active sex life. Contrary to popular belief, sex organs and drive do not wear
out with use. Sexual response capacity diminishes with *disuse*. Aging, taken
by itself, is no reason for sexual inactivity. Neither is aging a reason for physical inactivity. Physical response capacity also diminishes with disuse.

Statistically, good health declines with age. However, we do not yet fully
understand the role of the aging process in contrast to other factors that affect
this decline. Poor diet, overeating, smoking, excessive drinking, misuse of
drugs, accidents, and stress all affect our health. Some of the health problems
that the elderly have may be an inevitable consequence of the aging process.
Others clearly are not. Physical fitness and good nutrition are two factors that
can slow the aging process.

To best fulfill their individual potentials, people of all ages, especially
elders, need factual information about physical health and sexuality as these
factors relate to age. Let's look at these topics more closely: first, physical
health, and second, sexuality.

☀ The Aging Body

Aging is a gradual process beginning at birth. As a person ages, his or her
body parts may reach peak levels of operation or performance and their functioning then remains constant or begins a slow decline. Some peaks are
reached in youth; others in young adulthood or middle age; and some even
in old age, if the potential of the younger years was never developed.
Physical declines may result not from the aging process but from various
pathologies (diseases), lack of proper diet and exercise, cigarette smoking, or

other factors. Some declines that have generally been attributed to the aging process can take place at very different ages or not at all. Thus, we shall examine only those physical deteriorations that are *correlated* with age; they may or may not be *caused* by the aging process.

THE AGING BODY: A DESCRIPTION

Many changes that take place in the body are observable: the skin loses its elasticity and becomes more wrinkled, the hair grays and thins out, and the body becomes less erect. Individuals get tired more easily and quickly. As early as the thirties and forties, the eyes may develop presbyopia, a condition in which near vision is impaired and the fine print of a book or newspaper becomes difficult to see at close range. Hearing loss may occur. As the aging process continues, teeth may be lost or gums may develop disease. In addition, an older person tends to gain body fat, especially if he or she does not reduce caloric intake, and to lose muscle strength, especially if he or she does not exercise. In most cases, the older people become, the fewer calories their bodies need. Further, the ability of the body cells to absorb calcium declines. This loss of calcium results in bones that are more brittle and more easily broken. Aging brings more wear and tear to one's bones and joints; thus, the likelihood of rheumatism and arthritis increases with age.

Some health declines are not as apparent. The capacity of the body to achieve homeostasis (physiological equilibrium) declines with age. This means that older people have greater difficulty "getting back to normal," biologically speaking, after a stressful event. Blood pressure and heart rates, for example, take longer to return to their prestress levels. Various organs operate at reduced efficiency: the lungs decrease their maximum breathing capacity; the kidneys decrease the speed at which they can filter waste out of the blood; bladder capacity declines; and the level of sex hormones decreases. The nervous system also changes: Reflex action remains constant with age, but reaction time declines. As a result, tasks take longer to perform. The digestive juices decrease in volume; consequently, the body takes longer to digest its food. The body's **immune system** decreases in its ability to protect a person from disease; hence, the older individual is less immune to contagious diseases, such as the flu, and is likely to be harder hit by them.

Changes such as these often call into question the functional ability of older adults. One question often raised, for example, is whether older adults should be permitted to drive. Of the changes the aging body undergoes, visual changes are among the most pronounced. Peripheral vision decreases; cataracts or glaucoma become more likely; the ability to focus slows as the lenses lose flexibility; and pupil size decreases, impairing the ability to adjust rapidly from lightness to darkness as well as from darkness to lightness. New vision tests are being made available that can screen unsafe drivers (Colburn, 1992).

What effect does this have on the older adult's ability to drive? Although drivers aged 55 to 65 are the safest drivers on the road by almost every measure, after age 75, collision rates increase dramatically. Except for those between the ages of 15 and 19, those 75 and over are more likely than any other age group to be involved in fatal crashes (Rigdon, 1993).

Although these data suggest that physical changes may significantly affect the ability of some older adults to drive competently, improved structural changes in driving conditions would create a safer driving environment for older adults: larger road signs with more legible lettering, raised pavement reflectors, etc. As more and more of our citizens achieve late life, we will need to adjust traditional transportation practices to accommodate the mobility needs of this group.

All these physiological changes with age occur so gradually that they go unnoticed much of the time. The deterioration of body organs and systems with age may be fairly insignificant as it relates to an individual's ability to function independently, to get around, and to carry out normal activities. Nevertheless, the process of decline proceeds.

CHRONIC VERSUS ACUTE CONDITIONS

The key health problems facing middle-aged and older adults today are those that are chronic as opposed to acute. Young people tend to have **acute conditions,** that is, short-term illnesses in which the cause is known and the condition is curable. Chicken pox, colds, and influenza are examples of acute diseases. In contrast, the number and severity of chronic conditions increase with age, whereas acute diseases decline with age. **Chronic conditions** are long term. Their causes are typically unknown. Even if the cause is known, cures are not available. The goal of chronic health care is control, maintenance, or rehabilitation. The most prevalent chronic conditions affecting elders, in order of highest frequency are

1. arthritis
2. hypertension
3. heart conditions
4. hearing and visual impairments
5. cancer
6. diabetes

A chronic condition may or may not be disabling, depending on the type and severity of the condition. Loss of teeth can be considered a chronic condition, but is rarely disabling. A chronic condition may be progressively debilitating. Parkinson's disease is one example. An older person may have a number of chronic conditions but not be severely limited by any of them. Imagine the 65-year-old with mild arthritis, mild diabetes, minor visual impairment, loss of teeth, and a mild heart condition. Although this person has five chronic conditions, he or she may remain active, vigorous, and unaffected in a major way by any of them. Conversely, another older person might become completely bedridden by just one severe chronic condition.

Sometimes, the discovery of a medical cure for a disease can transform it from a chronic to an acute one. For example, some forms of cancer, now considered acute, were once thought to be chronic. Some chronic conditions do not seem to be the result of pathology (disease). Instead, they seem to be the result of the normal aging process. Several forms of arthritis fit into this category.

HEALTH STATUS

The majority of persons over the age of 65 are in fairly good health. The **health status of the aged** has improved throughout this century. Although the health status of the average 45-year-old and the average 65-year old differ, this difference is not great. People do not reach age 65 and suddenly become decrepit. However, physical decline does become more apparent with advancing age. Those aged 75 and over usually have noticeable physical declines compared with the middle aged, and those over 85 have even more noticeable declines. With advanced age come more numerous and longer hospital stays, more doctor visits, and more days of disability. But declines are typically very gradual.

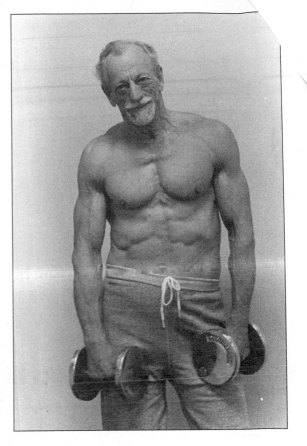

Ninety-five percent of the 65-and-over population live successfully or nearly successfully in the community. A smaller percentage are confined to institutions. Among noninstitutionalized elders, 86 percent have chronic conditions, but the vast majority of older people with chronic conditions suffer no interference with their mobility. Of the noninstitutionalized elderly with chronic conditions, which range from mild arthritis conditions to totally disabling ailments, 62 percent report no activity limitation whatsoever, 38 percent report some activity limitation, and 23 percent report limitation in a major activity (U.S. Bureau of the Census, 1993). Heart conditions and arthritis impose the most limitations on older people. Statistics which indicate that a high number of elderly suffer from chronic conditions hide the fact that most of the elderly manage quite well. The very old, those age 80 or older, are the ones who suffer most from disabilities.

Table 6.1 examines the functional limitations of older persons. Notice that those aged 65 to 74 have very few functional limitations and that those aged 75 to 84 do not, as a group, experience many limitations. And, although those 85 and over do have significant trouble managing everyday activities, a portion of them have no serious limitations.

☼ Major Health Problems

Though people tend to assume that old age brings sickness, this is not necessarily true. Most of the major health problems of old age result from pathology, the presence of disease, the causes of which, in many cases, lie outside the aging process. Poor living habits established early in life, inadequate diet, and too little exercise cause some of the "diseases of old age." With preventive measures, these diseases can be avoided. About seventy-five percent of all deaths are caused by heart disease, cancer, and stroke. Death rates from heart disease have declined significantly over the last 20 years, due to medical advances, modifications to diet, reduced smoking rates, and better exercise habits. However, cancer deaths have increased (Schick and Schick, 1994).

HEART DISEASE

Heart disease is a very general term covering many conditions. Some aspects of heart disease are pathological; that is, disease is present in the body. Other kinds of heart problems, although associated with aging, cannot be attributed to the aging process alone. Of all persons aged 65 and over, one-fourth (25 percent) are limited in their activities by heart conditions (U.S. Bureau of the Census, 1993).

Table 6.1

Functional Limitations by Age (Percent with Difficulty)

Activity	Age 65–74	Age 75–84	Age 85 and over
Walking	14.2%	22.9%	39.9%
Getting outside	5.6	12.3	31.3
Bathing/showering	6.4	12.3	27.9
Getting out of bed or chair	6.1	9.2	19.3
Dressing	4.3	7.6	16.6
Using toilet	2.6	5.4	14.1
Eating	1.2	2.5	4.4
Preparing meals	4.0	8.8	26.1
Shopping	6.4	15.0	37.0
Managing money	2.2	6.3	24.0
Using telephone	2.7	6.0	17.5
Doing heavy housework	18.6	28.7	47.8
Doing light housework	4.3	8.9	23.6

SOURCE: U.S. Bureau of the Census, *Statistical Abstract of the United States, 1988,* 108th ed. (Washington, DC: Bureau of the Census, 1989), p. 109.

The most widespread form of heart disease, *coronary artery disease,* so-called ischemic heart disease, is now the major killing disease in the United States and in other industrialized nations as well. Its incidence increases with age, and it is *the* most common cause of death in middle-aged and older individuals. With coronary artery disease, a deficient amount of blood reaches the heart. This deficiency, which results from the narrowing of the blood vessels, damages the heart tissue.

Although all the factors that lead to the narrowing of the blood vessels supplying the heart are not known, two major contributing factors are **atherosclerosis** and **arteriosclerosis.** Atherosclerosis occurs when fat and cholesterol crystals, along with other substances, accumulate on the interior walls of the arteries, thereby reducing the size of these passageways. Atherosclerosis, which occurs in large numbers of people in industrialized nations, occurs much less frequently in nonindustrialized nations, leading some observers to conclude that atherosclerosis is not a normal consequence of the aging process and that it can be avoided (even though it is statistically correlated with increasing age in the United States). High blood pressure **(hypertension),** another form of heart disease commonly found in older adults, impairs blood circulation and can lead to congestive heart failure. Blood pressure medications, exercise, and weight loss are generally effective means of maintaining blood pressure levels within acceptable limits.

A major health problem associated with atherosclerosis is *thrombosis,* or blood clotting. Blood clots occur when undissolved fatty deposits in the arteries cut off the blood supply to the heart. Some of the factors that lead to atherosclerosis are thought to be a high cholesterol count, a diet high in refined sugars and saturated fats, high blood pressure, obesity, stress, hereditary factors, lack of exercise, and cigarette smoking.

Arteriosclerosis, commonly called hardening of the arteries, also limits the supply of blood to the heart. People of all nations and cultures experience arteriosclerosis, and many researchers believe that this condition is a result of the aging process. Arteriosclerosis results in the loss of elasticity in the walls of the arteries. Although atherosclerosis and arteriosclerosis are separate and distinct conditions, an individual can suffer from both of them at the same time.

Coronary artery disease can vary in its severity. If a small portion of heart muscle is affected, cardiac reserves allow the work of the heart to continue and the individual recovers from the heart attack. Typical symptoms of a heart attack are shortness of breath, dizziness, confusion, and pain. A person recovering from a heart attack needs rest while the heart muscle heals. After a period of a few weeks, however, an attending physician can usually help the patient to design a program for resuming activity and work patterns. The heart attack victim need not be treated as an invalid. Exercise such as walking is commonly recommended to strengthen the heart.

CANCER

In reality a group of several hundred diseases, **cancer** may affect the breast, the skin, the stomach, bones, blood, or other parts of the body. Its common characteristic is an uncontrolled, invasive cell growth at the expense of normal body systems. There may be numerous causes of cancer. Some are thought to be the inhalation or ingestion of chemicals, smoking, diet, and radiation. Although the basic cause of cancer is not fully understood, a living cell somehow becomes a cancer cell. This cancer cell then transmits its abnormality to succeeding cell generations. When the wild growth of cancer cells is not eliminated from the body, tumors develop. Statistics show that the risk of cancer increases with age. Over one-half of all deaths from cancer occur in old age. Thus, cancer is the second leading cause of death among the elderly. However, like many other diseases, it is not an inevitable consequence of the aging process. Three forms of cancer treatment are surgery, radiation, and chemotherapy (treatment with drugs). Some forms of cancer can be successfully treated and effectively cured, especially following early detection. For example, breast cancer, if detected early, appears to be one of these treatable forms. Other forms of cancer, such as lung cancer, are more difficult to diagnose at early stages and are therefore more difficult to treat.

CEREBROVASCULAR DISEASE

This disease is common among middle-aged individuals, but more common in old age. **Cerebrovascular disease,** more commonly called stroke, is a killer; strokes also cripple thousands of older individuals each year. Some strokes, however, are so mild as to go unnoticed.

The most common cause of stroke is the same as that of coronary artery disease—atherosclerosis and arteriosclerosis. These conditions may result in either a malfunction or narrowing of the blood vessels serving the brain, or in

a blood clot that blocks an artery serving the brain. Two other causes of stroke are hemorrhage (bleeding inside the brain) and blockage of an artery serving the brain resulting from a clot that has broken off from a major clot elsewhere in the body. When brain cells do not receive blood from the heart, they die. The death of brain cells indicates the occurrence of a stroke.

The severity of a stroke depends on the area of the brain affected and the total amount of brain tissue involved. Strokes may affect various parts of the brain. When the left side of the brain is affected, the symptoms will differ from those that occur when the right side of the brain is affected. Depending on the particular area of the brain and the size of the area affected, paralysis in varying degrees, speech disorders, or memory impairment can result.

All strokes cause some degree of permanent damage to the brain. Sometimes, personality changes result that are difficult to understand or deal with. Formerly easygoing people may become impatient and irritable with little cause; their judgment may become impaired, confused, and befuddled; or they may become more emotional and break into tears easily. Some stroke victims lose interest in personal hygiene as well as in family and friends. Stroke is a leading cause of first admissions to mental hospitals.

Rehabilitation for stroke victims is successful in varying degrees, but it depends on the severity of the stroke. If treated promptly during the initial phases, the victim of a stroke has a better chance of recovery. Sometimes if clots have lodged in a major artery in the neck, they can be removed surgically and the normal blood supply to the brain can be restored.

ACCIDENTS

A health problem of major proportion is disability or death due to accidents. Although persons over 65 number 13 percent of the population, they represent 29 percent of all accidental deaths. Falls are the most common cause of accidental death among those 65 and over, followed closely by motor-vehicle accidents. Suffocation from an object that has been ingested, surgical and medical mishaps, fires, and burns are also major causes of accidental death among elders. The 90-and-over group has an alarmingly disproportionate share of deaths due to accidents in two of these categories: (1) falls, and (2) suffocation by ingestion of food (National Safety Council, 1993, p. 23). Such needless tragedy among advanced age groups illustrates a need for more preventive measures. A few concerned organizations, for example, have run "falls clinics" as a preventive measure. Not only are falls more likely, but hip fractures are increasingly likely as a result. There are solid reasons for the high occurrence of hip fractures, which can mean loss of mobility and independence or perhaps institutionalization. Because the hip is the area that instinctively absorbs most falls, and because bones are often weakened by osteoporosis (see below), a hip fracture is a common ailment to be feared. One-third of women (those most likely to have osteoporosis) and one-sixth of men who live to age 90 will suffer a hip fracture. About 90 percent of hip fractures are due to osteoporosis. Only 25 percent recover fully, and one in four die within six months of the injury (Schideler, 1994). Because recovery is so slow and painful, some never walk again, others gain mobility only with the use of a walker, and those that can heal well enough to resume a normal, active life take years to do so.

Some other factors of age that contribute to accidental death or injury are failing eyesight and hearing; reduced muscular strength, balance, and coordination; and increased reaction time. These limitations, combined with impaired judgment, make the very old especially vulnerable to accidents. They may try to lift loads that are too heavy or poorly balanced, or they may climb or reach overhead without sufficient strength to manage the task. Changes in automobile traffic conditions can happen too swiftly for them to react. The swallowing reflex diminishes with age, making choking on food or objects in the mouth, such as a safety pin, more likely. Danger signals of fire or leaking gas are not perceived readily, and the few minutes or seconds of delayed reaction often prove to be fatal. Accidental drownings of older persons result more often from activities around water rather than from actual swimming.

Most fatal accidents involving elders take place in the home. They also occur frequently in public places (including institutions), in and around motor vehicles, and at places of work.

ARTHRITIS

Arthritis, which results from the inflammation of a joint or a degenerative change in a joint, is one of the oldest diseases known and is widespread today, affecting all age groups, but mostly older persons. There are numerous types of arthritis, with different causes, different symptoms, and differing degrees of severity. Rheumatoid arthritis and gout, though rare, are painful and troubling forms. The type that most often pose problems for those age 65 and over is osteoarthritis.

Osteoarthritis, the most common form of arthritis, is fairly widespread in middle age and almost universal in old age. Most elderly have some degree of osteoarthritis. The joints most commonly affected are the weight-bearing ones: the hips, knee, and spine. The fingers and big toe are also commonly affected. With osteoarthritis, elastic tissue (cartilage) becomes soft and wears away, and the underlying bones are exposed, which causes pain, stiffness, and tenderness. For some, osteoarthritis starts early in life and affects mostly the small joints. For others, osteoarthritis results from injury or vigorous wear and tear (the athletic knee is an example). It occurs later in life in the large or overused joints.

OSTEOPOROSIS

Osteoporosis, another potentially severe and crippling skeletal problem, is characterized by a gradual loss of bone mass (density) that generally begins between the ages of 35 and 40. The number of victims and the severity of the disease increase with advancing age; millions of Americans suffer from this disease, and 75 to 80 percent are women. Loss of bone mass can result in diminishing height, slumped posture, the "dowager's hump," and a reduction in the strength of the bones, which makes them more susceptible to fractures. The bones may become so weak that a sudden strain will break them. The causes of osteoporosis are inadequate diet over a long period of time (lack of calcium is a major dietary factor), reduced absorptive efficiency due to an aging digestive system, cigarette smoking, lack of vigorous physical activity, and estrogen deficiency in women. The loss of estrogen at menopause contributes to about 80 percent of osteoporosis. But men can also get this disease.

An initial cause of osteoporosis is a decrease or upset in hormonal balance. In menopause and old age, the body may not have enough hormones to maintain its calcium balance. Osteoporosis can be slowed by a high-

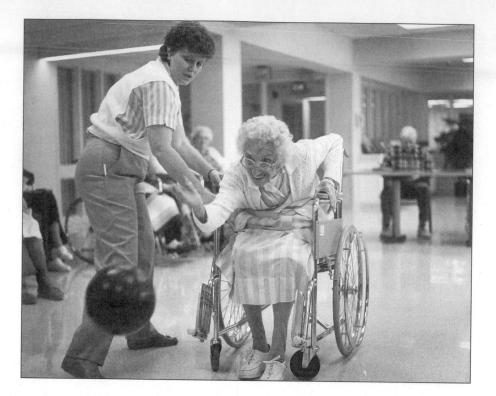

Exercise has been proven
to help maintain bone
strength.

calcium diet. Some doctors recommend calcium supplements. Estrogen treatment is typically recommended for women—but the side effect is a very slight increased cancer risk. Vitamin D has also been shown to help correct osteoporosis. National campaigns are being mounted to teach prevention of this disease. Weight-bearing exercise should start in younger years, as well as a good diet, and be continued in old age to slow this disease. Exercise has been proven to help maintain bone strength.

OTHER CONCERNS

Other health concerns more frequently found in older populations than younger ones are emphysema and chronic bronchitis (which often occur together), diabetes mellitus, and obesity. Emphysema is characterized by lung rigidity, thickening of the mucus of the bronchioles, and scarring of the lung walls. Smoking and inhalation of contaminants such as gases, industrial fumes, or traffic exhaust may increase the risk of emphysema. Bronchitis, on the other hand, is a condition in which the bronchial tube becomes inflamed and scarred, often resulting in chronic coughing and an excessive production of mucus.

Diabetes mellitus is a health-related problem that requires intervention and constant monitoring. Diabetes occurs when sugars and starches are not translated into energy, generally due to inadequate amounts of insulin (produced by the pancreas). Often, a change of diet may be sufficient to stabilize the condition; however, more severe cases may require insulin therapy. Although not considered a disease, obesity, which results from excessive food intake, strains the heart and exacerbates systemic disease factors such as emphysema, osteoporosis, and arthritis. About one out of three older adults is significantly overweight.

☼ Biological Theories of Aging

Must we grow old? Is there any way to stop aging? Human beings have asked these questions for centuries. The longest-lived persons on record are Shirechiyo Izumi of Japan and Jeanne Calmet of France, both of whom reached 120 years. This figure, then, represents the **maximum life span** of the human species, the greatest age reached by a member of a species. Biologists refer to biological aging as *senescence,* often described as the onset of the degenerative process—a process that usually becomes apparent between the ages of 40 and 45. Graying at the temples, crow's feet around the eyes, and the need for reading glasses to correct nearsightedness (presbyopia) are among the early indicators that the process is underway.

Medical technology is slowing the aging process by increasing our fitness and vigor along with our **average life span,** the average age reached by the members of a species. No physician, or anyone else, has ever saved another's life—they have only prolonged it. A child born today has a life expectancy of approximately 80 years. Someday, life expectancy may be 120 or more years, a span the accommodation of which will require profound social and cultural changes. The extension of life, although desirable, also challenges society to ensure that the quality of that life will justify the efforts to extend it. Why do we grow old? Although there are a number of biological theories of aging, there is, at this time, no one clear scientific reason why we age. Aging today is viewed as many processes, and the theories described here are not necessarily mutually exclusive.

AGING AS DISEASE

Aging may be entirely due to the disease processes in the body. If so, future medical science may be able to inhibit or eradicate **aging as disease.** By eliminating disease in the body as it occurs, medical intervention theoretically should be able to keep the body in good health indefinitely. Still, most scientists try to separate the aging process from disease, because people seem to age even when no disease is afflicting the body. Several ideas about the nature of aging have been put forth.

GENETICS

First, let us consider the genetics of aging. Scientific studies have demonstrated that human longevity runs in families. Investigations of twins confirm that human life span is inherited. Identical twins die within a relatively short time span of one another, whereas siblings have a greater variation in life spans. Evidence indicates that 10 to 15 percent of variation in age at death is genetically determined. Thus, the longevity of our parents and grandparents is an important indicator of our own longevity. A number of genetic theories have arisen to explain differential rates of aging. One group of theories is called programmed theories. They emphasize internal "programs." Some genetic theorists presuppose a **biological clock** within us that begins ticking at conception. This clock may be in the nucleus of each cell of our body, an idea that advances the proposition that the body is "programmed" by specific genes to live a certain length of time.

Scientists once speculated that the biological clock was governed by a single gene. They now believe that thousands of genes are involved. Aging appears to be a species-specific trait. Shrews live about 2 years; dogs, 20; tortoises, between 100 and 200 years; and so on for each species. Do we really know that the human life span cannot be extended well beyond 100 years? Scientists do not really know. What is the nature of the biological clock? How does it affect growth, development, and decline? Scientists in the fields of molecular biology and genetics continue to search for answers to these questions.

Related to the search for "longevity" genes is the search for genes that are responsible for hereditary diseases. More than 150 mutant genes have been identified. An example is the one responsible for a rare hereditary disease, a thyroid cancer. By the turn of the century, DNA tests are almost certain to be a part of medical exams. From a sample of the patient's blood, doctors will be able to spot genetic mutations that signal the approach of hereditary diseases and also breast cancer, heart disease, and diabetes. Today at least 50 genetic tests for 50 specific hereditary diseases are available. In the near future will be available a genetic test for the breast cancer gene (BRCA1), which is responsible for 1 in 10 of all breast cancers. Researchers are finding genes at a rapid rate, including mutations responsible for Alzheimer's and colon cancer. Most likely multiple genes are involved in Alzheimer's, and all these have yet to be found. Once a gene is found, laboratories soon develop a test to determine its presence or absence in the body. Ethical considerations as to genetic testing can hardly keep pace with the discoveries (Rubin, 1994).

IMMUNE SYSTEM

A most promising "programmed" theory involving aging is the immune system theory. Many aspects of immune function decline with age, and this decline is related to many kinds of disease, such as cancer. If the body's immune system becomes decreasingly effective with advancing age, harmful cells are more likely to survive and do damage. The theory is that cancer and other diseases attack the body with advancing age because the body progressively loses its ability to fight off disease. Some scientists are trying to revitalize the ailing immune systems of elders with hormone therapy, specifically the hormone DHEA. Studies of mice have shown that this hormone restored their immune systems to youthful levels in warding off certain diseases such as Hepatitis B. Experiments with testosterone show it to increase muscle strength and counter anemia. In addition AIDS research is bringing us more information about strengthening the immune system and hopefully will help prolong lives.

A related immunological theory of aging suggests that as the body ages, it develops more and more autoimmune antibodies that destroy cells, even normal ones. As age increases, the immune system seems to increase its capacity for autoimmune reactions. Several diseases, such as midlife diabetes, are related to autoimmune reactions, thus leading to the theory that such reactions cause aging.

Studies of diseases such as progeria, which ages individuals very rapidly, provide clues to the aging process. Individuals with progeria typically die in their teens, yet have the bodies of 80-year-olds. If gerontologists could find the key to curing progeria, they might also unlock a "cure" for aging.

CELLULAR THEORIES

A major group of theories, called "error" theories, direct attention to forces that damage cells (National Institutes of Health, 1993). If the forces can be controlled, the belief is that aging can be prolonged.

Thinking about Aging
No Purpose in Dying
■ KAREN F. SCHMIDT

According to Darwin's theory of natural selection, only those traits that interfere with reproduction get weeded out. Evolution basically doesn't care what happens to an individual animal once it has propagated, so genes that lead to disease or death later in life continue to flow down the chain of inheritance. As Michael Rose of the University of California at Irvine puts it, "We are genetic garbage cans for genes that produce bad effects at later ages."

Nevertheless, species can evolve to live longer, researchers have recently shown. For instance, Rose delayed the start of reproduction in laboratory fruit flies, thus allowing the forces of natural selection to operate longer. Seventy generations later, the flies were living on average 80 percent longer and were healthier. Apparently, natural selection eliminated some of the bad genes that had limited the population's life span.

Steven Austad of the University of Idaho has made a discovery in the wild that also validates the evolutionary theory of aging. On an island off the coast of Georgia, he has found a population of opossums that appear to age more slowly than their mainland cousins. Most female opossums in the South breed at a young age, then rapidly deteriorate and die by age 2 or 3. The island females, however, reach a second reproductive year twice as often as their mainland sisters do. Moreover, the oldest opossum Austad has tracked on the island is a year older than any he has followed in South Carolina.

Different Worlds

The aging and reproductive patterns of the two populations began to diverge about 4,000 years ago when the island broke off, creating two different evolutionary environments, Austad believes. On the mainland, opossums had to reproduce quickly before being chomped by an owl or a dog. But on the island, where there are far fewer predators, the animals survived longer and could afford to reproduce later, giving natural selection more time to sift out life-shortening genes.

These same evolutionary forces must also affect human longevity, researchers say. Indeed, if career-conscious couples continue to delay childbearing, people born several hundred generations from now might live longer because their genetic garbage cans will be less full. ☀

SOURCE: With permission of *U.S. News & World Report,* March 8, 1993, pp. 72–73.

One of the oldest and most enduring "error" theories is the cellular theory of **wear and tear,** the idea that irreplaceable body parts simply wear out. The cell is viewed as a highly complex piece of machinery, like an automobile. Some organisms live longer because they maintain themselves more carefully. Those who live more recklessly will wear out sooner. This idea is difficult to test and ignores the fact that cells can repair damage caused by wear and tear. The repair aspect returns the focus to the attempt to understand DNA, how it works, and why some cells get repaired and others do not. One theory would be that the person who lives longer has a more effective DNA repair system. This area of study is complicated by the intricate multiple phases of the repair systems.

FREE RADICALS

People seem to vary in their ability to fend off assaults to the body such as smoking, too much fat, and alcohol abuse. Some smokers, for example, manage to live long lives with no impact on their longevity. Winston Churchill is one example. Yet others who are very health conscious, such as Adelle Davis, succumb to cancer or other diseases before reaching old age. One theory is that some people are more susceptible to free radicals than others. "Free radicals" is a name given to molecules in the body that are highly reactive. They are the byproduct of normal metabolism, produced as cells turn food into energy. A way to combat aging is to trap the damaging molecules before they can do harm. Free radicals invade cells throughout the body, mangling vital protein enzymes and membranes, and in general damaging the body. Researchers are discovering chemical agents that absorb free radicals and thus prevent cell and tissue degeneration. For example, a compound called PBN administered daily to aged gerbils restored the function of oxidized proteins in their brains. Their ability to run through mazes improved, and they had fewer strokes from brain damage. The next step is to develop compounds for humans. In the meantime scientists are looking to vitamins such as A, E, and C as natural absorbers of free radicals. (Others warn of harm from taking too much vitamin C.)

☼ Longevity: The Role of Diet, Exercise, and Mental Health

There is a saying that all people want to live forever, but no one wants to grow old. And there is another: If I'd known I was going to live this long, I'd have taken better care of myself! Research on longevity holds a fascination for all of us—wondering whether science can find the key to knowledge that would keep each of us on the planet awhile longer. The previous section covered some biological theories that hold promise for understanding the mysteries of aging. Scientists are also looking at some other factors: as well as diet and exercise, social, emotional, and environmental factors. There is no one answer to living a good long life; it is a complex weave of many variables.

DIET

Research has come up with some astonishing findings regarding diet and longevity. Scientists at the University of Wisconsin—Madison found that reducing an animal's usual diet by 50 to 70 percent could extend its life span by 30 percent or more. The animals not only are living longer, but also are healthier, exhibit less cancer and heart disease, have better immune systems, and have a much lower incidence of diabetes and cataracts (Devitt, 1991).

"The outcome of caloric restriction is spectacular," stated Richard Weindruch, a gerontologist at the University of Wisconsin and a pioneer in this particular field. He has tested caloric restriction in animals from protozoa to rats to dogs to monkeys. The studies may be telling us we are tampering with fundamental aging processes. The animals act friskier and suffer fewer diseases. Tumor growth is reduced by at least 30 percent and some cancers are virtually eliminated. Thus, many usual causes of death are stripped away. A 22-year study of 19,297 men revealed that those at their ideal weight (determined by height) live longer than those who are 2 to 6 percent above their ideal weight. Those men 20 or more pounds above their ideal weight suffered a major loss in years lived (Manson and Gutfeld, 1994). And from another culture: Those who live on the island of Okinawa eat 60 percent of the normal Japanese diet. People live longer on Okinawa and have half the percentage of heart disease, diabetes, and cancer as in the main island of Japan. It would seem that by restricting food intake, scientists can cause age-sensitive biological parameters—such as DNA repair, glucose regulation, and immune functions—to work better and longer. The decline in the immune function is at the root of many of the health problems faced by elders. Flu, for instance, tends to be more severe with age because immune responses are less vigorous. Low caloric intake helps protect the immune response system.

NUTRITION

Only in recent years have we begun to understand the inadequacies of the food eaten by the average American. Studies have shown that nutritional adequacy in early life is related to health and well-being in later life.

Dietary patterns in the mind-twentieth century turned away from raw fruits, vegetables, dairy products, and whole grains. For too many, today's diet still is high in cholesterol, fat, sugar, refined grains, and processed food, and low in bulk, fiber, and nutrients. Data pertaining to this matter show that older persons often have a low intake of important nutrients, such as calcium, iron, magnesium, vitamins B, C, beta carotine, thiamine, and especially folic acid. In the 1990s, our awareness of the importance of fresh fruits, vegetables, and whole grains in our diet is increasing. Studies show that Americans are decreasing their intake of salt, red meat, and saturated fat. The statistics presented in Chapter 1, showing reduced rates of heart disease, bear this out.

The trace nutrient chromium, when given to rats, increased their life span by one-third. The chromium was thought to reduce the blood sugar level, which in turn reduces atherosclerosis and kidney disease (Schmidt, 1993). Author of a best-selling book *Longevity*, Kathy Keeton, along with many health-conscious Americans, eats large portions of complex carbohydrates, especially pasta, because they are fat free and have a calming effect on the brain (Keeton, 1992).

FUNCTIONAL AND BEHAVIORAL CHANGE

Physiological and sociopsychological factors can compound nutritional difficulties for the very old. Digestive processes slow down as part of the aging process. Dental problems can limit one to food that are easily chewed. Reduced keenness of taste, sight, and smell can diminish enjoyment of food and dampen the appetite. Physical handicaps, such as arthritis, can complicate the preparation and consumption of meals. Lack of transportation to markets poses further problems.

Less obvious, but also of great importance, are social and psychological factors. For example, a widow who has spent many years cooking for and eating with her family may find little incentive to shop and cook for herself when she is living alone. Older men living alone are even less inclined to cook for themselves than are women. Older adults on limited budgets who seldom leave their homes because of fear or disdain for shopping may settle for a diet of crackers, bread, or milk. Many have lost olfactory (taste and smell) acuity as well. Even those who live with families or in institutions may not find an atmosphere conducive to good eating habits. In some institutions, the hurried, impersonal atmosphere of meals served cold at 5:00 P.M. can discourage residents from eating as they should. And for those who do not live in institutions, we all know that American culture fosters the fast-food diet, which tends to be high in fat and lacking many needed nutrients.

PATHOLOGY AND DIET

Research on nutrition is now uncovering the way in which poor diet contributes to pathology (disease). Establishing the relationship between diet and disease is difficult, partly because the time that elapses before an inadequate diet results in disease can be substantial. Individuals may not be able to remember accurately their eating habits over a period of years. Nutritional cause and physical effect is difficult to determine.

Nevertheless, diet is increasingly being implicated as a factor in numerous conditions and diseases. Saturated fat contributes to atherosclerosis. A lack of fiber in the diet is thought to be one cause of cancer of the intestine or colon. With a low-fiber diet, the cancer agent remains in the intestine for a longer period of time. High fiber protects against constipation, intestinal disease, gallstones, and cancer. Diverticulitis, an infection or inflammation of the colon, may be caused by a deficiency of vegetable fiber in the diet. Research has shown that various nutritional anemias are almost certainly the result of poor diet. Similarly, studies have shown that proper dietary programs can control 80 percent of the cases of diabetes mellitus. As we grow older, our metabolic rate slows down. We require less energy intake, or fewer calories. Because of reduced kidney function, elders should eat somewhat less protein to help avoid kidney strain.

PHYSICAL FITNESS

Exercise is valuable for individuals of all ages. Older individuals are often wrongly considered unable to exercise or to profit from it. Actually, exercise helps maintain good health, improves circulation and respiration, diminishes stress, preserves a sense of balance, promotes body flexibility, and induces better sleeping patterns at any age. The person who exercises reduces the risk of heart attack and, should one occur, increases the chances of survival. Swimming, walking, running, bicycling, and tennis are all valuable and inexpensive forms of exercise. However, despite current publicity about physical fitness, some older people are not getting the exercise they need. Only 27 percent of older Americans exercise regularly ("Exercise Isn't Just for Fun," 1991).

Much of the deterioration and many of the health problems and physical disabilities associated with age have been thought to be inevitable. However, many of the problems found in older people result directly from disuse of body systems, which results in decline. Disuse may affect the skeletal system, heart, lungs, muscles, and almost every part of the body. We commonly associate youth with supple, strong, erect bodies and old age with weak muscles, drooped posture, and low energy. These polarized images are less true than we think. Older individuals in many parts of the world continue to be physically strong and active. One example is African tribal dancers, some of whom are between 70 and 80 years old. Much of the physical decline in the skeleton and muscles with age can be prevented; the cause is not the aging process but the sedentary lifestyle of older Americans.

Older individuals who participate in physical activity that constantly works the muscles will have a larger muscle mass than younger individuals who follow no physical fitness program. All unused tissues and functions atrophy. This can happen very quickly; it can occur in a matter of days while one is bedridden. With disuse, muscle tissue turns to fat tissue. Exercise prevents this from happening. But the exercise should be appropriate for the body's condition. For those who feel that high-impact aerobics are harsh, jarring, and harmful, low-impact aerobics may be ideal. Geriatric medicine should address these issues; unfortunately, there are not enough geriatric physicians in the United States at this time.

Many older people love to exercise to music.

An older person does not have to run marathons or enter competitions to get exercise, feel better, and stay fit. Many programs offer more moderate degrees of exercise. Light forms of yoga, stretching, and relaxing exercises, and all kinds of dance and aerobics have been standard fare for elderly fitness enthusiasts. Many older people love to exercise to music, and they love movement, contrary to what the stereotypes indicate.

People who exercise experience increased oxygen transport capacity, lung capacity, vital capacity, and physical work capacity. Body fat and blood pressure may decrease with regular exercise. Nervous tension also can be reduced with vigorous physical exercise.

People who become sedentary and who overeat lay the groundwork for the development of disease. Complaints of aches and pains in joints and muscles, low-back strain, high blood pressure, and other symptoms could be eased or eliminated with a physical fitness program.

A recent research report demonstrates scientifically what for health enthusiasts has long been an article of faith: regular exercise can indeed prolong life. People who are active and fit can expect to live a year or so longer than their sedentary counterparts. For each hour of physical activity, one can expect to live that hour over—and live one or two more hours to boot. The study, the most comprehensive ever to relate exercise and longevity, tracked the health and lifestyles of 16,936 men who entered Harvard from 1916 to 1950. The subjects were followed until 1978, by which time 1,413 had died. Correlating death rates with exercise habits, the researchers were able to quantify, for the first time, the relationship between various amounts of physical activity and length of life. Regular exercise, the researchers found, is a critical factor in determining longevity. Men who walked 9 or more miles a week (burning off at least 900 calories), for example, had a risk of death 21 percent lower than those who walked less than 3 miles a week. The optimum expenditure of energy seems to be about 3,500 calories a week, the equivalent of 6 to 8 hours of strenuous bicycling or singles tennis. The Harvard men who worked out that much had half the risk of death of those who did little or no exercise. Moreover, the study showed that a lifetime habit of engaging in energetic activity three to four times a week could reduce the negative health effects of cigarette smoking or high blood pressure. It even partly offset an inherited tendency toward early death (Elmer-DeWitt, 1986).

CHANGING EXERCISE HABITS

There are many physical activities, something appropriate for every age group. Speedwalking is an excellent routine for the middle aged and elderly. Dr. William Evans at Tufts University in Boston reports that it is never too late to start a strength training program. Study of participants 87 to 96 years old showed dramatic improvements after eight weeks, several no longer needed canes to walk and all experienced "three-to-fourfold increases in strength" (Evans and Rosenberg, 1991). Similarly, other experimental studies of nursing home residents lifting weights show them to greatly improve muscle strength, walking speeds, and mobility (National Institutes of Health, 1993).

The American College of Sports Medicine now recommends the following as minimum exercise routine: some kind of aerobic exercise for 20 minutes or more three times a week, and some form of resistance training at least twice a week, exercising all the major muscle groups in sets of 8 to 12 repetitions each (Segell, 1993, Part 1).

A study began in 1987 of almost 200 master athletes aged 40 and over who compete in one sanctioned event each year (e.g., runners, swimmers, field athletes) asks the question, "Just how old and how fit can one become?" The study is expected to continue 20 years but already has predicted the following: (1) speed and muscle strength will endure longer than assumed, (2) athletic performance will not decline significantly until age 60, (3) death rate will be reduced, (4) falls and injuries will be reduced, (5) the heart and lungs will not have to lose function as quickly as previously thought, and (6) the incidence of osteoporosis will be reduced. In general, we have underestimated the ability and potential of older people. The study also concludes to date that nothing can retard the aging process as much as exercise (Roan, 1993).

MENTAL HEALTH

Being a happy, optimistic person contributes to longevity. The 50-year study of Harvard graduates cited earlier found the following:

- Men who cope well with emotional trauma live longer. Men who denied their feeling or intellectualized personal problems suffered more rapid declines in health after age 50.
- Optimists have better health in middle and old age than pessimists.
- Good mental health (one measurement was the lack of need to take tranquilizers) predicts successful aging. (Segell, 1993, Part II)

A study by Costa at the National Institute on Aging found that a personality trait—"antagonistic hostility"—predicts premature death. This person is easily provoked to anger and is vindictive (reported in Segell, 1993, Part 1). Other related personality characteristics have been determined by social scientists to be life shortening: repressed anger, depression, egocentricity, shyness, and various other negative attitudes.

A whole set of findings revolves around stress. In a nutshell, some stress may be a positive factor in life but too much of the wrong kind is bad. And those who are good at coping with stress will live longer. In the same vein, a good sense of humor helps, as well as a strong sense of self and purpose and a zest for life. The feeling that one is in control of one's life also adds years. Even in a nursing home, those who have choices and assert their will live longer.

In the presence of disease, "guided imagery" has been shown to lengthen life for some. They imagine their body parts getting healed—perhaps their immune cells are warriors fighting off the evil enemy. Or a totally healed lung is pictured in their minds. Here, positive mental attitude is used to get the immune system activated and fighting. Hypnotism, meditation, and other relaxation techniques are being used, with some success, to prolong life.

SOCIAL AND ENVIRONMENTAL FACTORS

The environment we live in plays a role in how long we live. Noise and air pollution, pesticides, radiation, secondary smoke from cigarettes, and other adverse chemicals in our air, water, and food bring disease and shorten life. The ultraviolet rays of the sun age the skin and can cause skin cancer. Living in an area of high crime can be life threatening. For rats, overcrowding in cages alters behavior and shortens life. Likewise, living in overcrowded cities may be harmful for humans.

A positive, hopeful, stimulating social environment adds years to life. Rats in cages with lots of wheels and mazes live longer than those with no outlet for activity. Likewise an active physical and mental environment is important for humans. Social class is correlated with longevity. Those with more money for health care live longer.

A shortened life is statistically correlated with the following: divorce (for the man only); accidents (car, especially); a lifestyle that includes smoking, heavy use or abuse of alcohol or drugs, and too little or too much sleep; an imbalance of work and leisure; continual risk-taking/self-destructive behavior; and being a loner instead of having lots of friends.

CENTENARIANS

Rather than study animals in a laboratory, some scientists have focused their attention on centenarians as a way of learning about longevity. Twenty-five or so centenarians, the "oldest-old," with a balance of white and black Americans, were in the Georgia Centenarians Study (Poon, 1992). With regard to personality and coping, the oldest-old scored high on dominance, suspiciousness, and imagination, and low on conformity, personality traits that served as protective functions. The centenarians were described as assertive and forceful. There were a number of extraordinary persons who wrote, published, performed musically, gave guided tours, invested in the stock market, earned a living, and coped well in spite of poor support systems. In terms of cognitive skills, they rated high on practical problem-solving tests, but lower on intelligence and memory tests. Religion was important and a common coping device: "I don't worry about the future; it's in God's hands," said Charles C., 101 years old. Regarding nutrition, most were moderate, healthy eaters who did not go on diets. None were vegetarian; they did not smoke and drank very little; most ate big breakfasts. One negative is that they had high intake of saturated fat, especially the black men who consumed a lot of fat, pastries, soda, sugar, and whole milk. That goes against the grain of what was expected—but the sample size was very small. Further research of centenarians will provide us with more answers. A different study of centenarians, thousands in fact, correlated longevity with the following: optimism, good health habits, stimulating physical and mental activity, spirituality, moderation, tolerance, integrity, and interacting with others (Beard, 1991).

☼ Wellness

Advancements in medical science, along with new knowledge generated in the biological and physical sciences within recent years, have provided information that enables us to better understand the correlation between disease and disability in later life. This, in turn, enables us to learn to avoid high-risk behaviors. For example, the preceding discussion of physical fitness and nutrition documents the relationship among exercise, physical/emotional well-being, and increased stamina. Understanding proper nutritional intake allows us to avoid foods that correlate highly with heart disease, cancer, and related late-life health problems.

The **wellness** movement is based on anticipating and taking measures to prevent health-related problems as we age. Although modifying a person's lifelong behavior patterns is not always easy, it can be done. More and more of our young, middle-aged, and older citizens are losing weight, exercising, and monitoring their diet than ever before. Learning to avoid foods with higher levels of calories or fat, reducing hypertension, and discontinuing the use of tobacco, while simultaneously including a diet of nutritional foods and maintaining higher levels of physical activity reduces health-related risks in later life. Extending the number of healthy years of life, what has been called the **"health span,"** has become a viable goal for all Americans.

As science continues to document habits that increase stress and decrease nutritional and physical health, the wellness movement will gain strength, encouraging prevention and the adoption of good health-related habits. The long-term effects may well result in larger populations of older adults who will experience fewer debilitating illnesses and, as a result, higher levels of life satisfaction. Costs of medical care for older adults could also be reduced.

☼ Sexual Visibility or Invisibility

Younger people are often shocked when they learn that old people both want sexual contact and are capable of performing sexually. Stereotypes suggest that age imposes a decided disinterest in sexual contact—the belief, for example, that "My grandmother and grandfather would never do that!" Misinformation about the **sexuality** of older adults has no doubt been passed from generation to generation. Because adults who are older today were born and reared at a time when sexual expression was considered a very private matter, they received little information on sexual performance or expression in late life. As a result, elders in our society are "sexually invisible." More recently, however, studies have unfounded the idea that sexual interest is a thing of the past for older adults. The idea that sexual expression between two older adults is immoral or perverted is no longer valid. Negative stereotypes such as "dirty old man" reflect ageism or ignorance more than an awareness that an interest in affection and sexual contact lasts throughout the human lifetime. Unfortunately, for example, many view marriage between older people as an oddity or with amusement. Even old people themselves sometimes accept the stereotype of asexuality. If we can believe newspaper advice columns, many a newly married elder has been surprised to find that his or her new spouse expects more than companionship and a bridge partner.

MYTHS OF SEXUAL INVISIBILITY

The **sexual invisibility** of elders is basically rooted in the youth culture of our society. Some related themes are discussed here.

Physical Attraction and Youth

The idea that sexual tension is based mainly on physical attraction between the sexes and that very young men and women are the most physically or sexually attractive is widespread. Advertising, film, television, and stage promote the theme that good looks, youth, and sex go together. Models are generally young, and beauty contests usually involve those no older than their mid-twenties.

Many people consider only the young, perfectly proportioned body to be sexually attractive. The signs of age, especially when combined with obesity or socially unacceptable features, are assumed automatically to be unattractive. When people consider older bodies to be neither sexually stimulating nor desirable, the next step is to assume that no interest in sex or sexual activity occurs in old age. This assumption can produce a self-fulfilling prophecy in which old people feel devalued and thus lose interest in sex. Old people need self-confidence to avoid the frustration and dehumanization that our society fosters.

Romantic Love Is Only for the Young

Although romantic love has been variously defined, it has a number of generally accepted characteristics: idealization of mate, consuming interest and passion, fantasy, and desire for a blissful state of togetherness. Clichéd ideals—love at first sight and the idea that love conquers all—are often elements of romantic love. But there is no inherent reason why only young people should have exclusive access to romantic love. Yet in all forms of media, romantic love is predominantly an emotion for young people. From Shakespeare's *Romeo and Juliet* to the present, passion and romance is primarily for young lovers. Perhaps the concept came to be associated with young people because they are the ones most often involved in mate selection. However, with the increasing divorce rate and with increasing life expectancy, mate selection often continues throughout life. The belief that only young people are capable of strong passionate feeling invalidates the passions of older people.

Sexual Function Is for Procreation

Now fairly outdated, the concept of **sexual function for procreation,** which disassociates elders and sex, was embodied in the Christian religion by the teaching of St. Augustine (Feldstein, 1970). Accordingly, a woman's femininity was measured by her childbearing and mother role; a man's masculinity was measured by the number of offspring he produced. Because of the association between sexuality and procreation, men and women beyond the usual childbearing years were therefore believed to be less sexual. More and more, however, the sex act is considered an expression of love and happiness, with the reward being pleasure instead of children. Deeply rooted ideas take a long time to die, however. Some men still fear that a vasectomy will rob them of virility; some women fear that menopause or a hysterectomy will rob them of femininity.

Sexuality Is Hidden

Finally, a major factor perpetuating the idea that sex is the prerogative of the young might be lack of open display on the part of elders. Older people are not as candid in revealing an interest in sex as younger people. A survey of college students bears out this idea. The students were asked if their grandparents openly discussed their own sex life or displayed any show of **sexual interest** in their partner in the student's presence. Of 52 students who had two sets of living grandparents, 65 percent had never heard their grandparents discuss their own sexual relationship (Barrow, 1994).

Older people must struggle for more sexual visibility. Mae West, the actress and comedian, helped with that struggle. She was not afraid to poke fun at traditional norms that stifled older women. She died in 1980 at age 87, having been a sex symbol all of her adult life, even at age 85 in the 1978 movie, *Sextette*.

Old and Gay

Stereotypes of aging homosexuals maintain that they dread the onset of old age due to an overemphasis on youth, that they cannot find partners because of the age stigma, and that they are alienated from both homosexuals and traditional family support systems. The stereotypes overstate the case, yet the findings support the idea of ageism in the homosexual male subculture, which appears to emphasize youth even more than heterosexual society does. However, older gays express positive feelings about their age. Long-term relationships are much more frequent among gay men and lesbians than is commonly assumed. The AIDS epidemic has forced this fact into the open as the word *companion* is now published in obituaries across the country. Older lesbians and gay men typically live within a self-created network of friends, significant others, and selected biological family members. They tend to have more friends than do heterosexuals of similar age. Younger gays often look to older gays as role models and mentors (Kimmel, 1993).

In reality, the lifestyles and life choices of homosexuals and lesbians are similar to those of heterosexuals. In reports from older lesbians, the respondents were suffering from ageism, sexism, and homophobia, but did not regret their sexual orientation. They were able, with some therapy, to make a healthy adjustment and live their lives with high self-esteem (Schoonmaker, 1993).

☀ Findings on Sexuality

The **Kinsey studies** of the sexual practices of men and women were landmark, classic studies. *Sexual Behavior in the Human Male* appeared in 1948, followed by *Sexual Behavior in the Human Female* in 1953. No one had previously studied the sexual histories of so many individuals in such depth. Although very few of Kinsey's sample subjects were older men and women, Kinsey concluded that the rate of sexual activity gradually declines with age. The men in Kinsey's study were sexually most active in late adolescence (ages 16 to 20), the women in their twenties, and the rate for both genders gradually declined thereafter. Married men and women had a frequency of sexual activity higher than that of single persons.

Much research followed Kinsey's stepping-stone into aging and sexual behavior. A few of the most recent studies are explored here.

MASTERS AND JOHNSON'S STUDIES

Masters and Johnson's studies of human sexual behavior were considered revolutionary for their time period, just as Kinsey's were for his; they studied not just sexual histories but also observed and recorded the physiological responses of couples having sexual intercourse. This research resulted in their first book, *Human Sexual Response* (1966). Their second book, *Human Sexual Inadequacy* (1970), is based on their treatment program for those suffering from sexual dysfunctions. Although their technical language is rather difficult for the lay person to understand, the discussion that follows is taken largely from a very readable book that interprets their work and is endorsed by them (Belliveau and Richter, 1970). A problem with Masters and Johnson's study is that most of their "old" subjects were between 50 and 60. They studied few individuals over 60.

Masters and Johnson found that body processes slow down with age, but do not stop. They found that if a middle-aged husband and wife are aware of these changes and take them into account in their lovemaking, there is no reason why pleasurable sex cannot continue. For men, the body processes affected by the aging process include the length of time needed to get an erection and the firmness of the erection. The ejaculatory expulsion of semen is less forceful, and the erection may be lost faster after ejaculation. In addition, it may take longer to have another erection. If the older man is aware that these changes do not signal the end of his ability to have an erection, he can relax and enjoy sexual activity.

According to Masters and Johnson, men over 50 have many advantages over younger men. Their ejaculatory control becomes better, and they can maintain an erection for a longer period of time without the strong drive to ejaculate.

The aging female is subject to all the negative attitudes of our society regarding women and sexual matters: the beliefs that a woman's sex drive is not as strong as a man's, that women are more passive, that women are not supposed to enjoy sex as much as men. These myths become even stronger in terms of the older woman—for instance, the myth that it is unnatural for women to continue sexual relations after menopause. Masters and Johnson report that it is natural and beneficial for older women to continue sexual activity with no long periods of abstinence. Older women do, however, experience a slowing process, just as men do. Vaginal lubrication occurs more slowly with aging and less lubrication is produced. While younger women take 15 to 30 seconds for lubrication, older women may take as long as four or five minutes. The clitoris may get smaller with age, but it still receives and transmits sexual excitement. There is less increase in the size of the vaginal canal. And, with age, the lining of the vaginal walls becomes thin. Older women, like older men, generally experience a shorter orgasmic phase. Menopause may upset hormone balance; some older women benefit from hormone replacement therapy.

Masters and Johnson reported an increase in the rate of masturbation in older women. Many have become widowed, divorced and isolated from male sex partners. There were almost two unmarried women over 65 for each married man over 65. Husbands may be ill and not willing to participate in sex.

According to Masters and Johnson, there is no reason why these women who still need release from sexual tension should not provide it for themselves.

For women, as for men, aging has advantages. Postmenopausal women no longer need to be concerned about the risk of pregnancy or the side effects of contraceptives. They also may be free of the anxieties and pressures of motherhood. Masters and Johnson state that there is no reason why menopause should blunt the human female's sexual capacity, performance, or drive. They found no endpoint to female sexuality set by advancing years.

In their clinic, Masters and Johnson found at least a 50 percent chance of successfully treating sexual dysfunctions in people over age 50. Hope exists even for those with problems having lasted 25 years or more. A change of attitude is required more than anything else.

THE DUKE LONGITUDINAL STUDY

In spite of the small numbers of older people Masters and Johnson studied, their findings are of tremendous importance regarding the sexual *potential* of older people. But Masters and Johnson made no attempt to study just how many older people take advantage of their sexual potential and remain sexually active. The **Duke longitudinal study** tried to answer this question and to also assess the changes in sexual interest and activity that come with age (Verwoerdt, Pfeiffer, and Wang, 1969). The study, which began in 1954 at Duke University, still continues. Many different researchers involved in the study are still publishing their findings. One finding is that one in six of us will be even more interested in sex as we age (Witkin, 1994).

In the Duke study, sexual activity was one of many aspects studied in the lives of 254 older people. The sample was composed of nearly equal numbers of men and women whose ages ranged between 60 and 94. Four patterns of change in sexual activity were observed throughout the 10-year longitudinal study of 1954 to 1965: inactivity, sustained activity, decreasing activity, and rising sexual activity. The researchers found a great deal of variability in sexual behavior among the aging individuals. Approximately 15 percent of the sample fitted into the rising category, whereas unmarried women were almost totally inactive sexually. Ten years did not greatly decrease the number of elders who were sexually active. About half of the men and women who survived into their eighties and nineties reported having sexual interest. Among men surviving into their eighties and nineties, continued sexual activity was not rare; and about one-fifth of these men reported that they were still sexually active.

In summary, the Duke study shows enough sexual activity on the part of the old and the very old to illustrate the sexual potential Masters and Johnson found in older adults. On the other hand, the sexual interest of many Duke study participants exceeded their actual sexual activity. Although not clearly explained, this discrepancy was perhaps caused by ailing physical health, psychological reasons, or lack of an acceptable partner.

OTHER STUDIES

Starr and Weiner (1981) studied responses of older individuals to a lengthy sex questionnaire. Elders, even those in their seventies and eighties, reported being sexually active and stated that sex was as good or better than ever, though a little less frequent. Three-fourths of the elders studied said their lovemaking had improved with time. The researchers, who challenge the

Kinsey studies as to the rapidity of decline of sexual activity with age, state that Kinsey inaccurately compared old people raised in conservative times with young people raised in more permissive times and suggest that long-term longitudinal studies would show less decline in sexual activity than Kinsey's cross-sectional study.

Another opportunity for questionnaire response was provided by the Consumers Union (Brecher, 1984); 4,246 aged men and women responded. The responses indicated that age did not adversely affect enjoyment of sex and that most husbands and wives were currently having marital intercourse. Unhappy marriage reduced sexual activity for older couples, just as it did for younger couples. Rates of extramarital intercourse, though lower than those for younger couples, still occurred for the same reasons. Inattentive or uninterested spouses were major factors. Some couples had open marriages. Homosexual experiences were reported; some took place for the first time in old age. Such findings dash stereotypes of sexually inactive and uninterested elders, many of whom had struggled for sexual frankness and openness throughout their lives, fighting taboos that seem to have been more strict than those young people face today. Some elders had improved their sex lives over the years by breaking down psychological barriers; some had not. Some regretted being so sexually uninformed when they were young.

Overall, both men and women experienced only slight declines by decade in sexual activity. The percentage of sexually active married women in their fifties, sixties, and seventies is, correspondingly, 95, 89, and 81 percent. For married men, 98 percent are sexually active in their fifties; 93 percent in their sixties; and 81 percent continue to be active at age 70 and over.

Respondents found a variety of ways to compensate for sexual changes brought about by aging or poor health. They slowed down the lovemaking process, emphasized oral sex and manual stimulation of the genitals, and participated in lots of fondling and cuddling. Many reported that the sensation of touch was more important, meaningful, and appreciated than in their younger years. Some women used a lubricant to compensate for lack of vagi-

The possibility of intimacy and enchantment with another continues to the end of our lives.

nal moisture. The biggest problem for older, unmarried women was finding a partner; men their age are in small supply. Respondents generally showed a strong interest in sex and a large capacity for enjoying life.

For the very old, biological studies of changes in the male reproductive system reveal these findings: need for greater direct penile stimulation to achieve erection, slower erection (but only a few minutes slower), briefer stage of ejaculatory inevitability, reduced amount of seminal ejaculation, and reduced need for ejaculation at each and every sexual contact. If a man becomes impotent, the cause is illness or disease, not aging. There are various ways to help impotence, including implants. New knowledge and techniques are continually being made available in dealing with either impotence or premature ejaculation. In addition, sensations become less genital, more sensual, and more diffused. In the aging female, changes include slower lubrication, greater need for direct stimulation of the clitoris, shorter orgasmic phase, and irritability of vaginal tissue and outer lying tissue with low levels of estrogen. But these problems do not mean the end of one's sex life. According to Dr. Helen Singer Kaplan, sexuality is among the last of our faculties to decline with age (Witkin, 1994).

A study in the *Johns Hopkins Medical Letter* reports that 70 percent of 68-year-old men and the majority (over 50 percent) of women in their seventies regularly engage in sexual intercourse. One of the most debilitating factors related to diminished sexual activity is the self-fulfilling prophecy mentioned earlier; the belief that sexual prowess diminishes with age. The article suggests that knowing what changes to expect as a person ages as well as how to deal with those changes is a key to remaining sexually active. At any age health problems such as diabetes, alcoholism, depression, or anxiety can interfere with sexual function.

Like the studies cited earlier, the Johns Hopkins study generally finds no physical reason for refraining from sexual activity even during periods of chronic illness. Persons who have experienced heart attacks or who suffer from arthritis or diabetes can usually continue to engage in sexual intercourse without fear. In short, the article concludes, "age has little or nothing to do with continuing to enjoy sex" (Lobanov, 1990).

Bretschneider and McCoy (1988) studied the sexuality of a healthy population of individuals between the ages of 80 and 102. The most common activities in order of frequency were (1) touching and caressing, (2) masturbation, and (3) intercourse. Although 63 percent of the men had intercourse at least sometimes, only 30 percent of the women did. The researchers concluded that, for men, the frequency of sexual intercourse does not change greatly after age 80 compared to the previous decade. It is even possible that there is a moderate increase in the proportion of men in their eighties and nineties who are sexually active, but this may be due to the greater survival of the most biologically fit. For either men or women in general there is no decade this side of 100 in which sexual activity is totally absent. Of the men over 80, 61 percent reported problems of either achieving or maintaining an erection. The reasons were not clarified and were possibly more psychological than physical.

Such findings lead some researchers to the conclusion that women retain their physical capacity to enjoy sex more easily than men. Because women tend to marry men older than themselves, it is often the case that they stop having sex because the husbands are not interested, not because they wanted an end to the sex life. In another survey 48 percent of women ended sexual intercourse because their spouse died, but only 10 percent of men gave this as a reason. An interesting study revealed that older wives with younger husbands are more sexually active than are younger wives with older husbands (Christenson and Gagnon, 1965).

In general, findings on sexuality show that, given good health, a positive attitude, and an acceptable partner, even those in their eighties and nineties can remain sexually active.

Older people who are frightened by the aging process can be helped. In their second book, Masters and Johnson (1970) tell of a typical couple in their early sixties who came for treatment. While the couple had enjoyed sex throughout their many years of married life, the husband began to notice that getting an erection was taking a longer period of time. He panicked and became impotent. As so often happens at any age, once he began to doubt his sexual capacity he began to experience increasing difficulty. The couple went to a doctor who told them that this was a natural part of the aging process and that they should face it and accept it. A second doctor told them the same story. After five years of an unsatisfactory sex life, they came to Masters and Johnson's clinic. There, they became aware of the changes that come with age and were able to resume a satisfactory sex life. Masters and Johnson's studies suggest that just supplying basic education and information can be a major form of therapy for sexual dysfunctions.

Physically handicapped and terminally ill individuals sometimes need sexual counseling. The physically handicapped need reassurance that they are sexually attractive and capable, even though they may have become partially paralyzed or have had a limb amputated. Although they are not physically handicapped, women with mastectomies (breast removal) often need reassurance as to their sexual worth. Heart attack and stroke victims may require the same thing.

The terminally ill are often anxious about sex. Not enough doctors, nurses, and family members recognize the need to discuss sexual needs or are willing to do so. For elders who are "not supposed to have" sexual feelings, this is doubly frustrating; they want to enjoy what time is left. Sexual desires may increase to counter anxiety about dying. In contrast, the spouse of a cancer patient may even fear that he or she can catch cancer, that it is somehow contagious. Counseling in such instances is very important.

☼ Improving Attitudes About Aging and Sexuality

To encourage the fulfillment of sexual potential, society must broaden its definition of what is beautiful and sexually attractive. Not only the young should qualify. In European cultures, for example, the mature woman is viewed more positively than she is in the United States. One indication is Europe's greater demand and use of middle-aged actresses on stage and in film.

In spite of society's general taboo on romantic love for older adults, many are looking for romance. Many elders enjoy dating. They can and do talk about "steadies" and become possessive about their "friends" and partners. Indeed, retired older people may have more leisure time to dance, bicycle, eat out, and date than younger individuals, whose time is taken up with jobs and careers. Most dance clubs have a majority of members who are over 60 years old. Folk and country dancing, for example, can be vigorous exercise as well as fun, and an opportunity for romance as well.

Hearing from older people themselves is perhaps the best way to understand their desires and problems. One 63-year-old woman had a hard time turning age 60. But she said passing 60 was "no reason to pass up sexiness."

She and her friends all want to be sexually attractive to the opposite sex. "I don't think you ever lose that as a sexually oriented woman. Everyone I know has kept their figure . . . when skirts are short we wear them as short as we can get away with." "When you get older, there is more meaning to the touch," said Glenda Lee, a 70-year-old. "Even a shake of the hand has a different meaning. There's something about it that's a warm close feeling" (Ross-Flanigan, 1988). Thwarted sexuality and lack of intimacy can feed depression.

To heighten awareness that elders do indeed have and enjoy sex, a company that makes sex education films produced a film entitled *Ripple in Time* that shows an older couple making love. The couple in the film find each other's bodies attractive and stimulating. When this film was shown to a human sexuality class, the evaluations were overwhelmingly positive. Students of all ages said that they had never seen more tenderness and love expressed or thought sex could be more beautiful than the way it was portrayed by the couple in this film. Many remarked that the movie had changed not only their conceptions about sex but also their conception of elders.

In Ruth Jacobs' book, *Be An Outrageous Older Woman*, a chapter on sexuality relates her surprise and dismay at the shock evoked by her writings and seminars. Her writings, although not graphic, are open and candid about the sexual desires of older women. She believes that our definition of what is sexual has undermined older adults, and needs to be changed. If being sexy is measured by frequencies of orgasms and other quantitative counts, sexuality may show some decrease with age. But if sexuality refers to one's ability to be sensual, then one can become more sexual with age (Jacobs, 1993).

In one of her workshops an older woman who assumed her decreased interest in sex was due to aging, discovered that the tranquilizers she had been taking for four years were responsible. Other drugs, such as the relatively new ones for depression like Prozac and Zoloft, can severely affect the ability of a woman to have an orgasm. Individuals must check on the side effect of drugs. For example, sexual dysfunction is not an uncommon side effect for men who take certain medications for hypertension.

Jacobs discusses from "A to Z" the various needs, desires, and choices for older women regarding their sexuality. The present generation of women 65 and over are much less willing to have sex without marriage than are single men of the same age. Unmarried women do not have as much sexual activity because their values are more conservative and they tend to be looking for commitment. She encourages women to look at what they want and try to achieve it. Being celibate or being with another woman are viable, honorable choices. If a single older woman would like to be with a man and cannot find one, her advice is, "Don't feel there is anything wrong with you, it's the demographics. If you want a man, go where the men are" (Jacobs, 1993, p. 129). And further do not be embarrassed about dating younger men. It makes good sense: women live longer and thus the couple has more years together. The findings that older single men are more sexually active than their female counterparts should not be interpreted to mean that older women have lower sex drives. Generally speaking, older single men and women are equally interested in sexual relationships.

Moving into a nursing home can complicate sexual matters. Behavioral and psychological problems may result when residents are ridiculed or prevented from enjoying physical contact. When residents hold hands or say they want to marry, this may evoke laughter and sarcastic remarks, leading to humiliation. The lack of sexual contact hurts, as well as the lost sexuality.

Treating an aged man and women like children because they want to hold hands or embrace robs them of their manhood and womanhood. Nursing home staff may believe that residents should not be sexual or that sexual desire is a symptom of boredom or senility. Adult children may have trouble accepting that their nursing home parent wants intimacy with another resident. Hopefully, both nursing home staff and adult children are becoming more enlightened. As privacy for older residents, some nursing homes provide "do not disturb" signs and have rules that staff must knock before entering rooms.

We all need to know that the possibilities for intimacy and enchantment with another continue to the end of our lives. In summary, sex is for life. The frequency and vigor of sex may change with age, but sex in later life not only is possible, but also bolsters emotional health and self-image. Sexuality is a basic part of a person's makeup. Regardless of age, the loving expression of it says, "I value you. I appreciate you. I like having you in my life." A person who enjoys sexual expression when young will probably enjoy it when older, too.

Chapter Summary

The health status of the population aged 65 and over is higher than most people would predict. Most elders are able-bodied and not limited in a major way by physical impairments. Poor health in old age is not caused by the aging process; lack of exercise, inadequate diet, stress, and disease are contributors. Heart disease, hypertension, cancer, strokes, and accidents are the leading causes of death. With the elimination of these and other factors, longevity would increase. Exercise and nutrition are vital in maintaining health and longevity. Arthritis is the most common health problem among elders. Wellness is a concept that is useful for young and old alike.

In the United States, sexuality is viewed as the prerogative of the young. However, the findings generally show that the sex drive continues throughout life. Masters and Johnson found that a continuation of an active sex life is natural and beneficial. A longitudinal study at Duke University found great variation in the sexual activities and interest of elders. Some had decreased sexual activity from earlier years; others maintained or increased activity. Whether active or not, individuals maintain an interest in being sexual throughout their lives. A study of 80- to 102-year-olds revealed that intercourse is a definite possibility among the very old. Women outnumber men in old age and, thus, lack partners, but not necessarily desire.

Key Terms

acute condition
aging as disease
arteriosclerosis
arthritis
atherosclerosis
average life span
biological clock
cancer
cerebrovascular disease

chronic condition
Duke longitudinal study
health span
health status of the aged
heart disease
hypertension
immune system
Kinsey studies
Masters and Johnson's studies

maximum life span

osteoporosis

sexual function for procreation

sexual interest

sexual invisibility

sexuality

wear and tear

wellness

Questions for Discussion

1. Assuming that you are not yet 80 years old, examine your own lifestyle in terms of your everyday habits, exercise, diet, auto safety, smoking, drinking, and stress. How healthy will you be at age 80?

2. What is considered to be the age and shape of the "body beautiful" for males and females in our society?

3. What expectations do you have for your sex life at 65 and after? How will you deal psychologically with the changes in your body that come with age? Will the changes affect your sexual image of yourself? Will the changes affect your choice of partners?

Fieldwork Suggestions

1. Survey older and younger age groups about the kind and the quality of physical exercise they engage in. Which age groups are in better shape? Why?

2. Contact several elderly individuals at the close of day. Have them list everything they ate. Evaluate the nutritional quality of their food intake. Have a nutritionist help, if necessary.

3. Survey others on the question: When do the sexual drives of a person cease? Ask respondents to choose from the following age categories: 35 to 54, 55 to 64, 65 to 79, 80 to 94, 95 older, or never. What results do you find? How many "never" responses do you get?

4. Survey students about their thoughts on the sexuality of their grandparents. What do they think about or know of their grandparents' interest in sex?

References

Barrow, Georgia. "Study on Students' Opinions of Grandparents." (Unpublished). Santa Rosa Junior College, 1994.

Beard, B. B., et al., eds. *Centenarians: The New Generation.* Westport, CT: Greenwood Press, 1991.

Belliveau, Fred, and Lin Richter. *Understanding Human Sexual Inadequacy.* New York: Bantom Books, 1970.

Brecher, E. *Love, Sex and Aging: A Consumers Union Report.* Boston: Little, Brown, 1984.

Bretschneider, J. and McCoy, N. Sexual Interest and Behavior in Healthy 80 to 102 year olds, *Archives of Sexual Behavior,* 17:2, February, 1988, p. 102–129.

Christenson, C., and Gagnon, J. Sexual Behavior in a Group of Older Women, Journal of Gerontology, 20, 1965, p. 351–356.

Colburn, D. "Vision Tests Reduce Older Drivers' Deaths." *Washington Post* (30 June 1992): WH5.

Devitt, Terry. "Staying Young." *On Wisconsin Magazine* (September/October 1991): 21–26.

Elmer-DeWitt, Phillip. "Extra Years for Extra Effort." *Time* (17 March 1986): 66.

Evans, William, and Irwin H. Rosenberg. *Biomarkers: The 10 Determinants of Aging You Can Control.* New York: Simon & Schuster, 1991.

"Exercise Isn't Just for Fun." *Aging Magazine* 362 (1991): 37–40.

Feldstein, Ivor. *Sex in Later Life.* Baltimore, MD: Penguin Books, 1970.

Jacobs, R. *Be an Outrageous Older Woman: ARASP.* Manchester, CT: Knowledge, Ideas and Trends Publisher, 1993.

Keeton, K. *Longevity.* New York: Viking, 1992.

Keeton, K. "Mental Muscle." *Omni Magazine* 14:8 (May 1992): 40–45.

Kimmel, D. "The Families of Older Gay Men and Lesbians." In *Worlds of Difference,* edited by E. Stoller and R. Gibson. Thousand Oaks, CA: Pine Forge Press, 1993.

Kinsey, Alfred, et al. *Sexual Behavior in the Human Male.* Philadelphia, PA: W. B. Saunders, 1948.

Kinsey, Alfred, et al. *Sexual Behavior in the Human Female.* Philadelphia, PA: W. B. Saunders, 1953.

Lobanov, Igor. "Myths About Sex After 50 Shattered." *Senior Beacon* 2 (February 1990): 1, 16.

Manson, M., and G. Gutfeld "Losing the Final Five." *Prevention Magazine* 46:5 (May 1994): 22–24.

Masters, William M., and V. E. Johnson. *Human Sexual Response*. Boston: Little, Brown, 1966.

Masters, William M., and V. E. Johnson. *Human Sexual Inadequacy*. Boston: Little, Brown, 1970.

National Institutes of Health, National Institute on Aging. *In Search of the Secrets of Aging* (NIH Publication No. 93-2756). Bethesda, MD: National Institutes of Health, 1993.

National Safety Council. *Accident Facts*. Chicago, IL: National Safety Council, 1993.

Poon, L., ed. *The Georgia Centenarian Study*. Amityville, NY: Baywood Publishing, 1992.

Rigdon, J. "Car Trouble: Older Drivers Pose Growing Risk." *Wall Street Journal* (29 October 1993): A1.

Roan, S. "The Ponce de Leon Study." *Sunday Punch Section of the San Francisco Chronicle* (17 January 1993): p. 2.

Ross-Flanigan, N. "Sex and the Senior." *Detroit Free Press* (10 May 1988).

Rubin, K. "Tinkering with Destiny." *U.S. News and World Report* (22 August 1944): 58–67,

Schick, F., and R. Schick, *Statistical Handbook of Aging Americans*. Phoenix, AZ: Onyx Press.

Schideler, K. "Everybody Gets Osteoporosis." *Santa Rosa Press Democrat* (8 August 1994): D2.

Schmidt, K. "No Purpose in Dying: Staying Young Longer." *U.S. News and World Report* (8 March 1993): 66–73.

Schoonmaker, C. "Aging Lesbians: Bearing the Burden of Triple Shame." *Faces of Women and Aging,* edited by N. Davis, E. Cole, and C. Rothblum, New York: Haworth Press, 1993. 21–32.

Segell, M. "How to Live Forever, Part I." *Esquire Magazine* (September 1993): 125–132.

Segell, M. "How to Live Forever, Part II." *Esquire Magazine* (November 1993): 132–137.

Starr, B., and M. Weiner, *The Starr-Weiner Report on Sex and Sexuality in the Mature Years*. Briarcliff Manor, NY: Stein & Day, 1981.

U.S. Bureau of the Census, *Statistical Abstract of the United States, 1988*. 108th ed. Washington, DC: Bureau of the Census, 1993.

Winnick, M., L. Plumer, and H. S. Wang. "Sexual Behaviorism in Senescence." *Geriatrics* 24 (February 1969): 137–153.

Witkin, G. "Ten Myths About Sex." *Parade Magazine, Santa Rosa Press Democrat* (17 January 1994) 22–23.

Further Readings

Evans, R., et al., eds. *Why Are Some People Healthy and Others Not? The Determinants of Health of Populations*. New York: Aldine DeGruyter, 1994.

Inlander, C., and M. Hodge. *One Hundred Ways To Live to One Hundred*. Avenal, NJ: Wings Books, a division of Random House Value Publishing, 1994.

McCord, H. " 'C' Twice a Day." *Prevention* (March 1995) Vol. 47:3, p. 52.

Institute of Medicine. *Extending Life, Enhancing Life: A National Research Agenda on Aging*. Washington, DC: National Academy Press, 1992.

7 *W*ork and Leisure

CHAPTER OUTLINE

OLD IS NEWS

Maryland Man Decides 98 Is a Good Retirement Age

Thirty years ago, at an age when most people retire, Steve Minnich was just getting going in a new job as a salesman at a cooling-and-heating-equipment company.

Now that he's 98, he has reluctantly decided to take some time off.

"I retired because I did want some time, whatever time is left, to do some traveling, and whatever else will give me pleasure," he said.

He was still working eighteen days until he quit August 31.

Minnich began his lifetime of work early, near the farm in Lancaster, Pa., where he was born in 1894, the 10th of 11 children. One of his brothers lived to 102.

"I made my own living at the age of 10, when my father died," he said. His first job was on a neighbor's farm, where he was sent to work for room and board.

He was married for 35 years until his wife died in 1965. They never had children. He lives alone in an apartment in Hyattsville, Md.

"I have been asked many, many times why I do not retire. My answer is, I like meeting people who are meaningful to me," he said.

Before becoming a salesman, Minnich worked as an orange picker in California, a miner in Arizona copper mines and a machinist in a Philadelphia factory.

He got into sales in 1925 when he went to work in the Philadelphia branch office of the Cleveland Heater Co.

This group of retirees is enjoying a sunshiny day.

—Continued

When that company went out of business in 1962, he began working at William E. Kingswell Inc., now located in Beltsville, about 15 miles northeast of Washington.

Minnich said he's eager to share the wisdom he's gained from experience.

He offers some nuggets he's penned:

"Be not hypocritical. Be analytical."

"Be thankful being vertical and not horizontal."

His greatest fear is becoming idle—a so-far unfamiliar experience.

Even post retirement, he still shows up at the office, where he keeps fit by doing push-ups against boxes in the Kingswell warehouses.

He dresses nattily in a suit and tie, and Kingswell owner John Lenahan said customers love him. He's also always been punctual.

"I can count on him more than some of the other people today. He's never sick," Lenahan said. "We really don't like to see him go." ☀

SOURCE: Associated Press, *San Francisco Chronicle*, 16 November 1992, p. D6.

o work or not to work in old age: that is the question. The answer to this question has implications for both society and the older person. It also implies a choice that for many people is limited or nonexistent. Some people are forced to retire because of age discrimination or because of illness. Others must continue to work, often at menial jobs, because they cannot afford to retire. Further, the economics of supply and demand govern one's presence in or out of the job market. If there is a demand for your work, you stay; if there is not, you are encouraged to retire.

The issue of work and retirement is a thorny one. Retirees may feel either elated and free or devalued and depressed. Because of changes in routine, personal habits, and opportunities for social interaction, retirement can bring stress even when it is voluntary. Though studies show that most older people generally make a satisfactory adjustment to retirement, given good health and sufficient income, some do not have these benefits; and a minority are not satisfied with retirement, regardless of their health and financial status. *Retirement* is a dirty word to some; to others it represents freedom from a daily grind of work.

In this chapter, we will explore the options of retirement, analyze discrimination against the older worker, and examine the difficulties old people have in adjusting to retirement. We will also look at the meaning of leisure in our culture. When we are young, our time away from work is called "leisure"; when we are old, it is called "retirement." What is the difference?

☀ The Concept of Retirement

In 1900, nearly 70 percent of American men over age 65 were employed. By 1960, the figure had dropped to 35 percent; by 1976, to 22 percent; and by 1992, to 15 percent (see Figure 7.1). This figure is projected to be 14.7 percent by the year 2000 (U.S. Bureau of the Census, 1991). In 1992, the percentage of women in the workforce aged 65 and over was 9 percent; this number has remained fairly constant for the last two decades, but has experienced a 1 percent increase over the last five years and will rise further in the years ahead.

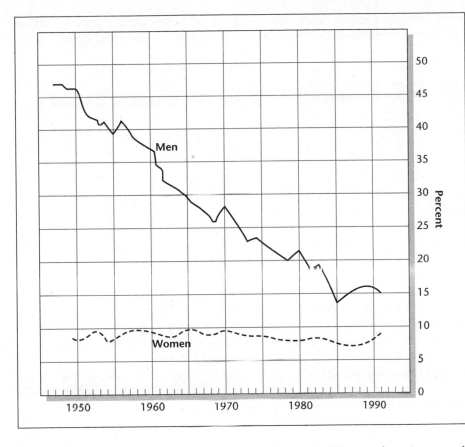

Figure 7.1

Working Less: Percentage of People Aged 65 and Over Who Still Work

SOURCE: Adapted from "Aging America," The Economist (16 September 1989): 18.

Most of the labor force growth in the 1990s has and will come from increased participation by minorities and middle-aged and older women (Rayman et al., 1993).

As the number of elders in the workforce has declined, the percentage of retired people has shot upward. For most people in the United States, **retirement** is an expected life event. Even though mandatory retirement has been abolished for many jobs, other factors are leading older men to favor retirement. On the other hand, more older women are entering or remaining in the workforce. However, not all workers retire completely. Studies show that more than one of every five older Americans who retire return to work at least part time.

In the agricultural era of the United States, few workers retired. Most workers were self-employed farmers or craftspeople who generally worked as hard as they could until illness or death slowed or stopped them. Stopping work, however, did not have to be abrupt. A gradual decline in the workload could occur simultaneously with a gradual decline in physical strength.

Older people who held property could usually support themselves in old age. For example, a homesteader who began to grow old and to experience difficulty in doing heavy work could usually pass the work on to family, retaining his or her authority as the children assumed more and more responsibility. Because he or she remained in charge, the older farmer did not have to quit producing entirely. No one could technically force "retirement."

Before 1900, few people lived past age 65. Those who owned property lived longer than those who did not own property or have helping family members. Older persons without economic resources had to do heavy work because of their need to support themselves. When they could no longer physically continue to work, they often ended up in alms houses or died of malnutrition and neglect. The "good old days" were not good for many old people.

The Industrial Revolution brought many complex changes. Increased productivity created great surpluses of food and other goods. More people ceased being self-employed and went to work in large factories and businesses. Government and bureaucracy grew. When civil service pensions for government workers were introduced in 1921, the retirement system began.

In 1935, with the passage of the Social Security Act, all conditions for institutionalizing retirement were met. The law dictated that persons over 65 who had worked certain lengths of time were eligible for benefits, and 65 became the age for retirement. Since then, employees in both the public and private sectors of the economy have retired in increasing numbers.

We also need a word about women and work. Women born in the early 1900s were not encouraged to enter the workforce. A Gallup Poll in 1936 found 82 percent agreement for the statement that wives of employed husbands should not work (Keating and Jeffrey, 1983). Not until the 1960s did the concept of work outside the home as other than a temporary role for women develop. Even then, wives' employment was often seen as a supplemental source of money for "extras." Before the 1960s, the majority of permanently employed women were single. Married women tend to have interrupted work histories—entering the labor force and then leaving it upon the birth of a child (the "mommy track"). Thus many women in their old age today (the married ones, at any rate) do not have the extensive work histories that older women in the future will have, even though many of them worked temporarily outside the home during the Depression and World War II.

Now more than 95 percent of all adults expect to retire some day. Although retirement has become an accepted feature of modern life, one must question whether retirement is wise for everyone.

☼ The Trend Toward Early Retirement

A different trend is usurping retirement at age 65. More and more companies are encouraging employees in skilled, semiskilled, or unskilled jobs to retire before age 65 without a substantial loss of pension benefits. American industry, which seems to presume that the young have greater vitality, has steadfastly worked for **early retirement** and restrictions on work opportunities for older workers. In industry, retirement at age 55 is not uncommon and 62 is typical.

This trend in industry has now become common in the white collar world of work. Whether blue or white collar, most baby boomers say they would like to retire by age 55. Some (about 40 percent) want to retire between the ages of 56 and 65, and some, after 65 or never. The desire for and expectation of early retirement has increased over the last several decades. From 1950 to 1990 the median retirement age dropped from 67 to 63.

In the 1970s the trend toward making pensions and other benefits available before age 65 greatly accelerated. One study indicated that those who were offered full pension benefits before age 65 were twice as likely to retire early. In 1992, 38 percent of early retirements from large companies were the result of incentive offers. For the most part, companies were seeking to cut their payrolls and at the same time avoid layoffs.

Studies of companies and educational institutions show that a majority have early retirement inducements in their pension plans. Only a handful offer incentives to continue working beyond age 65.

This excerpt illustrates the way in which Hewlett-Packard used early retirement to scale down its number of employees when business was off:

> Plagued by manufacturing problems that have hurt its earnings for the last two quarters, the company announced a corporate-wide plan to offer early retirement to 2,400 workers in plants across the country. The program is available to workers who are at least 55 years of age or older and have 15 or more years with the company. Those who opt for the program get a half-month's salary for each year of service up to a maximum of 12 months' salary. (Silver, 1990)

Likewise IBM's Japan unit needing to reduce the size of its workforce, offered an early retirement plan hoping to remove a significant number of employees aged 50 and over ("IBM's Japan Unit," 1993). These early retirement packages are typical of large corporations that wish to cut costs by downsizing their operations. Such downsizing is especially common in the cyclical high-technology industry, with its recurring booms and busts. Some workers like these packages, grabbing a retirement package at one company and then getting an equivalent or even better job elsewhere. Others wanted to retire anyway. The unhappy ones are those who feel forced to retire.

A few businesses are beginning to question the policy of encouraging workers to retire at or before age 62. The labor pool of young workers is declining, and they sometimes cost as much to train as to retain the older workers (McDonald and Chen, 1993). Some companies are studying **late-retirement incentive programs (LRIPs).** These studies show, however, that although most businesses are afraid that too many workers will take advantage of LRIPs, most workers still opt for early retirement. Incentives for early rather than late retirement are still the order of the day for business and industry. The only change is that many early retirees find the "good deals" not so good after all; buyout plans are growing skimpier, and new jobs are scarce (Lopez, 1993). Surveys show that older workers getting offers for buyouts are now turning them down (Salwen, 1993). Economic worries and inadequate pensions are slowing the trend toward early retirement.

EARLY RETIREMENT DISCRIMINATION

Some early retirement incentives are offers that older American workers cannot refuse, and many older workers are wondering whether they are being subjected to disguised **early retirement discrimination.** For example, at the age of 56, a man who had worked for 31 years for a large manufacturing company was hoping to work 6 more years and retire at age 62. But his corporation, like many others across the United States, decided to trim its payroll and abolish numerous jobs, including his. The company offered him half-pay retirement for the next four years, provided that he did not work elsewhere. He accepted these terms out of fear that other jobs were not available to him (Hey, 1988).

A one-time incentive is not the same as an early retirement option. An early retirement option offers the employee the choice to stay or to go. In contrast, with the one-time incentive, the employee either accepts or gets laid off. No clear-cut rules regarding legality have been established for the various early retirement incentives.

For every employee who gladly accepts an early retirement incentive, another feels that he or she is being forced out the door. Under the **Age Discrimination in Employment Act,** all early retirements must be voluntary (Quinn, 1991). The question is, what is voluntary? Do you leave of your own free will if your boss drops strong hints that you are not wanted and hints at a big bonus offer if you leave early? Or if you are told that in a year your job will be phased out? Before granting an early retirement bonus, some companies require the worker to sign a waiver agreeing not to sue. This requirement is illegal. Economists ask the question of induced retirement: is it retirement or is it unemployment (Osberg, 1993)? The tendency to ease older workers out of the labor market cuts across all industrialized nations. It is not a problem unique to the United States.

THE TAXPAYER VERSUS EARLY RETIREMENT

People are asking, "Can we afford old age?" (Meyer, 1992). Business and industry desire early retirement programs, and these programs are sometimes a boon for the older worker. But there is an irony involved. Life expectancy is greater than ever, and the supply of younger workers is shrinking, creating a larger percentage of older workers. Social Security, currently on the brink of financial collapse, would be more likely to stabilize if older workers stayed on the job longer; and the government, contrary to many companies' wishes, is attempting to see that they do. The Social Security retirement age will gradually become 67 (in other words, the normal retirement age will be 67 for those reaching age 62 after 2022), and those taking benefits early will receive 30 percent less (they currently receive 20 percent less) than those receiving benefits at the normal retirement age. In this way, federal policy is encouraging workers to extend their work lives. But the incentives from business and industry are too powerful in encouraging the older worker out of the market. Economics researchers make it very clear that most persons respond to economic incentives in choosing to retire. To keep older workers on the job and to thereby save Social Security funds, the government will need to strengthen its measures—to increase the amount of money older workers can earn without reducing their Social Security benefits, for example. And business and industry should try harder to find a place for the older worker, who may well offer a gold mine of experience, wisdom, and loyalty. Sadly, workers near retirement seem expendable to most large-scale employers. But as the number and percentage of younger workers shrink, private business may finally be motivated to retain and retrain older workers.

Paid part-time or volunteer work is a feature in the lives of most older Americans.

☼ Discrimination Against the Older Worker

Age discrimination in employment starts long before the traditional time for retirement. Even those still in their thirties have trouble getting into some training programs and schools, such as flight school and medical school. The problem of job discrimination is severe for older workers in spite of federal laws that prohibit it. The 1967 Age Discrimination in Employment Act (amended in 1974 and 1978) prohibits the following:

1. Failing to hire a worker between age 40 and 70 because of age.
2. Discharging a person because of age.
3. Discrimination in pay or other benefits because of age.
4. Limiting or classifying an employee according to his or her age.
5. Instructing an employment agency not to refer a person to a job because of age, or to refer that person only to certain kinds of jobs.
6. Placing any ad that shows preference based on age or specifies an age bracket. *Exceptions:* the federal government, employers of less than 20 persons, or jobs where youth is a "bona fide occupational qualification," such as modeling teenage clothes.

Prior to 1978, the Age Discrimination in Employment Act protected employees from age 40 through age 64. The amendments adopted in 1978 extended that protection to age 70. Though all upper limits were removed for federal employees, the law does include exceptions that allow the federal government to retire air traffic controllers, law enforcement officers, and fire fighters at younger ages. Nevertheless, the U.S. Supreme Court in 1985 ruled that the city of Baltimore could not force its fire fighters to retire at age 55, despite federal regulations requiring retirement at 55 for most government fire fighters. Other cities are easing their rules to allow fire fighters, police officers, and other public safety employees to stay on the job until 65 or older.

AGEISM IN THE JOB SEARCH

Age should not be a determining criteria in finding work. One's ability to do the job is what counts. Age discrimination in the labor market makes finding work more difficult. The skills and energy of older people are greatly under-utilized. More older people want to work than is commonly believed. One study found the following:

- As many as 5.4 million older Americans (55 and over)—one in seven of those not currently working—report that they are willing and able to work but do not have a job.
- More than 1 million workers aged 50 to 64 believe that they will be forced to retire before they want to.
- More than half of all workers aged 50 to 64 would continue working if their employer were willing to retrain them for a new job, continue making pension contributions after age 65, or to transfer them to a job with less responsibility, fewer hours, and less pay as a transition to full retirement. (Commonwealth Fund, 1993)

A 1992 Harris survey revealed these reasons for older people wanting to work: (1) financial, 37 percent; (2) bored with retirement, 21 percent; and (3) want to do something useful, 14 percent (Taylor, Bass, and Harris, 1992).

Older persons who feel that they have been denied employment or have been let go because of their age can take steps to get their job back or to receive compensation by making a formal written charge of discrimination against the employer to the Wage and Hour Division of the Department of Labor. Individual cases of age discrimination are difficult to prove, however. In the investigation of the employer's hiring, firing, and retiring practices, the government tries to reveal a pattern of discrimination. For example, if an employer has hired a good many people over the past several years—but nobody over age 30—a pattern of discriminating against older workers in favor of younger workers may be documented. The older worker will have a better chance of winning if he or she hires a lawyer. A class-action suit may be filed if a number of job applicants feel they have been denied employment because of discrimination.

Resources that work diligently to help the older worker find employment are few but multiplying. For example, in the past, employment agencies commonly violated the Age Discrimination Act by stipulating upper age limits or using words such as "junior executive," "young salesperson," or "girl" in advertising. Employment agencies also have been found guilty of failing to refer older workers to potential employers. Such violations, unfortunately, are still common practice. Now, however, employment agencies such as "Kelly Services: Encore" cater to people over 50 years of age. They advise older applicants that they do not have to give their date of birth on a resume, and they remind them that potential employers may not legally ask a person's age in an interview. Other employment resources are aimed specifically at elders. One example is Operation ABLE in Chicago, which has helped thousands of people between the ages and 50 and 70 to find work. It not only matches people with jobs but also teaches them skills such as word processing. Nevertheless age discrimination in employment is prevalent according to an AARP study ("Job Applicants," 1994) and older people are still laboring for acceptance (Fein, 1994, January 5).

In the mid-1970s, Jobs for Older Women, a branch of the National Organization for Women (NOW), began analyzing refusals to hire older women. Employers often base refusal on an older woman's appearance: a department or clothing store may be worried about projecting a youthful image, or a certain restaurant may hire only young women who will wear skimpy uniforms. Older women are also rejected in favor of younger women for the more visible positions of bank tellers, receptionists, and other such jobs. The sad refrain is "I'd love to hire you, but you just won't fit in" (Fein, 1994, January 4). But employers may soon lack the personnel to meet their youthful standards. As the U.S. population collectively ages, older women will begin to outnumber younger women in the job market (Crispell, 1993). The percentage of women aged 55 to 59 in the job market was 55 percent in 1993, compared to 27 percent in 1950 and 46 percent in 1983 (Perkins, 1994). Middle-aged women, often heads of households, have had to settle for low-paying jobs with little chance for promotion. Studies show that age discrimination is well established by age 40 for women. (One indicator is the large number of age discrimination lawsuits for women this age compared with men.) More women are in the labor force more continuously than ever before, yet 60 percent of these women are segregated into three occupations: sales, service, and clerical. Of the 27 percent in administration, management, and professions, many are teachers or nursing administrators. Further, women's earnings peak at age 35 to 44, whereas men's peak later in life at ages 45 to 54. One major reason is that women have the kinds of jobs that do not get rewarded with big raises (Rayman, 1993). In the very near future, many employers will need to change their attitudes toward these women or risk not only legal action on the basis of age and gender discrimination, but possibly understaffing as well if the predicted labor shortage occurs.

ON-THE-JOB DISCRIMINATION AND AGEISM IN LAYOFFS

Ageism in the labor market is deeply ingrained institutionally and culturally. Ageism in employment occurs in job categories of every kind. Studies of professionals, engineers, and scientists who are unemployed show age to be a significant variable in explaining their layoffs. Ageism is a factor in both blue-collar and white-collar occupations and for both sexes. Occupations in sales and marketing may suffer the most age discrimination, because they place more emphasis on youth and a youthful image than other occupations (Bass et al., 1993). Once out of work, older workers are likely to remain unemployed much longer than their younger coworkers and to find job hunting a nightmare. If they do find work, it is usually at a much lower salary and with fewer fringe benefits.

The number of age-discrimination charges filed with the U.S. Equal Employment Opportunity Commission (EEOC) has increased every year since the Age Discrimination in Employment Act went into effect. In 1992 30,604 cases of age discrimination charges were filed with the EEOC, 18% more than 10 years prior in 1982. Today, workers are more likely to press charges if they feel they have been victims of discrimination. Complaints of age discrimination have been growing faster than those concerning gender or race. In these recession years, the large numbers of layoffs and reassignments have angered all workers, especially older ones. These layoffs have also been a factor in the large number of age-bias suits. And, although few affirmative action programs address the concerns of middle-aged workers, a quirk in the age-discrimination law allows for jury trials, which seems to work in favor of those filing suits. In age-discrimination suits, jury members, who tend to be older, appear to see corporations as the "bad guys."

Age discrimination is still a tough charge to prove. In the last several years, thousands upon thousands of cases filed with the EEOC have led to only several hundred lawsuits, and not a high proportion have been won. However, in spite of mishandling many cases, the EEOC has obtained some very large settlements involving millions of dollars in back wages and pension benefits.

Blue-collar workers at the Kraft General Foods' plant in Evansville, Illinois, sued for bias when the plant closing led to the firing of workers (Geyelin, 1994). Sears was forced to change the age bias in its retirement package: early retirees no longer have to sign an illegal waiver that they would make no age-discrimination claims (Geyelin, 1994). In 1993 a suit against Southwest for age bias in the hiring of pilots was settled (Suit Over Alleged Age Bias," 1993). American Airlines and Delta have also been accused of age bias in hiring practices that discourage older pilots (O'Brian, 1993). An age-bias suit by 900 workers against McDonnell Douglas (aircraft builder) was settled in 1993 (New York Times, March 2, 1993). An NFL referee got an out-of-court settlement from the National Football League in his age-bias claim ("*Ex-N.F.L. Referee,*" New York Times, 1993). In other cases, workers at Michigan Bell won an age- and sex-discrimination case (Hagedorn and Dockser, 1991); General Electric was found guilty of age discrimination ("Award in G.E. Age Case," 1991); and Xerox settled an age-bias suit brought by ex-employees ("Xerox Settles Age-Bias Suit," 1991).

In the white-collar world ageism is a major issue, just as it is in the blue collar world. A news correspondent got a settlement from CBS on age discrimination (Lambert and Woo, 1994). Apple Computer has been sued for age discrimination in a "wrongful termination" suit ("Fired Executive Sues Apple," 1993). An ex-AT&T manager won 1.88 million dollars in an age-discrimination verdict (Sandecki, 1993). Other companies such as Nynex (telecommunications), Kidder-Peabody (stock brokerage), Saatchi and Saatchi Co. (advertising), and Doremus & Co. (communications) have age-discrimination suits against them (Stevens and Woo, 1994).

The following age-discrimination complaints are typical of those reported by older workers on the job:

1. Position terminated: older people are told their jobs are terminated; when they leave, younger workers are hired in their places.

2. Sales force downsized: the sales force is trimmed, and older workers are the ones eliminated.

3. Retirement credits refused: older workers reach a certain salary level, and there is no more potential for salary (or pension) increases.

4. Dropped for medical reasons: older people are told they are being dropped for medical reasons when it does not appear that their medical conditions would impose any limitations on their ability to work.

In some cases older workers are passed over for promotion or are the first fired, sometimes to protect a company's pension funds, sometimes to save salary costs. The reasons for and means of discrimination against older workers vary. Employers frequently prefer younger workers—sometimes because of age prejudice, sometimes because younger workers will accept a cheaper wage, and sometimes because the company feels it will receive more years of work before it must pay retirement benefits. Employers in a tight job market can get by without giving substantial salary increases, because the older worker, afraid of unemployment, will settle for a low salary. The older worker is highly vulnerable in a tight labor market.

Health and life insurance fees, which tend to increase with worker age, constitute a supposedly inordinate cost of retaining older workers. The older, tenured worker also tends to receive a higher salary and more vacation time. Surely, companies could deal more creatively and tactfully with older employees. For example, many older people would gladly contribute toward their health and life insurance costs if it meant keeping a job; in turn, companies could be more realistic—and less paranoid—about the older workers' health concerns.

MYTHS ABOUT THE OLDER WORKER

Negative stereotypes of the older worker still persist. The older worker is thought to be accident- or illness-prone, to have a high absenteeism rate, to have a slow reaction time, and to possess faulty judgment. Stereotypes contribute greatly to on-the-job discrimination. Common **myths about the older worker** include the following:

- Older workers cannot produce as much as younger workers.
- Older workers lack physical strength and endurance.
- Older workers are set in their ways.
- Older workers do not mix well with younger workers—they tend to be grouchy.
- Older workers are difficult to train—they learn slowly.
- Older workers lack drive and imagination—they cannot project an enthusiastic, aggressive image.

Retention of older employees in the labor force will require some changes in employer attitudes. Employers need to be aware of the following points:

1. Healthy older workers may not cost more in medical benefits than younger employees who have children at home.

2. Use of sick leave is more highly correlated with lifetime patterns developed at a young age than with age itself. A natural selection process operates to leave healthy older workers on the job. The less fit have quit.

3. Older persons retain their mental faculties, they can learn new skills, and they are not necessarily more rigid.

Age is not necessarily a determinant of the capacity to do well on the job.

OLDER WORKER PERFORMANCE

On-the-job studies reveal individual variations in the ability of older workers. Most importantly, however, such studies generally show that older workers are as good as—if not better than—their younger counterparts. One study indicated that older workers have superior attendance records (less absenteeism); that they are likely to be stable, loyal, and motivated; and that their output is equal to that of younger workers (Commonwealth Fund, 1993). The work ethic of older people tends to be very high, which leads to high job satisfaction.

Experience can often offset any decrements that come with aging. The ability to do heavy labor does decline with age, but this decline is gradual and jobs vary greatly in the physical strength they require. Furthermore, an older person in good physical condition is quite likely to outwork a younger person in poor physical condition. Studies of work loss due to illness how that workers aged 65 and over have attendance records equal to or better than those of most other age groups. The U.S. Bureau of Labor reports that workers aged 45 and over have better safety records than younger workers: the highest overall accident rates occur in the 18 to 44 age group (U.S. Bureau of the Census, 1991, 115). Older workers may take somewhat longer to train, but considering their careful work, the investment in time should be worthwhile. Some firms who recognize this say the problem is not "How can I get rid of the older worker?" but "Where can I find more?"

☼ Adjustment to Retirement

Just how difficult is adjustment to retirement? Though one myth claims that people get sick and die shortly after retirement, studies do not confirm this. Retirement in and of itself does not lead to poor physical health. Research shows, however, that adjustment to retirement can be difficult.

Studies of retirement adjustment show varying results in terms of adjustment, satisfaction, and happiness. A general finding is that a minority have serious problems with retirement, whereas the majority adjust reasonably well. The message here seems to be that of continuity. The kind of person you are does not change significantly just because of retirement. This man is typical of those who have no problem adjusting to retirement.

> I turn 80 next February. It's always a milepost, I suppose, but no big deal. I retired about 75 percent at age 65 and then fully retired at age 70. It was easy, very easy, for me to retire. I like the freedom to do what I want, go where I want. I never understood these people who are restless and unhappy in retirement. It seems to me they haven't got much imagination. (Colburn, 1987)

Financial problems top the list of reasons for unfulfilled retirement expectations. Those at a marginal or lower income level are affected most adverse-

Adjusting to retirement is much easier when health is good and income adequate.

ly by retirement. In fact, about one-third of retired men end up going back to work (Crudele, 1993), and many retirees worry that they will outlive their retirement funds ("Older Adults Concerned About Savings," 1993).

Clearly, if one's retirement income is adequate, retirement has a much greater chance of success. Good health is also a factor. If the retiree has the money and physical mobility to pursue the lifestyle of his or her choosing, adjustment comes more easily. The importance of these two factors suggests that adjusting to the role of retiree depends more on physical and monetary resources than on mental set. Lifestyle is another factor: if a person is involved with family, friends, and activities, then adjustment is usually more successful. Conversely, if a person has nothing to do and no associates, then adjustment may be poor.

Willingness to retire and attitude toward retirement are also important factors. Naturally, reluctant retirees show negative attitudes toward retirement. Those who retire voluntarily are healthier mentally and physically than those who did not feel control over the decision to retire (Herzog et al., 1991). A positive attitude toward retirement also depends on an individual's expectations. In general, those who expect to have friends and social activities, and who expect that their retirement will be enjoyable, usually look forward to retirement.

Gerontologist Anton Guillemard (1982) identified five types of retirement patterns:

1. Withdrawal—Extreme reduction of social activity; long "dead" periods exist between actions performed to ensure biological survival.

2. Third-age retirement—Professional activities give way to creative activities (artistic creation, hobbies) and cultural improvement. (This term is commonly used in France. Life has three stages: childhood, adulthood, and **"third age."** With each stage a new positive phase of living may begin.)

3. Leisure retirement—The focus is on leisure activities (vacations, trips to museums and other exhibitions, theater shows) with an emphasis on consumption.

4. Protest retirement—Characterized by political activism; much time is devoted to associations of the elderly to protect the interests of the retired.

5. Acceptance retirement—Acceptance of traditional retirement values; lengthy time periods spent in daily exposure to television and other forms of mass communication.

According to Guillemard, those with professional backgrounds tend to cluster in groups two and three. Those with working-class backgrounds are over-represented in the other categories.

Studies of white-collar/blue-collar differences in adjustment to retirement reveal various findings. Former top managers and executives can have difficulty adjusting because they feel a loss of power and status, on the whole, white-collar workers generally adjust fairly well because they have more resources at their command. Professional types, such as educators, often show a good adjustment to retirement. Because they are well-educated, they tend to have interests and hobbies, such as community affairs, reading, trav-

Retirement: First Day
■ *D. L. Emblen*

Do you know what it means
to a man of my age
to sit here, coffee cup in hand,
alone in the kitchen, cool first light,
back door open on the garden,
letting the undecided cats out or in,
and hear a quail call somewhere
maybe two houses over or the other way
from shrubbery in the park,
out there in all that April green?

That quirky call invites me out,
that is to say, invites me in,
a skinny boy, hip-deep in a pond,
calls another in from the bank—
all that burst of blossoms,
odorous whirl of grass and leaves
and tender, beckoning stems—
I'll hold my nose and take a running jump!

SOURCE: From *Cock Robin and Other Bird Poems* by D. L. Emblen. Santa Rosa, CA: The Clamshell Press, 1994.

el, and art, that lend themselves well to retirement. Some professional people write or act as consultants. They seem to have many ways to spend their time fruitfully.

Blue-collar workers indicate a greater readiness to retire because their work may bring them less satisfaction. For example, a man or woman with a dull, routine factory job may look forward to leaving. However, studies show that those with the least education and the lowest incomes have the most trouble adjusting to retirement. Socioeconomic status has been found to have a major influence on retirement rates. The lower one's socioeconomic status, the earlier one retires. Individuals with less education who are employed in occupations characterized by low skills and labor oversupply tend to retire early.

Retiring persons face several adjustments that relate directly to retirement: loss of the job itself, loss of the work role in society, loss of the personal or social associations that work provides, and loss of income. In addition, events such as declining health or the loss of a spouse may coincide with retirement. When all these events occur at the same general time, adjustment is stressful and difficult.

RETIREMENT PREPARATION PROGRAMS

Retirement preparation programs can aid adjustment to retirement. Anyone who is employed would be wise to prepare for retirement; yet few people do much beyond paying into Social Security.

Retirement preparation programs are growing. In addition to traditional programs, "Outplacement companies" have been created to assist with lay-offs and to offer assistance to laid-off employees (Mergenbagen, 1994). Most are offered by government agencies and by companies whose workers are covered by a private pension. These retirement programs fall into two categories: (1) limited programs that explain only the pension plan, the retirement timing options, and the benefit level associated with each option; and (2) comprehensive programs that go beyond financial planning to deal with topics such as physical and mental health, housing, leisure, and the legal aspects of retirement. Individuals exposed to comprehensive programs have a more satisfying retirement.

Favorable attitudes toward retirement are associated with planning, company counseling, personal discussion, and exposure to news media presentations about retirement. People need to be socialized into postwork roles just as they are socialized into other roles. Anticipatory socialization, which prepares a child for adult roles, is also necessary to prepare an adult for successful retirement in old age. We can prepare for retirement in several ways: by saving money, by deciding what our goals are, by beginning to care for and improve our health, by forming meaningful relationships with a sense of permanence, and by expanding our interests so that work is not our primary focus.

☼ Work and Leisure Values

Even though Americans are expected to retire, our traditional value system gives higher social esteem to those who work. In the past, leisure was an accepted lifestyle only for the extremely wealthy. Adherence to the traditional work ethic is not as complete as it once was. What value older people assign to leisure is a research question getting some interesting answers.

WORK

The **work ethic** is a traditional value that has given work a nearly sacred character. A long-standing American association between religious belief and work helped to form the firm conviction that it is immoral not to work. "Idle hands are the devil's workshop," a basic precept in the early American character structure, still influences our attitudes today. Work has high value not only because of its moral quality but also because of its practical and personal value. Many people truly enjoy their work and derive pleasure from it. Work can foster interest and creativity as well as a feeling of pride and accomplishment.

To some, work is not a value in and of itself but is, rather, a means to identify one's social standing. It is not work that matters but having a job. Indeed, everyone knows that the general question "What do you do?" requires a very specific answer: to have any status, one must name some type of occupation. Work provides a means of achieving self-identification and placement in the social structure. This very fact has made many American women second class citizens. Because work at home has not traditionally been considered an occupation. One problem with having a strong work ethic is that it may be difficult to reconcile it with retirement. Work attitudes can be so ingrained in retirees that they carry over to nonwork activities. A strong work ethic tends to be related to low retirement satisfaction. The least satisfied retirees tend to be those with high work values who do not perceive their retirement activities as being useful. Retirees with strong work values are not as active in social activities, because they have a hard time enjoying them. Although most eventually make a satisfactory adjustment, a 1993 survey found retirement to be one of the most difficult transitions in life: 41 percent of retirees said the adjustment was difficult. The younger the retiree, the more likely that retirement was a difficult adjustment (Mergenbagen, 1994).

Extreme devotion to the work ethic seems to be waning, however, and acceptance of retirement as a legitimate stage in the life course is increasing. As technology advances, the United States needs fewer workers to produce necessary goods and services, thus lowering the value of long work hours and increasing the value of other activities. In spite of this social change, though, some older people will still experience difficulty adjusting to retirement.

LEISURE

A Gallup Poll revealed that 8 out of 10 adults of all ages think time is moving too fast for them. One benefit of retirement is having more time. The older the person, the more content they seem to be with the amount of time they have. Only 44 percent of those younger than 50 said they have enough time, whereas 68 percent of those 50 and older believed they had time enough for their tasks. According to the poll, all Americans wish they had more time for personal exercise and recreation, such as aerobics, hunting, fishing, tennis, and golf (47 percent); hobbies (47 percent); reading (45 percent); family (41 percent); and thinking or meditation (30 percent). Given more time, most Americans would relax, travel, work around the house or garden, or go back to school. Workers generally agree that time spent off the job is more enjoyable than that spent on the job. Sixty percent of workers say they enjoy nonworking hours most, whereas only 18 percent prefer being at work ("People Feel Time is Running Out," 1990). These statistics imply that **leisure values**, i.e. the acceptance of leisure pursuits as worthwhile, are becoming stronger.

A study released by the Economic Policy Institute indicates, ironically, that a dramatic loss of leisure time during the past two decades has occurred. This is referred to as "the great American time squeeze" (Marshall, 1992). Americans have added a month of time to their annual work-and-commute load since 1969. For the first time since surveys of this issue began, significant numbers of people are saying they would be willing to accept lower incomes in return for more free time. Americans are troubled that paid time off (vacations, holidays, and sick leave) fell 15 percent in the 1980s. On the other hand, the unemployed and many part-timers want more work. The economy is creating too much work for some and not enough for others. The American population is apparently becoming more desirous of leisure time. This shift in values toward less work and more leisure should lead to greater contentment with retirement; we must take care that it does not lead to apathy as well.

Sociologists have observed that for the past several decades we have treated leisure as another commodity that is produced and consumed. The leisure industry is one of the largest segments of the American economy, and it keeps hundreds of thousands of persons employed. Ironically, Americans who become overly engrossed in working to attain the symbols and commodities of leisure must work harder to obtain them and end up with less time to enjoy them.

In some segments of American society, older people are becoming a visible and contented leisure class as they accept the new lifestyles of the retired. The retirement community concept has, no doubt, made the role of retiree more legitimate. Elders who choose the traditional symbols of leisure—the boat, recreation vehicle, or home in a warm climate with access to a golf course and swimming pool—seem to go beyond merely owning the symbols to enjoying the lifestyles that the symbols represent. On the positive side, recognizing elders as consumers gives them greater visibility and legitimizes their role as people enjoying life. On the negative side, some gerontologists are worried that consumerism directed at oldsters overemphasizes their role as "buyers of things" at the expense of their role as workers and their intrinsic value as people (Minkler, 1989). Targeting elders as consumers may emphasize their buying power and channel their lives into the pursuit of trivialized leisure, thereby perpetuating an undesirable aspect of American culture—that of valuing people in terms of their consumption patterns and exploiting their fears of aging to sell products.

☼ Expanding Work and Leisure Opportunities

In spite of age discrimination and retirement eligibility, a substantial number of elderly are employed. Many middle-aged women are entering into the job force for the first time in their lives. And, although men have been retiring in larger and larger numbers since the turn of the century, women have not. Indeed, although the labor-force participation of women 65 and over has remained at about 8 to 9 percent since 1990, middle-aged women have entered the labor market in increasing numbers.

More older people want to be employed full-time than are. Still, a more popular choice for older people is part-time work. But part-time jobs are relatively uncommon in many sectors; for example, professional, technical, administrative, and other high-paying jobs tend to be full-time. According to Social Security laws, those aged 65 to 69 are allowed to make only up to a prescribed amount (about $11,000 in 1994) without a cut in their payments. (The cut is one dollar off their social security for every two dollars earned.) And those younger than 65 suffer cuts at even a lower wage. These amounts are guidelines for many elders. Those who lack private pension coverage are more likely to continue working full- or part-time in their later years.

A nationwide study of 11,000 workers examined the work choices of those who retired. More than one-fourth of those workers who leave full-time employment will take up new employment within four years. (Typically, retirees return to work swiftly or not at all.) Most of the remainder will stay retired. The most likely work change is to take a new full-time job (11.4 percent of the sample); second, to take a part-time job (10.2 percent); and third, to work part-time at the job from which one retired (4.6 percent). Factors leading a retiree back to full-time employment included low pensions and personal savings and, in contrast, the offer of high wages. Those who were eligible for good pensions tended to retire completely (Myers, 1991).

Where and how do older people find jobs they want? Although jobs are hard to find for any age group, they are especially so for elders. Studies show that many elders who are not working want to do so. Yet they drop the idea. The original goal is to have leisure and a good paying part-time job as well. But they soon discover that part-timers are on track for some pretty rotten jobs. For example, some retail outlets recruit elders, but the pay is minimal. Fast-food chains might offer better wages, but flipping burgers has little appeal for retired professionals. And the common occurrence of being paid less per hour as a part-timer for the same work as a full-timer leads to low morale.

FULL-TIME WORK OPPORTUNITIES

An obvious and far-reaching way of expanding work opportunities for seniors has already been mentioned; that is for private business and industry to keep their older workers and discourage, not encourage, early retirement. More older workers should be retrained and motivated to stay in the labor force.

Older workers who want to change jobs or branch out on their own need support in achieving these goals. Rather than retire, able elders sometimes shift their focus or their employers. A nuclear engineer may become an expert witness on nuclear power. A lawyer may leave a large law firm set up practice on his or her own. A retired professor may become a lecturer, conduct workshops, or become a consultant. Consulting is a common job for "retired" managers, employers, and engineers.

Business leaders who look at demographics (shrinking young population, growing elders) have taken steps to hire older people. Days Inns of America currently employs many older persons; in fact, they are more than 30 percent of its labor force. Days Inns analyzed its Atlanta Center by comparing costs and benefits of hiring older versus younger workers. It found the following:

- After a half-day of computer familiarization training, older workers can be trained to operate sophisticated computer software in the same time as younger workers—two weeks.
- Older workers stay on the job much longer than younger workers— an average of 3 years compared with 1 year. This resulted in average annual training and recruiting costs per position of $618 for older workers compared with $1,742 for younger workers.
- Older workers are better salespeople: they generate additional revenue by booking more reservations than younger workers, although they take longer to handle each call for the reservations center.

■ Older workers are flexible about assignments and willing to work all three shifts. (Commonwealth Fund, 1993, p. 17)

All in all, the president of Days Inns reports a very positive experience hiring seniors as reservations agents. Other companies that recruit elders for full-time positions are Bay Bank Middlesex of Boston and Aerospace Corporation of Los Angeles.

Many elders turn to self-employment as a way to earn money. Creativity, initiative, capital, and sometimes past business experience are needed to start a business in old age. Still, self-employment is often easier than getting hired to work for someone else. Slightly over 40 percent of all employed elders are self-employed. One "retired" man at age 62 started a travel agency that eventually expanded into three more. At age 60, another started an equipment leasing business. A 60-year-old woman started producing how-to videos on more than 150 subjects ranging from watercolor painting to foreign language instruction to being a magician; the videos are now distributed nationwide (Croft, 1991). Some retirees have businesses in arts and crafts, such as real grandfathers who make grandfather clocks (Duff, 1994).

A way of assisting older people in finding work is to encourage self-employment, whether by helping them to start new businesses or by providing the means for advertising and selling the goods they make. One urban senior citizens' center established a shop to provide local artisans with a sales outlet for quality handmade goods. Rural towns, too, offer stores selling quilts, stichery, wooden carvings, and other crafts made by local elders.

PART-TIME WORK OPPORTUNITIES

Some older people welcome the opportunity to work part-time and companies such as McDonalds, Wal-Mart, and Walt Disney World are recruiting older workers. Some "young-at-heart" retirees have found part-time work in the summer at amusement parks (Harper, 1994). Some companies, such as Travelers Insurance at Hartford, Connecticut, and Aetna Life and Casualty, offer an early retirement program to the long-term workers who command

Some companies such as McDonalds, Wal-Mart, and Walt Disney World are recruiting older workers for full- and part-time work.

the highest salaries. But Travelers hires back pensioned workers part-time when they are needed. Retirees are recruited regularly at "unretirement parties" hosted by the company. Open to all retirees is a job bank, which offers flexible part-time temporary work. The company profits by not having to train new workers and by not having to create new pension funds for them. Thus, one place to look for work is in the company that retired you (Commonwealth Fund, 1993).

One company that hires older workers for new assignments is the F. W. Dodge Company, a data-gathering firm headquartered in Kansas. Until recently, the firm hired temporary, part-time workers to assist in filling out forms. Because these temporary workers were not always dependable, the company redesigned the jobs as part-time permanent positions and recruited retirees. The response by oldsters was extraordinary: 90 percent of the positions were filled. Employees work several days every month. The older employees have proven to be more reliable and the accuracy of the data has increased (American Association of Retired Persons, 1990).

The federal government has several small-scale work programs designed to aid retired persons by providing work to supplement their Social Security benefits. For example, the Green Thumb Program pays older people living near or under the poverty level minimum wage to plant trees, build parks, and beautify highways. The Foster Grandparent Program also employs old people near the poverty line to work with deprived children, some mentally retarded and physically handicapped, others emotionally disturbed. The older workers try to establish meaningful relationships with the children. For their efforts as foster grandparents, the elderly receive an hourly wage, transportation costs, and one meal a day.

Work opportunities could expand if employers were more flexible in scheduling the hours and days older employees worked per week. Management consultants have suggested that workers aged 55 and over be allowed gradually shrinking workweeks, with final retirement not occurring until age 75 or later. Another suggestion is that companies allow employees the option of reducing their work load to two-thirds time at age 60, one-half at 65, and one-third at 68. Still another alternative would allow the older person near retirement to work six months and to "retire" for six months, alternating work and "retirement" periods until permanent retirement. Flexible work/retirement plans enable older persons to gradually retire and at the same time remain productive on the job even into their seventies and beyond, if they desire.

Part-time work is sometimes possible through **job sharing.** Job sharing has generally been found not only to please workers by giving them more options, but also to benefit employers. One employer stated that it increases productivity: "When people know they're working only two or three days a week or only up to four hours a day, they come in all charged up. You can bet they're much more productive." Although studies have shown that job sharing increases job interest and lowers absenteeism, employers' arguments against job sharing are (1) people may have less commitment to part-time work than to full-time work; and (2) training and administrative costs might increase because of the greater number of people involved. But neither of these points are necessarily true.

Polaroid has a program offering part-time work to employees aged 55 and over. Permanent part-time opportunities are available through job sharing. Varian Associates, a high-tech firm in California's Silicon Valley, offers reduced work schedules before retirement. As a rule, the reduction entails a four-day work week the first year of transition and a three-day schedule in the second year. A third year of half-time work is possible. At Corning, Incorporated, the "40 Percent Work Option" enables persons to retire, collect their pension, and work two days per week at 40 percent of their preretirement salary. To qualify, they must be age 58 or older and have been with the company 20 years or more.

Polaroid also has a "rehearsal for retirement program" allowing individuals to take unpaid leaves of absence. Leaves can run as long as six months. At Kollmorgen Corporation in Massachusetts, employees may reduce their time on the job to do volunteer community service while receiving full pay and benefits 12 months before retiring (American Association of Retired Persons, 1990).

RETRAINING

If new technology makes older workers obsolete, they should have options for updating their knowledge and skills. In the past, people assumed that professionals and their skills naturally and unavoidably became obsolete. Now, however, **retraining** and mid-career development programs have proven effective; and national training programs have trained older workers as successfully as younger workers, despite the fact that these training programs could work harder to consider the unique problems of adult retraining.

Career development programs for middle-aged and older workers are far too few. In our society, which generally punishes those who make job changes, the older worker who changes jobs loses most of the retirement benefits from his or her previous job. People would have much more career flexibility if retirement benefits were transferable. They would feel freer to change jobs, and companies would be more inclined to hire the middle-aged. For those whose careers require working so intensively that one becomes hardened and emotionally drained, spending a few years in a related field would actually increase one's effectiveness in the original career, if one chose to return to that field of work.

Under Title V of the Older Americans Act and with the help of the Job Training Partnership Act (JTPA), older workers are receiving some job training. The JTPA offers special training programs for economically disadvantaged older workers aged 55 and over; 3 percent of the funds allotted to the act must be spent on such training.

Some businesses are offering more than severance pay to laid-off workers: a change to start a new teaching career. Pacific Telesis, Chevron, AT&T, Rockwell, IBM, and Kodak, as a part of their severance program, pay tuition and expenses for retirees to go back to school to become teachers in kindergarten through twelfth grade. At PacTel, managers with undergraduate degrees in math or science who are bilingual are given priority ("Severance Offers Chance to Teach," 1991).

Other diverse businesses offer continuing education and retraining. General Electric and AT&T have classes to teach employees the latest changes in technology. Pitney Bowes has a retirement educational assistance program in which employees and their spouses over age 50 are eligible for tuition reimbursement up to $300 per year per person, continuing for two years after retirement for a maximum of $3,000 per person. These same retirees often become teachers for classes as Pitney Bowes (American Association of Retired Persons, 1990). The examples given here may be a "drop in the bucket," but they serve as examples of how older people can be retrained, reeducated, and encouraged to stay in the workplace.

Thinking about Aging

A Trek on the Wild Side

■ MARC SILVER

A new wave of old thrill seekers is roughing it—and loving it

Greg Williams, 59, was beginning to feel jittery as he hiked along an 8-foot-wide sandstone fin amid the towering rocks of Arches National Park in Utah. To either side of the ridge, the drop is a few hundred feet; to Williams, it seemed like a thousand.

A vacation meltdown in the making? "The trip was great," says Williams, of Winfield, Kan., of the 10-day excursion for travelers ages 50 and up, which was run by Walking the World in Fort Collins, Colo. The former IBM sales manager and his 11 fellow trailblazers (three of them in their 70s) camped out and covered more than 50 miles of wilderness parkland on foot, 14 of them on a single day. The rain didn't stop them—nor did a later hailstorm—as they marveled at dinosaur tracks, Indian ruins and a sea of wine-red cactus flowers that burst into bloom after the downpour. "It was the kind of experience that keeps you alive," he reflects. "The older you get, the more concerned you are about that."

Stouthearted seniors like Williams are flocking to adventure vacations—one of the hottest niches in the travel business. No one has yet taken a census of these hoary trekkers, but many adventure firms say at least a third of the people who fork over $100 to $250 a day to rough it on white-water rafts, snowmobiles, horses and the like are in their 50s, 60s and 70s. Trips in unluxurious style to the wilds of Borneo, Vietnam and other distant lands, with plenty of treks and time spent with the natives, are attracting seniors.

Adventure travel, of course, is not for those whose idea of a vacation challenge is a grudge match in shuffleboard on a cruise ship. You might find yourself facing a rattlesnake in the brush, a trail wiped out by a landslide or temperatures that plunge below zero. Bradford Washburn, 84, an eminent mountaineer and cartographer, paraphrases Goethe to explain the willingness to face adversity and outhouses: "If there is something that you think you can do, or even dream that you can, begin it. Boldness has mystery and power and magic in it."

Some older adventurers may have longed for wild and woolly jaunts in their youth but not have had the time or money. Mary Norman of Lakeland, Fla., 81, recently donned a wet suit to make her white-water rafting debut. "The 8-foot waves were thrilling."

Adventure trips to exotic locales test body, mind *and* taste buds. In Indonesia, Leslie Foss, 54, of Santa Barbara, Calif., breakfasted on a porridge of chopped tree pulp, climbed a volcano and spent three nights on a primitive island, sleeping on the floor of a jungle hut on stilts while pigs and poultry roamed below. "I didn't want a trip that was a flying wedge into the Holiday Inn," says Foss, who says her visit was "profound and wonderful."

The 18-to-40 crowd often wants to blast through a place rather than soak up ambience, says ElderTreks President Tov Mason. They think they're tough enough to stay in a joint with no electricity—until they get there. And they chafe at delays. Travelers over age 50, by contrast, are more realistic and more patient. It may be because of a lifetime of travel experience. Then again, it may just be that they can't move as fast as the young fry. Whatever the reason, most senior globe-trotters have mastered the Zen of adventure travel: Don't hurry, be happy. ☀

SOURCE: Marc Silver. Copyright, June 13, 1994, U.S. News & World Report.

LEISURE OPPORTUNITIES

As we discussed before, Americans generally use leisure for keeping busy with something, so that we rarely *relax* or refresh ourselves. Time away from work at any age should be a time for *being*, not doing. We all need conditioning to learn to be, to express our individual talents and interests, and to find fulfillment in the pleasure of self-realization.

Boredom does come with nothing to do, but real leisure is self-satisfying. Meditation, reflection, and contemplation are fun when divorced from the necessity to do them. Playing with ideas, trying to resolve puzzles, or brainstorming new inventions can be relaxing and pleasurable. A group of older citizens could meet daily for lunch to share their ideas and experience: "We solve the problems of the world, but no one listens." All of us have undeveloped personal resources, talents, and abilities that could be realized. We need not limit our self-development only to what is necessary to hold a job. For example, a particular college professor likes to sit quietly and speculate. Students coming to her office say, "I see you are not doing anything." Much that can be enjoyed cannot be seen!

We should try to see the role of retiree as a valid and legitimate one, well deserving of leisure in its real sense. Our work values need to be examined and put into perspective. Passively watching television, a common activity of both young and old, is hardly a form of self-realization. Our educational system, both formal and extended, should prepare us not only to work, but also to find fulfillment as human beings.

Chapter Summary

Retirement has not always been characteristic of American life. Ceasing work at a given age and receiving a pension has become more and more common for Americans after the Great Depression when Social Security was enacted. Most now expect to retire and many take an early retirement. Orientation to work and leisure are important factors influencing the other person's decision to retire. The older person with a strong work ethic who enjoys status and friends on the job may continue working. Age discrimination operates against older people in employment. There are negative stereotypes of older workers. Employers may want more years of work than the older person has to give. "Youth cult" values encourage hiring the young instead of the old. Finding work in old age can be difficult.

Many factors affect one's adjustment to retirement, and the capacity to enjoy leisure is not a given. Sufficient retirement income appears to be of great significance in retirement. Work and leisure opportunities for elders in our society could be greatly expanded. More part-time options and gradual retirement programs would give older persons more choice, and hence, satisfaction with postcareer plans.

Key Terms

age discrimination in employment
Age Discrimination in
    Employment Act
career development program
early retirement
early retirement discrimination
flexible work/retirement plans
job sharing

late-retirement incentive
    programs (LRIPs)
leisure values
myths about the older worker
retirement
retirement preparation program
retraining
third age
work ethic

Questions for Discussion

1. Are we becoming a more leisure-oriented society?

2. Do you see positive or negative values (or both) in retirement communities that place great emphasis on leisure activities?

3. Why would someone want to continue working beyond age 65?

4. Will discrimination in jobs on the basis of age ever be eliminated? Why or why not?

5. What do you envision for yourself in old age in terms of work and leisure?

6. Imagine yourself isolated in a cabin in the mountains for two weeks with only pencil and paper—no visitors, television, or radio. Would you enjoy it?

Fieldwork Suggestions

1. Study adjustment to retirement by surveying a number of retired persons.

2. Interview older people in low-wage jobs, such as restaurant workers. Why are they working? If they had another source of income, would they quit?

3. Observe elderly workers in government programs such as the Foster Grandparent program. How do such programs work? How do the elderly persons feel about their activities?

4. Interview older people who have remained in their professions—entrepreneurs, lawyers, writers, teachers, executives, managers, or doctors, for example. Why do they continue working? Do they have any "retirement" plans?

References

American Association of Retired Persons (AARP). *Using the Experience of a Lifetime* (booklet #D13353). Washington, DC: American Association of Retired Persons, 1990.

Bass, S. et al., eds. *Achieving a Productive Aging Society*. Westport, CT: Auburn House, 1993.

Colburn, D. "Facing the Certainty of Death." *Washington Post* (14 April 1987): 16.

Commonwealth Fund. *The Untapped Resource: Americans Over 55 at Work*. New York: Commonwealth Fund, November 1993.

Crispell, D. "Rank of Older Wives Swell in Work Force." *Wall Street Journal* (13 September 1993): B1(W), B11(E).

Croft, N. "It's Never Too Late." Article no. 18 in *Annual Editions: Aging*. Guilford, CT: Dushkin, 1991.

Crudele, J. "Odd Jobs." *Washington Post* (28 February 1993): v. 116, pp. 1–2.

Duff, C. "These Big Clocks Actually Are Made by Grandfathers." *Wall Street Journal* (6 April 1994): A1(W), A1(E).

"Ex-N.F.L. Referee Settles Bias Claim." *New York Times* (6 January 1993): v. 142, p. B9(L).

Fein, E. "Frustrating Fight for Acceptance." *New York Times* (4 January 1994): v. 143, p. B1(L).

_____. "Older People Laboring for Acceptance." *New York Times* (5 January 1994): v. 143, p. A7(N).

"Fired Executive Sues Apple." *Washington Post* (27 September 1993): v. 116, p. NB17.

Geyelin, M. "Age Bias Verdict." *Wall Street Journal* (17 May 1994): B7(W), B5(E).

Guillemard, Anton. "Old Age Retirement and the Social Class Structure." In *Aging and Life Course Transitions*, edited by T. Haraven and K. Adams. New York: Guilford Press, 1982.

Hagedorn, A., and M. Dockser. "Michigan Bell Loses." *Wall Street Journal* (15 April 1991): B3(W), col. 2.

Harper, L. "Young-at-Heart Retirees Work at Amusement Parks." *Wall Street Journal* (28 June 1994): A1(W), A1(E).

Herzog, A., et al. "Relation of Work and Retirement to Health and Well-Being in Old Age." *Psychology and Aging* 6:2 (May 1991): 202–211.

Hey, Robert R. "Age Bias in the Workplace." *Christian Science Monitor* (5 January 1988): 1.

"IBM's Japan Unit Offers Early Retirement Plan." *Wall Street Journal* (19 February 1993): B12(W), B2(E).

"Job Applicants Face Age Bias, Study Finds." *New York Times* (23 February 1994): v. 143, p. A7(N), p. A15(L).

Keating, N., and B. Jeffrey. "Women's Work Careers." *Gerontologist* 23 (August 1983): 416–421.

Lambert, W., and J. Woo. "CBS Settlement." *Wall Street Journal* (29 April 1994): B5(W), B4(E).

Lopez, J. "Out in the Cold." *Wall Street Journal* (25 October 1993): A1.

Marshall, M. "Report on Great American Time Squeeze." *San Francisco Chronicle* (17 February 1992): A3.

McDonald, L., and M. Chen. "The Youth Freeze and the Retirement Bulge." *Journal of Canadian Studies* 28 (Spring 1993): 75–102.

Mergenbagen, P. Rethinking Retirement American Demographics, June 1994, p. 28–34.

Meyer, J. "Can We Afford Old Age?" *USA Today Magazine* (January 1992): v. 120, 22–26.

Minkler, M. "Gold in Gray: Reflections on Business' Discovery of the Elderly Market." *Gerontologist* 29:1 (February 1989): 17–23.

Myers, D. "Work After Cessation of Career Job." *Journal of Gerontology* 46:2 (March 1991): S93–102.

O'Brien, B. "American Airlines Sues EEOC to Block Fine in Age-Bias Case." *Wall Street Journal* (26 March 1993): A4(W), A5G(E).

"Older Adults Concerned About Savings."*Christian Science Monitor* (20 July 1993): V85:163, p. 8.

Osberg, Lars. "Is It Retirement or Unemployment? Induced Retirement Among Older Workers." *Applied Economics* 25:4 (April 1993): 505–520.

"People Feel Time Is Running Out." *San Francisco Chronicle* (5 November 1990): B3.

Perkins, K. "Older Women Forced Back to Work." *Santa Rosa Press Democrat* (12 July 1994): A1.

"Planting a Bumper Crop for Your Retirement." *Dollar $ense* (Winter 1989/90): 6.

Quinn, J. "What to Look for When Considering Early Retirement." *San Francisco Chronicle* (16 March 1991): B3.

Rayman, P., et al. "Resiliency Amidst Inequity: Older Women Workers." In *Women on the Front Lines*, edited by A. Pifer. Washington, DC: Urban Institute, 1993.

Salwen, K. "Older Workers: University of Michigan Survey." *Wall Street Journal* (28 September 1993): A1(W), A1(E).

Sandecki, R. "Ex-AT&T Manager Wins Verdict." *Los Angeles Times* (5 July 1993): v. 112, p. C18.

"Severance Offers Chance to Teach." *USA Today* (26 November 1991): 4B.

Silver, M. "Retire Early at Hewlett-Packard." *Santa Rosa Press Democrat* (30 January 1990): B1.

Stevens, A., and J. Woo. "Nynex Discrimination Suit by More Than 70 Former Employees." *Wall Street Journal* (9 May 1994): B7(W), B8(E).

"Suit Over Alleged Age Bias in Hiring of Pilots Is Settled." *Wall Street Journal* (7 September 1993): B8(E).

Taylor, H., R. Bass, and L. Harris. *Productive Aging: A Survey of Americans Age 55 and Over.* New York: Louis Harris and Associates, 1992.

U.S. Bureau of the Census, *Statistical Abstract of the United States, 1990,* 110th ed. Washington, DC: Department of Commerce, Bureau of the Census, 1991.

"Xerox Settles Age-Bias Suit." *Wall Street Journal* (27 February 1991): B8(W).

Further Readings

Fyock, C. and Dorton, A. *Unretirement: Still Working and Loving It.* New York: AMACOM, 1994.

Gross, D. *Beyond the Gold Watch: Living in Retirement.* Louisville, Kentucky: John Knox Press, 1994.

8 Finances and Life Styles

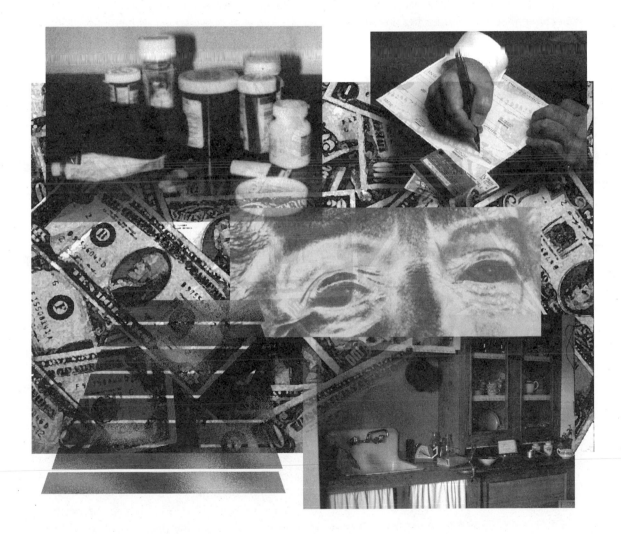

CHAPTER OUTLINE
- Financial Status
- Social Security or Social Insecurity?
- Medical Expenses, Medicare, and Medicaid
- Private Pensions
- Lifestyles of the Poor
- A Piece of the Good Life

Oakland's Mother of Mercy: 'The need is there all the time, not just Christmas'

■ DON MARTINEZ

OAKLAND—Thirteen years ago this Christmas, Mother Mary Ann Wright had a vision. "I just woke up, sat straight up in bed and heard the Lord calling me to feed the hungry," she said. "That's what I've been doing ever since."

Since she cooked that first meal of donated beans and vegetables in her kitchen in 1980, Wright has become a local legend for her tireless work on behalf of the needy. She has come to be known as Oakland's "Angel of the Poor" and has received commendations from everyone from local officials to U.S. presidents—two of them.

Her commitment has never wavered, and she isn't even fazed when heartless thieves steal the donated food, clothing and toys out of her crowded home/headquarters in West Oakland, as happens occasionally.

"We never complain," she said. "We just make our locks stronger and our fences higher . . . I never worry because I know the Lord will get them in the end."

Wright, 72, is diminutive with sparkling eyes, salt-and-pepper hair and a bottomless reservoir of energy. Just a partial list of the things she does on a regular and voluntary basis reads like a full agenda for a harried public assistance agency:

■ She distributes 1,000 donated loaves of bread daily.

■ She provides a hot lunch for up to 500 every Saturday at Jefferson Park, a downtown gathering spot for the homeless, jobless and destitute.

■ She manages an 18-bed shelter—on the second floor of her house—for men in transition from alcohol and drug abuse.

■ She combs the city for secondhand clothes and other goods to be refurbished and reused.

In addition to her local work, Wright has made pilgrimages to Africa and native American reservations in Arizona and in other states on relief missions.

"And the need for this kind of help is growing," she said recently.

"I've seen more and more people in need of help in the last couple of years than ever before," she said in a voice cracking with emotion. "So many more people have lost their jobs and their homes … It's so very sad. I'm always going full-steam ahead."

A native of New Orleans, Wright settled in Oakland more than 40 years ago. She and her husband raised 12 children of their own—six boys and six girls— and nine foster sons.

She has worked as a farmer, a domestic and a nurse, among other jobs, and often held more than one at a time.

"But the work I'm doing now is much harder than anything I have ever done . . . and much more rewarding and fulfilling," she said.

The nickname "Mother" came not from her own huge family—which now includes 30 grandchildren and 31 great-grandchildren—but from colleagues who are drawn in by her maternal spirit.

"The reason we call her mother is out of love and respect, because she's such a great lady," said colleague Addie Mae Mitchell. "She's a mother to all of us and to all the needy."

A vacant lot on the side of Wright's home is now crammed with donated goods, from a children's swing set to furniture to sacks of vegetables. Every room in her house is piled with secondhand goods in various stages of repair—even the bathroom is used for storage space.

"She's become an institution in this city," said Loretta Chisom, Oakland's director of health and human services. "Many people depend on her and her programs always attract so many volunteers." ☀

SOURCE: Reprinted with permission from the *San Francisco Examiner.* © 1994.

I n the early 1900s, older Americans were almost all poor or near-poor. They faced a variety of economic hardships that were not justified, given the generally high standard of living among the rest of the population. With the advent of Social Security and other pension programs, the financial status of the elderly has improved throughout the twentieth century. Changes in Social Security in the 1960s and 1970s provided more comprehensive coverage. Still, the bulk of elders live relatively modest lifestyles. To cope with inflation, a big problem in the 1970s and early 1980s, the government raised interest rates. In the early 1990s when the recession hit, interest rates were dramatically lowered. Interest sensitive monies are savings accounts, bonds, and utilities stocks. In the 1990s, as a result of low interest rates, many people have seen the returns on these investments decrease.

☼ Financial Status

The financial status of the average older American is rather ordinary. The household income of those over age 65 is not much different than the average for all adult households. Figuring average household income by age is a complicated matter. At first look it would seem that the household incomes of the 65-and-over group are lower than all other adult household incomes. But when we examine after-taxes income for households whose sizes remain the same, we find that the household income of the 65-and-over group is slightly higher than for households of adults under 65. The median household income of a single person aged 65 and older was $13,500 in 1990 (Shick and Shick, 1994). Middle-aged individuals have an average income considerably higher (income tends to peak in middle-age), but young adults (18–34) have a lower income. Figure 8.1 charts median income for families by age of household head. Notice that the decline beginning between age 50–54 continues on throughout extreme old age.

On average, the poverty level of elders has improved over the last several decades. The poverty rate for persons aged 65 and older declined from 24.6 percent to 12.4 percent between 1970 and 1991, whereas the rate for persons under 65 rose from 11 percent to 15 percent (U.S. Bureau of the Census, 1993, p. 470). A major reason for the increased income of elders is that Social Security payments are higher because of automatic cost of living adjustment. And they now cover more women. The number of young and middle-aged women in the workforce who pay into the system has steadily increased since the 1960s. As these women retire they receive greater benefits than women from previous generations.

WIDE DIVERSITY IN FINANCIAL STATUS

Analysis of recent census data suggests that the spread of wealth is great among older people. That means those 65 and over have a great diversity of rich and poor. The poorest one-fifth (often unmarried women, minorities, and the physically impaired) receives 5.5 percent of the elderly's total resources, whereas the one-fifth that is best off receives 46 percent (see Figure 8.2). Equalizing effects of Social Security are more than outweighed by private pensions and asset income (interest on savings), which are received mainly by those in the upper income brackets. Inequality throughout life is cumulative and becomes magnified in old age. In other words, the advantages of good education and/or good jobs leads to better pension coverage and savings in the later years (Crystal and Shea, 1990).

Figure 8.1

Median Family Unit
Income, by Age of
Head, 1990

SOURCE: F. Schick and
R. Schick, *Statistical
Handbook of Aged
Americans* (Phoenix, AZ:
Oryx Press, 1994),
p. 213.

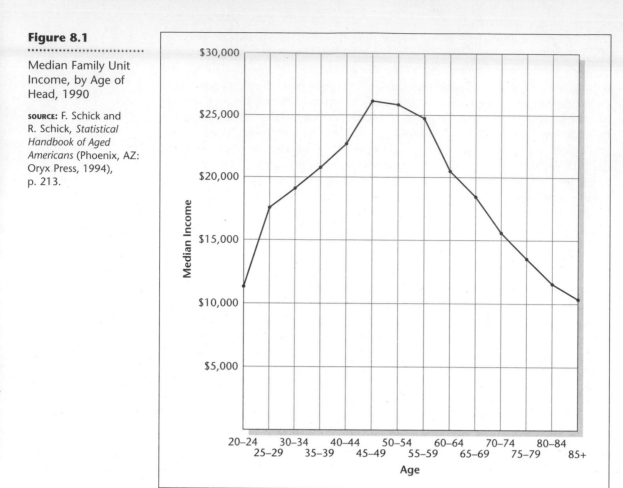

Women, ethnic minorities, those who live alone, and the oldest-old compose 90 percent of the elderly poor. We will discuss women and ethnic minorities in more detail in Chapter 13. Their financial distress is a function not only of aging, but also of education, race, and past employment. The single, widowed, and divorced have a difficult time, because living alone is the most expensive way to manage. Because women live longer, and because they have not paid as much into Social Security, older women are many times more likely than older men to live alone in poverty. Figure 8.3 reflects differences by age, sex, race, and Hispanic origin. Black females 75 and over have the highest rates of poverty. White males aged 65–74 have the lowest rates of poverty.

Many elders live just barely above the poverty level. They have been variously described as near-poor, deprived, or **economically vulnerable.** To most persons, such income is inadequate to have a full life. According to recent studies, 10 million, or nearly 30 percent of all those 65 and over in the United States, are in poverty or economically vulnerable.

The incomes of elders have improved over recent years, but not extraordinarily. Gerontologists are concerned that older Americans are being unfairly blamed for the country's huge economic deficits. The myth that all elders are down-and-out has transformed into the myth that elders are well-to-do and depriving the young of their fair share. But only 10 percent of those aged 65 and over had an annual income of $50,000 or more in 1991

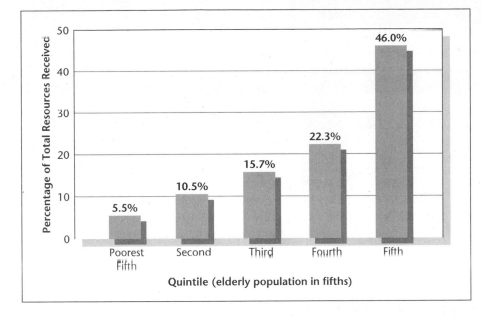

Figure 8.2

Shares of Total Income Aged 65 and Over Population

SOURCE: Graph based on information from S. Crystal and D. Shea, "Cumulative Advantage, Cumulative Disadvantage, and Inequality Among Elderly People," *The Gerontologist* 30:4 (August 1990): 441.

(U.S. Bureau of the Census, 1993, 458). Most older people are struggling in the lower- to middle-income ranges, as shown in Table 8.1 on page 180.

HOME OWNERSHIP

The overwhelming majority of the American population saves little for old age, does not maintain significant savings accounts, and does not hold other financial assets. However, around 76 percent of the elders owned their own homes in the early 1990s, a figure that is 10 percent higher than a decade before. Although more older people own their homes than do younger

Inequality throughout life becomes magnified in old age.

Figure 8.3
....

Poor Elderly in 1990,
by Age, Sex, Race,
and Hispanic Origin

[1]Hispanic origin may be
of any race.
SOURCE: Mark Littman,
U.S. Bureau of the
Census, Poverty in the
United States: 1990,
*Current Population
Reports.* Series P-60, No.
175. Washington, D.C.:
U.S. Government
Printing Office, 1991,
table 5. Reprinted in:
F. Schick and R. Schick,
*Statistical Handbook of
Aged Americans*
(Phoenix, AZ: Oryx
Press, 1994), p. 249.

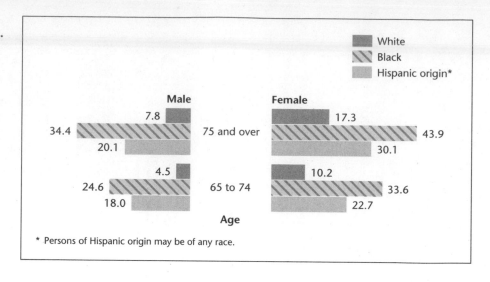

adults, the problem for older home owners is to remain in their homes and
stay financially solvent. High energy costs and the generally high cost of living, can lead to difficulties. Nevertheless, most older people do not want to
sell their homes or leave their community.

In 1988, the federal government introduced a plan of **reverse mortgages,**
whereby payments are made to older home owners for a period of time.
When a home is sold, the government gets its money back plus interest. Other
similar innovations allow elders to cash in on the equity in their homes,
which is typically their only source of wealth.

A number of elders own mobile homes, which are typically cheaper than
houses. Many have found the mobile-home park lifestyle to be an affordable
one. A rundown of mobile-home facts and figures reveals the following:

- Six percent of older Americans live in mobile homes.
- Almost half the residents of manufactured housing are age 50 or
older.
- More than one-third of manufactured home residents are retirees or
part-time workers.
- More than 90 percent of older residents own their manufactured
homes; 23 percent own their lots.

Table 8.1
....

1991 Distribution of
Income for Those 65
and Over

Income Level	Percent Distribution
Under $5,000	5.6%
$5–9,999	21.4
$10–14,999	17.4
$15–24,999	23.4
$25–34,999	13.0
$35–49,999	9.2
$50–74,999	5.8
$75,000 and over	4.1
	100.0%

SOURCE: U.S. Bureau of the Census, *Statistical Abstract of the United States, 1993,* 113th ed.
(Washington, D.C.: Commerce Bureau, 1993).

- More than half the older residents of manufactured homes live in mobile-home parks.
- States with the most manufactured homes are California and Florida.
- In the first 11 months of 1993, 93 corporations produced 223,000 manufactured housing units in 245 plants nationwide.
- "Double-wides"—composed of two sections—and even larger mobile homes are growing in popularity, accounting for nearly half of all units produced in 1993.
- Average price for a single-section home in 1992: $20,600; for a multi-section home: $37,200. (Glasheen, 1994)

These figures speak for themselves as to the popularity of mobile homes and their affordability. Also is implied a modest lifestyle of the owners.

However, residents must pay rent for the space, and these rents have risen in recent years. In many areas of California, elders are called "prisoners of paradise," because their rents have escalated at a frightening pace. Mobile-home owners and even condominium owners who pay maintenance fees are subject to cost increases over which they have no control. Older people would benefit from legislation controlling these costs.

HOME RENTAL

A worse situation for older persons than home ownership is to rent a home or apartment. About 25 percent of all elders rent their dwelling. A renter is more subject to inflation, enforced living conditions, involuntary moves, and other forms of control by others. Some cities have adopted rent-control ordinances, but such policies are rare.

☀ Social Security or Social Insecurity?

Social Security began in the 1930s to counteract the effects of the Great Depression, which forced many elders and disabled persons into lives of extreme poverty. With Social Security, many have been able to survive financially, but many others still have trouble paying for even basic necessities.

Social Security is the nation's basic method of providing income to the elderly and the disabled. Many studies have shown how important Social Security is in providing cash support for an individual's retirement years. These studies indicate that Social Security benefits are the major source of income for most retirees.

Social Security was designed to supplement pensions or retirement savings, rather than to provide the total income of aged people. Although everyone seems to agree that Social Security should not be and was never designed to be the sole source of retirement income, for most people it continues to be just that. If it were not for Social Security benefits, nearly half of our aged, rather than the current 12.4 percent, would live in poverty. In general the lower one's income level, the more important Social Security becomes as a component of the household budget. As evidenced in Figure 8.4 Social Security is the most common source of income for all races. For either blacks or Hispanics, it is much less likely to be accompanied by other forms of income. Obviously, for the individual with no income from earnings, savings, stock and bonds (asset income), or pensions, Social Security is a much higher

Figure 8.4

Receipt of Income of Aged from Various Sources, by Race and Hispanic Origin: 1990

SOURCE: F. Schick and R. Schick, *Statistical Handbook of Aged Americans* (Phoenix, AZ: Oryx Press, 1994), p. 212.

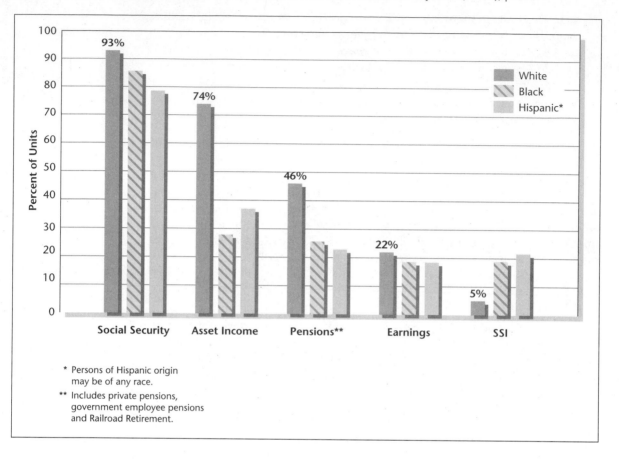

* Persons of Hispanic origin
  may be of any race.

** Includes private pensions,
   government employee pensions
   and Railroad Retirement.

percentage of the total income (Crenshaw, 1992). Under these circumstances, there is no universal agreement on the adequacy of the benefits or the appropriate level of benefits. Social Security benefits currently begin at age 65, but they may begin at age 62 if the recipient chooses to accept 20 percent less per month.

The United States was one of the last modern, industrial nations to introduce a major public system of social insurance against old-age dependency. By 1935, 27 other countries already had well-developed national retirement systems. The Social Security Act of 1935 required that employer and employee each pay 1 percent on the first $3,000 of the worker's wages. (Workers in 1991 paid 7.65 percent of their paychecks into Social Security.) Congress eventually amended the act to extend benefits on the basis of social need in addition to earned right. Amendments adopted in 1939 made certain dependents of retired workers and survivors of deceased workers eligible, too. In 1960, amendments extended benefits to all disabled persons. Over the years, the amount of money a retired person may earn before forfeiting part of the benefit has also increased.

FEWER WORKERS TO SUPPORT MORE RETIREES

Social Security operates on a principle of sharing: some individuals die before they are able to collect benefits, whereas others live long enough to get back much more than they contributed. The budget supposedly balances. However, the increasing percentage of elders and their increasing life expectancy has greatly strained the Social Security system.

In 1945, for instance, 42 workers paying into Social Security supported one retiree. Today, each retiree is supported by just three active taxpayers. In about 30 years, the huge baby-boom generation will begin to retire, creating even bigger strains. In the year 2030, there will be only two workers for every retiree. Most citizens believe that their payroll taxes go into a kind of insurance pool, which is held and invested until the day they retire. In fact, Social Security taxes are transferred almost immediately to retirees: The system takes money from workers and hands it to retirees. Americans have been receiving far more than they and their employers ever paid into the system. Most young people now will collect less after retirement than they contribute over their working lives (Roberts, 1995).

CHANGES

Social Security benefits do rise with the cost of living. This change was brought about by Social Security amendments instituted in 1972. Under the current law, this **cost-of-living adjustment,** or **COLA,** occurs automatically whenever there is an increase in the Consumer Price Index in the first quarter of the year (in comparison with the same period in the previous year). Effective January 1995, for example, Social Security benefits increased 3 percent based on the 1994 increase in the Consumer Price Index from the previous year. However, even with the COLA provision, many who now receive Social Security are still living below the poverty line.

How to keep Social Security solvent has been a major issue over the last decade. Some changes in Social Security have been made to restore the system's fiscal health. In 1983, compromise amendments were painfully worked out by a bipartisan committee and were subsequently adopted by Congress. For example, since 1988 college students between the ages of 18 and 22 can no longer draw benefits on a deceased parent who paid into Social Security. The practices designed to protect the Social Security system include:

1. Accelerating Social Security tax rate increases.
2. Gradually raising the eligibility age for full benefits (in the year 2000, the retirement age will begin to slowly increase from 65 to 67). This change affects people born in 1938 or later. For example, those born between 1943 and 1954 will not receive full benefits until age 66.
3. Substantially increasing tax rates for the self-employed.
4. Levying an income tax on higher-income Social Security beneficiaries.
5. Expanding coverage to newly hired federal employees.
6. Creating sharper decreases in starting benefits for early retirees—to a 30 percent reduction at age 62 by the year 2000.

In short, people are now paying more into the system and getting less back. Changes were necessary to keep the system from defaulting. Between 1975 and 1983, the system ran at a deficit. With the new changes, the system is less strained, but more cuts or increased Social Security taxes may be necessary in the future. As long as the U.S. government budget is operating at a huge deficit, there is continued pressure to cut back Social Security in a number of ways. A freeze on COLAs, for example, is one typical suggestion. A more radical suggestion is to eliminate social security for young adults entering the job market and instead, require mandatory IRAs; in other words, privatize retirement benefits (Roberts, 1995). Increasing medical costs are the biggest problem of Social Security, and this topic is discussed in a later section.

INEQUITIES IN SOCIAL SECURITY

Under Social Security, people under age 65 and between ages 65 and 69 are penalized for working, although after age 70 there is no penalty on wages earned. In 1994, for every $2 earned over approximately $8,000 for persons age 62 up to age 65, (or over approximately $11,000 for those ages 65 to 69, for every $3), $1 in Social Security benefits was deducted. Earned income is subject to both income and Social Security taxes, although Social Security payments are subject to neither. Nor is there a penalty for income earned through capital gains or interest on savings. The "idle rich," do not pay as much in taxes as the "working folks." This situation has lead to minor reforms, as very well-to-do elders are now paying taxes on their Social Security.

Salaried workers are penalized the most by the present system. Older workers who need money often settle for hourly part-time jobs at minimum wage or even less so their wages will not be docked. In fact, most federal government employment programs for elders provide income only as a supplement to Social Security and pay minimum wage or less. However, military, federal, and state government and other pensioned retirees generally face no penalty against their pension earnings after retirement, because salaries and wages are the only income subject to the penalty. Before complete retirement, some employees receive retirement benefits (other than Social Security) from one job while receiving full salary from another—a practice called "double dipping." The end result of one of the changes in Social Security—an income tax levied on higher-income Social Security beneficiaries—is that about 20 percent of people who get Social Security have to pay taxes on their benefits. This provision affects the more well-to-do who typically have income from a variety of sources such as salaries, interest from savings, and dividends from stocks and bonds.

Congress has considered reforming the Social Security law to eliminate the ceiling on earnings. However, this change has never been enacted. The reluctance of Congress to remove all limits on extra benefit income is due in part to uncertainty as to the effects of such a move. Congress has reasoned that an older person who could earn more than the yearly amount of unpenalized income probably does not need full Social Security benefits, thus reducing the strain on the system for the benefit of others. But this ruling works a hardship on those making a very modest living. Further, if there were no ceiling, it might reduce the number opting for early retirement by keeping them employed full time. All that would ease the strain on the system.

Still another criticism of Social Security involves the two-career family. The law favors one-earner households. Working couples pay up to twice as much in Social Security taxes as single-earner families, yet they seldom collect twice as much in benefits. A woman who has contributed throughout her working years may find that, because of her lower earning capacity, she may fare better with 50 percent of her husband's benefits than with 100 percent of her own. (She is not entitled to both.) In essence, many working women receive none of the money they paid into Social Security. Another problem:

Divorced men and women, particularly those who have not worked outside the home, may be left totally unprotected. To draw on an ex-spouse's benefits, a man or woman must have been married to that spouse for 10 years. For example, a woman married to one or more husbands, each for 9 years, who has not paid into Social Security, is not eligible for benefits. A man or woman married 10 years to one person and 10 years to another would not qualify for benefits from both. Divorced women suffer more than divorced men because they are more likely to have worked at home and to not have paid into Social Security.

A federal program formerly known as Old Age Assistance, which was intended to aid those not covered adequately by Social Security, was renamed **Supplemental Security Income (SSI)** in 1974. Instead of being managed by local offices, it is run by the Social Security Administration. Funds, however, come not from Social Security, but from general U.S. Treasury funds. The program provides a minimum income for elders, blind, and disabled by supplementing Social Security benefits if they are below the amount stipulated by SSI. In essence, it is a guaranteed annual income, and that is very important for those who get little or no Social Security. The monthly amounts vary from state to state. Complaints about the program are (1) the amounts are too low; (2) people who work and earn over a set amount experience a reduction in their SSI check; (3) eligible people who live in someone else's house get reduced checks; (4) in some states, those receiving SSI are not eligible for food stamps; and (5) one can have no major assets outside one's home to qualify for SSI. (Savings must virtually be used up.)

RETIREMENT WINNERS AND LOSERS

Social Security payments are determined according to detailed guidelines and legislated formulas and are not based solely on need. Depending on a person's personal circumstances or work history, the amount of a monthly Social Security check can be adequate or inadequate. Here are some hypothetical examples of people who fared differently in retirement:

■ Once relatively well off, Ed earned $75,000 per year as a chemical engineer. But he never stayed long enough at one job to qualify for a private pension. He spent his full salary every year on his wife and four children, hobbies and travel, and their home. He retired at age 65, with a Social Security benefit of $1,733 per month, making his annual income $18,396. How will he handle the giant financial step downward?

■ Jim, a former construction worker, earned an average yearly salary of $30,000; so did his wife, Jane, a teacher. Both retired in 1994. Their combined monthly Social Security check is $2,028; their union pension checks provide another $1,500; they also have a joint savings account that yields $600 in monthly interest. Now they earn almost as much as they did while working. (Their combined working salary after taxes, was $50,000). They are now making $49,536 annually and are moving to a condo in Hawaii.

■ Wilona still misses her husband who died in 1975. She was age 61 at the time and eligible for Social Security benefits as his widow. In 1994, she is 80 years old, is healthy, and wants to go on some boat cruises. But her yearly income, in spite of cost-of-living adjustments (COLA), is less than $6,000 a year—income hardly sufficient for living, let alone traveling.

■ Former Senator Calvin Bigg was in the Air Force for 20 years before joining a law firm and then entering politics. He has an annual $25,000 military pension; for his years as a lawyer, he qualifies for Social Security; and he qualifies for a civil service pension for his years of public service as senator. His three combined pensions total more than $80,000 a year, not including interest on his savings and dividends from real estate holdings, which bring his yearly total to $130,000.

At its inception, Social Security was meant to provide a stable future and a safety net for all citizens. It was never meant to be the sole source of income, which unfortunately it is for many older Americans.

☼ Medical Expenses, Medicare, and Medicaid

Medical expenses rise with age. Although elders represent only 13 percent of the population, they spend 25 to 30 percent of the money used for health care. Contrary to popular belief, Medicare and Medicaid do not cover all medical expenses when one is over age 65. Actually, these programs do not cover many chronic conditions, leaving the individual to pay for treatment. The "Medicare Handbook" lists the following expenses as not covered:

- Dental care and dentures
- Over-the-counter drugs and most prescribed medicine
- Eyeglasses and eye examinations
- Hearing aids and hearing examinations.
- Routine foot care
- Most immunization shots
- Custodial care in the home
- Custodial long-term care (nursing homes)

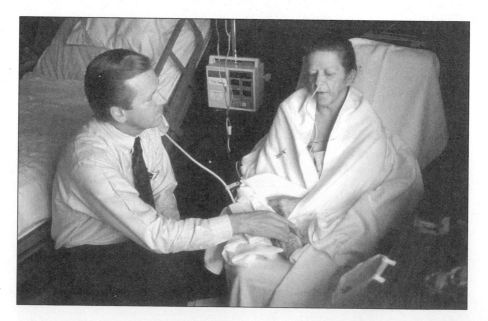

Steadily rising medical costs are a threat to elderly individuals.

Examine the list carefully. The program's coverage excludes most parts of the body that tend to change with age and require care. As medical costs rise, one's standard of living declines.

MEDICARE AND MEDICAID

Medicare is a part of the Social Security system, and those eligible for Social Security benefits are also eligible for Medicare. Steadily rising medical costs are a threat both to the Social Security system and the elderly individual. In 1993 close to 20 percent of the Social Security budget went for Medicare and another 10 percent for Medicaid (Anderson, 1993), and that budget faces the prospect of huge deficits: Soaring medical costs coupled with the overall aging of the population and the steady increase in life expectancy have strained the program. Estimates are that during the next 25 years, hospitalization fund deficits will grow to hundreds of billions per year. Spiraling health-care costs have far outpaced the COLAs in Social Security. If medical providers could bring these costs under control, the economic implications for our aging population would not seem so dire.

Medicare has two parts. Part A, called Hospital Insurance, covers a portion, averaging about 50 percent, of short-term hospital bills. Most people on Social Security pay no premiums for Part A. In 1994, hospital insurance paid for all covered services for the first 60 days in a hospital, except for a deductible of about 700 hundred dollars. For days 61 to 90 in a hospital, Medicare pays a portion and the older patient pays a daily coinsurance amount. If you need inpatient skilled nursing or rehabilitation services after a hospital stay, Medicare pays for up to 100 days. Medicare does not pay for "custodial" care given in a facility that lacks appropriate medical staff. Some hospice care is also covered. If you are confined at home, Medicare can also pay for limited visits from home health workers. Part B, called Medical Insurance, consists of optional major medical insurance for which the individual paid a monthly fee of about $40 in 1994. Medical insurance helps pay for necessary doctor's office visits, outpatient services for physical and speech problems, and many medical services and supplies that are not covered by Part A. After the patient pays a deductible, medical insurance pays 80 percent of covered services.

To qualify for Medicare payments under Part A hospital care must be "reasonable and necessary for an illness or injury." Congress established Medicare to pay a restricted portion of a citizen's medical expenses that resulted from only the most serious illnesses. That is why the most common health needs of seniors, such as routine checkups, drugs, and dentures, are not covered. In addition, the program places both a dollar limit and a time limit on what is covered. Recall, for instance, that Part A has a deductible that the patient must pay. Other restrictions and limitations get rather elaborate. Suffice it to say that many frail, sick oldsters pay thousands of their own dollars for medical care. Medicare does not usually cover all expenses, especially for long-term, chronic conditions, and private insurance plans such as Blue Cross, Kaiser, and EmCare cover only portions of either office visits or a hospital stay. Therefore medical expenses can get costly and a person may be just a major illness away from financial disaster. Over the past several years, Medicare has "tightened" its system covering less, not more, of hospital and medical costs. The patient has to pay the difference between what the doctor charges and what Medicare pays the doctor. Figure 8.5 indicates the increasing dollars that elders must pay. The future holds more cuts in Medicare because of skyrocketing costs.

Figure 8.5
....

Elderly Out-of-Pocket
Health-Care Expenses
as a Portion of After-
Tax Income

SOURCE: Families USA
Foundation, Washington,
D.C. Reprinted in F.
Schick and R. Schick,
*Statistical Handbook of
Aged Americans* (Phoenix,
AZ: Oryx Press, 1994),
p. 245.

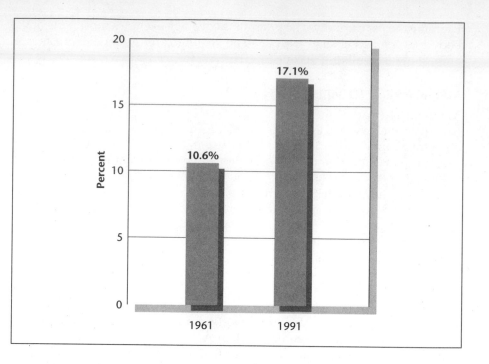

Extremely low-income individuals who qualify for SSI are also eligible
for **Medicaid.** To be eligible in 1994, one had to have a limited income and
have less than $3,000 in savings, excluding one's home and automobile,
household goods, and $1,500 in burial funds. For those who qualify, Medicaid
helps pay for a wide variety of hospital and other services. Medicaid often
pays for services Medicare does not cover, such as eyeglasses, dental care,
prescription drugs, and long-term nursing home care.

MEDIGAP POLICIES

"Medigap" insurance policies are popular among elders who can afford
them. In spite of continually rising policy costs, a majority of those on
Medicare are estimated to also have a **Medigap policy.** Such policies are sold
by private companies to help cover the "gaps" in health-care protection for
which Medicare does not provide. In summary, there are four basic gaps:

1. Medicare deductibles and co-payments.

2. Limits set on days of covered hospitalization.

3. Noncovered items such as hearing aids and prescription drugs.

4. Charges exceeding the amount approved by Medicare (also called
"allowable or reasonable charges").

All states have laws to protect consumers from bogus insurance policies, and
federal law sets minimum standards for Medigap policies. Elders should
comparison shop for additional medical coverage and read policies carefully.

Medigap policies do not cover nursing home care. Policies for long-term
nursing care are generally very expensive. Some elders are biting the bullet
and buying insurance for long-term nursing care regardless of the cost. The
reason is that the government provides limited coverage in a skilled nursing
facility and does not cover most custodial care, such as for stroke victims. As

many as 7 percent of elders now carry such policies ("Many Buying Insurance," 1993), a figure that has tripled since 1987.

NO PLACE TO GO

The out-of-pocket costs for nursing home care have dramatically increased, as indicated in Figure 8.6. For many older Americans, the high cost of long-term health care is insurmountable. In just months they use up all their assets. If their income is sufficiently low, they can apply for Medicaid to cover nursing home care. This is a devastating experience, one that tends to happen to the oldest-old (those aged 80 and over), to women, and to those living alone.

In terms of medical coverage, the forgotten minority are those whose income is just above the Medicaid cutoff, yet too low to cover the cost of nursing home care. Medicaid is administered by states; eligibility and dollars per month coverage vary widely. In Delaware, one of the best states for coverage, nursing homes are well reimbursed: therefore, good homes are available and willing to take even "heavy care" patients. In contrast, a study of working, in middle-class Florida residents just above the Medicaid level of eligibility found that these elders were experiencing severe emotional, physical, and financial hardships trying to cope at home. Nursing home care, unavailable or unaffordable, was urgently needed for many (Quadagno et al., 1991).

With no adequate government programs to pay for nursing home care, older patients suffer, as do hospitals and frustrated care providers. Many low-income elderly patients who cannot get into nursing homes remain in hospitals even if they no longer need the very expensive hospital care. Hospitals that keep older patients for longer periods than Medicare or Medicaid will fund rack up huge losses. The "boarder elderly" problem affects about 25 percent of the nation's hospitals, with urban hospitals hurt the most. Seventy-

Figure 8.6

Distribution of Out-of-Pocket Health-Care Costs per Elderly Family

SOURCE: Families USA Foundation, Washington, D.C. Reprinted in F. Schick and R. Schick, *Statistical Handbook of Aged Americans* (Phoenix, AZ: Oryx Press, 1994), p. 245.

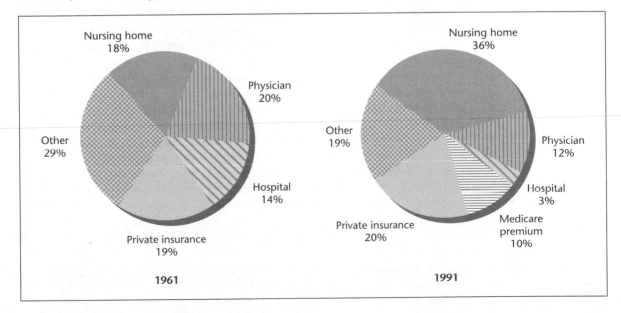

five percent of hospitals say that moving patients into nursing homes is difficult. Although "buyers" regularly visit some hospitals shopping for "profitable" elders on Medicare or Medicaid to fill their nursing homes, they have trouble finding them. Patients such as 70-year-old Lucille Arrington, who suffered from seizures and was on a ventilator, do not interest them. The reimbursement for heavy-care patients does not meet the true cost of care, so nursing homes such as Stoddard Baptist limit the heavy-care patients they take. (Bacon, 1990).

The message here for older people is this: Do not stay too long in a hospital or nursing home unless you can pay for it yourself. If you are poor and there is no government subsidy, nobody wants you and there is nowhere to go.

☼ Private Pensions

A pension is money received upon retirement from funds into which an individual usually has paid while working. Some employers have plans to which the employee contributes; others have plans to which the employee does not have to contribute. An employee may have both a pension plan and Social Security or only one of these programs. On the average, **private pensions** provide a much lower percentage of the income of elders than Social Security (which is, overall, 38 percent of the income of elders).

TRENDS IN PRIVATE PENSIONS

Private retirement plans created in the 1980s have become popular, such as Individual Retirement Accounts (IRAs) and 401(K) pension plans. In both plans, the benefit amounts are proportionate to the amount of money the employee contributes (and the employer matches in the case of a 401(K) plan), as well as by how long the money is invested in the plan at the bank or with the employer. These plans transfer more of the retirement costs directly to the individual employee. For cost-cutting reasons, U.S. employers, in droves, have eliminated traditional pension plans in which they footed the bill. These plans guaranteed retirees a specific income based on salary and length of employment. Many employers offer no substitute; the others offer 401(K) plans or similar types of individual plans (IRA's), which may or may not have a limited contribution by the employer. And they do not guarantee a monthly income for one's retirement life. Such studies show that the current generation of workers is not going to have large retirement benefits unless they save their own money. There is also a definite shift away from fully paid health care for retirees by private employers.

Tax incentives further encouraged this avenue of retirement planning. However, the Tax Reform Act of 1986 eliminated some tax advantages, and uncertain interest rates (on which IRAs are based) have made these alternatives less reliable over the long term. When interest rates were high in the 1980s, the IRA and 401(K) (along with other savings plans such as certificates of deposit) were seen as good sources of supplementary income to Social Security or employer pension plans. When interest rates came down in the early 1990s, these saving plans did not seem as good or as reliable as they were in the 1980s. Also the earnings can be tied to the stock market, which carries risk for the individual who is participating. In any case whatever is in the account when the worker retires is what he or she gets. And if it runs out before the retiree dies, too bad. One good thing is that a worker who changes jobs can take the IRA or 401(K) along—they are portable—unlike the company-sponsored pension.

PROBLEMS WITH PENSIONS

Numerous gaps exist in private pension plan coverage. Temporary or part-time employees do not typically have a pension plan offered by their employers. Some companies simply have no pension plans. And to be eligible for pension benefits in many companies, the individual must have worked for a considerable number of years. Thus, the person who changes jobs every 7 years might work for 40 or more years but accrue very small or no pension benefits from any job. Thus, the worker who changes jobs several times will typically get less in total pension income than a long-term worker, even if both earned the same pay, worked the same number of years, and were in similar pension plans. In spite of a pension reform bill passed in 1974, many loopholes in pension plans continue. Before the Pension Reform Act of 1974, a person who lost a job before retirement might have lost all the money he or she had paid into the company's pension fund. The Employee Retirement Security Act of 1974 established minimum funding for private pension plans and offered termination insurance to protect employees if their company ended the plan for any reason. As shown in Figure 8.4 in a previous section of this chapter, only 46% of whites, 27% of Hispanics, and 24% of blacks have private pensions.

Congressional investigation of private pension plans has revealed that too many workers, after a lifetime of labor rendered on the promise of a future pension, found that their expectations were not realized. As more giant companies fall on hard times, retirees face a wave of broken promises. When Pan Am entered Chapter 11 bankruptcy, the pension plan was terminated. The federal government stepped in to cover (according to the Pension Reform Act of 1974), but determined that they were obligated to pay workers only $596 per month of the $1,000 per month they were expecting from Pan Am. A major problem is that Pan Am and many other financially strapped companies "underfund" their pension programs intending to make up for it later. General Motors is one such company among numerous well known large companies. (Karr, 1993). The problem is that, for companies who go bankrupt, later never comes.

As previously stated, the person leaving employment before an established retirement age may receive only rather small benefits. Typically, if a person leaves a job before 30 years of service or before reaching the retirement age the company specifies, benefits are drastically cut. There are other reasons for getting small pension benefits. Sometimes, a company will stipulate that an employee's years of service must be uninterrupted. For example, a truck driver who belonged to the Teamsters Union for 22 years and retired anticipated that he would receive pension benefits of $400 per month. Upon retirement, however, he was told that he was ineligible for a pension because he had been involuntarily laid off for three and one-half months during one of his work years. Denied a pension he thought was rightfully his, this Teamster sued the union, claiming that he was never told of the pension plan risks. He won his case.

When not completely denied, benefits from a pension fund may be small because the recipients are either widows or widowers. Most private pension plans require the wage earner to sign a form, if he or she wishes, to allocate survivor benefits, usually considerably less than those the employee would receive, to his or her spouse. An employee who refuses to do this need not inform his or her spouse, and the spouse may have no way of learning the details of the pension. The federal government and private companies, because of privacy laws, may not divulge pension information to anyone but the employee. A widowed homemaker, consequently, cannot always count on getting something from her husband's pension.

Some retirement plans base pensions heavily on wages earned during the final three years of the worker's employment. Thus, in spite of pension plan reforms, loopholes prevent many elders from receiving equitable benefits. For example, a teacher who worked full time for 30 years, but who worked on a half-time basis for the final three years, might draw a pension largely based on the salary received during those last three years. Thus, the teacher's pension benefit would be considerably less per month because he or she had worked part time rather than full time—a severe penalty for trying to ease into retirement. Teacher retirement differs from state to state, and teachers must investigate those provisions and restrictions. Anyone employed where there is a pension plan should become fully acquainted with the provisions of the plan.

Even after reform, current pension laws and provisions *do not* encourage job change. Yet, data from the field of occupational psychology indicate that with advancing technology college graduates today will *have* to change careers, on an average, three times in their lives. What can be done? Young people, eager to get a job, rarely question or quibble about retirement policies, and too many young people still cannot imagine themselves getting old. However, young people *will* become old; and they must concern themselves with the retirement benefits of the jobs they accept. Perhaps, in time, all private plans will merge into one federal plan of Social Security, with each individual's account showing total earnings regardless of occupational mobility.

A potential problem with private pensions is that they do little to contend with inflation. How can companies offering pensions take inflation into account? That is a grave challenge for financial planners. An opposite problem in the 1990s is the recession and the dramatic lowering of interest rates. Many elders use the fixed interest on savings accounts to pay for living expenses. When interest rates are cut from say 10 percent to 5 percent, the income from the accounts is cut in half. Today's times bring fear and anxiety to retirees, which can only be alleviated by a certainty of financial security.

☼ Lifestyles of the Poor

What does poverty mean to you? You might say it is low spendable income, and that would certainly be true, but how does income translate to lifestyle? It is the housing in which you cannot live, the food you cannot afford, the stores in which you cannot shop, the medical care you cannot get, the entertainment you cannot enjoy, the luxury items (color TV, VCR, car) you cannot possess, the clothing you cannot buy, the places you cannot go, the gifts you cannot give, the holidays you cannot celebrate. These and other deprivations are the essence of poverty.

Inner cities and rural areas both contain disproportionately high shares of the older poor, yet these elders' lifestyles are different. About 4 million people in the United States are poor and old. Each day, about 1,600 people aged 65 years old enter this group.

A PROFILE OF POVERTY

Rather than a sudden displacement from an upper- or middle-class economic situation to a lower class, the overall picture of the aged poor is typically a descent from a lifelong lower economic class to the lowest, culminating in total dependency on a government paycheck that is far too small.

The study of poverty among elders is more a woman's story—70 percent of the aged poor are female. Though numbers show that this woman is typically over 75 years old and white, the poverty rate among African-American females is three times as high as it is for white females.

Below is a discussion of the poorest poor—the homeless.

THE HOMELESS: AN URBAN DILEMMA

Close to three-fourths of all older persons live in urban areas. Of these urban seniors, nearly half live in central cities. Although younger people are more likely to abandon a deteriorating city area, older people are more attached to their area; for both emotional and financial reasons they have been unable to move to the suburbs. Urban issues such as crime, pollution, transportation, housing, and living costs in a large city are the issues of older people. The bulk of the older population in a central city lives in neighborhood communities, often racially segregated and/or ethnic enclaves of European or Asian ancestry.

Large cities across the United States suffer from an American tragedy that hit with a jolt in the early 1980s: homelessness. Defying solution, the problem is growing ever faster in the 1990s. High inflation in the 1970s, economic policies favoring the rich, greed and corruption in the savings and loan industry, high unemployment in some industries, budget crunches at all levels of government, and lack of low-cost housing have all worked to swell homelessness. A new feature of poverty in the 1980s and 1990s has been the large number of homeless women and children. Though homelessness received considerable media attention, formal studies of the homeless focus more on the young than on the old despite the fact that an estimated 27 percent of the homeless in shelters are over age 60 (Kaufman, 1991). On any given day there are about 10 percent of the homeless on the streets.

In Boston, a study of homeless elders revealed an average age of 77. Having lived on the streets an average of 12 years, obviously many have been chronically homeless before old age. They had an average of four chronic diseases and suffered from chronic alcoholism, severe mental illness, or both. Most resisted all efforts to place them in nursing homes (Knox, 1989). More than one-third of Philadelphia's 252,000 elders report they live below the federal poverty line. This is especially true for women, African Americans, and Hispanic Americans (Kaufman, 1991). A study in Detroit, "Aged, Adrift, and Alone," found an estimated 2,000 to 3,000 elders walking the streets and living in vermin-ridden abandoned homes—hungry and unable to find help. Most had incomes of $200 to $300 a month, which they got by retrieving discarded bottles and cans; most have fallen prey to crime, including rape. The study named three causes of homelessness: poverty, substance abuse, and improper release from mental hospitals and prisons (Tschirhart, 1988).

The Bean Eaters
■ *By Gwendolyn Brooks*

They eat beans mostly, this old yellow pair.
Dinner is a casual affair.
Plain chipware on a plain and creaking wood,
Tin flatware.

Two who are Mostly Good.
Two who have lived their day,
But keep on putting on their clothes
And putting things away.

And remembering . . .
Remembering, with twinklings and twinges,
As they lean over the beans in their rented back room that
 is full of beads and receipts and dolls and cloths,
 tobacco crumbs, vases and fringes.

SOURCE: From "BLACKS," by Gwendolyn Brooks, © 1991. Published by Third World Press, Chicago, 1991.

NOTE: *Gwendolyn Brooks was awarded the Pulitzer Prize for Poetry in 1946, was inducted into the National Women's Hall of Fame in 1988, received a Lifetime Achievement Award from the National Endowment for the Arts in 1989, and in 1990, the Gwendolyn Brooks Chair in Black Literature and Creative Writing was founded in her honor at Chicago State University.*

Older men and women suffer homelessness in essentially the same way. Often labeled "bag ladies," homeless women cannot afford even the most inexpensive shelter, often shun the confinement of an institution, and carry their few possessions with them, eating from garbage cans or wherever they can get a free meal. Their very existence says something profoundly tragic about the role of elders in our society. For older, homeless men "skid rows" are common living environments. Estimates are that one-fifth of the homeless live in such areas. A skid-row resident is essentially homeless, even though he or she may not live exclusively on the streets. When they can afford it, they get cheap accommodations in run down hotels or boarding houses. Typically, the men live on the street, periodically abuse alcohol or other drugs, may be physically or emotionally impaired, lack traditional social ties, and are poor.

A study of 281 homeless men aged 50 and over in the Bowery area of New York City provides us with a look at survival strategies (Cohen et al., 1988; Cohen and Sokolovsky, 1989). The men were paid $10 upon the completion of a two- to three-hour interview. Fifty may not be very old, but in the Bowery men look and act 10 to 20 years older than they are. Of the final group interviewed, 177 lived in flophouses, 18 in apartments, and 86 on the street. The oldest man living on the street was 78.

The men had developed skills that enabled them to survive in a treacherous environment. One-half of the non-street men had spent 2 or more years at their current address, suggesting considerable stability. The median number of years residing in New York was 13. Approximately half of the street men had been living on the streets for 3 years. One had been on the streets for more than 25 years. Most had very little income. One man bragged, "Sometimes I live on two bucks a month." Their lives revolved around getting food, cigarette butts, some wine, a bench to sleep on, a bit of hygiene, and a degree of safety. One man said, "I'm really tired; I'm worn out. You walk back and forth from 23rd to 42nd Street. I must walk 30 miles a day." Income sources were welfare or SSI, friends or relatives, panhandling and hustling, and odd jobs. Quite a few had long work histories. Some sought food from garbage cans or obtained scraps from restaurants. The men had their friendships with each other, counting on each other for help in times of trouble. Crimes such as muggings were their biggest fear. Though many of these men were eligible for government aid of some type, they did not apply for it, relying first on themselves, second on each other, and last on local charities such as missions. The researchers suggest that flophouses offer a better chance of survival than streets; they suggest that supporting and strengthening local service groups would help these men (Cohen et al., 1988). Project Bowery in lower Manhattan has been partially successful in providing assistance—food, clothing, job and housing referrals—to older residents (Cohen et al., 1992, p. 467).

Marginal and poor elders also live in single room occupancy (SRO) hotels. The Tenderloin area of San Francisco fits the stereotyped image of the decaying central city. Although unique in some respects, it characterizes sections of all large cities. The Tenderloin is primarily a residential neighborhood where most inhabitants occupy cheap single rooms in apartment buildings, rooming houses, and hotels. The area seems to house society's discards; it is a dumping ground for prisons, hospitals, drug programs, and mental institutions. Many residents are simply transients who drift in, stay awhile, and drift on. The most numerous and yet least visible of those who live in the 28-block area are the elderly; most of them live alone in small rooms. During the day, they go out on short walks and for meals. A few never make it past the hotel lobby, where they sit. Others barricade themselves in their rooms and are not seen for long periods of time. Very few leave the buildings at night.

Higher-priced rooms usually include a private bathroom. The cheaper rooms may include a sink and toilet, but more often the bathroom is down a dimly lit hallway. Many hotel managers take no responsibility for meeting special needs of older people; their job is simply to operate the hotel at a profit. Many of the buildings do not have cooking facilities. Some residential hotels maintained specifically for elders provide food on the "continental plan," which includes three meals per day, six days per week. On Sundays, only brunch is served.

Some of the residents are alcoholics; others are simply lonely and detached. Both men and women, reluctant to trust, tend to present a "tough" image and protect their privacy. The death rate is high in the Tenderloin, with common causes of death including malnutrition, infection, and alcoholism, all of which hint at neglect, isolation, and loneliness. In spite of the negatives, some elders seem to like the independence and privacy that a hotel room in the Tenderloin can offer, much preferring their SRO quarters to an antiseptically clean room in a nursing home. A survey of 485 aged SRO residents in New York City had similar findings. Many of the elderly residents had weak family ties, strong preferences for independence, and long-standing attachments to central city neighborhoods. The SRO hotel, although run down, was an acceptable solution for housing because more "standard" accomodations were not affordable (Crystal and Beck, 1992). Some are able to find meaning and purpose in life despite rough circumstances; others are not.

Many downtown urban areas have undergone urban renewal. The older hotels in these marginal areas have been torn down, and the residents, with their low incomes and limited housing options, face a crisis. For example, by the late 1980s the skid row in Chicago no longer existed. SRO hotels were eliminated. Although an alcohol treatment center was built, no affordable housing remained; and the residents left to seek cheap shelter in other areas. Eliminating the skid row destroyed a community and a way of life. The area had been a settled community in that 30 percent of its residents had lived there 4 years or more. And 37 percent drank no alcohol. About 60 percent had the meager economic means to make independent life in an SRO hotel a viable living arrangement, and the inhabitants needed the proximity to employment that the urban downtown environment provided. They might have liked a more pleasant room and perhaps better food, but if the hotel had a TV, lobby, working elevator, housekeeping services, and was reasonably clean, they were satisfied with the convenient location, the autonomous lifestyle, and the affordability. But they had no power to resist redevelopment (Hoch and Slayton, 1989). Social scientists suggest that such hotels should be improved, not torn down, and that planners and professionals must honor the rights of hotel dwellers to choose their own lifestyle.

RURAL ELDERS

Rural is defined by the U.S. Census Bureau as territory outside places of 2,500 or more inhabitants. It includes ranches, farms, other land, and towns that are smaller than 2,500 persons. The term *nonmetropolitan* is much more general and refers to counties that are not metropolitan. A metropolitan county (or counties) contains an urban area of 50,000 or more and the surrounding counties totaling at least 100,000 people.

Elders in rural areas represent all social classes. Some are owners of large farms or ranches; others own oil fields, factories, businesses, or have been professionals such as doctors, lawyers, and teachers. Their only commonality may be a love of the rural lifestyle, which in itself varies from the South to the Midwest to the North and East coasts, and varies by population density. Some rural areas contain small towns; others, acres and acres of farms and ranches with no towns for miles. The map in Figure 8.7 reflects the poverty rates for persons aged 75 and over. Notice that the rates are highest in the South, and higher than average in the farm belt states of the Midwest.

The lifestyle of the rural poor is potentially more isolated than that of the urban poor. We imagine the rural elders living in comfortable homes close to neighbors and family in small towns, shopping at nearby stores, and busily involving themselves in the social activities of the community; but this is not necessarily so. The older person may live miles from town or from neighbors. Housing in rural areas is often more run down than in urban areas and more likely to be substandard.

Numerous studies have found that incomes for the rural elders are often lower than those of their urban counterparts. Compared with urban elders, a greater percentage of rural elders are poor and an even higher percentage are **near-poor.** This is especially true in the South. Yet income in and of itself may

Figure 8.7

Poverty Rates for Persons Aged 75 and Over, 1990

SOURCE: F. Schick and R. Schick, *Statistical Handbook of Aged Americans* (Phoenix, AZ: Oryx Press, 1994), p. 251.

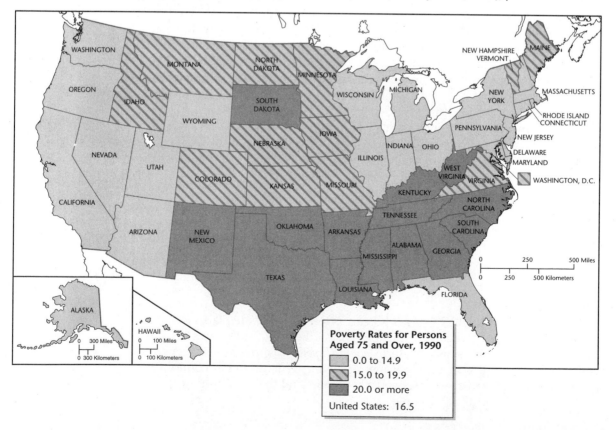

CHAPTER 8   *Finances and Life Styles*

not be the most appropriate indicator of this group's well-being. The rural elderly have a somewhat lower cost of living and tend to be more satisfied and more able to make do with what they have. Rural elders are likely to have lived 20 or more years in their communities; they have commonly developed low expectations with regard to services, both social and medical. Studies indicate that rural and urban elders construe health differently, with rural persons more tolerant of health problems (Thorson and Powell, 1992).

The rural crisis of the last decade continues: Small farmers are being forced to abandon farming because they cannot make a living. The cost of supplies and equipment has far outpaced the price increases for beef, pork, and grain. Young people have been leaving the farm life for years. Many towns and counties in the Midwest have been slowly losing population for the last 50 years. These rural changes have threatened the survival of towns, many becoming ghost towns (Norris-Baker and Scheidt, 1994). Those who own businesses and homes in these now-defunct towns have lost a sense of strong, thriving community, not to mention a lot of money as buildings are abandoned.

Older people constitute a relatively high and increasing percentage of the population in rural areas, being left behind as young people are forced to the city to look for jobs. The 1990 census showed that a large number of those 85 and older live in Iowa, South Dakota, Nebraska, North Dakota, and Kansas— all farm belt states of the Midwest (Otter, 1991). Individuals who lived a marginal lifestyle as farm workers rather than owners tend to exist on Social Security as their only source of income when they retire.

A survey of 56,000 households showed that elders in nonmetropolitan areas have higher rates of poverty and the disparity increases with age. The differences are attributed to poorer employment experiences, lower educational attainment, and poorer employment opportunities. Lifetime earnings were lower resulting in lower Social Security benefits and lower pension benefits (McLaughlin and Jensen, 1993). Rural elderly have more medical conditions and are more likely to have falls than those living in the cities or suburbs (Hospitals & Health Networks, 1993). Interviews with rural Southern elders indicate that they believe they are worse off in comparison with other elders (Dinkins, 1993). Elderly black farm women are a population at risk: They are isolated and underserved (Carlton-LaNey, 1992).

Government-sponsored low-income housing is less available in rural areas. Rural residents are likely to migrate to cities simply to improve their housing circumstances. Yet retirement complexes in large cities often do not offer a viable way of life to longtime rural dwellers. They do not really want to sacrifice the advantages of rural living, such as peace and quiet and longtime friendships, for better medical care and a more modern home. Studies of rural life tend to document a marked resilience and strength. Interviews reveal rural elders to be self-sufficient, proud, and able to survive on small Social Security checks.

THE CULTURE OF POVERTY

Location is only one way in which the lifestyles of the poor can vary. Their degree of independence, pride, dignity, and happiness, and their ability to meet their physical needs and provide meaning in their lives, can also differ. The **culture of poverty** refers to the abject hopelessness, despair, apathy, and alienation in poverty subcultures. The concept, which has been used to describe minority subcultures, has application to poor elders who are hopeless and despairing about their situation. Some have trouble living life with dignity, hope, happiness, and meaning. This tends to be more the case in inner cities where elders are fearful and alienated. Elders in rural areas seem to be more content with their lifestyle.

RELATIVE DEPRIVATION

According to the theory of **relative deprivation,** a person is deprived if his or her resources come up short in comparison with another's. This theory, which has been applied to financial adequacy, holds that the older person who compares his or her income with the income of another and feels relatively deprived is not satisfied with the income regardless of its actual amount. Applied in another way, the older person who looks back on past income and considers the former a better income than the present one may also feel relatively deprived and therefore dissatisfied.

One study hypothesized that not only real income, but the older person's subjective interpretation of that income affects financial satisfaction. The theory ties in with the symbolic interactionist definition of a situation: If people perceive a situation as real, its consequences become real. An older person can examine relative deprivation both in terms of comparison of self with others, as well as in terms of comparison between one's present and past financial circumstances. Objective income influences financial satisfaction only indirectly: Feelings of relative deprivation directly affect subjective financial well-being. Subjective feelings allow some to be satisfied with low incomes and others to be dissatisfied with high incomes. A study substantiated this theory of relative deprivation as applied to the financial well-being of elders (Liang, Kahana, and Doherty, 1980).

☼ A Piece of the Good Life

In reflecting on what old people deserve in later life, we must conclude that they deserve a fair share of the "good life"—respect, dignity, comfort, and resources for experiencing new or continuing pleasures. Actually, a select number of aged in our society's upper echelons are doing quite well, having amassed great assets over their lifetimes. But they account for only 5 to 6 percent of the population aged 65 and over. Many elders, especially those at the very bottom of the economic ladder, struggle to enjoy—or to simply get—their piece of the American pie.

One obstacle to attaining this good life is that older people typically have less income in retirement than when they were working. A rationale for this is that the older person is not doing anything; therefore, little money is necessary. However, this rationale is based on a negative image of nonactivity, which often becomes self-fulfilling. Actually, the retired person with plenty of leisure time needs an adequate sum of money to enjoy it. During our working years, we spend 8 hours per day on the job; we spend more time traveling to and from work; and we spend still more time resting up from work. After the working years, one may justifiably need more money for pursuing leisure activities, such as travel, school, and hobbies. Elders without money most commonly fit the negative stereotypes of aging.

Businesses in cities and towns recognize the modest means of many older persons and offer discounts of all kinds. Local programs provide seniors with token assistance such as free banking service and discounts in theatres, restaurants, and transportation. In the Richmond, Virginia, area, for example,

local merchants initiated a **senior discount program.** All elders who wanted to participate were issued photo identification cards. After nine months, over 600 merchants and over 10,000 older persons were participating. The AARP has a national discount directory, and some cities have a "Silver Pages" section of the Yellow Pages that lists special services and shops that cater to the "senior citizen."

Under senior discount programs, elderly individuals receive discounts from 10 to 15 percent on drugs, groceries, baked goods, taxi fares, haircuts and hairstyling, TV and radio repairs, auto tires, shoe repairs, restaurant meals, banking services, movie and theatre tickets, miniature golf, cassettes and compact discs, jewelry, hearing aids, dry cleaning, electrical work, furniture and appliances, hardware, flowers, books, clothing, auto repairs and supplies, art supplies, services at health spas, and pest extermination. Merchants, who offer a variety of explanations for their voluntary participation in such programs, often join because they believe such programs will promote their goods and services. In short, programs such as these indicate the awareness of the need to ease the financial burden on older persons. Though Maggie Kuhn, founder of the Gray Panthers, described contemporary programs for the elderly as "novocaine treatment" that dulls the pain without really changing anything, some are more optimistic. They feel that discount programs are a step in the right direction and are greatly appreciated by older people.

We might easily wonder why our society seems so unwilling to allow its members a comfortable passage through middle and old age. In *Critical Perspectives on Aging* (1991), Vicente Navarro, professor of health policy at Johns Hopkins University, poses this question:

> Why is there no debate about the morality of an economic system that does not provide security, joy, and relaxation for those citizens who have built the country through their sweat and toil?

Navarro believes that most Western populations would like to see their countries' resources distributed according to need and that the unrestrained capitalism of the United States is failing in this area. He poses another question:

> How can the U.S. proclaim that it is the society of human rights when basic rights such as access to health care are still denied?

Those with a critical perspective (see Chapter 1) call for a restructuring of our society to meet the needs of the whole populace, not just a select few.

Chapter Summary

The financial status of aged individuals varies, with a considerable percentage being poor or near-poor. The bulk of older persons live modest lives in the lower- to middle-income bracket; few are rich. Social Security coverage has improved over the years; nevertheless, it remains a program that meets only minimum needs. Loopholes in pension plans result in inadequate coverage for some elders. Medical expenses are probably the most feared and the most likely expenses to cause poverty. The financial needs of older women, especially those who are single, divorced, or widowed, are much greater than the financial needs of older men. Close to one-third of women living alone are poor. The lifestyles of the older poor vary; some feel despair, whereas others have a keen instinct for survival and optimism. More commitment is needed to see that the minority of homeless and poverty-stricken elders are attended to.

Key Terms

cost-of-living adjustment (COLA)

culture of poverty

economically vulnerable

SRO Hotels

Medicaid

Medicare

medigap insurance

near-poor

private pension

relative deprivation

reverse mortgages

senior discount programs

Social Security

Supplemental Security Income (SSI)

Questions for Discussion

1. What is the general purpose of Social Security for older persons?

2. What are some loopholes in pension plans?

3. Why do older women have more financial problems than older men do?

4. Within the population of elders, compare the urban poor with rural poor.

Fieldwork Suggestions

1. Go to your local Social Security office and find out about the minimum and maximum amounts an elderly person can receive from Social Security and SSI. What are the determining variables? How do the elders make ends meet if they have no other source of income? Give some examples of where they might live, what their rent might be, and how much they could spend for food, entertainment, and travel.

2. Interview an older person who lives below the poverty line. Describe his or her lifestyle and outlook on life.

3. Try depriving yourself for a week of food you want (have only peanut-butter sandwiches for lunch, or go without snack foods, or without meat, or spend a limited amount of money on food). Imagine that you cannot ever have what you deprived yourself of because you cannot afford it. Write about your feelings during your period of deprivation.

References

Anderson, J. "Why Should I Pay for People Who Don't Need it?" *Parade Magazine* (21 February 1993): 4–7.

Bacon, K. "Ailing System: Poor Elderly Patients with no Place to Go Burden City Hospitals." *Wall Street Journal* (23 November 1990): A1.

Carlton-LaNey, I. "Elderly Black Farm Women: A Population at Risk." *Social Work* 37:6 (November 1992): 517–524.

Cohen, C., et al. "Project Rescue: Serving the Homeless and Marginally Housed Elderly." *Gerontologist* 32:4 (August 1992): 467–471.

Cohen, Carl I., et al. "Survival Strategies of Older Homeless Men." *Gerontologist* 28 (February 1988): 58–65.

Cohen, C., and J. Sokolovsky. *Old Men of the Bowery.* New York: Guilford Press, 1989.

Crenshaw, A. "Retirement Is Getting Tougher." *San Francisco Chronicle* (13 December 1992): C2.

Crystal, S. and Beck, P. A Room of One's Own: The SRO and the Single Elderly, *Gerontologist* 32:5, October, 1992, pp. 684–692.

Crystal, S., and D. Shea. "Cumulative Advantage, Cumulative Disadvantage, and Inequality Among Elderly People." *Gerontologist* 30:4 (August 1990): 437–443.

Dinkins, J. "Meeting Basic Needs of Rural Southern Elders." *Journal of Home Economics* 85:1 (Spring 1993): 18–25.

Glasheen, L. "On the Drawing Board: Better Mobile Homes." *Bulletin of the AARP* (March 1994): 15–17.

Hoch, C., and R. Slayton. *New Homeless and Old.* Philadelphia, PA: Temple University, 1989.

Kaufman, M. "Study: Poverty, Inadequate Care Afflict City's Elderly." *Philadelphia Inquirer* (15 January 1991): B1.

Karr, A. "Imperiled Promises: Risk to Retirees Rises as Firms Fail to Fund Pensions They Offer." *Wall Street Journal* (4 February 1993): A1.

Knox, R. "Crisis Predicted in State's Elder Care." *Boston Globe* (14 March 1989): A2.

Liang, J., E. Kahana, and E. Doherty. "Financial Well-Being Among the Aged: A Further Elaboration." *Journal of Gerontology* 35 (1980): 409–420.

"Many Buying Insurance for Long Term Nursing Care." *Los Angeles Times* (4 February 1993): D11.

McLaughlin, D., and L. Jensen. "Poverty Among Older Americans: The Plight of the Nonmetropolitan Elders." *Journal of Gerontology* 48:2 (March 1993): S44–55.

Navarro, V. "Introduction: The Unique Contributions of this Volume." In *Critical Perspectives on Aging,* edited by M. Minkler and C. Estes, v–vii. Amityville, NY: Baywood Publishing, 1991.

Norris-Baker, C., and R. Scheidt. "From 'Our Town' to 'Ghost Town'?: The Changing Context of Home for Rural Elders." *International Journal of Aging and Human Development* 38:3 (April 1994): 181–203.

Otten, A. Farm Belt Holds Onto the Oldest Americans." *Wall Street Journal* (9 September 1991): B1.

Quadagno, J., et al. "Falling Into the Medicaid Gap: The Hidden Long-Term Care Dilemma." *Gerontologist* 31:4 (August 1991): 521–526.

Roberts, P. It's Time to Privatize Social Security. *Business Week* (February 20, 1995): 22.

Schick, F., and R. Schick, Statistical Handbook of Aged Americans. Phoenix, AZ: Oryx Press, 1994.

Study: "Rural Elders Living Alone at Greater Risk for Health Problems." *Hospitals and Health Networks* 67:18 (20 September 1993): 58.

Thorson, J., and F. Powell. "Rural and Urban Elderly Construe Health Differently." *Journal of Psychology* 126:3 (May 1992): 251–261.

Tschirhart, D. "The Desperate Elderly." *Detroit News* (23 December 1988): B6.

U.S. Bureau of the Census. *Statistical Abstract of the United States, 1993,* 113th ed. Washington, D.C.: Commerce Bureau, 1993.

Further Readings

Bull, N., ed. *Aging in Rural America.* Newbury Park, CA: Sage, 1993.

Church, G. and Lacayo. "The Case for Killing Social Security." *Time* (March 20, 1995): 24–32.

Riley, M. et al. *Age and Structural Lag: Society's Failure to Provide Meaningful Opportunities in Work, Family and Leisure.* New York: Wiley, 1994.

9

Living Environments

CHAPTER OUTLINE

My New Small Town

■ F. CHAMPION WARD

North Branford, Conn.
I had assumed my retirement community—call it Sycamore Woods—would be like a hotel, a base for excursions, with anonymous transients in the next room. Not so. It is more like a small town. You know and meet everybody daily at the mail room, bank and stores, on surrounding roads and trails, at Saturday night movies in the community room and, if female, at the hairdresser's. There is even traffic: carts coursing through the corridors, dodging ambulatory but unsteady pedestrians.

Indeed, intimacy extends further here, induced by a swimming pool, common dining room and hobby groups: cabinet makers, trailblazers, bird watchers and poetry lovers.

Nor is government lacking. An elected residential council calls the loftier shots, hears complaints (however trivial), negotiates with the owner and forms subcommittees to oversee the library, planting of patio borders, display of art in the corridors and the food. There is even a "town meeting," at which views are aired, awkward amendments put forward and decisions occasionally reached.

Before moving in, I wondered what one would talk about at Sycamore Woods. The answer was soon clear: Sycamore Woods. No small town ever took itself more seriously. And self-preoccupation is intensified by the presence of a large number of strong-minded former executives, professors, nurses and doctors. During their life work they formed a habit of command, which is now directed at the less far-reaching affairs of Sycamore Woods.

If this suggests an inescapable and intrusive atmosphere, it has yet to materialize. We are free to welcome or avoid any or all neighbors or activities. This might have left us feeling crowded or lonely if our fellow residents had not proved to be an interesting and congenial lot. Rather, my wife and I have made many ninth-inning friends, and it is easier to entertain here than it was in Greenwich.

In a retirement community, people can make many 9th-inning friends

This may be the last American generation consisting largely of married couples, now in the autumn of long lives together. The mutual loyalty and determined cheerfulness are moving. The health—physical or mental—of one partner is often impaired, but brave fronts are gallantly maintained, fortified by the unfailing solicitude of other residents and the staff.

Comparison with old elephants, retreating into the jungle to expire together, is inviting. But I've avoided black humor since enduring the reproachful reception that greeted my suggestion that Sycamore Woods be renamed "The Semi-Finals." Meanwhile, a recent spell in drydock due to repairs to sundry body parts may appear to bear out de Gaulle, "Old age is a shipwreck." But I still like to think that Santayana got it right when he wrote that "the last years of life are the best, if you are a philosopher." ☼

SOURCE: *New York Times*, Sept. 24, 1993. Copyright © 1993 by the *New York Times Company*. Reprinted by permission.

*T*hink of the one place where you can be yourself, keep the things that mean the most to you, live in the way you prefer, and shut the world out when you feel like it. There are lots of names for it, but they all mean the same thing—home. In this chapter, we will discuss the problem of housing, which to some may mean a home or to others may mean only a shelter. Psychologically, there may be a big difference between *housing* and *home*.

☼ Living Environments

The diversity of the aged population underscores the need for many housing options. Compared with other industrialized nations, the United States has been slow to acknowledge the housing needs of its older citizens and slow to offer the needed options. The housing market for older people is continually changing as the older population ages and grows. Elders need appropriate housing that offers safety and comfort in a convenient, desirable location and at a cost within their budgets. Gerontologists are becoming increasingly concerned with the effect of the **living environment** on older people—not only in terms of the house structure, but in terms of the environmental context as well. The features of a residential area and its surrounding community help to determine whether an older person is going to be happy. Because older people are typically in their homes many more hours per day than younger people are, their living environments must make a positive, meaningful contribution to their lives.

DIVERSITY IN LIVING ARRANGEMENTS

The kinds of problems elders face in housing depend to an extent on the location and type of housing they have. Of those who are not institutionalized, 69 percent live in family settings, typically a husband/wife household. More than one-quarter (31 percent) live alone. Those remaining individuals live in group quarters as shown in Table 9.1. The tendency for older couples or individuals to maintain independent housing arrangements has increased over the past 20 years.

The trend in the 1980s showed a modest increase in the rate of home ownership for elders, whereas it showed a decrease in home ownership rates for young adults, minorities, and other first-time buyers. Rates of home ownership for elders in the 1990s has stabilized, or, according to some reports, declined slightly. From 75 to 80 percent of elders own their own homes. For elders, these statistics reflect both their better health (enabling them to live in

Table 9.1
....

Living Arrangements of Persons 65 Years Old and Over by Sex, 1992

Living Arrangements	Total	Male	Female
Living in household	99.7	99.7	99.8
Alone	31.1	16.3	41.8
Spouse present	54.1	73.8	39.8
Living with someone else	14.6	9.6	18.1
Not in a household*	.3	.3	.2

*In group quarters other than institutions.
....

SOURCE: Adapted from U.S. Bureau of the Census, *Statistical Abstract of the United States, 1993,* 113th Ed (Washington, D.C., U.S. Government Printing Office, 1993, p. 45, table 48.

their own homes longer) and a better financial situation (enabling them to afford homes of their own).

The older population is scattered throughout the United States, although some areas and states have disproportionately high numbers. Florida has been the most popular state for older migrants, where the proportion of elders is 18.6 percent of the total population and where many counties have proportions of elders 25 percent and more. Large proportions of elders can be found in all the southern states and the Midwest as well. In the Midwest, disproportionate numbers are the older-old, those 75 and older (Crispell and Frey, 1994). Inner-city areas with high percentages of elders typically house those who have "aged in place." In such areas the people have aged along with their houses.

Older people tend to reside in ordinary houses in ordinary neighborhoods, rather than in institutions or in age-segregated housing. Thus, the housing needs of elders are obscured because many are dispersed and invisible as a distinct group. Those who live alone tend to have fewer financial resources than married couples, and their housing tends to be of poorer quality. Single men have the poorest housing, in spite of having higher incomes than single women, who, after fulfilling roles as homemakers, often seem to have more of an emotional investment in their housing.

AMERICA'S OLDER HOMELESS

Some elders have no home at all. Homelessness was addressed in Chapter 7 in more detail, but this chapter on housing addresses the problem once again. Between 15 percent and 28 percent of the homeless are age 50 to 65; they can be seen on the streets and, periodically, in shelters and SROs (single

GRAMMA IS DETERMINED TO AGE IN PLACE

room occupancy hotels). An unknown but substantial number are 65 and over (Elias and Invi, 1993).

Although the *proportion* of men who are homeless is declining because of the increased number of women and children in this situation, the *number* of homeless men is increasing. A study of 35 chronically homeless older men in Seattle found them to have serious health-care needs, to be subject to violence and crime, and to be facing loneliness and alcoholism. Public homeless shelters provided them a temporary sanctuary, but the rigid routines and the loss of self-esteem they suffer in such places are not conducive to their staying (Elias and Inui, 1993). Older homeless women, increasing in number and proportion, like the men, often suffer from alcoholism and/or mental health problems (Keigher, 1991). Outreach agencies such as Project Rescue in New York have been successful in providing respite and health care to the homeless. But little funding is available for such programs (Cohen et al, 1992).

In one's old age, a home of one's own fosters the maintenance of personhood and integrity. A home not only provides shelter, but also is a symbol of permanence and identity. The loss of home is devastating to one's being. Along with the loss of self is often the loss of friends and neighbors, loss of support, and loss of a platform from which to reach out and restructure one's life. When bodies age, the desire to remain settled and safe is strong. Homeless elders symbolize the tragic nature of a competitive society where the less fit are ignored and neglected. Lack of a place to call home in one's old age is tragically incomprehensible.

DISSATISFACTION WITH HOUSING

Compared to the homeless, those who have a place to live are doing well and counting their blessings. Yet older people can be dissatisfied with their housing situations for a number of reasons.

Personal Changes

Changes in one's life may lead to a housing situation that does not match one's needs. First, as the older persons' needs change, a house may become too large. A large proportion of older individuals are widows or widowers living alone. When a house that once was the appropriate size for a family is unnecessarily large and empty, a smaller house or an apartment may be more suitable.

Those with physical disabilities may not want to put their energies into keeping up a big house. Limited mobility and agility make it hard for older people to climb stairs, stand on stepladders, use bathtubs, and reach high cupboards. The person who loses a driver's license due to failing health or as a result of forgoing car ownership may be unhappy if the home is also isolated from friends and stores.

Financial Changes and Increasing Maintenance

Shrinking personal finances lead to difficulties in paying required housing costs. The older person who retires may receive only half the income he or she received when working. For home owners, property taxes and insurance premiums take ever-increasing chunks out of fixed income; sizable rent increases may force them to move to less adequate dwellings. In addition to housing costs, rising rates of utilities such as electricity, gas, and telephone service create hardships for persons living on a limited budget.

The home ages with the person. Older people may have lived in their homes 20, 30, 40, or more years. The older house requires more maintenance; hiring others to perform the work is often costly. Leaking roofs must be fixed, appliances repaired, lawns mowed, and windows washed.

Housing that requires little upkeep is ideal, but an estimated 10 to 15 percent of elders live in dwellings that are substandard, with rural areas having the highest rates.

Urban Blight

The calm, quiet residential neighborhood in which inner-city residents choose to grow old often becomes a run-down area of high crime. Elders may be afraid to go out at night or may be afraid in their own homes. What was once an attractive residential area can deteriorate or become a "concrete jungle" of commercial buildings or factories, with extensive air and noise pollution. Drug trafficking, burglary, theft, muggings, and assault as well as rape occur with greater frequency in these areas.

Desire to Pursue Leisure

Old people who have no financial or health problems may wish to relocate closer to recreational amenities. Some want milder climates; others want to live among those in their own age group. These people, who must go through the difficult decision of whether or not to uproot, often select a retirement community or center. Many such places exist, especially in Florida, Arizona, and southern California, were the climate is mild; but there are others scattered across the United States.

☼ Problems in Relocating

According to an AARP study quoted by Braus (1994), the most common reasons for relocating are:

1. want to be closer to family, 15%
2. want a change, 10%
3. no longer able to afford current housing, 9%
4. buying better housing, 8%
5. retirement, 7%

Whatever the reasons for deciding to relocate, there are a number of issues associated with making the move. Four of those issues are discussed here.

SHORTAGE OF APPROPRIATE HOUSING

The availability of adequate housing for elders is, in some communities, woefully inadequate. A shortage exists in both low-cost housing and in housing that meets the special needs of the oldest-old.

One of the biggest shortages is in low-cost housing. Demand far exceeds supply in all areas of the United States. Those with low incomes—for example, those who must live entirely on Social Security or Supplemental Security Income—often have substandard housing. Rural elders often live in housing that is both inadequate and substandard.

Government housing programs for elders lost their funding in the 1980s, due to budget cuts. The National Affordable Housing Act of 1990 has some provisions to help older home owners. A home equity provision allows use of home equity to make home repairs (Redfoot and Gaberlavage, 1991). The equity provision is available to all home owners, regardless of income. Budget constraints at the federal, state, and local levels, however, offer little hope that other funds for housing will be forthcoming.

Public pressure to cut federal spending and reduce the national debt has resulted in down-funding many of the support programs for older adults. Housing for lower income elders has not been spared the carving knife in spite of the lobbying efforts on their behalf. Currently, for example, Congress is considering reducing funds for housing available through Titles 202 and 236 of the Housing Act. Title 202 enables elders with moderate incomes to afford adequate housing, and Title 236 provides housing for low- and moderate-income elders by reducing the cost of housing through lower interest rates (and consequently, lower monthly payments), or by providing rent supplements for those who qualify. To allow elders to remain in their original homes, some states provide property tax relief by not taxing property after the owner is a given age. When the older person dies, the tax bill is deducted from the estate.

Ideally, the physical structure of a house for the older person would include the following: wide hallways and doors to allow wheelchairs to move freely, protective railings and dull-surfaced floors to reduce the probability of falls, low-hung cabinets to eliminate climbing on stools, increased brightness in lighting fixtures to accommodate failing eyesight, and acoustical devices to increase the volume of doorbells and telephones. The very-old have little physical tolerance for extreme temperatures; thus, the thermal environment must be carefully regulated. The house should have no change of levels, not even a step down into a living room. Walk-in, sit-down showers rather than bathtubs are a must. Housing designed especially for the elderly seldom takes into account all of these factors.

Nearly as important as services and facilities of the living environment is the **surveillance zone**—the visual field outside the home that one can view from the windows or glass doors inside. A surveillance zone provides an important source of identity and participation with one's environment. The concept has implications for location, design, and landscaping.

UPROOTING

Relocation is difficult for both voluntary and forced moves as it involves leaving close friends and associates as well as a familiar environment; it also poses many uncertainties associated with moving into a new and alien neighborhood. Forced moves, however, are generally far more traumatic because, in most cases, the older adult has no desire to move and views the move more negatively.

Notwithstanding the physiological impact of relocation discussed above, its psychological-emotional aspects are important as well. Often, a person who has long lived in the same environment finds it difficult to effectively readjust after a move. A change of housing may also affect one's sense of independence and identity. Most of us have warm feelings for "home" and its pleasant memories. Even an essential or desirable move requires in-depth soul searching with respect to a new and changing lifestyle if the move is to represent an exciting change in the quality of one's life.

Downsizing, that is, moving into a smaller dwelling, is often very difficult for many older adults because the smaller unit will not accommodate many of their relics collected over a lifetime. Parting with these items is often traumatic and produces conflicting emotions—the need to move versus the inability to "let go."

MIGRATION

More than 60 percent of older people living in their own homes have lived there 20 years or longer (Redfoot and Gaberlavage, 1991). Living in an area for a long time fosters a feeling of neighborhood integration and security, and closeness to friends and family. Yet many older persons can and do move, some very happily.

A first move typically occurs around retirement for the young-old. In any five-year period, about 5 percent of the population over age 60 makes a long-distance move. Long-distance moves are more popular among "sixty something" couples who have both the financial resources and the desire to relocate during their early elder years. Some retirees have planned their move for years and have vacationed in the spot many times. Though the reasons for relocation vary, they typically involve the attractive leisure amenities retirement communities offer—whether it be arts/crafts, music, golfing, boating, fishing, tennis, or social activities. Elders from the Northeast and Midwest still migrate toward the Sunbelt of the West and South. Migration may be either permanent or seasonal (Hogan and Steinnes, 1993b). For several decades now, Sun City, Leisure World, and other large retirement communities of the Sunbelt states have offered housing and amenities at reasonable prices. Over half the popular retirement communities are in southern states, or in the southern parts of states: Florida, Texas, Arkansas, Arizona, and California. The northern and western states of Michigan, Wisconsin, Minnesota, Oregon, and Nevada also have clusters of retirement communities. Florida still has the largest percentage of elder residents of all states.

Some older persons are **snowbirds**, living in the north for several months during the summer and going south for the winter. The opposite, those who live in the south and move north in the summer, have been labeled **sunbirds**. Sunbirds have been understudied, yet the tendency for older Arizona residents to leave in the summer is comparable to the tendency of older Minnesotans to go south during the winter. Researchers find a trend toward the snowbird eventually making a permanent migration to the South, then becoming a sunbird. This finding about sunbirds would no doubt be replicated throughout the southern United States if studies were done in other states (Hogan and Steinnes, 1993a). Studies show that seasonally migrant elders compared to nonimmigrants are more likely to be married and retired; they also tend to report higher levels of education and white-collar as opposed to blue-collar work. Studies of Sun City and similar retirement communities show that the stereotype of the older person moving away from family and friends to a foreign and unfamiliar world is largely false. Elders hear about such places from relatives and friends and visit the community before moving to it.

The pressure for a second move occurs when older people develop chronic disabilities that make it difficult to carry out everyday tasks. The presence of a spouse is helpful and may act to postpone the move which, when made, may place the disabled elder nearer to adult children who can offer assistance or nearer to medical facilities. With urbanization and industrialization, many grown children have moved to cities for jobs. Older parents from rural areas, if they are to be near their children, must move to the city. An example is that of a middle-aged Iowa farmer who gave up farming after years of drought and moved to the city to secure a more financially stable livelihood for his family. In the process, he left his parents, both in their seventies, behind on the farm. With increasing age and/or declining health, these older parents will need to move closer to their displaced son and his family or make arrangements for local services (if any are available). Sometimes the second move is to some type of congregate or assisted housing, where the older person can maintain a degree of independence.

The 1990 census repeated the 1980 census finding that more older persons live in the suburbs than in central cities. Declining health and the need for health care are often associated with migration to suburban areas. Given the closing of rural hospitals and the inadequacy or nonexistence of rural health-care systems, worry about well-being often acts as a strong stimulus for an unwanted move to the city. The young-old who do not have to worry as much about health care tend to migrate to rural areas. The old-old tend to come to the suburbs or city from rural areas for necessary social and medical services.

INTEGRATION VERSUS SEGREGATION

The issue of **age-integrated housing** versus **age-segregated housing** revolves around the question of whether it is better to have elders segregated and to thus encourage the severing of their ties with the larger society, or whether it is better to integrate them into the larger society and thereby encourage interaction among all age groups.

Age-concentrated retirement housing has strong support from middle- to high-income elders. Interviews with elders in three apartment buildings with low, medium, and high densities of older adults revealed that residents associated high-density senior citizen housing with larger numbers of friends, more active friendships, and slightly better morale (Hinrichsen, 1985). However, the hypothesis that age-concentrated housing is the best and most desirable situation has not been proved conclusively. A study, in contrast, revealed that living environments with high densities of elders had little effect on morale, either positive or negative.

Many are in age-concentrated housing because they like the accommodations and amenities. Others are simply in "old" neighborhoods: age-concentration is high because everyone has been there for years. They do not, by choice, limit their interactions to other old persons. Researchers conclude that, in general, though age-concentrated housing is a desirable alternative for some, it should not serve as a guide for housing policy at large. Some sociologists are predicting more age integration in the years to come (Riley and Riley, 1994). If the young-old stay in the job market longer and continue their activities of middle age, they will not gravitate toward age-segregated housing. Some social critics view age-segregated housing as a means of insulating older people from the ageism in the larger society. Here again, if ageism decreases, one would predict a decline in age-segregated housing.

✹ Housing Options

We can view types of housing as ranging on a continuous scale from independent to dependent. Living in one's own home is the most independent lifestyle; living in a hotel-type residence is semi-independent; and living in an institution is the most dependent lifestyle.

Generally speaking, the more dependent the new lifestyle, the more difficult the adjustment. Sometimes the problem in institutionalized group housing is not the quality of care provided, but the fact that the older person really does not want to be there. Many elders are dedicated to a lifestyle of self-reliance and self-direction and have little tolerance for the regulations of a nursing home. They would like better food and shelter, but not in exchange for the freedom to decide their life's course. A truly independent person might choose to live on a menu of eggs, beer, and ice cream in a cockroach-infested hotel, rather than live in a nursing home.

On the other hand, an isolated, frail, disabled elder might welcome the safe haven of institutionalized care. Acknowledging the diversity in age, personality, and health of those age 65 and older opens up more and more housing alternatives for older people. The needs and requirements of the young-old in good health are vastly different from the frail elders in poor health. In this section, housing options for both the young-old and the oldest-old are considered.

AGING IN PLACE

Aging in place has become a popular phrase indicating staying in one's home as long as possible with no strong desire to permanently relocate. With the development of so many retirement communities in the 1970s and 1980s, it seemed, on the surface, that most elders wanted to relocate. But in the 1990s attention is being drawn to the fact that the bulk of elders choose to "age in place" (Ravo, 1992).

Aging in place offers freedom and independence.

More older people are showing a powerful preference to stay in their homes rather than move elsewhere, according to a 1990 survey (Downey, 1990) sponsored by the American Association of Retired Persons (AARP). About 84 percent of the more than 1,500 people age 55 and older said they want to stay in their longtime homes rather than move to senior citizen projects. When they are forced to move, 63 percent prefer to remain in the same city or county and only 11 percent prefer to move to a different state. "Their dominant preference is to stay in their homes, and not move, never move and stay there forever," said Lea Dobkin, a housing specialist with AARP. " [For developers], it means use caution. It's a more competitive environment."

Many older people already live in informal retirement communities known in the senior housing industry as **naturally occurring retirement communities (NORCs)**. These are buildings or neighborhoods where the residents have aged over the years. There are many cases in point, both in the suburbs, the rural Midwest, and inner cities (Roberts, 1991). The neighborhood, like the individual, goes through a life cycle of young to middle aged to old.

Aging in place is not always easy. As people age into their eighties and nineties and beyond, more and more tasks may pose difficulties, even for those in good health—writing checks, driving a car, shopping, or bathing. Public or private agencies must be available to provide services that elders themselves and their families and friends cannot provide. A need exists for home-nursing services and homemaker services, including cooking, housecleaning, bathing and grooming assistance, laundry, and transportation. Also, social services are needed for emotional health and support. In more and more areas, volunteers are calling older people once a day to check on their health and safety. These calls are especially important for those living alone.

DOWNSIZING

The move to a smaller home, say a condominium or a mobile home, if it is in the same town or general area, is a form of aging in place. The reasons for such a move were discussed earlier in this chapter: The upkeep is easier, taxes are lower than for a large house, and the location may be more convenient.

Mobile homes, typically smaller than conventional homes, can provide a comfortable living environment. Perhaps the most significant factor in opting for a mobile home is related to its affordability. Mobile homes provide older adults with a sense of home ownership, privacy, and security.

Life in a mobile home may not be without problems, however. Historically, the quality of mobile homes has been suspect. In the past, owners have had little success in influencing manufacturers to correct deficiencies. There has been general agreement that, overall, the quality of mobile homes has improved in recent years. In a move to protect mobile-home buyers, recent congressional proposals would require that buyers be provided with a five-year warranty, building (manufacturing) standards be raised, and "mandatory" funds designed to pay for repair costs not reimbursed by unscrupulous or bankrupt businesses be required from state funds.

An additional potential problem for the majority of older mobile-home residents is related to the fact that they must purchase space in a **mobile-home park** where they have little control over actions made by park owners. For example, in Washington State, an owner of a lush mobile-home park is planning to close his park and redevelop it for more lucrative commercial use (Glasheen, 1994). The effect will be to dislodge all of the current tenants! Other problems include space rental increases, restrictive rules, and the lack of parity between the mobile-home owners and park owners (Glasheen, 1994).

Enough people live in their RVs (recreation vehicles) the year around for the term **full-timing** to have evolved. This is one more choice that older people have. Some fulfill a lifetime retirement dream when they "hit the road" in their RVs and see all the places in Canada, the United States, or Mexico that draw them. It is a lifestyle that has not gone unnoticed by sociologists and gerontologists.

ADULT DAY CARE

Adult day care offers medical and social services at a center to elders who commute from home. Centers may be nonprofit organizations, government-run centers, or profit organizations run by insurance companies such as: Elderplan, Kaiser, SCAN, and Seniors Plus. Multipurpose senior centers provide health-care facilities where older persons are brought in the morning and taken home in the afternoon. These might be day hospitals that offer medical or psychiatric treatment or day-care centers that provide social and recreational services. Studies show that persons who can avail themselves of adult day care reduce their risks of hospitalization.

Some nonprofit organizations provide multiple services to elders. Through the Older Americans Act, the federal government now funds a number of multipurpose senior centers. One such organization, the Minneapolis Age and Opportunity Center, largely government-funded, provides services such as daily meal deliveries, laundry, and transportation. Insurance programs are now being offered to assist the older person in staying at home. Such plans are becoming affordable and workable. A variation of the health maintenance organization (HMO) is the SHMO—social health maintenance organization. Elderplan in New York, Kaiser in Oregon, and Seniors Plus in Minnesota offer health insurance programs that provide personal care and household assistance services at home or in day-care settings.

A new variation of health insurance policies offers LCH (Life Care at Home). Insurance agencies are tailoring LCH insurance policies that cover medical and personal costs for the older person who wishes to stay at home. One must proceed with caution in purchasing a LCH plan because the LCH involves a large initial entry fee, a monthly fee, and at least a one-year contract. Such private long-term care insurance policies are expensive and may have restrictions that limit coverage.

The On Lok Health Center in San Francisco, patterned after the day-care system in England, provides day-care services to elders in Chinatown. A van with a hydraulic lift transports the elderly to the center, where each day begins with exercise and reality orientation. People are introduced to each other in both English and Chinese. On Lok assumes responsibility for providing all services needed by the functionally dependent. If not for On Lok, the participants would need institutional care. Though the cost per person for this service is about the same as that for institutional care, the psychological benefits and the social facilitation make the service well worth the price.

GRANNY UNITS AND SHARED HOUSING

A housing concept currently being proposed and enacted on a limited basis in the United States is actually an old concept to the Japanese and Australians: the **granny unit,** also called the granny flat or elder cottage. A granny unit, by U.S. definition, is a small living unit, built on the lot of a single-family home, where adult children can care for aging parents. Older people can also install granny units in their backyards. They can rent their home or their granny unit for income or trade for services such as nursing or homemaking.

Advocates of the granny-unit concept, such as the American Association of Retired Persons (AARP), must fight zoning laws in some towns and cities. Areas zoned for single-family homes may not welcome added granny units. The desirable features of granny units are that they allow the older person a choice of living independently. If the older person can live in a granny unit rather than in the adult child's house, there is more privacy and freedom for everyone. The "granny flats" experience in Great Britain suggests that "they have an important but limited role" in enabling people to live close to their families (Tinker, 1991). But, despite cost and regulations, this housing alternative is gaining support in more countries worldwide. Canada, for example, has endorsed the granny-unit concept (Lazarovich, 1991).

Shared housing that involves some type of group living is another concept being developed by and for elders. In Great Britain, there are over 700 Abbyfield homes—homes in the community that house several elders and are run by specialists in aging. This kind of program is being developed in the United States. Another alternative is renting a room of one's house to another person and sharing such rooms as the kitchen and living room. Such an arrangement is usually predicated by the need for financial relief, services, and companionship. Many variations are possible. An older person could rent a room of the house in return for income or services.

The difficult part is to find a good tenant–home owner match. More and more community agencies, such as Share-a-Home in Memphis, Tennessee, and Independent Living in Madison, Wisconsin, are helping to coordinate shared housing. One study, unfortunately, showed that matching is problematic. A majority of the matches dissolved in the first three months.

ADULT COMMUNITIES

Many towns and cities have **adult communities** for those over age 50. Typically, children under 18 are prohibited from living in these places; court cases have upheld the legality of the age limit. Adult mobile-home parks with age limits on younger persons are also quite popular. An adult community may have a grocery store, bank, medical clinic, and convenience stores within its boundaries. The sizes of adult communities within cities vary. A recent trend is for older folk with interests in common (for example, artists or gay retirees), to form their own communities (*Wall Street Journal*, 1994).

RETIREMENT CITIES

Some older people seem to like the age-segregated **retirement cities,** because such communities offer so much. Sun City, Arizona, after which many other retirement towns have been patterned, has a population of over 46,000 and a minimum age of 50 (others, such as Youngstown, Arizona, have set the lower limit at age 60). Located 20 miles northwest of Phoenix, Sun City is a large complex on 8,900 acres with a number of social and leisure activities, such as tennis, bridge, quilting, wood carving, and language classes. The lure is the affordability and the weather. Prices for homes in 1991 started at $65,000 in Sun City West, a development started in 1978 when all of the original Sun

City units had been built and sold. Residents tend to be upbeat about cities made up of all senior citizens. They get involved more easily because of the many activities shared by persons in their own age group.

Several million older people have bought or leased property in the retirement cities that have mushroomed around the country since 1905. One of the most successful retirement community developments has been Leisure World, with locations in several sections of the country. Most retirement villages have swimming pools, clubhouses for dancing or crafts, symphonies, golf courses, and free bus rides to shopping centers and entertainment. One community excludes dogs and puts a three-week limit on visits by children. Such features make age-segregated housing more desirable to some older persons.

ASSISTED LIVING

Assisted living (or assisted housing), an alternative to institutionalization typically indicates community-based residential group living with supportive services to assist in the activities of daily living. They include features such as meals, housekeeping, health and personal services, and transportation. Directories of assisted housing show a growing number and variety of facilities. As an example, a middle-income, high-rise apartment building might have an infirmary, a long-term nursing care facility, a dining room, or a community area. Some assisted housing creates a real sense of community among elders giving them support and a renewed zest for living. Other planned housing, however, shows rather isolated elders whose main support is relatives on the outside. Research is needed to learn ways to encourage the former.

Recently hotel and hospital industries have become involved in developing assisted-living facilities. Marriott Corporation, for example, has opened several 100-unit assisted-living residences and plans a national chain of them (Kalymun, 1992). Also still around are **board and care homes** like the old "mom and pop" operation in a large family home where unoccupied bedrooms become available to boarders. The board and care facility offers a bedroom in a private home, whereas an assisted-living facility offers self-contained housing units. Operators of board and care homes are typically middle-aged women who live in the homes with their spouses, many of whom have worked as nurses or aides in health-care settings (Kalymun, 1992).

Sunrise Retirement Homes and Communities is the country's largest operator of assisted-living centers, operating more than 30 such communities (Estrada, 1994). When a husband-wife team started their first Sunrise Center by renovating a nursing home, the term *assisted living* did not exist. Now more than 2,000 elders live in their centers. One example of their efforts is the Sunrise Retirement Home near Washington, D.C., a three-story "Victorian mansion" with 42 one- and two-room units The building has the feeling of a country inn with a fireplace, large bay windows, and a sun room filled with wicker furniture. Residents' rooms are grouped around common living rooms and lounges. Units rent for $1,000 to $2,000 a month, which includes housekeeping, meal services, and minor medical care.

Marie Morgan, 73 years old, was withdrawing and deteriorating in a nursing home when she opted for assisted living and moved to Rackleff House in Canby, Oregon (McCarthy, 1992). Despite incontinence and a heart condition, she is thriving in her assisted-living quarters. She gets out and about using her walker to circle the grounds, does her own laundry, and is able to keep her dog, a Lhasa Apso, in her private apartment. For about $2,000 a month she also gets housekeeping, meals, laundry facilities, transportation, social activities, and regular visits from nurses. Some residents have mild to moderate Alzheimer's disease, like the one who loiters by the copy machine in the office. She was a bookkeeper most of her life and finds the office bustle comforting. The staff understands and works around her. In Oregon assisted-living centers have become so widespread that nursing home population has been reduced by 4 percent even though the over-65 population rose by 18 percent. There are more than 20 assisted-living units in Oregon.

Rackleff House, which opened in 1990, was created by a professor at Portland State University, motivated by her mother's needs, not profit. Renting a room in Rackleff House is affordable to lower-middle-income elders. The average age is 89 and half are on Medicaid. They can furnish their rooms with their own things. Rackleff looks like a big yellow farmhouse. It is not lavish yet it has a cathedral ceiling in the dining room and a secure enclosed courtyard. A fireplace flickers in the front parlor. Traditional nursing homes have a staff–patient ratio of about ten to one: Rackleff's is one worker per three residents.

CONTINUING CARE RETIREMENT COMMUNITIES (CCRCS)

The **continuing care retirement community (CCRC)** represents an upscale form of congregate housing that requires a strong commitment on the part of the resident. CCRCs, also known as **life-care communities,** require a large entry fee ($50,000 to $500,000), monthly fees of $500 to $2,000 (depending on the area of the country, quality of housing, and number of services available), and commitment to at least a year-long contract. In return, the entrant is provided with housing, health care, social activities, and meals. A typical CCRC has a campus consisting of independent living units, such as one- or two-bedroom apartments, a nursing facility, and possibly a nursing home. Long-term care costs are fundable through a "pooled risk fund" derived from residents' entry and monthly fees. Because different CCRCs offer different services and accommodations, costs vary widely.

An even deeper commitment is made in life-care communities where the elderly resident consigns all possessions and savings to the CCR community. In return, no monthly fee is charged. Legislation and other policies in some states discourage these plans because of possible abuses to the participants.

The life-care industry has grown dramatically in the last few years: there were over 700 communities in 1992 (Neuman, 1992). Dozens of big-name developers and corporations are looking to build CCRCs. If older people can sell their homes, that money will generally cover a CCRC entry fee. Those with adequate pensions can afford the monthly fee.

Legislation is being passed in many states to protect the older consumer. Contracts and rental agreements are regulated, and most states have certification and registry requirements. California and Florida, for example, require extensive disclosure statements prior to certifying facilities; Indiana and Colorado require that the potential resident receive copies of such disclosure statements. Those considering life-care communities must protect themselves as much as possible by examining the facility and contract very carefully before signing.

Still, unexpected problems can occur. A poorly managed CCRC can experience financial difficulties and declining service, and may head for bankruptcy, creating a dilemma for the elder residents who have given their possessions to the institution. There is a need for government regulation of CCRCs to ensure that they remain in good financial condition, capable of honoring their commitment for lifetime care. Efforts are currently underway in California to introduce legislation that would require owners of continuing-care communities to disclose their financial condition ("Tireless Warriors," 1990). A study showed that facilities offering full nursing care displayed poorer financial profiles than those offering less comprehensive care (Ruchlin, 1988). Thus, one should beware of facilities that promise too much; such promises could portend financial instability.

These communities offer the older adult control of his or her fate. The promise of care for the remainder of one's life assures the older person of not being a burden to adult children. But it represents security only if the financial position of the CCRC is sound. CCRCs are available only to those who are at least moderately wealthy. Even the middle class has trouble affording them (Somers and Spears, 1992.)

Some continuing care communities are being built near college campuses, giving residents with free time an easy commute to college classes and other cultural benefits such as musical productions, concerts, sports events, lectures, libraries, films, and discussion groups. These CCRC villages may give preference to alumni, but any qualified person is eligible. Some have up-front fees as high as $200,000, and monthly fees for food, lodging, and medical care in the $3,000 range. Other communities near campuses are on a pay-as-you-go basis (Sherrid, 1993).

☼ Nursing Homes: What Do They Offer?

Meeting the needs of the infirm is the responsibility of society, not just the responsibility of service providers, the government, or their families. Here we will consider what nursing homes can offer. How well they meet needs ultimately depends on how well the public informs itself concerning the problems of nursing homes and the rights and services to which residents are entitled.

WHO NEEDS A NURSING HOME?

The typical nursing home patient is female, white, widowed, and over age 80. Most of the patients come to the facility from another institution, usually a general medical hospital, rather than from their own homes. Most patients have multiple problems such as arthritis, heart trouble, diabetes, or vision/hearing impairment. In addition to physical impairments, there are usually mental health problems, such as disorientation (confusion), impulse control (anger), and emotional affect level (depression). Many patients need help dressing, eating, toileting, and bathing. Given these amounts of personal needs and limitations, it is not surprising that most of these patients are in the care of nursing homes.

MAKING THE DECISION

Whether an older parent, relative, or friend will need nursing home care can often be anticipated some months before the individual actually enters the facility. The limitations in behavior brought on by chronic illness or age may be progressive as well as irreversible, usually allowing the individual and the family time enough to make a thoughtful and careful selection of homes and to ease the transition from one living arrangement to another.

Unfortunately, too few people are willing to entertain the possibility of a nursing home and simply wait for circumstances to force a quick, hurried decision, usually one filled with emotional trauma for all concerned. Statistics indicate that the typical nursing home patient enters the facility from a hospital rather than from a private home. This signifies that nursing home care has become a necessity rather than a choice. Families often burden themselves for long periods of time trying to care for an elderly parent who could receive care as good or even better in a nursing home. They often associate guilt, and even shame with any attempt to consider nursing home care until the need becomes absolutely critical.

Families can anticipate eventual need and involve all members in the decision-making process. All concerned can discuss the advantages and disadvantages of nursing home care and together can inquire about and visit potential facilities. A grandparent living with adult children may not be happy to be in the midst of bustling young people or to be the cause of unusual alterations or deviations in a family routine. Families can and should discuss these problems in an atmosphere of mutual love and concern. The older person "dumped," without discussion or plan, in a nursing home after a sudden medical crisis may well feel deserted and hurt. The American Health Care Association has published three brochures for those considering nursing home care: "The Nursing Home Dilemma," "Thinking About a Nursing Home?", and "Welcome to Our Nursing Home, A Family Guide." Available upon request, these brochures, which detail the many aspects of the decision-making process, can be the basis for beginning conversations about future needs (American Health Care Association, 1994).

FINDING A NURSING HOME

Many nursing homes provide excellent patient care and make special efforts to meet the psychosocial needs of their residents. Others are skilled in the delivery of medically related services but lack the foresight, knowledge, and skill to address the psychological and emotional needs of their residents. The better homes generally have long waiting lists, so early planning is essential to eventual placement.

Unfortunately, most families spend little time in visiting a variety of nursing homes in order to secure a satisfactory placement. There are, however, available resources that can assist in the search for the right nursing home. The local Council on Aging and the local chapter of the state Health Care Association can provide the locations of licensed facilities in the area and factors to consider in choosing a home. The Office of Nursing Home Affairs can provide information on characteristics of good homes. Finally, the local chapter of the Gray Panthers typically has a nursing home committee; various other watchdog groups publish information on how to choose a nursing home. In the meantime, social workers and nursing home professionals have compiled the suggestions provided below, which should provide some preliminary ideas about how to select a nursing home.

- Make at least two visits to a particular nursing home, once at a mealtime and again in mid-morning or mid-afternoon. Visit several other facilities, so you can make comparisons.
- Make sure you know what the basic rate covers. Investigate extra charges for professional services and medications.

Thinking about Aging

'Heavy Duty' Postcards Delight Elderly

■ JOE RUFF

The postcards aren't fancy and their messages aren't deep. But the mysterious missives from a truck driver known as "Heavy Duty" have residents of Nebraska nursing homes eagerly awaiting the next day's mail.

"We look forward to his cards and wonder when he will drop us a card again. They are so interesting to see the different states he's going through," said Ida Kramer, 77, who lives at Schuyler Nursing Center in Schuyler, a town of 4,100 people about 50 miles west of Omaha.

For months and even years, postcards signed "Heavy Duty" or "The Nebraska Trucker" or "Bob H." have been arriving at three nursing homes from New York, Washington, Alabama and other states in the East, South and Midwest.

At the Schuyler nursing home, activities director Dorothy Zwick has formed a Heavy Duty fan club and keeps a scrapbook of the 18 cards received since May. A sign outside says: "Truckers Come and Go; Stop, Heavy Duty, and Say Hello."

"I kind of figure him to be a big fat guy," said Kramer, one of 70 residents. "Some truckers are that way, you know. They do a lot of sitting, don't get much exercise."

Heavy Duty also writes to the Mount Carmel Home in Kearney, a south-central Nebraska city of 22,000, and to Wilber Nursing Home in Wilber, a town of 1,600 about 40 miles south of Lincoln.

Residents speculate that he sees the nursing homes from the highway. Others think he has relatives in each home.

"It makes them feel good that somebody is thinking of them and caring enough to let them know what is going on in the world," said Tish Sigler, social services director at Mount Carmel, which has 76 residents.

Heavy Duty's first card to the Schuyler home summed up his motives:

A postcard is like a hug for a nursing home resident.

"Hi, just trying to send a little bit of the USA to anyone interested."

"As both my parents used to be in a rest home, I would visit and notice some people never had much company. Just maybe somebody will appreciate these cards. I don't live in Schuyler, but not too far away. Heavy Duty."

Sigler figured out the trucker's identity when his aunt began stopping by to gather up his postcards, but she keeps the secret because he wants it that way.

His aunt, who gave her name only as Angeline, said Heavy Duty used to write letters to her husband at Mount Carmel. "His uncle was so proud of the cards that he shared them with other residents," she said.

When his uncle died in 1989, the trucker started writing to everyone in the home.

Heavy Duty is an independent trucker in his 50s, has a wife and three children and lives in York, a town of 7,700 west of Lincoln, Angeline said.

SOURCE: Ruff, Joe. "'Heavy Duty' Postcards Delight Elderly," *San Francisco Chronicle* (30 November 1991): C1. Used with permission of The Associated Press.

■ Ask to see a copy of the month's menu. Is it varied and interesting? Does the food on the menu actually get served? How many hours a month does a registered dietician spend in the facility? Experts believe four hours a week should be the minimum.

■ Is there a registered nurse on duty on the afternoon and evening shifts? This is required by law for facilities of 100 beds or more; such facilities are required to have an RN or licensed vocational nurse on those shifts. All facilities with more than six beds should have an RN on the daytime shift.

■ Is there an activities director? This is required for Medicare-certified homes. The activities director should spend at least 20 hours per week in the home, unless it has fewer than 50 beds. There should also be activities for bedridden patients.

■ Look for activities geared to adults, not children. There is no excuse for only finger-painting and television. Why not poker games, adult education classes, or movies?

❂ Nursing Homes: How Bad Are They?

Virtually all of us are either directly or indirectly affected by nursing home care. Although at any given point in time only 5 percent of the nation's elders are in long-term care institutions, this figure is deceptive. Recent data provided by Kemper and Murtaugh (1991) indicate that of all people turning age 65 in 1990 one-third of the men and one-half of the women will spend some time in a nursing home. Furthermore, for couples who turned 65 in 1990, approximately seven out of ten will experience one of their members spending time in a nursing home (Smyer, 1993). Families are also affected. Nine out of ten children can expect that one of their parents (or their spouse's parents) will spend time in a nursing home. According to recent estimates, nursing home populations will increase from the 1990 level of 1.8 million to 4 million within the next 24 years—an increase of well over 50 percent (Braus, 1994). The question, then, of the availability of adequate resources with high quality of care is one of prime importance.

The question remains: are all homes as bad as we imagine them to be, or is a bad nursing home relatively rare? This question is quite difficult to answer. No one knows what conditions exist in all homes, and standards for measuring good and bad vary. Most homes seem to provide adequate care, but there is much room for improvement. The remainder can be filthy and unsafe, cheerless and depressing. The worst of homes are firetraps, with unhealthy living conditions and neglect of patients. Cleanliness is only one indication of whether a nursing home is "good" or "bad."

What kinds of conditions do investigators find in substandard homes? Nursing home violations have included the following:

■ Patients tied in chairs for hours at a time.

■ Patients lying in urine-soaked bedding for hours at a time.

■ The use of styrofoam drinking cups and plastic utensils, which impose a hardship on those with arthritis and tremors.

■ Meals being served cold and unappetizing.

■ Nonavailability of assistance.

- Patients having trouble eating.
- No attempt being made to get patients out of doors.

The above complaints reflect neglect and indicate a lack of staffing and limited monies being spent on the residents. Some apparently "senile" patients in nursing homes are suffering from no more than a lack of stimulation and some human interaction. Others may be in a state of profound depression because they feel they have been brought to the nursing home to die.

Bad nursing homes tend to be understaffed and to hire poorly qualified personnel. Nurses are often required to fill the role of doctors; nurses' aides, the role of nurses. Nurses are burdened with administrative duties that leave them little time for patients. Untrained aides and orderlies, who are often paid minimum wage and who evidence a high turnover rate, administer between 80 and 90 percent of all patient care.

A study of physician visits to nursing homes revealed some thorny problems which persist in the 1990s. Most physicians have little contact with patients in nursing homes for the following reasons: low reimbursement levels of Medicaid and Medicare; excessive administrative requirements in processing payments; and the opinion that both the patients and their nursing home environments are hopeless, gloomy, and depressing. Other federal regulations may keep physicians away. Medicare and Medicaid require that patients in skilled nursing homes be visited at least once per week; intermediate-care patients must receive physician visits every 30 days. Physicians often do not like the time and expense involved in traveling to a home. The average nursing home visit takes twice as long as the office visit. Perhaps more extensive geriatric training for physicians would stimulate their interest.

In addition to the understaffing of doctors and nurses and a shortage of dental care, social services, and psychiatric care, patients are often overmedicated. Good nutrition and sanitary conditions can be lacking, and activities more stimulating than watching television are deadening when absent.

The financing of nursing homes creates other problems. The government reimburses nursing homes through two systems, both of which allow corrupt owners to make huge profits. On the flat-rate system, the nursing home is paid so much per patient. The operator who wants to make a large profit on this system keeps costs as low as possible by providing cheap food, having as few registered nurses on the staff as possible, and providing no physical therapists or psychiatric counseling. Healthy patients are the most desirable under this system. Basically healthy old people who simply have nowhere else to go can get pushed unnecessarily into these nursing homes.

The second system is called the cost-plus system. Here, the nursing home is reimbursed for its costs, plus a "reasonable" profit. The way to make money under this system is to pad the bills; in other words, to bill the government for more goods and services than the facility received, or to bill for goods and services never delivered. Doctors and nursing homes gain if doctors perform "gang visits," stopping just long enough for a quick look at patients in the nursing home. The government is then billed as if the doctor had visited each patient separately, a task probably requiring days instead of hours. The ABC news show *20/20* (ABC News, 1991) exposed a Fort Worth, Texas, nursing home with a history of horrible abuses to patients. Informants interviewed by Tom Jarrell told stories of these shocking conditions: patients bound to their beds and chairs; patients drugged; patients unwashed, dirty, and hungry; and cockroaches in the beds. The nursing home, surrounded by barbed wire and a fence with locked gates, made a profit of $300,000 annually, funded almost totally by Medicaid. The owners, instead of spending the money appropriately on the patients, pocketed as much as they could.

A watchdog group in California reported that California nursing homes received more than 1,500 citations in 1993 for health and safety violations, 16 of which led to the deaths of residents, and in some cases led to severe maggot infestation (Bjorhus, 1994). The same report stated that millions of dollars in state fines to nursing homes go uncollected.

A more emphathetic look at nursing homes was provided by a long-term nursing home administrator who assumed the identity of an alcoholic wheelchair-bound patient and signed himself in for a ten-day temporary stay at a large Boston-area nursing home. From the insights he gleaned, he wrote a book about nursing home life (Bennett, 1980). Here are some of his observations:

1. The patient may feel admittance to be a life sentence.
2. The mandated size of room is too small.
3. There are barriers to easy access in a wheelchair—carpeting, for example.
4. The need for ties with the outside world is great.
5. The present standard of hours of care per resident per day should be upped.
6. There should be in-service training for all new staff in geriatrics/gerontology.

Bennett believes that encouraging competition among nursing homes might eliminate poor homes (Bennett, 1980).

The debate over whether proprietary (for-profit) homes offer a lower quality of patient care than nonproprietary (nonprofit) homes goes unanswered. One study, using strict quality control measures, found no difference in the quality of care between profit and nonprofit facilities (Duffy, 1987). Close to three-quarters of all nursing homes are operated on a for-profit basis.

Those in the business who are really concerned about elders and provide quality care deserve credit. Credit also must be given to all the honest doctors, pharmacists, nursing home inspectors, social workers, and therapists. A number of nursing homes are excellent by any standards. The Jewish Home for the Aged in San Francisco is considered to be among the best. The residents are not called "patients." The living quarters resemble rooms in a nicely furnished college dormitory. Virtually all residents are out of bed and dressed. The home has a beauty shop, and there are many activities and opportunities for therapeutic exercising on stationary bicycles and other equipment. "They take care of me from head to toe," said one resident.

☼ New Trends in Nursing Homes

The elder population is rapidly increasing, especially at the upper age levels. Because the oldest-old develop chronic ailments and a frailty that decreases independence, the housing market has developed more and more assisted housing to help them remain at home. Increasingly, those who stay in nursing homes have more serious problems that only institutional care can address. The majority of nursing home patients have disabling psychiatric conditions, such as depression or Alzheimer's disease; many nursing home patients present behavior problems, such as agitation, abusiveness, or wandering.

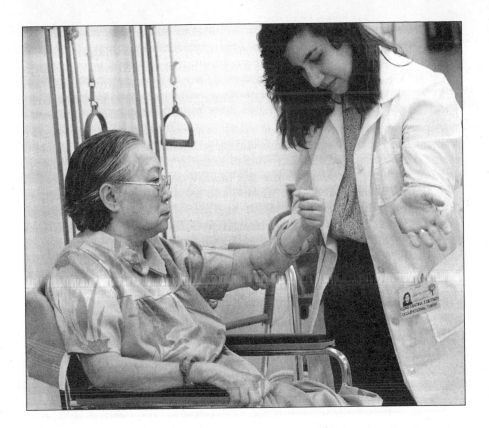

Nursing homes are becoming more involved in rehabilitation.

Nursing home care presents an increasing challenge for staff, family, and residents alike. In the past, the health-care system provided scant rehabilitation for frail elders and held low expectations for older people in nursing homes. Now, however, there are positive new trends for both the physically and the mentally disabled.

Those over 65 are more likely than any other group to suffer strokes, lower limb amputation, hip fractures, and heart disease. With rehabilitation, many can achieve a level of independence that allows them to live in their own homes. Rehabilitation units represent a departure from the traditional nursing home. A nursing home with a rehabilitation unit revealed that 57 percent of its patients were discharged after an average stay of three months in the unit. The unit had a team composed of a geriatrician, psychiatrist, physical therapist, social worker, nurse, occupational therapist, and nutritionist. The conclusion was that patients discharged "quicker and sicker," without rehabilitation, are likely candidates for relapse and readmission. The rehabilitation unit brought a sense of triumph to all who participated (Adelman et al., 1987).

According to Strahan and Burns (1991), 65 percent of all nursing home residents have at least one mental disorder. The mentally ill, who present far more behavioral problems than other nursing home residents, need rehabilitative services. Such services have been found to be generally effective. But, according to Shea et al. (1994), less than 25 percent in nursing homes with a mental disorder actually received such services in the year of the study. Furthermore, only about 5 percent of those residents with a mental disorder received *any* mental health treatment in the last one-month period. One-half of the services they received was provided for by general practitioners who usually have very little training in geriatric psychiatry. Obviously, although services for those who receive them tend to be somewhat effective, much more must be done to provide the quality and quantity of services for those who need them. If, indeed, as Shea et al. (1994) contend, nursing homes, in fact, should be mental health facilities, more in-depth preparation of staff is necessary and a wider range of mental health professionals must be utilized.

Family and community involvement can improve life for elders in a nursing home. Both resident-only counseling groups and resident/family counseling groups reduce anxiety and increase feelings of internal control for those in institutions. Family members who strive to keep family connections, offer optimism for recovery, and help the resident to maintain dignity can do much to uplift spirits. Family members tend to judge a nursing home not so much by its technical care as by its psychological care. The views of involved family members provide the staff with good feedback that hopefully can lead to improvements. Families of nursing home residents are often unfamiliar with ways to assist their relatives. Nursing homes that establish a "partnership" with families in sharing responsibilities for the nontechnical aspects of care enhance the psychological and emotional welfare of the resident as well as that of family.

Typically, nursing homes participate in an ombudsman program. An ombudsman is usually a specially trained volunteer who acts as an advocate for clients' rights and quality nursing home care. The ombudsman performs tasks such as making information available to residents and their families about policies, procedures, and their rights, and helps them to identify other helpful resources. On occasion, the ombudsman may also investigate complaints and seek relief on behalf of nursing home residents or their families.

❖ The Omnibus Budget Reconciliation Act of 1987 (OBRA)

With the enactment of the **Omnibus Budget Reconciliation Act of 1987,** major nursing home reforms were introduced. In addition to tightening survey and certification procedures, the act strengthened patients' rights when planning their care and making treatment decisions. Other requirements, such as written care plans, required training for nurses' aides, and the employment of certified social workers, were designed to upgrade the quality of patient services and to insure their participation in planning their care. OBRA also intensified requirements for survey teams making routine and unscheduled audits. As a result, many past procedures, such as placing patients in restraints without medical authorization or denying patients full disclosure of their medical records and diagnoses, and failing to assure patients of their rights may become grounds for censure or, ultimately, the closing of a facility by regulatory agencies. Although OBRA does not purport to correct all problems related to the quality of care, it represents a concerted effort to upgrade and enrich services to institutionalized elders. Enforcement of the provisions of OBRA is generally left in the hands of State Health Departments that are generally woefully understaffed, which results in only occasional audits of nursing homes to ensure that OBRA mandates are being carried out. Although it is hoped that the enactment of OBRA has led to a higher quality of care for residents, empirical evidence does not confirm that those outcomes have been achieved.

Chapter Summary

Theoretically, there are many acceptable kinds of housing currently available to those who must relocate:

- home of a relative
- public housing
- deluxe high-rise apartment
- retirement village
- mobile home
- apartment complex or duplex
- hotel-type residence with meals or a board and care home
- intermediate day care/own home at night
- assisted living (a residential complex with many services and facilities)
- small group residential home
- institution

But reality does not keep pace with theory. Old people are often forced into housing that is inadequate or that needlessly increases their dependence. Most prefer to live in their own homes where possible, but others enjoy the stimulation of living in retirement communities, shared housing arrangements, community care retirement centers, or similar living environments. For older adults with limited incomes, public housing or mobile homes may provide a practical alternative. Although the percentages are declining, many continue to live with relatives—usually a daughter or son and their families. Regardless of the type of living situation, most prefer to remain as independent as possible.

For those who decide to relocate (either voluntarily or involuntarily), problems may arise with respect to housing shortages, downsizing, decisions over whether to live in an integrated or segregated environment, or finding a community in which to live that is compatible with their lifestyles. Relocation is never a simple matter, although under optimal conditions it can enhance both the lifestyle and life satisfactions of those who elect to do so.

For a small percentage of older adults—those who are debilitated—the nursing home is often the only viable housing option. The lack of personalization often creates dependency and the loss of personal freedoms for the resident. OBRA legislation was enacted to increase the quality of life in nursing homes by providing for resident input and by offering a broader range of higher quality services.

Everyone *needs* a home. The older we get, the more important a safe harbor becomes. Home is not just a place to exist, but a place to *be*. More needs to be done to meet this most important psychological requirement. We all deserve to live out our lives in dignity, pride, and comfort.

Key Terms

adult community
adult day care
age-integrated housing

age-segregated housing
aging in place
assisted living

board and care home
continuing care retirement communities (CCRCs)
downsizing
full-timing
granny units
life-care community (LCC)
living environment
mobile-home park

naturally occurring retirement communities (NORCs)
Omnibus Budget Reconciliation Act of 1987 (OBRA)
public housing
retirement city
snowbirds
sunbirds
surveillance zone

Questions for Discussion

1. Identify at least three reasons that adequate housing is important for older adults.

2. Think of your parents as older adults. In what type of housing environment would you like to see them live? Why? Imagine that you are 70 years of age. Where would you like to live? Why?

3. What are some of the issues associated with living in public housing? What steps would you take to increase the quality of public housing?

4. What are the disadvantages of living in a segregated community? Advantages?

5. What would you look for in selecting a nursing home for your father or mother? What alternatives, other than the nursing home, would you consider? Why?

Fieldwork Suggestions

1. Visit a senior center and interview at least five older adults. Ask each of them where they live, who lives with them, and what problems (if any) they have with housing. Compare and contrast their responses to ascertain any consistent themes. How consistent are the responses to material presented in this chapter?

2. Visit a public housing complex in your community. What are your first impressions? Talk to residents to find out how they feel about living there. Interview the director of housing with a focus of identifying the positives and negatives associated with that particular complex.

3. Volunteer at a local nursing home. Observe what you consider to be the major strengths and weaknesses with respect to how the environment promotes quality of life for residents.

References

ABC News. "Victims of Greed." *20/20,* (25 October 1991).

Adelman, Ronald, et al. "A Community-Oriented Geriatric Rehabilitation Unit in a Nursing Home." *Gerontologist* 27 (April 1987): 143–146.

American Health Care Association. *The Nursing Home Dilemma, Thinking About a Nursing Home?* and *Welcome to Our Nursing Home, A Family Guide.* Washington, D.C., 1994.

Bennett, C. *Nursing Home Life: What It Is and What It Could Be.* New York: Tiresias Press, 1980.

Bjorhus, J. "Nursing Homes Blasted in Report." *San Francisco Chronicle* (4 August 1994): A15.

Braus, P. "Groceries over Grandchildren." *American Demography,* (June 1994): 33.

Braus, Patricia. "When Mom Needs Help." *American Demographics* (March 1994): 41.

Cohen, Carl I., Hal Onserud, and Charlene Menaco. "Project Rescue: Serving the Homeless and Marginally Housed Elderly." *Gerontologist* 32:4 (1992): 467–471.

Crispell, D., and W. Frey. "American Maturity." *American Demographics* 15:3 (March 1993): 31–43.

Downey, Kirstin. "Senior Housing Losing Appeal, Poll Shows." *Santa Rosa Press Democrat* (6 May 1990).

Duffy, Joann Miller. "The Measurement of Service

Productivity and Related Contextual Factors in Long-Term Care Facilities." Unpublished doctoral dissertation. Austin, TX: The University of Texas, 1987.

Elias, C., and T. Invi. "When a House Is Not a Home: Exploring the Meaning of Shelter Among Chronically Homeless Older Men." *Gerontologist* 33:3 (June 1993): 396–402.

Estrada, L. "At the Dawn of Assisted Living Centers." *Washington Post* (9 May 1994): WB11.

Glasheen, L. "Mobile Homes." *Bulletin of the American Association of Retired Persons* (June 1994): 1–16.

Hinrichsen, Gregory. "The Impact of Age-Concentrated, Publicly-Assisted Housing on Older People's Social and Emotional Well-Being." *Journal of Gerontology* 40 (November 1985): 758–760.

Hogan, T., and D. Steinnes. "Comparing the Flights of Arizona Sunbirds vs. Minnesota Snowbirds." Paper presented at the Annual Meeting of the Gerontological Society in New Orleans, LA, November 1993a.

Hogan, T., and D. Steinnes. "Elderly Migration to the Sunbelt: Seasonal vs. Permanent." *Journal of Applied Gerontology* 12 (December 1993b): 246–260.

Kalymun, M. "Board and Care vs. Assisted Living." *Adult Residential Care Journal* 6:1 (Spring 1992): 35–44.

Keigher, S. *Housing Risks and Homelessness Among the Urban Elders.* New York: Haworth Press, 1991.

Kemper, P., and C. M. Murtaugh. "Lifetime Use of Nursing Home Care." *New England Journal of Medicine* 324:9 595–600.

Lazarovich, N. Michael. "Granny Flats in Canada." *Journal of Housing for the Elderly* 7:2 (1991): 31–40.

McCarthy, M. "Home of One's Own." *The Wall Street Journal* (4 December 1992): A1.

Neuman, E. "Golden Years without a Care." *Insight,* (Jan. 13, 1992), p. 14–16.

Ravo, N. "For Retirees, No Place Like Home; They Prefer to Remain Near Roots and Family." *New York Times* 141 (2 August 1992): R1.

Redfoot, D., and G. Gaberlavage. "Housing for Older Americans: Sustaining the Dream." *Generations Journal* (Summer/Fall 1991): 35–38.

Riley, M. and J. Riley, "Age Integration and the Lives of Older People." *Gerontologist,* Feb. 1994, p. 110–115.

Roberts, S. "Lesson in Aging: Penn South, a NORC." *New York Times* (9 December 1991): B3(L).

Sherrid, P. "It's Back to the Old Alma Mater." *U.S. News and World Report* 114: 23 (14 June 1993): 101–104.

Smyer, Michael. "Mental Health Services in Nursing Homes: Still Crazy After All These Years." Presidential Address for Division 20 of the American Psychological Association, Toronto, Canada, April 29, 1993.

Somers, A., and N. Spears, *The Continuing Care Retirement Community.* New York: Spring, 1992.

Strahan, G. W., and B. J. Burns. "Mental Illness in the Nursing Home." *U.S. Vital Statistics* 13:105 (1991).

Tinker, Anthea. "Granny Flats—The British Experience." *Journal of Housing for the Elderly* 7:2 (1991): 421–456.

"Tireless Warriors for the Elderly." *Santa Rosa Press Democrat* (23 December 1990): E1.

Wall Street Journal Gay Retirees Retirement Community, April 12, 1994, p. A1.

Further Readings

....

Enright, Robert B., Jr. *Perspectives in Social Gerontology.* Boston: Allyn and Bacon, 1994.

Gubrium, J. *Speaking of Life: Horizons of Meaning for Nursing Home Residents.* New York: Aldine De Gruyter, 1993.

Kidder, T. *Old Friends (Two Friends in a Nursing Home).* New York: Houghton Mifflin, 1993.

Savishinsky, J. *The Ends of Time: Life and Work in a Nursing Home.* New York: Bergin and Garvey, 1991.

10 Mental Health

CHAPTER OUTLINE

OLD IS NEWS

The Man Who Makes Bach Swing

■ KEN RINGLE

It is more than a little humbling for anyone on the downhill side of 30 to realize that Dave Brubeck, the man who gave jazz a college education, has been recording for more than 40 years. Had anyone been recording that long when Brubeck started out, he would have almost had to know Tom Edison. Yet what is almost as startling as the $3.95 price tags on those well-worn LPs from the 1950s is how fresh and dynamic the music of them sounds today.

Thousands of jazz groups have come and gone since "Jazz Goes to College," the Dave Brubeck Quartet's landmark 1953 Columbia album, rewrote the rules of American music even more profoundly than the Beatles' "Sgt. Pepper" would 14 years later. Few of those groups are more than a memory today, and none has had as great and enduring a cultural impact as Brubeck's.

Brubeck, on the other hand, is still playing, still writing, still trying new things. At age 73, unslowed by a cardiac triple bypass, he remains one of the rare and enduring jazz superstars, jetting off to European tours with a quartet that for many years has included his sons: the embodiment of musical (and generational) fusion long before people used that term.

Over the decades Brubeck has toyed tirelessly with rhythms, and seems to feel his greatest musical achievements lie in his experiments with tempos. His most influential album, he believes, was "Time Out" (1959), the first instrumental jazz album to sell a million copies, which he says "helped liberate jazz from the straightjacket of 4/4 time," and presaged his improvisations of such unimagined tempos as 7/4, 9/8 and even 13/4. Yet unlike those of more rarefied jazz musicians, his improvisations seldom lost sight of melody. And, as in "La Paloma Azul" from his 1967 Mexican album, "Bravo Brubeck," he could create something as lovely and lyrical as anything ever put on record.

"Time Signatures," a stunning 1993 four-CD retrospective includes stories and photos from Brubeck's long career.

Dave Brubeck chats with Harry Belafonte at the White House after receiving the National Medal of Arts from President Clinton.

—Continued

There are pictures and cuts of great black artists like Jimmie Rushing, Carmen McRae and the often difficult and always demanding Charlie Mingus recording with Brubeck; stories of soldout Brubeck concerts at black theaters like the Apollo in Harlem and the Howard in Washington.

A highlight of the booklet is a photo of Willie "The Lion" Smith with Brubeck at a joint appearance in Rotterdam in the 1960s, where a journalist asked Smith if it was true no white man could really play jazz. Gesturing at Brubeck, Smith replied: "I want you to meet my son."

Brubeck was, quite literally, raised as a cowboy, son of a rodeo roping champion (possibly part Indian) and a piano teacher. His fascination with tempos, he says, grew out of the changing rhythms of his horses' hooves.

Visually impaired from birth (he was born cross-eyed), he bluffed his way through college music courses on the strength of his astonishing ear, never really able to read the music. His success in the 1950s followed almost a decade of stubborn hand-to-mouth struggle against failure in which he not only perfected his craft but managed simultaneously to support a wife and five children on a jazzman's meager, uncertain pay, as well as recover from a near-fatal neck injury.

Brubeck's been married more than 51 years to his wife, Iola, whom he decided to wed 20 minutes into their first date in college. She was with him at the Kennedy Center. They were still having fun. ☼

AUTHORS NOTE: This article was written while Brubeck was performing at the Kennedy Center in January 1994.

SOURCE: © 1994 *The Washington Post* Reprinted with permission.

Social scientists are continuing to unravel the effects of aging on the mind. The fate of an elderly person was once considered to be senility—whatever that meant. No one was surprised if Grandpa forgot where he put his glasses, that cousin Herman was coming to visit, or even that he was married. No one became too alarmed if old Mrs. Jones down the street saw angels in the sky or was hiding in a cave because she thought the world was going to end in 6 months. The reasoning went: "This is what happens when people get old—their minds go. At the very least, they become set in their ways, stubborn, and cranky." Nonconformist, bizarre behavior was tolerated and rationalized: "What can you expect at her age? Old age must take its course. What can you do but accept?" These ideas about old age still persist.

Today, scientific evidence suggests that declining mental health is not a natural consequence of the aging process. The vast majority of those aged 65 and over are in good mental health. If they are not, specific causes other than the aging process itself usually can be pinpointed. This chapter will examine the psychology of aging and the most common mental health problems of older adults.

☼ The Psychology of Aging

In this chapter, we will discuss areas traditionally covered in the behavioral aspect of the psychology of aging. These are changes with age in perception, motor performance, intelligence, learning, memory, and personality. Gerontological psychologists also study changes in the brain and central nervous system. Many psychologists have backgrounds in physiology, biology, physics, math, or some combination thereof. Others are more interested in personality characteristics and social behavior and, thus, may have social psychology backgrounds.

In the psychology of aging, one must distinguish between **age-related changes** and **biologically caused changes**. For example, a scientist may find a positive correlation between age and depression—the older the age group, the higher the incidence of depression. In this case, depression is an age-related phenomenon. Once this statistic is staring the scientist in the face, the scientist must interpret it. Can the scientist say that the biological aging process causes depression? Certainly not without further investigation. What would be some possible causes of the correlation? Are society's values the cause? Are there cumulative stresses that some persons resist in their younger years but to which they finally succumb in old age? How do events such as retirement, poor health, or the death of a spouse affect aging? There may be other possible causes for the correlation.

The important thing to remember is that some psychological states that initially appear to be caused by the biological aging process are, upon closer examination, really related to age, in which case the scientist must look further for the cause of the correlation. For example, studies of the incidence of depression in the United States show some surprising and contradictory results. Several studies found the highest rates of depression in young adults and elders, but not in middle-aged groups. In contrast, in three other studies the oldest group showed a lower rate of depression than all younger groups, when variables such as income, socioeconomic status, and gender were held constant. These studies suggest that the initial findings of increased depression are a consequence of the social changes that accompany aging, rather than due to the biological aging process itself (Bliwise et al., 1987). A social scientist must go beyond assumptions; preconceived notions should undergo objective testing.

☼ Cognitive Processes

Cognition is awareness of the world around us, how we absorb stimuli and information, and how we make sense of it. Did you see the traffic accident? Did you hear the crash? What happened? Do you know who was at fault based on what you saw? What was your response? Did you think to call the police or 911? How quickly did you react? Cognitive processes involve the use of our senses, our arousal, attention, information processing, reaction time, and motor performance. Gerontologists want to know whether older people see and hear things differently, whether their attention span or speed changes, or whether their information processing is altered in any way by their aging.

Psychologists have compared our brains to computers. Information enters our brain, is coded, and then is stored at various levels. If our brains are working efficiently, we can retrieve information when we need it. This section deals with cognitive functioning. First, the basic senses, sensory memory, and steps of information processing are described; second, studies of intelligence are reported; and, third, learning and longer-term memory are analyzed.

BASIC COGNITIVE FUNCTIONS

Information processing in the brain is a complicated matter. Many factors are involved, such as genetics, overall health, mood, motivation, and alertness.

Psychologists are attempting to study these factors along with the factor of aging in order to understand how the mind works.

The Senses

The five senses (vision, touch, hearing, smell, and taste), which relay environmental information to the brain, generally lose their sharpness with age (Plude, 1987). Some very old people, however, experience no sensory declines. The social and psychological consequences of sensory declines can be enormous. For a person who "lives to eat," the loss of smell and taste could mean the end of the person's will to live. The five senses decline in different degrees for older individuals. The old-old, that is, those over age 75, are more likely to experience noticeable declines than are the young-old, those between 65 and 75 years of age.

Older persons vary in how they deal with sensory loss. Some persons can compensate for losses in one area by stressing enjoyment from another. For example, a person losing vision might become an avid fan of symphony music. Compensation by habit and routine is probably even more frequent. Though their adaptability may vary, most older people can compensate very well for minor sensory losses. For example, vision loss can be compensated by following the same paths through the house or always placing objects in the same places.

Those who care for the elderly could easily respond inappropriately to such sensory decline: Why fix a nice meal for one who cannot taste it, or why take a vision-impaired elder outside? Rather than encouraging withdrawal, sensory decline should challenge caretakers to find ways of enhancing life for those who have suffered losses. Perhaps the person might like spicy Mexican food, or stronger hugs, or a windy day, or a warm fire in the fireplace. Sensory decline may call for stronger responses on the part of the caretakers, rather than weaker ones.

Sensory Memory

Each memory starts as a sensory stimulus. You can remember certain aspects of things you see and hear for only a fraction of a second. This initial short-term sensory experience is called a **sensory memory**. Sensory memory takes in large amounts of information so rapidly that most of it gets lost. Do you recall what is on a one-dollar bill or a dime? Could you draw the details? Much information that passes through sensory memory is never processed to a storage place in the brain because we cannot pay attention to everything hitting our senses. Few researchers have studied sensory memory, but initial studies show that the amount of visual information that one can handle at a time seems to decline with age.

Attention

Paying attention is an important part of information processing. Because of the many stimuli bombarding us, we have to be selective in what we attend to (**selective attention**). If we pay attention to a stimuli, then the experience goes from our sensory memory and is stored in our working memory. Compared to sensory memory, working memory can handle a very small amount of input. We vary in the capacity of information that can get to our working memory at any one point in time. Very old people have a smaller capacity to absorb stimuli into working memory and thus to maintain concentration over a long period of time.

Studies of **divided attention** (doing two things at once such as watching television and reading) show that when divided-attention tasks are easy, age differences are typically absent. But when the tasks become more complicated, age differences emerge. Attention studies show that older people are more distractible and cannot disregard the clutter of irrelevant information. Age-related differences in vigilance also exist. Older adults tend to have lower physiological arousal (Plude, 1994), which lowers their alertness. Vigilance does not appear to be age related unless the task is sustained over an extended period of time, when, beyond age 60, fatigue can result in notable performance loss.

Perception

The process of evaluating the sensory information carried to the brain is called **perception**. Individuals may perceive the same stimuli differently; further, the same person may react differently at different times. The psychologist is interested in what is perceived, why it is perceived in a given fashion, and the perceptual variations that may occur. Mood, activities, and personality may all influence perception.

Sensory decline affects perception significantly. Given sensory decline, evaluating a stimulus is more labored and time consuming. Perceptual differences among age groups are frequently reported, but the research does not explain their cause. The differences may be caused by biological changes, or they may be age related. Social isolation also tends to affect perception; therefore, isolation, not aging per se, may cause perceptual changes.

Psychomotor Speed

A person first experiences the environment through the five senses; second, a person perceives what is happening; and third, a person may react. A physical reaction to stimuli is called motor performance. Motor performance may be simple, that is, a reaction requiring very little decision making or skill. Pressing a button to turn on the television and turning off a light switch are simple motor skills. Some motor performance, such as dancing, riding a bike, playing tennis, or driving a car is more complex.

Very old drivers, for example, may be affected by losses in vision and hearing. They do not adapt as well to dark and are more affected by glare. Studies show that they take longer to read road signs. However, when a picture for "men working" or "divided highway" sign accompanies the words, the age difference in reading the sign disappears (Cavanaugh, 1993). Researchers suggest designing cars with older adults in mind: headlights with less glare, well-lit instrument panels, easy entry, and so on. They recommend large letters on signs with pictures if possible. Training programs for those with sensory declines are also advised.

Figure 10.1 reflects the high rate of automobile accidents for those 75 and over, and Table 10.1 indicates some of the reasons the rate is so high.

One aspect of motor performance is reaction time—the length of time between the stimulus and the response, directly related to psychomotor speed. Studies show that reaction time increases with age, at about age 26 for some tasks and not until the seventies for other tasks. The general slowing of behavior with age is one of the most reliable and well documented age-related changes. This includes slowed **psychomotor speed** and the resultant lengthened reaction time. The more complex the task, the greater the difference in reaction time by age, generally speaking. However, individuals can differ

Figure 10.1

Crash Involvements per Million Vehicular Miles of Travel, by Age

SOURCE: Schick, F. and Schick, R. *Statistical Handbook of Aging Americans.* Phoenix, AZ: Onyx Press, p. 106, Table B6–7.

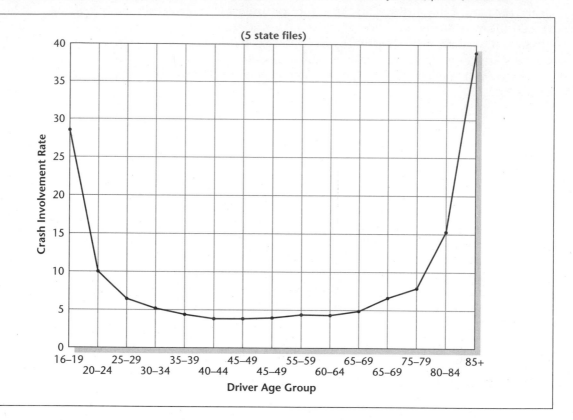

substantially; for example, an individual 70-year-old might respond more quickly than a 30-year-old.

The many possible variables involved in the age-related slowing of information processing continue to be formulated (see Table 10.2). A noted researcher in this area of study has introduced two terms to categorize the variables affecting cognition:

1. **Cognitive mechanics**—the hardware of the mind—reflect the neurophysiological architecture of the brain. It involves the speed and accuracy of elementary processing of sensory information.

2. **Cognitive pragmatics**—the software of the mind—reflect the knowledge and information of one's culture. It involves reading, writing, education, professional skills, and life experiences that help us master or cope with life. (Baltes, 1993).

The first term represents the genetic–biological influence and the second represents the cultural–social influence. In Table 10.1 the biological factors are separated from the cultural–social factors. The cultural–social factors tend to be more reversible than the genetic–biological ones.

Many of these variables in Table 10.1 do not accompany aging universally. The pathologies mentioned (e.g., high blood pressure) do not go hand-in-hand with aging. Neither does lessened activity. Aerobic exercise and other

Table 10.1

Variables Hypothesized to Be Related to the Slowing of Information Processing in Old Age

Genetic–Biological Factors

- Changes in the acuteness of the senses—vision and hearing, for example.
- Changes in physiological arousal to stimuli.
- Changes in ability to be attentive.
- Changes in perceptual ability.
- Changes in motor capacity, such as increased stiffness of joints and muscles and reduced muscle strength.
- Lower levels of physical activity.
- Changes in blood flow to the brain leading to neural malnutrition.
- Changes in the central nervous ystem.
- Changes in cortical levels of the brain.
- Gradual loss of brain mass.
- Neural/metabolic changes.
- Declines in physical health, such as increased blood pressure and cerebrovascular or cardiac disorders.

Cultural–Social Factors

- Changes in self-esteem and self-confidence.
- Lower levels of mental activity.
- Lessened familiarity and experience with the task.
- Lifestyle characteristics, such as divorce, lengthy marriage to a non-intellectual partner, lack of travel, and lack of stimulating environments.
- Lack of recent educational activities and lack of recent test-taking skills.
- Self-reported poor health.
- Financial worries.
- Fear of tests or other debilitating anxieties.
- Lack of motivation.

forms of physical activity have been shown to increase blood flow and increase speed of reaction. Activities such as tennis and dancing are helpful. Physically fit older people have shorter reaction times than less fit young adults (Spirduso and MacRae, 1990). Practice at a task can compensate for slowness. Many a grandchild has been amazed, for example, at the speed with which a grandparent can peel a potato or whittle a wooden object.

Table 10.2

Self-Reported Driving Difficulties of Older and Younger Drivers

Reported Difficulty	Percentage by Driver's Age (N = 446)	
	55+	35–44
Reading traffic signs	27	12
Seeing while driving at night	40	32
Turning head while backing	23	5
Reading instrument panel	9	3
Reaching seat belt	22	10
Merging and exiting in high-speed traffic	32	15

SOURCE: Schick, F. and Schick, R. *Statistical Handbook of Aging Americans*. Phoenix, AZ: Onyx Press, 1994, p. 106, Table B6–6.

The thinking of psychologists now is that the slower reactions of older people have more to do with changes in the mental processes of interpretation and decision rather than at the initial level of sensory input (Thomas, 1992). In other words, the course of slowing has a lot to do with the brain and central nervous system. Again, we must mention that not every older individual experiences a slow down in reaction. It is a pattern of aging that has many exceptions. The implications of this slowing for the everyday life of the older person are various. Experience and familiarity are great levelers—giving the older person an edge on the job or at various tasks at home. Very old people may need more time to get a job done, and they may need to be more cautious to avoid accidents. A speedy reaction is needed to avoid falling objects, to drive a car safely, to escape a fire, to get across a busy street, or to play a good game of ball. Many older adults would benefit from education or retraining to minimize the consequences of reduced cognitive efficiency. Environmental modifications may be in order—for example, stronger lighting, brighter colors, grab bars, hand railings, door handles as opposed to knobs, louder telephone ring, larger sturdier step stools. And people should not be so ready to assume that if an individual cannot think quickly, he or she cannot think well. That is a form of ageism.

INTELLIGENCE

As we compare the learning abilities of babies, elementary students, college students, or people in general, we find that within each group, some are better able to learn than others. **Intelligence** is an abstract term used to describe differences in the "sharpness" of minds. Although tests have been devised to measure one's intelligence quotient (IQ), the validity of such tests has been debated for years. Two major questions arise. Is there any such thing as intelligence? Do IQ tests really measure intelligence? The tests actually measure a number of specific intellectual abilities rather than a general concept. Twenty-five **primary mental abilities** have been established, but measuring all twenty-five in the same study is difficult. Researchers typically concentrate on a subset of five: number, word fluency, verbal meaning, inductive reasoning, and space. Researchers have also developed tests of six or so secondary mental abilities—skills composed of several primary abilities. Most research focuses on two secondary mutual abilities: fluid and crystallized intelligence (Cavanaugh, 1993, 220–221). IQ tests can be, to some extent, culturally biased by the words, phrases, and questions they employ. Nevertheless, IQ tests remain an important tool for measuring differences among individuals.

Intelligence is most often measured by a standardized test with many multiple-choice items on vocabulary, reasoning, and the ordering of numbers and spaces. Using such a test represents the **psychometric approach** in contrast to other tests that examine thought processes—the quality and depth of thinking and the ability to solve complex problems (the **cognitive process** approach). The most widely used psychometric test of intelligence for older adults is the Wechsler Adult Intelligence Scale (WAIS), developed in the 1950s. This test compensates for increasing age. The test norms assume declining speed with age; an older adult can perform worse than a younger adult and still have the same IQ! Critics point to the fact that this test emphasizes skills learned in school and not skills of everyday life. For this reason, all things being equal, the test favors the younger adult. This test has been revised (WAIS-R) and is used widely in clinical settings. Another IQ test, the Primary Mental Abilities Test (PMA) has often been used to examine adult intellectual development. The WAIS test measures a "verbal intelligence" aspect that involves comprehension, arithmetic, similarities, vocabulary, and the ability to recall digits; and a "performance intelligence" aspect that involves completion, block design, and assembly of objects. On the performance scale, speed is important. Bonus points are awarded for rapid solutions.

Both the WAIS-R and the PMA include tasks that evaluate fluid and crystallized intelligence. **Crystallized intelligence** is a measure of knowledge you have acquired through experience and education. Vocabulary tests are a clear example. **Fluid intelligence** refers to innate ability—the information-processing skills described in the previous section. Each of these types of intelligence taps a cluster of primary abilities. No standardization test measures one alone, although a given test can emphasize either crystallized or fluid intelligence.

We once assumed that a decline in intelligence with age was to be expected. Scientists are now questioning this assumption. Longitudinal studies have found that some IQ components such as verbal skills remain stable with time and some can even increase with age. Schaie (1990) reports that virtually no individuals show deterioration on all mental abilities, even in their eighties. At age 60, 75 percent of subjects maintained their level of functioning on at least 80 percent of the mental abilities tested (as compared to seven years prior). More than 50 percent of those aged 80 had maintained 80 percent of their mental abilities over the seven-year period.

Fluid intelligence does appear to decline some with age, whereas crystallized intelligence does not (see Figure 10.2). Similarly, the verbal scores of the WAIS show no declines with age, whereas the performance scores do decline with age. The high verbal score and declining performance score of older adults is so consistently found that it is called the "classic aging pattern" (Thomas, 1992). The drop in fluid intelligence indicates a decline in the ability to process information and complete tasks in an efficient manner. There are many theories to account for this drop: Basically, all the items presented in Table 10.1 have been postulated to account for declines in performance, which includes something as complex as changes in neurophysiological processes and something as simple as lack of practice or fear of tests.

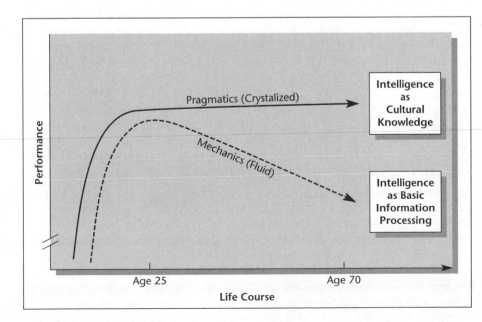

Figure 10.2

Cognitive Change with Age

SOURCE: P. Baltes, "The Aging Mind," *Gerontologist* 33:5 (October 1993): 580–594.

To understand fully what happens to intelligence with age, we need to know exactly what primary mental abilities decline with age and why. We need to know at what age the onset of decline happens and the rate of decline. We need to know whether such changes are inevitable and whether they can be reversed. And we need to account for individual differences. Schaie (1990) found that it is not until people reach their seventies that declines in intelligence take on significance. Speed of response is the major decline. There is mounting evidence that perceptual speed may be the most age-sensitive mental ability (Stokes, 1992). Older people are as proficient as ever when it comes to situations that demand past experience or knowledge—given that they have enough time.

Though nonlongitudinal cross-sectional "one-shot" studies of different age groups often find that older people have lower IQs than younger people, such studies may not acknowledge that young adults may have benefitted from upper-level schooling. Many of the elderly studied in the 1950s and 1960s had not attended either high school or college. Some had had no formal schooling at all. Thus, cross-sectional studies that infer a decline in IQ with age are suspect. Test makers should distinguish between actual IQ (the quotient the test actually measures) and potential IQ for the young as well as for the old.

We emphasize that intelligence tests must be used with caution. IQ tests measure specific skills to generalize about an all-inclusive concept of intelligence. Their results may be biased, and scientists must continue to investigate why, how, and in what direction such instruments are biased. The evidence today supports the finding of little decline with age in skills that one acquires through education, enculturation, personal experience. We do not really know what happens to IQ as one approaches extreme old age, say after age 85. Although researchers believe that IQ begins to decline at some point in very old age, they have yet to determine the typical course it follows.

A problem with cross-sectional studies for the future is that the new generation of young students today are not doing as well on standardized tests in their general education. If this translates into lower scores on IQ tests, then it appears that IQ increases with age because older generations today do better at test taking, and it is not necessarily true that IQ increases with age. To avoid the problems in cross-sectional research, longitudinal studies appear desirable. A few words of caution, about longitudinal studies: Sample size tends to be small; repeat presentation of material, which brings about improved performance, can produce a learning effect; and attrition of the less healthy and less able subjects occurs. In one study only one-sixth of the sample was left after 7 years (Savage et al., 1973). One must be aware of the research methodology employed and recognize that any one study is bound to have some inadequacies in addressing issues of age-related changes.

A new area of intelligence study is practical problem solving. Researchers have done studies using tests such as the Everyday Problem Solving Inventory (Denney and Palmer, 1987) to measure ability to solve problems such as a grease fire breaking out on top of the stove. When the problems are familiar to older people, they do extremely well on these tests, but not necessarily better than middle-aged adults. Once again, let it be said that intelligence comes in various forms. Also, retraining is becoming a major focus of study. The decline in primary abilities in old age can be slowed or even reversed in many cases. Future studies will clarify which abilities can be maintained or improved and the circumstances under which it is possible (Stokes, 1992).

Further research is needed to clarify the relationship between age and intelligence. A theory of terminal decline or **"terminal drop"** has been proposed by a number of gerontologists. According to this theory, a decrease in cognitive functioning is related to the individual's distance from death rather than to his or her chronological age. "Critical loss" in cognitive functioning is supposedly experienced up to two years before death. The theory is controversial and has not been fully substantiated by research.

LEARNING AND MEMORY

Learning and memory, important components of mental functioning, are separate yet interrelated processes.

Learning

Learning is the process of acquiring knowledge or understanding. For purposes of psychological research, scientists speak of learning in terms of cognitive processes, which are intellectual or mental. As in studies of intelligence quotients, learning is measured by tests of performance, particularly verbal and psychomotor performance. Again, the same sort of question surfaces: Do such tests really reflect learning?

Stimulating conversation keeps the mind active, which in turn, enhances learning and memory

Let us consider two general questions related to age: Do learning skills change with age, and how do older people's skills compare with younger people's? The answers to these questions depend on the skills being learned and the conditions under which they are being learned. Up until 1960, and even later, members of the scientific community generally assumed that learning declined with age.

Many factors affect learning abilities. Pacing (the rate and speed required for learning) is an important factor. Older adults learn better with a slower pace; and they perform best with self-pacing. They also do better with a lengthened time to respond. Another factor is anxiety. Some studies suggest that older adults are more uncomfortable with the testing situation and therefore experience increased anxiety. The meaningfulness of the material makes a difference, too. Older people do better when nonsensical or abstract syllables and words are replaced with actual, concrete words. They tend to be more interested if the material makes sense to them. Further, they are more susceptible to distraction. Motivation and physical health are contributing factors as well. Here again the factors in Table 10.1 may inhibit learning. The finding that younger adults are better learners than older adults should be viewed cautiously. Under certain conditions, older people can learn as well as or better than younger people.

Memory

Memory varies enormously among individuals of all ages; and types of memory vary greatly in the same person. An interesting cross-sectional study of a population between age 50 and 96 showed slight and progressive deterioration in memory efficiency as people grow older (Plude and Rabbitt, 1988). That is a general conclusion of many studies.

Researchers have distinguished among four levels of memory. They are diagrammed in Figure 10.3 and are as follows:

1. *Sensory memory.* Sensory memory is the initial level at which all sensory information is registered but not stored. It is fleeting, lasting less than a second, unless deliberate attention is paid to the information and it is transferred to primary memory (see previous section on Basic Cognitive Functions). Countless numbers of stimuli bombard us every fraction of a second in our waking hours.

Figure 10.3

Levels of Memory

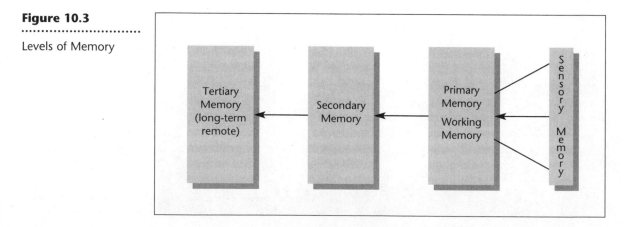

2. *Primary and working memory.* Primary memory is our current consciousness. We have only a small capacity to deal with what is being paid attention to at the moment. It may be forgotten rather quickly—for example, a phone number or joke; or it may be transformed for longer storage. The processing of our current sensate information is our working memory.

3. *Secondary memory.* Secondary memory, once called recent memory, refers to remembering the details of everyday life—friends' telephone messages, directions to the new shopping mall, the movie you saw last week, what you studied for the exam, what you need to do at work, and so on. It is the major basis for the research on memory. Hundreds and hundreds of studies are reported in this area.

4. *Tertiary memory.* Tertiary memory is long-term memory, sometimes called remote memory. It is the stored facts and words, learned years ago—the past life experiences such as weddings, births, deaths, and episodes from childhood. Tertiary memory is studied much less often than secondary memory.

The findings on sensory memory are contained in a previous section of this chapter, Basic Cognitive Functions. The findings on the other levels of memory follow.

Primary Memory and Working Memory **Primary memory** shows little change with age. Once information is stored in primary memory, people of all ages seem equal in being able to recall it. But age differences are found in **working memory**—the processing of sensory stimuli to give it meaning and get it transferred to longer-term storage. If information does not get to storage, it cannot be recalled. Two examples of using working memory are (1) remembering a phone number given to you orally long enough to dial the number a few seconds later, or (2) unscrambling letters of a word in your head. One researcher believes that working memory is vital to understanding declines in the cognitive functioning of older adults. He believes a major portion of the decline is due to decreased speed of working memory to process information (Salthouse, 1991). Research on working memory is relatively new but holds great promise in solving some of the mysteries of the mind.

Secondary Memory Research indicates that **secondary memory** is another major source of age-related decline. Younger adults are superior on tests of secondary memory, which is the major memory function in everyday life. The processing involved is deeper than primary memory, enabling recall to take place over a longer period of time. If the processing is too shallow, a person will not be able to recall the information a year, month, or even a day later.

Numerous kinds of memory tasks have been developed to study secondary memory. For example, in "free recall," people are given 20 words and asked to recall as many as they can in any order they wish. The results from hundreds of studies are that younger people do better on this task. There is great variation with the type of task and pace involved. In tests of "recognition," people are given a list of 20 words to look at, and then given a list with those 20 words plus 40 new words. They are then asked which are old and which are new. Older people do as well as but not better than young people on this test. On some memory tests, such as those that require the subject to recall facts out of context, older persons do worse than middle-aged persons.

Starting somewhere in middle age, many persons suffer from "tip-of-the-tongue" syndrome, which places them on the verge of recalling a name, date, or event and unable to do it. Later, when they are not trying to remember, they will recall the information. One finding generally agreed upon is that, in old age, interference hinders secondary memory. For example, if a neighbor rings the doorbell while an older person is reading the paper, he or she may forget what was just read. Studies suggest that eliminating distractions could optimize short-term memory for the older person. Still some older people have excellent memories. Steven Powelson, in his seventies, is capable of reciting Homer's *Iliad* by memory—24 books and 15,693 lines, a recitation that would take about 18 hours. He undertook the memorization to keep his mind active (Furst, 1988).

Future studies of secondary memory should involve more "naturalistic" topics, that is, more real-life topics and situations. Older people do not usually have to engage in free recall because they have external cues, such as date books or notes of reminder on the refrigerator. A psychometric test situation may not have "ecological validity" in a real-life setting. Older people may do better in real-life situations than the tests indicate. This matter needs further exploration (Stokes, 1992).

Where the Black Begins

D. L. Emblen

A teacher, graying locks, or few, above old brows,
remains on his feet, as always,
to keep the students on their toes,
forgets the title of the book he talks about.
He pauses, smiles at the waiting toe-dancers,
at the hesitant ring-master, at falling leaves
outside the window where late the sweet birds sang.
He leaves the room.

Later, in his crowded office,
he thinks briefly of senility
(doesn't think much of it);
remembers with utter clarity a cat
he has or used to have. Sveä is her name,
and he recalls precisely where the orange stops
across that owlish face
and where the black begins.

Tertiary Memory   Information is stored for years in **tertiary memory**. The study of this memory has some problems: if the person constantly recalls the old days, say, going to college, is it still tertiary memory compared with someone who has not thought about his or her college days for years? Some people may retrieve certain events of the past often, whereas others never do. Another problem is knowing the accuracy of long-term memories. Re-searchers often have no way to validate the memories.

One method of study is to ask people of all ages about a historic event—such as a major earthquake, a space disaster (such as the Challenger in 1986), a past presidential election, or a popular television show. Typically, no age differences exist in these studies. Some autobiographical information can be verified, naming high-school classmates, for example. Again, no age differences appear in tertiary memory. Memory for skills does not vanish with age: musicians can still perform with power, and grand masters can still play strong chess games. Teritary memory is related to crystallized intelligence, which also does not decline with age.

Exercising the mind is important. Learning and recalling what is learned (in other words, keeping the mind active and stimulated) is a good way to preserve memory. Learning and memory are related; memory is the ability to retain what is learned. The more one learns, as a general rule, the more one can remember. Reading books, talking to friends, and going out are fun ways to exercise the mind. People adapt differently to recent memory loss. Some might compensate very well by carrying a notepad to jog the memory—keeping a written record of phone numbers, plans, and appointments. Another person might give in too easily and permit what he or she perceives as "senility" to become a self-fulfilling prophecy. As is so often the case, positive attitudes and self-evaluations can lead to constructive, corrective actions.

According to memory expert Tony Busan (1991), memory may decline with age but only if it is not used. If used, memory will be maintained or even improved throughout one's lifetime. Busan advocates the use of mnemonics, that is, memory techniques to improve memory. One technique is to use a vivid imagination, calling forth wild, colorful, and exaggerated images, even sexual ones, and associating them with important dates or items on a shopping list. A second technique is to use a linking system with a special list of key words to which all other items are linked.

Studies of memory view the person as a machine that acquires, processes, stores, and retrieves information. Using this image, older adults generally show a pattern of decline in the speed and efficiency with which they can process, store, and recall information. If one changes the image to exclude speed and include philosophy of life and the ability to integrate a lifetime of experiences, the older person makes gains with age. There may be a trade-off: losing some details but gaining the broader outlook. This has been referred to as the race between the bit and the bite, with older adults giving up the bit for the bite. We have just begun to explore the potential of the aging mind. Using our increased cultural–social knowledge, we will be able to "outwit" the biological limitations and deficits of old age (Baltes, 1993).

☼ Psychopathology and the Myth of Senility

Psychopathology is the study of psychological disease or, in other words, of mental disorders. Some mental disorders have a physical cause; others seem to be entirely emotional in nature. In still others, the physical and emotional aspects seem intertwined. A specific diagnosis, though difficult, is critical in the treatment of patients at any age.

Unfortunately, the term **senility** has been used as a catchall term for any mental disorder of the elderly. Any symptoms of confusion, anxiety, memory loss, or disorientation may too readily receive this label. Given the complexity of mental health in the elderly, senility is not a useful term. In some cases, for example, persons diagnosed as senile actually suffer from acute thyroid deficiencies. Thyroid hormone treatment eliminates the "senility." In other cases, the "senile" patient may be suffering from anorexia or emotional problems that antidepressant medication can alleviate.

Senility is not an inevitable consequence of growing old, and it is not a disease. It is an overly generalized term used to label the inexplicable mental health problems of older persons. It masks both the possibility of multiple causes of certain mental disorders and the fact that treatment for them may be available.

A danger exists when doctors and other health-care professionals accept the stereotype that the elderly become senile as a result of the aging process. Both families and medical personnel have a tendency to use suspected senility as the basis for ignoring an older person's complaints, rather than attempting to diagnose the problem thoroughly. The symptoms of "senility" have many causes. Older patients can show confusion and disorientation as a result of infection, pneumonia, heart failure, heart attack, electrolyte imbalance, anemia, or dehydration, to name only a few causes. Furthermore, older people tend to react more pronouncedly to drugs than do their younger counterparts. Depression may also be a reason for pseudo-senility. Most mental illnesses can be more precisely described—and thereby treated—than the label "senile" suggests.

☼ Functional Disorders

A reference book by the American Psychiatric Association (1994), designed to improve the diagnosis of psychiatric disorders is the *Diagnostic and Statistical Manual of Mental Disorders* (4th ed.), called *DSM-IV* for short. Psychologists use the term **functional disorder** to denote emotional problems of psychological, rather than physical, origin that interfere with daily functioning. Such disorders are more serious than the emotional problems (such as those based on widowhood or other loss) previously described. To differentiate among functional disorders, psychologists use the following terms: *anxiety disorders, depressive disorders, personality disorders, affective disorders*, and *schizophrenia*.

Anxiety Disorders

Persons with **anxiety disorders** tend to be anxious, hysterical, rigid, or insecure personality types. There are numerous types of anxiety disorders.

Generalized Anxiety Disorder When a person becomes so anxious that fears and dreads of things or events begin to impair his or her ability to function, a **generalized anxiety disorder** is present, exaggerating any real danger. An older person may fear being robbed or mugged. Consequently, he or she may not leave home; the person may get dozens of locks and constantly check them. Therapy would help this person face the threat—if actual—rationally and realistically. Necessary precautions should be taken, but the person should still get out and enjoy life.

Obsessive-Compulsive Disorder A person obsessed with one act, such as washing hands, walking back and forth across a room, looking for something, or touching something, exhibits **obsessive-compulsive disorder**. Persons who continually wash their hands may think they are dirty when they are

Most older individuals have good mental health.

not. The "dirt" may be internal—for example, repressed feelings of guilt that need to be resolved.

Phobia   A **phobia** is a fear that displaces fears that a person cannot face. Claustrophobia, the fear of being closed in, may, for example, mask a more potent fear, such as fear of death. Numerous kinds of phobias can manifest numerous fears.

Depressive Disorders

The primary mental disorder suffered by the elderly is **depressive disorder**. A depressed person feels sad, has low self-esteem, is lethargic, and believes that life is confusing, hopeless, or bereft of meaning. Physical symptoms may be insomnia or drowsiness, sharp increase or decrease in appetite, self-neglect, decreased interest in sex, or the onset of constipation. Depression can be triggered by the deaths of family members, the loss of memory, or other major disappointments. The person may or may not have had bouts of depression throughout his or her life. Surveys indicate that most persons over age 65 suffering from depression are not receiving any formal psychiatric treatment.

Many individuals, including older ones, frequently suffer from clinical depression independent of any apparent reason. Usually this condition can be treated, but first it has to be recognized. Roughly 15 percent of elders are depressed, and 2 to 3 percent are severely depressed. More than three-quarters respond well to treatment. New anti-depressants have proven to be effective for adults of all ages.

Hypochondria   A hypochondriac is someone who is overly concerned about his or her health. The person generally has bodily complaints for which no physical cause exists; he or she may be depressed, fear physical deterioration, need attention, want to punish "sickness" role. Although the complaints may be real, the appropriate treatment involves dealing with the underlying emotional problem.

Personality Disorders

Another category of functional disorders is **personality disorders.** People who have developed extremely rigid styles of coping that make adaptive behavior difficult or impossible fall into this category. Such a person typically had held long-standing, maladaptive, and inflexible ways of relating to stress and the environment throughout adulthood. We can describe a number of personality types that lend themselves to disorders.

The *paranoid* personality is extremely suspicious and mistrustful, preoccupied with being alert to danger. A person with this personality tends to be stubborn, hostile, and defensive.

The *introverted* personality tends to be a solitary person who lacks the capacity for warm, close social relationships. Situations that call for high levels of social contact are especially stressful for the introverted individual.

The *antisocial* personality is characterized by a basically unsocialized behavior pattern that may conflict with society. Such people have difficulty with social situations that require cooperation and self-sacrifice.

These personality types and others involve behavior from childhood or adolescence that has become fixed and inflexible; for each, certain situations cause stress and unhappiness.

Affective Disorders

Affective disorders are sometimes called "mood disorders" because depression and mood swings are typical. *DSM-IV* uses the term *bipolar disorder* to describe behavior that includes both a depressed phase, of sadness and slowed activity, and a manic phase, characterized by high levels of excitement and activity. An individual generally first manifests this type of disorder in his or her twenties and thirties. *Depression*, without the manic phase, is more common. Depression is most severe as an affective disorder; as an anxiety disorder, it is moderate. Some event—great disappointment, for example—sets it off. For the older person, depression might follow the loss of a spouse or the onset of a terminal illness. In nonclinical depression, sad feelings are normally appropriate for the situation; normally, the feelings will eventually wane. An inappropriate duration of depression and intense, continued sadness mark clinical depression.

Schizophrenia

Schizophrenia, another category of functional disorder, is more complicated, severe, and incapacitating than any of the disorders previously described. Typically suffering serious disturbances in thinking and behavior, schizophrenics are often unable to communicate coherently with others. Their language seems to be a means of self-expression rather than communication, and their talk is filled with irrelevancies. Feelings have no relation to verbal expression: fearful topics may be discussed with smiles; a bland topic may incite rage. Schizophrenia is characterized by an impaired contact with reality, at least during the disorder's active phases, that often takes the form of hallucinations or delusions. Late-life onset of schizophrenia is fairly rare; typically, the sufferer has evidenced the disorder in earlier years. Studies of elderly schizophrenics show that improvement or remission is sometimes possible, even after many years of illness.

☼ Organic Mental Disorders

Organic disorders arise from a physical origin that impairs mental functioning. Studies indicate that about 11 percent of older adults have mild disorders of this type (Hinrichsen, 1990, 77), and geriatricians estimate that 6 percent of Americans over 65 have severe intellectual impairment based on physical causes. This rises to 20 percent for those over age 80 (Cohen, 1990); some estimate as high as 50 percent. A general estimate is that more than half of elders in institutions (mental hospitals, nursing homes, or residential care facilities) suffer from organic mental disorders, either acute or chronic.

An acute disorder is short-term and reversible. An infection, heart condition, drug reaction, liver condition, or malnutrition may cause an acute disorder. Anything that interferes with the nourishment of the brain—the supply of oxygen or food by the bloodstream—can produce an acute disorder. If not treated promptly, it may become chronic.

Chronic organic disorders are brain disorders with a physical cause for which no cure is known. Thus, such disorders characterize an irreversible, chronic, and progressive deterioration of the brain. One should not assume, however, that these disorders go hand-in-hand with old age; they do not. Organic brain disease is so debilitating for the minority who suffer it that we should direct our efforts to finding cures, rather than merely fostering acceptance. Of those with chronic brain disorders, 50 to 60 percent are living at home rather than in institutions and are being cared for by relatives and neighbors. More geriatric services would be helpful to all concerned.

The two manifestations of organic brain disorders are delirium and dementia, which are general terms for two syndromes or symptoms of organic brain disorders. Delirium is characterized by a lack of awareness about oneself and the surroundings, hallucinations, delusions, and disorientation. Caused by the atrophy and degeneration of brain cells, **dementia** was once labeled as senility and was thought to accompany normal aging. Now no longer "normal," dementia syndromes can result from many disorders, through, for some cases, causes are still unknown. More than ten forms of dementia have been identified. For example, years of substance abuse, especially alcohol, can lead to dementia. However, the largest contributor by far is Alzheimer's disease.

In the early stages of dementia, emotional responses to ordinary daily affairs, previously handled without difficulty, may be extreme to inappropriate. Memory, judgment, social functioning, and emotional control is impaired. Problems become more difficult to solve, and decisions become harder to make. One may lose interest in life and become apathetic or irritable. Further declines come as one has trouble receiving, retaining, and recalling new information. A newly acquired fact may be forgotten in minutes: a person may forget, for example, what he or she saw on a television program minutes after the program ends. As time passes, progressive disorganization of personality follows, accompanied by disorientation with respect to time, situation, and place. Some patients can no longer recognize even family, friends, and neighbors. An estimated 10 to 20 percent of dementias and deliriums are reversible (Elias et al., 1990). They have a specific, treatable cause and are acute, not chronic, brain disorders.

Alzheimer's Disease

The most common form of chronic organic brain disease, accounting for 70 percent of all such disease, is **Alzheimer's disease**. It affects 4 million middle-aged and older persons in the United States, about 100,000 die every year. Ex-president Ronald Reagan at age 83 announced that he was in the early stages of Alzheimer's disease. The results of a major study found that 10 percent of those 65 and older, and nearly half of those 85 and older, were suffering from "probable" Alzheimer's disease (Gelman et al., 1989). Named after the German neurologist Alois Alzheimer, who, in 1902, diagnosed the condition in a 51-year-old woman, the disease was thought to be rare and was relatively unknown as late as the 1970s. In the 1980s, it emerged as the fourth leading cause of death among adults. As a result of this disease, the brain gradually atrophies, shrinking in both size and weight; neurons are lost; fibers become twisted in the neuron cell bodies; and abnormal masses develop. Affected individuals gradually lose their memory; their thought processes slow; their judgment is impaired; they develop speech disturbances; and they become disoriented. In the disease's more advanced stages, the individual suffers emotional disturbances, delusions, deterioration of personal and toilet habits, failing speech, and finally total loss of memory. This disease, which heightens anyone's fear of brain disorders, is tragic for all concerned.

The major symptoms of Alzheimer's disease are gradual declines in cognitive functioning (memory, learning, reaction time, word usage), disorientation, declines in self-care, and inappropriate social behavior such as violent outbursts. In the beginning the symptoms are mild and may mimic depression or mild paranoia.

The cure for Alzheimer's disease continues to elude scientists, although they are working on several leads. Evidence suggests that the cause of the disease may be genetic, because the disease clusters in some families. In fact, from 10 to 30 percent of cases are believed to be hereditary (Gelman et al., 1989). In the late 1970s, researchers found that sufferers had below-normal amounts of a chemical neurotransmitter called acetylcholine; however, attempts to restore the amounts to a normal level have had mixed results at best. Aluminum has also been implicated as a possible culprit. During postmortems, Canadian investigators found the metal at above-normal levels in the brains of some Alzheimer's disease victims. In 1988, researchers found clues to suggest that a virus causes Alzheimer's; other investigations suspect that Alzheimer's is triggered by an environmental toxin. Some think a specific gene causes Alzheimer's—similar to the one linked with Down's syndrome.

Still others have observed that the brains of Alzheimer's patients are dotted with a brain protein called beta amyloid. In a healthy brain the amyloid protein is located only in the outer shell of a nerve cell. In Alzheimer's, bits and pieces of amyloid appear throughout the brain in microscopic globs known as plaques. Researchers have injected diseased laboratory rats with a human protein, known as substance P, that protected them from developing what would be full-blown Alzheimer's in humans. These researchers are now attempting to replicate the results in monkeys; they hope to eventually apply the treatment to humans (Booth, 1991).

Researchers in 1993 found that a defect in a gene on chromosome 19 occurs in late-onset Alzheimer's, the most common type. This is not consistent with the finding that plaques of beta amyloid plaques cause the disease, a theory that is gaining increased acceptance. It could be that the gene defect acts as a "helper" that increases the beta amyloid, which in turn kills brain nerve cells. Researchers are working on a beta amyloid blocking drug to begin testing within a few years (Snider, 1993).

Some medical experts think it unlikely that Alzheimer's disease is the result of a single, underlying cause. Focus on environmental preventions (e.g., removing neurotoxic substances at the workplace such as those found in organic solvents and pesticides) and self-health promotion strategies involving education, exercise, and diet would delay the onset of the disease. They caution that a genetic basis for the disease, if it does exist, does not negate the need for looking at other social and environmental factors that hasten its onset and intensify its effects (Gatz et al., 1994).

Several experimental drugs are becoming more widely available. THA, for example, seems to have improved the ability to think and function in about 12 percent of patients (Recer, 1993). However, it has shown mixed results in clinical tests and has been suspected to cause liver damage.

Because a prevention or cure for Alzheimer's disease has yet to be discovered, attention must be directed toward improving the functioning of the ailing person and helping family members to cope. The disease is gradual and progressive; the length of survival ranges from 2 to 20 years. Several stages are involved—some say seven stages: (1) normal; (2) forgetfulness; (3) early confusional; (4) late confusional; (5) early dementia; (6) middle dementia; and (7) late dementia.

In the first stages, cognitive declines are not readily apparent. A midway stage is characterized by recent memory loss and personality changes. For example, a person may become hopelessly lost while walking to a close and familiar location. Abstract thinking can also become impaired; the difference between an apple and an orange can become confusing, for example. Ailing individuals are typically aware of their intellectual decline, becoming anxious, depressed, or angry.

The next stages of Alzheimer's disease advance the deterioration of thought processes. Further memory loss and drastic mood swings are common. Speaking may become difficult, and paranoid symptoms may appear. During this stage, complications often force the patient to relocate to housing where care is provided. He or she may have trouble remembering close family members.

The final stage is terminal and usually very brief, lasting one year or less. Though many Alzheimer's patients at this stage stop eating and communicating and are unaware of surroundings, years, or seasons, they are still sensitive to love, affection, and tenderness. This is an enormously stressful time for friends and relatives; at this stage, they are most in need of support groups and counseling. (The "Old is News" article contained in Chapter 11 gives the story of one person's battle with the disease.)

Multi-infarct Dementia (M.I.D.)

Rising from problems with blood flow to the brain, this vascular dementia is caused by a series of small strokes (infarcts) that damage brain tissue over time. The disease is typically chronic, and a person may live with it for many years. For most, impairment is intermittent, occurring when a stroke occurs. The strokes are so small that one is unaware of them. A patient may have sudden attacks of confusion but then recover. Another may remember something one minute, then forget it the next. Gait difficulty, urinary incontinence, and palsy may accompany dementia symptoms. The brain area in which the stroke occurs corresponds with the impaired ability.

Alcoholism

Lifelong alcoholism or the onset of alcoholism in late life may yield changes that indicate a dementia syndrome. For example, chronic alcoholism may cause Wernicke-Karsakoff's syndrome, a type of dementia resulting from the lack of vitamin B_{12}, which results in memory loss and disorientation.

Creutzfeld-Jacob Disease

Creutzfeld-Jacob brain disease, though less common and much more rapid than Alzheimer's, follows a similar course. Within a year, the cerebral cortex degenerates to a fatal point in the sufferer. Scientists suggest that an infectious agent, possibly a virus, may be involved.

Parkinson's Disease

Parkinson's disease, which can lead to dementia, affects close to 1 million individuals in the United States. Rarely diagnosed before age 40, it increases in prevalence in those between the ages of 50 and 79. Tremors and rigidity of movement characterize the disease. Parkinson's progresses through stages, and some sufferers are eventually confined to bed or a wheelchair. Between 20 and 30 percent of patients develop dementia. Parkinson's has been treated with some success using the drug L-dopa, which relieves symptoms but is not thought to slow the progression of the disease (Elias et al., 1990).

Huntington's Disease

A rare disease, Huntington's disease is inherited as a defective gene. Its most famous victim was Woody Guthrie (1912–1967), a popular folksinger and

composer. The disease starts unnoticed in one's thirties or forties and proceeds over a 12- to 15-year period, ending like Alzheimer's disease with total
deterioration of memory and bodily functions.

☼ Caring for the Mentally Ill

Care for mentally ill elders can be provided in clinical settings of mental
health professionals, hospitals, institutions for the mentally ill, nursing
homes, or the homes of relatives. Studies show that some environments are
supportive of mentally ill elders, whereas others are hostile or indifferent.
Mentally ill, whether in group homes or boarding homes, have been shown
to benefit by (1) activities to keep them busy, such as music, dance, cards, and
handiwork; (2) activities to get them outside the setting and into the community—even if only to have a cup of coffee; and (3) programs and goals of
reducing dependency and getting them out of a conforming, passive rut.

Comparisons of U.S. and Canadian funding and organization of psychiatric services for elders find services to be more accessible in Canada because
of universal health insurance. For acute mental health problems, hospital
benefits are free of charge in Canada. The many limitations posed by
Medicare in the United States do not exist there. However, in both countries,
the small number of professionals trained and interested in the mental health
of the elderly limits such services. In both countries, long-term care is generally inadequate, especially for those with serious behavioral disturbances.

Beginning in the mid-seventies, institutions running high costs and
offering basic, nontherapeutic care "dumped" the mentally ill. The ousted
older persons wandered around trying to find a place in the community, or
they were placed in nursing homes where they often received inadequate
treatment for mental illness. Elders who were once treated custodially in
mental hospitals are now cared for in nursing homes, often with not even a
pretense of psychiatric care.

For families caring for the mentally ill elderly at home, the burden can be
great: Caretakers can expect no expanded government programs in the
immediate future; if anything, programs are being curbed. Gerontologists are
looking to volunteer programs and family support groups to help the elderly infirm and their families. Fortunately, support groups for caretakers of
patients with Alzheimer's and other dementias are often available and highly beneficial.

Outreach programs can serve the mental health needs of elders very
effectively. A program in Iowa, for example, sent workers on request to the
homes of rural mentally ill aged, most of whom were single women between
the ages of 65 and 85, living alone and experiencing depression, some form of
dementia, or adjustment problems. The program, which assessed clients, then
treated them or referred them to more professional help, was deemed a success in helping older persons and in keeping them out of institutions
(Buckwalter et al., 1991).

Volunteer programs designed to consider the unique needs of mentally
ill elders are effective in organizing the assistance of friends, other residents,
and family members. Through network building, programs can expand to
involve churches, schools, and senior citizen groups in caring for the mentally ill in institutions or at home.

Peer counseling is a somewhat similar concept. Older persons are trained
by a professional to reach out to other elders in need of mental health services. These volunteer peer counselors are taught to deal with a variety of

problems, to offer advice, and to serve as a bridge, through referrals, to more formal mental health services. In some communities, peer counselors have organized hotlines for elders in crisis.

☼ Good Mental Health

Most older persons have good mental health. One safeguard against emotional debilitation in later years is good mental health in youth and middle age. Many mental disorders in old age represent continuing problems that have gone untreated. A second safeguard against emotional debilitation in old age is to maintain an active interest in life and to keep one's mind stimulated. A third safeguard is to seek professional health-care services when they are needed.

Getting mental health care is less likely in the older years. The mental disorders of elders have been too often viewed as untreatable, and the problems of younger persons have often received more priority in mental hospitals and other care facilities. Older people are also more reluctant to seek help. But the mental health of the elders is beginning to receive more attention. For example, as you recall, a major research effort is underway to find a cure for Alzheimer's disease. And more geriatric specialists are offering encouragement and assisting those older individuals with mild emotional problems or more severe disorders. Older persons do not have to tolerate depression, anxiety, or other disorders any more than younger persons do. Depression and anxiety are pathologies that can be treated and cured.

At every point in our lives, we can have the goal of maximizing our potential. Even a person in a very debilitated mental state can generally respond to help. For example, individuals suffering from advanced organic brain syndrome can benefit from "reality orientation": reviewing the day of the week, one's location, and one's name. Human contact, a touch or hug, also adds meaning to life.

Caretakers in the field of mental health can work toward maximizing a patient's potential. In the On Loc Nursing Home in San Francisco, even the most impaired attend programs, form friendships, and are encouraged to attend music groups, old movies, and arts and crafts workshops. They are fully dressed in street clothes every day, even though most are incontinent. In this hospital, the worker's goal is to help patients reach and maintain maximum functioning potential. With a constant deteriorating patient, specific goals may have to be adjusted downward; but if the goal is to see Mrs. Smith smile, or to hear Mr. Juarez sing, the task remains rewarding.

Community Mental Health Clinics (CMHCs) have been mandated to serve the old as well as the young, yet a disproportionately small number of older persons use these services. Medicare pays only a minimal amount for outpatient mental care. A tragic irony exists in that although nursing homes represent a major setting for mentally ill elders, they receive, for the most part, inadequate mental health care in these homes. Geriatric mental health is an evolving field desperately in need of growth and improvement.

Chapter Summary

The psychology of aging is a broad field covering cognition and its many aspects: perception, sensory input, information processing, psychomotor speed, intelligence, learning, and memory. Older persons generally suffer a decline, in reaction time, but not necessarily in intelligence, learning, memory, and other areas. Mental health problems may be functional (have no physical basis) or organic (have a physical basis). Functional disorders may be moderately debilitating as with a temporary emotional problem, or they may be quite severe, as with a psychotic breakdown. The most common form of organic brain disease is Alzheimer's disease. The bulk of the aged have good mental health. A substantial minority need mental health care by a professional.

Key Terms

affective disorders
age-related changes
Alzheimer's disease
anxiety disorders
biologically caused changes
cognition
cognitive mechanics
cognitive pragmatics
cognitive process approach
crystallized intelligence
dementia
depressive disorder
divided attention
fluid intelligence
functional disorders
generalized disorders
information processing
intelligence
learning

memory
obsessive-compulsive disorder
organic disorders
perception
personality disorders
phobia
primary memory
primary mental abilities
psychometric approach
psychomotor speed
schizophrenia
secondary memory
selective attention
senility
sensory memory
tertiary memory
the five senses
working memory

Questions for Discussion

1. How does age affect intelligence, learning, and memory? How would you design a training program that would permit the capable older worker to retrain under the least stressful circumstances and to demonstrate capability?

2. What personality variables would you choose to examine in a longitudinal study of adults throughout their lives? Why?

3. What emotional problems do you anticipate in your old age based on your present personality?

4. How would you respond to being told you had a chronic brain disease?

5. Why do high numbers of older men commit suicide?

Fieldwork Suggestions

1. Put on a thick pair of glasses that do not fit your eyesight, and wear ear plugs and a thick pair of gloves as you go through your daily routine. Note the loss of sensory perceptions and how these losses influence your ability to function and to do things for yourself. Are you treated well by other people? Are you hesitant about going out in public? How long are you able to withstand the sensory loss? Did you find any ways to compensate for it?

2. Call your county mental health agency to find out what services are available for elders.

3. Interview a mental health worker. Ask him or her what mental disorders older people seek treatment for. Is there a percentage breakdown?

4. Interview the caretaker of an elderly person who suffers from an organic brain disorder. What is the personality profile of the elder? What are the disease manifestations? What is the caretaker doing to help? How is the family reacting?

5. Call an alcohol treatment center. Find out what percentage of its patients are older. Interview a worker to analyze the problems and prognoses for working with elderly alcoholics. How many have a lifetime drinking problem? For how many is the problem a recent one? Why?

References

American Psychiatric Association. *Diagnostic and Statistical Manual for Mental Disorders (DSM-IV).* 4th ed. Washington, DC: American Psychiatric Association, 1994.

Baltes, P. "The Aging Mind: Potential and Limits." *Gerontologist* 33:5 (October 1993): 580–594.

Bliwise, N., et al. "The Epidemiology of Mental Illness in Late Life." In *Serving the Mentally Ill Elderly,* edited by Lurie, E. and Swan, J., 73–89. Lexington, MA: D. C. Health & Co., 1987.

Booth, W. "Protein Shows Promise in Treating Alzheimer's." *Santa Rosa Press Democrat* (15 August 1991): A3.

Buckwalter, K., et al. "Mental Health Services of the Rural Elderly Outreach Program." *Gerontologist* 31:3 (June 1991): 408–412.

Busan, T. *Use Your Perfect Memory.* New York: Plume Division of Penguin Books, 1991.

Cavanaugh, J. *Adult Development and Aging.* Pacific Grove, CA: Brooks/Cole, 1993.

Carpenter, B. "A Review and New Look at Ethical Suicide in Advanced Age." *Gerontologist* 33:3 (June 1993): 359–365.

Cohen, G. "Psychopathology and Mental Health in the Mature and Elderly." In *Handbook of the Psychology of Aging,* edited by J. Birren and K. W. Schaie. San Diego: Academic Press, 1990.

Denney, N. W., and A. M. Palmer. "Adult Age Differences in Traditional and Practical Problem Solving Measures." *Psychology and Aging* 4 (1987): 438–442.

Doussard, Roosevelt. "Aging, Selective Attention, and Feature Integration." *Psychology and Aging* 4 (1989): 98–105.

Elias, M., et al. "Biological and Health Influences on Behavior." In *Handbook of the Psychology of Aging,* edited by J. Birren and K. W. Schaie. San Diego: Academic Press, 1990.

Furst, Alan. "Unforgettable. . . . That's What He Is." *50 Plus* (June 1988): 72.

Galz, M., et al. "Dementia: Not Just a Search for the Gene." *Gerontologist* 34:2 (April 1994): 251–255.

Gelman, D., et al. "All About Alzheimer's." *Newsweek* (18 December 1989): 54–63.

Hinrichsen, G. *Mental Health Problems and Older Adults.* Santa Barbara, CA: ABC-CLIO, Inc., 1990.

Humphrey, Derek. *Let Me Die Before I Wake.* Los Angeles, CA: The Hemlock Society and Grove Press, 1985.

Humphrey, Derek. *Final Exit.* Eugene, OR: The Hemlock Society, 1991.

Kaplan, M., et al. "Trends in Firearm Suicide Among Older American Males." *Gerotologists* 34:1 (February 1994): 59–65.

Osgood, N. *Suicide in the Elderly.* Rockville, MD: Aspen, 1985.

Plude, Dana. "Sensory, Perceptual, and Motor Function in Human Aging." In *The Elderly as Modern Pioneers,* edited by P. Silverman. Bloomington: Indiana University Press, 1987.

Plude, D. J. "Attention and Memory Improvement." In *Memory Improvement: Implications for Memory Theory,* edited by D. Herrmann and A. Weingartner. New York: Springer-Verlag, 1994.

Plude, D. J., and P. Rabbitt. "Social Psychology, Neurosciences, and Cognitive Psychology Need Each Other." *The Psychologist* 1:12 (1988): 500–506.

Recer, P. "Drug Raises Hopes for Elderly." *Santa Rosa Press Democrat* (19 March 1993): A3.

Savage, R. D., P. Britton, N. Bolton, and E. H. Hall. *Intellectual Functioning in the Aged.* London: Methuen, 1973.

Schaie, K. W. "Intellectual Development in Adulthood." In *Handbook of the Psychology of Aging,* 3d ed., edited by J. Birren and K. W. Schaie. San Diego: Academic Press, 1990.

Snider, M. "Alzheimer's Drug Possible by Year 2000." *U.S.A. Today* (21 June 1993): D1.

Spirduso, W. W., and P. G. MacRae. "Motor Performance in Aging." In *Handbook of the Psychology of Aging*, 3d ed., edited by J. Birren and K. W. Schaie. San Diego: Academic Press, 1990.

Stokes, G. "On Being Old: The Psychology of Later Life." London: The Falmer Press, 1992.

Thomas, J. *Adulthood and Aging*. Boston, MA: Allyn and Bacon, 1992.

U.S. Bureau of the Census, *Statistical Abstract of the United States, 1990*, 110th ed. Washington, DC: Department of Commerce, Bureau of the Census, 1991.

Whitlock, F. A. "Suicide and Physical Illness." In *Suicide*, edited by A. Roy. Baltimore: Williams and Wilkins, 1986.

Further Readings

Birren, J. R. B. Sloan, and G. Cohen. *Handbook of Mental Health and Aging*. San Diego, CA: Academic Press, 1992.

Cerella, J., et al. eds. *Adult Information Processing: Limits on Loss*. San Diego, CA: Academic Press, 1993.

Cohen, U., and K. Day. *Contemporary Evvironment for people with Dementia*. Baltimore, MD: John Hopkins University Press, 1993.

Gard, R. *Beyond the Thin Line: A Personal Journey Into the World of Alzheimer's Disease*. Madison, WI: Prairie Oak Press, 1992.

Light, L., and D. Burke, eds. *Language, Memory and Aging*. New York: Cambridge University Press, 1993.

Sinnott, J., ed. *Interdisciplinary Handbook of Lifespan Learning*. Westport, CT: Greenwook Press, 1994.

CHAPTER 10 Mental Health

11

The Oldest Old and Caregiving

CHAPTER OUTLINE

■ The Oldest-Old   ■ Informal Caregiving   ■ Solving Caregiving Problems

Alice's Story

■ SHANNON BROWNLEE

The Early Warnings

In the beginning there were the misplaced keys and missed appointments, little lapses of memory that seemed to be nothing more than the ordinary slowing of mental processes that almost inevitably comes to a person who has reached the age of 73. When Alice Zilonka forgot to record checks she had written, her son Roland and daughter-in-law Pat patted her arm and told her not to fret. "Everybody your age forgets once in a while," they said. Alice went to visit her sister and lost her wedding ring. Then she couldn't find her safe-deposit-box key. Don't worry, we all lose things, they said. Alice wrote little notes to herself: "Remember! Address is 6202 Marluth. . . . Today is Thursday. . . . Find safe-deposit-box key!" Who doesn't do that, her son and daughter-in-law said. She forgot to add baking powder while making a cake . . . mislaid three hearing aids in as many months . . . lost her way walking the 10 blocks home from church one Sunday. Don't worry, Alice, they said, but Alice was frightened: "My mind is like a dark thunderstorm. . . ."

The Note Writing

The Huebners' walls are now plastered with notes to jog Alice's fractured memory. "It's Tuesday. Your room is upstairs." For every new source of confusion, Pat painstakingly writes another note. Once shy and placid, Alice has become agitated. By night, she paces her room. By day, she roams the house, stopping only at the refrigerator to gobble food. Alice never gains weight, but the Huebners' dog does. Alice has been feeding it dinner rolls.

The notes multiply and grow ever more insistent. "Turn off the water." "Do not leave the house." The Huebners chain the refrigerator shut. Her granddaughter, Kerri, is just out of diapers when Alice must begin wearing them. Alice and Pat wrestle with clothing and diapers every morning, as Alice shakes her head like a willful child. One morning, Alice strikes Pat across the face. "I was so mad I was shaking," Pat recalls. "But by the

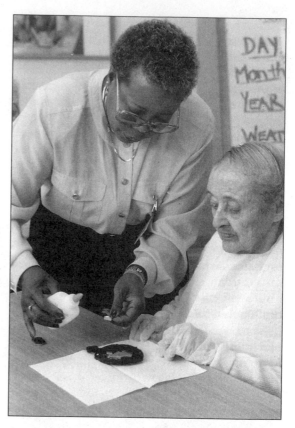

An occupational therapist works with a patient in the Alzheimer Disorder Program.

time we got in the car, Mom had forgotten all about it."

The Final Days

The average cost of a nursing home is $40,000 a year, and Alice's estate had dwindled to just a few thousand. The director of a home instructs her son Roland to "spend down," to deplete Alice's funds below $1,800 so that Medicare can kick in. But there are no beds available, and there may not be for another two years. Pat wonders if she will go crazy along with Alice.

Alice almost never recognizes her family when they come to visit her. Kerri stands apart, watching her father feed his mother. A year ago, Alice would sometimes smile at Pat, or stroke her granddaughter's cheek, but now she sits rigid in her wheelchair, compulsively pinching her skin.

Roland knows Alzheimer's sometimes runs in families, and if he has forgotten a name or an appointment he often finds himself lying awake at night. He turns to Pat and says, "If I get this disease, put me in a nursing home right away. I don't want Kerri to go through this again." ✸

SOURCE: Shannon Brownlee, "Alzheimer's: Is There Hope?" © *U.S. News & World Report* (12 August 1991): 40–49.

*A*s the population of the old-old has mushroomed, caregiving to an older person within a family setting has become more common. Informal caregiving usually precedes and sometimes accompanies or replaces the formal caregiving offered by hospitals and other institutional settings. We have no clear-cut norms or customs dictating care for older family members who need help in caring for themselves. This chapter examines the oldest-old population and the caregiving that is offered in a family context.

✸ The Oldest-Old

Recently, researchers have begun separating old-age groups in their studies. As early as 1974, Bernice L. Neugarten separated the older population into the young-old (age 65 to 74) and the old-old (age 75 and over). Before that, studies considered all the elderly together, obscuring important differences and offering little insights into the social realities of the **oldest-old**. Other terms for the oldest-old have also come into use, and they may have slightly different meanings: the very old, the extreme aged, the dependent elderly, and the frail elderly. These terms, often used interchangeably, need to be clarified when they are used. There is no clear-cut time at which gerontologists all agree that one joins the "oldest-old." The discussion in this chapter reflects that fact. Here age 75 and over and age 85 and over are both used at different times to demark the oldest-old, depending on the studies cited. Figure 6.1 shows the percentage distribution of three age groups among those 65 and over, the two oldest groups being 75 to 84, and those 85 and over. Those age 75 and over (which includes these two groups from the figure) are the fastest growing segment of the older population. Those 75 and over represent over 13 million persons, or nearly 43 percent of all elders in 1991. By the year 2000, those age 75 and over will comprise 48 percent, or nearly half of the aged population. Thus, the needs of the oldest-old will weigh more heavily in the future as their number and percentage of the population increase. We as a society will need to provide a viable lifestyle for this burgeoning group. Women dominate the men at the upper age levels in terms of numbers. Of those aged 75 and over, 8.5 million or 65 percent are women. Of those age 85 and over, 73 percent are women (U.S. Census Bureau, 1993, p. 15, table 14).

PHYSICAL HEALTH

The 75 to 84 age group is, by and large, healthier and happier than stereotypes would have us believe. In fact, the general consensus seems to be that physical losses in old age do not begin taking a heavy toll until after age 85. The 85-and-older group uses approximately ten times as many hospital days

Figure 11.1
....
Three Age Groups of Elders: The Percentage of Those 65 and Over, 1991

SOURCE: Adapted from U.S. Bureau of Census, *Statistical Abstract of the U.S.*, 113th ed. (Washington, D.C.: U.S. Government Printing Office, 1993), p. 15, table 14.

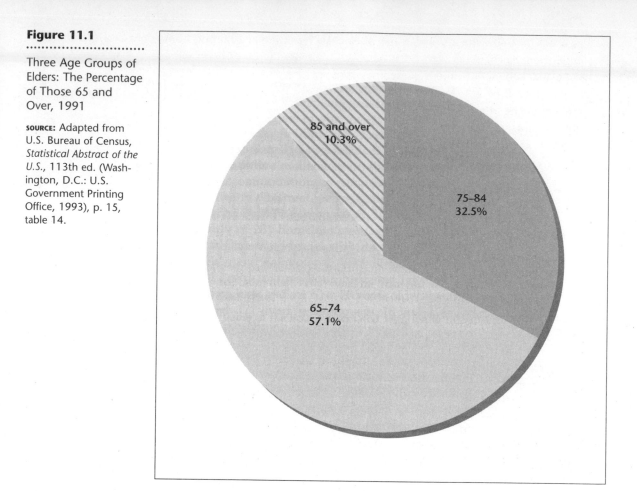

as those 45 to 64, whereas those 75 and over use about 4.5 times as many (U.S. Census Bureau, 1993, p. 125). An 85-year-old is 2.5 times more likely to enter a nursing home than is a 75-year-old.

In a longitudinal study, a ten-year follow-up conducted on 279 elderly found little or no decline in social and economic function, and only moderate declines in mental, physical, and daily living functions (Palmore et al., 1985). At the time of the follow-up, the men were age 72 or older, and the women were age 75 or older. The mean age was 88.8 years. The findings contradict the gloomy view that the old-old experience rapid decline: the declines were moderate and gradual overall, with considerable variation from individual to individual.

The health of the oldest-old is a basic concern. A critical measure of health is whether they can manage daily activities alone, or whether they need the help of others. A measure of functional disability is the ability to do **personal activities of daily living** (PADLs or ADLs) without help. These include bathing, eating, dressing, toileting, transferring oneself in and out of a bed or chair, and walking or getting around inside the home (see Figure 11.2). A second measure of functional disability is the ability to do **instrumental activities of daily living** (IADLs) such as shopping, housework, money management, and meal preparation (see Figure 11.3). Less than half of the oldest-old (85 and over), need some help in performing ADLs, and about 60 percent need help with IADLs.

CHAPTER 11   The Oldest Old and Caregiving

Physical Self-Maintenance Scale (PSMS)

Subject's Name_____ Rated by_____Date_____

Circle one statement in each category A-F that applies to subject.

A. Toilet

1. Cares for self at toilet completely, no incontinence.
2. Needs to be reminded or needs help in cleaning self, or has rare (weekly at most) accidents.
3. Soiling or wetting while asleep more than once a week.
4. Soiling or wetting while awake more than once a week.
5. No control of bowels or bladder.

B. Feeding

1. Eats without assistance.
2. Eats with minor assistance at meal times and/or with special preparation of food, or help in cleaning up after meals.
3. Feeds self with moderate assistance and is untidy.
4. Requires extensive assistance for all meals.
5. Does not feed self at all and resists efforts of others to feed him/her.

C. Dressing

1. Dresses, undresses, and selects clothing from own wardrobe.
2. Dresses and undresses self, with minor assistance.
3. Needs moderate assistance in dressing or selection of clothes.
4. Needs major assistance in dressing, but cooperates with efforts of others to help.
5. Completely unable to dress self and resists efforts of others to help.

D. Grooming (neatness, hair, nails, hands, face, clothing)

1. Always neatly dressed, well-groomed, without assistance.
2. Grooms self adequately with occasional minor assistance, e.g., shaving.
3. Needs moderate and regular assistance or supervision in grooming.
4. Needs total grooming care, but can remain well-groomed after help from others.
5. Actively negates all efforts of others to maintain grooming.

E. Physical Ambulation

1. Goes about grounds or city.
2. Ambulates within residence or about one block distant.
3. Ambulates with assistance of (check one) a. another person_____ b. railing_____
   c. cane_____ d. walker_____ e. wheelchair_____
   1. gets in and out without help.
   2. needs help in getting in, out.
4. Sits unsupported in chair or wheelchair, but cannot propel self without help.
5. Bedridden more than half the time.

F. Bathing

1. Bathes self (tub, shower, sponge bath) without help.
2. Bathes self with help in getting in and out of tub.
3. Washes face and hands only, but cannot bathe rest of body.
4. Does not wash self, but is cooperative with those who bathe him/her.
5. Does not try to wash self, and resists efforts to keep him/her clean.

....

SOURCE: Adapted by M. Powell Lawton, Ph.D. Director of Research, Philadelphia Geriatric Center, Philadelphia, from *Older Americans Resource and Assessment Multidimensional Functional Assessment Questionnaire.*

The oldest-old have a number of common chronic disabling conditions. The most common problems are bone and joint problems, heart disease, vision and hearing problems, mental impairment, drug intoxication (from prescribed drugs), falls, and urinary incontinence. Selected chronic conditions of those under age 75 and over age 75 are shown in Table 11.1.

In spite of these numbers many of the oldest-old have no functional limitations: that is, their chronic diseases do not keep them from living alone and doing their own personal and household chores. In a large sample of elders aged 80 and over, 33 percent were described as "robust" (Suzman, 1992). They were active and healthy, needing no help with ADLs or IADLs. In fact, they were able to perform at even higher levels of functioning than represented by ADLs and IADLs. This sample did not include institutionalized elders.

Figure 11.3

....

Instrumental Activities of Daily Living (IADL) Scale

Name _____ Rated by _____ Date _____

1. Can you use the telephone
   without help,   3
   with some help, or   2
   are you completely unable to use the telephone?   1

2. Can you get to places beyond walking distance
   without help,   3
   with some help, or   2
   are you completely unable to travel unless special arrangements are made?   1

3. Can you go shopping for groceries
   without help,   3
   with some help, or   2
   are you completely unable to do any shopping?   1

4. Can you prepare your own meals
   without help,   3
   with some help, or   2
   are you completely unable to prepare any meals?   1

5. Can you do your own housework
   without help,   3
   with some help, or   2
   are you completely unable to do any housework?   1

6. Can you do your own handyman work
   without help,   3
   with some help, or   2
   are you completely unable to do any handyman work?   1

7. Can you do your own laundry
   without help,   3
   with some help, or   2
   are you completely unable to do any laundry at all?   1

8a. Do you take medicines or use any medications?
   Yes (If yes, answer Question 8b.)   1
   No (If no, answer Question 8c.)   2

8b. Do you take your own medicine
   without help (in the right doses at the right time),   3
   with some help (if someone prepares it for you and/or reminds you to take it), or   2
   you are completely unable to take your own medicine?   1

8c. If you had to take medicine, could you do it without help (in the right doses at the right time),   3
   with some help (if someone prepared it for you and/or reminded you to take it), or   2
   would you be completely unable to take your own medicine?   1

9. Can you manage your own money
   without help,   3
   with some help, or   2
   are you completely unable to manage money?   1

The IADL Scale evaluates more sophisticated functions than the ADL Index (see Figure 6.2). Patients or caregivers can complete the form in a few minutes. The first answer in each case—except for 8a—indicates independence; the second, capability with assistance; and the third, dependence. In this version the maximum score is 29, although scores have meaning only for a particular patient, as when declining scores over time reveal deterioration. Questions 4–7 tend to be gender-specific: Modify them as you see fit.

SOURCE: Adapted with permission from M. Powell Lawton, Ph.D. Director of Research, Philadelphia Geriatric Center, Philadelphia, from *Older Americans Resource and Assessment Multidimensional Functional Assessment Questionnaire.*

     CHAPTER 11 The Oldest Old and Caregiving

Percent Distribution

Table 11.1

Table Prevalence of Selected Reported Chronic Conditions by Age and Sex, 1990

| | Male | | Female | |
Chronic Condition	65–74	75 & Over	65–74	75 & Over
Arthritis	37.3	37.7	47.2	62.9
Cataracts	8.1	12.9	13.7	27.1
Other uncorrected visual impairment	7.3	11.0	3.4	10.5
Hearing Impairments	35.0	48.0	19.5	37.0
Heart conditions	27.5	40.5	24.3	29.2
Hypertension	28.5	30.4	41.0	44.4

SOURCE: Adapted from U.S. Census Bureau, *Statistical Abstract of the United States,* 113th ed. (Washington, D.C.: U.S. Government Printing Office, 1993), p. 135, table 206.

LIVING ARRANGEMENTS AND MARITAL STATUS

Only a small percentage of the oldest-old are institutionalized. Of the oldest-old, those age 85 and over, more than 50 percent still live at home. More than 35 percent live alone at home; in fact, about 75 percent of those 85 and over are widowed. An estimated 25 percent of the oldest-old live in the household of an adult child or other person (usually a relative), and another 21 percent reside in nursing homes. For the oldest-old, the most critical need in the future will be for programs and policies that reduce the risk of dependence and promote self-determination. If housing were more affordable and home help services more available, more people could live in their own homes.

From Figure 11.4, one can see that most people live in their own homes. Not until elders reach age 90 are there more than 50 percent who cannot live independently. However, much of the help needed is not covered by Medicare. For example, if a medical diagnosis is osteoarthritis of the knees, the primary problem is trouble with walking. Although the problem is medical, and some help involves pain medication (to control but not cure), major help is needed with shopping and self-maintenance. Such categories of help are not "treatments" and therefore, are not covered by Medicare.

The marital status of men and women at the upper age levels afford a dramatic comparison with the oldest-old women much more likely to be widowed, and the oldest-old men, married. From Table 11.2 one can compare the percentage of single, married, widowed, and divorced men and women under 75 and 75 and over. The number of widowed men more than doubled (from 10 percent to 24 percent). For women in both age groups, the percent of

Table 11.2

Marital Status for Two Age Groups: 1992

Sex and Age	Percent Distribution				Percent Total
Male	Single	Married	Widowed	Divorced	
65–74	4.6	79.1	10.2	6.1	100%
75 and over	3.5	70.2	23.7	2.6	100%
Female					
65–74	4.4	53.0	35.9	6.7	100%
75 and over	5.4	25.6	65.0	4.0	100%

SOURCE: Adapted from U.S. Census Bureau, *Statistical Abstract of the United States,* 113th ed. (Washington, D.C.: U.S. Government Printing Office, 1993), p. 54, table 61.

Figure 11.4
···

Which Problems Hit at Which Age

SOURCE: Adapted with permission from Andrus Gerontology Center, University of Southern California, as appeared in Brian O'Reilly, "How to Take Care of Aging Parents," *Fortune Magazine* (May 18, 1992), p. 108–112. Reprinted with permission of *Fortune* magazine.

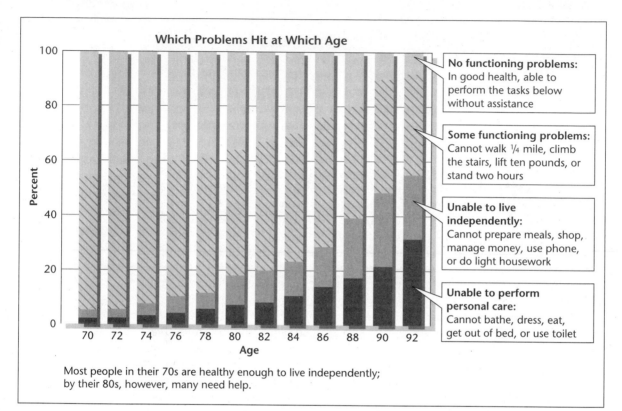

Which Problems Hit at Which Age

No functioning problems: In good health, able to perform the tasks below without assistance

Some functioning problems: Cannot walk ¼ mile, climb the stairs, lift ten pounds, or stand two hours

Unable to live independently: Cannot prepare meals, shop, manage money, use phone, or do light housework

Unable to perform personal care: Cannot bathe, dress, eat, get out of bed, or use toilet

Most people in their 70s are healthy enough to live independently; by their 80s, however, many need help.

widows are dramatically higher than the men. Nearly 36 percent of women aged 65 to 74 are widowed. The majority of women 75 and over are widowed (65 percent), whereas the majority of men (70 percent, in fact) in the same age group are married. Widowhood is the predominant lifestyle for women 75 and over.

EVALUATION OF LIFE

A study of the oldest-old, those age 85 and over, reveals that at some point between 80 and 90 years of age, individuals are willing to describe themselves as "old" (Bould et al., 1989, 1). There is a definite awareness that the spirit is willing, but the body is unable to cooperate. Malcolm Cowley (1980) who wrote of his personal experience with aging in *The View from Eighty* describes this reality:

> Everything takes longer to do—bathing, shaving, getting dressed or undressed
> Travel becomes more difficult and you think twice before taking out the car
> Many of your friends have vanished . . .
> There are more and more little bottles in the medicine cabinet . . .
> (You hesitate) on the landing before walking down a flight of stairs
> (You spend) more time looking for things misplaced than using them . . .
>   It becomes an achievement to do thoughtfully, step-by-step, what (you) once did instinctively.

Thinking about Aging

Pushing the Limits of Longevity Hundred Fold: Many More Reach the Century Mark

■ NEAL THOMPSON

Reaching the age of 100 this year? Join the club.

While still an impressive feat, becoming a centenarian is not quite the landmark it once was.

Between 1980 and 1990, the number of centenarians in the United States more than doubled, reaching nearly 40,000. Census officials expect about 100,000 Americans to be celebrating triple-digit birthdays by the end of this decade.

But pushing the limits of longevity is a costly feat. To survive decades past retirement exacts a price, both in terms of a high cost of living and a declining quality of life.

It's a trend that raises some troubling questions: How can a person who has been retired for 30 years afford a 10-year stay in a nursing home at costs exceeding $100 a day? How will doctors meet the physical and emotional needs of someone who outlives a spouse, friends, and sometimes children?

Gaetano "Guy" Salvo, who turned 101 last week, sees both sides of living into one's second century, the good and the bad.

"It's nice here. They take care of me," Salvo said, reclining in the easy chair his children bought him. "But I enjoyed working. I liked to drive . . . Now, I don't do nothing. I'm lazy."

Salvo recently moved into a room in Bergen Pines' nursing home, which he shares with three other elderly men. He had been living with his son, Ron, in Old Tappan until the family decided he needed professional care.

Salvo's wife, Margaret, died 10 years ago at 87. And although he worked until he was 82, retirement has lasted a long time, 19 years. But he can still walk with the help of a walker, his hearing isn't too bad, and he enjoys watching Saturday-morning wrestling on television, occasional music shows, especially opera, and game shows such as "Jeopardy" and "Wheel of Fortune."

"I'm just lucky," said Salvo, who quit smoking a pack a day at age 75. "One hundred and one, ooh,

that's a lot of years. I'm surprised."

As baby boomers age, and life expectancy grows, there could be 1 million centenarians in 50 years, said Bonnie Damon, a census researcher.

For doctors, the growing number of centenarians presents a challenge.

Some doctors lump anyone over 65 into the "elderly" classification, Aronson said. But that age group can now include three separate generations with three unique sets of medical needs.

The problem is that people don't know enough about what happens late in life.

Studies show that some mental decline, memory loss, impaired judgment is inevitable at extreme ages. And the decline can be magnified by loneliness or depression. But centenarians say it's their bodies rather than their minds that betray them most.

They want to drive, walk, and shop, but are frustrated by physical limitations. Poor eyesight is common. Weakened bones and muscles often prevent them from supporting their own weight, robbing them of independence.

Even so, some centenarians said they actually feel better now than they did at 90. They say they've put surgery and hospital stays behind them. Doctors are reluctant to perform surgery or other invasive procedures on centenarians because of their weakened condition and have learned to live within their limits.

Margaret D'Angelo, who turns 100 next month, walks to and from Mass each morning, exercises for 15 minutes, and then goes to work in the cafeteria of her senior-citizens complex.

"As far as my health is concerned, I don't feel 99," said D'Angelo, who has a strong voice but says she doesn't like talking about herself.

D'Angelo thanks God and her six children, ages 67 to 83, for keeping her happy and healthy. She walks with a sturdy gait, always looking like she's in a hurry. When she's not working, she cleans her apartment, sews, visits with family, and watches some television. "I don't like to stand around and gab," she said.

Her eyesight isn't great, but the rest of her works fine, only slower. She refuses the drugs her doctor prescribes, and only takes an occasional Tylenol.

"I see people come here who are 15 to 20 years younger than I am, and they're all stooped over and can't get around. I feel sorry for them. So I count my blessings for every minute I'm here," she said. ☼

SOURCE: *The Record (New Jersey)*, 25 May 1994, p. A1.

Evaluations of reality vary with one's age and life view. To those age 85 and over who are in good health, living at home, and still driving—the absence of limitations keeps them feeling lucky in life.

Some elderly at age 100 and beyond have remarkably good health and a positive outlook on life (see "Thinking about Aging" on page 263). Lives of the extremely old are potentially rich if their health problems are not major. Joy in living is reported by the "frail elderly" at the upper age limit in spite of limiting health conditions that typically require at least some help in coping with day-to-day living.

Most life satisfaction studies have focused on the young-old. One exception, which focused on the stability of life satisfaction for the old-old over a three-year period (Baur and Okun, 1983), found that life satisfaction remained stable over time for the oldest-old, even through the nineties. Forty-six percent of the 91 respondents were between ages 81 and 94; the study found that the elderly correlated good health and not being neglected by friends with high life satisfaction.

More longitudinal studies of the old-old would help us to better understand this age group. Life may or may not be different as one progresses from age 75 to 85 to 95 to 100. For the "one hundred over 100" (Heynen, 1990) interviewed for a book about centenarians, full and meaningful lives were the norm. No single factor predicted who would live to be over 100—some were smokers, worrywarts, or nonexercisers. Some were homebodies, others travelers; some were religious fanatics, others skeptics. The only commonality was a desire to live. A study of 165 elders (48 of them centenarians) in the state of Georgia discovered a theme of good health, good coping patterns, and consistently high life satisfaction among the centenarians. A surprising finding was that the centenarians also tended to score high on the psychological variables of hostility and suspicion (Poon, 1992). As we learn more about aging in the very advanced years, we must put aside our assumptions, including the belief that contentment or satisfaction automatically implies having a sunny or trusting nature.

Generally speaking, studies of the very old show that their world does become smaller as physical and mental decline occurs. For example, an older woman who used to prepare a special dinner two evenings a week may now do so once a week, once a month, or less. However, coping skills seem good at this age level; and increased isolation and frailty is not necessarily associated with depression and unhappiness. There is joy in surviving and in enjoying what one has.

☼ Informal Caregiving

A great number of elders receive in-home care from relatives. Depending on definitions, at least 17 percent of all noninstitutionalized elders are in need of help. This percentage more than doubles for those age 85 and over. For every disabled person who resides in a nursing home, two or more equally impaired aged live with and are cared for by their families (Brody, 1990). An even larger number of people provide help to old people who do not share their households.

There is a myth that the extended family, especially the three-generation family, was common in the 1700s and 1800s. In fact, the three-generation family is more common in the 1900s than it was then. The primary reason is due to demographics. There are more elders alive today. Five percent of U.S. children today live with their grandparents or other relatives. In a third of these homes neither parent is present (Minkler et al., 1993). Fifteen percent of all those 65 and over live with someone other than their spouse. However, the preferred living arrangement of elders is independence from adult children. The trend over the last several decades has been to encourage such independence with more care being provided in the homes of elders, not in the homes of the adult children.

Informal caregiving is caregiving at home by nonpaid, nonprofessionals as opposed to **formal caregiving** which is caregiving provided by physicians, hospitals, day care centers, nursing homes, or other paid, professional care providers. Informal caregivers are predominantly female and older themselves. Role strain is most evident among middle-aged caretakers, with many reporting child care responsibilities, some reporting work conflicts, and others quitting jobs (Monson, 1993). But caretakers of all ages report stress and strain.

MORAL OBLIGATIONS OF ADULT CHILDREN TO PARENTS

The **modified nuclear family** concept describes the typical American situation. There is a great deal of family interaction, for example visiting and

HELLO... CARE GIVER HOTLINE ... WHAT ARE THE SYMPTOMS OF OVER-EXTENDED CARE GIVER STRESS?!

exchanges of gifts and services, but no extended family household. Most elders live in separate households, but they are not cut off from their families. However, the standard indicators used to measure family interaction do not measure emotional closeness; nor do they measure how responsible the family feels for frail, older parents.

Gerontologists observe that there are no clear cultural guidelines, no specific norms for behavior, in the area of intergenerational relationships between elderly parents and adult children. Some older parents expect that: (1) married children should live close to parents; (2) children should take care of sick parents; (3) if children live nearby, they should visit their parents often; and (4) children who live at a distance should write or call their parents often. Indeed, that is why the phrase "modified extended family" has been used; it describes families that keep close ties even though they do not share households. These norms or expectations of close relationships are adhered to in the typical American family.

Extreme financial or physical dependence of aged family members, however, tests the limits of adult children's sense of responsibility. In seeking to determine whether there is a solid moral underpinning for filial responsibility, Canadian researchers used the vignettes in Figure 11.5 to elicit adult children's sense of responsibility for physically ill or disabled parents (Wolfson et al., 1993). Respondents were first asked what levels of assistance adult children *should* provide in each case. Second, adult children were asked to imagine that it was there own parents described in the vignettes. They were asked what levels of financial assistance, emotional support, and physical assistance that they *could* provide if the elders in the vignettes were their own parents.

Figure 11.5

....

Vignettes to Elicit Sense of Responsibility of Adult Children for Dependent Parents

SOURCE: C. Wolfson et al., "Adult Children's Perceptions of Their Responsibility to Provide Care for Dependent Elderly Parents," *Gerontologist* (June 1993): 318.

Vignette 1

A 64-year-old woman had a major stroke 8 months ago causing paralysis of her right side. Because of this weakness, she is unable to get out of bed and into her wheelchair or onto the toilet without physical assistance. Her 71-year-old husband, who has some minor health problems, finds it very difficult to do this for her and is only just managing. Also, he is obviously having trouble coping emotionally with seeing his wife in such a weak condition.

Their only source of income is the government old-age pension, so they are unable to afford private help.

Vignette 2

A 76-year-old man has had Alzheimer's disease for the last 4 years. He presently lives with his wife in an apartment where a community nurse visits him every week. Besides poor memory, his major problem is that he has no understanding of his illness. He gets quite upset, and at times aggressive, when anyone tries to get him to do something against his will. He tends to get more agitated at night and has trouble sleeping. He has reached the stage where he requires supervision for most activities and so cannot safely be left alone for any length of time.

His wife, who is 72 years old, is in reasonable physical health but is becoming exhausted with having to take care of her husband. She is unable to get a good night's sleep and cannot rest during the day because she is afraid her husband will get into trouble.

They are living on their old-age pension supplemented by a small amount of savings.

Vignette 3

An 82-year-old widower lives alone in a small second-floor apartment with no elevator. He has quite bad arthritis causing pain in his knees and deformity in his hands. He can get about his apartment safely with specially designed canes but is unable to get outside without help. Even though he has few visitors he claims not to be lonely, but the visiting social worker thinks that he must be.

Two years ago he had an operation to remove a cancer from his bowel. Unfortunately, he required a permanent colostomy, which means that he has to wear a plastic bag on the side of his abdomen to collect his stool. Because of the arthritis in his fingers he needs help to empty and maintain the bag.

He receives the old-age pension along with a small pension from his former employer.

A study of adult children found that almost all of them felt they should provide emotional support for aged parents.

The overwhelming majority (almost all) felt that emotional support *should* be provided by adult children in general and *could* be provided by them for their parents. Not quite as many, but still a substantial majority, believed adult children *should* provide physical assistance; a somewhat lower percentage *could* provide physical assistance. And a majority believed adult children *should* help out financially. The lowest figure in the study was the degree to which adult children *could* help financially, and even these scores were reasonably high. The researchers concluded that adult children feel a strong moral obligation to provide care for their disabled parents. They concluded that more government programs encouraging home care would be a desirable and workable policy direction.

Another study in a similar vein asked respondents to agree or disagree with statements such as the following:

> If an old man has a medical bill of $1,000 that he cannot pay, his son or daughter is morally obligated to pay the debt. (Mangen and Westbrook, 1988).

The purpose of the study was to reach a deeper understanding of **intergenerational norms** which are the standard, expected behaviors of one generation towards another. Interestingly, on the above item older generations were more likely to disagree than younger generations. Their pride may well keep them from expecting adult children to pay their bills for them. The majority of adult children agreed with the above statement.

Not all studies show similar expectations of aid to older parents from adult children. Intergenerational conflict was revealed in a survey of three generations of women, this study used a hypothetical story about a widowed mother to ask each generation what adult children *should* do for an elderly parent (Brody et al., 1984). Respondents from each generation recommended in general that adult children not share a household with the mother. (The youngest group of women was most in favor of sharing the household, a feeling the researchers interpreted as a youthfully idealistic view of the caregiver role.)

Older parents judged female family members as acceptable to provide personal care such as meal preparation, housework, and grocery shopping, whereas male family members were judged unacceptable. Middle-aged daughters reluctant to change family schedules or give up jobs outside of the home were somewhat reluctant to become caregivers. The oldest generation of women in the Brody study expected their daughters to adjust schedules, including work schedules, to help widowed mothers. Because each generation's parent-care expectations were different conflict could eventually ensue. The middle-aged daughters, who were the busiest, were the very ones the mothers expected to assume the caregiving responsibility.

WEAKENED FAMILY SUPPORT SYSTEMS

Treas (1977) accurately predicted that the family would be more and more strained by caring for its oldest members. She cited three factors that contribute to the **weakened family support system,** which remain relevant in the 1990s: (1) demography; (2) women's changing roles; and (3) changing intergenerational relationships.

Demography

Long-run trends in morality and birthrates have startling consequences for the kin network. In the 1990s, the aging parent, having raised fewer children, will have fewer offspring to call upon for assistance than did his or her own parents. Middle-aged children without siblings to share the care of the elderly parents will feel increased strain.

Kin networks offer fewer options and resources when the younger generations have fewer members. Generally speaking, an aging couple will fare better when several children can contribute to its support. And having a number of grown children increases an aging widow's odds that one will be able to accomodate her.

With more and more people living into their eighties and beyond, more of the old will become frail elderly or the old-old. The burden of their physical, financial, and emotional support may be considerable, especially for the young-old children of old-old parents, children whose own energy, health, and finances may be declining.

Women's Changing Roles

Traditionally, providing older parents with companionship and services has produced a sexual division of labor. The major burden for physical care and social activity has traditionally fallen on female relatives' shoulders. However, social roles for women are undergoing dramatic change. Increasingly, women are working for pay outside the home. Middle-aged wives are returning to the job market when the children leave home. In 1970, only 54 percent of women between the ages of 45 and 64 worked outside the home; in 1990, close to 70 percent did so (U. S. Bureau of the Census, 1993). In fact, more than half the women who care for elderly relatives work outside the home; nearly 40 percent are still raising children of their own. The average American woman will spend 17 years raising children and 18 years helping aged parents (Beck et al., 1990). The employee role for women conflicts with caring for aging parents, which can be time-consuming—especially if the parents live in the adult offspring's home.

Changing Intergenerational Relationships

In other societies, and to an extent in this society's recent past, children are, and have been, expected to tend to their aging parents in return for inheriting the family farm or business. This exchange creates economic interdependence. Parents have insured control of children through the threat of disowning them.

Children are now less likely to take over their parents' farm or business. They are taking jobs elsewhere or establishing careers independent of their parents, and the parents have lost their power to control. Emotional ties, however, remain strong in the American family. Affection, gratitude, guilt, or a desire for parental approval still motivate adult children to care for their aging parents. Thus, the basis for helping is now less for economic and more for psychological reasons.

We may view these changes either as positive or negative. On one hand, the power of elders to ensure family support is reduced. On the other hand, Social Security and other governmental programs have also reduced the dependence of the old on family-support systems. As we experience the postindustrial society and the welfare state, both grown children and aged parents have been liberated from complete economic dependence on one another.

The family's declining ability to support the aged is resulting in more governmental and formal intervention in their care. Programs like day care centers, hot meals, and housekeeping services can help relieve overburdened family-support systems. However, these programs still suffer from high cost and limited availability.

SPOUSAL CAREGIVING

Spouses provide a large percent of caregiving, with wives being more likely to be caregivers than husbands. About 40 percent of all caregiving is provided by spouses, 14 percent by husbands, 26 percent by wives (Harris, 1993). Living to very old age as a married couple represents a biological and social achievement. Nevertheless, the consequence of marriage in late life is not always blissful. If illness and chronic impairments loom large, heightened anxiety, interpersonal difficulties, and economic strains may result. Older married women often become part-time nurses for their husbands, who tend to be older and in worse health than themselves. Of noninstitutionalized elders in the community, some are homebound, and of those, a portion are bedridden. A husband or wife is most often the primary caregiver. If the couple is lucky, paid helpers and children provide additional assistance.

Wives caring for disabled husbands are often strongly preoccupied with the husband's health. Such women are often worried, frustrated, and impatient; working wives typically experience "work overload." Both husband and wife feel isolated when they cannot maintain previous social contacts. Sometimes the caretaking role is assumed for years and years. In this example the husband has Alzheimer's disease.

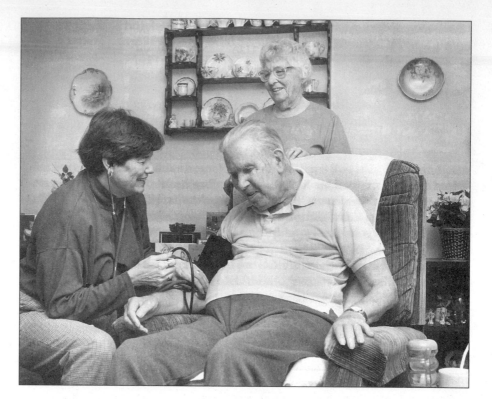

Wives caring for disabled husbands are often strongly preoccupied with the husband's health.

For nearly a decade, Hildegarde Rebenack, 69, has watched her 78-year-old husband, Robert, deteriorate from Alzheimer's disease. Robert was a bank examiner, a man proud of rising above his eighth grade education. Now, he spends his days staring at a collection of stuffed animals in their Louisiana home. . . . Robert was diagnosed in 1982. By 1984, he could no longer be left alone, and, two years later, Hildegarde had to put him into a nursing home. . . . Last March, the latest price hike forced her to bring him home. "We had 37 good years together," says Hildegarde, her voice breaking. "But the last six years have been hell." (Beck et al., 1990)

For the spouse of an impaired person, declines challenge long-established patterns of interaction, goals, and behavior. Spouses meet with circumstances that bring up the most intense emotional issues: life and its meaning, freedom, isolation, and death. One study, which showed that caregiving wives are more depressed and more burdened than caregiving husbands, found that women were more likely to be actively helping a spouse with daily living activities. In contrast, the husbands in the sample were more likely to receive help from others with hands-on care for their spouses. Interestingly, in this study of 315 caregivers, the men were more emotionally committed to helping their wives (e.g., she's always taken care of me; now I can repay her) than the women were to caring for their husbands (Pruchno and Resch, 1989). Different styles of caregiving bring different problems and issues. The women in the study seemed "burned out" by giving too much of themselves over the years, both before their husbands' health began to fail and after. One implication of the study is that wives of frail, ailing husbands would be wise to seek more outside help—and that such help should be available. Other studies indicate also that female caregivers are more likely to be involved in daily personal care of husbands and likely to report greater burdens than male caregivers (Miller and Cafasso, 1992).

In a study of husbands who were caregivers, four types were named. They are described as follows:

1. The worker—He models his role after the work role. He plans his work schedule every day. He reads everything he can about Alzheimer's disease and has a desk to organize the insurance papers and other materials.

2. Labor of love—He caretakes out of deep feelings of love. He often holds his wife's hand and embraces her. Caring is out of devotion, not duty.

3. Sense of duty—Caregiving stems from commitment, duty, and responsibility. He says, "she would have done the same for me. I will never abandon her."

4. At the crossroads—This is typical of a new caregiver who hasn't oriented to the role. He is floundering and in crisis. (Harris, 1993, p. 554)

The study showed that many husbands relied on their clergy for social support. The study recommended a variety of supports: (1) educational groups led by a male caretaker and nurse clinicians, (2) support groups for men only (because they were not comfortable discussing personal matters in predominantly female groups), (3) computer networking programs for men who would not join groups, and (4) more quality and affordable in-home respite services.

ADULT CHILDREN AS CAREGIVERS

Nearly 30 percent of aging persons who need home care are receiving it from adult daughters, and about 10 percent of ailing elders receive home care from adult sons (Stoller, 1990). The most sacrifices seem to come from "women in the middle" (Brody, 1990)—middle-aged women who have children and jobs, and who also are responsible for the home care of parents. In fact, just when women are getting off the "mommy track," they are finding themselves on the "daughter track" (Beck et al., 1990).

Unmarried adult children who share a household with the ailing parent provide the most care. Being married and being employed decreases the amount of help given. Living apart further reduces the amount of help elders receive. Adult children caregivers most commonly offer help with the following activities: getting out of bed and going to the bathroom, shopping for food, traveling, doing laundry, preparing meals, doing housework, bathing, taking medicine, dressing, getting around the house, and providing personal, supportive communication.

In examining the effect of family size on parent care, one study compared older parents with an only child with parents of two or three children and also with parents of four or more children, with regard to helping expectations and actual assistance (Hays, 1984). The results indicated that a larger number of children is related to increased frequency of contact with children and more assistance from children. Parents of only children, as one might expect, did not receive as many visits or as much aid. Regardless of family size, elderly parents' expectations were moderately high, which often left parents with one child feeling disappointed.

Studies show that approximately 25 percent of elders have no surviving children or siblings residing close enough to provide regular assistance.

Because of high employment rates for daughters and the stresses of family life for middle-aged adults, the overall levels of help suffer. Daughters from blue-collar families provide more assistance and have more interactions with their parents than do sons. Traditional sex roles are thought to be the explanation. In general, elders with a higher income receive greater contact and assistance from children. Exchange theory would explain that these elders are in a position to reciprocate with financial rewards. Another explanation might be that the children themselves have more resources than do adult children of low-income families.

A study of caregiving by adult daughters to mothers revealed that the daughters perceived the experience as much more than a series of chores. It was an emotional experience in which they assumed responsibility for their parents' lives and were dedicated to preserving their dignity and self-respect (Abel, 1991). This statement of the researcher summarizes their experiences:

> Parent care involves a constant tension between attachment and loss, pleasing and caring, seeking to preserve an older person's dignity and exerting unaccustomed authority, overcoming resistance to care and fulfilling extravagant demands, reviving a relationship and transforming it. (Abel, 1991, p. 112)

The daughters discovered they could not "go home again" in the sense that roles had reversed. Caregiving punctured the illusion of maternal omnipotence. The experience led to a mix of emotions. Some wanted outside help to gain relief from the physical burden and also to achieve emotional detachment.

Unlike caregiving for children, who become more independent with age, caregiving for the severely impaired requires more effort as the years go by. A study that interviewed 30 women caring for a chronically ill parent or parent-in-law along with the person receiving care observed two kinds of parent-caring roles: care provision and care management (Archbold, 1983). A care-provider was one who personally performed the services an older parent needed, whereas a care-manager was one who identified and obtained needed services, then supervised their provision by others.

The care-providing individuals tended to be more strained, to have lower income and less knowledge of available resources, to be more involved in the heavy physical work of daily care, and to be less apt to provide stimulating activities and entertainment. In contrast, though the care-managers did not totally avoid strain and stress, they experienced less than the care-provider. The expenses care-managers incurred were greater, but financial expenses were high for care-providers as well.

We might note here that the Tax Reform Act of 1986 entitles anyone who works and who pays for the care of a dependent to a federal tax credit. However, care must be for a child or other relative for whom the taxpayer provides *more than half* the needed support, and the maximum credit allowance is only 30 percent of care expenses per dependent. Therefore, the act provides very little actual relief.

CHILDLESSNESS

As the rate of childlessness increases in the United States, gerontologists have begun to examine its impact on elders. Children were once described as one's "old-age insurance." Yet today, 20 percent of the population over age 65 have no children; and this trend is accelerating. A basic question arises: Who is in the social-support system of the childless elderly? Childlessness has been related to isolation (Soldo et al., 1990). Other researchers have found that childless elders follow the "principle of substitution" by turning to other kin for help. But they receive less help from other kin. Nieces and nephews, for example, are not as willing to help as children. Childless married couples tend to rely primarily on each other and to remain otherwise isolated. Unmarried individuals, having established lifetime patterns for seeking assistance, are more resourceful in using a variety of people and social resources to meet their needs. The childless elderly require more highly available substitute supports (Chappell, 1991).

ELDER CAREGIVING TO ADULT CHILDREN AND GRANDCHILDREN

The number of older parents who care for dependent adult children and grandchildren is increasing. One reason is that the parents of those released from state and county mental hospitals in the 1970s are now 65 and over and in the caregiver role. Another reason is the increasing ability to prolong the lives of those with disabilities. The older parent may be caring for a mentally or physically disabled adult child. Perhaps an 85-year-old parent in good health is caring for a 65-year-old offspring who has cancer or a grandchild who has been abandoned by parents. Oftentimes the older parents assume the caregiver role because no one else is available to care for their dependent children or grandchildren. Support groups for elderly parents have become more available in recent years to help them with their caregiving in times of stress and crisis. A study investigated the impact of later-life caregiving on 105 mothers of adult children with mental illness and 208 mothers of adult children with mental retardation (Greenberg et al., 1993). The elderly mothers had the most problems with mentally ill adult children. The mentally ill children posed greater behavior problems and were less likely to have day care outside the home or be employed. The mothers' social networks of helping friends and relatives was smaller. The study emphasized the large numbers of elders in society who are on the giving rather than the receiving end of intergenerational exchanges and the gratifications of caretaking for both sets of older mothers.

☼ Solving Caregiving Problems

The stresses and strains of caregiving have drawn considerable attention over the last decade. The discussion that follows summarizes some of the solutions that have been offered.

STRESS AND STRESS MANAGEMENT

A fierce tangle of emotions comes with parenting one's parents: anguish, frustration, inadequacy, guilt, devotion, and love. Stress comes not only from these emotions, but also from work overload. "Caregiver distress" indicates the negative stresses of caretaking, including role strain, subjective burden, depression, anxiety, hostility, and other troublesome emotions. Scales such as the Zarit Burden Interview (ZBI) have been developed to measure degrees of caregiver distress (Knight et al., 1993). One specific emotion that has been widely studied is depression. Gerontologists are seeking to understand how much of the depression precedes the caregiving distress and how much is solely the result of the new added role. Those who are not depressed to begin with cope better than those who are. Personality factors have been examined, using personality inventories, for their role in one's ability to cope (Hooker et al., 1994).

Coping has been conceptualized as a response to the demands of specific stressful current situations. Coping techniques and abilities vary from person to person. These variations in ability need attention and explanation so that persons with poor skills can be helped. In one study the specific stressors imbedded in caring for severely impaired elders were specified. The most commonly identified characteristics of the person with Alzheimer's disease that caused stress to the caregiver were memory defects, loss of ability to communicate, and unrelenting decline (Williamson and Schulz, 1993). Coping strategies for depressed caregivers were wishfulness and stoicism. In these cases, caregivers dreamed and hoped the situation would change and fought their battles alone. Coping strategies for less depressed caregivers were relaxation, acceptance, and the seeking of social support. In these cases, caregivers accepted the reality of the disease and reached out to others for help.

Problems in caregiving tasks come from (1) the strain of responsibility for direct personal care of the elder, (2) the caregivers' own current personal and health problems, (3) role strain from the demands of other work and the need for leisure, (4) intersibling problems and other strained family relationships, and (5) arranging outside help and coping with bureaucratic mix-ups.

A social support network is very important to caregivers. Face-to-face interviews with 50 older women caring for husbands with dementia revealed that these women, who experienced frustrations and disrupted life plans, were gratified if a feeling of marital closeness continued through difficult times. In this particular study, marital closeness and a good support network offset the severity of patient symptoms and the duration of caregiving (Motenko, 1989).

Although helping parents can be rewarding for many adult children, it can be accompanied with enormous burdens, both financial and emotional. The principal caregiving adult children are "women in the middle," pulled in many directions from competing demands on their time and energy. Brody (1990) reports that three-fourths of these women said that they felt they were not doing enough for their mothers. She offers the hypothesis that adult children feel guilty as caregivers because they have a deep feeling that they should give as much care as their parents gave them in their childhood and infancy. This is impossible, and guilt is the result. She believes adult children should not fall for the myths that families provided better care in the "good old days."

To alleviate stress, caregivers are well advised to educate themselves by reading books about others with similar problems and/or by reading self-help books (see Further Readings). Books such as *Taking Time for Me: How Caregivers Can Effectively Deal with Stress* (Karr, 1992) help caretakers deal with their feelings: love, compassion, indifference, hostility, or guilt. Community services for the aged are described, and families are shown how to work together more effectively to reduce stress and strain. Caregivers are also encouraged to form social support networks of friends and neighbors (Clipp and George, 1990).

PSYCHOSOCIAL INTERVENTIONS AND RESPITE CARE FOR CAREGIVERS

The 1980s was a time for drawing attention to the burdens of caregiving. Gerontologists have documented the problems over and over again, but

The Pianist

■ *Carolyn J. Fairweather Hughes*

Gnarled fingers of hands
that were once beautiful
fondle the yellowed keys.

When no one is listening,
she randomly strikes
a few dissonant notes.

Sometimes, I have to turn away
to keep from weeping
at her altered state.

But then, I see
the grey, wrinkled face smile
as chords, precise and graceful,

drop from her hands
like ripened plums.

SOURCE: *When I Am an Old Woman I Shall Wear Purple*, Papier-Mache Press, 1987. With permission of author Carolyn J. Fairweather Hughes.

are still studying what kind of help is most useful. A controlled study of psychosocial interventions (psychological help from paid professionals) and respite programs (programs that allow the caregiver time off) showed them generally to be moderately effective (Knight et al., 1993). The kinds of **psychosocial interventions** for the caretakers were varied: individual counseling, family counseling, support groups, educational groups, problem-solving groups for the caretaker and patient, social worker visits, and family consultants.

Support groups are typically available in larger communities at mental health clinics, and also from individual counselors. They usually meet once a week for eight weeks or so, in which individuals share problems and help each other with emotional support, friendship, and ideas. A paid professional leads the group. We should keep in mind that group interventions such as these work for some, but not for everyone. Counseling, either individual or family, can also be helpful if families can afford it; although for some families suffering from poor relationships, no amount of professional help can "fix" the problem. In this case, emotional distancing may be the only stress-management technique that would alleviate guilt and despair. Organizations are available in most communities to offer services to caregivers or to refer them to individuals who do.

In the study cited earlier by Knight et al. (1993), respite care was somewhat more effective than psychosocial interventions. **Respite care** can mean placement of the dependent elder in a nursing home for two weeks or so, or it may involve bringing a hired home-care worker into the home for one to two weeks or more while the caregiver goes on a vacation. Time off for the caregiver is very important in relieving distress. Intervention and respite care should not measure its success by the alleviation of caregiver distress only. Other important outcomes have been found: improved functioning of the dependent elder, reduced use of hospital days for the elder, and improvements in patient mortality.

Future research should direct attention to how much and what kind of intervention is necessary to achieve a desired effect (Knight et al., 1993). If interventions and respite care work, which they often do, the appropriate question becomes, What works best at what levels of strength with which kinds of caregivers for elders with which kinds of impairments? Studies are also underway to encourage support groups in African-American and Hispanic populations (Henderson et al., 1993). One finding shows that recruiting ethnic minority caregivers to participate in support group activities requires an enormous amount of personal contact. Understanding the local ethnic minority cultures is crucial to providing a comfortable and useful setting for offering support.

THE HOME-CARE CRISIS

As the percentage of frail elders increases and as more family members work outside the home, a crisis is emerging. Who will care for the very old in our society? Many gerontologists believe that developing a paraprofessional labor force for long-term care of the aged and disabled is a national priority. Present trends toward increased numbers of elders and the desire for independent living accentuate the importance of paid caregiving by qualified workers.

Too often, workers have been poorly paid, overworked, and undertrained. They are disproportionately ethnic minority, middle-aged women

(Feldman, 1993). Wages, job conditions, and opportunities for caregiving work have typically been at the lower end of the employment scale, with no chance for advancement. Outstanding **paraprofessional caregivers** in such job categories as nurse's aid, home health aide, personal care attendant, chore worker, and homemaker should receive prospects for increased responsibility and advancement. Poorly paid **paraprofessional home-care workers** are a transient work group with a high turnover rate. Paraprofessionals at present have little training. They must undergo about 75 hours of training and pass a competency test. In many states the requirements include fewer hours of training and no test. In the face of easy entry into the field one might expect a large labor pool, but this is not the case (MacAdam, 1993a). Many states report having trouble delivering state-funded home-care services because of worker shortages and high turnover. With increased wages and better working conditions, turnover can be reduced and continuity of care improved (Feldman, 1993).

Paraprofessional home-care wages lag behind those with similar jobs in nursing homes and hospitals. Homemaker rates in Massachusetts are at the higher end of the pay scale, running from $11.50 to $12.50 per hour. However, large cuts in state home-care funding have resulted in the loss of 500 paraprofessional homemaker jobs in that state. Another problem in the industry is the poor job image associated with the long-term care of chronically disabled elders (MacAdam, 1993b). More attention needs to be paid to upgrading the job image and recruiting, training, and retaining quality home-care workers for elders (Eustis et al., 1993). The number of elders is expected to increase by 40 percent over the next 30 years, and the utilization of home care is expected to increase by 60 percent over this time (Burbridge, 1993).

Many families do not qualify for state-funded home-care workers. Studies show that nearly 46 percent of all Medicare users of home health care must purchase services in addition to those Medicare offers (Kane, 1989). Only 25 percent of the disabled elderly population getting home assistance receives skilled nursing care at home. When they have to pay out of their own pockets, many go without care. Those in need who have enough income and access to services do seek paid help (Stoller and Cutler, 1993).

Although private insurance should be available at affordable prices to cover home care, it typically is not. In the words of gerontologist Nancy Kane, "Society should be compelled to come up with better ways to both pay for home care and provide the services" (Kane, 1989, p. 24). She proposes a managed long-term care insurance program focused on maintaining older people in their homes, a program similar to most HMOs. She estimates that 40 to 50 percent of the very old could afford such an insurance policy. The federal government could assist in a number of ways, such as subsidizing low-income elders who want to buy into the program.

The private sector has a stake in care for elders. There were 33 million Americans aged 65 or older in 1990; 70 million will reach old age in the next century when life expectancy may increase to 90 years. Currently, about 80 percent of all in-home care received by frail elders is being provided by family members. This elder care costs business billions of dollars per year in absenteeism, lost productivity, and increased turnover (Scharlach et al., 1990 and Scharlach, 1994).

Businesses are run better if caregiving adult workers receive outside help in caring for aged parents. To date, only about 3 percent of U.S. companies have policies that assist employees who care for the elderly; but many more are considering such programs. Such programs need to develop, and quickly; for the growth in the labor force in the 1990s will come primarily from women aged 35 to 54, Brody's stressed "women in the middle."

Researches suggest that employers could provide more policies, benefits, and services for employees who are caregivers. They recommend:

1. part-time job options such as job sharing, voluntary reduced time, or shared retirement;

2. flexible work hours, such as a spread during the day and evening, or a compressed workweek with a day or two off;

3. policies encouraging working at home;

4. paid sick, vacation, and personal leave;

5. parental/family leave—paid or unpaid;

6. medical/emergency leave;

7. dependent-care reimbursement plan in which the employer directly subsidizes a portion of the employee's caregiving expenses;

8. long-term care insurance that includes home care by paraprofessionals and respite for family caregivers;

9. education about caregiving;

10. resource and referral;

11. counseling;

12. on-site day care; and

13. more tax relief for caregivers (Neal et al., 1993).

The point is that, as a society, we should make it easier for family members to assume care of their elders. It would reduce government costs and give individuals the satisfaction of helping their own kin.

One company that recognizes the importance of care from the viewpoint of both employee and care receiver is the Stride Rite Corporation in Massachusetts, which has a corporate day-care center for both children and elders. Employees pay according to their income, and the company's charitable foundation makes up the difference. The elders and children spend some time together but do have separate activities. Elders who are able to read stories to the children; both young and old seem to enjoy each other (Kantrowitz, 1990). Large companies such as IBM and the Travelers Insurance Company also have elder care programs. They offer flexible work schedules to allow employees time to care for older relatives and further, pay for leave up to 26 weeks for elder care. Adult day-care costs can be lower than bringing in home health care aides, depending on how much care is needed. We need many more such creative efforts to insure proper care and attention for all persons in their frail years.

Chapter Summary

This chapter is an extension of the chapter on social bonds with an emphasis on the old-old and caregiving. Norms governing intergenerational relationships are not clear-cut. This leaves room for elders to feel disappointed when adult children do not live close by and act in a supportive manner. Aged women far outnumber aged men, especially at advanced ages. The existing studies show the old-old to be healthier and more active than stereotypes would have us believe. Most manage to live outside nursing homes, either in their own homes or with adult children. Chronic conditions are common but most are not totally disabled by them. Caregiving by adult children is becoming more and more common as more elders live into their 80s, 90s, and 100s. The largest percentage of caregiving is provided by older wives and middle-aged daughters. A smaller but substantial percentage of caregivers are older husbands and sons. Caregiving places a great deal of stress on families because more women are employed outside the home and families have fewer children than they once did. In spite of the burdens, the family in the United States remains strong and a major source of aid to its members. More paraprofessionals are needed in the home-care field to offer quality care at a reasonable price to the oldest-old.

Key Terms

caregiver distress
coping
formal caregiving
informal caregiving
instrumental activities of daily living
intergenerational norms
modified nuclear family

oldest-old
paraprofessional caregiver
paraprofessional home-care worker
(personal) activities of daily living
psychosocial interventions
respite care
weakened family support system

Questions for Discussion

1. How would you compare the lifestyles of childless older couples with the lifestyles of older couples with children?

2. What kind of life do you hope to live when you are one of the oldest-old?

3. Based on your relationship with your parents now, what will your relationship be like if and when they become very old and need care?

4. What satisfactions could one enjoy from serving in capacities such as nurse's aide, home health aide, personal care attendant, chore worker, or homemaker?

Fieldwork Suggestions

1. Interview older people about their friendship networks. How many friends do they have? How many are close friends? Are they of the same gender? How many are relatives?

2. Contrast the daily life of a very old person who is frail and ill with one who is active and fit.

3. Interview a family in a caregiving situation. Are there stresses and strains? Is there love and affection? Explain.

References

Abel, E. *Who Cares for the Elderly: Public Policy and the Experience of Adult Daughters.* Philadelphia: Temple University Press, 1991.

Archbold, P. "Impact of Parent-Caring on Women." *Family Relations* 32 (January 1983): 39–45.

Baur, P., and M. Okun. "Stability of Life Satisfaction in Later Life." *Gerontologist* 23 (June 1983): 261–265.

Beck, M., et al. "Trading Places." *Newsweek* (16 July 1990): 48–54.

Bould, S., et al. *Eighty-Five Plus: The Oldest Old.* Belmont, CA:

Wadsworth Publishing, 1989.

Brody, E. *Women in the Middle: Their Parent Care Years.* New York: Springer, 1990.

Brody, E., et al. "Caregivers, Daughters and Their Local Siblings. Perceptions, Strains, and Interactions." *Gerontologist* 29:4 (1984): 529–538.

Burbridge, L. "The Labor Market for Home Care Workers." *Gerontologist* (February 1993): 41–46.

Chappell, N. "Living Arrangements and Sources of Caregiving." *Journal of Gerontology* 46:1 (January 1991): S1–8.

Clipp, E., and L. George. "Caregiver Needs and Patterns of Social Support." *Journal of Gerontology* 45:3 (May 1990): S102–111.

Cowley, Malcolm. *The View from Eighty.* New York: Viking Press, 1980.

Eustis, N., et al. "Home Care Quality and the Home Care Worker: Beyond Quality Assurance as Usual." *Gerontologist* (February 1993): 64–73.

Foldman, D. "Work Life Improvements for Home Care Workers: Impact and Feasibility." *Gerontologist* (February 1993): 47–54.

Greenberg, J., et al. "Aging Parents of Adults with Disabilities: Gratifications and Frustrations." *Gerontologist* (August 1993): 542–550.

Harris, P. "The Misunderstood Caregiver? A Qualitative Study of the Male Caregiver." *Gerontologist* (August 1993): 551–556.

Hays, J. "Aging and Family Resources." *Gerontologist* 24 (April 1984): 149–153.

Henderson, J., et al. "A Model for Alzheimer's Disease Support Group Development in African American and Hispanic Populations." *Gerontologist* (June 1993): 409–414.

Heynen, J. *One Hundred Over 100.* Golden, CO: Fulcrum Publishing, 1990.

Hooker, K., et al. "Personality and Coping Among Caregivers of Spouses with Dementia." *Gerontologist* (June 1994): 386–392.

Kane, Nancy. "The Home Care Crisis of the Nineties." *Gerontologist* 29:1 (February 1989): 24–31.

Kantrowitz, B. "Day Care: Bridging the Generation Gap." *Newsweek* (16 July 1990): 52.

Karr, K. *Taking Time for Me: How Caregivers Can Effectively Deal with Stress.* Philadelphia: Temple University Press, 1992.

Knight, B., et al. "A Meta-analytic Review of Interventions for Caregiver Distress." *Gerontologist* (April 1993): 249–257.

MacAdam, M. "Paraprofessional Home Care Workers." *Gerontologist* (February 1993a): 41.

———. "Home Care Reimbursement and Effects on Personnel." *Gerontologist* (February 1993b): 55–63.

Mangen, D., and G. Westbrook, "Measuring Intergenerational Norms." In *Measurement of Intergenerational Relationships,* edited by D. Mangen et al. Newbury Park, CA: Sage, 1988.

Miller, B., and L. Cafasso. "Gender Differences in Caregiving: Fact or Artifact?" *Gerontologist* (August 1992): 498–507.

Minkler, M., et al. "Community Interventions to Support Grandparent Caregivers." *Gerontologist* (December 1993): 807–811.

Monson, Gordon. Caught in the Middle, *L.A. Times,* May 12, 1993, p. E1.

Motenko, A. "The Frustrations, Gratifications, and Well-Being of Dementia Caregivers." *Gerontologist* 29:2 (April 1989): 166–172.

Neal, M., et al. *Balancing Work and Caregiving for Children, Adults, and Elders.* Newbury Park, CA: Sage, 1993.

Palmore, E., et al. "Predictors of Function Among the Old Old. A Ten-Year Follow-Up." *Journal of Gerontology* 40 (March 1985): 244–250.

Poon, L. W., et al. *The Georgia Centenarian Study.* Amityville, NY: Baywood Publishing, 1992.

Pruchno, R., and N. Resch. "Husbands and Wives as Caregivers: Antecedents of Depression and Burden." *Gerontologist* 29:2 (1989): 159–164.

Scharlach, A. "Caregiving and Employment: Competing or Complementary Roles." *Gerontologist* (June 1994): 378–385.

Scharlach, A., et al. *Elder Care and the Work Force.* Lexington, MA: Lexington Books, 1990.

Soldo, B., et al. "Family Households and Care Arrangements of Frail Older Women: A Structural Analysis." *Journal of Gerontology* 45:6 (November 1990): S238–249.

Stoller, E. "Males as Helpers: The Role of Sons, Relatives, and Friends." *Gerontologist* 30 (April 1990): 228–236.

Stoller, E., and S. Cutler. "Predictors of Use of Paid Help Among Older People Living in the Community." *Gerontologist* (February 1993): 31–40.

Suzman, R., et al. "The Robust Oldest Old." In *The Oldest Old,* edited by R. Suzman et al., 341–358. New York: Oxford University Press, 1992.

Treas, J. "Family Support Systems for the Aged." *Gerontologist* 17 (1977): 486–491.

U.S. Census Bureau, *Statistical Abstract of the United States,* 1993, 113th ed., Washington, DC: U.S. Government Printing Office, 1993.

Williamson, G., and R. Schulz. "Coping with Specific Stressors in Alzheimer's Disease Caregiving." *Gerontologist* (December 1993): 747–755.

Wolfson, C., et al. "Adult Children's Perceptions of Their Responsibility to Provide Care for Dependent Elderly Parents." *Gerontologist* (June 1993): 315–323.

Further Readings

....

Coughlan, P. *Facing Alzheimer's: Family Caregivers Speak,* Ivy: Ballantine Books, 1993.

Kahana, E., et al. eds. *Family Caregiving Across the Life Span,* Newbury Park, CA: Sage, 1994.

San Francisco Examiner/Chronicle, Series on Caregivers, section A, six articles by various authors: March 5, 12, 19, and 26; April 2 and 9, 1995.

Wright, L. *Alzheimer's Disease and Marriage: An Intimate Account,* Newbury Park, CA: Sage, 1993.

Zarit, S., et al., eds. *Caregiving Systems: Informal and Formal Helpers.* Hillsdale, NJ: Lawrence Erlbaum Associates, 1993.

12 Special Problems

CHAPTER OUTLINE

OLD IS NEWS

Stale Elder Abuse Reports Increase

■ SUSAN BARBER

The neighbors heard Mary's cries.

When Eau Claire police found the 72-year-old woman locked in the bathroom, they found she had been in the room three days and two nights. She was caked in her own feces and urine.

Mary, whose caregiver daughter had died, was living with her son-in-law and granddaughter. When she refused to turn over her $68 Social Security check, she was locked in the bathroom, check hidden in her bra.

The police brought Mary to Bolton Refuge House, an Eau Claire shelter, where workers cleaned her and called her other daughters.

When the women arrived, they peered down their mother's bra for the Social Security check, which a Bolton Refuge House worker had stored for safe keeping.

Instead of going home with loving children, the Eau Claire County Department of Human Services placed Mary in an apartment for the elderly.

All for $68.

•

Reality can shatter the Norman Rockwell-image of Grandma and Grandpa sitting on the porch swing sharing a glass of lemonade.

"A marriage license is a sentence to life imprisonment for some women," said Louise Garvey, a counselor with Bolton Refuge House who holds a weekly Elder Abuse Support Group for women age 55 and older.

That's how 73-year-old Elizabeth would describe her 53 years of marriage. "Neither one of us are well," she said. "This is the time that we should be the happiest of our life. It's just been really plain hell."

Elizabeth said the mental abuse was worse than the physical violence she endured.

That is typical in elder abuse situations, Garvey said.

"Older men don't hit," she said. "They use silence or swearing. . . . These women have been called every single dirty name in the book. They use those words because they know it bothers (them). These are men they love, not some stranger in a bar."

Today Elizabeth and her husband are at a turning point. After attending Al-Anon, a group for the families of alcoholics, and getting involved with Garvey's support group, she found the courage to leave her husband and stay at Bolton Refuge House for a time.

Her husband agreed to get counseling.

"He knows I mean business," Elizabeth said. "Right now I've never been happier in my whole life.

"He's not changing with everything. But the things that he doesn't (change), I'm able to cope with it.

"This is the only help I've ever found," Elizabeth said of the support group. ☀

SOURCE: *Eau Claire (Wisconsin) Leader-Telegram,* 27 March 1994, pp. E1–E2.

---

*R*ight at this moment, an older person is being robbed or mugged. Right at this moment, an elder is being abused by caretakers, cheated of his or her savings, or victimized by medical quackery. Some abuses against elders are committed by street thugs; others are perpetrated by presumably reputable business people and professionals; and still others are committed by adult children or by paid caretakers. And some of the abuse is self-inflicted. Every 83 minutes an elderly American commits suicide (McIntosh, 1992).

With regard to crime, the actual commission is only one aspect of the problem; the fear of crime brings its own set of problems. Law enforcement and social agencies now recognize the crime patterns most likely to affect elders. Older people themselves are devising ways to fight back, and they are taking initiative, both as individuals and as a group, to protect and defend themselves.

As we develop our understanding of what it means to be old in our society, we must understand that it brings a vulnerability due to ageism and, for some, further vulnerability due to physical and financial limitations. Here we discuss some special problms that, if not unique, occur in high frequency within the aged population. And let us not forget that older persons are not always victims; they can also be perpetrators. This topic will be covered briefly.

☼ Suicide

Suicide is one of the ten leading causes of death in the United States. The annual national **suicide rate** is about 12 persons per 100,000 (U.S. Census Bureau, 1993). The rate is the reported rate but may be underestimated because many suicides go undetected and some are actually concealed. Accidents, especially those involving motor vehicles, overdoses of prescribed medication, or the long-term self-neglect found with alcoholism can mask deliberate self-destruction.

The United States witnessed a decrease in the suicide rate for the 65-and-over population from 1933 to 1969, not much change in the 1970s, a dip in the early 1980s, only to be followed by a considerable rise in the mid and late 1980s. The rate has remained stable in the 1990s. In 1933, the first year the National Center for Health Statistics kept suicide statistics, the suicide rate among elders was 45.3 per 100,000 as against a national average of 15.9. In 1981, it was 17.1 against a national average of 12. Since then it increased to 22 in 1986 against a national average of 12 and was at 21 against a national average of 12 in 1990.

DIFFERENCES BY GENDER AND RACE

The suicide rate of those 65 and older is the highest of any age group, even teenagers. Women 65 and over, however, have a disproportionately low rate of suicide; suicides peak for women in middle age rather than old age at a rate of 7.8. The rates in old age for white and black women combined are about 6.5. But in the United States the risk of suicide for men, although high starting in the teen years, continues to increase with age. Older men have a rate several times the overall average rate of suicide. Furthermore, in old age, the proportion of **successful suicides** to **attempted suicides** is higher than in younger age brackets. This suggests that older men are more determined to end their lives. The high rate of suicide among aged men is not a universal pattern; in the Scandinavian countries, and in other countries as well, suicide peaks in middle age (Lester and Tallmer, 1994).

The high suicide rate for men in the United States is a critical problem. Over the last few years suicide rates for women have dropped, whereas they rose among men (1992). Table 12.1 shows the suicide rates for the older population. Notice the dramatically high suicide rates for older white males.

Several reasons for a higher male suicide rate have been offered such as loneliness, ill health, anger, and depression. Men tend to be more combative

	Male			**Female**		**Table 12.1**
	Total	*White*	*Black*	*White*	*Black*	
55–64	16	27.5	10.8	8.0	2.6	Suicide Rates of Older Population by Sex, Race, and Age Group, 1991
65–74	17	34.2	14.7	7.2	2.6	
75–84	24.9	60.2	14.4	6.7	Unknown	
85 & Over	22.2	70.3	Unknown	5.4	Unknown	

SOURCE: Adapted from U.S. Bureau of Census, *Statistical Abstract of the United States,* 113th ed., Washington, D.C.: U.S. Government Printing Office, 1993, p. 99.

and aggressive, and more action oriented. In 1988 nearly 8 out of 10 suicides by males 65 and over were committed with a firearm (Kaplan et al., 1994). Men are more adversely affected by retirement and less willing to endure illness and inactive status. At home and out of the workplace, they may feel diminished. Women are more used to secondary status; if an older woman is poor, she often can better handle the situation, whereas a man feels that he is at fault and a failure. Women also tend to have a larger and more intimate circle of supportive friends. Men tend to be more socially isolated and have more trouble asking for help. Divorced aged men, for example, have a suicide rate that is quite high: 102 per 100,000 (McIntosh, 1992). Notice the comparatively low rates of suicide for older black men and women. The reasons for these low rates are not entirely clear, but they are thought to be related to positive views of aging, a developed tolerance for suffering, and the lack of a giant step downward in status that white males experience in retirement.

CAUSES OF SUICIDE

Some experts speculate that the technological advances bring a quality of life that elders cannot accept. These advances give people longer lives, but the quality of that life is not always good. Medical costs may be extremely high, and the person may be helpless and/or in physical pain.

Suffering and loss are factors known to be related to suicide, and these experiences may accompany advanced aging. Table 12.2 reflects some major factors related to suicide, both its causes and its prevention. The most significant factor is the loss of a loved one by separation or death. When children leave home, when friends and relatives die, and especially when a spouse dies, the survivor is often beset with the desperate feeling that there is no reason to continue living. Downward social mobility is related to suicide at all ages. The experience is profound if retirement forces a lifestyle change to a lower standard of living and lower social status. Social isolation has been related to suicide, and the fact is that elders are all too often isolated both socially and psychologically by attitudes and practices of ageism in society at large. A study of suicide notes indicates that males tend to write about painful problems in their interpersonal relations (Leenaars, 1992).

Perhaps most important, physical illness, pain, or disability can prompt suicide. Aversion to the bodily changes that illness brings and worry over medical bills, coupled with the possibility of becoming a burden to one's family or to society, are typical reasons for older persons to take their own lives. Studies show that a high percentage of elders who commit suicide had seen a doctor the previous month. Physical illness as a cause of depression may be a common precipitating factor in completed suicides. Studies generally show that more than 60 percent of older suicide victims have extreme medical prob-

Table 12.2	**I. Ego Weakening Factors**
Suicide Recognition and Recovery Factors: The Most Frequent Signs	Major mental, physical, or neurological illness. Depression. Paranoia or a paranoid attitude. Alcoholism or heavy drinking. Intractable, unremitting pain, mental or physical, that is not responding to treatment.

II. Social Isolation

Living alone.
Living in the inner city, or a socially disorganized area.
Few or no friends.
Isolation or social withdrawal of a couple.

III. Psychodynamic Factors

A major loss, such as the death of a spouse.
*A history of major losses.
A recent suicide attempt.
A previous history of suicide attempts.
A family history of suicide.
Major crises or transitions, such as retirement or imminent entry into a nursing home.
Major crises or changes in others, especially among family members.
Age-related blows to self-esteem, such as loss of income or loss of meaningful activities.
Loss of independence, when dependence is unacceptable.

IV. Attitudinal and Communication Factors

Rejection of help; a suspicious and hostile attitude towards helpers and society.
Expressions of feeling unnecessary, useless, and devalued.
Increased irritability and poor judgment, especially following a loss or some other crisis.
Expression of the belief that one is a burden, in the way, or harmful to others.
Expression of the belief that one is in an insoluble and hopeless situation.
The direct or indirect expression of suicidal ideation or impulses. Included, too, are symptomatic acts, such as giving away valued possessions, storing up medication, and buying a gun.
Feelings of hopelessness and helplessness in the family and social network.
Feelings of hopelessness in the therapist or other helpers, or a desire to be rid of the patient.
Feelings of being trapped with no way out, and finished with life.
Acceptance of suicide as a solution.

V. Recovery Factors: Resources and Abilities

A potential for:
  Understanding,
  Relating,
  Benefitting from experience, and
  Benefitting from knowledge.
  Acceptance of help.
A potential or capacity for:
  Loving,
  Wisdom,
  A sense of humor,
  Social interest,
  A caring and available family,
  A caring and available social network,
  A caring, available, and knowledgeable professional and health network.
*or cumulative recent losses

Joseph Richman, *Preventing Elderly Suicide: Overcoming Personal Despair, Professional Neglect and Social Bias* (New York: Springer, 1993), pp. 5–6.

lems (Lester and Tallmer, 1994). Depression appears to be a factor in many suicides. Studies show that the vast majority of older suicide victims have suffered from depression or some other form of mental illness.

CHOICES

The Hemlock Society in Los Angeles was founded by Derek Humphry in 1980 to help people make choices about how they would deal with terminal illness. The motto of the society is "Good life, good death through control and choice." Humphry gained international fame after writing *Jean's Way*, the personal account of how he helped his terminally ill wife kill herself in 1975. Humphry's book *Let Me Die Before I Wake* (1985) describes methods and recommended drug dosages for a nonviolent, painless death. It has sold more than 100,000 copies. Humphry, aged 61 in 1994, comes to Florida every year to visit each of the state's 13 Hemlock chapters. More than 4,000 of the society's 40,000 paid members (annual dues: $10) live in Florida, second in size only to California. Until recently, most members were older people. Now with AIDS in our midst, many younger people are joining. Humphry's book *Final Exit* (1991), shares with the public methods to use to die a gentle, painless death; it, too, has been a best-seller. His most recent book is *Dying with Dignity* (1993). The Hemlock Society does not believe that suicides are necessarily the result of poor mental health. They can be the result of a sound decision based on good mental health, what Humphry called a **rational suicide**. Thus, the relationship between suicide and mental health is not as clear-cut to some as it is to others.

Therapeutic intervention by skilled professionals is certainly recommended for a suicidal person. Depression is treatable with psychotherapy or drugs. Many communities have established suicide-prevention centers that maintain 24-hour crisis lines for helping persons in distress. The National Center for Studies of Suicide Prevention has assigned a high priority to the problem of suicide among those 65 and older. There is, however, a shortage of skilled therapists to treat self-destructive elders, and of all calls to suicide hot lines, those over 65 make only 3 percent of them. Even though suicide is more common in the elderly than in other age groups, it is still a relatively rare event. What is missing in the discussion of suicides among elders is why some can cope with stress and loss and others cannot (Lester and Tallmer, 1994). Society may not sufficiently recognize the mixed picture of (a) the hardy survivorship qualities of old people and (b) the isolating effect of relentless loss of peers (Kastenbaum, 1992). All in all, the viability and allegiance to life of elders in general should not be underestimated.

SELF-DESTRUCTIVE BEHAVIOR

Both in the population as a whole and in all age groups, *attempted* suicide is most prevalent among females. One implication here is that females exhibit a greater number of total suicidal behaviors than do males at all ages. With increasing age, the percentage of successful attempts (the ratio of successful attempts to the total number of attempts) among females rises from 8 percent in very early adulthood (age 20 to 29) to 38 percent for those 65 and over. But they do not come close to the success rate of men. About 68 percent of all suicide attempts of men 65 and over are successful (McIntosh, 1992). The approximate 6,500 suicides per year of those 65 and over leaves a large number of survivors who grieve and mourn. This issue, too, must be considered in any discussion of suicide. For those who cannot cope, a growing trend toward **double suicides** has been observed. Of double suicides the most common pattern is a mercy killing with the husband as the instigator, followed by his suicide. Those in nursing homes are especially vulnerable to self-destructive behavior. Although the suicide rate is

Thinking about Aging

Partners for Life Took Death into Their Own Hands

■ CHRIS COURSEY

They lived together for 54 years, and they died together two weeks ago on a bench in Santa Rosa's Howarth Park.

Just after midnight on Aug. 24, Mervyn Adams twice shot his 83-year-old wife in the chest with a .38 caliber revolver. Then the 81-year-old grandfather put the gun to his own head, and pulled the trigger.

Police classify the Adams' deaths as a murder/suicide. But Peter Adams has no doubt that his parents' deaths were a carefully planned, "rational act" committed by two people fully aware of what they were doing.

"It was an act of love," he said.

Gladys Adams, a retired elementary school teacher, and Mervyn Adams, a self-taught, "brilliant man" who had been an English police officer, a Mendocino County timber worker and a Seattle land salesman, both suffered from severe arthritis, their son said. An active couple, they had enjoyed hiking in Howarth, Spring Lake and Annadel parks until the pain in their joints and Gladys Adams' Parkinson's disease slowed them down in recent years.

For the past year, they had been mostly housebound.

While psychiatrists say that the vast majority of suicides result from treatable depression, Peter Adams said his parents do not fit into that category.

"This was not a situation of temporary despondency," said Peter Adams, a 52-year-old theoretical physicist. "It was something that they'd thought long and hard about.

"They were very independent people, but they were losing their independence, and they resented that very much. Both of them were in considerable pain all the time; even casual motion was painful."

At an annual family reunion in July, when the Adamses gathered their two sons and their wives and four grandchildren around them in Santa Rosa, the old couple "was physically much worse, but mentally all there," he said. "It was a genuinely happy reunion. But even with that, Dad took me aside and told me that he and Mother felt the end was not far off.

The Adamses apparently meticulously planned their deaths. They made arrangements for their cremation, paid their rent, cleaned out their apartment, wrote letters to their children, their grandchildren and the police. To make sure the gun he used didn't fall into the wrong hands, Mervyn Adams chained the weapon to his wrist.

"They covered all the bases," said Peter Adams, who came to Santa Rosa as executor of their estate. "There wasn't much for me to do. All I found in their apartment was one cobweb and a little glass hummingbird hanging from the chandelier. ☀

SOURCE: *Santa Rosa Press Democrat,* Sept. 6, 1993, pp. D1, D6.

---

only 16 per 100,000, the attempted rate is 63, the rate of death from indirect self-destructive behavior is 79, and the rate of nonlethal, indirect self-destructive behavior is 228 per 100,000 (Osgood, 1991). Methods included self-mutilation, ingestion of foreign substances, refusal to eat or drink, or any repetitive act bringing physical harm or tissue damage.

FUTURE TRENDS

Suicide is twice as prevalent in western states as in the East and Midwest. Older persons in the West are more likely to have moved away from friends and family, and the divorce rate is higher there. These facts imply that meaningful social interaction is more difficult to come by in the West. Meaningful personal relationships are the most potent antisuicide remedies; failures and losses are burdens easier to bear when people have close friends and family nearby. Studies also show that people with strong religious beliefs are less likely to commit suicide. We would do well to take into account the current status and treatment of elders in our society as we formulate suicide-prevention programs in the future.

Health experts anticipate an even higher rate of suicide as the post–World War II baby boomers reach age 65. Statistically, baby boomers have had higher rates of mental illness than their predecessors; after age 65, this group may suffer a tragically high suicide rate.

Crimes Against Persons

Though attacks on elders have drawn increasing media attention in recent years, national surveys show that they are less likely to be victimized than younger adults. When one considers **crimes against persons,** such as robbery, rape, and assault, only one specific area shows elders victimized as frequently as younger adults—the personal larceny of purse and wallet snatchings and pocket-picking (U.S. Census Bureau, 1993, 192). Researchers are studying crime against elders in an attempt to reduce it and to reduce the fears regarding it.

Gerontologists are aware of the wide variations in victimization rates. Surveys show that a majority of violent victimizations of older people occur in or near their homes. The converse applies to younger adults, who are more likely to be attacked when away from their homes. Unlike younger adults, elders tend to avoid places of danger and to restrict their use of public streets. But, in spite of precautions and their tendency to stay home more, some elders still are victimized.

Their particular vulnerability may well be a reason for attacks on older individuals. Many are poor, living on fixed incomes, and dependent on public transportation. They may live in neighborhoods with relatively high crime rates, or in changing neighborhoods where unemployed youths prey on them. Often, they are not physically strong enough to defend themselves against their assailants. Further, they are often unable to identify attackers, or may be unwilling to report crimes or press charges for fear of reprisal. Crimes against the elderly are often called **crib jobs,** because robbing an old person is supposedly like taking candy from a baby.

A 33-year-old woman decided to experience victimization by "becoming old" herself. Donning a gray wig, wearing semi-opaque glasses, and putting splints and bandages on her legs, she created, at various times, three characters: a shopping bag lady, a middle-income woman, and an affluent woman. She traveled through 116 big cities and small towns across the United States, walking the streets, eating at restaurants, and living in motels. While some people were sweet and kind to her, she was overwhelmed at the abusive and neglectful attitudes of others, and by the constraints she suffered because of transporation systems inadequate for those who have difficulty walking or seeing. She was mugged twice in New York City. Today she lectures to designers and gerontologist on the needs of elders. A TV movie based on her experience is in the works (Ryan, 1993).

Some oldsters are unwilling to report crimes or press charges because of fear of reprisal.

Some elders defy the stereotype of being weak and easily threatened. A 73-year-old woman in New York City battled an intruder and foiled a rape attempt in her apartment ("Woman, 73, Battles Intruder, 1991"). In an elder housing project, the tenants got involved when gang members had been arrested and charged with attacking 12 older women over a three-week time period, choking them from behind, punching them, and stealing their money. Older tenants got involved in helping police set up a stakeout, and in being witnesses to identify those arrested. Anger won out over fear as the residents who "didn't want to take this" came forward (Hevesi, 1994). In another case a 74-year-old woman got into her car and outdrove would-be carjackers (Lyons, 1992).

These examples are not meant to advocate fighting back in every circumstance. It is not widely recommended that anyone fight an armed assailant. These accounts merely remind us that not all old people are easily intimidated. If this fact were more widely known, the number of attempted attacks might decrease.

The damage an attack can do to an older person is hard to measure. Crime can destroy one's possessions, body, and emotional well-being. Attacks against persons can shatter pride and self-esteem. They can change one's view of the world from trust and security to bitterness and paranoia and can change one's concept of humanity from good to bad. The memory of an attack can disturb sleep and rest and cause continuous anxiety during waking hours. Recouping financial losses because of crime can be difficult or impossible for the older victim. And, although a bodily attack may be fatal to anyone, the danger of serious injury is even greater for frail oldsters, whose bones break more easily and for whom the shock of assault may trigger heart or respiratory failure. Sensory acuity diminished by age may be completely lost by a blow to the head.

FEAR OF ATTACK

The National Opinion Research Center (NORC) has conducted national surveys on the **fear of crime.** When asked "Is there any area right around here (your home) that is within a mile where you would be afraid to walk alone at night?" more than 50 percent of those over age 65 answered yes. In fact, studies show that fear of crime outweighs the actual rate of crimes against older persons.

NORC surveys find older persons to be more fearful than younger persons. Four variables help determine who is most fearful:

1. Sex—Women are more afraid than men.
2. Race—Blacks are more afraid than whites.
3. Social class—Those with less money are more afraid of crime than those with more money.
4. Community size—Residents of large cities tend to be more fearful than people in smaller towns and rural areas.

In spite of considerable documentation, the full effects of fear have not been clearly established. But fear does lead to a certain amount of "house arrest"—that is, staying at home for fear of going out. And it dampens or lowers one's sense of well-being.

In high-crime neighborhoods, many older Americans are afraid to use public streets for exercise and enjoyment, to go shopping for food or other necessities, or to use public transportation. Studies reveal that fear of crime is greatest in the inner city, where the threat is the greatest. Perceptions of a neighborhood's safety level and of the reliability of social support systems are two important variables in predicting degrees of fearfulness.

The manner in which fear of crime should affect social policy is not entirely clear. On the surface, it would appear that one way to reduce fear of crime among elders would be to segregate them in walled and guarded retirement communities. But age segregation in our society could have undesirable consequences. Studies show generally that the more integrated one is in community activities the less one fears crime. Related to this is the finding that one feels less threatened by crime if one knows and trusts one's neighbors. The social implications are that developing cohesive, close-knit communities reduces fear of crime. These two alternatives are opposites, but either may be needed depending on the possibility of developing a close-knit, friendly neighborhood.

A consistent finding over the years has been that although older women fear crime more than older men, they are less likely to be victims. And though older people are more fearful than younger people, they are less likely to be victims. One explanation for this paradox may be that women and elders, considering themselves to be more vulnerable, do not as often expose themselves to risk. An additional explanation may be that they associate more minor offenses with more serious ones. For example, an older person, thinking that begging is a pretext for mugging, might be more afraid of a beggar than a younger person is. A woman might fear burglary more than a man because of the threat of rape in addition to theft. Thus, the possible consequences of the criminal act can be as frightening as the fear of victimization itself.

FIGHTING BACK

In many cities, new programs aimed at preventing crime against the elderly, helping those older persons who have become victims, and teaching them what they can do to help themselves are receiving priority. For example, one common approach is the use of police units trained in the problems particular to older people. Such units tip off the elderly to the latest trends in crime, help them to be on the alert for suspicious activity, and instruct them how to be effective witnesses against criminals caught in the act. Programs like **Neighborhood Watch,** which emphasizes crime awareness in residents of all ages, have resulted in crimes being spotted while in progress.

In many cities "granny squads" of older persons patrol neighborhood blocks and give lectures on how to avoid being raped, robbed, and burglarized. Granny squads, organized under titles such as Heaven's Angels and Gray Squads, recommend such precautions as the following:

- Report all suspicious persons and all crimes to the police.
- Use automatic timers to turn on radios and lamps when you are away from home.
- Do not carry a purse. Make a band to wear inside clothing to carry money.
- Have Social Security and pension checks mailed directly to the bank.
- Join a Neighborhood Blockwatch, in which neighbors in a block meet each other and watch out for one another's person and property.

Some cities provide escort services to older people when they are the most vulnerable to attack—such as on trips to stores and banks. For example, one Chicago police district supplies a bus and driver on the day that Social Security and relief checks arrive to pick up people from two housing projects, take them to a bank and a grocery store, and then return them safely home. New York City police, hoping to bridge the gap between young and old, use teenage volunteers to provide escort services for elderly persons. In Milwaukee, Wisconsin, neighborhood security aides patrol the streets in high-crime areas that house many older residents, walking in pairs to offer safety in numbers. Although they have no power to arrest, they carry two-way radios to call police or firefighters if they encounter suspicious persons (Zevitz et al., 1991).

Efforts to protect elders from crime exist at the state level as well. Many states offer reimbursement programs for crime victims, and some of these programs give priority to older persons. A New York state law makes a prison sentence mandatory for anyone, including a juvenile, who commits a violent crime against the elderly. Many states have extended child-abuse laws to include elders. Other states are currently considering legislation that does not allow probation for those who commit crimes against older persons.

✺ Aging Criminals

Although studies find that younger adults are at least ten times more likely than elders to commit crimes, elderly crime is very much a reality. Most crimes committed by elders are misdemeanors—petty theft, sleeping on the sidewalk, alcohol violations, and traffic violations. Shoplifting is a frequent misdemeanor charge, and most shoplifters are white females. But felonies occur as well, most frequently in the form of grand theft and narcotic charges.

There is not necessarily a relationship between economic hardship and crime. Typically, older people are caught stealing lipstick, perfume, night creams, even cigars. They are not necessarily stealing to eat. Shoplifting among elders represents the combined influence of stress, age, and merchandising; fear for the future may compel some to shoplift in order to conserve money for anticipated expenses. Some steal to ease fear; others do it to get attention. Psychologically, stealing may reflect feelings of deprivation in human relationships (Dullea, 1986). Only a minority of elder shoplifters have been engaged in criminal activity throughout their lives.

In general, the older perpetrator accounts for only a minority of all crimes committed. Arrest statistics by category of crime for 1986 showed that those over 65 committed no more than 1.5 percent of crimes involving murder or manslaughter and as little as 0.1 percent of motor-vehicle thefts and 0.7 percent of forcible rapes (U.S. Census Bureau, 1993). Most crimes are committed by men between the ages of 16 and 24. In terms of age, studies reflect that "burn out" sets in after age 30, leading older individuals to curb their criminal tendencies.

OLDER PROFESSIONAL CRIMINALS

Professional criminals, however, tend to remain active because crime represents their life's work. The longevity of some professional thieves is incredible. Joseph (Yellow Kid) Weil, a prototype for Paul Newman's role in The Sting, lived to be over 100 years old and was last arrested at age 72. Willie Sutton, professional bank robber, was into his eighties and still on parole when he died (Newman et al., 1984). Most leaders of organized crime are in the upper registers of the age scale. Organized crime is age-stratified, and the heads of "families" tend to be well over 50. Vito Genovese died in prison at age 71, still commanding his organization from his cell. Older offenders also play an important role in white-collar crime. And, as the percentage of elders increases in the total population, their percentage of criminal arrests will probably increase as well.

GROWING OLD BEHIND BARS

More people are being sent to prison and receiving longer sentences, increasing the number of older prisoners. In California, for example, the number of prisons has grown from 12 in 1983 to 26 in 1993 with 7 more approved for construction (Taylor, 1993). Older convicts can be (1) chronic offenders who have grown old in a steady series of prison terms; (2) those sentenced to long mandatory terms who have grown old in prison; or (3) first-time offenders in their old age. Those 85 and older are a rapidly growing segment of the prison population. Prison costs for eyeglasses, dentures, heart surgery, and other age-related needs are growing. And most prisons are not equipped to provide quality care for Alzheimer's patients and others with severe health problems. Experts say an old prisoner, with increasing health problems, costs three times as much to house as the average young prisoner (Aday, 1994).

The routine of prison life starkly separates the old from the young and middle aged. The young men tend to be muscled and heavily tattooed, have an "in-your-face" attitude, and form groups, even gangs, for friendship and safety. The old men tend to stay to themselves trying to find quiet. The gang tensions, the chaos, the constant chatter, the televisions going from early morning to late at night take their toll over the years. In California the average age of a prisoner is 31 (Taylor, 1993). Little consideration is given to older prisoners.

Being institutionalized causes premature aging. There is serious degradation, physical strain to the body, cigarette smoke, extreme tension, and lack of quality health care. According to a doctor on staff at a national center for correctional health care, incarceration ages a person 10 years (Taylor, 1993). A 55-year-old inmate is going to look and act 65.

State governments spend as much as $60,000 a year for each older prisoner (Fisher, 1992). An Iowa study of 119 male inmates 50 and older revealed this incidence of health problems: hypertension—40 percent; missing teeth—97 percent; gross physical impairment—42 percent; cigarette smokers—70 percent (Colsher et al., 1992). Experts say that a reexamination of present policies toward older prisoners is needed. Older prisoners are low-risk repeat offenders and early release for them may make sense (Himelstein, 1993).

☼ Elder Abuse

One category of violence that tends to go unreported and unprosecuted is violence in the home. Though we are familiar with the "battered baby syndrome," evidence increasingly indicates a corresponding syndrome at the other end of the age scale—**battered parent syndrome**—in which parents are attacked and abused, sometimes fatally, by their own children. At the far end of this age scale is the battered elder—sometimes abused by adult children, but possibly by a "friend," spouse, or caretaker.

How common is this kind of violence? More than one million elders are victims of physical or mental abuse each year, most frequently by members of their own families. In 1988, a nationwide survey showed that such incidents are increasing. The national rate is difficult to compute because of variation in interpretations of what constitutes abuse. Several measures of abuse have been identified:

1. *Physical abuse* is the willful infliction of pain or injury and may include beating, choking, burning, inappropriate medication, tying or locking up, and sexual assault.

2. *Psychological abuse* includes threats, intimidation, and verbal abuse.

3. *Financial/material abuse* means taking financial advantage of frail or ill elderly. It is the misuse of an elder's money or property: theft, deception, diverting income, or mismanagement of funds.

4. *Violation of rights.* Old people have the right to vote and the right to due process. A conservator, for example, may take away all the rights of an older person.

5. *Neglect* occurs when a caregiver's failure to provide adequate food, shelter, clothing, and medical or dental care results in significant danger to the physical or mental health of an older person in his or her care.

6. *Self-abuse and neglect.* Some old people do not adequately care for themselves. Sometimes it is intentional; other times they simply cannot adequately provide for themselves. Table 12.3 shows types of elder abuse in 29 and 30 states, 1990 and 1991 respectively. Neglect is by far the most common form of abuse, followed by physical abuse, then financial and material exploitation.

Granny dumping is indicative of the abuses to elders and is an active form of neglect. This term is used by emergency workers at hospitals to refer to abandonment of frail elders. It is most noticeable in Florida, California, and Texas. A Tampa, Florida, emergency room staff found a woman sitting in a wheelchair with a note that said, "She's sick. Please take care of her." More commonly, the older person is brought to the hospital by family members or a nursing home. When the patient has recovered, there is no one in sight to take the patient home (Locke, 1991). Elder abandonment has become more widespread over the last few years (Economist, 1992).

Table 12.3
....
Types of Elder Abuse:
1990 and 1991
(Reports from 29 and
30 States)

Type of Maltreatment*	Percentage	
	FY90 (N=29)	FY91 (N=30)
Physical abuse	20.3	19.1
Sexual abuse	0.6	0.6
Psychological/emotional abuse	11.6	13.8
Neglect	46.6	45.2
Financial/material exploitation	17.4	17.1
All other types	3.3	4.0
Unknown/missing data	0.2	0.2
Totals:	100.0	100.0

*This analysis includes *only* the substantial reports involving abuse victims and does *not* include self-neglect reports.

....

SOURCE: Toshio Tatara. Summaries of the Statistical Data on Elder Abuse in Domestic Settings for Fiscal Years 1990 and 1991. Released by the National Aging Resource Center on Elder Abuse. Washington D.C. February 1993. Reprinted in F. Schick and R. Schick, *Statistical Handbook on Aging Americans* (Phoenix, AZ: Ornyx Press, 1994), p. 98.

Police officers, lawyers, and community mental-health workers report numerous cases involving verbal and emotional abuse—situations in which the very old are treated like children, humiliated, and undermined in their dignity and self-worth. Physicians, morticians, or medical examiners confirm suspicions of physical violence unrelated to a single episode such as a fall. Nurses and caseworkers say victims often do not report abuse for fear of reprisal. Victim support groups are a new development for elders (Wolf and Pillemer, 1994).

We can offer several theories for the causes of abuse or neglect. The social exchange theory, which focuses on power imbalances and on the vulnerability and dependency of the victim, is one explanation for the cause of abuse. The developmental approach presents the idea that mistreatment is handed down from generation to generation, whereas the situational explanation

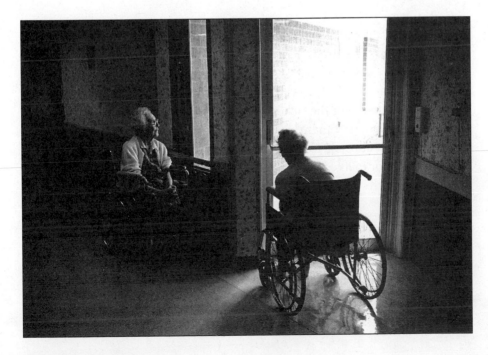

The most common form of abuse suffered by elders is neglect.

suggests that caretakers get overwhelmed during this particular time period. The stresses of caring for a frail parent, for example, can cause a life crisis for an adult child. It also can rekindle a long-standing negative relationship or unresolved conflict.

Researchers say that sudden dependency is not tolerated well in the United States by either the older victim or the family caretaker. Based on its life history, the family may or may not be able to handle the crisis. The policy implication is that strained families need to have more help available to them—help from social services, home-care services, protective services, personal-care homes, and family counseling.

A son or spouse is the most likely abuser of an elder, followed by a daughter who is providing care. Table 12.4 indicates that adult children are the most common abusers, followed by spouses.

Some of the abusers' typical characteristics are

1. A relative who has looked after the elder for many years—average 9½.
2. Lives with victim
3. 50–70 years old
4. Short of money, stressed
5. Socially isolated
6. Past violent behavior—at least to property
7. Depression, hostility, or anger
8. Alcohol or drug addiction
9. Parent-child hostilities early in life (Decalmer, 1993, 60–61)

These profiles suggest that violence within the family is a major cause of elder abuse.

The average age of the abused elder is 75 or older, and victims are more often female and/or dependent on others for care. The following profile of the typical victim was drawn from a number of studies:

1. Female
2. Over 75 years old
3. Physically impaired, often chair or bedridden
4. Mentally impaired
5. Socially isolated
6. Depressed
7. Ready to adopt the sick role
8. Have thwarted many attempts for help in the past
9. Been an abusing parent in the past
10. Too poor to live independently
11. Stubborn—last attempt to have some independence (Decalmer, 1993, 60)

Table 12.5 shows that the older the person, the more likely abuse will occur.

In some cases, offspring keep parents confined, neglecting all but their most minimal needs. Qualitative studies of elder abuse reveal complicated interdependent relationships that defy easy explanation. Oftentimes the victim is financially and emotionally supporting the abuser. In one case, an older woman lived with her son and supported him while he drank all the time and abused her. In another case, an older mother cared for her epileptic daughter

Type of Abuser	Percentage	
	FY90 (N=21)	FY91 (N=21)
Adult children	31.9	32.5
Grandchildren	4.0	4.2
Spouse	15.4	14.4
Sibling	2.6	2.5
Other relatives	13.0	12.5
Service provider	6.6	6.3
Friend/neighbor	7.3	7.5
All other categories	16.7	18.2
Unknown/missing data	2.5	2.0
Totals:	100.0	100.1*

*Due to rounding errors, the total is not exactly 100.0%.

Table 12.4

Abusers of the Elderly: 1990 and 1991 (Reports from 21 States)

SOURCE: Toshio Tatara. Summaries of the Statistical Data on Elder Abuse in Domestic Settings for Fiscal Years 1990 and 1991. Released by the National Aging Resource Center on Elder Abuse. Washington D.C. February 1993. Reprinted in F. Schick and R. Schick, *Statistical Handbook on Aging Americans* (Phoenix, AZ: Ornyx Press, 1994), p. 101.

who stole money from her. In some cases, wives were abused by the severely disabled husbands they were caring for. Abusers are rarely stable individuals, brought to the brink by the excessive demands of an elderly dependent; rather, these caretakers are suffering emotionally and barely able to meet their own needs. The older person who stays in an abusive situation can see no better alternative. Under the social exchange theory, the abuser's lack of power is a factor in the abuse. The caretaker's dependency, especially his or her financial dependency, rather than the dependency of the victim, correlates most strongly with abuse.

Abuse can and does take place in nursing homes by staff. Older persons are more at risk in institutions than in their own homes because of their exceptional frailty and danger of retaliation by caretakers (Sengstock et al., 1990). Abuse in institutions is not necessarily reported or reflected in national statistics. A survey revealed that 36 percent of the staff at serveral nursing homes had observed other staff psychologically abusing patients and had witnessed physical abuse that included employing excessive restraints; pushing, grabbing, kicking, or shoving patients; or throwing things at them. Over 70 percent of the psychological abuse included yelling and swearing at

Age Category	Percentage	
	FY90 (N=22)	FY91 (N=25)
60–64	7.8	7.6
65–69	11.2	10.5
70–74	15.0	15.5
75–79	17.4	17.1
80–84	19.2	19.4
85 and up	22.2	23.1
Missing data	7.2	6.8
Totals:	100.0	100.0

Table 12.5

Age of Elder Abuse Victims: 1990 and 1991 (Reports from 22 and 25 States)

SOURCE: Toshio Tatara. Summaries of the Statistical Data on Elder Abuse in Domestic Settings for Fiscal Years 1990 and 1991. Released by the National Aging Resource Center on Elder Abuse. Washington D.C. February 1993. Reprinted in F. Schick and R. Schick, *Statistical Handbook on Aging Americans* (Phoenix, AZ: Ornyx Press, 1994), p. 99.

patients; this abuse also included isolating patients, threatening them, and denying them food and/or privileges (Pillemer and Moore, 1989). Violation of individual rights is also a common problem in nursing homes. There is a need to more closely monitor both physical and chemical restraints.

Although penalties have been stiffened, county and state agencies are receiving more power to investigate and prosecute, and people are being encouraged to report suspicious happenings, elder abuse still appears to be increasing. Signs of abuse include abrupt negative changes in physical appearance; inappropriate behavior, such as extreme fear, asking to die, or extreme anger; a bad attitude on the part of the caregiver; and deteriorated or isolated living quarters. More and more of us are living to extreme old age and, thus, to the point of becoming physically dependent on someone else—sometimes with tragic consequences.

☼ Fraud

Any person with money is a potential victim of the huckster and the con artist. Although victims of confidence schemes and consumer frauds who file crime reports are not normally required to give their age, accounts of fraud state that the elders who constitute approximately 13 percent of the population represent approximately 30 percent of those who are swindled. Many elders have accumulated a nest egg over the years or have recently come into a large lump-sum pension or life insurance benefit. Some may be seeking investments they can make with relative ease; for some, low returns on passbook savings accounts motivate the search for new investments (Bekey, 1991). And they are more likely to be at home when a con artist calls. The following descriptions summarize some of the major kinds of fraud.

SOCIAL REFERRAL

Some dating and marriage services seek out the lonely and the widowed to lure them into paying big fees for introductions to new friends or possible mates. A victim may pay hundreds of dollars for a video to be shown to prospective dates (and then it is never shown) or for a computerized dating service that never generates any dates. Religious cults also have targeted elders and even entire retirement communities as recruitment areas for new members (Collins and Frantz, 1994).

LAND AND HOME-EQUITY FRAUD

In one type of **land fraud,** real-estate developers may offer lots for sale in a still-to-be-built retirement community, promising all kinds of facilities, such as swimming pools and golf courses, and describing the site in glowing phrases. None of the descriptions and promises may be accurate.

Home-equity fraud has left some elders homeless (Wallace, 1992). Swindlers pose as financial experts who offer help in refinancing a home. The swindler ends up with the cash from the home-equity loan or actually gets the owner to unwittingly sign papers transferring title.

FRAUD THROUGH MAIL ORDERS AND TELEVISION

Mail-order catalogs and television advertising can be misleading and result in **mail-order fraud.** Current ads that may be hoaxes or wild exaggerations, tout nutritional miracles, breast developers, and weight-reducing and exercise devices. Mail ordering and phone ordering from television ads are particularly attractive for those who no longer have transportation. Although many firms are honest, the mail-order and television industries have yet to eliminate the racketeers in their midst.

Mail-order health insurance has, in the past, proved to be worth little. Fraudulent hospitalization policies can be filled with small-print exceptions—ifs, ands, and buts that will eliminate the policyholder when a claim is made. Coverage for the person may not exist at the very time of failing health and hospitalization.

In 1986, a national consumers' group filed a complaint charging 19 insurance companies with trying to sell extra health insurance to elders using deceptive mailings that bore official-sounding names and Washington, D.C., addresses. These companies sent out hundreds of letters warning people about Medicare cutbacks. Those who returned a response card, thinking they were dealing with a concerned government group, were solicited by insurance agents. The companies were given cease-and-desist orders (Reich and Morrison 1986). In a similar case, California is now conducting mail-fraud investigations on a direct-mail kingpin of the political right who exploits the fears of elders by telling them their Social Security benefits are being taken away (Stone, 1993).

The "contest winner" fraud is ever present in our mail system. In some, the "winner" of a vacation, car, stereo, or other prize must either send money for postage or registration or pay to make a long-distance telephone call for more information.

TELEPHONE FRAUD

Telephone fraud is also a problem. A suburban couple in their seventies were swindled out of $350,000 by a "financial expert" who phoned two or three times per week for months, encouraging them to invest in real-estate deals and limited partnerships, which left them virtually empty-handed. Telephones are now the vehicle of choice for committing fraud. Telemarketing fraud accounts for $10 billion in investor losses annually, and southern California alone has as many as 300 **boiler rooms** (offices from which the telephone calls are made) functioning at any one time. The telephone vacation scam has lured may retirees. Callers tout fantastic-sounding Hawaiian packages for an unbelievably low price—$179 for two people for a week, for example. The "lucky traveler" need only provide their credit card number for reservations. But the trip is either postponed indefinitely or uses sleazy hotels with untold extra charges. Other popular scams involve oil and gas drilling and gold investments (Bekey, 1991).

CREDIT CARD FRAUD

Credit card fraud, in which swindlers find ways to get your card number and charge items on your account, has become widespread.

DOOR-TO-DOOR SALES

Peddlers of various kinds of merchandise often target the homebound because their loneliness makes them eager for conversation. Some salespeople are honest; others sell shoddy goods or offer useless services. For example, a salesperson might scare a person into contracting for unnecessary home repairs and then flee with the down payment. Or one salesperson may make a pitch while the other robs the house (Bekey, 1991).

Life Alert, a company whose television ads used the memorable line "Help! I've Fallen and I Can't Get Up!", has been sued for deceptive advertising. The lawsuit, which contends that the company uses high-pressure sales tactics (including sales presentations that last up to six hours!) and misleading ads to bully old people into buying the product, alleges that salespeople lied to senior citizens and disabled persons during sales pitches and refused to leave until a sale—the system's cost ranged from $1,700 to $5,000—was made. Misrepresentations included the claim of an emergency hotline more reliable than the public 911 system (Holding, 1991).

INVESTMENT FRAUD

There are many "get-rich" schemes used to fleece older people. Older people eager to invest their savings as a hedge against inflation may become victims of numerous investment frauds involving bogus inventions or phony businesses. Or the older person may fall victim to a work-at-home scam—the promise of substantial income if he or she will only purchase costly start-up materials. In reality, the income is not guaranteed; and the work may be tedious and difficult.

ESTATE RIP-OFFS

Some scam artists contact elders to offer services in preparing living trusts. They charge high fees, make phony pledges, and make off with money, and no living trust is provided (Crenshaw, 1992). Court-selected guardians or conservators assigned to look after older persons are in a position to steal from them, and some do. To preserve an inheritance, children will sometimes force adult parents to live in inferior dwellings; in Texas, a 90-year-old deaf and blind woman was being fed only oatmeal while her son pocketed the $1,300 monthly income allotted for her care. Some authorities are urging the government and the courts to more closely audit estates, so that abuse can be discovered. They also suggest a limit on the yearly fees that conservators can charge.

A study of guardianship revealed the following:

1. Elderly in guardianship courts are often afforded fewer rights than criminal defendants.

2. The overburdened court systems puts elders' lives in the hands of others without enough evidence that such placement is necessary.

3. The more than 300,000 persons 65 and over who live under guardianship are "unpersons" in that they can no longer receive money or pay bills, marry, or choose where they will live or what medical treatment they receive.

4. Though most appointed guardians are dedicated, caring people, there are not enough safeguards against the minority who are corrupt and greedy (Associated Press, 1987).

MEDICARE AND MEDICAID FRAUD

One kind of medical hoax involves outrageous abuses of the federal Medicare and state Medicaid programs. The violators are licensed physicians and registered pharmacists who file exaggerated claims for reimbursement.

Despite an elaborate system of safeguards, some experts say that the Medicare program is being bilked millions of dollars a year. Vague regulations, overworked investigators, swamped claims processors, and gullible consumers all play a part. These are typical frauds:

- A cardiac specialist who performs EKGs, which last 20 minutes, bills for a 24-hour procedure.
- A doctor does unneeded eye surgeries.
- A dermatologist who removes a single growth bills for multiple growth removal.
- A doctor submits bills for treatment on patients who died five years ago.

Fraud and abuse account for 10 to 25 percent of Medicare spending, the National Health Care Anti-Fraud Association estimates. The most common abuses are overcharges or bills for services that were never provided. In addition, medical equipment, some of which is ineffective, is sold at outrageous prices and Medicare picks up 80 percent of the tab (Cole, 1990). Fraud not only inflates the cost of medical aid, but also results in legitimate medical needs not being met.

CONFIDENCE GAMES

Con artists use various tactics. In a **confidence game,** the victim is tricked into giving up money voluntarily. Several games are common. Some examples are (1) the "block hustle," in which the con artist sells the victim a worthless item that he or she claims is both stolen and valuable; (2) the "pigeon drop," in which the victim is persuaded to put up money on the promise of making much more; and (3) the "lottery swindle," in which the victim pays cash for counterfeit lottery tickets. In one case a man was arrested for bilking older tenants by dunning them with fake water bills (James, 1994).

SUMMARY

Frauds, schemes, and exploitation techniques are limitless; and fleecing the fleecers is a complicated and difficult task. In 1990, a federally funded multiple-state law enforcement program raided 15 boiler rooms and launched 30 prosecutions against swindlers. As of 1991, California telemarketers were forced to post a $50,000 bond to operate legally. Florida has made the act of defrauding five people for $50,000 or more a first-degree felony. More safeguards are needed because the abuse continues (Ravitz, 1994).

MEDICAL QUACKERY

Though **medical quackery,** the misrepresentation of either health or cosmetic benefits through devices or drugs that are presumably therapeutic, can victimize both young and old, older people tend to be more prone to this kind of victimization. For one thing, older persons often have more ailments than younger persons; for another, the "youth culture" in the United States sometimes leads older persons on a medical quest for more youthful looks.

Many who offer medical goods and services are honest. Some are not, however; and the elderly are often cheated. Americans spend about $27 billion a year on quack products or treatments. Here are the top five health frauds in the United States, as listed by the FDA: (1) ineffective arthritis products, (2) spurious cancer clinics (many of which are located in Mexico), (3) bogus AIDS cures (offered at underground clinics in the United States, the Caribbean, and Europe), (4) instant weight-loss schemes, and (5) fraudulent sexual aids ("The Top Ten Health Frauds," 1990). We will cover four topics here: medical devices, youth restorers and **miracle drugs,** cancer cures, and arthritis cures.

Medical Devices

According to the Federal Trade Commission, many older Americans who need such medical devices as eyeglasses, hearing aids, and dentures frequently are victims of overpricing, misrepresentation, and high-pressure sales tactics. And because Medicare does not cover the cost of eyeglasses, hearing aids, or dentures, many persons cannot pay for devices and must do without them. Some findings are as follows:

- Surveys of retail firms show a 200 to 300 percent variation in the cost of identical pairs of eyeglasses.
- Identical dentures range in price from $100 to $1,000.
- The retail price of hearing aids is often 2.5 times the wholesale price.
- Heart pacemakers may sell for four times the manufacturing cost (Schmid, 1988).

Youth Restorers and Miracle Drugs

Elders are likely targets for products that promise to restore the appearance of youth—cosmetics, skin treatments, hair restorers, male potency pills, wrinkle and "age spot" removers, and the like. In a society like ours, which glamorizes youth, the desire to remain young is strong.

Like the medicine shows that once traveled from town to town offering miracle tonics and multipurpose cures, those who today provide cosmetic surgery and breast implants are enjoying a booming business. Unfortunately, the cosmetic surgery field contains may quacks. Poorly trained "surgeons" have mutilated faces and bodies and endangered lives.

Even ads for beauty products that promise to restore wrinkled skin border on quackery. But even though the Federal Drug Administration (FDA) believes that claims such as the following are misleading if not absolutely false, the interpretation of the law is fuzzy, and there's not much that can be done.

The skin-care market has grown into a huge money making industry. Dermatologists say that despite the claims of all the antiaging creams and lotions, there is no substance that can alter the structure or functioning of your living skin. The only thing that any product can hope to do is add some moisture to the top layer of skin. Nevertheless, advertisers are having a heyday because the FDA spends its time regulating more harmful substances.

Even products that have been FDA-approved tend to be advertised with exaggerated claims. A product called Retin A (generic name: tretinoin), originally used to treat acne, is now touted as a miraculous cure for wrinkles. Actually it is not a permanent cure. Further, use of the product carries some risks and side effects. The FDA-approved antibaldness medication minoxidil, under the brand name Rogaine, may not produce a perfect head of hair and does not work for everybody (Adelson, 1988).

Cancer Cures

Cancer victims have been offered "cures" ranging from sea water at $3 per pint to irradiated grape juice to machines alleged to cure cancer. Scientific studies have not shown Laetril, a substance extracted from apricot seeds, to have value in treating cancer. The FDA's disapproval of Laetril has caused many states to ban it. Yet, many cancer sufferers claim to have been helped by the drug.

Many factors account for the popularity of proven "cures" like Laetril. Because hundreds of thousands of new cancer cases are diagnosed each year and because two out of three victims will ultimately die of it, people are rightfully afraid of cancer. Conventional treatment is neither simple nor pleasant—surgery is often extensive, radiation can burn, chemotherapy can cause hair loss and vomiting. Laetril, for example, offers a far more easy treatment. It comes in tablets to be taken with large doses of vitamin C on a low-sugar diet that avoids all foods containing additives.

Fraudulent cancer "cures" rob the sick not only of their money. Cancer quacks also rob their victims of the most precious thing they have: time for proper treatment.

AIDS patients who can perceive no cure in the traditional medical establishment are especially willing to try unconventional treatments. In desperate efforts to prolong their lives, AIDS patients are prime targets for medical quackery. Some have spent thousands of dollars on worthless cures.

Arthritis Cures

Arthritis is the most common chronic condition of elders. An inflammation that makes joints stiff and painful to move, arthritis appears in a hundred or so forms, the most severe and crippling of which is rheumatoid arthritis. Some forms of arthritis are painless; others cause severe pain.

Because no one knows exactly what causes arthritis, doctors can do little more than prescribe pain relievers. This lack of certainty leaves the field wide open for all kinds of fake cures. Copper bracelets have been sold to cure arthritis. Wearing two kinds of metal in each shoe purportedly sets up "chemical impulses" that ward off pain. Various diets, cod-liver oil, brown vinegar with honey, "immune" milk, alfalfa tablets, mega vitamins, and snake or bee venom have all been sold to "cure" arthritis.

☼ Drug Abuse

Elders can be victims of drug abuse. Our society offers drugs—both legal and illegal—as a solution to a host of problems. The abuses discussed here are not those involving illegal drugs, such as heroin and cocaine, but those that involve legal drugs: prescription drugs, over-the-counter drugs, and alcohol.

PRESCRIPTION DRUGS

Though persons of all ages need prescription drugs for various health problems, elders need them in much greater proportions, because they are more likely to suffer from chronic illnesses or pain. The elderly, who comprise 13 percent of the population, consume 30 percent of all prescribed drugs (Blazer, 1990). More than 30 percent of all prescriptions for Seconal and Valium, two potent and potentially addictive sedatives, are written for persons over age 60.

With high drug usage, a more significant chance exists for adverse drug reactions and drug abuse. Health professionals are responsible for some of the drug abuse suffered by the older population. Their errors can be of two types: (1) not prescribing a drug correctly, or (2) prescribing less or more drugs than necessary. A study from Harvard University found that almost one-fourth of seniors are prescribed drugs that by themselves or in combination are dangerous or wrong (Stolberg, 1994). But such errors can sometimes seem intentional. Health professionals in nursing homes, for example, may over-prescribe drugs so that patients become calm and easier to manage. When overused, drugs can stupefy, injure, and kill. Educational intervention is advised, not only for older drug consumers, but for practicing physicians and pharmacists as well.

The nearly two million nursing-home residents are perhaps the nation's most medicated people, often suffering depression and disorientation from receiving too high a dosage of drugs such as Valium, Calpa, and Elavil or a combination of such drugs. Elderly patients both in and out of nursing homes may get prescriptions from several doctors and have reactions from their combined ingestion. Friends may exchange prescription drugs without regard to side effects or combination (synergistic) reactions with other medications. They also may mix prescription and over-the-counter drugs without realizing that the interactions can be harmful. Or they may take the wrong amounts of their own medications. Adverse drug reactions occur more frequently in old age, and multiple drug use should be closely monitored.

Studies show that stereotypes and the negative portrayal of older people have a considerable impact on a physician's prescribing habits. In ads in physicians' magazines, such as *Geriatrics*, elders tend to be pictured as inactive and described in negative terms: aimless, apathetic, disruptive, insecure, out of control, and temperamental. Drug advertising influences the medical professional to offer drugs as a first solution to emotionally disturbed elders; viewing old people in this manner may result in a physician giving increased prescriptions.

OVER-THE-COUNTER DRUGS

Although over-the-counter (OTC) drugs may seem harmless, they are overused and consequently abused. One can either blame the drug companies, who push their products through advertising, or the poorly informed consumer. Aspirin is the most widely used OTC drug. Many old people use very high doses of aspirin for arthritis, even though aspirin is a stomach irritant and can deplete the body of essential nutrients. (Some doctors use a milder drug, suprofen, rather than aspirin, to treat arthritis; but suprofen is not available over the counter.) And, though laxatives have been advertised as "nature's way," nothing is further from the truth. Prolonged laxative use can impair normal bowel function. Nature's way is plenty of water and fiber in the diet; many people, however, get "addicted" to laxatives, thinking they are making the best choice. The same is true of those who take sleeping pills, which must be taken in escalating doses to be effective. Consequently, they can cause rather than cure insomnia (Kolata, 1992). Because people need less sleep as they get older, many are better off to accept this fact rather than to try to force themselves to sleep eight or more hours a night. Antacids such as Alka-Seltzer contain sodium bicarbonate, which may harm kidney function. Hemorrhoid medication ads exaggerate the effectiveness of their products, and mouthwash does little more than add to the complaints of dry mouth. These OTC drugs can be a waste of money, cause bodily harm, and delay proper treatment of potentially serious ailments.

ALCOHOLISM

Alcoholism as a problem for elders has been largely ignored until recent years. If, after retirement, older persons lead much less visible lives, alcoholism can remain well concealed, becoming a self-generating cycle of abuse:

diminished contacts and a sense of loss may trigger drinking that goes unrecognized. The well-to-do, especially, have the means to hide their drinking. Elders *do not* have higher rates of alcoholism than younger adults, but the problems that some have are more serious because the alcoholism has taken a tremendous toll over the years.

Some older alcoholics began their drinking early in life; others do not drink heavily until old age. The "early onset" alcoholic has had alcohol-related problems for years and typically engaged in abusive drinking in early adulthood. In contrast, the "late-life onset" alcoholic, who begins abusive drinking in his or her fifties or sixties, is often viewed as a reactive drinker, one whose problem began after traumatic events such as the death of a spouse, retirement, or moving from an original home. He or she will have fewer chronic health problems and is likely to drink alone at home. In cases where alcoholism first occurs in old age, the alcoholic will often respond readily to intervention—help for depression or loneliness, for example, may reduce the need for alcohol. Treatment focuses on rebuilding a social support network and overcoming negative emotional states. Long-term alcoholics are more difficult, but not impossible, to help. A substance abuse program for elders started in Florida revealed that, before treatment, early onset alcoholics were intoxicated more days out of the month than late onset alcoholics: sixteen days for the early onset alcoholics, compared to eight days per month for the late onset alcoholics. Those in the early onset group were also more likely to drop out of treatment. But both groups had similar reasons for drinking: to offset loss, loneliness, depression, and boredom. But the early onset alcoholics who stayed in the program had more success in recovering (Schonfeld and Dupree, 1990).

Studies of admissions to psychiatric hospitals and outpatient clinics show that admission for alcoholism peaks in the 35-to-40 age group. Some researchers believe that alcoholism may be a self-limiting disease; that is, the decrease in alcoholism in the older age groups results not from treatment but

Books and magazines offer consumer information aimed at elders.

from a spontaneous recovery with age due to factors such as a lowered social pressure to achieve. Others think that alcoholism kills many of its victims before they reach old age. Still, about 10 percent of elders manifest symptoms related to excessive use of alcohol. Older men are more at risk than older women. And two-thirds of older alcoholics are severe chronic alcoholics whose symptoms tend to be obvious and profound (Hinrichsen, 1990).

Heavy drinking causes both psychological and physical damage and may cause either acute or chronic brain syndrome. Wernicke-Karsakoff's syndrome, an advanced brain disorder, can occur after a long history of drinking associated with malnutrition and vitamin deficiency. Alcoholism can complicate problems such as gastritis, cancer, hepatitis, and heart disease, and can cause cirrhosis and blackouts. In addition to disease, heavy drinkers suffer from numerous other problems. A fairly major one is nutrition; when food becomes secondary to drink, malnourishment results. Serious psychological problems, such as anxiety, melancholy, and depression, often surface. For those with marginally sufficient incomes, chronic drinking brings about poverty.

Alcoholics Anonymous (AA) and other groups can be instrumental in stopping heavy drinking. Countless people have benefited from AA. Addiction can touch even the powerful and the famous. Former First Lady Betty Ford described her cross-addiction to alcohol and pain-killers as "insidious." She went public about her mutiple drug abuse and eventually founded the Betty Ford Rehabilitation Center. Many people, including Mary Tyler Moore, Elizabeth Taylor, and Tony Curtis, have attended the clinic and gotten help for their drug abuse.

☼ Promoting Consumer Education

Consumer education is vital in helping individuals to avoid fraud, medical quackery, and drug abuse. Adult education programs are one way of reaching the public. Videotape systems now provide advice on a variety of topics, such as how to buy a used car without being swindled, how to handle the estate of a deceased relative, or how to recognize and avoid con artists. Books and magazines offer consumer information aimed at the older population, covering topics such as prescription drugs and their side effects, as well as the use and abuse of over-the-counter drugs and alcohol. Consumer action groups are available for persons of all ages who want to support the creation of stricter consumer-protection laws and the enforcement of existing laws.

Chapter Summary

Suicide continues to be a significant problem among those 65 and over. The suicide *attempt* rate for older women is much higher than for older men, yet older men (white males, that is), have the highest rate of *actual* suicides of any age group. Many factors may be involved, especially dependency, depression, physical illness, and social isolation.

The dimensions of the problem of crime against the elders are being studied by law enforcement and social agencies. National surveys show that elders are less likely to be victimized than younger adults, except in the area of personal larceny (e.g., purse and wallet snatchings), where attacks on elders are considerable. Over half of the violent victimizations occur in or near one's home. Fear of crime is widespread among elders and exists in a greater degree than the actual crime rate against them would suggest. It is the metropolitan elderly for whom fear of crime takes its greatest toll. Elders, themselves, can be the victimizers. Older criminals come from two groups: (1) those who started at a young age engaging in illegal activities, and (2) those who committed offenses for the first time in their later years. The older prison population is growing, but adequate medical care is lacking in jails and prisons.

Elders are potential victims of the huckster and con artist. Land fraud, mail-order fraud, mail-order health insurance, and confidence games are used to deceive and cheat people out of money. Medical quackery often entices the sick and ailing. Medical devices, youth restorers, and cancer and arthritis cures have robbed many of their money. Elders are sometimes victims of drug abuse—both prescription and nonprescription drugs.

Education, self-help groups, and professional help should be available to assist elders with their special problems. Consumer education is useful in learning to detect frauds and gaining knowledge about over-the-counter and prescription drugs.

Key Terms

attempted suicide
battered parent syndrome
boiler room
confidence games
credit card fraud
crib job
crimes against persons
double suicide
fear of crime
granny dumping

home-equity fraud
land fraud
mail-order fraud
medical quackery
miracle drugs
Neighborhood Watch
rational suicide
successful suicide
suicide rate

Questions for Discussion

1. How does fear of crime affect one's behavior?

2. Imagine that you are an old person and that your adult offspring is taking advantage of you in some way. How would you handle the situation?

3. Why might some elders be susceptible to con artists?

4. Imagine that you have just been cheated of $1,000 by a con artist who has promised that your money will be quadrupled in four days. What would you do?

Fieldwork Suggestion

1. Clip articles from magazines and newspapers that advertise goods and health insurance that are probably fraudulent. Find other evidence of fraud, such as letters from funeral homes, that borders on the unethical.

References

Adelson, B. "Hope in a Bottle: The Billion Dollar Baldness Race." *New York Times* (13 March 1988): F5 (L).

Aday, R. "Golden Years Behind Bars." *Federal Probation* 58:2 (June 1994): 47–54.

Associated Press. "Elderly Unpersons." *Santa Rosa Press Democrat* (20 September 1987): 1, A11.

"At the Races: Death in Life." *Economist* 323:7753 (4 April 1992): A29.

Bekey, M. Special Report on Fraud. *Modern Maturity* (April/May 1991): 31–64.

Blazer, D. *Emotional Problems in Later Life.* New York: Springer, 1990.

Cole, A. "The $10 Billion Dollar Blank Check: Medicare Abuse." *Modern Maturity* (April/May 1990): 38–43.

Collins, C., and D. Frantz. "Let Us Prey: Cults & the Elderly." *Modern Maturity* (June 1994): 22–26.

Colsher, P., et al. "Health Status of Older Male Prisoners." *American Journal of Public Health* 82:6 (June 1992): 881.

Crenshaw, A. "Living Trusts Lure Some People Not To Be Trusted." *Washington Post* (27 September 1992): H3.

Decalmer, P. "Clinical Presentation." In *The Mistreatment of Elderly People.* edited by P. Decalmer and F. Glendenning, 35–61. Newbury Park, CA: Sage, 1993.

Dullea, S. "When the Aged Start to Steal." *New York Times* (10 February 1986): B12.

Fisher, K. "Senior Scoundrels: Another Look." *State Legislators* 18:3 (March 1992): 10–12.

Hevesi, D. "Anger Wins Out Over Fear of a Gang." *New York Times* (27 March 1994): 31(L).

Himelstein, L. "The Case for Not Letting 'Em Rot." *Business Week* 3322 (16 August 1993): 89.

Hinrichsen, J. "The Heart of Treatment for Alcoholism." *Aging Magazine* 361 (1990): 12–17.

Holding, R. "'Help! I've Fallen' Firm Sued." *San Francisco Chronicle* (12 September 1991): A19.

Humphry, D. *Dying with Dignity.* New York: St. Martin's Press, Inc. 1993.

——————*Final Exit.* New York: Dell Trade, 1991.

James, G. "Man Is Held in Swindles of Elderly." *New York Times* (29 March 1994): B3(L).

Kaplan, M. et al. "Trends in Firearm Suicide among Older American Males 1979–1988." *Gerontologist* 34:1 (February 1994): 59–65.

Kastenbaum, R. "Death, Suicide, and the Older Adult." In *Suicide and the Older Adult,* edited by A. Leenaars et al. New York: Guilford Press, 1992.

Kolata, G. "Elderly Become Addicts to Drug-Induced Sleep." *New York Times* (2 February 1992): E4.

Leenaars, A. "Suicide Notes of the Older Adult." In *Suicide and the Older Adult,* edited by A. Leenaars et al., 62–79. New York: Guilford Press, 1992.

Lester, D., and M. Tallmer, eds. *Now I Lay Me Down: Suicide in the Elderly.* Philadelphia: Charles Press, 1994.

Locke, M. "Elderly Being Abandoned at Hospitals." *Santa Rosa Press Democrat* (11 November 1991): A3.

Lyons, R. "Woman, 74, Outdrives Carjackers, Police Say." *New York Times* (27 November 1992): B5(L).

McIntosh, J. "Epidemiology of Suicide in the Elderly." In *Suicide and the Older Adult,* edited by A. Leenaars et al., 15–35. New York: Guilford Press, 1992.

Newman, E., et al. *Elderly Criminals.* Cambridge, MA: Oelgeschlager, Gunn, and Hain, 1984.

Osgood, N., et al. *Suicide Among the Elderly in Long-Term Care Facilities.* Westport, CT: Greenwood Press, 1991.

Pillemer, K., and D. Moore. "Abuse of Patients in Nursing Homes: Findings From a Survey of Staff." *Gerontologist* 29:3 (June 1989): 314–320.

Ravitz, J. "The Elderly Need Safeguards Against Con Artists." *New York Times* (7 April 1994): A26(L).

Reich, K., and P. Morrison. "Deception in Insurance Mailers." *Los Angeles Times* (1 October 1986): 3.

Ryan, M. "Undercover Among the Elderly." *Parade Magazine* (18 July 1993): 8

Schmid, R. "Fear Tactics Defrauding the Elderly, FTC Told." *Santa Rosa Press Democrat* (17 March 1988): A7.

Schonfeld, L., and L. Dupree. "Older Problem Drinkers— What Triggers Their Drinking?" *Aging Magazine* 361 (1990): 5–11.

Sengstock, M., et al. "Identification of Elder Abuse in Institutional Settings." *Journal of Elder Abuse and Neglect* (February 1990): 31–50.

Stolberg, S. "Many Elderly Too Medicated, Study Finds." *Los Angeles Times* (27 July 1994): A1.

Stone, P. "Just Another Con Job on the Elderly?" *National Journal* 25:36 (4 September 1993): 2141–2144.

Taylor, M. "Aging Inmates—A Growing Prison Presence."

San Francisco Chronicle (2 August 1993): A1, A6.

"The Top Ten Health Frauds." *Consumer's Research Magazine* (February 1990): 34–36.

"Till Death Them Do Part." *Economist* 325:7789 (12 December 1992): 64.

U.S. Census Bureau, *Statistical Abstract of the United States, 1993,* 110th ed. Washington, D.C.: U.S. Government Printing Office, 1993.

Wallace, B. "Elderly Cheated Out of Homes by Scam Artists." *San Francisco Chronicle* (10 February 1992): A13.

Wolf, R. and Pillemer, "What's New in Elder Abuse Programming? Four Bright Ideas." *Gerontologist* 34:1 (February 1994): 126–129.

"Woman, 73, Battles Intruder and Foils Rape in Apartment." *New York Times* (14 August 1991): A12(N).

Zevitz, R., et al. "Factors Related to Elderly Crime Victims' Satisfaction with Police Service: The Impact of Milwaukee's 'Gray Squad'." *Gerontologist* 31:1 (February 1991): 92–102.

Further Readings

McNamara, R. *Creating Abuse-Free Caregiving Environment for Children, the Disabled, and the Elderly.* Springfield, IL: Charles C. Thomas, 1992.

Richman, J. *Preventing Elderly Suicide.* New York: Springer, 1993.

Shiferaw ,B. et al. "The Investigation and Outcome of Reported Cases of Elder Abuse: The Forsyth County Aging Study." *Gerontologist* 34:1 (February 1994): 123–125.

13 Women and Ethnic Groups

CHAPTER OUTLINE
- Women
- African Americans
- Hispanic Americans
- Asian Americans
- Native Americans
- Improving the Status of Ethnic Elders

Muyu Angelou Offers the Grace of Good Advice

■ PAUL CRAIG

The scope of Maya Angelou's life is breathtaking.

She has been during her 65 years an actress, dancer, journalist, educator, author, screenwriter and TV and movie director-producer. She also has served on federal commissions and, at the inauguration of President Clinton, delivered her poem, "On the Pulse of Morning."

Angelou's new book, *Wouldn't Take Nothing for My Journey Now,* offers some of her thoughts on what the years have taught. From her comparatively tranquil vantage point as a professor at Wake Forest University in Winston-Salem, N.C., Angelou (pronounced AngeLOW) comments on everything from the status of women to tired phrases she hates.

Above all, Angelou issues a plea for honoring diversity as the country grows into a more varied mixture of peoples and creeds: "It is a time for the preachers, the rabbis, the priests and pundits and the professors to believe in the awesome wonder of diversity so that they can teach those who follow them. It is a time for parents to teach young people early on that In diversity there is beauty and there is strength."

Angelou admits she ponders death "with alarming frequency" but fears the loss of others more than her eventual demise, recommends forgiveness but no patience with fools and heartily recommends taking a day off now and then just for fun. She even suggests a paranoia can have its valid uses.

On the less serious side, Angelou, always a women who dresses in cheerful colors she says make her happy, writes of fashion's intimidation of those who "are imprisoned by powerful dictates on what is right and proper to wear. Those decisions made by others and sometimes at their convenience are not truly meant to make life better or finer or more graceful or more gracious. Many times they stem from greed, insensitivity and the need for control."

She also warns the whiners of the world, "Whining is not only graceless, but can be danger-

Poet Maya Angelou recites her poem on Capitol Hill during the presidential inauguration.

ous. It can alert a brute that a victim is in the neighborhood."

Some of her accomplishments?

She toured Europe with the cast of *Porgy and Bess* in 1952; has been an editor and writer in Cairo and in Ghana's capital, Accra; was northern coordinator of Martin Luther King Jr.'s Southern Christian Leadership Conference at the start of the 1960s; worked on commissions under Presidents Ford and Carter; acted in TV's *Roots;* and has seen her autobiographical works, such as *I Know Why the Caged Bird Sings,* adapted for television.

Additionally, she appeared in such plays as *Mother Courage* and *The Blacks,* was nominated for a Tony Award for her stage role in *Look Away,* and received a Pulitzer nomination for her book *Just Give Me a Cool Drink of Water 'Fore I Diiie.* (Yes, "i" three times is how she wanted to spell it.)

—Continued

Her career in education has included teaching in Italy, Ghana and Israel, as well as in American universities, including an appearance as distinguished visiting professor at California State University, Sacramento. And she has clear-cut evidence of her welcome at Wake Forest—the professorship is for life.

Her thoughtful work soars far above most "what I have learned" books. Angelou has things to say and says them gracefully. Her book is an excellent learning investment for any reader. ☀

Author Note: In addition to writing several other books such as *I Know Why the Caged Bird Sings,* in Cairo Egypt she was the first woman editor of *The Arab Observer,* and she was feature editor of *The African Review* in Ghana. She has a son and 19-year-old grandson. Angelou is the last name of an ex-husband, and "Maya" was the name given to her by her brother Bailey who as a child called her "Mya sister" rather than her first name Marguerite. She grew up in the Depression in Stamps, Arkansas, and moved to San Francisco as a young person where she studied dance, and then on to New York where she launched her stage career. A poem of hers is on page 312 of this chapter.

SOURCE: © Copyright , *The Sacramento Bee,* 1995.

*M*ulticulturalism has become a central focus of the social sciences. This focus corrects a past tendency to ignore the diversity and richness that ethnic groups have added to American life. Until recently the study of aging America was a study of the older white Americans who made up nearly 90 percent of America's elderly population; while the many ethnic groups were ignored. Generalizing from the population to all subcultures of elders is misleading, incorrect, and insensitive. As researchers become more aware of ethnic differences, more attention will be drawn to their unique situations and needs.

In future years there will be marked increases in the racial and ethnic diversity of those 65 and over. Presently the ethnic aged comprise 13 percent of all those 65 and over, but they will grow to 22 percent of all elders in 2020 and be 33 percent of the older population by the year 2050. Thus, with every passing year they become a larger component of aging America. The proportion of all elders who are African-American will increase slowly from 8 percent in 1990 to 10 percent by 2050. The American Indian population will increase from .1 million to .5 million in that time span. It is the Asian and Hispanic populations that will swell the ranks the most swiftly. Asians will increase from 1 percent to 8 percent of the elder population, and Hispanics from 4 percent to 16 percent of the elder population by 2050. Immigration is a big factor contributing to the rise in the elder population of these two later groups. Increases in all the groups are related to past fertility patterns and to increasing life expectancy (*National Institute on Aging, 1993*).

The exploration of ethnic minorities must begin with basic definitions of what constitutes an ethnic group and what constitutes a minority. If an ethnic group has a shared identity based on language and cultural tradition, the Asian, Hispanic, or American Indian groups might each be defined as one ethnic group or many ethnic groups, depending on one's interpretation. And African Americans, if they had no interest or knowledge of their African heritage, might not fit the definition of an ethnic group. Acknowledging the limitations of the "ethnic" concept, we consider here four groups: African

NO THANKS GENTLEMEN... I AM MEDITATING ON MY INTRINSIC VALUE AS A HUMAN BEING ... RATHER THAN JUST A CONSUMER.

Americans, Hispanics, Asian, and Native Americans. A minority elder is someone 65 or over who is discriminated against by the dominant group in a society. That person suffers from both ageism and racism. Women are not necessarily an ethnic minority, but they hold a lower status in our culture than men. Therefore, women, have been judged a minority group, not in terms of numbers, but in terms of status. Older women are considered first in this chapter and the section on ethnic minority elders follows.

✸ Women

The minority status of women is based on the sexism that pervades U.S. society. For older women sexism is compounded by ageism. Older women have trouble finding acceptance and equality in the work world, in politics, and in romance. Women are making progress in these areas; however, hundreds of years of established patterns cannot be changed overnight.

One advantage for women is their willingness to reach out and get help: from each other, from books and seminars, from re-entry programs at colleges, and from various counseling services. Models of positive aging such as Meryl Streep and Susan Sarandon, in their 40s; Jane Fonda, Erica Jong, in their 50s; and Gloria Steinhem, who turned 60 in 1994, are looked to for advice and inspiration. Dr. Ruth Jacobs (1993), a university professor and author of books for older women is also one who offers support to aging women. She recommends books such as hers and the following:

Be an Outrageous Older Woman (Jacobs, 1993)
I Am Becoming the Woman I've Wanted (Martz, ed., 1994)
Flying Solo: Single Women in Midlife (Anderson and Stewart, 1994)
Moving Beyond Words (Steinhem, 1994)
Going Strong (York, 1991)
Women, Aging and Ageism (Rosenthal, 1991)

Look Me in the Eye: Old Women, Aging and Ageism (Macdonald and Rich, 1991)

Old and Smart: Women and Aging (Nickerson, 1991)

suggest that the present generation of older women is receiving more attention and validation than previous generations. Roles for older women, which formerly have been narrowly constructed in the U.S., are broadening. According to Gail Sheehy (1993), American women are beginning to view the approach of menopause not as a marker to the end, but as a bridge to a new stage of adulthood. Increasingly, older women have more options to experience a rewarding and fulfilling later life. Two areas of struggle for older women are discussed in this section of the text: finances and the double standard of aging.

On Aging

■ *Maya Angelou*

When you see me sitting quietly,
Like a sack left on the shelf,
Don't think I need your chattering.
I'm listening to myself.
Hold! Stop! Don't pity me!
Hold! Stop your sympathy!
Understanding if you got it,
Otherwise I'll do without it!

When my bones are stiff and aching
And my feet won't climb the stair,
I will only ask one favor:
Don't bring me no rocking chair.

When you see me walking, stumbling,
Don't study and get it wrong
'Cause tired don't mean lazy
And every goodbye ain't gone.
I'm the same person I was back then,
A little less hair, a little less chin,
A lot less lungs and much less wind.
But ain't I lucky I can still breathe in.

From *And Still I Rise* by Maya Angelou. © Copyright 1978 by Maya Angelou. Reprinted by permission of Random House, Inc.

Financial Status

Some have called the high percentage of women and their children among the poor the "feminization of poverty." Just as for younger cohorts, poverty after age 65 is heavily concentrated among women. Of all individuals poor enough to receive Supplemental Security Income (SSI), two-thirds are women. Women comprise more than 70 percent of the older poor. Poverty rates have fallen more slowly over the last two decades among older women living alone than for older men or for older married couples.

MIDDLE-AGED DISPLACED HOMEMAKERS

Financial problems for women frequently originate in middle age, or even earlier. A typical displaced homemaker is middle-aged and has been a homemaker for most of her adult life, dependent on her husband for her income and security. She finds herself suddenly alone with little or no income and with limited marketable skills. In 1993, 30 percent of all women in the 45-to-64 age bracket were single, widowed, or divorced.

Most divorced women do not receive alimony. Many widows are left with few funds; they are ineligible for unemployment insurance because they have been engaged in unpaid labor in their homes. As more young women get educations and start careers before middle age, the displaced homemaker problem will become smaller.

The middle-aged woman who can save some money (or at least pay into Social Security) improves her chances for a fulfilling old age. Though middle-aged women are now in the workforce in large numbers, a pay gap persists for these women and for older women. They tend to be in low-paying "women's jobs," working as secretaries, sales clerks, waitresses, nurses, or teachers.

SINGLE, WIDOWED, AND DIVORCED OLDER WOMEN

Single Women

More than 25 percent of women 65 and older who live alone or with nonrelatives live below the poverty level (U.S. Bureau of the Census, 1993, 470, table 738). This percentage would almost double if the Federal Poverty Index were updated as experts recommend. In contrast, 8 percent of those living with their husbands are poor. Those married and living with their husbands have the benefits of another income. Those single women receiving Social Security receive lower pensions than men because the earnings on which they contributed to the program tend to be lower than the earnings of men of their generation. Women who are 65 years old today are still paying for the wage and social discrimination they suffered in their earlier working years.

Widows

Widows constitute nearly one-half of all women 65 and over. Of women 65 and over who live alone, 85% are widows. Some widowed women depended on their husbands' incomes, and, when retired, on their husbands' private pension plans or Social Security. More often than not, private pension plans fall sharply when a retired spouse dies. The death of a spouse also lowers the amount of Social Security benefits. If this is the case, widows' low incomes expose them to greater social and economic risks than other segments of the white population. Data from a national sample of widows of all ages found that widowhood decreased living standards by 18 percent and pushed into poverty 10 percent of women whose prewidowhood incomes were above the poverty line. Not surprisingly, economic status prior to widowhood is the strongest prediction of status during widowhood (Bound et al., 1991). A major social issue is how to meet the needs of older widows.

The opportunity for older widows to remarry is quite limited, due to the relatively small number of eligible males in their age group. Older females who are eligible for marriage outnumber eligible males by a ratio of three to one. In addition, males who marry after age 65 tend to marry women from younger age groups. The number of men aged 65 and older who marry during a given year is twice as high as the number of brides in that age category. Over half of the older grooms marry females under the age of 65.

Older couples tend to live by themselves. The death of a woman's spouse thus assumes great significance. More than 60 percent of widows continue to live alone. This can be expensive and isolating, even if it is a preferred lifestyle.

Divorcees

The socioeconomic well-being of divorcees is significantly below that of married or even widowed women. Given current statistics and expected trends in marriage, divorce, and widowhood, the numbers of married and widowed older women will decline, but the proportion of divorced older women will dramatically increase. Included in the increasing divorce rate are divorces involving women over age 40. And, although 7 percent of women over age 60 are divorced (and not remarried), this statistic is expected to increase. Viewed from another angle, 18 percent of all married women 40 and over (based on recent trends) will experience a divorce from their first marriage. From still another perspective, 11 percent of those who have been married for 20 years will divorce (Uhlenberg, 1990).

For women, the probability of remarriage after divorce declines steeply with age and is quite low after age 45. In 1990, for example, fewer than 5 out of every 100 divorced women between the ages of 45 and 64 remarried within the year. The remarriage rate for divorced women between 45 and 64 is only one-tenth of that for those under age 25. If current rates persist, few women who enter midlife divorced, or who divorce after midlife, will ever remarry. Remarriage rates have fallen dramatically since 1965; they have fallen by half for women between the ages of 45 and 64.

According to rough projections, by 2025 no more than 37 percent of women between the ages of 65 and 69 will be in their first marriage. Half will not be in any marriage; this figure could be considerably higher if the divorce rate after age 40 continues to increase and the remarriage rate continues to decline (Uhlenberg, 1990). There is good reason for public concern over these statistics. Older women living outside marriage, especially those who are divorced, have much lower standards of living than married women. Unless this fact changes, the economic well-being of older women will continue to deteriorate. The high divorce rates of adult children strains family resources as well. Divorced sons and daughters have more trouble finding time and money for their aging parents. Older divorced women, financially vulnerable, are often forced to look for work and to share residences. They must be creative to make ends meet.

Upgrading the Financial Status of Older Women

In our society, in spite of positive steps toward equality, women in the workforce and in politics remain in inferior positions. Their lower incomes reflect this fact. Inequalities in income for older women will not totally disappear until women achieve equality in the workplace from the beginning of their careers.

Today, women on their own and as a part of the women's movement are attempting to upgrade their status. As more women get good-paying jobs in their younger years, they acquire built-in protection for their older years by becoming entitled to their own Social Security at maximum benefits.

If women are homemakers or caretakers of children or elder parents during their working years, they suffer financially in old age. Being removed from the paid labor market reduces their Social Security benefits (Kingson and O'Grady-LeShane, 1993). They could be compensated in a number of ways. One way would be for women to receive full credit for their nonmarket labor in pension plans, including Social Security (Quadagno and Meyer, 1993). Another plan suggests combining the wage earner's 100 percent benefits with the dependent homemaker's 50 percent benefits. The wage earner and the homemaker could then divide the resulting 150 percent into equal shares of 75 percent that they would receive regardless of gender or family earning roles, and they could place the equal shares in separate accounts under their own names and Social Security numbers. The funds would thus remain unaffected by possible divorce or separation.

Some centers provide job counseling, training, placement services, legal counseling, and outreach and information services to middle-aged and older women. Policies that encourage work and insure adequate survivor benefits improve the financial status of older retired women.

DOUBLE STANDARD OF AGING

In 1972, Susan Sontag coined the term **double standard of aging.** By implication, the standard of aging for a woman progressively destroys her sense of beauty and self-worth, whereas the standard of aging for a man is much less wounding.

Society trains women from an early age to care in an exaggerated way about their physical beauty. As a result, women spend much more time and money on their appearance than men. They may disappear periodically at parties and other social gatherings to see that their makeup and hairstyle are still intact. Their role, society tells them, demands this behavior. Women must be more concerned about being "fat" or "ugly." Cosmetic and plastic surgery and face-lifts are performed more often on women than on men. Many women's exercise programs emphasize appearance rather than strength or endurance: In the self-help section at any local video store, note the number of cassettes that promise shapelier breasts, thighs, or buttocks. Or attend an aerobics class at a local health club and note the female clients' concerns about their exercise clothing.

The youth culture in our society exerts an intense social pressure for women to remain young. In a personal account of her own aging Ruth Thone, an activist from Lincoln, Nebraska, gave her reason for writing her book. It was the "subtle, deep, pervasive, unspoken distaste and derision" for old Americans in general and old women in particular (Thone, 1993, xi). She wrote of her own "internalized aging" in which she is filled with self loathing and anxiety about aging. She is also furious at being sexually invisible to men and being patronized by younger people. She is sensitive about any jokes putting down older women. She gave this account.

> My husband found a joke in a magazine, that he added to his repertoire, about two women in a nursing home who decided to streak their fellow residents. Two startled old men looked up and one asked, "What was that?" "I don't know," the other replied, "but whatever they were wearing sure needs ironing." My husband did not understand how hurt I was by that joke, by that ridicule of women's aging skin and by the double standard that does not make a mockery of men's aging skin. He insisted it was my feminism, not any ageism in him that kept me from knowing the joke was harmless. (Thone, 1993, 54)

She wondered, "Am I an object of scorn as my body ages?" She dealt with self-criticism, self-rejection, and self-hate, coming to terms with aging by writing in her journal, meditating, and becoming more spiritual. In a chapter on "The Grief of Aging" she described working through her sadness at the loss of her youth.

Not all women can confront their aging so directly and honestly. They buy into the idea that they must stay young and beautiful in appearance forever. According to researcher Goodman (1993), dieting programs have become a national obsession and cosmetic surgeries are greatly escalating in the 1990s. Older women in her study assigned more importance to their faces, and young women measured self-worth by body size—especially breast size. Older women were concerned with wrinkles, "saggy" jowls, and "droopy" eyelids. These concerns led to face- and neck-lifts and to chemical peels to "smooth" the skin. The successful exploitation of women's fears of growing older has been called **age terrorism.** Women are so frightened of being rejected or abandoned at home by romantic partners and in the workplace by their bosses that they will buy any product to prolong a youthful look (Pearlman, 1993). Pearlman speaks of **late midlife astonishment**—a developmental crisis in which women aged 50 to 60 work through society's devaluation of their physical appearance. Women suffer a loss of self-esteem, depression, and

words never spoken
■ *Doris Vanderlipp Manley*

walking through the city I saw the young girls
with bodies all silk from underthings to eyebrows
legs shaven
heels pumiced
nails glossed
hair lacquered
thighs taut
eyes clear
gladbreasted tittering girls

and I wondered how even for an hour
you could love a woman who has no silk
no silk
only burlap
and that
well worn
tattered
and frayed
with the effort of making a soul

Sandra Martz, ed., *When I Am an Old Woman I Shall Wear Purple* (Manhattan Beach, CA: Papier-Mache Press, 1987), p. 89.

feelings of shame and self-consciousness. Feminist therapists believe that body image disturbances are not limited to eating-disordered clients and occur to women of all ages (Chrisler and Ghiz, 1993). One example is Helen Gurley Brown, former editor of Cosmopolitan Magazine, the "Cosmo Girl," who at age 71 referred to age as the great destroyer. She admits to silicone injections, cosmetic surgery, shrink sessions, endless dieting, and a 90-minute daily "killer" exercise regime. She says:

> I'm afraid of losing my sexuality. I'm desperately afraid of retirement. I fear that with age, I'll cease being a woman, that I'll be neuter. I fear losing my looks and ending up looking like . . . like an old crumb. (quoted in an interview with Marian Christy, 1993)

The perception that only youthful women are beautiful perpetuates the older man-younger woman syndrome and isolates the older woman. Women who base their self-worth on signs of youthful beauty have problems aging. Some inroads have been made, for example, by older women who date and marry younger men. But the double standard still endures.

In terms of diet and exercise, our society emphasizes health and fitness like never before. In one sense this has been positive as older women join the trend and live healthier lives. But as long as society's definition of being beautiful sets expectations that are unrealistic, women will continue to suffer.

☼ African Americans

African Americans constitute the largest minority group in the United States, totaling 30 million in 1990 (U.S. Bureau of the Census, 1993, 32, table 33). About 2.5 million of these African Americans are 65 or over. They are a diverse group, yet, some overall pictures do emerge. A majority of elder African Americans (53 percent) live in the South. There are fewer males than females. Older men tend to be married; women tend to be divorced or widowed. African-American elders are less likely to be married than any other ethnic group, but all ethnic elderly, including African Americans, are more likely to live with other family members (not counting the spouse) than whites.

African Americans as a group differ widely in socioeconomic factors. As a result of the civil-rights movement, African Americans have gained a large middle class, a class having grown so greatly that it now outnumbers the African-American poor. As comparatively well-off African Americans move to better neighborhoods, they leave behind an African-American "underclass"—chronic welfare recipients, the unemployed, high-school dropouts, and single-parent families. Although many moved into the upper middle class in the 1980s, one-third remained locked in deprivation. There now exists a deep class division among African Americans (Frisby, 1991). Elders in inner cities are often left to cope with deteriorating neighborhoods, high crime rates, and the threat of violence.

INCOME AND HOUSING

Compared with Caucasian elders, **African-American elders** have less adequate income, and poorer quality housing. Although the income level for older African Americans has improved over the past 25 years, the improvement rate has not been as rapid as that for older whites. In 1959, 62.5 percent of African-American elders were living in poverty, double the percentage for

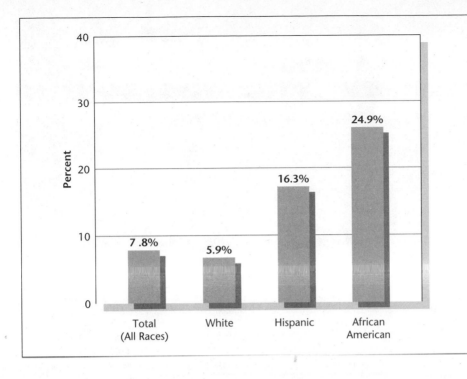

Figure 13.1

Percentage by Race of Persons Aged 65 and Older Living below the Poverty Level, 1992

SOURCE: U.S. Bureau of the Census, *Statistical Abstract of the United States.* 1994, 114th (Washington, DC: U.S. Bureau of the Census 1994), p. 478 (selected information from table 734).

whites. In 1992, 24.9 percent of African Americans aged 65 and over were living below the poverty level, a figure more than triple that of whites (see Figure 13.1). Unemployment rates for African Americans of all ages tend to be higher than those for whites, and have been for many years.

A small percentage of retired African Americans are from the upper class, having owned large businesses or real estate, headed large corporations, or worked in the highest levels of industry. Other retired African Americans are middle class, having been schoolteachers, owners of small businesses, or government employees. Still others are retired from manual labor or domestic service jobs. Overall, however, they have not paid as much into Social Security as whites have; therefore, they will be eligible for less in old age. They are also less likely to have accumulated savings, assets such as real estate, or pensions.

African-American elders are slightly more likely to be looking for work after age 65, due to inadequate retirement income. Older African-American men have higher unemployment rates than older white men. Elders in the lower socioeconomic groups, regardless of race, have a different understanding of retirement. Health permitting, they often must work at lower-paying jobs well beyond retirement age in order to meet basic expenses for food, medical care, and housing. Studies of work patterns among African Americans revealed a large group of "unretired retirees" aged 55 and over who need jobs but cannot find them. They do find occasional work well into old age—but this work is usually part-time and temporary. Those under age 62 are not eligible for Social Security or other pension programs and, therefore, without work, are more financially needy than those eligible for pensions.

Studies of African-American retirees aged 65 and over show that those who receive Social Security have relatively high morale—higher, in fact, than that of their counterparts who are still working. This finding is reversed for

Relatively few older African Americans are admitted to nursing homes.

whites. One explanation for the high morale of retired African Americans is the undesirable work they often face should they remain employed (Gibson, 1993).

Older African Americans are more likely than older whites to reside within decaying central cities and to live in substandard housing. They are also more likely than whites to live in public housing. Those who work with minority elders must be able to advise them accurately on low-cost public housing, low-interest housing loans, and other forms of available property relief.

Older African Americans are admitted to nursing homes at between one-half and three-quarters of the rate of whites. This underutilization cannot be explained only with the statement that African Americans prefer to care for elders within their families. In many cases they cannot afford the long-term care they need. Thus, racial disparities in institutional care must be considered (Belgrave et al., 1993).

HEALTH CARE AND LIFE EXPECTANCY

Low-income African Americans tend to have health-care problems. They lack the money required for good health care, and this inadequate care results in a life expectancy rate that is much lower than that for whites. The average African American's life expectancy was 69.1 years in 1991, 7 years below the average of 76.1 years for whites (U.S. Bureau of the Census, 1994, 88, table 116). Given an average retirement age of 65, the average African-American *male*, whose life expectancy in 1991 was 64.5 years, cannot realistically expect to live long enough to collect benefits from Social Security and Medicare. The lower life expectancy does, however, equalize with whites at age 80 and after.

The differences in life expectancy between African and white Americans fade away if a number of social variables are held constant, these being marital status, income, education, and family size. (Marriage, high income and education, and small family size are correlated with longevity). Thus, longevity appears to be more socially than racially determined (Guralnik et al., 1993; Bryant and Rakowski, 1992).

Between 1986 and 1991, life expectancy for African Americans actually *dropped*. Though African Americans had been sharing in life expectancy increases over the decades, the trend reversed in the late 1980s. One major reason is the high number of African-American babies who die in their first year. But this is only one factor. Thousands of African Americans die in the prime of life from illnesses that could be cured or treated by routine medical care: appendicitis, pneumonia, hypertension, cervical cancer, tuberculosis, and influenza are examples. Given early detection and good treatment, all these illnesses are curable; nobody should be dying of these things (Hilts, 1990).

Older African Americans have endured a lifetime of "the color barrier." Operating under a theory that low social status generates repressed negative emotions and inner tensions, some gerontologists believe the high incidence of hypertension reflects the pressures of low social status. They believe that both physical and mental illness can result from the ongoing prejudicial attitudes and behavior of others. Others believe hypertension to be genetic.

Whatever the cause, the incidence of high blood pressure among African Americans is nearly two-and-a-half times that of whites, and the mortality rate from high blood pressure is higher for African Americans than for whites (U.S. Bureau of the Census, 1993, 25). Though yoga, aerobics, and biofeedback programs to reduce blood pressure have typically been attended by white, middle-class persons, African Americans are now joining these programs.

FAMILY AND SOCIAL RELATIONSHIPS

More than 40 percent of African-American women 65 and over live in poverty. The high mortality rate of African-American males and the high divorce rate alienate these women from a traditional family lifestyle. More effort needs to be directed toward unifying African-American women and channeling their efforts to improve their socioeconomic conditions. Consequently, political activists urge women to join organizations, such as the National Association for the Advancement of Colored People (NAACP) and the National Black Women's Political Caucus, that can speak and work effectively for them.

Despite racism and economic woes, African Americans have possessed a resolve to persevere. The solid family ties, which are one source of this strength, is indicated in the concept of **familism.** The notion of family often extends beyond the immediate household. Within the family network, roles are flexible and interchangeable. A young mother, an aunt, a grandfather, or an older couple may head a family. Grandmothers often help raise children while the parents work (Strom et al., 1993). The high divorce rate has encouraged reliance on older relatives. Families tend to value their elder members because they have survived in the face of hardship and because they play important roles within the family (Luckey, 1994). A study of 60 African-American grandmothers and grandfathers rearing their children's children as a consequence of the adult children's drug addiction showed that grandparents bore a large burden. It was emotionally rewarding but exacted many costs, psychological and financial (Burton, 1992). Similar findings were shown in grandmothers raising grandchildren in the crack cocaine epidemic (Minkler et al., 1992).

Religion has also been a resource of support (Nye, 1993; Walls, 1992). The African-American church has been a source of strength for coping with racial oppression and has played a vital role in the survival and advancement of African Americans. The church has provided a place of importance and belonging. Within the church, elders receive recognition as members, choir vocalists, deacons, and treasurers. A study of a Pennsylvania church, which revealed that church membership contributed to feelings of well-being among older African Americans, recommended that these churches act as a link between families and aging agencies. The church is a likely information and referral institution because so many older individuals are active participants (Walls and Zarit, 1991).

A spirit of survival has seen older African Americans through hard times. Thankful to have survived, they are more likely to appreciate aging; thus, they accept it more easily than those who have not experienced such hardship.

FUTURE OUTLOOK

Though data on the lives of African-American elders are becoming more available, our knowledge is still far from adequate. We are gaining knowledge about their lifestyles, roles, and adaptations to living environments, but the information on whites that pertains to these topics still far exceeds that about minorities.

Studies of *fear* of crime and victimization show much higher rates of fear for African Americans than for whites; and, in fact, their rates of victimization are significantly higher than those for whites. The major reason is thought to be geographic locations—more of them compared with white American elders, live in high-crime areas such as the inner city and in or near public housing. And because feelings of alienation and mistrust of police may have existed from their youth, these elders are less likely than their white counterparts to reach out for help. Social policy experts suggest neighborhood watch programs to unite residents and also recommend age-segregated housing with more safety features (Barazan, 1994).

Despite recent affirmative action plans in the United States, the economic outlook for large numbers of older African Americans is bleak. Table 13.1 reflects some characteristics that are related to their economic inequality. African Americans and other minorities are still disproportionately clustered in peripheral industries that pay lower wages: agriculture, retail trade, nonunionized small businesses, and low-profit companies that pay minimum wage. In contrast, white Americans are still clustered in better-paying "core" industries, such as the automobile industry, construction, and other high-profit, unionized industries. Although some improvement can be expected by

Table 13.1

Social and Economic Characteristics of White and African-American Population (percent), 1992

Characteristic	Percent	
	White	Black
Age 65 and over	13.0	8.3
Homeowner	67.5	42.3
College, 4 years or more	22.1	11.9
Income of $50,000+	34.1	14.9
Unemployed	4.3	8.9
Person below poverty level	10.3	33.8

SOURCE: U.S. Bureau of the Census, *Statistical Abstract of the United States,* 1993, 113th (Washington, DC: Bureau of the Census, 1993), p. 46, table 49.

This Hispanic-American migrant worker is of Mexican descent.

the twenty-first century, it will be small: Between 1982 and 1992, the ratio of African-American family income to white family income actually declined, from 62 to 56 percent. In 1992, the average income of whites was $37,783 a year; the African-American average was $21,548 (U.S. Bureau of the Census, 1993, 46, table 49). If young and middle-aged working African Americans cannot fare as well as whites, they will not compare much better in old age. Only through major economic changes that promote the hiring of minorities in major businesses and industries will they begin to achieve economic parity in middle and old age.

☼ Hispanic Americans

Older Hispanics, the "ancianos," are not a homogeneous group. Researchers are often unprepared for the cultural and socioeconomic diversity of the Hispanic community. One of the many obstacles preventing **Hispanic elders** from being understood and served is the lack of a clear-cut definition of who they are. Census counting often uses two inclusive terms that increase the problem: Spanish heritage (having Spanish blood or antecedents) and Spanish origin (having been born in a Spanish-speaking country or having antecedents who were). Theoretically, then, a person could be of Spanish origin but not of Spanish heritage and vice versa. The term *Hispanic* will be used here to mean Spanish people in a broad sense including either term.

DEMOGRAPHICS

In 1990, more than 22 million persons in the United States were of Hispanic origin. Of these, 5.5 percent were aged 65 or older, and this figure will rise to 7.2 percent by 2010 and 10.9 percent by 2025 (U.S. Bureau of the Census, 1993, 22, 25). Mexican Americans are the largest Hispanic group in the United States—more than half of all Hispanics combined. The percentage breakdown is shown in Figure 13.2.

Figure 13.2
....

Hispanic Population
by Nation of Origin

SOURCE: Data for Circle
Graph from National
Institute on Aging,
"Profiles of America's
Elderly," Washington,
DC: U.S. Dept. of Health
and Human Services,
November 1993, p. 2.

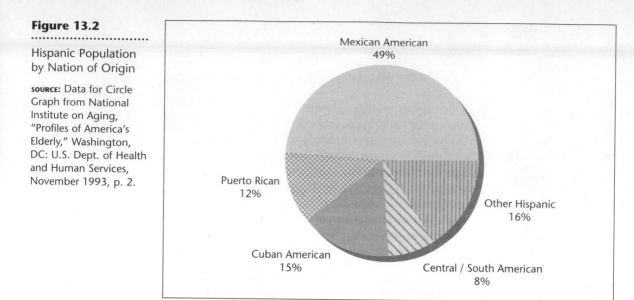

The 1970 and 1980 censuses identified only four categories of Hispanics: Mexican, Puerto Rican, Cuban, and Other. The 1990 census, reflecting the large influx from still other countries, identifies 14 categories.

Mexico
Cuba
Puerto Rico
Dominican Republic
Central America
   El Salvador
   Guatemala
   Nicaragua
   Ecuador
   Honduras
   Panama
   Other Central Americans
South America
   Peru
   Columbia
   Other South Americans

The Hispanic population, one of the fastest-growing ethnic groups, is expected to be the largest U.S. minority group after the year 2000.

MINORITY STATUS

Several social factors indicate the minority status of Hispanic elders: (1) the high percentage that live below the poverty level; (2) the inadequate health care; (3) the second highest illiteracy rate among U.S. racial/ethnic groups—only the rate for Native American elders is higher; and (4) low occupational levels such as operatives, artisans, unskilled laborers, and farm workers. Because they receive fewer social services than whites, Hispanics tend to stay in the workforce longer than whites. Some Mexican-American elders are unlikely to seek social services support because they entered the country illegally; by seeking government help, they risk detection and expulsion.

MIGRATION PATTERNS

Most Hispanic immigrants are from Mexico, Cuba, and Puerto Rico. (Their portion totals 76 percent of all Hispanics.) The majority of Mexican Americans were born in this country, yet other Hispanic elders are more likely to be foreign born. The foreign-born Hispanics are not as acculturated as native-born citizens: They need more help in understanding and utilizing services. Further, programs developed for them must acknowledge the traditions and values they have retained.

Differing patterns of migration have brought Hispanics to various locations in the United States. Hispanic-American immigrants tend to live in urban areas. Immigrants from 6 of the 12 Hispanic nations identified in the 1990 census have more than 80 percent of their populations in the nation's 20 largest cities (New York, Los Angeles, Chicago, Miami, Washington, D.C., Boston, Philadelphia, and San Diego, for example), and three others have between 70 percent and 79 percent in the 20 largest cities. Because so many Mexican Americans are born in the U.S., they are not as extensively urbanized as other Hispanics. Some became citizens when the rural Mexican territory in the Southwest was incorporated into the United States. It is still very rural and heavily populated with Mexican Americans.

However, Hispanics who immigrate (including Mexican immigrants) tend to locate in urban areas. In Texas, for example, the older urban immigrants outnumber their rural counterparts by a ratio of five to one. San Antonio, Houston, and Dallas have large numbers of Mexican Americans who are foreign born.

Puerto Rican and Cuban elders are almost exclusively city dwellers. The Hispanic populations of Florida and the Northeast are more urbanized than those of the Southwest.

THE AMERICAN EXPERIENCE

Hispanic elders today are an ethnic composite that has suffered major linguistic and cultural barriers to assimilation and has occupied a low socioeconomic status. Forty-five percent of Hispanic elders are not proficient in English (Applewhite and Daley, 1988). In 1992, 16.3 percent of persons of Hispanic origin aged 65 and over lived below the poverty level (see Figure 13.1). A major reason for the financial disadvantages of older Hispanics is the lack of pension plan coverage during their working lives: Their coverage rates are lower than those for whites or African Americans. Health problems such as diabetes and obesity are more common among Hispanic elders than in the aged population as a whole.

UTILIZATION OF SERVICES

As a rule, Hispanic elders tend to be somewhat suspicious of governmental institutions and of service workers and researchers not of their culture. Their suspicion, along with a lack of education and money, results in isolation and nonutilization of available services. This underutilization tends to conceal their very real need. Further, because the census undercounts minorities, underutilization is even greater than is generally recognized. One example is in nursing home care, where Hispanic elders are greatly underrepresented

(Mui and Burnette, 1994). Social program providers need to develop a sensitivity to, and communication skills with, Hispanic seniors. Popular beliefs characterize Mexican Americans as living in extended families and, in fact, Hispanic families do tend to be larger than white families in the United States. But that does not mean that the extended family system runs smoothly. Generally speaking, the more acculturated the family members, the less extensive the family interaction, and the more the breakdown of extended family. Traditionally, adult children provide a great deal of support to Hispanic parents in terms of chores such as laundry, housework, transportation, and shopping; both cultural values and economic need dictate these close family ties. Moreover, for those who do not speak English, adult children are needed to provide a link to American culture. But changes are eroding the extended family concept and replacing it with the nuclear family group (Lubben and Becerra, 1987).

STUDYING ETHNIC VARIATIONS

For all Hispanic groups, researchers are studying the types of ethnic communities and institutions that tend to develop in given localities and their impact on the lives of elders. Mexican Americans, for example, participate heavily in senior citizen clubs. Actually, the senior citizen culture is strong in the various representations of Hispanic community (Torres-Gill, 1988). Though minority elders tend to underutilize government and health services, high ethnic population density seems to correlate with higher rates of utilization. The status of the elders in the various Hispanic groups is better in large, fully developed ethnic communities than in small or scattered ones. Here are some statistics about high ethnic population density:

- Eighteen percent of all Hispanics live in Los Angeles.
- Twelve percent of all Hispanics live in New York.
- New York's Puerto Rican population is double that of San Juan, Puerto Rico.
- Seventy-seven percent of immigrants from the Dominican Republic live in urbanized New York.
- Laredo, Texas, is 94 percent Hispanic. The percentage is nearly that high in several other Texas border towns.
- Cubans are clustered in Miami and other cities of southeastern Florida.
- Panamanians are the most geographically diverse. Other groups cluster in enclaves of large cities, by national origin. (Winsberg, 1994)

Another area of research is the unique cultural traditions that are maintained in each Hispanic group. Cuban elders, for example, tend to be much more politically active than Mexican Americans. A professor from Miami describes some unique aspects of Cuban culture as they affect elders (Hernandez, 1992): Cuban culture is a blend of whites from the Iberian Peninsula and blacks from Africa. The Afro-Cuban culture emphasizes respect for elders, stemming from their folk healing beliefs and practices. "Familism" (adherence to strong family values) is strong in Cuban culture and evokes guilt when members do not fulfill expected roles. For example, adult children are filled with guilt if they do not care for aged parents. Cuban women tend to marry older men who care for them financially. Eventually the younger wife cares for the aged husband. Complete dependence on family members, such as adult children or spouses, is welcomed and encouraged by the culture and not interpreted as pathology.

Neglected areas of research are social stratification within ethnic groups, rate of return migration, and degree of cultural adaptation. Hispanic elders who lived most of their lives in their native countries and do not immigrate until late adulthood no doubt experience more culture shock and isolation, but this phenomena needs to be explored.

☼ Asian Americans

Asian American refers in the broadest sense to persons of Chinese, Korean, Japanese, Filipino, East Indian, Thai, Vietnamese, Burmese, Indonesian, Laotian, Malayan, and Cambodian descent who live in the United States. Most **Asian-American elders** are concentrated in California, Hawaii, New York, Illinois, Washington, and Massachusetts. The total U.S. population of Asian and Pacific Islanders was 7.3 million in 1991 (U.S. Bureau of the Census, 1993, 22). Of this number, 6.3 percent are aged 65 and over, or nearly .5 million persons. Of the Asian elders in 1990, about 30 percent were Chinese; 24 percent Japanese; 24 percent Filipino; 8 percent Korean; and 14 percent other Asians and Pacific Islanders.

A single description cannot encompass the Asian communities in the United States. Differences of culture, language, and religion make each group unique (see Table 13.2). Asians are alike, however, in the sense that they all have encountered language barriers and racism.

That Asian elders have nothing to worry about because Asians always care for their own is a misconception. The current generation of Asian Americans, which has been conditioned to our social and cultural folkways and mores, may regard their elders as an unwelcome burden, just as many middle-class white Americans seem to do. According to traditional culture in China, Japan, and Korea, the eldest son assumes responsibility of his elder parents. Filial piety is a custom demanding that family members respect and care for elders. Because of the high proportion of single Asian immigrants, this custom has weakened. Further, a considerable moral "generation gap" often exists between young Asian Americans and their elders. Older family members tend to hang on to traditions, especially those concerning moral propriety, whereas the young move away from them.

Because health and welfare agencies have few bilingual staff members, and because they therefore have difficulty publicizing their available services to the Asian community, outreach programs to Asian-American seniors have been limited in their success. These deficits, in addition to their socially conditioned reluctance to seek aid from their adopted land, result in neglect of Asian-American elders.

JAPANESE AMERICANS

Most of the Japanese who first came to the United States were single men, often younger sons who did not inherit any family wealth. The bulk of the Japanese immigration, which took place between 1870 and 1924, consisted primarily of men who wanted to have traditional families. Many waited until they could afford a wife, who was generally much younger, and then paid for one to come from Japan. This pattern reinforced traditional values of high status for men and elders. The survivors of that earliest immigration period, called *issei*, are now mostly women because the men, being much older, have died.

Table 13.2
. . . .

Asian/Pacific Persons in the United States by Subgroups

Asian
  Chinese
  Filipino
  Japanese
  Asian Indian
  Korean
  Vietnamese
  Lao
  Thai
  Cambodian
  Pakistani
  Indonesian
  Hmong
Other Asians
Pacific Islanders
  Polynesian
    Hawaiian
    Samoan
    Tongan
  Micronesian
    Guamanian
  Melanesian
Other Pacific Islanders
. . . .

The first generation worked primarily on farms or as unskilled laborers or service workers. However, within 25 years of entering the United States, they showed great economic mobility. Though their internment during World War II was economically as well as morally devastating, Japanese Americans as a group rebounded remarkably. First-generation Japanese, the *issei*, learned to live socially segregated from American culture. The children of the *issei*, the *nissei*, generally born between 1910 and 1940, are more likely to be integrated into the American mainstream. Most *nissei* are now over 65 and doing well economically and socially.

Japanese-American elders, on the whole, have adequate savings or family support in their retirement years. Japanese Americans have largely replicated the traditional pattern of family care for elders; 46 percent live with an adult child in addition to or in lieu of a spouse. In traditional Japanese society, when retirement occurred, the retiree joined the ranks of elders and assumed religious duties in the community. This particular tradition is lacking in the United States (Markides and Mindel, 1987).

CHINESE AMERICANS

Because past restrictive immigration laws denied entry to wives or children, a disproportionate share of Chinese- and Filipino-American elders are men. Male immigrants have outnumbered females by at least three to one in census counts. These Asian men were valuable as cheap labor in U.S. mines, canneries, farms, and railroads, but their wives and children were neither needed nor wanted. Though we cannot fully assess the damage to the family life of the elderly Chinese American, such damage has no doubt been extensive, traumatic, and demoralizing.

The immigration law of 1924, which halted Asian immigration, forbade males of Chinese descent from bringing their foreign-born wives to the United States. As a result, many Chinese men in the United States could not marry. Although the men who originally came in the early 1900s are a rapidly vanishing group, a few can still be found, typically living in poverty and without close family ties.

Chinese Americans retain a tradition of respect for elders based on Confucian ethics. Traditionally, the Chinese family was embedded in a larger system of extended family and clans than was the Japanese family. Older family members held wealth and power, not only in their immediate family but all the way up the family hierarchy to the encompassing clan. Though this traditional structure has never been reproduced in the United States, respect for elders persists. The Chinese pattern is for adult children to bring a widowed parent into their household.

Chinese elders are increasingly second-generation. This generally means that they are more educated, more acculturated, and have a more comfortable financial situation. There is a vast difference between the lifestyles of those who are foreign born and who have never learned English and those who were born in the United States. The second generation is retiring with pensions and savings, reaping the harvest of their hard work in this country. Despite discrimination, Chinese Americans have achieved a high rate of occupational mobility; many have gone from restaurant and laundry businesses to educating children who have entered professional and technical occupations.

SOUTHEAST ASIAN AMERICANS

The settlement of Vietnamese, Cambodians, and Laotians in the United States has included a small percentage of elders, who enter a world alien in all facets of life, from language, dress, and eating habits to religious beliefs. Family ties are strong for most of these people. Traditionally, extended families are standard. Southeast Asians have a special respect for their elders, especially for fathers and grandfathers.

Though immigration procedure initially places Southeast Asians throughout the entire United States, once on their own, many have gradually migrated to areas where the weather is similar to their native countries. California has by far the largest number of Southeast Asians. Studies of Southeast Asian refugees show that, like other Asian groups, they adjust fairly well to U.S. culture. Older first-generation immigrants who have suffered, living near or below the poverty line, take pride in children or grandchildren who have achieved financial and other successes.

In Los Angeles, a study that interviewed 19 older Hmong refugees and their families clearly demonstrated the pain and culture shock of displacement (Hays, 1987). In Laos, they lived in extended families with households containing as many as 35 members. Order and authority were maintained through respect for age. The oldest male of each clan sat on a governing council that handled all problems. Both male and female elders experienced a high degree of status within the village.

The Hmong believed that they would be resettled in the United States in a large group, possibly on a reservation. It was a major blow to be scattered in cities. They were shocked to learn about American housing standards; they were unable to understand, for example, why a family of ten could not live in a two-bedroom apartment. One elder Hmong recalled, "When I found out that some of my children would not live with me, my life stopped." The older Hmong had had no formal education in Laos, and many could not face the rigors of learning English in an American classroom.

The role of elders in the Hmong family has changed. In Laos, the elders acted as counselors for adult children experiencing marital difficulties. In the United States, in contrast, they are more out of touch with young couples' marital problems; and they rarely act as advisers and mediators. The older women try to help with child care, but the men don't have much to do. Many would like a farm and animals to tend. Elderly Hmong have experienced loss of function, loss of mobility, loss of religious customs, and loss of status. Some are very depressed. Studies of Southeast Asian refugees find that, because of the language barrier and lack of communication with the larger society, displacement is more difficult for the elderly than for their young (Yee, 1993).

☼ Native Americans

Measured by numbers alone, **Native-American elders** constitute a small percentage of American society: In 1991, there were 1.8 million Native Americans, slightly more than 6 percent of whom were age 65 or over (U.S. Bureau of the Census, 1993, 22). By any social or economic indicator of living conditions, however, they are possibly the *most* deprived of all U.S. ethnic groups.

Many of the problems of Native-American elders are due to minority status rather than to age. American Indians on reservations and in rural areas

Very few Native Americans live to old age.

experience extremely high unemployment rates. Few jobs exist on the reservations, and those who leave in search of work pay the high price of losing touch with family, lifestyle, and culture. Many houses on reservations are substandard, and, despite substantial improvements in health, disparities still exist, especially in sanitation and nutrition. More than 140 years of federal programs have done little to improve the lives of Native Americans.

CULTURAL UNIFORMITY AND DIVERSITY

Though Native Americans are a diverse group, they do share some values that set them apart generally from the larger society. Their lifestyle and spirituality dictate a deep reverence for the land, animals, and nature; and, generally, they believe in attaining harmony between human beings and nature.

Family structure, values, and norms among Native-American tribes are diverse. Generally speaking, Native Americans have close family ties. Though many family structures are patriarchal, a wide variety of descent systems exist. The largest tribe, the Navajo, follows a matrilineal structure. The position of the elderly varies from tribe to tribe, as does emphasis on peace versus war and many other values. And, although some tribes are rivals, there exists today an extensive pan-Indian network that promotes intertribal networking, visiting, and cooperation. Marriage between members of different tribes is also more common (Kitano, 1991). The United States has approximately 278 federally recognized reservations, more than 300 recognized tribes, and around 100 nonrecognized tribes (John, 1991). This includes Eskimo and Aleut populations.

POPULATION DATA

For many years, despite rapid growth in the population of the country as a whole, the Native-American population declined. At the time of the first European settlement in what is now the United States, the number of Indians is estimated to have been between 1 and 10 million. By 1800, the native population had declined to approximately 600,000; by 1850, it had shrunk to 250,000. This mortifying decrease, the result of malnutrition, disease, and an all-out military assault on Native Americans, was a unique occurrence in our national history. However, the population eventually stabilized and is now increasing (Kitano, 1991, 173). Because of early childbearing, it is common for Native Americans to become grandparents in their mid to late thirties. By comparison, grandparenthood usually comes to whites in their mid fifties.

Many older Native Americans live on reservations, tending to stay behind while the young seek work in the city. Young or old, those who go to the city often expect to return to rural reservations to retire. Although the American population as a whole is more urban than rural, the reverse is largely true for the Native-American population. Native Americans are the most rural of any ethnic group in the country. Fifty-three percent live in non-metropolitan areas; 22 percent live in central cities; and the rest live in suburban areas outside central cities (Schick and Schick, 1994).

Life expectancy among Native Americans is substantially lower than that for whites. The Native-American population is largely young; in 1991 nearly 50 percent were under the age of 25 (U.S. Bureau of the Census, 1993, 21, table 22). Elders constitute slightly more than 6 percent of the total Native-American population; by comparison, they represent 12 percent of the total U.S. population. As in the white population, Native-American women live longer than Native-American men.

Native Americans who leave the reservations are usually scattered throughout urban areas, rather than forming ethnic enclaves. Over 48,000 Native Americans, for example, live throughout the Los Angeles area. San Francisco, Tulsa, Denver, New York City, Seattle, Minneapolis, Chicago, and Phoenix all have sizable Native-American populations; Minneapolis has a Native-American enclave. Although a multitude of tribes are scattered throughout the United States, 44 percent of all Native Americans reside in California, Oklahoma, Arizona, and New Mexico (Kitano, 1991). Findings for one tribe cannot be generalized to include all others; values and behavior vary greatly. Specific patterns of aging need to be examined in each tribe.

EDUCATION, EMPLOYMENT, AND INCOME

The educational attainment of Native Americans today is behind that of whites. A sizable percentage of unemployed Navajo adults, for example, cannot speak English; nor can they read or write it. Among Native-American youths, the school dropout rate is twice the national average. Because education has been a traditional means of social advancement in the United States, these data suggest that future generations of Native-American elders may continue to suffer from functional illiteracy. A high percentage of Native-American elders have graduated neither from elementary nor from high school.

Unemployment creates a problem in the Native-American community. An extremely high percentage of the Native-American workforce is unemployed, and most of those who work hold menial jobs with low pay and few, if any, fringe benefits. Because they have often paid only small amounts into Social Security, retirement for Native Americans is a great hardship. White Americans often associate major difficulties of growing old with retirement from the workforce. Native Americans usually have no work from which to retire. For most over 65, old age merely continues a state of poverty and joblessness that has lasted a lifetime.

HEALTH CHARACTERISTICS

Native-American elders are more likely to suffer from chronic illnesses and disabilities than any other ethnic aged group, and they have the lowest life expectancy. However, though the mortality rates for younger Navajos are relatively high, mortality rates among elder Navajos are lower than those for non-Indians of the same age. This paradox represents an instance of the mortality "crossover" (Kunitz and Levy, 1989, 216). Native Americans are more likely than the general population to die from diabetes, alcoholism, influenza, pneumonia, suicide, and homicide ("The Health of America's Native Tribes," 1990). Lack of finances leads to poor nutrition and health care. Further, the Native-American accident rate is high. Native Americans are more likely than the general population to be killed in motor-vehicle accidents; and death from other types of accidents is also more likely. And, although research is underway to study the high rates of alcoholism, minority status is thought to be a major cause. Health problems are compounded by the alien nature of the dominant health-care system to the traditional culture of Native Americans.

Older Native Americans remain an enormously needy group. Today, Native Americans suffer both from dependency on the federal government and from the impact of conflicting federal policies. They are sometimes denied assistance from various government agencies under the excuse that the Bureau of Indian Affairs (BIA) is responsible for providing the denied service. According to the *United States Government Manual 1989/90*, the principal objectives of the BIA are to "actively encourage and train Indian and Alaska Native people to manage their own affairs under the trust relationship to the Federal Government; to facilitate, with maximum involvement of Indian and Alaska Native people, full development of their human and natural resource potential; to mobilize all public and private aids to the advancement of Indian and Alaska Native people for use by them; and to utilize the skill and capabilities of Indian and Alaska Native people in the direction and management of programs for their benefit." The BIA has 12 area offices in the United States, so that the distance between the service provider, the work site, and the reservation (place of residence) compounds the difficulties of eligibility and availability of assistance.

☼ Improving the Status of Ethnic Elders

A large number of minority elders spend their last years lacking income, adequate housing, decent medical care, and needed services. Aging accentuates the factors that have contributed to a lifetime of social, economic, and psychological struggle. Rather than achieving comfort and respect with age, minority persons may get pushed further aside.

Upgrading the status of ethnic elders in the short term requires, first, recognition of the various factors that prevent them from utilizing services and, second, outreach programs designed to overcome those factors. The object should be to expand present programs, to develop more self-help programs, to increase the **bilingual** abilities of social service staffs, and to recruit staff members from the ethnic groups they serve.

With these goals in mind, the Administration of Aging (AOA) has funded four national organizations to improve the well-being of minority elders.

1. The National Caucus and Center on Black Aged (NCCBA) in Washington, D.C.

2. The National Indian Council on Aging (NICOA) in Albuquerque, New Mexico.

3. Asociación Nacional Pro Personas Mayores (National Association for Hispanic Elderly) in Los Angeles, California.

4. National Pacific/Asian Resource Center on Aging (NP/ARCA) in Seattle, Washington.

These centers educate the general public and advocate for their groups.

Ultimately, though, spending a bit of extra money and adding a few services will not solve the real problem. The disadvantages tend to derive from economic marginality that has lasted a lifetime. One's work history is a central factor in how one fares in later life. A work history that allows for a good pension or maximum Social Security benefits is a big step toward economic security in old age. Also, those who have made good salaries have had a chance to save money for their retirement years—a safety net not possible for low wage earners. Until members of minority groups are from birth accorded full participation in the goods and services our society offers, they will continue to suffer throughout their lives. The critical perspective in sociology calls for addressing these basic inequalities and taking major steps toward making all citizens equal.

Chapter Summary

Women, including older ones, in the United States, are in a minority status. They do not participate equally in the political and economic structures. Older women are victims of the double standard of aging—a standard that judges them more harshly as they age. A large percentage of elders in poverty are female.

Ethnic elders suffer from inequality in the United States. Older blacks are poorer than older whites and have a lower life expectancy, poorer health, more inferior housing, and less material comforts. Although some older African Americans are well-to-do, others are impoverished. Family ties, religion, and a resolve to persevere are special strengths. Hispanic elders are not a homogeneous group. About half of all Hispanic elders are Mexican Americans; others come from Cuba, Puerto Rico, and various Central and South American countries. Hispanic elders have suffered major linguistic and cultural barriers to assimilation and have occupied low socioeconomic status. Asian-American elders come from many countries, also. They, too, have encountered racial hatred, language barriers, and discrimination. Native-American elders are a small group. But by any social or economic indicator, they are, possibly, the most deprived group in the United States. More efforts need to be directed at correcting inequities for ethnic minorities and women.

Key Terms

African-American elders

age terrorism

Asian-American elders

bilingual

familism

double standard of aging

ethnic group

Hispanic elders

late midlife astonishment

minority elder

Native-American elders

Questions for Discussion

1. What special problems do older women experience? Older African Americans? Hispanics? Asian Americans? Native Americans?

2. What generation-gap problems exist between the young and the old of each minority group?

Fieldwork Suggestion

1. Interview an older person from a racial minority. Note carefully the person's lifestyle and outlook on life. What past and present discrimination has he or she experienced?

References

Applewhite, S., an R. Daley, "Cross-Cultural Understanding for Social Work Practice with the Hispanic Elderly." In *Hispanic Elderly in Transition*, edited by S. Applewhite, 3–16. New York: Greenwood Press, 1988.

Barazan, M. "Fear of Crime and Its Consequences Among Urban Elderly Individuals." *International Journal of Aging and Human Development* 38:2 (March, 1994): 99–116.

Belgrave, L. L. et al. "Health, Double Jeopardy, and Culture. The Use of Institutionalization by African-Americans." *Gerontologist* 33:3 (June 1993): 379–385.

Bound, J. et al. "Poverty Dynamics in Widowhood." *Journal of Gerontology* 46:3 (May 1991) 115–124.

Bryant, S., and W. Rakowski. "Predictors of Morality Among Elderly African-Americans." *Research on Aging* 14:1 (March 1992): 50–58.

Burton, L. "Black Grandparents Rearing Children of Drug Addicted Parents." *Gerontologist* 32:6 (December 1992): 774–751.

Chrisler, J., and L. Ghiz. "Body Image Issues of Older Women." In *Faces of Women and Aging*, edited by N. Davis et al. Binghamton, NY: Haworth Press, 1993.

Christy, M. "At 71 She's Still a Cosmo Girl." *Santa Rosa Press Democrat* (15 April 1993): D1.

Current Population Reports, Series P-20, No. 444, Table 1, 1990.

Fowler, M., and P. McCutcheon, eds. *Songs of Experience: An Anthology of Literature on Growing Old*. New York, NY: Ballantine, 1991.

Frisby, M. "Gap Among Blacks Widening." *The Boston Globe* (9 August 1991): 1.

Gibson R. "Reconceptualizing Retirement for Black Americans." In *Worlds of Difference*, edited by E. Stoller, and R. Gibson. Thousand Oaks, CA: Pine Forge Press, 1993.

Goodman, M. "Culture, Cohort, and Self-Worth in Women." A paper presented at the 46th Annual Meeting of the Gerontological Society, New Orleans, November 1993.

Guralnick, J., et al. "Educational Status and Active Life Expectancy Among Older Blacks and Whites." *The New England Journal of Medicine* 329:2 (8 July 1993): pp. 110–117.

Hays, C. D. "Two Worlds in Conflict: The Elderly Hmong in the United States." In *Ethnic Dimensions of Aging*, edited by D. Gelfard and C. Barresi. New York: Springer, 1987.

"The Health of America's Native Tribes," *Washington Post Health Section* (13 February 1990): 5.

Hernandez, G. "The Family and Its Aged Members: The Cuban Experience." In *Hispanic Aged Mental Health*, edited by T. Brink, Binghamton, NY: Haworth Press, 1992, pp. 45–58.

Hilts, P. "Life Expectancy for U.S. Blacks Drops Again," *San Francisco Chronicle* (29 November 1990): A14.

Jacobs, R. *Be An Outrageous Older Woman*, Manchester, CN: Knowledge Ideas, & Trends, 1993.

John, R. "The State of Research on American Indian Elders." In *Minority Elders*. 38–50. Washington, D.C.: Gerontological Society of America, 1991.

Kingson, E. and R. O'Grady-LeShane. "The Effects of Caregiving on Women's Social Security Benefits," *Gerontologist* 33:2 (April 1993): 230–239.

Kitano, H. *Race Relations*. Englewood Cliffs, NJ: Prentice-Hall, 1991.

Kunitz, S. and J. Levy. "Aging and Health Among Navajo Indians." In *Aging and Health: Pespectives on Gender, Race, Ethnicity and Class*, edited by K. Markides 211–245. Newbury Park, CA: Sage, 1989.

Lifshitz, L. *Only Morning in Her Shoes: Poems About Old Women*, Logan, UT: Utah State Univ. Press, 1990.

Lubben, J. E., and R. M. Becerra. "Social Support Among Black, Mexican, and Chinese Elderly." In *Ethnic Dimensions of Aging*, edited by D. Gelfand and C. Barresi. New York: Springer, 1987.

Luckey, I. "African American Elders: The Support Network of Generational Kin." *Families in Society: The Journal of Contemporary Human Services* 75:2 (February 1994): 82–90.

Markides, Kuriakos S., and Charles H. Mindel. *Aging and Ethnicity*. Newbury Park, CA: Sage, 1987.

Minkler, M., et al. "Raising Grandchildren in the Crack Cocaine Epidemic." *Gerontologist* 32:6 (December 1992): 752–761.

Mui, A., and D. Burnette. "Long-term Care Service Used by Frail Elders: Is Ethnicity a Factor?" *Gerontologist* 34:2 (April 1994): 190–198.

National Institute on Aging, "Profiles of America's Elderly: Racial and Ethnic Diversity," Washington, D.C.: U.S. Dept. of Health and Human Services, November, 1993.

Nickerson, B. *Old and Smart: Women and Aging*, Eugene, OR: All About Us, 1991.

Nye, W. "Amazing Grace: Religion and Identity Among Elderly Black Individuals. *International Journal of Aging and Human Development* 36:2 (March 1993): 103–105.

Pearlman, S. "Late Mid-Life Astonishment: Disruptions to Identity and Self-Esteem." In *Faces of Women and Aging*, edited by N. David, et al. Binghamton, NY: Haworth Press, 1993.

Porcino, J. *Growing Older, Getting Better*, Redding, MA: Addison-Wesley, 1983.

Quadagno, J. and M. Meyer. "Gender and Public Policy." In *Worlds of Difference*, edited by E. Stoller and R. Gibson. Thousand Oaks, CA: Pine Forge Press, 1993.

Rosenthal, E., ed. *Women, Aging and Ageism*. Binghamton, New York: Harrington Park Press, 1991.

Schick, F. and R. Schick, eds. *Statistical Handbook on Aging Americans*. Phoenix, AZ: Oryx Press, 1994.

Sheehy, G. *Preface Women on the Front Lines*, edited by J. Allen and A. Pifer. Washington, D.C.: The Urban Institute Press, 1993.

Sontag, S. "The Double Standard of Aging" *Saturday Review* (23 September 1972).

"Special Report: Black and White in America." *Newsweek* (7 March 1988): 18–45.

Strom, R. et al. "Strengths and Needs of Black Grandparents." *International Journal of Aging and Human Development* 36:4 (May/June 1993) 255–259.

Taylor, R., and L. M. Chatters. "Correlates of Education, Income, and Poverty Among Aged Blacks." *Gerontologist* 28 (August 1988): 435–444.

Thone, R. *Women and Aging: Celebrating Ourselves*, Binghamton, NY: Haworth Press, 1993.

Torres-Gill, F. "Interest Group Politics: Empowerment of the 'Ancianos.'" In *Hispanic Elderly in Transition*, edited by S. Applewhite, 75–94. New York: Greenwood Press, 1988.

Troll, I. "Issues in the Study of Older Women." In *Health and Economic Status of Older Women*, edited by A. Herzog, K. Holden, and M. Seltzer. Amityville, NY: Baywood Publishing, 1989.

Uhlenberg, P. "Divorce for Women After Midlife." In *Journal of Gerontology* 45:1 (January 1990): 53–61.

U.S. Bureau of the Census. *Statistical Abstract of the United States, 1993*, 113th ed. Washington, D.C.: U.S. Department of Congress, Census Bureau, 1993.

Walls, C. "The Role of Church and Family Support in the Lives of Older African Americans." *Generations* (Summer 1992) 16:3, 33–37.

Walls, C., and S. Zarit. "Informal Support from Black Churches and the Well-Being of Elderly Blacks." *Gerontologist* 31:4 (August 1991): 490–495.

Winsberg, M. "*Special Hispanics*." American Demographics, February, 1994, pp. 44–53.

Yee, B. K. W. "Elders in Southeast Asian Refugee Families." In *Worlds of Difference*, edited by E. Stoller and R. Gibson. Thousand Oaks, CA: Pine Forge Press, 1993.

York, P. *Going Strong*, New York, NY: Arcade Pub. Inc., 1991.

Further Readings

Banner, L. *In Full Flower: Aging Women, Power, and Sexuality*. New York: Random House, 1993.

Blakemore, K. and Boneham, M. *Age, Race and Ethnicity*. Buckingham, England: Open University Press, 1994.

Gelfand, D. *Aging and Ethnicity: Knowledge and Services*. New York: Springer Publishing, 1993.

Holden, K. "Continuing Limits of Productive Aging: The Lesser Rewards for Working Women." *Achieving a Productive Aging Society*, ed. by Bass, S. et al. Westport: Auburn House, 1993, pp. 269–284.

Holstein, M. "Women's Lives, Women's Work: Productivity, Gender, and Aging," *Achieving a Productive Aging Society*, ed. by Bass, S. et al. Westport: Auburn House, 1993, pp. 235–244.

Narduzzi, J. *Mental Health Among Elderly Native Americans*. New York: Garland Pub. Inc., 1994.

Savishinsky, J., ed. Special issue on ethnicity and aging, *Ethnic Groups* 8:3 (1990): 143–214.

14 Death and Dying

CHAPTER OUTLINE

A Death Doctor's Strange Obsessions

■ JAMES RISEN

He was a bright young doctor at a time when the United States was just beginning its post–World War II ascent, and Jack Kevorkian, University of Michigan Medical School Class of 1952, could have—should have—had it all.

But he had this nagging, inexplicable fascination with the dying and the dead, a personal obsession, really, one that was all the more peculiar because it first appeared during an optimistic era of limitless possibilities and unquestioning faith in the resiliency of American life.

Perhaps it was reinforced during his brief time as a U.S. Army doctor in Korea; certainly it was there during his residency at the University of Michigan Medical Center in the mid-1950s. . . .

"I don't like to watch someone die," he insists. "It is a traumatic, wrenching experience. . . ."

Over the years, Kevorkian's obsession would cost him dearly. On the fringes of medicine, he would become permanently unemployed in his mid-50s—rejected even for a job as a paramedic.

His last patients were acquaintances who would stop him in the street to ask his advice on minor ailments. He would complain that American medical journals refused to publish his ideas. By the onset of the 1990s, Kevorkian had retreated into a private world. . . .

And so when Janet Adkins came to him eager to end her life, eager to stop the suffering of Alzheimer's disease before she became mentally incompetent, Kevorkian was ready.

He already had traveled the slippery ethical slope that leads from medicine to euthanasia. In his own mind, he was no longer a practicing pathologist.

Instead, he printed up new business cards. On them, he called himself an "obitiatrist," with its root in the word "obituary"; a doctor of death. "The world's first," he says.

On June 4, 1990, Adkins, a 54-year-old mother of three from Portland, Oregon, climbed into the back of Kevorkian's rusting old Volkswagen van in a rural Michigan park not far from Pontiac and allowed Kevorkian to connect her to his homemade "suicide machine."

Dr. Jack Kevorkian in a Michigan courtroom.

She then pushed a button three times to ensure the machine's death-inducing drugs would course through her veins. According to Kevorkian, "Thank you, thank you," were her last words. ☀

Authors Note: In 1991, at age 63, Kevorkian lost his license to practice medicine in Michigan. In the years from 1990 to 1994, Jack Kevorkian publicly acknowledges assisting in 21 suicides (See page 353 of this text for a list). In 1993, Michigan passed a law banning assisted suicide. In 1994, Kevorkian, at age 66, went on trial for violating Michigan's law banning assisted suicide. The court ruled in May of 1994 that the law banning assisted suicide was not enacted properly and therefore Kevorkian could not be found guilty of violating it, but that he can be tried for murder under Michigan law. In December 1994, the Michigan State Supreme Court ruled that assisted suicide had always been a crime under common law; no ban against it is necessary to enforce the law against assisted suicide. In April, 1995, the United States Supreme Court refused to hear the Kevorkian case, which paved the way for Kevorkian to be tried in Michigan for 2 murder charges and 3 suicide assists.

SOURCE: James Risen, "Death Doctor's Strange Obsession," *San Francisco Chronicle* (26 June 1990): A8. Copyright © 1990 Los Angeles Times. Reprinted by permission.

*D*eath is one of the few certainties of life. This statement is neither pessimistic nor morbid. Despite our wildest fantasies about immortality, no one has yet escaped death permanently. Despite its universality, however, death is not easily discussed in American society. People tend to be sensitive and shy about discussing the topic openly.

Facing death, dealing with the fact of death in a rational way, and exerting control over the manner of one's dying are all difficult situations in a society that denies death. Just because one is old does not mean that one does not fear death or that one welcomes dying. In this chapter, we will examine the ability of the older individual to experience a "good" death to the extent our society permits it.

☼ A Death-Denying Society?

Our words, attitudes, and practices suggest that ours is a **death-denying society** (Hoefler, 1994 p. 2). Have you ever used the word *died* and had the uncomfortable feeling that those with whom you were talking considered the word too direct and in bad taste? "Passed away" is the preferred phrase—or "passed on," "expired," "departed," or "sleeping"—but not "dead." There are dozens of euphemisms for the process of dying. Funerals, presenting an embalmed and painted body, try to project an illusion of life. There even exists a sort of prescribed script that mourners follow: "She looks just like she did yesterday when I was talking to her" or "He looks so natural." Death is denied. Those selling cemetery plots advise us not to buy a grave but to invest in a "pre-need memorial estate." Cemeteries often try to avoid the image of death with pleasant names or "sunrise" burial plans.

Watching death on television or killing after killing in the movies is not facing death. Violent deaths portrayed in cartoons and action films do not evoke the full range of human emotions—the deep sorrow, anger, and guilt—that the actual death of a loved one would. "Sensitive" television dramas that depict the death of a family member tend to be just as unrealistic. Even the news media and the U.S. government were criticized during the 1991 Gulf War for presenting a too-sanitized picture of war. Thus, in many cases, the media does not help us come to grips with death.

However, the AIDS epidemic has forced us to look at death more honestly. AIDS has brought death and dying issues out in the open as thousands of victims and their families grapple with illness, death, grief, and loss. Shanti, for example, is a nationwide grief counseling organization composed of staff and volunteers funded by government and private sources, which has channeled almost all of its time and efforts into counseling AIDS victims and their families.

At the turn of the century, dying and death were household events that encompassed not only elders, but the young and middle aged as well. Whereas, then, the body remained in the home until everyone had paid their respects, now, the average individual rarely, or never, sees an untreated dead body. How to deal with a corpse was a piece of domestic know-how familiar in most nineteenth-century households, know-how that has vanished from lack of practice. Sociologists observe that death in modern societies is characterized by prolongation, bureaucratization, and secularization (Hoefler, 1994 p. 67). In other words, chronic diseases and increased technology keep people in a prolonged state of dying, bureaucracy makes the setting impersonal, and a secular society robs a person of the religious significance of dying. These three trends make it difficult for a dying individual to construct an identity.

Because people now typically die in hospitals, the final moments of life are seldom observed, even by family. Of the nearly 2 million patients currently residing in nursing homes, only 20 percent will ever return home; the vast majority will die in the nursing home or be sent to a hospital to die. Health professionals, rather than family, care for the dying. Dying in institutions is depersonalized, and it serves to dissociate society from death and dying. The body goes to a funeral parlor rather than home. We no longer stay after the graveside service to see the earth shoveled back into the grave, let alone do it ourselves. Serving a meal to all who attend the rites or holding a wake is becoming less common.

However, despite society's increasing disassociation with death and dying, interest in the topic has escalated in the last decade or so. College courses on death and dying, seminars instructing health professionals and clergy in understanding the dying person, and many books on the subject have become available. More informal memorial services have become common in contrast to impersonal, rigid funeral services.

☼ Fear of Death

Old people are commonly stereotyped as waiting fearlessly for death. And, although studies concerning the relationship between age and a **fear of death** have been largely inconclusive, the data indicate that elders in general do seem to be somewhat less fearful about death. Though any given individual may be an exception to the rule, elders as a group seem less fearful than younger persons. Gerontologist Kalish (1987) attributes this difference to three things: (1) elders often feel they have completed the most important tasks of life, (2) they are more likely to be in pain or to be suffering from chronic diseases, and (3) they have lost many friends and relatives, losses that have made death more of a reality for them.

However, other researchers think that old people may fear death more because they are closer to it. Others believe that fear is the greatest in late middle age, when midlife transition brings a heightened awareness of aging and death (Gesser, Wong, and Reker, 1988). Once that transitory phase passes, however, fears usually decline. A number of philosophers assert that fear of death is innate in all individuals, regardless of age, and that it provides direction for life's activities. Is one more ready to die at age 20 than at age 10? Will you be less fearful of death at age 95 than at age 55?

In one study, a majority of elders reported fearing death at least sometimes (Barrow, 1967). The sources of fear varied. Death as the unknown was a common source of apprehension. One man elaborated:

> I think it's incredulous. It's hard to believe what could happen, where I would be. I can't think of it as just going to sleep. There must be something else. It's very difficult. It's the uncertainty of the thing. The hereafter is perhaps awesome and fearful.

Many in the sample were afraid that the act of dying might be long, painful, or difficult. An 85-year-old Jewish man, who thought going to sleep and never waking up would be a wonderful way to go, said, "I pray when the time comes, to go quick." A 76-year-old man who was a diabetic amputee said, "I tell you, it's a bad thing to have to think about, but there are worse things than dying—like being in great pain. Dying—it don't take too long when the time comes." One 66-year-old Baptist woman was afraid of being watched while she died:

> If I should go I want to go right now. I wouldn't want to struggle with death. I don't want anybody standing over me, (to) see me go. My pastor's wife died all of a sudden. She feared her troubles herself.

Others feared how their death would affect their family. One man said:

> The day has to come. It's unknown. My family would cry and carry on. My wife would tear her hair out.

One 79-year-old woman dreaded her own death because her 30-year-old mentally ill daughter would have no one to turn to. Still another feared death because he did not have the means to pay for funeral expenses.

Given painful experience and the power of imagination, people can find dozens of reasons to fear death itself or to have fears about dying. Fear of a long, painful death; fear of illness, such as cancer; fear of senility; fear of the unknown; fear of judgment in the afterlife; fear about the fate of one's body; fear of dying alone or, conversely, the fear of being watched; fear of dying in a hospital or nursing home; and fear of the loss of bodily control are some of the more common. Some of these fears are of death itself; others are fears about the process of dying, such as the imagined pain, helplessness, and dependence. Both are important areas of study.

Some fears seem normal, that is, justified and within reason. Others seem to be exaggerated. The term *fear* (in this case, fear of death) is usually used when such apprehension has a specific, identifiable source. In comparison, **death anxiety** denotes feelings of apprehension and discomfort that lack an identifiable source. Scales have been developed to measure death anxiety (Neimeyer, 1994) as well as fear of death (e.g., the Collett-Lester Fear of Death Scale). **Death competency,** our capabilities and skills in dealing with death, has been measured using Burgen's Coping with Death Scale and Robbins's Death Self-Efficacy Scale. Scales have also been used to analyze "death depression" and "death threat" (Neimeyer, 1994). As taboos lift in studying death and dying, more will be known about helping people personally grapple with the topic.

Researchers are aware that scales asking subjects to agree or disagree with statements such as "Death is an experience to look forward to," "I don't fear death," or "I am very much afraid to die" may not probe respondents' true feelings. Social norms dictate that we not admit being afraid of death. Indeed, certain religious groups teach that one should look forward to death.

LIZ... YOU'RE SO BUSY... WHAT ARE YOU DOING?

DON'T WORRY, I'M DOING MY NECESSARY LIFE ASSESSMENT!

Clinical in-depth interviews might yield more accurate results than scaled response tests.

Though the experience of death will be different for every person, research indicates that, in general, our fears about the suffering death involves may be at least somewhat unfounded. In Connecticut, a study of the deaths of 1,000 persons over age 65 found that most died peaceful and relatively painless deaths. In most cases, health did not deteriorate until near the end. More than half of those whose deaths were studied were in good or excellent health a year before they died. About 10 percent were in good health the day before they died (McCarthy, 1991).

Elders' fears and concerns about dying should be dealt with as openly as possible. Because of their own anxieties about death, adult children often will not allow parents or grandparents to fully express their views on the subject. Yet this "death talk" can be realistic, practical, and therapeutic; family members would be wise to listen.

☼ Living Fully Until Death

The marginal status of elders in our society affects their ability to live fully until death. Kalish (1969) discovered that though, in U.S. society, the death of an elder is much less disturbing than the death of a younger person, this attitude is not universal. He told this story:

> I once asked a group of about two dozen Cambodian students in their mid-twenties whether, given the necessity for choice, they would save the life of their mother, their wife or their daughter. All responded immediately that they would save their mother, and their tone implied that only an immoral or ignorant person would even ask such a question. I doubt whether 10 percent of a comparable American group would give that response.

He also reported that the Mangalase, an Oceanic society, believe that remaining alive into old age indicates a strength of soul. Their elders receive more respect than the aged in most other societies (Kalish, 1987).

Although we all hope we will live fully from the moment of birth until death, for elders, depending on their circumstances, living fully until death may not be possible. Many spend their final years confined to nursing homes or other care-taking institutions. Oddly, researchers have generally found a seemingly more positive attitude toward death among institutionalized elderly than among those living in their own homes. Upon closer examination, however, this positive attitude may not represent an acceptance of dying as much as it represents a desire not to continue living in a depersonalized, unstimulating environment. Some institutionalized persons may earnestly prefer the real thing over the living deaths to which they are consigned.

Although many believe that death is welcome to those in old age, this is not necessarily true. Instead of being at a stage of acceptance, many have simply reached a stage of resignation, where life is no longer meaningful.

For the terminally ill, who may have only a few years, months, or days to live, living fully until death is important, whatever the time span. Many people have written books chronicling their last months with someone they love who is dying. When death is faced squarely, this time period is filled with intense mutual appreciation and love. Dying persons have also written books about their last days. Gilda Radner wrote about facing her final days in *It's Always Something* (1990). Because of our society's efforts to deny and avoid death, we have trouble knowing what to say or do when a friend or family member falls victim to a terminal illness, and everyone has difficulty coping with the situation. Terminal illness delivers a death sentence, but it can be coped with in a positive way. One woman with terminal cancer had a "going-away" party attended by close friends and family. Those who attended the celebration said it was a very moving experience (DeSpelder and Strickland, 1991).

During her pioneer work in hospitals with death and the dying, Elisabeth Kübler-Ross invited dying patients to share their wants, anxieties, and fears with professionals involved in the care of the terminally ill. These interviews often gave these patients great relief, because they could openly discuss their impending death. (Kübler-Ross does not specify, however, how many of her sample of 200 were 65 or over.)

The following synopses summarize the Kübler-Ross theory of the **stages of dying** through which a patient proceeds. Though, in theory, the simplest and most logical course would be for the patient to begin at the first stage and to progress step-by-step to the final one, patients may be in any stage or in several stages simultaneously—and they may or may not achieve the final stage of acceptance (Kübler-Ross, 1969).

Stage 1: Denial and Isolation

Of more than 100 dying patients interviewed, most reported first reacting to the awareness of a terminal illness with statements such as, "No, not me, it can't be true." Denial behavior might include insisting that x-rays or other evidence is incorrect, going from doctor to doctor hoping for a more favorable diagnosis, assuming that the illness is really a minor one, talking about continuing life and avoiding any discussion about death or any type of change, or approaching treatment with the expressed belief that it will offer a complete cure. Such denial, which is simply a way of dealing with an uncomfortable and painful situation, eventually gives way to at least partial acceptance. Kübler-Ross states that maintained denial (which is rare) does not necessarily increase distress if it remains until the end. Of the 200 patients in her sample, only three attempted to deny the approach of death until they died.

Stage 2: Anger

Denial gives way to a new reaction: anger, rage, envy, or resentment. The patient, who may be demanding or have temper tantrums, asks, "Why me?" Their anger is often displaced: the doctors are no good, the nurses do everything wrong, the family is not sympathetic, and the world is a mess.

Stage 3: Bargaining

Dying people arrive at the bargaining stage in an attempt to postpone the inevitable. If their lives can only be extended until they can do the one thing they have always wanted to do, or until they can make amends for something they have regretted, or until they can see someone again, they promise to accept death. Some pledge their life to God or to service in the church in exchange for additional time. Others in the Kübler-Ross study promised to give their bodies to science, if the doctors would first use their medical knowledge to extend the dying patient's life. Bargaining is the compromise stage that follows the realization that impending death cannot be denied or escaped.

Stage 4: Depression

When terminally ill patients can no longer deny an illness because of its advancing symptoms, they experience a profound sense of loss. The loss may be of physical parts of the body removed by surgery, of money that is being spent on treatment, of functions that no longer can be performed, or of relationships with family and friends. Depression results from facing these losses. Kübler-Ross identifies depression as either reactive (the reaction to loss) or preparatory (preparation for one's impending loss of life; such preparation facilitates a state of acceptance).

Stage 5: Acceptance

The patient who has been given the time and assistance he or she needs to work through the previous stages will usually reach the final stage of acceptance. The patient will have expressed anger and envy and will have been lifted from depression. Grief will normally give way to contemplation of the coming end with quiet expectation.

The stages that Kübler-Ross has identified apply to persons of all ages. Old age alone is not a factor that necessarily induces positive attitudes toward dying. The patients in her sample clearly struggled with dying. Facing death must be a difficult task upon which age, status, and experience have little bearing, if any. Lofland (1979) proposes that the following four dimensions of choice shape the role of a dying person:

1. Space—how much "life space" to devote to the dying role; the degree of activity involved with dying;

2. Whether to surround oneself with others who are dying;

3. Whether to share information about the facts and feelings of one's death with others;

4. What kind of personal philosophy one wishes to express in the dying role.

☼ The Life Review

Preparing for death is at least partially a psychological process. Butler (1974) postulates that approaching dissolution and death generates a life review process in individuals of advanced age. The aging person progressively remembers more of past experiences and reexamines and reintegrates unresolved conflicts. This process—which can bring new significance and meaning to one's life, reduce fear and anxiety, and prepare one for death—may well be universal, occurring in all individuals in the final days of their lives. One may or may not be aware of it and, if aware, may consciously deny it is happening. Though a life review can occur at a younger age, the drive to put one's life in order seems strongest in old age. Psychologist Erik Erikson wrote of the last stage of life as a time to look back on one's life and integrate its meaning.

According to Butler and Lewis (1991), at some point in late life, the individual develops a particularly vivid imagination and memory for the past and can recall with sudden and remarkable clarity events of early life, seemingly moving thoughts from their subconscious to their conscious mind. Such developments allow them to understand their vulnerability and mortality as they reassess the meaning of life. The resulting **life review** may be told to others, or it may be preserved as private reflection. Finding the process of expression therapeutic, some older people will tell their life history to anyone who will listen; others share their thoughts with no one. Those who cannot resolve the issues their life review uncovers may become anxious or depressed, or even enter a state of terror or panic. Those who cannot face or accept the resolution of their life conflicts may commit suicide. Others gain a sense of satisfaction, a sense of tranquillity, a capacity to enjoy to the utmost the remainder of their life. Counselors are advised to be attentive and ready to openly discuss death with patients who present cues that such conversation is desired (Aiken, 1991).

Butler's ideas have generated much research, and though the terms *life review* and *reminiscence* have often been used interchangeably in the accompanying literature, some researchers have separated the concepts by considering the life review to be one of many forms of reminiscence. **Reminiscence** may provide materials for life review or it may be just storytelling for fun or social activity. By comparison, life review can be defined as that form of reminiscence in which the reviewer actively evaluates the past and attempts to resolve conflicts. However, reminiscence is not unique to old age; but it is possible that it is more common and more meaningful in the later years. Butler contends that thoughts of death initiate the life review, which is, developmentally, then, more expected as one nears the end of life.

Although it often seems that older people, whether close to death or not, are wasting time by talking of the past and dwelling on details that are meaningless to younger listeners, these elders may be engaging in life review. Disengagement theory may accurately describe what happens just prior to death: people turn inward, mentally evaluate their lives, and gradually disengage. In contrast, activity theory, which emphasizes external activity for older persons, may potentially damage the self-concept of the dying by discouraging this reflection, reevaluation, and resolution in favor of maintained social involvement.

One study of disengagement asked 120 residents of old-age homes to estimate the time they had remaining before death, a variable the researchers called "awareness of finitude." The researchers found this awareness to be a better predictor of disengagement than chronological age: The residents who gave a shorter estimate had altered their behavior by constricting their life space and had already become more introverted (Still, 1980). Some researchers actually believe that individuals have a certain amount of personal control over the timing of their death (Phillips and Smith, 1990).

☀ Care of the Dying in Hospitals

Care of the dying in hospitals calls for an understanding of the stages of dying and for a sensitivity to patients' needs. In the past, doctors were reluctant to tell patients of a terminal diagnosis, let alone help them proceed through the process of dying. In their pioneer study of patient–staff interactions in a number of hospitals, sociologists Barney Glazer and Anselm Strauss (1966) created a typology of **awareness contexts of dying** for terminally ill patients. During the first of these, "closed awareness," the patient does not yet know that he or she is going to die. The physician in charge decides to keep the patient from knowing or even suspecting the actual diagnosis, and the rest of the staff do all they can to maintain the patient's lack of knowledge. The physician gains the patient's trust and at the same time avoids revealing the fact of his or her impending death.

The second context is "suspicion awareness," during which the patient suspects the truth, but no one will confirm his or her suspicions. Because the patient is afraid to ask outright questions, he or she therefore receives no clear answers. Still, the patient, who wants evidence, tries to interpret what the staff says and does. Peeking at medical charts, eavesdropping on medical conversations, and watching listeners' reactions after declaring, "I think I'm dying," are typical behaviors.

The third type of awareness is the "ritual drama of mutual pretense." Both patient and staff now know that death is impending, but both choose to act as if it is not. The patient tries to project a healthy, well-groomed appearance, and behaves as if he or she will be leaving the hospital soon; the staff makes comments such as "You're looking well today"; and both follow the script as if acting out a drama. Blatant events that expose the mutual pretense are ignored.

However, during the fourth context, "open awareness," which may or may not extend to the time of death and mode of dying, both patient and staff openly acknowledge that the patient is dying. Game playing is eliminated.

The trend in recent years has been to encourage more open awareness in the context of dying. Doctors and nurses for whom daily encounters with dying patients produce painful and bewildering emotions can be distant and tense with dying people. To face a dying person is to be reminded of one's own mortality, and when one's predominant attitude toward dying is fear, avoidance of those close to death becomes one's operative behavior. Some hospital staff members react by withdrawing emotionally at a time when the patient most needs their support. Along with this is a "doctor-patient disconnection." An erosion of trust has undermined the doctor-patient relationship in recent decades (Hoefler, 1994, p. 71).

If health professionals can face their own mortality, they can more easily face mortality in others and are less likely to transmit their fear, shock, or horror to the dying person. The goal for the hospital staff is to maintain as much of an open awareness context as the patient seems to need. Sometimes other contexts are called for; closed awareness, for example, may be appropriate if the patient indicates a strong desire not to know any details about his or her condition and clearly denies his or her own illness.

Care of the dying in a hospital involves more than the decision to tell or not to tell a patient of his or her fate. A number of other problems are evident. One is that doctors and nurses often tend to stereotype or label a terminally ill person as "the dying patient." The word *dying* fades all other facets of the individual's personality and colors others' behavior toward him or her. Forgetting that the person is still alive, aware, and unique, staff members may talk as if the patient were insensate or absent. The patient is often handled without regard for his or her feelings or intelligence by staff who must learn to treat the dying person as a full human being.

How much hope to offer the dying patient is another task health-care professionals must face. Some degree of hope is helpful to the terminally ill. Even the most accepting, most realistic patients leave the possibility open for some cure, for the discovery of a new drug, or for new research developments. A glimpse of hope can maintain them through tests, surgery, and suffering. Patients show the greatest confidence in doctors who offer hope without lying, who share with them the hope that some unforeseen development will change the course of events.

The "Dying Person's Bill of Rights," drawn up by those who nurse cancer patients, includes this statement about hope: *"I have the right to be cared for by those who can maintain a sense of hopefulness, however changing this might be."* A study of survivors of recently deceased persons found that, even in their last month, 65 percent of those who died had maintained a positive quality of life. And many experienced a feeling of hope. Hope did not mean that they believed they would live. It meant they had something to live for a little while longer (McCarthy, 1991).

Timing is essential for those helping the terminally ill through the process of dying (Kübler-Ross, 1981). There seem to be particular times to offer hope, to relate bad news, to allow denial of death, and to help in facing reality. Those who work with the dying must be sensitive to the stages of death and the terminal patient's special needs at various points in the dying process.

For nearly two decades, the National Cancer Institute has offered a seminar to physicians planning to specialize in the care of cancer patients. The physicians meet to come to grips with their own anxieties about death and to better understand their interactions with dying patients and their families. At Grady Memorial Hospital in Atlanta, Georgia, which used this seminar as a model to develop one for both physicians and nurses, the seminar director has noted that doctors and nurses often feel an involuntary anger at the dying patient, who comes to represent their own sense of failure and helplessness: "When you've exhausted everything you can do for a patient medically, it becomes difficult to walk into the room every day and talk to that patient." The seminar seems to relieve stress on the cancer ward's nurses, who used to regularly ask for transfers to other wards. It also teaches the staff to be more comfortable in discussing death and other potentially sensitive topics with the patient. Other training seminars are operating across the country. The University of California Medical Center at Berkeley, for example, offers a counseling service to train volunteers who work with dying patients. The hospice program at New Haven, Connecticut, offers a similar service.

Courses in death and dying are now available at Harvard, Tufts, and other medical schools. A survey of medical schools revealed that nine of ten medical schools had at least one or two lectures for students on the topic, but only 20 percent of medical schools offered an entire course on death and dying. In only half of the schools with such a course was it required; in the other half it was an elective. Personal involvement of students with dying patients was minimal in almost every course at every medical school. One exception is the Yale School of Medicine, which developed a course enabling medical students to interact with very sick patients. They learn how to show compassion without being afraid (Mermann et al., 1991).

Elders, as we might expect, have a higher death rate than any other age group. Morbidity and mortality statistics indicate that health declines and the death rate increases at the upper age levels. Care of the dying, then, has special relevance to older persons, especially the very old, who stand to benefit the most from improved care for the dying.

☼ A Matter of Choice

More and more individuals who face the prospect of imminent death are seeking to expand their rights in determining the manner of their dying. Deciding to die at home or to not prolong life by artificial means are becoming two areas of choice for terminally ill patients. In addition, suicide and funeral plans, which also involve the matter of choice, have special implications for elders.

THE HOSPICE MOVEMENT

Hospices were virtually unheard of in this country until the mid-1970s. Created by the British, they have now spread throughout the United States. The hospice program, which stresses effective pain relief for terminal cancer patients, is designed to care for the dying person—the whole person, not just the disease. The goal is to meet the emotional, social, and spiritual needs of a dying person along with his or her medical needs. There are three basic hospice models: (1) houses that provide counseling and facilities for short- or long-term stay; (2) home-care service only, which provides support for the dying person and his or her family; and (3) hospice care in a hospital. Hospice facilities encourage a warm, homey atmosphere where one can be surrounded by family and friends. Often, overnight accommodations are available for a spouse or close relatives. Death is spoken of openly, and individuals are allowed to die with a maintained sense of self. Morphine has long been in standard use, and some hospices have worked toward legalizing the use of heroin in combating pain. The hospice program works to make the patient's comfort and needs a major priority by eliminating the clinical, impersonal hustle-bustle and high-tech atmosphere common in hospitals. Dramatic medical intervention is avoided when death approaches; rather, hospices have been responsible for many recent advances in pain control, particularly in cases of advanced cancer.

The first U.S. hospice, Hospice of Connecticut, in New Haven, offers a model of care for the dying. The New Haven hospice began as a home-care program. Outreach workers visited and counseled patients, and they also provided home nursing to the dying. Family members could receive individual or group counseling throughout the dying process to get support from others experiencing the same shock and grief. When possible, clients could die at home among the comfort and familiarity of family members and friends. In 1980 an inpatient unit was christened for those who needed more medical facilities than a home setting could provide. But the focus was the

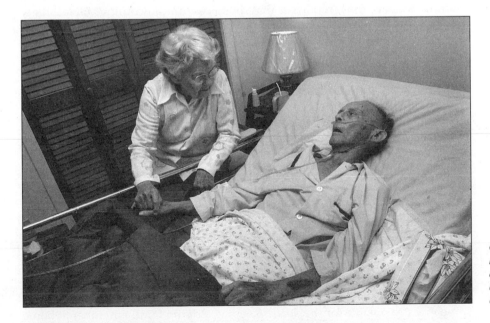

One's own fear of death must be faced squarely to deal empathetically with another person who is dying.

same—meeting the emotional and comfort needs of the dying person. Studies show that those nurses and others who are drawn to hospice work tend to be devout persons who want to engage in holistic, independent nursing (Gentile and Fello, 1990). Medical intervention takes a back seat to nursing intervention in hospice care.

An interdisciplinary team of workers includes nurses, aides, counselors, physical therapists, nutritionists, chaplains, volunteers, doctors, and administrators. Volunteers provide care so family members can get out of the house. They also may do light housekeeping, laundry, meal preparations, and errands.

Some hospitals have hospice programs, and such programs are becoming available at nursing homes as well. These programs offer an integrated approach to death in which medical and nursing staffs, chaplains and visiting clergy, and social service staff members work together to meet the physical, spiritual, and psychological needs of the dying. Awareness of hospitals as potentially grim and depersonalized places to die has encouraged a trend toward dying at home. Some health-care organizations enable patients to go home to die by providing doctors and nurses who will counsel the family, monitor the patient's drug intake, and provide emotional support.

A dying person often takes a renewed interest in life when he or she finds people who are sensitive to both medical needs and emotions. The hospice or the hospice wing of a hospital does not have to appear to be an institution for the terminally ill. In the visitors' lounge, the radio may play upbeat music while rambunctious children play in the hallways. Visitors are welcome over a wide range of hours. If patients have not been told their diagnosis or expected fate before entering the program, the hospital hospice policy is to encourage openness. Frankness with patients is a major hallmark of the hospice program, along with a relaxed, personalized atmosphere.

Hospice care in the 1990s has focused a great deal of attention on AIDS patients. Nursing homes that, until recently, have cared mostly for elders now provide facilities for young adult AIDS patients (Allers, 1990). Hospice care, though stretching to meet the needs of all clients, is, nevertheless, overburdened in areas where the numbers of AIDS patients are high. One researcher, Josefina Magno, has reported that hospices are becoming increasingly bureaucratized and regulated by the government, especially where Medicaid and Medicare reimbursements apply. At the same time, conventional hospitals have responded to the hospice influence, becoming less institutionalized and less depersonalized in their approach to the dying (Magno, 1990). The AIDS epidemic, with no cure in sight, has underscored the need for the hospice orientation, an approach that emphasizes care when there is no cure. Hospice care underscores the idea that comfort and quality of life are worthwhile and essential goals to the end of one's life.

Although most people, when asked, express a desire to die at home, only a small percentage actually do. Not everyone should die at home. For a patient who has an unhappy or unstable family, or who needs complicated nursing care, a hospital or nursing home may be a better option. Parents and grandparents sometimes choose to die in hospitals to avoid traumatizing young children. However, some psychiatrists believe that the very fact of a death occurring at home can ward off psychological damage to the family. The child who is involved throughout the dying process does not have to face the sudden, unexplained disappearance of a parent or grandparent. In contrast, children who are not involved may believe, for example, that they are somehow responsible for the death. Keeping a dying family member at home can both make it easier for relatives to accept the death and prevent the patient from being alone in the dying process.

REFORMING THE CRAFT OF DYING

Lynne Lofland (1979) refers to the hospice movement and a number of other groups that work toward improving attitudes and conditions surrounding death as **the happy death movement.** This movement opposes the conventional view that the dying person be stoic, strong, and silent. The movement began in academia and filtered out to ordinary citizens who are embracing the "happy death" concept (Hoefler, 1994). Lofland notes that although the new movement has helped some people to freely express their fears, others still refuse to express their concerns. The new movement has advocated the view that dying can be a learning, growing, and positive experience; Lofland observes that this emphasis, in itself, may pressure all dying persons to assume this way of thinking. Those who will not or cannot share their thoughts and feelings, or who do not develop positive attitudes, may feel like failures. She believes that alternative ideologies should be available to provide dying persons maximum choice in their mental preparation for death. In a similar vein, others have criticized the phrase "death with dignity" as putting too much emphasis on being proper or accepting (Nuland, 1994). Individuals should be free to approach their dying in their own uniquely personal way.

THE RIGHT TO DIE

We have grappled with the **right-to-die issue** for more than two decades. In the 1970s, the parents of Karen Quinlan, a young woman in a permanent vegetative state, initiated a court battle in the state of New Jersey for the right to disconnect the life-support machines to which Karen was attached. After taking the case to the New Jersey Supreme Court in 1975, the Quinlans were allowed to have the machines removed; nonetheless, Karen lived on until 1985. Families in other states are still fighting similar court battles today. Doctors have traditionally felt they must prolong life as long as possible without questioning the circumstances, an idea that constitutes an intrinsic part of the Hippocratic oath. However, values and laws have traditionally lagged behind technological advancements; and the value system doctors have followed for centuries is now in a state of flux. The right to die is but one of many issues confronting **medical ethics** in the 1990s. In the following sections, we will discuss that issue and several others. The issues are complex: At what point should the decision not to prolong life be made, who should make the decision, and does an individual have the right to choose death when life could be extended in some fashion? Some of the right-to-die issues can be stated as specific questions:

1. What is the difference between killing and allowing a person to die?
2. What is the difference between stopping treatment and not beginning it?
3. Are there reasonable and unreasonable treatments?

The answers to these questions, which cannot be easily answered, vary on both moral and legal grounds.

Theoretically, there are a number of ways that medical personnel could hasten the end for patients who wish to die. They could simply kill the terminally ill patient by injection. They could decide not to begin, or could simply stop, an intravenous drip or a respirator. They could wait until the weakened body was infected with pneumonia and then avoid using antibiotics. If the person was in pain or unable to sleep, they could administer fatally high doses of a narcotic or barbiturate. The legal consequences of the alternatives vary, and doctors vary as well in their attitudes and behaviors. Some use code words on charts for "hopeless case" patients. Such a patient may be labeled "Code 90 DNR" (Do Not Resuscitate), for example, or "CMO" (Comfort Measures Only). Both indicate that extraordinary lifesaving measures should not be applied (DeSpelder and Strickland, 1991).

A number of states have initiated natural-death legislation, which varies from state to state. Generally speaking, such legislation affirms the patient's right to refuse treatment while still fully conscious. Some states recognize previously prepared documents stating that an individual in his or her right mind has requested death with dignity and that life shall not be prolonged beyond the point of meaningful existence. A few other states have established a line of authority, beginning with the spouse, to make the decision to end the life of a person incapable of making the decision for him- or herself. In 1987, a paralyzed man who starved to death after his wife removed his feeding tube was the first person to die under the New Jersey Supreme Court's landmark right-to-die decision ("First Death," 1987). Idaho legally permits the terminally ill or their families to actively hasten death, and doctors who cooperate are fully protected under the law. In 1986, Florida courts ruled that the removal of artificial feeding tubes from persons with no prospect of regaining cognitive brain function was permissible.

However, given society's deeply ingrained abhorrence of suicide and the legally sanctioned taking of human life under any circumstances, the right to die can still be extremely difficult to obtain. In 1990, the Supreme Court ruled, in *Cruzan v. Missouri*, that the parents of a comatose woman did not have the right to insist that hospital workers stop feeding her. They ruled that a *conscious* patient has the right to refuse all medical treatment, but that a family cannot speak for an unconscious child. The 5 to 4 decision meant that the 32-year-old, Cruzan, who had been involved in an auto accident in her teens, would remain on life support. They also ruled that the right to die would continue to be decided on a state-to-state basis. Eventually the state of Missouri heard enough testimony to be convinced that she would not want life-support devices, and they ruled in favor of Cruzan. After being unhooked, she died several days later. In Missouri, and other states as well, Cruzan would have been allowed to die without a court battle had she signed a **living will,** or what is now called an "advance directive." Her case prompted thousands to make out such advance directives.

States with natural-death legislation do not concur as to the binding quality of a signed document requesting death with dignity, and court cases in several states are now testing the legality of such documents. If documents requesting natural death are not legally binding, those who sign them hope they will be *morally* binding. As of 1993, 47 states have adopted "living-will" statutes, or what is called natural-death legislation.

As of 1985, individuals in California can complete a form giving a friend or family member durable power of attorney for their health care in case they are incapacitated by illness or injury; further, they can specify exactly what attempts they approve or disapprove as lifesaving measures. The form has bite because doctors who follow the wishes of those with the power of attorney are not legally liable and are therefore more likely to follow right-to-die

Figure 14.1
....

Living Will Example

SOURCE: "Your Wishes
Made Known,"
Extension publication
C–722. Manhattan, KS:
Kansas State University,
Cooperative Extension
Service, April 1991.
Used with permission.

Living Will
(Declaration)
....

Declaration made this _____ day of _____ (month, year).
I,_____ , being of sound mind, willfully and voluntarily make known my desire that my dying shall not be artificailly prolonged under the circumstances set forth below, do hereby declare:

If at any time I should have an incurable injury, disease, or illness certified to be a terminal condition by two physicians who have personally examined me, one of whom shall be my attending physician, and the physicians have determined that my death will occur whether or not life-sustaining procedures are utilized and where the application of life-sustaining procedures would serve only to artificially prolong the dying process, I direct that such procedures be withheld or withdrawn, and that I be permitted to die naturally with only the administration of medication or the performance of any medical procedure deemed necessary to provide me with comfort care.

In the absence of my ability to give directions regarding the use of such life-sustaining procedures, is is my intention that this declaration shall be honored by my family and physician(s) as the final expression of my legal right to refuse medical or surgical treatment and accept the consequences from such refusal.

I understand the full import of this declaration and I am emotionally and mentally competent to make this declaration.

My additional instructions, if any, are listed on the reverse side.

Signed_____

(Declarant)

City, County and State of Residence_____

The declarant has been personally known to me and I believe him or her to be of sound mind. I did not sign the declarant's signature above for or at the direction of the declarant. I am 18 or older, not related to the declarant by blood or marriage, not entitled to any portion of the estate of the declarant according to the laws of intestate succession or under any will of the declarant or codicil thereto, and not directly financially responsible for the declarant's medical care.

_____   _____
Witness   Witness

_____   _____
Address   Address

See reverse side for any Optional Additional Instructions.

The declaration and optional additional instructions may be revoked or changed by declarant at any time.

directives. (However, doctors are not bound by the new form and can follow hospital policy or their own consciences if they choose. In turn, family members can opt for another doctor.)

In 1989, Kansas, which has had a natural-death act since 1979, passed a bill, similar to the one in California, giving individuals the power to appoint an agent with a durable power of attorney to make medical decisions on their behalf if they become unable to do so (see Figure 14.1). Notice that life-sustaining procedures can be withheld or withdrawn, and also notice the optional instructions in the living will.

New Jersey adopted in 1991 an Advance Directives Health Care Act, which became effective in 1992. It is the most comprehensive and progressive natural-death legislation in the United States. New Jersey's legislation, by its

Optional Additional Instructions

I make these optional additional instructions to my living will to exercise my right to determine the course of my health care and to provide clear and convincing proof of my treatment decisions **when I lack the capacity to make or communicate my decisions.**

> **If there is a phrase, statement or section below with which you do not agree, draw a line through it and add your initials.**

- I direct all life-prolonging procedures be withheld or withdrawn when there is no hope of significant recovery, and I have:
  - a terminal condition; or
  - a condition, disease or injury without hope of significant recovery and there is no reasonable expectation that I will regain an acceptable quality of life; or
  - substantial brain damage or brain disease which cannot be significantly reversed; or_____
  - other
- I choose to have withheld or withdrawn the following life-prolonging procedures, when the above conditions exist:
  - surgery
  - heart–lung resuscitation (CPR)
  - antibiotics
  - mechanical ventilator (respirator)
  - dialysis
  - tube feedings (food and water delivered through a tube in the vein, nose or stomach)
  - other_____
- If my physician believes that a certain life-prolonging procedure or other health care treatment may provide me with comfort, relieve pain or lead to a significant recovery, I direct my physician to try the treatment for a reasonable period of time. However, if such treatment proves to be ineffective, I direct the treatment be withdrawn even if so doing shortens my life.
- I direct I be given health care treatment to relieve pain or to provide comfort even if such treatment might shorten my life, suppress my appetite or my breathing, or be habit-forming.
- I make other instructions as follows: (you may describe what an acceptable quality of life is for you)

_____

_____

- I have discussed my wishes with the following person(s) and authorize my physician to discuss my treatment and this document with them: **(If you have used a Medical Durable Power of Attorney to appoint an agent, initial here   and include that person on the first line below.)**

Name (agent)   Address
Telephone

Name   Address
Telephone

I have read these instructions and have given them careful consideration. As I have indicated, they are in accordance with my wishes.

Date _____ Signed _____
                                                                     Declarant

Witness _____ Witness _____

wording, gives the most expansive autonomy to the "designated health-care agent" (another name for the person given "durable power of attorney" in the Kansas and California legislation) to make decisions for the dying person without physicians and hospitals worrying about lawsuits (Cantor, 1993). In fact, the physicians have to worry more about lawsuits for not following the advance directives.

Polls show that adults of all ages support the right to die by refusing treatment. However, when it comes to actively hastening death, older people are less supportive than younger people, quite possibly because of the cohort effects of the older group's greater religiosity and less education, rather than because of aging per se. One can still wonder, however, if the older person takes the topic more personally and worries that someone would hasten his or her death without consent.

Two terms are important to a discussion of the right to die: (1) **passive euthanasia,** the process of allowing persons to die without using "extraordinary means" to save their lives; and (2) **active euthanasia,** performing a deliberate act to end a person's life—administering a fatal injection or shooting them with a gun, for example. A husband or wife chooses active euthanasia in performing the mercy killing of a spouse. As a rule, however, people are more willing to accept the idea of passive rather than active euthanasia. One form of active euthanasia is an assisted suicide, which is discussed in the next section. There are acts between active and passive euthanasia that are hard to categorize as either. Not treating a person for their pneumonia is one example.

One study of age and the acceptance of euthanasia found that women and nonwhites, because of their religiosity, are less accepting of euthanasia than are men. Nonwhites also tend to have less formal education but greater distrust of institutional decisions, both decisive factors in a group's level of acceptance. Among older people, acceptance of euthanasia is greater among those who are generally more dissatisfied with their own lives.

SUICIDE AND ASSISTED SUICIDE

Whether anyone has the right to take his or her own life is another complicated issue with moral implications. Older persons may first contemplate, then commit, suicide because they feel life no longer holds meaning. For example, Arthur Koestler (author of *Darkness at Noon* and other works), suffering from leukemia and Parkinson's disease, committed suicide, along with his wife, in March 1982 by taking an overdose of barbiturates. Similarly, a California man, who had told neighbors he was depressed by his and his wife's pain and physical deterioration, killed himself and his wife (Smith, 1993). Other deaths of elders lie between accident and suicide. Older people who are disappointed and frustrated with life may refuse to eat, keep to themselves, and refuse care, with fatal consequences. Such deaths may not be officially regarded as suicides.

Suicides such as these pose this question: Do old people have a right to choose death by suicide? Several groups, such as the Hemlock Society, founded in England, and EXIT, its affiliate in the United States, advocate control over one's dying, which includes committing suicide, if necessary, to escape terrible pain or great bodily deterioration. Katherine Hepburn, concurring with this idea, produced with her own money, *The Ultimate Solution of Grace Quigley,* a 1984 film about an older woman who wants to end it all by killing herself. Hepburn has been an outspoken proponent of right-to-die stances for many years. Derek Humphrey, the founder and president of the Hemlock Society, has advocated the right to commit suicide for the last 30 years; his book, *Final Exit* (1990), basically outlines methods for painless suicides using drugs, mostly barbiturates and muscle-paralyzing medications. AIDS advocates also tend to favor the right to commit suicide; it is not uncommon for them to assist AIDS patients in ending their lives. But no one has received as much publicity in terms of assisted suicide as Dr. Jack Kevorkian (see Old Is News article this chapter and Table 14.1). After publication of the book from which Table 14.1 is derived, Kevorkian helped his twenty-first patient commit suicide. She was Margaret Garrish, a 72-year-old woman who was in constant pain from severe rheumatoid arthritis and advanced osteoporosis. She had suffered the amputation of both legs and the removal of one eye. Dr. Kevorkian is a central figure in the controversy over the thorny issue, which hits home for many oldsters, of whether individuals have the right to end their lives if they believe that life is no longer meaningful.

Assisted Suicide

Law in the United States did not uphold an **assisted suicide**—whether the assistant is a physician, friend, or family member until November 1994, when Oregon became the first state in the U.S. to pass a law that allows doctors to hasten death for the terminally ill. Betty Rollin, who wrote in her book *Last Wish,* actually violated the law of helping her mother die (Rollin, 1985). About half the states have laws that make assisted suicide a felony. In other states, the assistant might be prosecuted under a general charge of murder or manslaughter. In Oregon, the only state where it has become legal, a patient with six months to live can ask a doctor to prescribe a lethal dose of drugs to end unbearable suffering. At least two doctors must agree that the patient's condition is terminal. The patient must request the drugs in writing and administer the drugs to him or herself.

There are several arguments against assisted suicide. First, it could put society a step closer to involuntary euthanasia, in which doctors or the state decide when someone should die—such as a "medically defective" person, or someone who is "too old" or "too poor" to warrant expensive medical care. Ethicists worry that the power to decide who should live and who should die will get into the hands of the wrong person. Second, some believe that the doctor's duty is to heal and save lives and alleviate suffering, but never to "play God" by participating in an assisted suicide. Third is the argument that very few would opt for suicide if they knew for certain that their pain, comfort, and expenses would be under control. These opponents of assisted suicide believe that our time, efforts, and money should be spent developing more effective systems of comfort, care, reassurance, and human support such as that offered by good hospice programs.

On the other side are the proponents of assisted suicide. A January 1991 Gallup Poll found that a majority—58 percent of Americans—say that a terminally ill patient has the right to end his or her life "under any circumstances" and 80 percent agreed "under some circumstances" (Ahronheim and Weber, 1992, 75). At the extreme end of the proponents is Jack Kevorkian and his supporters who believe in "death on demand" as a public service and public policy for those who wish to die. Kevorkian would like to establish national death clinics or "obitoria" (singular is "obitorium") staffed by "obiti-atrists," suicide specialists trained in helping people commit "medicide" (a doctor-assisted suicide). His suicide assists have been criticized because he

Table 14.1

Jack Kevorkian and Assisted Suicide

Patient's Name (Age)	Date of Suicide	Patient's Condition	Comments
1. Janet Adkins (54)	6/4/90	Alzheimer's disease	▪ first suicide and a member of the Hemlock Society ▪ homicide charges filed and dismissed ▪ judge barred Kevorkian from using "mercitron" ▪ Michigan suspended Kevorkian's medical license
2. Sherry Miller (43)	10/23/91	multiple sclerosis	▪ first double suicide ▪ homicide charges filed and dismissed
3. Marjorie Wantz (58)	"	uncontrolled pain in in the pelvis	▪ tried and failed at a Hemlock suicide first ▪ autopsy revealed no clinical cause of pain
4. Susan Williams (52)	5/15/92	multiple sclerosis	▪ blind and wheelchair-bound for 12 years
5. Lois F. Hawes (52)	9/26/92	lung and brain cancer	▪ technically, first patient considered "terminally ill"
6. Catherine Andreyev (46)	11/23/92	breast cancer	▪ considered acutely ill
7. Marguerite Tate (70)	12/15/92	amyotrophic lateral sclerosis (ALS)	▪ second double suicide ▪ both patients considered acutely ill
8. Marcella Lawrence (67)	"	heart disease, emphysema, and arthritis	▪ on same day, Governor Engler signed bill making assisted suicide illegal in Michigan (effective 4/1/93)
9. Jack Miller (53)	1/20/93	bone cancer and emphysema	▪ first male patient
10. Stanley Ball (82)	2/4/93	pancreatic cancer	▪ third double suicide ▪ Ball was blind, in constant pain, and the oldest suicide
11. Mary Biernat (73)	"	breast cancer	
12. Elaine Goldbaum (47)	2/8/93	multiple sclerosis	
13. Hugh Gale (70)	2/15/93	heart disease and emphysema	▪ Gale had second thoughts, aborted suicide attempt at least once before going ahead as planned
14. Jonathan Grenz (44)	2/18/93	neck, lung, and chest cancer	▪ fourth double suicide ▪ Governor Engler signed a new bill making assisted suicide illegal immediately
15. Martha Ruwart (41)	"	ovarian cancer	
16. Ronald Mansur (54)	5/16/93	bone and lung cancer	▪ Kevorkian arrested under new law ▪ judge struck down law on 5/20 ▪ law reinstated on appeal
17. Thomas Hyde (30)	8/4/93	ALS	▪ youngest suicide ▪ Kevorkian arrested; released on bond to await trial
18. Donald O'Keefe (73)	9/9/93	bone cancer	▪ Kevorkian arrested again and released on bond
19. Merian Ruth Frederick (72)	10/22/93	ALS	▪ patient unable to talk; fed through a stomach tube ▪ Kevorkian jailed on 11/5 for assisted suicides of Hyde and O'Keefe and began hunger strike ▪ an opponent of Kevorkian bailed Kevorkian out of jail, against Kevorkian's will, on 11/8
20. Dr. Ali Khalili (61)	11/22/93	bone cancer	▪ Khalili was prominent pioneer in rehabilitative medicine, assistant professor of rehabilitative medicine, Northwestern University, and former chair of the Department of Rehabilitation, Grant Hospital, Chicago ▪ Kevorkian rearrested on 11/30 for death of Frederick. Bail set at $50,000, and Kevorkian began another hunger strike (taking in only water, juice, and vitamins)

SOURCE: James M. Hoefler. *Deathright* (Boulder, CO, Westview Press 1994). Used with permission.
Author Note: The 21st suicide assist was for Margaret Garrish, 72, on November 26, 1994. She had severe rheumatoid arthritis and advanced osteoporosis. Previously, both legs were amputated and one eye removed.

did not have a long-term relationship with the patients he helped. Therefore, he was not able to assess completely how depressed they may or may not have been; he may not have thoroughly investigated pain control possibilities as an alternative; and some of the patients were not yet in great pain, totally disabled, or near death. He has also been criticized for being a publicity hound.

Those in the center of the argument tend to be doctors who believe the stage is set for an assisted suicide if a good, long-term relationship with the patient has developed, if doctor and patient have thoroughly explored all other options, and if the patient is not depressed. If the patient is terminally ill, is near death, and cannot face either the pain of the disease or the agonizing efforts of more useless treatments, then a physician-assisted suicide is acceptable. They caution that this would rarely be necessary if good pain control methods were readily available. Other medical experts are quick to point out, in agreement with Kevorkian, that adequate pain control is simply not available in all cases and that there are many forms of suffering besides physical pain (Kasting, 1994). Further those in the center position (often medical professionals) accept physician-assisted death on a case-by-case basis but feel the danger of abuse would be too great if it became a matter of public policy. A major argument for assisted suicide is that the individual has a right to autonomy and self-determination in both living and dying.

Assisted Death in Holland

Notice that the phrase ("assisted death" carries less stigma than "assisted suicide.") Holland is the only country in the world where physician-assisted deaths are out in the open. A **physician-assisted death in Holland** is conducted only under certain conditions. If (1) the patient is suffering intolerably with no chance of improvement; (2) the patient requests assistance in dying repeatedly over a reasonable length of time and is near death; (3) the patient is competent to decide; and (4) two physicians, one not involved in the patient's care, agree that help is appropriate, then the assisted death can take place. About 2,500 or 1 percent of all deaths per year are physician-assisted. Approximately 25,000 requests per year are submitted; obviously, the bulk of these are denied. Studies do show that in Holland, patients would prefer comfort, pain control, and a natural death to the quick, unnatural death from an assisted death (Ahronheim and Weber, 1992, 90). Even in Holland, some of Jack Kevorkian's suicide assists would not be acceptable. For example, some of his clients were not near death. The first was only in the beginning stages of Alzheimer's, one was debilitated from multiple sclerosis, but not terminal, another was in great pain from a pelvic disease but not in a terminal stage of the disease. The seventeenth assisted suicide was performed by Kevorkian in August 1993 in Detroit, Michigan, for a young man with Lou Gehrig's disease who had lost all motor function except use of his left hand, but death was not imminent. Kevorkian has pushed to the forefront the questions of assisted suicides for the disabled, for those who *expect to become* mentally or physically debilitated, or even those who simply find no reason to live. The ethics behind these questions will be debated for years to come.

INFORMED CONSENT TO TREATMENT

Patients do not always realize that they have the right to accept or reject any treatment or prescription that their physician may offer them. Those suffering a serious or life-threatening illness for which several treatment plans are possible or optional should gather as much information as possible and then select what they believe to be the best plan. Though this may put an additional burden on an ailing individual, such research is ultimately in the patient's best interest.

In terms of cancer, for example, surgery, radiation, chemotherapy, and special diets are all available as treatment options. Patients should become aware of the risks involved with each option and then base their consent to treatment on three principles.

1. The patient is competent to give consent.

2. Consent is given freely (e.g., not coerced by economic situation or relatives).

3. Consent is given with a full understanding of the situation (DeSpelder and Strickland, 1991).

Informed consent means that patients share in their health-care decision making by becoming informed and by basing their choice, acceptance, or rejection of treatment on the information available to them.

THE PATIENT SELF-DETERMINATION ACT

The **Patient Self-Determination Act,** which took effect December 1, 1991, requires hospitals and other medical institutions to tell patients that they have the right to refuse treatment or artificial life-support procedures. Hospitals must also ask patients whether they have living wills or other documents that spell out their wishes in the event they become incapacitated. Nursing homes that receive Medicare or Medicaid funding must also inform patients of these rights. Although proponents believe that this act educates patients about their rights and options, detractors maintain that the real purpose is cost containment for the health-care system.

MORE ETHICS ON AGING

Other ethical issues have been increasingly debated now that medical technology has the capacity to prolong life almost indefinitely, and disease control keeps more people alive into advanced age. Here are some of those issues:

1. How paternalistic should family members and society be when dealing with a person who is losing competency? For example, is the person with early Alzheimer's allowed self-determination in deciding whether to drive a car? With more advanced Alzheimer's, how is a "wanderer" restrained and who makes the decision? (Moody, 1992)

2. With regard to the ethics of nursing home placement and ethical dilemmas in the nursing home, how much self-determination and autonomy is allowed the older person to make decisions and act for himself or herself?

3. Should we ration health care on the grounds of age? Using formulas of cost and age, who decides when the cost gets too high and when the very old are not saved?

4. What kind of research can legally and morally be conducted on older subjects? Effects of various drugs and therapeutic procedures are

constantly under study. Yet ethical guidelines for research with aged patients is not discussed nearly as much as with younger patients (Wicclair, 1993).

5. What obligations do adult children have for the financial, physical, and emotional support of frail elderly parents?

These and other related ethical questions are growing in urgency.

FUNERALS

Old and young alike can be victims of coercion when arranging funerals for themselves or for their loved ones. Commercialization, unnecessary extravagance, and deception are criticisms leveled at the modern funeral industry. An individual, vulnerable after the death of a spouse or relative and wanting to do the very best for the deceased person, is easily persuaded to spare no expense for a funeral.

Some funeral directors play on the emotions of the bereaved. They may, for example, persuade a grief-stricken relative to buy an expensive casket to show how much he or she loved the deceased. The cost of the casket can be one financial trap; embalming can be another. Funeral directors are hesitant to mention that no law requires embalming or that no casket is required for cremation. The cost of cemetery plots also can be high. Charges for limousines, burial clothes, use of the viewing room, and a headstone are not necessarily devious; mortuaries are in a business for profit. However, consumers should not be pressured into spending thousands of dollars on a funeral that will create financial hardship. Some organizations help to provide simple, dignified funerals for their members. Cremation, which involves about one-eighth the cost of a conventional funeral, is becoming more common, appealing especially to those who believe that cemeteries are a needless waste of land. Individuals should be aware that they do have

A funeral in mid-America.

choices in these matters. Cremation doubled in popularity between 1980 and 1990; nevertheless, it still represents the method of choice in less than 15 percent of all American funerals. In contrast, in Japan, 90 percent of those who die are cremated (Aiken, 1991).

Because of complaints about the funeral industry, the Federal Trade Commission (FTC) ruled in 1984 that funeral directors must provide itemized lists of goods and services and their prices. This may keep prices from varying depending on a client's vulnerability, and it shows clearly that a price range exists. The FTC also ruled that misrepresentation of state laws concerning embalming and cremation is against the law. In addition, funeral parlors must itemize on a funeral bill every charge—the cost of flowers, death notices in newspapers, the provision of hearses and limousines, guest registers, and other related services (Aiken, 1991).

Consumer groups still need to educate the public abut the laws governing the funeral industry and to inform individuals about their rights and choices. An individual needs to know about the itemized price list, for example, to ensure that he or she asks for and receives one. The average cost of a funeral is now more than $5,000. But no one has to spend that much. For example, inexpensive caskets are available; but family members of the deceased may not know this. Sometimes they feel guilty if they purchase one made of, say, particleboard rather than wood, not realizing that a particleboard casket can be just as beautiful as a wooden one. It's helpful to family members if these matters can be discussed before death occurs. Some people buy their plots and tombstones long before they are near death. In good health with a clear mind is the best condition in which to discuss funeral decisions with one's family. If a person can give specific instructions about the kind of funeral and burial he or she wants, a surviving spouse and children are less likely to be led into agonizing and/or expensive choices they will regret.

☼ Near-Death Experiences

Over the years, many people have reported psychological experiences that occur at a point near death, but from which they recover. Known as **near-death experiences,** they often involve similar images and recollections. In fact, researchers estimate that one in three who recover from coming close to death or becoming clinically dead report having had a near-death experience (Underwood, 1992).

Cardiac patients participating in one of the first studies of near-death experiences reported experiencing an out-of-body sensation—being aware of all that went on around them when they "died," but watching as if from a distance or as if they were suspended above the scene (Sabom, 1982). In recording the recollections of those who nearly died under a variety of circumstances, following studies have established a pattern for near-death experiences: The restrictions of time and space disappear. The dying person sometimes enters darkness or a tunnel, at the end of which is a warm, engulfing golden light. Some experience a flashback stage, during which they experience a panoramic view of their lives; some see angels or encounter another supernatural personality. Usually the near-death experience involves a feeling of peace and well-being and a sense of separation from the physical body. Almost always, individuals interpret the experience in a positive way.

A near-death experience can give a person a fresh sense of what is important or unimportant in life and a new resolve to live according to this revela-

Bright Soul
■*Teresa Spencer*

Nimble fingers, be still.
Rest.
You've earned your peace.
I miss you
I wasn't ready
I hurt.
But good bye is not forever:
Hello waits down the road.

So, gentle heart, lie quiet.
Your love still shines softly
In the part of me
That is you.

SOURCE: Previously unpublished poem used by permission of the poet. Teresa Spencer is a photographer and systems analyst. She still mourns the loss of her parents in 1990 and 1992.

tion. Researcher Kenneth Ring (1984) went further by suggesting that near-death experiences are a step in a lifelong evolutionary process of spiritual development. More research is needed to evaluate this common, but phenomenal, area of study.

☼ Facing and Preparing for Death

Realizing that death is the ultimate destiny for each of us, we need to understand, regardless of our age, the importance of preparing for it. Facing death, or at least easing personal anxiety about it, can improve the quality of an individual's life. Whether you have thought about or have already answered any of the following questions tells something about your degree of preparation for dying.

1. Do you have a will?
2. Do you have life insurance?
3. Did you prepare advance directives?
4. Are you willing to have an autopsy done on your body?
5. Are you willing to donate the organs of your body for use after you die?
6. Do you know how you want your body disposed of (burial, cremation, donated to a medical school)?
7. What kind of last rites do you desire (funeral, memorial services, a party)?

When we reduce our own fears of death and dying, we can offer others, including the terminally ill, better care and help them cope. If our thoughts of death elicit thoughts of satisfaction with a life well-lived, we have reached what psychologist Erik Erikson means by integrity, his final stage of psychosocial development. In the later years of life, those with a sense of integrity reflect on their past with satisfaction; those filled with despair dwell on missed opportunities and missed directions. With luck and understanding, the path each person takes will prepare them for death, which Kübler-Ross calls "the final stage of growth."

☼ Bereavement

The loss of a loved one is generally the most tragic event an individual experiences in a lifetime. It is an experience that occurs some time or another in nearly everyone's life. In old age, these events occur with increasing frequency. The author's 82-year-old mother, for example, who is the second to the youngest of ten siblings, has experienced the deaths of nearly all her siblings and their spouses, not to mention many other friends and relatives. Social scientists believe that their goal, after empathizing with another person's suffering, is to step aside from the maze of emotion and sensation and to make sense of it. Studies of grief in the past have been too simplistic. Studies now show it to be complicated and variable.

Bereavement theory and research is expanding into unknown areas, such as the puzzle of why some bereaved themselves die soon after their loved one. Research tends to indicate that the majority of the bereaved recover over a 2-year period, yet a high-risk minority simply cannot make a recovery (Stroebe et al., 1993). Self-help groups and individual counselors and therapists are offering higher quality grief therapy because bereavement is better understood than it was a few years ago. Some of this understanding comes from analyzing accounts of those who lost friends and partners to AIDS.

Chapter Summary

Death is one of the few certainties of life, yet denial of death is common. We have euphemisms for the word "death;" we protect children from hearing about it; and death on TV is not real. Instead, death is disassociated with everyday events by typically occurring in a hospital setting. Elders, just as any other age group, may have fears about dying. The stages that a terminally-ill person goes through are: 1) denial and isolation, 2) anger, 3) bargaining, 4) depression, and 5) acceptance. Efforts must be made so that terminally ill patients are given care, concern, and support. Elders are being given more choices in dying, but suicide is still not socially accepted. Yet changes are slowly taking place to broaden choices for the dying. Physician-assisted suicide has become a topic of wide debate and has been legalized in Oregon. The hospice movement has supported people in their choice to die at home and to refuse life extending measures that bring pain and discomfort. Medical ethics are challenging the assumption that lives should be extended at any cost. Patients are being informed of their rights, especially the right to refuse treatment. The "right-to-die" movement has gained momentum. Social scientists are now seriously exploring the issue of near death experiences. It is important for elders to face death and prepare for it.

Key Terms

active euthanasia
assisted suicide
awareness contexts of dying
bereavement
death anxiety
death competency
death-denying society
physician-assisted death in Holland
   (conditions of)
fears about dying
fear of death
hospice

informed consent
life review
living will
medical ethics
near-death experiences
passive euthanasia
Patient Self-Determination Act
reminiscence
right-to-die issue
stages of dying
the happy death movement

Questions for Discussion

1. Why do death and dying evoke fear? Why might a person fear death?

2. What is the function of the life review?

3. What are the arguments for and against euthanasia?

4. Imagine being told that you have six months to live. What would be your reaction? Explain in depth. What would you think? Where would you go? What would you do?

Fieldwork Suggestions

1. Go to a cemetery, walk around, and examine your own feelings about death and dying.

2. Survey attitudes toward specific kinds of euthanasia. Do older people seem more or less opposed to active euthanasia than younger people? Explain.

3. Interview several people concerning their fear of death. Try to include persons of varying ages.

References

Ahronheim, J., and D. Weber. *Final Passages*. New York: Simon and Schuster, 1992.

Aiken, L. *Dying, Death, and Bereavement*. Boston: Allyn and Bacon, 1991.

Allers, C. "AIDS and the Older Adult." *Gerontologist* 30:3 (June 1990): 405–407.

Barrow, G. "The Aged's Attitudes Toward Death." Unpublished. St. Louis, MO: Washington, University, 1967.

Butler, Robert N. "Successful Aging and the Role of the Life Review." *Journal of the American Geriatric Society* 22 (1974): 529–535.

Butler, R., and M. I. Lewis. *Aging and Mental Health*. New York: Macmillan, 1991.

Cantor, N. *Advance Directives and the Pursuit of Death with Dignity*. Bloomington: Indiana University Press, 1993.

DeSpelder, L. A., and D. L. Strickland. *The Last Dance*. Mountain View, CA: Mayfield Press, 1991.

"First Death Under N.J. 'Right to Die' Ruling." *San Francisco Chronicle* (21 July 1987): A18.

Gentile, M., and M. Fello. "Hospice Care for the 1990s: A Concept Coming of Age." *Journal of Home Health Care Practice* (November 1990): 1–15.

Gesser, G., P. Wong, and G. Reker. "Death Attitudes Across the Life Span." *Omega: Journal of Death and Dying* 18:2 (1988): 113–28.

Glazer, Barney, and Anselm Strauss. *Awareness of Dying*. Chicago: Aldine Publishing, 1966.

Hoefler, J. *Deathright: Culture, Medicine, Politics and the Right to Die*. Boulder, Colorado: Westview Press, 1994.

Kalish, Richard A. "The Effects of Death Upon the Family." In *Death and Dying* edited by Leonard Pearson. Cleveland, OH: Case-Western Reserve, 1969.

——. "Death and Dying." In *Elderly as Pioneers*, edited by G. Busse, 360–385. Bloomington: Indiana University Press, 1987.

Kasting, G. "The Nonnecessity of Euthanasia." In *Physician-Assisted Death*, edited by J. Humber et al., 25–46. Totowa, NJ: Humana Press, 1994.

Kübler-Ross, Elisabeth. *On Death and Dying*. New York: Macmillan, 1969.

——. *Living with Death and Dying*. New York: Macmillan, 1981.

Lofland, Lynne H. *The Craft of Dying: The Modern Face of Death*. Beverly Hills, CA: Sage Publications, 1979.

Magno, Josefina. "The Hospice Concept of Care: Facing the 1990s." *Death Studies* 14 (1990): 109–119.

McCarthy, A. "The Country of the Old." *Commonwealth* (13 September 1991): 505–506.

Mermann, A., et al. "Learning to Care for the Dying: A Survey of Medical Schools and a Model Course." *Academic Medicine* (January 1991): 35–38.

Moody, H. *Ethics in an Aging Society*. Baltimore: Johns Hopkins University Press, 1992.

Neimeyer, R., ed. *Death Anxiety Handbook*. Washington, D.C.: Taylor and Francis, 1994.

Nuland, S. *How We Die: Reflections on Life's Final Chapter*. New York: Alfred A. Knopf, 1994.

Phillips, D., and D. Smith. "Postponement of Death Until Symbolically Meaningful Occasions." *Journal of the American Medical Association* 263:14 (1990): 1947–1951.

Radner, G. *It's Always Something*. New York: Avon Books, 1990.

Ring, Kenneth. *Heading Toward Omega: In Search of the Meaning of the Near Death Experience*. New York: William Morrow, 1984.

Rollin, Betty. *Last Wish*. New York: Warner Books, 1985.

Sabom, M. *Recollections of Death: A Medical Investigation*. New York: Harper & Row, 1982.

Smith, C. "Santa Rosa Couple Carefully Planned Their Deaths." *Santa Rosa Press Democrat* (25 August 1993): B1.

Still, J. S. "Disengagement Reconsidered: Awareness of Finitude." *Gerontologist* 20 (1980): 457–462.

Stroebe, M., et al. *Handbook of Bereavement*. New York: Cambridge University Press, 1993.

Underwood, N. "Between Life and Death." *Maclean's* (20 April 1992): 34–37.

Wicclair, M. *Ethics and the Elderly*. New York: Oxford University Press, 1993.

Further Readings

Cleiren, M. *Bereavement and Adaptation*. Washington, D.C., Hemisphere Publishing, 1993.

Cundiff, D. *Euthanasia is NOT the Answer*. Totowa, NJ: Humana Press, 1992.

Doukas, D., and W. Reichel. *Planning for Uncertainty: A Guide to Living Wills and Other Advance Directives for Health Care*. Baltimore: Johns Hopkins University Press, 1993.

DeSpelder, L. and Strickland, D., eds. *The Path Ahead*. Mountain View, CA: Mayfield Publishing, 1995.

Enck, R. *The Medical Care of Terminally Ill Patients*. Baltimore, MD: Johns Hopkins University Press, 1994.

Humber, J., R. Almeder, and G. Kosting, eds. *Physician-Assisted Death*. Totowa, NJ: Humana Press, 1994.

Logue, B. *Last Rights: Death Control and the Elderly in America*. New York, NY: Lexington Books, 1993.

Lundquist, K., and V. Nelsen, eds. *Ethnic Variations in Death, Dying, and Grief*. Bristol, PA: Taylor and Francis, 1993.

Richman, J. *Preventing Elderly Suicide*. New York, NY: Springer Publishing, 1993.

15 Aging in Other Cultures

CHAPTER OUTLINE

■ The Cross-Cultural Approach   ■ The Graying of the Planet   ■ Social Modernization and Elder Status   ■ Variation in Nonindustrialized Societies   ■ Third World Countries: A Test of Modernization Theory   ■ Case Study of an Industrialized Nation: Japan   ■ Aging in Scandinavia   ■ Applying the Findings

Mandela's Journey Perhaps Unsurpassed in History of Human Spirit

■ **RENER TYSON**

On trial for sabotage at Pretoria's Palace of Justice, Nelson Mandela knew he faced the gallows. But he would have his say even if it cost him his life.

That was April 20, 1961. Mandela was 45 years old. The charge against him, which carried the death sentence, was sabotage with intent to overthrow the white government. It was a charge he readily admitted.

Thirty years later, Mandela used the exact words he spoke to the judge during that 1961 trial as he campaigned for the presidency of South Africa.

"During my lifetime I have dedicated myself to this struggle of the African people," Mandela told the Pretoria court. "I have fought against white domination, and I have fought against black domination.

"I have cherished the ideal of a democratic and free society in which all persons live together in harmony and with equal opportunities. It is an ideal which I hope to live for and to achieve. But if it needs be, it is an ideal for which I am prepared to die."

Mandela lived to achieve that ideal. At the age of 75, he became South Africa's first black president—the victor in the country's first all-races election that sounded the death knell of apartheid.

Born into African aristocracy (July 18, 1918), Mandela was groomed to rule from childhood.

When Mandela was 12, his father died. The youngster was placed under the care and instruction of his guardian uncle, Chief Jonquintaba, at the nearby village of Maekezweni.

"In my youth in the Tranaei, I listened to the elders of my tribe telling stories of the old days," Mandela told the Pretoria court back in 1961.

Eager to learn and always a good student, Mandela enrolled at the University of Fort Mars in South Africa's eastern Cape Province, where he met a reserved but highly intelligent student named Oliver Tambo. Their friendship was to prove a pow-

On May 10, 1994, Nelson Mandela became South Africa's first black president.

erful force in the struggle for freedom. Later they opened South Africa's first black law firm in Johannesburg.

But after two years at Fort Mars, both Mandela and Tambo were expelled for protesting poor food and living conditions.

In Soweto, a sprawling black township on the southwestern edge of Johannesburg, Mandela took refuge in the modest home of real estate agent Walter Sisulu. It was a move that shaped his life forever.

Sisulu encouraged Mandela to attend law school in Johannesburg. Mandela, Sisulu, along with Tambo and other young turks, took over direction of the moribund ANC (African National Congress– the major native African political organization) through its youth league. At that time the Afrikaner-dominated National Party had just come to power and began imposing apartheid.

Tall, handsome, an amateur boxer, Mandela, now a lawyer, quickly emerged as the liberation movement's main man.

He led the passive resistance Defiance Campaign of 1952, which aimed at getting white officials to hear black grievances about discrimination. White officials banned him from public activities. A court convicted him under the Suppression of Communism Act, but gave him a suspended sentence. He was tried and acquitted for treason.

In 1960, the government of Prime Minister Henrik Varwoard, apartheid's architect, declared the ANC unlawful and banned it. The ANC went underground. . .

Mandela was captured near the Natal town of Howick. Last year, Mandela made a visit to Howick and remarked how after his arrest, "I went on a long holiday."

On July 12, 1961, Mandela, Sisulu and six other leaders were sentenced to life in prison. Mandela's powerful and emotional speech in court probably saved his life and the lives of his compatriots.

In prison, Mandela excited the passions of human rights activists around the world. Even though he was behind bars, he gained stature year by year as a symbol of the fight against apartheid.

On February 11, 1990, President F. W. de Klerk, who was to share the Nobel Peace Prize in 1993 with his former political prisoner, released Mandela from prison to make the walk to freedom and into the presidency, completing a journey perhaps unsurpassed in the history of the human spirit. ☼

eople everywhere tend to believe that the way they live is the "right" way to live and should be typical of the whole world. In other words, they tend to be ethnocentric. As Americans, we fall too easily into the habit of thinking that our ways are the only ways. We can learn a great deal about ourselves as a culture and the value we assign to old age by looking at value systems, families, and cultures around the world.

☼ The Cross-Cultural Approach

Anthropologists using the **cross-cultural approach** study values and norms affecting elders in other cultures. A cultural **value** is a widely held belief that a quality is good or bad, right or wrong. A culture may value privacy, financial success, nudity, certain animals, close mother-daughter relationships, or selected sports. Values reflect the importance of various activities, relationships, feelings, or goals, and are deeply rooted; they form the description of a culture and even the nature of its reality.

Value systems vary from culture to culture, affecting every aspect of the culture, including the society's expectations for the older person. In turn, these expectations shape the self-perceptions of elders. There is always an interplay between the individual and society, each influencing the other. Some cultures foster views of old age that are conducive to happy, contented later years. Other cultures foster feelings of worthlessness, despondency, and futility.

Values can be continuous or discontinuous throughout the life cycle. Where there are **continuous values,** the transitions from childhood to adulthood to old age are smooth, natural, and comfortable. In a society where **discontinuous values** exist, sharp or abrupt changes in the life cycle can subject individuals to severe trauma and strain. Consider our own society, where the onset of adolescence causes an upheaval in behavior. We are expected to suddenly become an adult at the age of 21, and from 21 on we are expected to assume varying adult roles until we reach age 65. At that time, we are considered old and encouraged to retire. Our society offers little preparation for these life changes.

Cultures vary in the extent to which they emphasize individual achievement and self-reliance. The more these values are emphasized, the lower the status of elders who are dependent or incapacitated. In societies that stress the work role, striving, and competition, older individuals eventually lose ground.

Cultures also vary in the way they define old age. Some societies use **functional age:** One is old when he or she is unable to perform certain physical functions—when the body no longer possesses either the strength or the mobility required to do adult work. Other societies use **formal age:** Old age depends on some external symbolic event. The entrance to old age might be the birth of a first grandchild. In such a culture, a person might therefore be old at age 40, at age 70, or never. The definition of old age in the United States is formal rather than functional. Chronological age is the determining factor, not one's ability to function; and the arbitrary mark of old age in the United States is still circa age 65. Our society uses this purely chronological fact to classify many able-bodied, well-functioning people as old.

Cultural values vary from familial to religious, from economic to political. We can estimate a culture's ageism by the extent to which its values work against the self-esteem and social status of elders. Examining the phenomenon of aging in other cultures allows comparisons of ageism. How many cultures are ageist? By comparison, how widespread is ageism in the United States? What causes ageism? How can it be avoided?

Nonindustrialized societies usually have proportionately fewer elders in their populations, because the birthrate is higher and more people die at earlier ages. But they may do a better job of dealing with their older members in terms of the tasks, status, and power accorded them. But first, let us examine the fact that the percentage of elders is increasing in almost every country around the world, both in the developing and the already developed nations.

☼ The Graying of the Planet

The world's older population is growing faster than the total population. In 1991 there were about 332 million persons aged 65 and over worldwide; by the year 2000 that total will reach 426 million. Sweden is the "oldest" country in the world (see Figure 15.1), with 18 percent of the population age 65 and over. By the year 2025 Sweden is expected to have 25 percent of its population age 65 or over. Developing nations have lower life expectancy and smaller percentages of their populations aged, as reflected in Figure 15.1.

The rate of growth of the aged in the developing countries is faster than in the developed nations. The two rates of growth are compared in Figure 15.2. Until recent years, the biggest factor contributing to population aging around the world has been the drop in fertility. This reduces the number of births and therefore increases the ratio of old to young. Only in the last several decades has the fall in mortality significantly increased in the developing nations. (It has been a fact in the United States, a developed nation, since the

Figure 15.1

Life Expectancy and Percentage of Population 65 and Over: Selected Developed and Developing Countries (*), 1993

SOURCE: Adapted from: World Population Data Sheet of the Population Reference Bureau, Inc. Prepared by demographers Carl Haub and Yanagishito Machiko. Washington, D.C., 1993.

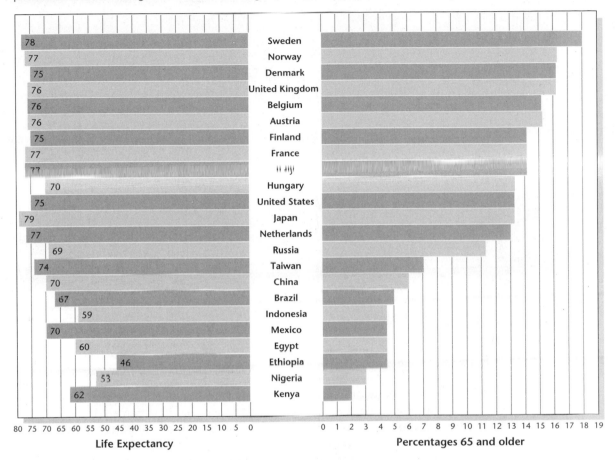

beginning of the century.) The lower mortality rate means that more people survive to old age, a major contributing factor to "aging" a country. As one gerontologist said, "Mass longevity is a gift of industrialization" (Kinoshita, 1992). But the "gift" comes with strings attached.

The European countries took 150 years from the time they entered the "demographic transition" that accompanies industrialization to reach an older population of 12 percent. The developing countries as a whole are expected to reach it in 75 years. In countries such as China, where fertility has fallen dramatically, this percentage will have been reached in less than 50 years, some time between 2005 and 2010. Fifty-seven percent of all older people in 1991 lived in the developing world. This percentage will increase to 69 percent by the year 2020 because fertility and mortality rates are continuing to decline in developing countries. Developing countries have scant resources with which to face up to the problems of old age; therefore, their explosion of numbers represents a great challenge. In 1950 those over 70 years of age in the Third World accounted for 30 percent of elders; in 1990, 37 percent; and in

Figure 15.2

Average Annual Percent Growth of Elderly Population in Developed and Developing Countries

SOURCE: F. Schick and R. Schick, *Statistical Handbook on Aging Americans* (Phoenix, AZ: Ornyx Press, 1994).

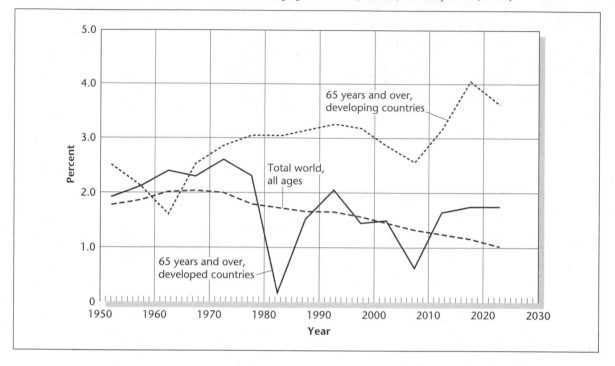

2025 they will be 40 percent of Third World elders (Chasteland, 1992). The developed nations, too, will continue to increase their percentage of elders, especially the very old. But their rates will not be as great because their birthrates are stable rather than declining. (Only their mortality rates are still showing decline.) These rapidly expanding numbers of persons around the world is a phenomenon without historical precedent. Every month the net balance of the world's population of elders is increasing by a million; 70 percent of this increase is occurring in developing countries (National Institute on Aging, 1993).

☼ Social Modernization and Elder Status

In their classic study Cowgill and Holmes (1972) developed a formalized theory of aging from a cross-cultural perspective. Their **theory of social modernization** holds two tenets: (1) the **status of elders** in the community declines as the society's degree of **modernization** increases, and (2) their status goes down in proportion to the rate of social change. These statements suggest that the more modernized a society is and the more rapidly modernization has come about, the lower the status of the elderly.

Additional tenets to their theory explain why lower status accompanies modernization. **Nonindustrial societies** tend to emphasize tradition and ceremony, and the elders within such societies know the most about these customs. Therefore, especially in preliterate societies, their status is high. Older

Having more freedom than at any other time in their lives, elderly people can opt to enjoy a variety of activities.

people function as historians, genealogists, vocational instructors, researchers, and often as doctors and priests. According to Cowgill and Holmes, the status of the elders is always higher in societies where they continue to perform useful and valued functions. In most agrarian societies, for example, old men and women continue their accustomed economic roles as long as they are physically able. Retirement is a modern invention found only in industrialized, high-productivity societies.

Societies that embrace the extended family system offer their older members a stronger familial role and, therefore, higher status. Old people are not as central in the nuclear family of industrial societies, which often relegate care of the dependent aged to the state or other outside agencies. Cowgill and Holmes hypothesize that "modernization tends to decrease the relative status of the aged and to undermine their security within the social system." Numerous studies have supported their modernization theory. One example is employment studies that indicate lower economic status for older members as the shift occurs from agriculture to industry.

In examining historical and anthropological work, Cox (1990) expanded on modernization theory to describe an "S" curve. This pattern suggests a low status for the aged in primitive **nomadic society,** a high status for those in settled agricultural communities, a low status for those in societies experiencing industrialization, and, ultimately, a higher status for elders within postindustrial societies. According to Cox, postindustrial society is so highly technical and automated that fewer workers are needed. Thus society accords importance to leisure as well as work. Cox's definition, the **postindustrial period,** the time the United States is supposedly experiencing, places less emphasis on labor and more emphasis on recreation and leisure. The efficient technology of the 1990s and in 2000 and beyond is expected to reduce working hours and usher in the four-day workweek. With less emphasis on the work ethic, society's older members will have a wider range of nonwork roles and higher status as they enjoy their retirement years. Having more freedom than at any other time in their lives, they may opt for more family involvement, education, volunteer work, local politics, athletic club membership, or just relaxation. The postindustrial society, its productivity insured, can emphasize the quality of life (Cox, 1990). This may sound utopian. We can only hope the postindustrial era brings high status and quality of life not only to elder citizens, but also to all members of societies everywhere.

☼ Variation in Nonindustrialized Societies

The status and role of elders in industrially undeveloped cultures vary widely. The diversity of social and economic roles for older people in societies around the world make generalization difficult. Broadly speaking, Cowgill and Holmes's modernization theory explains elders' high status in nonindustrial societies, but high status may be related to other factors as well. And their modernization theory cannot explain the low status of elders in some nonindustrial societies.

The role of the aged in technologically primitive societies depends partially on resources. Scarcity or abundance of resources can determine the position of elders in hunting-and-gathering societies, in agrarian societies, or in any nonindustrial society. With abundance, societies can afford to indulge their dependent, nonproductive members. With scarcity, societies cannot afford to be so generous and must, at times, make difficult choices.

Egalitarian societies are, by definition, the oldest, smallest, and technologically most simple. Examples are the !Kung of the Kalahari Desert and the Aleuts of Northern Canada and Alaska. Economically egalitarian because no one individual or group has more material goods and resources than another, these peoples subsist by hunting and foraging in small nomadic bands. The !Kung have an esteemed elderly population, which maintains control over water holes. They act as repositories of information about plant and animal life in the region. Further, long after their productive years, they are cared for and respected for their participation in ritual curing. By comparison, among the Aleuts, who nonetheless respected their elders, geronticide was an accepted practice. These people led a harsh life with a small margin of safety, and those who could not contribute simply forfeited their right to live (Halperin, 1987).

Cox, as mentioned previously, believes that nomadic societies in general have the lowest esteem for their senior members. Such societies have the fewest material resources and are usually located in harsh environments, which favor youth and vigor. Because of the high geographic mobility nomadic life requires, individual autonomy is a primary value. There is no reason for younger members to secure the favor of parents and grandparents. The Serono of the Bolivian rain forest offer an opinion that Cox considers typical of nomadic peoples:

> Actually the aged are quite a burden; they eat but are unable to hunt, fish or collect food; they sometimes hoard a young spouse, but are unable to beget children; they move at a snail's pace and hinder the mobility of the group. When a person becomes too ill or infirm . . . he is abandoned. (Holmberg, 1969, quoted in Cox, 1990, 59)

By comparison, another group of traditional societies, whose economic bases centered around agriculture or animal husbandry, provided their older members high esteem. Societies that settled permanently in one place and established property rights gave elders economic power through ownership and control of land. In addition, elders had the power to arrange marriages, thereby discouraging individualism. In such traditional societies, older people pass on legends, myths, and ethical principles. The Aleuts in northern Russia are an example:

> .. every village had one or two old men at least, who considered in their special business to educate the children, thereupon, in the morning or evening when all were home these aged teachers would have the young folks surround them and listen. (Elliott, 1987, quoted in Cox, 1990, 60)

The printing press destroyed the strong need for this type of teaching and, consequently, undermined the status of elders where the oral tradition was used.

☀ Third World Countries: A Test of Modernization Theory

Third World is a term used to designate countries in the early stages of modernization, such nations, also called developing or **less-developed countries (LDCs),** are not yet as industrially advanced as the United States, Western Europe, and other technology-oriented areas, which are considered to be developed countries. Though the proportion of those 65 and over is increasing in Third World countries, we have as yet, few studies of aging from these areas. According to Cowgill and Holmes's modernization theory, within the agrarian LDCs that have not undergone modernization, the status of elders should be high. But this may or may not be the case.

In Turkey, a study of the status of older men affirmed the modernization theory. Old men headed households in villages with low levels of urbanization and industrialization. Further, their labor force participation was higher in these villages than in cities. This particular study provides strong support for the major tenets of modernization theory (Gilleard and Gurkan, 1987).

A study of older Hindus in Kathmandu, Nepal, showed them to still be living in extended families, but to be suffering from changes caused by urbanization and industrialization (Goldstein et al., 1983). Unemployment and inflation were widespread. The sons' salaries were insufficient to support their extended families, and financial choices were made in favor of children rather than parents. The extended family structure was intact yet modernization altered family relationships, creating stress. The Igbo of Nigeria provide another example. They have extended families with great respect for the authority of the aged. Their culture does not reject the aged or disengage them from society (Shelton, 1972). But recent changes such as mass migration to towns and cities have reduced the authority of elders and lessened the ritual value of land. As the young receive formal education, the spiritual power of the elders has been eroded (Ohuche and Littrell, 1989).

The developing nation of China has the largest number of elders in the world. In 1991, China was home to more than 20 percent of the world's total number of elders, with more than 60 million persons 65 years of age or older. India had close to 40 million; Russia and the United States each had close to 30 million. Half of all elders in the world live in these four countries (National Institute on Aging, 1993). In China the unprecedented decline in fertility since the 1970s when the one-child-per-family policy was instituted, accompanied by a decline in mortality, has brought a rapid rise in the percentage of older people. So much attention has been paid to population control in China that little attention has been paid to population aging, which is becoming a major problem. The Chinese have about 30 years to prepare for one of the most massive aging processes in human history. By the year 2030 about 24% of China's population will be 65 and over.

Overall, 82 percent of Chinese elders lived with adult children in 1987, the first time such a survey was even conducted. Furthermore 53 percent lived in households with three or more generations, but these figures are expected to gradually decline with time. The traditional role of grandparents is to supervise grandchildren in return for board and care. But recent social changes that have created more jobs, wealth, and mobility are leading to the decline of extended family. As adult children move to the city for jobs, grandparents left behind lose their important family roles of watching grandchildren and other household tasks. These social changes, as well as current population policy, believed to be essential to China's goal of modernization, is straining the traditional values of family solidarity and mutual responsibility. The only answer for the future may be a more extensive pension program for elders such as the Social Security program in the United States. But only 10 percent of retired workers, largely in cities, now get a pension. China does have a social welfare system, which includes the Confucian ideal of respect and care of the aged. The Confucian *Book of Rites* states that "at 50 one is privileged to carry a cane at home, at 60 in the village, at 70 in the capital, at 80 in the royal court, at 90, to be visited by the emperor and presented with delicacies when he is asked for advice" (Hsia, 1993, 61). As a socialist country, it wants to care for all who need it, but only a very small proportion get help. Widows and widowers get special care from local and state government programs. In rural areas 80 percent of elders are still cared for by family. In urban areas the figure is somewhat lower and on a gradual decline throughout the country (Kwong and Guoxuan, 1992). Limited health and social services are provided by the government. Entertainment for elders is a required service of all state-run organizations, but China's annual budget allocation for its older population is small.

A major problem in developing nations where family support systems are breaking down is that pension systems are difficult to initiate. Older workers may not have been part of a work-based economy and may not earn enough to make payroll contributions. Governments are often unstable, and inflation is a typical problem. A study of five countries—China, Kerala, Mexico, Nigeria, and Turkey—indicated that the adoption of industrial social welfare programs runs counter to traditional values of filial piety or family reciprocity systems or religious beliefs (Tracy, 1991). Every country is unique, however, and those responsible for initiating government pension programs must be sensitive to the cultural traditions of the country. The aged are the "transition generation" in developing countries. They are experiencing a decline in family support, but the state cannot afford to fill the gap (Hugo, 1992).

In contrast, a few studies show that modernization does not affect the status of the aged. A study of aging in American Samoa (an island territory of the United States since 1900) shows that rapid and extensive social changes have not eroded their status. Historically, Samoa has given its elderly strong respect and prestige, and they report being very happy (Rhodes, 1984). The explanations seem to be that the traditional family system continues to function and that traditional values continue to thrive. Further, the Samoans accept the idea of dependency in old age because they are taught throughout their lives to rely on the group, especially the kin-group, rather than on the individual.

In a study of old age on Java, an Indonesian island, three-fourths of elders reported being very happy. Their dependence on kin was not a source of unhappiness (Rudkin, 1994). A source of unhappiness for some was too much stress from dependent children burdening them in old age. Actually, the traditional family care of elders is much more cost effective than the modern system of pensions and nursing homes. Social gerontologists encourage policies that support the traditional family system, even if the inevitable modernization is rolling forward (Nugent, 1990). The Thinking About Aging box on "babushka power" is an example from Russia of traditional family roles for elders holding a developing nation together.

Both modernization itself and the economic failure of modernization can threaten the traditions of a culture. Hardship and poverty are typically a way of life in poorer nations. Countries in which the family structure and value system have been kept intact are the lucky exceptions. Even there, we can ask, "For how long?" We need to find ways to assist families in less-developed countries as their traditional way of life vanishes.

☼ Case Study of An Industrialized Nation: Japan

Many of us in the West think of Japan as a country that grants its elder members high status. Nevertheless, reality reveals a changing Japan in which elder status may be declining. The stereotypes surrounding aging in Japan concern love, honor, and respect. The Confucian ideal is one of **filial piety,** which dictates that children show devotion, warmth, and respect to parents and a high regard for their wishes. Filial piety means being responsible for one's parents and one's family honor, encouraging family harmony, and making sacrifices for one's parents and one's family honor. In Asian societies that practice filial piety, older people are revered and valued, not alienated. Confucius said, "Filial piety nowadays means to support one's parents. But dogs and horses are nourished, too. If care for parents is not accompanied by respect, what is the difference between them and the animals?" (Sung, 1990, 611). Palmore (1975) wrote that the Japanese are the only exception to the theory that the status of the elderly declines with industrialization.

However, Palmore has been accused of idealizing Japan. Evidence indicates that reality may not match the idealized stereotypes of old age in Japan. Even in premodern Japan, a belief that elders who become burdensome have an obligation to leave this world countered the Confucian ideal of filial piety. And, in modern Japan, many older men, for example, are rudely labeled *sodaigomi,* or "unwieldy refuse" (Berger, 1987). A similar translation of the word is "big trash," which describes retired men who are overly dependent on their wives and who expect to be waited on. The term has even more negative connotations than the American term *couch potato* (Martin, 1989, 13).

The Japanese concept of filial piety has an economic basis. Traditionally, the eldest son cares for his aging parents in return for inheriting their land and possessions. This arrangement is much more pragmatic than the Confucian philosophy of filial piety would suggest. Nevertheless, a tension between the pragmatic and the ideal, between affectionate care and formal obligation, pervades Japanese culture.

HISTORY

World War II brought many changes to Japan. The old social establishment and traditional value system were overthrown in much the same way that nonindustrialized or Third World cultures are undergoing change. Japan's reform of the Civil Code in 1948 changed the father–eldest son arrangement

Thinking about Aging

Russia's Good Gray Ladies: Babushka Power Holds a Sick Society Together

■ C. BOGERT

Muza Sorminskaya certainly isn't a typical *babushka*. At 63, winner of Moscow's Super-Babushka '91 competition, she is svelte, speaks fluent English and plays a wicked game of volleyball. Pageant judges gave her top marks for her "charm, intelligence and erudition," her execution of the waltz and the lambada and her knowledge of Moscow's history, architecture, and painting. But despite the worldly polish, Muza Sorminskaya shares the same drudgeries as millions of babushkas (grandmothers) across Russia. She lives in a tiny two-room apartment with her divorced son and 10-year-old grandson and devotes her life to little Dmitry's well-being. She cooks, cleans, sews his clothes, stands in endless lines, takes him to school every day and helps him with his homework every evening. "Our society is relying on its older generation," says Sorminskaya. "We don't work for money; we work so hard because we think it's the right thing to do. When this generation goes, things will be a lot worse."

As Russian society comes crashing down, one pillar stands fast: the babushka. In fact, the term connotes not so much a familiar relationship as an informal institution made up of stalwart, patient, forbearing women of grit. They are the indomitable survivors who keep Russian families afloat during hard times. Many Russians grow up with a babushka in the house, or nearby: only 83,000 people in Russia live in retirement homes, compared with more than 4 million in the United States. As guardians of tradition, babushkas may soothe the national consciousness—or act as a brake on progress. Or they may just be champion busybodies. In any case, they represent practically the only remaining moral authority in post-Soviet society.

Babushkas play a pivotal role in Russian society partly because there are so many of them. The average Russian woman marries at 22 and becomes a babushka in her 40s. With birthrates falling, Russia is experiencing major demographic distortions: some villages are entirely populated by pensioners—women over 55 and men over 60—as able-bodied young people escape the countryside in increasing numbers. Moscow and St. Petersburg also have unusually high proportions of retired people, putting a desperate strain on municipal budgets. Nationwide, more than 20 percent of the population has reached retirement age—almost twice as many as in the United States. Says sociologist Yuri Levada: "Our society will face some major new burdens caring for this unproductive sector."

. . . Yet babushkas make a real economic contribution, both to individual families and to the society as a whole. Most food lines are composed almost exclusively of older women, and in Russia, standing in line is practically a full-time job. Babushkas thus free other people to pursue productive activity. They often work to supplement their meager pensions, doing underpaid menial jobs such as shoveling snow or washing floors. "We're tough, that's for sure," says Lyudmila Ivanova cheerfully; at 64, she rises daily at 5 A.M. to wash cars for foreign diplomats in Moscow. But a babushka's chief contribution to society is spiritual. Russian Orthodox congregations have always consisted mostly of kerchiefed babushkas, who kept the faith alive during decades of official censure. ☼

SOURCE: *Newsweek,* 14 February 1992, p. 33–34.

by providing equal inheritance to all siblings; by breaking the legal foundations for the eldest son's sole inheritance, the code fundamentally altered the age-old care system.

Because the accompanying social change has been gradual, the role of the eldest son is not yet clear, however. If anything, a generation gap seems to be developing, with tradition-minded elders on one side and younger, nontraditional family members on the other. A 1988 survey indicated that, although 47 percent of those 60 and older thought it an eldest son's duty to look after his parents, only 32 percent of those younger than 60 thought so (Martin, 1989, 15).

Modernization favored the younger generation, particularly after 1960, by making jobs abundant in cities. But it affected the older population negatively, especially in rural areas, where elders were left behind to work the land alone. Although those in the rural areas had to cope with a changing and disintegrating lifestyle, older people who moved to the city with their children had problems adapting to a new life in the city. Such rapid change in ways and values has had a significant and sometimes devastating impact on the mental health of the Japanese people, especially the older population.

However, for Japan, modernization has had positive effects as well. Industrialization has dramatically increased the life expectancy at birth, raising it from 50 to 79 years. In 1991, the average life expectancy was 76 years for Japanese males and 82 for females—the highest life expectancy in the world. Thirteen percent of the Japanese are 65 or over, and demographers predict that, by 2025, 20 percent of the Japanese population will be composed of elders, half of whom will be over age 75. The numbers of the very old are a staggering 40 percent of the aged population now. They present an overwhelming problem to caretakers. Surprisingly, 75 percent of Japanese men smoke (only 14 percent of women). An end to smoking would further increase life expectancy in Japan (Baba, 1993).

The number of very old in Japan has mushroomed, straining caretakers.

PROBLEMS OF MODERNIZATION

Business and marketing agents are trying to find ways of cashing in on the growing number of elders in Japan. For instance, though old people usually are called *rojin*, businesses have created a catchier phrase, *jitsunen* (age of fruition), to advertise private retirement residences, day care centers, medical equipment, drugs, travel, education, social clubs, and even a "love hotel" for those who want a rendezvous (Berger, 1987). The term *silver selling* has been used to describe these attempts to target the older market ("The Silvering of Japan," 1989).

Even though some Japanese workers are mandatorily retired as early as age 55, most pension payments do not begin until age 60. A considerable percentage of Japan's companies release workers at age 55; a smaller percentage between the ages of 56 and 59; and the largest percentage at age 60 (over 50 percent); only 5 percent of Japanese companies allow employees to work past the age of 60. However, in spite of these mandatory retirement policies, Japanese elders are more than twice as likely to keep working as elders in any other developed country (see Figure 15.3). Those Japanese who continue to work often hold occupations in agriculture, forestry, and fisheries. Many who are mandatorily retired from high-paying jobs in large firms accept work in these lower-paying industries. Some sociologists believe that the strong work ethic in Japan does not allow men to enjoy retirement; thus they continue working because it provides them with identity and meaning in life.

Not all of Japan's elder workforce is automatically barred from big business. A number of Japan's large firms have systems for extending employment. The aging employee, however, usually must agree to a pay cut, a loss of title, and no guarantee of continued employment. Unemployment is a troublesome fact of life for older Japanese men. Some who would like to work simply cannot find work, even in the lower-paying industries. However, in spite of the difficulty of finding employment, Japanese elders tend to have large savings, a high rate of home ownership, and economic well-being.

Though Japan's health-care and social programs are modest compared with those in Scandinavian countries (discussed in the next section), they are rapidly becoming a burden.

A key question facing all industrialized nations is how much national income to spend on health care, public pensions, and other benefits for elders. Japan currently spends approximately 41 percent of its national income to fund its universal health insurance and pension systems, more than half of which goes to those over 65. By the year 2020, Japan plans to spend 50 percent of its national income on such systems, with two-thirds going to programs for the elderly. (Although this sounds like a great deal of money, welfare states such as Norway and Sweden currently spend 60 percent of their national revenues to fund such programs.) However, private Japanese economists project that the percentage of national income spent on health care and welfare could soar to 60 percent or higher if present benefit systems, such as pensions beginning at age 60 and virtually free health care for those 40 and older, continue. The government is already planning to have older people absorb some of the increasing costs by increasing the fees they pay for health care.

The government is also hoping that families will continue to be highly involved in care of the aged, but these hopes are in question. Although more than 60 percent of Japan's aged live with their children or extended families (compared with 10 percent in the United States), this represents a decrease from 77 percent in 1970. The percentage will continue to fall as more women

Figure 15.3

Labor Force Participation Rates for Men Age 60 to 64 and 65 and over in Selected Countries, 1988

SOURCE: Organization for Economic Co-operation and Development (OECD), Labor Force Statistics, 1988 (Paris: OECD, 1990). Reprinted in F. Schick and R. Schick, *Statistical Handbook on Aging Americans, 1994 Edition* (Phoenix, AZ: Ornyx Press, 1994), p.184.

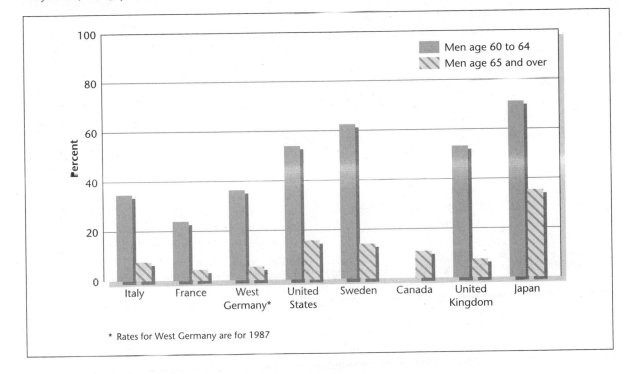

work outside the home and as the declining birthrate produces fewer adult children to care for aging parents (Dentzer, 1991).

Even though fewer elders are living in three-generation households, 60 percent is a high figure compared with 10 percent in the United States. The custom persists and the tendency to live with the oldest son is strong. In that case, the financial responsibility rests with the son and the caretaker responsibility with the daughter-in-law. The life of Japanese elders is still intricately tied to their children. One gerontologist states:

> Given the rapid social change that has occurred in Japan over the past decades, it is remarkable that the solutions to the problem of old age are still largely found within tradition. (Hashimoto, 1992, 41)

Major reasons for this reliance on tradition are (1) small pensions, (2) lack of affordable and acceptable housing, (3) ethics of filial piety legitimate and entitle the aged to family care, and (4) the Japanese are more willing than others to forgo independence in exchange for protection and security.

A lower birthrate also means increased government costs for elder care. As in the United States, the number of retirees in Japan is growing faster than the number of laborers in the workforce. Japan's baby boomers (the 8 million babies born between 1947 and 1949) provided the country with a vast, cheap, young workforce in the 1960s and 1970s—one reason for Japan's phenomenal economic growth. But the tables will turn around by the year 2010, when these baby boomers start to receive their pensions. The birthrate in Japan has

Thinking about Aging

Number of Centenarians Rises to 4,802

The number of people aged 100 or more in Japan is now a record 4,802, comprising 3,859 women, or 80.4%, and 943 men, the Health and Welfare Ministry said.

The number is up 650 from last year and has increased for the 23rd consecutive year, the ministry said in issuing a list of those who will be 100 or older by the end of this month. The list marks Respect for the Aged Day on September 15, a national holiday.

Tane Ikai, 114, of Nagoya, central Japan, is the oldest person in Japan for the second consecutive year, followed by 113-year-old Hide Ohira of Tanabe, Wakayama Prefecture, western Japan.

Of 35 people aged 107 or older, only four are men.

The oldest man is Gengan Tonaki, 108, of Okinawa Prefecture, who is 13th on the list.

Yoshikazu Murakami, 103, of Innoshima, Hiroshima Prefecture, western Japan, attributed his long life to clean air and good digestion. Murakami celebrated his 103rd birthday with his 97-year-old wife Kuma recently, bringing their combined ages to 200.

He said he drinks medicinal spirits with his evening meal, but Kuma joked, "he always drinks too much after saying only a bit."

Murakami said he is determined to see Kuma become a centenarian, and he "wants to live longer happily (with Kuma) although (we) sometimes quarrel."

The number of centenarians per 100,000 people in Japan now averages 3.86, up 0.5 from last year.

Okinawa topped the list with 16.64 centenarians per 100,000 people, followed by Shimano Prefecture with 10.71, Kochi Prefecture with 9.91 and Kagoshima Prefecture with 8.17.

The top 10 prefectures in the list are all located in western Japan. The lowest is Saitama Prefecture, neighboring Tokyo, with 1.46, followed by Akita with 1.89 and Osaka with 1.96. ☀

SOURCE: *Kyodo News International, Inc., 7 September 1993.*

---

declined considerably since the postwar years, and there will be a shortage of workers and a corresponding abundance of retirees after the year 2000. To save costs, the government is working to raise the age of eligibility for public pensions from 60 to 65. But many businesses, who fear being saddled with costly older workers, are opposed. This sounds remarkably like the ageism in American business (Schultz, et al., 1991).

Despite these somewhat stalemated efforts to control costs, Japan has done reasonably well so far in providing medical care and social education for elders, but government costs are increasing rapidly. Free physical examinations are offered annually to everyone over age 65. Public health insurance programs cover most medical expenses, and local governments are beginning to pay for the remainder. Thousands of senior citizen centers have developed across the nation, offering educational and recreational programs at little cost. However, many of the severely impaired—those who are completely bedridden or totally incontinent—are cared for at home. The sheer number of impaired elders and the lack of family to care for them dictates the need for more outside help. Although Japanese custom still declares that children must provide support for aging parents, more and more adult children are seeking home help or retirement homes for their dependent elders.

To maintain tradition as well as to save money, Japanese government policy supports the concepts of family care for older members. Caretakers may receive the following assistance:

1. Tax deduction or exemption. (Income tax credit is given to all taxpayers who are supporting a family member aged 70 or older. If the older person is functionally impaired, the caretaker is eligible for additional tax credits.)

2. Loans to build or remodel a home in which an older parent is to live.

3. Provisions of special equipment, such as special beds, bathtubs, and telephones.

4. Short-term stay service at a nursing home when a caretaker becomes ill or must leave home.

5. Community care centers.

The government has adopted a ten-year Gold Plan for the Aged that adds more geriatric rehabilitation centers and training for 60,000 "home helpers," a kind of housekeeping assistant or nurse's aid who visits several times a week (Baba, 1993). But even in Japan these low-paying jobs are considered "3-D"—dirty, demanding, or dangerous. Although the government is planning to build many more nursing homes, at present, nursing home demand is so high that some have a two-year waiting period. Also, Japanese nursing homes are presently so crowded that overmedication of residents is common. On the positive side, hundreds of programs have been initiated to meet the leisure, social, and educational needs of elders in Japan (Campbell, 1992).

The "welfare" retirement centers are much needed, but at the same time, resisted. Most Japanese still believe that family care is the most desirable arrangement for the well-being of the aged and that it is basically wrong to segregate old people. The Japanese are far more suspicious of retirement communities and homes for the aged than are Americans. Retirement communities have not been popular, especially low-income welfare housing called *yūryō* homes. It is shameful to be there with no family and little money. The image and status of such homes is gradually improving. An ethnographic study of such a community revealed some positives and some negatives for the residents (Kinoshita and Kiefer, 1992). Interaction among men was limited and shallow. Their vocabulary indicated the highest level of politeness and formality. Two norms were "don't cause trouble to others" and "exchange respect." The women "dressed to impress" and gossiped a lot. They were a bit more friendly with each other in terms of talking casually, but few close friendships formed. Health and economic needs were met, but the residents did not have norms or expectations for intimate, meaningful relationships.

There are thousands of community centers and old people's clubs throughout Japan. In 1990 there were more than 130,000 old-age clubs with 8,280,000 members, more than 40 percent of those 60 and over in all of Japan. The healthy retired Japanese are expected to keep quietly busy with household duties. Their favorite activities are watching television, traveling, and gardening. In the centers and clubs they are offered training in these "arts":

haiku—very short poem of 17 syllables

tanka—a short lyric poem of 31 syllables

bonsai—live miniature trees in small pots

haiga—simple but philosophical painting

A CROSS CULTURAL DELEGATION IS HERE TO SHARE
THEIR CULTURAL DIVERSITY

shodō—calligraphy

shigin—poem recitation

sado—tea ceremony

Japanese classical dancing

These activities can be done alone, and they bring deep satisfaction (Maeda, 1993).

The answer to the question "Is aging really better in Japan?" is mixed. Health and longevity have dramatically improved. Income adequacy and government care has improved. Elders receive somewhat more respect than in the United States. But industrialization gradually continues to take its toll on the traditional family relationships. And the very old population is growing faster than the ability of the society to accommodate them.

To summarize, the increasing percentage of frail elderly, combined with the decreasing capability of families to care for older parents, is placing increasing strain on Japan. The government is struggling to meet the escalating financial demand while remaining, economically, a leading world power. The older Japanese themselves, showing many parallels to their counterparts in the United States, are organizing to seek more privileges and rights.

☼ Aging in Scandinavia

Aging in the Scandinavian countries is of special interest because Denmark, Sweden, and Norway have very large aged populations. In 1991, for example, 18 percent of Sweden's population was 65 or over. The number of people aged 90 and older will nearly double in the next 30 years (Hedin, 1993). In addition, these countries are more welfare oriented, imposing higher tax rates to provide social services and financial support to those who need it. Are older individuals better off in Scandinavia in terms of medical care and finances? Are attitudes toward elders improved as a result? Is ageism, therefore, reduced?

The Scandinavian countries, like the United States, are highly industrialized. Per capita real incomes are high, and the standard of living in Scandinavia is higher than in most other countries, though not as high as that in the United States. These countries, like Japan, are world leaders in the proportion of citizens over age 65 and in life expectancy in general.

Though the basic pension, or social security, rate in Denmark is very modest, the retiree may add pensions from a former employer and special housing or rent supplements. Some who compare the financial situations of the elderly in Denmark with those in the United States conclude that Danish are better off. In Denmark, the difference between rich and poor is not as great, and elders have incomes more equal to those of younger groups. Yet absolute comparisons show that those in the United States still fare slightly better because of a higher standard of living overall. On the basis of income, Scandinavian elders are not affluent; at the same time, neither do they suffer minimal deprivation or live in poverty. Slums do not exist in the Scandinavian countries. Elderly people are neither homeless nor destitute. Their welfare system works very well in this regard.

Both Norway and Sweden have experimented credibly with flexible retirement plans. In Sweden, the practice of partial retirement is widespread. The Norwegian system opposes mandatory retirement and other work barriers; many elders there, however, choose a partial retirement system. Public policy formation in the United States would benefit through examination of these systems.

Sweden implemented its flexible retirement system in 1976, and the system has been working reasonably well ever since. Under Swedish law, persons between the ages of 60 and 64 may reduce their work hours and receive partial compensation for their loss in earnings from a national pension fund. The law stipulates that partial retirees must work at least 17 hours per week and reduce their average weekly hours by at least five. This provides a fair amount of leeway for those who find full-time work too demanding or otherwise undesirable. For example, under this system a 60-year-old could work

A major goal of Scandinavian governments is to prevent financial and physical problems that can force seniors into institutions such as the one in this typical American scene.

half-time, or perhaps a four-day week. The average reduction in workload is 13 to 14 hours per week. Under this flexible plan, older workers can retain valued employment with the same company; they do not have to turn to self-employment or part-time employment in an undervalued job. Working the number of days per week that the mind and body can tolerate and enjoy offers health benefits as well (Wise, 1990).

Unlike U.S. health care, Scandinavian medical care is provided by the government. In Denmark, for example, 95 percent of the population receives medical care through health insurance societies established by local and state governments. Membership, which is free to elders living on pensions, provides lifesaving drugs and medical and hospital treatment at no cost. The elderly receive free physiotherapy, pedicures, and dental and eye care. The state even pays for funeral expenses. In Sweden, pensioners are reimbursed for most of their doctors' fees and for travel to and from medical facilities. Health care is comprehensive and offered at virtually no cost to older individuals. All the Scandinavian countries provide extensive services that enable elders to maintain themselves in their own homes. Family members in Sweden and Norway, for example, receive government pay for helping aging relatives at home. A home helper (a trained worker paid by the government) may visit regularly to clean, shop, and cook, and to offer assistance with personal activities such as letter writing or bathing. In some cases, hot meals are delivered daily. For the municipal governments, which also provide home nursing for the sick who do not require hospitalization, a major goal is to prevent the financial hardship or physical deterioration that forces seniors into institutions. National policies offer workers up to 30 days of paid leave to care for ailing elder relatives. (The Scandinavian countries had extensive family leave policies long before the United States enacted its limited family leave policy.)

In addition to providing health care, many Scandinavian countries encourage and sponsor fitness programs and holidays for seniors. Sweden, for example, annually sponsors the Vasa Race, a cross-country ski race in which many older people compete. The RiksKommitten, a Swedish local community agency, supervises and encourages fitness programs for all ages. Every year, Swedish elderly enjoy two pensioners' holidays and two special pensioners' weeks (one in spring and one in the fall) during which senior citizens receive public recognition and attend special functions.

In addition to health-care and other public programs, Scandinavia also offers its elder population a variety of housing options, ranging from "sheltered villages" for the elderly to integrated housing for both young and old. In Sweden, for example, it is not uncommon for an old-age home to be next to a youth hostel. There, old and young share a common cafeteria. In comparing Scandinavia to the United States, a journalist wrote:

> My instant impression was that there are fewer old people in Scandinavia who just stare vacantly into space as they await death. There are more elderly who walk, talk, and smile. (Szulc, 1988)

In Stockholm, Copenhagen, and Helsinki, daytime community centers for elders are open to all who care to walk in from their homes in the neighborhood. Such centers offer classes in dance, English, French, weaving, and other skills, in addition to providing care tables, books, magazines, and inexpensive meals.

Government officials are dedicated to eradicating the warehousing of frail elders. A half hour from downtown Stockholm is the Hagstrata, an integrated housing project where more than 1,000 older people, averaging 85 years old, rent apartments alongside young families with children. Hagstrata has a social center that houses a library, a wood and textiles workshop, and a photography lab, as well as a school, hospital, hockey rink, tennis court, gym, and sauna. This complex gives older inhabitants a sense of living in the "normal" world and allows them to live, in the words of Mauno Koivisto, the 68-year-old president of Finland, "active, self-reliant, and free" lives (Szulc, 1988).

The elder care system in Sweden has a guiding principle of independent living and freedom of choice. Large institutions are being phased out; small-scale housing such as group dwellings are being developed. It usually means a small housing collective for six to eight persons, in which each resident has his or her own room, shares communal areas, and has 24-hour-a-day access to staff. **Group homes** actually cost less per resident than large-scale institutions. These homes are most common for persons with senile dementia, but are used for older and younger persons with other physical and mental disabilities. By 1992 there were 5,300 residents of group homes and plans to develop facilities for another 6,400 people. A study of one group home showed a very calm, homey environment. Residents' rooms were filled with their furniture and memorabilia. Staff satisfaction was high and resident turnover low. The familiar atmosphere of home was a great positive for those with senile dementia. The group home concept is a great success in Sweden (Malmberg and Zarit, 1993).

In Scandinavian countries, aging parents do not typically live with adult children, but they do remain in close contact. A survey of persons aged 60 and over found that only 4 percent of Danes and 3 percent of Americans thought it best for older and younger generations to live together as compared with 58 percent of the Japanese surveyed (Martin, 1989, 15). Studies of family relationships in Scandinavian countries have found that, in general, elders have frequent contact with their children. However, Danish elders involve themselves relatively less in the daily lives of their children and have greater independence. Sociologist H. Johansen (1987) found limited help and support between the generations in Denmark. Family relations in Denmark are fairly formal; spontaneous gatherings at the home of an older parent, for example, are rare. Adult children are not traditionally responsible for supporting their parents financially or housing them in their own homes. Denmark's extensive system of support developed partly because care of aging parents was not considered a family obligation.

Despite such comprehensive public programs, life for Scandinavian elders still has its negative aspects. Social mobility has separated younger and older family members, and the stressful lifestyle of the middle class has left less time to help older family members. The Norwegian term *gammel*, which means "old," is associated with negative traits; old people prefer the word *eldre*, which means elderly. Loneliness, isolation, and a feeling of uselessness are serious problems for Scandinavians just as for Americans.

In Sweden, a study of adults and their aging parents revealed a high degree of contact between aging parents and their adult children who have remained in the same social class and who live nearby (Sundstrom, 1986). However, a recurrent theme in Swedish fiction—that "socially arrived" children tend to sacrifice their parents and their cultural heritage—was borne out in the study. Middle-class adult children of working-class parents tend to move away from home and to have a lower degree of contact with their parents, whereas adult children who remain in the working class live closer to their parents and maintain more contact.

The future for Sweden's system is that resources will become more scarce. There have already been some cutbacks in home-help services. There is almost universal support for the concept of the state as primary provider of care for the aged, but new, more cost-effective means of care may need to be sought. A social scientist visiting Sweden said, "I was told that requiring family members to perform caregiving tasks is illegal at present, but at some point in the near future, this may be reevaluated" (Boise, 1991, 5). The language and tone of this statement does not sound as though it would dare be uttered in the Asian countries. Even the thought of mandating family care of elders would probably be an insult. Some individuals think that the strong state support of the aged has undermined family support. Others think that Sweden has the best care of the aged in the world.

☼ Applying the Findings

Industrialization does not dictate socially debilitating loss of status for elders in every case, but it does appear to be a very strong trend. The rate of loss may slow as the rate of modernization slows or when the proportion of elders reaches a certain peak. In many nonindustrialized societies the satisfaction of older members seems greater than it does in more developed nations. One must wonder whether technology really adds significantly to the quality of life. A simple diet, continuing exercise, and a genuine place (i.e., role, status, respect) in the ongoing life of the community seem to bring fulfillment and a zest for living. Too often, in "modern" societies such as ours we tend to believe that we can solve a problem by throwing money at it. No amount of money can buy self-esteem, pride, a sense of worth, and a feeling of well-being.

Though we are learning about elders in other cultures, more research is needed. In addition to an overall lack of research, much of the work done by researchers in other cultures has not been translated into English. Journalists are filling some of the gaps, but their work needs corroboration through a scientific approach that gerontologists, anthropologists, and sociologists must provide.

Findings from other cultures have many uses. For example, we can use them to test our theories of aging, which may be culturally biased. In the United States, gerontologists have developed the disengagement theory, which proposes that old people inherently and gradually disengage from society and that society, in turn, disengages from them. Yet, studies of peasant societies offer little support for the universality of this theory: their members never disengage.

Sometimes in other cultures we can see new ways to improve the status of elders in our own country. In socialistic countries such as Scandinavia, health care is essentially provided to one and all through government-subsidized national health insurance, and the Scandinavian health-care system is generally more innovative and progressive than our own. Extensive homemaker services, such as those in Sweden, are also lacking in the United States. We have also been slow to offer many integrated hospice services for the dying. And several European countries provide more comprehensive social security than the United States does.

We can look beyond our society for other patterns of improvement. The British pension system, for instance, issues a standard payment, regardless of previous earnings. Germans receive social security benefits at age 65 even if they are working full time. In countries with the best coverage, the government usually contributes to social security through its general tax revenues. The U.S. government at present does not, although it may do so in the future. In some other countries, pension deductions from wages are proportionately higher than those in the United States. If Americans want comprehensive social security coverage equal to that of many European nations, they can find ways to accomplish that goal. But these ways will generally involve more taxes. What kind of commitment do we have?

In addition to providing seniors with better care, what might we do to increase their status? Integrating—or reintegrating—them into the mainstream of society by providing more job opportunities is an important first step. Palmore, in *Honorable Elders Revisited* (1985), suggests a national annual Senior Citizen Day similar to Japan's Annual Respect for the Elders Day. They recommend a special celebration of the 65th birthday and gestures of social respect such as reserving special seats on buses and trains for elders.

In closing, we should consider the viewpoint of Margaret Mead, the noted anthropologist who traveled the world observing the process of aging in many cultures. Mead questioned the great emphasis we place on the independence of elders in our society. Our preoccupation with independence compels our elderly to live apart from their families and from the younger generation. Mead observed:

> The young need to know about their past before they can understand the present and plot the future. Young people also need reassurance that change does not mean an end to the world, but merely an end to the world as they first saw it. (Mead, 1972)

Integrating older people into the mainstream of our lives, rather than excluding them, allows them to be valuable role models, and lets them share their experience for the benefit of youth.

Chapter Summary

The cross-cultural approach compares value systems and social structures across cultures. Value systems and social structures reflect on the status of elders and vary widely from culture to culture. In some countries, the elders have a central place in the social structure and are held in high esteem. Social scientists are testing the hypothesis that modernization decreases the status of the elderly. Undeveloped, developing, and developed countries offer a test of the hypothesis, which generally speaking, is supported. However, one can over generalize on this subject because exceptions do exist.

We think of Japan as a country honoring elders, yet industrialization and other socioeconomic changes have eroded the concept of filial piety. Aging in Scandinavia seems to have advantages over other countries in the comprehensiveness of its health care. Scandinavian countries are more socialistic and have more tax dollars to spend on programs that tend to be progressive and enlightened.

Key Terms

continuous values
cross-cultural approach
developed countries

discontinuous values
filial piety
formal age

functional age
group home
less-developed countries (LDCs)
modernization
nomadic society

nonindustrial societies
postindustrial period
status of elders
theory of social modernization
value

Questions for Discussion

1. What cultural factors are possibly involved in longevity?

2. What aspects of modernization affect the elderly adversely?

3. How does growing old in nonindustrialized countries compare with growing old in America?

4. How does growing old in Japan and Sweden compare with growing old in America?

5. Describe the ideal culture in which to grow old. Describe yourself living in this ideal culture and your attitudes toward aging and toward life in general.

Fieldwork Suggestions

1. Interview the oldest living member of your family. Were any born outside the United States? Find out about their childhood and their experiences growing up.

2. In the library, find descriptions of the status of the elderly in nonindustrial or developing nations. Is this status high or low? Why?

3. Interview an older person born in another country. Ask him or her to compare old-age experiences in his or her birth country with those of the United States.

References

Baba, S. "The Super-Aged Society." *World Health* 46:3 (May/June 1993): 9–11.

Berger, M., with C. Gaffney. "The Rush Is On: Mine the 'Silver Generations.'" *Business Week* (15 June 1987): 52–53.

Bogert, C. "Russian's Good Gray Ladies: Babushka Power Holds a Sick Society Together." *Newsweek* (24 February 1992): 33–34.

Boise, L. *Family Care of the Aged in Sweden.* New York: Swedish Information Service, February 1991.

Campbell, J. *How Policies Change: The Japanese Government and the Aging Society.* Princeton, NJ: Princeton University Press, 1992.

Chasteland, J. "The Graying of the Planet." *UNESCO Courier* (January 1992): 40–44.

Cowgill, Donald, and Lowell Holmes. *Aging and Modernization.* New York: Appleton-Century-Crofts, 1972.

Cox, H. "Roles for Aged Individuals in Post-Industrial Societies." *International Journal of Aging and Human Development* 3:1 (1990): 55–62.

Dentzer, Susan. "The Graying of Japan." *U.S. News & World Report* (30 September 1991): 65–73.

Elliott, H. *Our Arctic Province: Alaska and the Sea Islands.* New York: Scribner, 1987.

Gilleard, C., and A. Gurkan. "Socioeconomic Development and Status of Elderly Men in Turkey: A Test of Modernization Theory." *Journal of Gerontology* 42 (July 1987): 353–357.

Goldstein, M., et al. "Social and Economic Forces Affecting Intergenerational Relations in Extended Families in a Third World Country: A Cautionary Tale from South Asia." *Journal of Gerontology* 38 (November 1983): 716–724.

Halperin, R. "Age in Cross-Cultural Perspective: An Evolutionary Approach." In *The Elderly as Modern Pioneers,* edited by P. Silverman. Bloomington: Indiana University Press, 1987.

Hashimoto, A. "Aging in Japan." In *Aging in East and South-East Asia,* edited by D. Phillips. London: Edward Arnold Publishing, 1992.

Hedin, B. *Growing Old in Sweden.* Stockholm: The Swedish Institute, 1993.

Holmberg, A. *Nomads of the Long Bow.* Garden City, NY: Natural History Press, 1969.

Hsia, Lian Bo. "China." In *Developments and Research on Aging: An International Handbook,* edited by E. Palmore, 59–72. Westport, CT: Greenwood Press, 1993.

Hugo, G. "Aging in Indonesia." In *Aging in East and South-East Asia,* edited by D. Phillips, 207–230. London: Eward Arnold Publishing, 1992.

Johansen, H. C. "Growing Old in an Urban Environment." *Continuity and Change* 2 (August 1987): 297–305.

Kinoshita, Y., and C. Kiefer. *Refuge of the Honored*. Berkeley: University of California Press, 1992.

Kwong, P., and C. Guoxuan. "Aging in China." In *Aging in East and South-East Asia*, edited by D. Phillips. London: Edward Arnold Publishing, 1992.

Maeda, D. "Japan." In *Development and Research on the Aging: An International Handbook*, edited by E. Palmore. Westport, CT: Greenwood Press, 1993.

Malmberg, B., and G. Zarit. "Group Homes for People with Dementia: A Swedish Example." *Gerontologist* 33:5 (1993): 682–686.

Martin, L. "The Graying of Japan." *Population Bulletin* 44:2 (July 1989): 13–39.

Mead, Margaret. "Dealing with the Aged." *Current* (January 1972).

National Institute on Aging and the U.S. Bureau of the Census. *Wall Chart on Global Aging*. Washington, D.C.: U.S. Department of Commerce, 1991.

Nugent, J. "Old Age Security and the Defense of Social Norms." *Journal of Cross-Cultural Gerontology* 5 (May 1990): 243–254.

Ohuche, N., and J. Littrell. "Igbo Students' Attitudes Toward Supporting Aged Parents." *International Journal of Aging and Human Development* 29:4 (1989): 259–267.

Palmore, Erdman. *The Honorable Elders*. Durham, NC: Duke University Press, 1975.

Palmore, Erdman, and Daisaku Maeda. *Honorable Elders Revisited: A Revised Cross-Cultural Analysis of Aging in Japan*. Durham, NC: Duke University Press, 1985.

Rhodes, E. "Reevaluation of the Aging and Modernization Theory: The Samoan Evidence." *Gerontologist* 24 (June 1984): 243–250.

Rudkin, L. "Dependency Status and Happiness with Old Age on Java." *Gerontologist* 3:2 (April 1994): 217–223.

Schick, F., and R. Schick, eds. *Statistical Handbook on Aging Americans*. Phoenix, AZ: Ornyx Press, 1994.

Schulz, J., A. Borowski, and W. Crown. *Economics of Population Aging: The "Graying" of Australia, Japan, and the United States*. Chicago: Auburn House Greenwood, 1991.

Shelton, Austin J. "The Aged and Eldership Among the Igbo." In *Aging and Modernization*, edited by D. O. Cowgill and L. D. Holmes. New York: Appleton-Century-Crofts, 1972.

"The Silvering of Japan." *Economist* (7 October 1989): 81–82.

Sundstrom, Gerdt. "Intergenerational Mobility and the Relationship between Adults and Their Aging Parents in Sweden." *Gerontologist* 26 (August 1986): 367–371.

Sung, Kyu-taik. "A New Look at Filial Piety." *Gerontologist* 30:5 (October 1990): 610–617.

Szulc, Tad. "How Can We Help Ourselves Age with Dignity." *Santa Rosa Press Democrat* (29 May 1988): 4–7.

Tracy, M. *Social Policies for the Elderly in the Third World*. Westport, CT: Greenwood Publishing Group, 1991.

Wise, L. "Partial and Flexible Retirement: The Swedish System." *Gerontologist* 30:3 (June 1990): 355–361.

Further Readings

Albert, S., and Cahill, M. *Old Age in Global Perspective*. New York: G. K. Hall Division of Macmillan Publishing, 1994.

Butler, R., and K. Kiikuni, eds. *Who Is Responsible for My Old Age*. New York: Springer, 1993.

Jerigan, H., and M. Jerigan. *Aging in Chinese Society*. New York: Haworth Pastoral Press, 1992.

Palmore, Erdman, ed. *Developments and Research on Aging*. Westport, CT: Greenwood Press, 1993. (Chapters on 25 countries including China, Japan, Norway, Sweden, and Denmark.)

Shi, L. "Family Financial and Household Support Exchange between Generations: A Survey of Chinese Rural Elderly." *Gerontologist* 33:4 (August 1993): 468–480.

Silverman, G. "Ageing Asia: Honour Thy Father." *Far Eastern Economic Review*, March 2, 1995, pp. 50-55.

16 *Senior Power:* Politics, Policies and Programs

CHAPTER OUTLINE

- Early Rumblings
- Senior Power Today
- The Older Americans Act and Other Programs
- Activism and Advocacy
- The Equity Issue
- Epilogue: Change and the Future

The Invisible People: The Sebastopol Pomos

■ JEFF ELLIOTT

The oldest name for Mr. Young's property—and all of the city of Sebastopol—is Batikletcawi, which roughly means "The Village Where Elderberries Grow." The blood ties of the Sebastopol Pomos to this place are deep, hallowed by the graves of their dead. Last spring, when the Sebastopol City Council again denied the landowners permission to build an upscale subdivision on the site, Grant Smith (an 88 year old Pomo) spoke at the public hearing. "This whole Laguna was the Indians', our babies died here," he told the hushed council and audience. "Their bodies are buried on the shore of this Laguna. What will they find when they build this? They will find the bodies of our children."

At issue in Sebastopol is a Pomo identity with homeland, a place to show their children where ancestors lived and died. Becerra [A Native American child-welfare activist] is clear that taking this step has nothing to do with building casinos, what has recently become the most contentious issue with Indians in Sonoma County and elsewhere. "Gaming is an economic development, and that is completely different from the spiritual sense of connecting with the land," she says.

It is a subtlety lost on bureaucrats and developers, to whom land is merely property. But listen to Grant Smith and a single message comes loudly through: this area is his home, and part of his very being. Not the modern-day town of Sebastopol, not the county of Sonoma, but right here: the "shore of this Laguna."

. . . Not until 1908 did the United States attempt to identify and count native people in California; by that time, much was lost. Within a few short years of California's 1850 statehood, the American engine of genocide was at full throttle.

"The Americans were the worst," says Grant Smith firmly. "They drove my grandmother up north."

The people call it the Death March. Starting around 1857, horse-riding whites with bullwhips—

Grant Smith recalls the genocide of his Pomo tribe: "These pictures I'll carry with me until I die: I see the people on the riverbanks and their fires, so many things."

either local militia or vigilantes, there being at the time only a breath of difference between the two—forced the people to walk some 120 miles north to the newly established reservation at Round Valley, near Covelo. Says Smith, "They herded them like cattle, like animals. Old people couldn't make it, couldn't keep up, and died on the road. [When I was a boy] they talked about it, they would talk about what happened on the road and they would cry, go all to pieces. It was misery, it was hardship. It was death."

When Round Valley began in 1856, there was no venereal disease among the people; two years later, 20 percent were afflicted. Also common was kidnapping of their children; Pomo children were highly esteemed as house servants, fetching $50 for a child who could cook, and up to $100 for a "likely young girl," according to an 1861 news clip.

Not surprisingly, the people began to escape. Grant Smith continues: "They were there in Covelo and they began to die off, sick. My great-grandfather brought the people together, said we're going
—Continued

387

home. They went up, walked along the tops of the ridges, traveled all night, but they got back home." Asked where "home" was, Smith explains, "Anywhere around here. Our people came down; they suffered to come home."

Once home, they faced a devil's choice of options. Some Indians sought refuge in the wild; Grant Smith's niece remembers her great-grandmother forever talking about "hiding," and how anxious she was when in public. Many resigned themselves to work on ranches or in the orchards that were being planted around Sebastopol.

Young and the Ghilottis have sued Sebastopol after the City Council turned down the fourth construction project in 13 years on this site. An attempt to mediate the dispute is planned. Sebastopol already has a hefty legal bill from a just-concluded suit brought by another thwarted developer. A citizen's group has offered to contribute $60,000 toward acquiring the land for open space.

"I remember when old folks would get together in camps and cry and cry," says Grant Smith. "These pictures I'll carry with me until I die: I see the people on the riverbanks and their fires, so many things."

Meanwhile, the last remnant of Batikleteawi lies quiet. ☀

SOURCE: *Sonoma County Independent* 16:6 (August 11–17, 1994), pp. 10–12. Reprinted with permission from *The Sonoma County Independent,* Santa Rosa, CA.

*T*o judge strength by size alone, the older population of the United States is stronger than ever before. Numbers command political power at the voting booth and in lobbying efforts. Yet the 1990s, largely because of harsh economic turns, have brought forth a general political environment that is increasingly hostile to the aged or, for that matter, to any group that makes a request of local, state, or federal budgets. Though elders have made significant steps over the last 50 years in gaining the wherewithal to maintain healthy and meaningful lives, their progress, like that of our society in general, depends essentially on the condition of the U.S. economic system. When that system is mired in massive debt and other problems, as it is now, progress grinds to a halt; established groups are forced to work toward preserving benefits and gains, rather than toward acquiring new ones.

The same situation of threatened cutbacks in government programs exists in most of the nations of Europe and will grow larger in the next 20 years as the baby boomers of the World War II era reach age 65. The Netherlands provides a clear example of threatened cutbacks; their social welfare policies provide substantial benefits to elders that they have come to take for granted. Now conservative political parties are challenging these policies. In a country of 11 million, some 15,000 Dutch senior citizens marched into a soccer stadium to rally, shouting to opposing political parties, "Keep your hands off our pensions" (Drozdiak, 1994). In that country the General Old People's Union, along with another senior citizens' party, won six seats in parliament, and the political awakening of the elderly is gathering momentum. The cost of social welfare in Holland has gone off the charts. The Dutch now spend $100 billion a year on health and social security costs, about ten times what they pay for their military defense. The older population fears a decrease in their standard of living as cost-cutting measures become inevitable. They support political candidates who do not advocate the reduction of their entitlements.

We begin this chapter by briefly reviewing periods during which elder political activism in the United States flourished. Today's political climate can then be examined in the light of these earlier decades of struggle and progress.

☼ Early Rumblings

Political movements are the combined result of social, economic, and historical events. Circumstances develop that make political action imperative. Those who are affected respond by joining forces and asserting their need to improve their situation. This happened in the early 1900s, when a large proportion of the elderly were living in poverty. Although retirement had become increasingly mandatory, pensions were not yet generally available, which often left the elderly with neither work nor money. In 1921, though a limited pension system was established for federal employees, the vast majority of elders still had no pensions at all. During the Depression, millions of those age 65 and over suddenly left without resources became the age group hardest hit. Their plight created the social environment for the nation's first elderly uprising, which took political form as the **Townsend plan.**

Named after the retired physician, Francis E. Townsend, who headed the program, the Townsend plan was organized through Townsend Clubs, which numbered 7,000 at their peak in 1936 (Kleyman, 1974). The Townsend plan proposed placing $200 of government funds per month in the hands of persons aged 60 and older, with the requirements that the recipients retire from work and spend the money within 30 days. The plan's appeal lay in its twofold purpose: to raise the status of the elders and to stimulate the depressed economy by rapid circulation of money. However, the political atmosphere toward age issues in the 1930s and 1940s was hostile and unreceptive. Only 3.8 percent of the electorate approved the Townsend plan, according to a 1936 Gallup poll (Pratt, 1974). Eventually, conflict arose among top leaders, whose personal financial gains from the movement were exposed. The conflict and charges of graft helped lead to the Townsend plan's gradual demise. In addition, the Roosevelt administration vigorously opposed the plan.

The Social Security Act, part of the New Deal legislation, adopted one of Townsend's main objectives—a pension for elders. However, the Social Security Act was a more conservative measure. Rather than "giving" pensions to the retired, it paid pensions out of sums collected from workers; and the amount of each pension was determined by each individual's employment record. Those who did not work were not eligible for benefits. In the decades that followed, amendments to the Social Security Act added coverage for more kinds of workers and their dependents.

Other political movements, many of which originated in California, attempted to help the elderly during this era. Even before the Townsend plan, there had been EPIC (End Poverty in California). The EPIC movement was based on campaign promises Upton Sinclair made when he ran for governor of California in 1934. His platform of sweeping social reform included a monthly $50 pension for the elderly.

Also from California, the **Ham and Eggs movement** proposed that the government issue a large amount of special script, the value of which would expire at the end of a year; therefore, the elderly pensioners who received it would spend it promptly and stimulate the economy. In the late 1940s, George McLain, a leader of the Ham and Eggs movement, lobbied the California state legislature and advocated his reforms through a daily radio program. He believed that all elderly were entitled to pension increases, low-cost government housing, medical aid, and elimination of the financial means test (a questionnaire that the applicant would "fail" if income reported was too high and benefits were denied). Before any of his proposals were widely adopted, the McLain movement, which drew a membership of about 7 percent of those aged 65 and over in California, ended in 1965 with McLain's death.

A significant characteristic of the various movements in the 1930s and 1940s, including McLain's, was that they extracted great sums of money from the elderly themselves. Indeed, although the movements set a precedent for political organization, they nonetheless demonstrated how vulnerable the elderly could be to powerful leaders who actually preyed on their trust: "Certainly old-age power was helped to grow because of them; however, the secretiveness, greed, and paranoia with which the advocates held power stymied grassroot growth" (Kleyman, 1974, 70).

Although the civil-rights movement began in the 1950s, this decade is often described as a time of political inactivity and apathy, an era of general economic prosperity chiefly characterized by inattention to needy groups. The early 1960s brought more fervor to the civil-rights movement and President Lyndon B. Johnson declared the War on Poverty. The high incidence of poverty among some groups—racial minorities, the rural, and

Political awareness leads to empowerment.

elders—began to attract public attention. With the advent of the antiwar movement and the hippie lifestyle, the 1960s also saw increasing political activism among students and other adults. Gay liberation and the women's movement evolved in the 1970s as civil libertarian ideals gathered support. The women's movement, in particular, dealt with the issue of aging by attacking job discrimination against middle-aged and older women. The National Organization for Women (NOW) established a task force of older women. In addition, the 1970s ushered in the advocacy of rights for the disabled. These humanistic movements created an environment in which one movement could combine forces with another. In this sense, all of the social movements of the 1960s and 1970s contributed to the social movement of **senior power.** A number of pro-senior interest groups and programs materialized in the 1960s; their chief accomplishments were the passage of the Older Americans Act (1965) and Medicare (1966).

The early 1970s brought forth a more visible and vital seniors movement. For the first time since the Great Depression, older people, with cries of "gray power" and slogans such as "Don't Agonize—Organize," showed evidence of considerable political activism. Demonstrations, sit-ins, and sleep-ins by oldsters wearing "Senior Power" buttons made the headlines. The new militancy of old-age groups such as the Gray Panthers presented a surprising and exciting image for those who had once been stereotyped as powerless, dependent, slow, and unenthusiastic. The name "Gray Panthers" captured the new consciousness of the elderly. It suggested strength, power, and radical—if not revolutionary—political and social behavior.

☼ Senior Power Today

VOTING

When enough older people turn out to vote on a given issue and vote as a bloc, they wield considerable power. Approximately 90 percent of Americans over age 50 are registered to vote, compared with an overall national figure of less than 75 percent. In all recent elections, older people are more likely to vote than younger ones (Binstock, 1992). Citizens in their eighties are more likely to vote than those in their early twenties. Older voter turnout (those 65 and over) tend to be double the voter turnout of young adults under 25 years of age. Thus, the voting power of older people is greater than their actual numbers in the population would indicate, even though disability and lack of transportation keep a few elders from the polls. Longitudinal studies indicate that those who vote in their younger years continue to vote for as long as they are able. Cross-sectional studies show that voter turnout tends to be relatively low for young people, to increase in middle adulthood, and to remain stable in old age. Only one subgroup of elder voters shows low turnout—homemakers, virtually all of whom are women. Older women are advised to become more politically aware through leadership training workshops, where they can learn about the legislative process and advocacy techniques. This political empowerment would allow them more say in protecting their rights and in advancing their interests (Jirovec and Erich, 1990).

Despite generally large voter turnout among elders, studies show that they do not generally vote as a bloc on any issue, not even on old-age issues. In national politics, age has not yet become a factor that unites people regardless of their differences. Social class as a variable outweighs the effects of age. The wealthy older person, for example, might not support welfare measures for older people living in poverty. Elders come from a wide variety of ethnic backgrounds, and they are widely dispersed in urban and rural areas. Political organization and mobilization are necessary to encourage them to use their potential power by voting as a bloc.

An interesting finding that violates a stereotype of old age is that older people are neither more nor less conservative than younger people. The elderly are spread fairly evenly between Republican and Democratic leanings: In the 1980 and 1984 elections, about half of the voters aged 65 and over voted for Ronald Reagan; in 1988, more than half voted for Bush, but that is because he won by a larger margin among all age groups. And in the 1992 election the older vote was fairly evenly divided between Bush and Clinton.

OFFICE HOLDING

Another measure of political power is the ability to be elected or appointed to public office. Only two U.S. presidents have entered office after the age of 65: William Henry Harrison (age 68) and Ronald Reagan (age 69). Many more have turned 65 while in office. For example, George Bush turned 65 in 1989, not long after his inauguration. Because life expectancy has increased greatly since George Washington's time, one might guess that presidents have entered office at increasingly older ages. However, this has not happened. Though the first four presidents were 57 or older, in the following years, the nation has seen some very young presidents. The youngest was Theodore Roosevelt (age 42), followed by John F. Kennedy, who was 43 years old at his inauguration in 1961. President Bill Clinton was aged 47 at his inauguration in 1993. Vice-presidents have, on the average, been considerably older than the presidents of the United States (Kiser, 1992).

Members of Congress, because they are elected officials, are not subject to mandatory retirement laws. Some members have served into their eighties and, occasionally, into their nineties. Until the Ninety-fourth Congress in 1974, when many senior members retired, their average age remained over 50. Since 1974, the average age has risen again to over 50; in 1994, many congressional members were over age 65. The seniority system in Congress allows older members who have served many years to wield the most power, often as heads of important committees.

Some U.S. citizens and politicians would like to limit the number of congressional terms members can serve, not so much to reduce the power of older senators and representatives, but to ensure that they remain responsive to their electorate. As it stands, some are tempted to take their reelection for granted because they have been reelected so many times. And, although older men are overrepresented in Congress (compared to their population numbers), only a handful of women are in the Senate and House of Representatives. More women would be a welcome addition to the U.S. political scene.

Cabinet members and ambassadors tend to be older, perhaps because they are appointed by the president rather than elected. These positions, which imply years of experience, are often filled by men and women who, in any other area of work, might have been forced by age alone to retire. Supreme Court justices also tend to be older. There is no mandatory retirement for them, and they generally serve as long as their health allows. In 1991, the controversial appointment of Clarence Thomas, age 43, made him the youngest justice to serve on the Court. In 1995, two justices were over age 65: Paul Stevens, 79, and Chief Justice William Rehnquist, 71. In 1995, Sandra Day O'Connor was 65, and the most recent appointee, Ruth Bader Ginsberg, was 62.

Thinking about Aging

What Goes Around: His Views Are Back

■ JONATHAN YENKIN

For decades, John Kenneth Galbraith etched his opinions into the nation's psyche as a prolific writer, as a presidential adviser and, as some colleagues call him, "the most famous professor at Harvard."

His liberal views haven't always been embraced especially in the 1980s when the White House sought to shrink the role of government.

At age 85, he's back in vogue.

"His influence has been great," says Labor Secretary Robert Reich. "Ken Galbraith's influence can be felt not only in the insistence that every American have access to high quality health care, but also in the confidence that we as a nation can accomplish that feat."

"People are seeing that some things can only be accomplished by the state, the government," he said.

Galbraith's basic philosophy, outlined in books such as his 1958 best seller "The Affluent Society," says capitalism cannot survive in a country that fails to help its needed through social programs such as housing, public schools and welfare.

To his admirers, Galbraith stands out for his ability to put a human face on economic theories. "Galbraith quite correctly understands the reason why capitalism survives is because government humanizes it," said historian Arthur Schlesinger, Jr., a longtime friend.

Galbraith insists he doesn't take an adoring view toward government.

"I don't see government as good or bad," he said. "I see it as indispensable."

After he graduated from the University of Toronto in 1931, Galbraith moved to the United States, where he saw a country in the throes of the Great Depression, desperately needing government help.

Of all the public figures he has known, Galbraith said he revered FDR the most.

"Most of my generation did," he said. "We didn't make up our minds on an issue until we knew what Roosevelt wanted."

John Kenneth Galbraith, 85, is still writing books.

But the person for whom Galbraith had the greatest affection was John F. Kennedy. Galbraith was his ambassador to India.

The admiration was mutual. Colleagues have described how Kennedy enjoyed Galbraith's prose so much that he would insist on seeing all his cables, regardless of whether they were directed at the president.

After Galbraith came back from India, he returned to teaching at Harvard, where he had rejoined the faculty in 1948 and remained a professor of economics until his retirement in 1975.

It was in this role that Galbraith did much of his writing, gaining national acclaim.

In retirement, Galbraith keeps producing best sellers like "The Age of Uncertainty" and "Almost Everyone's Guide to Economics."

All told, Galbraith has written about 30 books and is now finishing up another that will recount his personal views of economic history since World War I. And once he's done with that book, he plans to start another one, describing his encounters with famous figures such as Roosevelt, Kennedy and Charles de Gaulle.

Paul Samuelson, the Nobel-winning economist from the Massachusetts Institute of Technology and another longtime friend, said he is astounded by Galbraith's energy.

—_Continued_

"He's an amazingly imaginative and creative hard-working person," Samuelson said. "There's no day that goes by that he doesn't write every morning, and it adds up to a lot."

Galbraith, who lives a few blocks from Harvard Yard and still regularly attends events at the university, says he doesn't see himself kicking back and relaxing.

"I'm afraid I might not die of boredom, but I might wish that I would," he said. ☀

SOURCE: Reprinted with permission from the *Sonoma County Independent*, Santa Rosa, CA. Vol. 16:6 (August 11–17, 1994), 10–12.

Despite the preponderance of elders in elected and appointed positions, we do not seem to be headed toward a gerontocracy—rule by the old. Both young and old are involved in the political arena. Although it has long been acceptable for members of Congress to be middle aged or older, a political youthful image has been favorable since the time of Teddy Roosevelt. In addition, even among old politicians, age does not appear to be a major variable affecting their position on political issues. A presidential candidate or Congress member does not support old-age measures simply because he or she is near age 65. Ross Perot, for example, who in 1995 turned 65 years old, is influenced more by his business background than his age in formulating his political positions. The support that members of Congress give to issues should reflect not only their political ideology but the wishes of their constituents as well. Supreme Court justices make decisions based on philosophy and ideology; impartiality dictates that age not be an influencing variable. Older politicians and other elders involved in the political process provide good role models and typically work hard at their jobs.

POLITICAL ASSOCIATIONS

Now able to exert tremendous political pressure, interest groups representing older Americans have increased in number and political effectiveness over the past several decades.

One type of specialized interest group is the trade association. Trade associations represent specific concerns and lobby to achieve their purposes and goals. Some examples are the American Association of Homes for the Aging, the American Nursing Home Association, the National Council of Health Care Services, and the National Association of State Units on the Aging. There are also professional associations, such as the Gerontological Society, the Association for Gerontology in Higher Education, and the American Society of Aging, composed primarily of academicians in the field of aging. Other interest groups, such as the National Association of Retired Federal Employees (NARFE) and the National Retired Teachers Association (NRTA), are composed of retired persons.

A few organizations representing older persons have enjoyed special growth, success, and media attention. Here we consider six of them: the American Association of Retired Persons, the National Committee to Preserve Social Security and Medicare, the National Council of Senior Citizens, the National Council on the Aging, the National Caucus and Center on the Black Aged, and the Gray Panthers.

American Association of Retired Persons (AARP) The largest and most powerful group of older persons in the United States, the **American Association of Retired Persons (AARP)**, which already boasts nearly 30 million members aged 50 and over, has been growing at the astonishing rate of 6,700 persons a day. Although the goals of some groups have always been to exert political influence, the primary goals of AARP, originally directed toward individual and social betterment, have only recently become political. The group's founder, Ethel Percy Andrus, was concerned with improving the image of retirees and raising their status. As a California educator, she founded the National Retired Teachers Association (now called NRTA) in 1947. By 1955, the organization had grown to 20,000 members. In that year, the association added a health insurance program to its benefits, and its membership grew even more rapidly. So many persons outside the teaching profession were interested in the health insurance option that the AARP was founded as an expansion organization in 1968. Besides insurance, its services now include travel packages, special prescription rates, an auto club, education, income tax counseling, and training services. The AARP's growing array of services ranges from widows' counseling to driver re-education, and the association produces television and radio shows that are broadcast nationwide.

Its membership makes the AARP one of the largest voluntary organizations represented in Washington and one of the nation's largest lobbying groups. The group, which tries to remain nonpartisan, has directed its political efforts at improving pensions, opposing mandatory retirement, and improving Social Security benefits, widely shared goals that unite the association's members. Their congressional lobbyists support causes for poor elders, and their magazine *Modern Maturity* stresses an image of well-to-do, healthy aging. Plans are under way to provide an AARP political organization in every congressional district.

The National Committee to Preserve Social Security and Medicare Founded by James Roosevelt (son of President Franklin Roosevelt) in 1983, the **National Committee to Preserve Social Security and Medicare** is concerned about the solvency of the Social Security Trust Funds. Now boasting 5 million members, it is a nonprofit organization funded entirely by membership fees and donations. Its 59-member staff works to protect and improve Social Security and Medicare benefits. Many of the staff are full-time lobbyists.

National Council of Senior Citizens (NCSC) The **National Council of Senior Citizens** (NCSC) originated in 1961 as a pressure group to support the enactment of Medicare legislation. Its leadership has always come from labor unions, mainly the AFL-CIO and other industrial unions. From a small, highly specialized group, the NCSC has grown to include a general membership of about one million in 1994. It is now an organization of autonomous senior citizens clubs, associations, councils, and other groups. Their aims are to support Medicare, increases in Social Security, reductions in health costs, and increased social programs for seniors.

The organization's stated goals are broad and straightforward: "We work with, persuade, push, convince, testify, petition, and urge Congress, the Administration, and government agencies to get things done on behalf of the aged." The council, located in Washington, D.C., lobbies for Social Security revision, a national health insurance program, higher health and safety standards in nursing homes, and adequate housing and jobs for elders. The membership base is composed primarily of labor union retirees, but membership is open to anyone aged 55 or older.

National Council on the Aging Founded in 1950, **the National Council on the Aging,** a confederation of social welfare agencies and professionals in the field of aging, has been at the forefront of advocacy, policy, and program development on all issues affecting the quality of life for older Americans. The organization, which has its headquarters in Washington, D.C., has regional offices in New York and California. The council publishes books, articles, and journals on aging, sponsors seminars and conferences, and funds eight special-interest groups.

- National Association of Older Worker Employment Services (NAOWES)
- National Center on Rural Aging (NCRA)
- National Institute on Adult Day Care (NIAD)
- National Institute on Community-Based Long-Term Care (NICLC)
- National Institute of Senior Centers (NISC)
- National Institute of Senior Housing (NISH)
- National Voluntary Organizations for Independent Living for the Aging (NVOILA)
- The Health Promotion Institute (HPI)

The National Caucus and Center on Black Aged (NCCBA) Formed in 1980 when two groups—the National Caucus on Black Aged and the National Center on Black Aged—joined, the **National Caucus and Center on Black Aged** attempts to improve the quality and length of life for senior African Americans. The NCCBA, which believes that problems can be resolved through effective and concentrated political action on behalf of and by older African Americans, was initially formed as an ad hoc group of African-American and white professionals who shared a concern for older African Americans. NCCBA activities have been largely national, focusing on such areas as income, health, and housing. An annual conference is held every May. The National Center on Black Aged in Washington, D.C., established by the NCCBA through federal funding, is the location for various activities: training, research, legislative development, and assistance to black elders.

The five groups discussed so far are neither revolutionary nor radical. Rather than advocating a redistribution of wealth, they work to improve the status of the elders by ensuring that more federal money is channeled to them. For example, they have successfully lobbied the Department of Health and Human Services, the Department of Education, the Office of Economic Opportunity, the Administration on Aging, and other government agencies to increase resources for the older population.

The Gray Panthers One pro-age political group that identifies itself as nonviolent yet radical is the **Gray Panthers**, a loosely organized group that includes young people as well as old ("age and youth in action") to fight ageism in U.S. society; it received a great deal of media attention when it was formed in 1970.

The late Maggie Kuhn, a dynamic woman who was mandatorily retired at age 65, founded the movement in her search for new ways to constructively use her energies. She and the group's other members describe themselves as a consciousness-raising activist group. Drawn together by deeply felt concerns for human liberation and social change, the Gray Panthers operate out of an office in a West Philadelphia church. From that office, a small staff and a group of volunteers maintain a center for the entire organization—thousands of concerned persons in several hundred chapters in cities and towns across the nation. Their goals are to bring dignity to old age, to eliminate poverty and mandatory retirement, to reform pension systems, and to develop a new public consciousness of the aging person's potential.

Describing themselves as a movement rather than an organization, the Gray Panthers have no formal membership requirements and collect no membership dues. They have opposed the national budget deficit, the nuclear arms race, and cuts in Social Security. Currently, the group advocates a national health insurance program. These views are similar to those who espouse the critical perspective in sociology.

In a newsletter called Network, the Gray Panthers espouse their views. Writes one member:

> We stand firm in our commitment to oppose all forms of discrimination and to challenge harmful prejudiced attitudes and values. Now, we reaffirm our pledge to help create a world that is fair to *all* people regardless of their gender, race, ethnicity, nationality, sexual orientation, religion, income, physical or mental abilities, or age. (Kerr-Layton, 1993)

Another member writes that too much emphasis on age results in the suffering of both young and old and that ageism has three components: stereotyping, trivializations, and blaming the victim. All three of these behaviors have to stop (Better, 1993). Gray Panthers also defend the rights of gays, lesbians, and AIDS victims and their friends. They are opposed to violence and abuse of any kind and draw special attention to the presence of hate crimes in our society. They also sponsor jointly with other organizations an international "People's Summit for Peace" and work for world peace in any way they can.

Researchers offer divergent views on the political impact of the "gray lobby." In some areas they are organized and strong. The AARP, along with

NOTICE THE CONGRESSMAN EATING HIS SUBSIDIZED LUNCH... HE VOTED TO CUT THE ELDERS FOOD PROGRAM

the other organizations, has been effective in staving off large cuts in Medicare (Weisskopf, 1993). A Social Security freeze proposed by the Clinton administration was abandoned as politically dangerous because of the "gray lobby" groups (Risen, 1993). And because of senior power, higher taxes on Social Security benefits is also viewed as a politically risky move by politicians (Rosenblatt, 1993). On the other hand, the state of the economy (the national debt, the trade imbalance, worldwide recession), and the growing number of elders, along with the shrinking workforce are not factors the "gray lobby" can control. Assessing the impact of the senior movement is difficult because it is so diverse and so vast (Wallace and Williamson, 1992). There are many more interest groups than those listed in this chapter. A recent book sketches 83 national, private, nonprofit advocacy organizations that focus primarily on aging (Van Tassel and Meyer, 1992).

☼ The Older Americans Act and Other Programs

The **Older Americans Act** (OAA) authorizes taxpayer funds to be spent on programs for the elderly ($1.3 billion was appropriated by the act in fiscal year 1991). Although Social Security and Medicare are self-supporting public insurance programs, taxpayers foot the bill for programs under this act, which comes to Congress for refunding every four years. The U.S. political and economic climate determines increases or decreases in the act's funding.

The OAA was adopted by Congress in 1965, a period very favorable to programs for the aging. For example, Medicare was enacted during the same general time period. However, whereas the 1960s and 1970s saw budget increases and expanded programs under the OAA, the 1980s brought decreases in funding. The 1980s were considered a time of "retrenchment," and the 1990s are experiencing more of the same. In fact, in the 1990s, the OAA intends to target the needy—the frail and minority aged, knowing that the act's scant resources cannot reach every person in the mushrooming older population. Still, as before, the major portion of OAA funds will be devoted to congregate meals, senior centers, and transportation programs.

The Older Americans Act contains six major sections, called titles, which outline the intentions and objectives of the act. Title II establishes the Administration on Aging (AOA) in Washington, D.C., the organization that administers the programs and services that the act mandates. Title III provides for the distribution of money to establish state and community agencies; in 1991, there were 57 state units and 672 area units on aging, or AAAs. These agencies disseminate information about available social services and are responsible for planning and coordinating such services for the elderly in local settings. A local community that has a council or center on aging is probably receiving federal funds through Title III. Title IV, its funding slashed in the 1980s, and not increased in the 1990s, provides funds for training people to work in the field of aging as well as for research and education on aging. Other titles provide funds for multipurpose senior centers to serve as community focal points for the development and delivery of social services. All in all, the specific titles of the act are intended to achieve the following objectives for older citizens, as spelled out in Title I:

1. Adequate income.
2. Good physical and mental health.
3. Suitable housing at reasonable cost.
4. Full restorative services for those who require institutional care.

5. Equal employment opportunities.

6. Retirement with dignity.

7. A meaningful existence.

8. Efficient, coordinated community services.

9. Benefits of knowledge from research.

10. Freedom, independence, and individual initiative in the planning and management of one's life.

The act's major programs are developed to meet these goals at local levels, with guidance from state units and the federal Administration on Aging. Funding comes partially from the federal government and partially from state and local governments and charity organizations. The term **aging network** is often used to refer to the complex web of services the act provides (Gelfand, 1993). Some of the programs are described here.

MEALS AND NUTRITION

The success of pilot projects in the 1960s resulted in federal funding for home-delivered meals and, in 1972, funding for congregate, or group, dining projects. Under the Older Americans Act, funds are available to all states to deliver meals to the homebound elderly or to serve meals in congregate sites. Meals on Wheels, for example, delivers meals to the homebound at a minimal charge. Congregate dining is aimed at getting the elderly out of their homes and into a friendly environment where they can socialize with other people as well as enjoy a hot meal. Meals and activities take place in churches, schools, restaurants, or senior centers. Besides serving hot meals, some agencies provide transportation to and from the dining site, information and referral services, nutrition education, health and welfare counseling, shopping assistance, and recreational activities. The act establishing the congregate dining program specifies that participants not be asked their income; they may make a contribution if they wish, but there is no set charge.

Meals on wheels delivers meals to the homebound at minimal charge.

FRIENDLY VISITING AND TELEPHONE REASSURANCE

The OAA provides limited funding for volunteer community services such as friendly visitor and telephone reassurance programs. Because of decreasing funds, however, local staffs have had to become increasingly adept at fund-raising to keep programs afloat.

The Friendly Visitor Program has improved the quality of life for many people. Visitors are volunteers of all ages who have an interest in developing a friendly relationship with older persons. They are matched with elderly persons in their community on the basis of such things as common interests or location. In some cases, the Friendly Visitor has proved to be a lifeline. The program has a small paid staff that organizes and instructs volunteers.

Telephone reassurance programs have staff, either paid or volunteer, to check on older persons daily by phone at a given time. For the homebound, this call may be an uplifting and meaningful part of the day. If the phone is not answered, a staff member immediately goes in person to check on the elder's welfare.

EMPLOYMENT

The Title V employment program is small but is one of the most politically popular programs. The major program, the Senior Community Service Employment Program (SCSEP), which provides community service work opportunities for unemployed low-income persons aged 55 and over, employs 62,500 older applicants in part-time minimum-wage community service jobs throughout the United States.

A related program is Green Thumb. Men and women aged 55 and older who live in rural areas may work up to 20 hours per week at minimum wage in public projects which include landscaping, horticulture, and highway maintenance.

DAY-CARE CENTERS

The Older Americans Act partially funds multipurpose day-care centers to provide services on an outpatient basis to the many older people who need services on a daily or weekly basis but do not need 24-hour institutional care. Older people may come to such centers for health care, meals, social activities, physical exercise, or rehabilitation. Practitioners from the centers may, on occasion, deliver home services. These centers allow people to enjoy the advantages of both institutional care and home living.

OTHER SERVICES

Local agencies on aging may offer legal services to low-income elders for civil matters such as landlord disputes; other agencies may offer home health services as well. Still others may offer housing services such as counseling regarding housing options, home equity conversion information, and assistance in locating affordable housing. Information and referral is a hallmark of agencies on aging.

Considering the budget constraints within which the AOA must work, fulfilling all the goals of the OAA is largely impossible. In 1994, for example, Social Security and Medicare payments to older persons totaled between $300 & $400 billion, vastly more than the $15 billion OAA appropriation. Nevertheless, the OAA provides an excellent outreach structure for elders across the United States. Vast numbers have enjoyed and appreciated the services the act offers. Those who think they might be eligible for any of these programs are advised to call their local agency on aging. Though the limited funds cannot reach far enough to include those above the poverty line as well as those below it, many elders living in modest if not meager circumstances do meet eligibility requirements.

TWO PROGRAMS NOT FUNDED BY THE OAA

Elderhostel   Certainly not all successful programs for older persons have been funded by the Older Americans Act. Some have sprung up locally and are funded by local tax dollars. Others are funded by private donations or charity organizations or sponsored by churches or various federal or state government agencies separate from the Administration on Aging. **Elderhostel** is a program made available through state colleges and universities.

Offering special one-week or summer residential academic programs for citizens age 60 and over, the very successful Elderhostel program is an innovative idea designed to meet some of the educational needs of older people. From its Boston headquarters, the program, inspired by the youth hostels and folk schools of Europe, directs a network composed of several thousand high schools, universities, national parks, environmental education centers, and many other educational institutions throughout the United States, Canada, and more than 100 overseas locations. Hostelers can go to school (a different school every week, if desired) as many weeks as they wish and take up to three courses per week. The college or university finds room and board for these older students and appoints regular faculty members to teach the classes, which encourage intellectual stimulation and/or physical adventure. Noncredit courses with no exams, no grades, and no required homework are offered in multitudinous subjects; no-cost extracurricular activities are also provided. Scholarships are available, and students are charged a reasonable flat fee for class, room, and board. Elderhostel offers personal assistance with overseas travel arrangements. The program has been enormously popular among older "students of life." Many classes have waiting lists.

The Foster Grandparent Program   Funded through participating states and ACTION (the principal federal agency that administers volunteer service programs), the **Foster Grandparent Program** (FGP) allows low-income citizens of age 60 or oder to use their time and talents to provide much needed love, care, and attention to disadvantaged youngsters. Begun in 1965, FGP was the first federally sponsored program to offer challenging activity to retirees. The FGP provides opportunities for close relationships to two different groups: low-income elders who want to feel needed and who want to participate in and contribute to the lives of institutionalized children and/or children with special or exceptional needs.

Foster grandparents exist in every state. Participating elders receive 40 hours of orientation in the specific area of their choice. In most cases, they work 4 hours a day, 5 days a week, assisting youngsters in physical or speech therapy or with their homework. Their main task is to provide for the emotional, mental, and physical well being of children by affording them intimate and continuing relations through uncomplicated activities such as going for a walk or reading stories, or within family intervention structures. Foster grandparents receive a nontaxable stipend of an amount per hour that is approximately minimum wage, transportation if needed, a meal each day that they work, accident and liability insurance coverage, and an annual physical exam. Sometimes, nonstipended volunteers may enroll in the program under certain conditions. Many seniors work in this program for years both because they need the extra income and, more importantly, because their "grandchildren" love them.

☼ Activism and Advocacy

Activism connotes more than simply voting or joining an organization. The term *political activist* brings to mind an individual who is politically involved in a fuller, more energetic way and who uses a variety of means to push for social change. Effective political activities include:

- Political campaigning in support of local, state, and federal officials and legislators who support the interest of the older population.
- Registering nursing-home and old-age home residents as absentee voters.
- Lobbying.
- Organizing petition drives.
- Providing political education for the older population.

Elders and those interested in their causes participate in community activities by serving on boards of trustees, advisory councils, and committees in all kinds of social service agencies. Interested persons may get involved in police/community relations, join voluntary organizations, and enter local politics as either campaign workers or as candidates. They may lobby to maintain or increase funding for federal programs, including those of the Older Americans Act. Legal activity is another area for activism. Class-action lawsuits can be brought against organizations and institutions that discriminate against or do not properly serve elders. Individual lawsuits can also be filed, if necessary, for fraud, malpractice, and recovery of small claims. Voter registration drives are important. They ensure that older persons can support those who support Social Security, Medicaid, home-delivered meals, public housing, employment programs, improved transportation, health benefits, and dozens of other programs for the elderly. Grievance procedures can be initiated to aid complaints against Social Security or welfare departments. Collective activity is a good tactic for the activist who joins with others in membership drives, marches, and demonstrations. Such activity may include the following public events:

- Visiting facilities serving older consumers.
- Loading of buses to show a need for reduced fares.
- Marching in streets to emphasize the need for freedom from crime or local lack of services.
- Squatting in abandoned buildings to dramatize housing shortages.
- Monitoring court hearings that involve elders.

An example of a political and social action group is Seniors for Justice. It was started by a recreational therapist in a large nursing home of 550 residents. The group advocates for improvements in nursing-home care, and in the process, enhances residents' sense of control and self-identity (Hubbard et al., 1992). The group addresses many issues. One project was a petition drive urging state and federal elected officials to keep abortion legal. Another task was to launch letter writing campaigns to continue funding for programs such as the Retired Senior Volunteer Program. They have organized food drives to help local hungry children. And as a direct result of their efforts, the nursing home started a recycling program.

Other individuals across the country keep busy advocating for seniors. Elder advocate Sue Harang has been called a crusader and gadfly of nursing homes because someone burned down a bunkhouse on her rural property containing case records and computer files with information on nursing-home abuses. Featured in a national magazine, she continues her fight for better nursing-home care (Beck, 1992). She has taken on some industry giants with the help of her lawyer-husband and been very successful in winning cases.

Another advocate is Florence Rice of Harlem who in 1991 at age 72 received an award from the AARP for her efforts on behalf of older consumers. Ms. Rice has battled businesses, utility and phone companies, food and furniture stores, credit companies, and banks. For decades she was virtually a one-woman consumer movement known as the Harlem Consumer Education Council (Meier, 1991).

Resistance activity may be effective. It includes boycotts, rent strikes, wheelchair sit-ins, mass resistance to paying regressive property taxes, and voting against bond issues. Designated individuals may act as watchdogs on agencies that serve the elderly. In any type of organized activity, the media can provide an important tool in airing the interests and concerns of elders.

Advocacy is a term widely used in the field of aging, perhaps because of numerous individuals and organizations doing just that. Advocacy involves using one's resources and power for the benefit of a special-interest group, such as the elderly. The activist activities mentioned above qualify as advocacy. So does the work of the organizations mentioned in the Political Associations section of this chapter. Stereotypes of the 1950s and 1960s portrayed elders as dependent and passive, in need of someone to advocate for them (Brown, 1990). The 1970s and 1980s changed that idea. The Gray Panthers were in the forefront of creating a stronger, more forceful image for elders. The poem by Marilyn Zuckerman in this chapter captures this image. It is becoming quite clear that older persons are capable of advocating for themselves; nonetheless, they do appreciate all the help they can get. In the

After Sixty

■ *Marilyn Zuckerman*

The sixth decade is coming to an end
Doors have opened and shut
The great distractions are over—
passion ... children ... the long indenture of marriage
I fold them into a chest
I will not take with me when I go

Everyone says the world is flat and finite
on the other side of sixty
That I will fall clear off the edge into darkness
That no one will hear from me again
or want to

But I am ready for the knife slicing into the future
for the quiet that explodes inside
to join forces with the strong old woman
to throw everything away and begin again

Now there is time to tell the story
—time to invent the new one
Time to chain myself to a fence outside the missile base
To throw my body before a truck loaded with phallic images
To write Thou Shalt Not Kill
on the hull of a Trident submarine
To pour my own blood on the walls of the
Pentagon
To walk a thousand miles with a begging bowl in my hand

There are places on this planet
where women past the menopause
put on the tribal robes
smoke pipes of wisdom
—fly

SOURCE: With permission of the author. *Poems of the Sixth Decade*, Garden Street Press, Cambridge, MA, 1993.

1990s, advocacy will, ideally, combine the efforts of individuals, regardless of age, who desire to promote a more satisfying later life for all U.S. citizens.

☼ The Equity Issue

Generational equity is a controversial issue that appeared in the mid-1980s and continues into the 1990s. Critics of elder proponents, who fear that the older generation is advancing at the expense of the younger one, have described older people as "greedy geezers" and as pampered, coddled babies (Lacayo, 1990; Fairlie, 1988). The organization called **Americans for Generational Equity** (AGE), founded by Senator David Durenberger (R.-Minnesota), believes we spend resources on current gratification at the expense of future generations. The group criticizes the high percentage that Social Security takes out of wages, as well as the high cost of medical care for elders, especially expensive medical procedures that prolong the lives of elders without adding to the quality of life. Age-based health-care rationing is still being proposed by some professionals (Callahan, 1994). Smith (1992) calls it the "tyranny of the old," stating, "By clinging to an outsize share of governmental goodies, the elderly are unintentionally forcing the nation to short-change its young." These critics demand generational equity—a correction to perceived imbalances ("Aging America," 1989).

Those who advocate generational equity suggest that all age groups and generations have a right to fair treatment and that benefits for one group (e.g., the elderly) should not be advanced without doing the same for other groups. They believe that younger generations will suffer because of the older population's unprecedented size and affluence. Around the country suburbs are home to a growing number of older residents. Older residents have no direct stake in the public school systems. The constituency for supporting schools and other youth services is shrinking (Gaines, 1994). In some cases school bonds to expand and improve schools have been voted down and elders blamed for ignoring the needs of young students. The entire state of Florida, with its large older population, has been viewed as a place of generational conflict over the issues of increased taxes for schools (Button, 1992). Hundreds of Floridians were interviewed (535 in 1990 and 556 in 1991) in a Florida study of generational conflict. The results were mixed (see Table 16.1) with the finding that the higher the percentage of elders in a community, the more negative the images were of them. This does not bode well for the future (Rosenbaum and Button, 1993).

AGE is also complaining about the proportion of the federal budget that the aged population commands. Though elders, they argue, are only 13 percent of the population, they consume more than 30 percent of the U.S. health-care budget. Whereas poverty among elders has decreased, the incidence of poverty among children has increased. They argue for less spending on elders and more on children.

But we must view all these arguments with caution. This subject is complex, and the assumption that our policies for the old unfairly burden the young is questionable. The idea that increased affluence for elders (and the increase lately is intangible) leads to decreased moneys for children is unsound. The improved financial status of elders is due largely to better Social Security coverage; and indeed, benefit increases should keep pace with inflation. Although dramatically reducing poverty rates among seniors, such essentially small increases in benefits are not the basic reason for poverty among children and other younger generations. Nor is the increased cost

404
CHAPTER 16 Senior Power: Politics, Policies and Programs

"Older residents generally help to improve the quality of life in my community."		Percentage of Respondents		
		All	<55	55+
	Strongly disagree	1	1	–
	Disagree	26	34	10
	Don't know	6	4	9
	Agree	62	57	70
	Strongly agree	6	4	11

"Older persons in my community tend to oppose paying for local public services which do not directly benefit them."		Percentage of Respondents		
		All	<55	55+
	Strongly disagree	1	1	2
	Disagree	36	33	42
	Don't know	12	12	10
	Agree	47	48	46
	Strongly agree	4	6	1

"Suppose the local public schools said they needed much more money. As you feel at this time, would you vote to raise taxes for this purpose, or would you vote against raising taxes?"		Percentage of Respondents		
		All	<55	55+
	For taxes	47	47	49
	Don't know	4	2	8
	Against taxes	49	51	43

SOURCE: Adapted from W. Rosenbaum, and J. Button. "The Unquiet Future of Intergenerational Politics," *Gerontologist* 33:4 (August 1993): 485.

of medical care for elders. If, as some suggest, Medicare premiums tripled in cost for the well-to-do and expensive surgeries were rationed for the very old, women and children would still be poor in this country. The growing number of older people is hardly the major reason for spiraling health-care costs. It is only one contributing factor that needs to be put in perspective (Cohen, 1994).

The basic reasons for the poverty of children are their parents' unemployment or underemployment and the increasing number of female-headed families with low incomes. Our economic system is the major factor in such poverty, not elders. To protect children, we need to get our economic house in order. We need industrial policies that provide jobs to all working Americans, regardless of age and sex. And we need policies to increase our competitiveness in world markets. Further, by reducing the government's interest payments, the lessened national debt would make more federal money available to both children and elders. If one generation is pitted against another, fighting for crumbs, no one has time to look at the real source of the problem. Placing blame is counterproductive.

In the words of William R. Hutton, executive director of the National Council of Senior Citizens:

> We must realize that Social Security and Medicare are not responsible for the poverty of children ... social programs assisting the young have been gutted as the direct result of enormously rising defense spending since 1983 and (because) of tax loopholes. (Hutton, 1990)

Social Security actually provides benefits to many different age groups, and every worker can rest easier knowing that, despite recent doubts about the program's continued solvency, he or she will likely be covered in retirement. Social Security is, in reality, an intergenerational program. According to gerontologist Fernando Torres-Gil, it is critical to dispel the myth that the needs of children are not being met because older Americans are taking more than their fair share. He and many others have observed poverty to be a cross-generational issue that affects us all (Torres-Gil, 1991).

In *Ties That Bind: The Interdependence of Generations* (Kingson et al., 1986), the authors strongly argue against any conflict between the generations. Age groups have a mutual obligation to help each other, and interdependence binds all generations. Until we understand that, public policy will be ineffective. Moody (1987) believes *Ties That Bind* to be a landmark in the politics of aging: "No longer can we assume that old people will automatically be viewed as 'the deserving poor'." In Moody's view, creative policy analysts will look toward defining programs, such as home care and day care, that meet the combined needs of the young and the old. **Generations United** is a group seeking to merge concerns of the young and the old. This group owes its existence to the generational equity controversy. Generations United is opposed to divisive rhetoric that separates generations. It supports intergenerational programs uniting old and young. If schools want the support of elders, they may find ways to integrate them into programs and enlist their support. In one school, students perform tasks for seniors in their homes, and seniors serve as teaching aides in the schools (Gaines, 1994).

The issue of what one generation owes another has been called the "contract between generations." It is the human dilemma of defining the expected benefits and obligations between older and younger age groups. One such obligation was stated in the bible, "Honor thy father and thy mother." A perspective in gerontology that goes beyond parents and children is the negotiation of exchanges between the working and the retired: who owes what to whom and how, and when is it transferred. These exchanges are called **intergenerational transfers**. An economist has suggested that unless we can control the budget deficit, unborn generations of Americans will pay a 21 percent larger share of their lifetime incomes in Social Security taxes than today's wage earners (Kotlikoff, 1992). Kotlikoff's studies indicate that a 70-year-old male in 1989 will receive $42,700 more in benefits than he paid out, whereas a 40-year-old man (who will be 70 in 2019) will pay $76,200 more than he will take out. The implication is that older people today are taking more than their share. Critics of his assessment state that older people today make other intergenerational transfers. They pay taxes for schools and get nothing back, they give money and gifts to children and grandchildren, and they leave inheritances. Intergenerational transfers do not revolve around Social Security alone. And when the Social Security system stabilizes (i.e., the ratio of workers to retirees levels off), there will be equity in amounts of Social Security received across generations.

Historians look more broadly at intergenerational contracts, asking socially and politically as well as economically, "To what extent do we hold older generations accountable for the effect of current policies on future generations?" Should members of current generations compensate future generations for past injustices of prior generations (Laslett and Fishkin, 1992)? Without answering specifics, today's younger generations should act with concern about the effect of their political policies on future generations, and older generations should be concerned enough to want the best social, political, and ecological environment for the young people who will replace them. In this sense the "contract between generations" is a humanistic commitment to keep the world a desirable place in which to live.

☼ Epilogue: Change and the Future

What does the future hold for older individuals? In some respects, the future looks bright. Elders are living longer and healthier lives, and they are becoming more visible not only in numbers but also in their political activism. They have demanded, and to some degree have received, a bigger slice of "the American pie." The quality of life for the average older person has improved over that of several decades ago.

On the other hand, the future looks clouded. The challenge of finding viable roles for the growing numbers of older people has not been met. A healthy 65-year-old, with a life expectancy of at least 15 more years, still has contributions to make to society. In the United States, the percentage of elders will grow from the current 13 percent to more than 18 percent in 25 years. Many of these seniors will be healthy, fit, and looking for activities rewarding to themselves and to society. We need to address this issue by changing our patterns of employment, changing work and leisure opportunities, and raising the status of this group, which has so much to contribute. Perhaps we could emphasize the role of sage and/or social critic for elders, who have a lifetime's experience and the time and freedom to elaborate on their observations and philosophies.

Not only will more elders be vigorous, but more will also be frail. Gerontologists have observed that we do not know enough about the aging process and what is considered normal—physically, mentally, and socially— for the very old. Until recently, death was the "norm"; persons in their eighties were somehow "abnormal." With so many now living into their eighties, we are pushing harder toward the genetic limit imposed by the mysterious mechanisms of the biological clock. With time, research will allow us to get even closer to this limit and perhaps even to surpass it.

We will be thinking more and more about the meaning of frailty and of being very old. Society faces a challenge in finding the means to provide good care for frail or disabled elders when they become unable to manage for themselves. A major question of very old age is why one should want to survive if life is not meaningful. This is a great challenge that the United States and other nations must face—meeting the financial and moral burden of fostering a quality life for the very old. At this writing health-care reform has not been enacted and long-term care remains a problematic issue for older Americans.

In the 1970s, we witnessed the birth of a social movement aimed at raising the status of the seniors and creating for them a more powerful, more positive image. Though its initial militancy has ebbed, this movement leaves in its wake new aspirations for many individuals and the hope of change yet to come. Even after a social movement has peaked and media attention dies away, large numbers of people continue to change their attitudes and behavior. As a result, more people are coming to face, understand, and accept the experience of aging. Rather than continuing to fear or dread old age, they look forward to and plan for productive and happy lives as older people. And elders now, and even more so in the future, can live out the last stages of their lives without the limitations imposed by the stereotypes and adverse social conditions that stifled the potential of generations before them.

Chapter Summary

Judging by numbers, the political power of elders is stronger than ever before. However, numbers do not tell the whole story. The political environment for elders in the 1990s is rather harsh because of the recession and budget deficits.

In earlier times, there have been examples of social movements by and for elders. The Townsend plan and Ham and Eggs movement in the 1930s are two examples. The activism of the 1970s symbolized by the Gray Panthers is a third example.

Today there are a number of indicators that older people have reasonable political clout. They vote in larger numbers than do younger persons. We have recently seen two presidents (Reagan and Bush) over 65, and the seniority system in Congress insures power to elder members. A number of political associations are strong—the leading one being the American Association of Retired Persons. The Older Americans Act of 1965 authorizes taxpayer spending on elders. However, funding is <u>not</u> increasing in the 1990s. The major funding goes to congregate meals, senior centers, and transportation programs. Only if there is effective advocacy and activism can these programs remain in place.

The question of generational equity will continue to raise its head as the percentage and number of elders continues to increase while funding for social programs decreases. It is unfortunate when old are posited against young. People of all ages should unite to improve the quality of life for everyone.

Key Terms

activism
advocacy
aging network
American Association of Retired Persons
Americans for Generational Equity
Elderhostel
Foster Grandparents Program
generational equity
Generations United
Gray Panthers

Ham and Eggs movement
intergenerational transfers
National Caucus and Center on Black Aged
National Committee to Preserve Social Security and Medicare
National Council of Senior Citizens
National Council on the Aging
Older Americans Act
senior power
Townsend plan

Questions for Discussion

1. Evaluate the social movements for the elders in the 1930s and 1940s.

2. What do you predict for future social movements for seniors? Why?

3. Do you think ageism will be reversed in the future? Why or why not?

4. What are the political implications of the growing numbers of older people?

5. Do you expect to be politically active as an elder? Is so, why? Why not?

6. What organization(s) would you join? What measures would you support? Would you be an activist? Explain.

Fieldwork Suggestions

1. Examine pending state and federal legislation that has a bearing on elders. What issue or issues does it address? What are its chances for passage?

2. Interview the head of the AARP in your area. How politically active is this person?

3. Locate the nearest chapter of the Gray Panthers. Write for information on their activities. Attend meetings and interview members.

4. Interview an old person who considers himself or herself to be an activist or radical.

References

"Aging America: They've Got To Eat So Let Them Work." *Economist* (16 September 1989): 17–19.

Deely, M. "The Flames of a Crusader." *Newsweek* (October 1992): 58.

Better, M. "Explaining Ageism." *Gray Panther Network Newsletter* (November 1993): 2.

Binstock, R. "Older Voters and the 1992 Presidential Election." *Gerontologist* 32:5 (October 1992): 601–605.

Brown, A. *Social Processes of Aging and Old Age.* Englewood Cliffs, NJ: Prentice-Hall, 1990.

Button, J. "A Sign of Generational Conflict: The Impact of Florida's Aging Voters." *Social Science Quarterly* 73:4 (December 1992): 786–798.

Callahan, D. "Setting Limits: A Response." *Gerontologist* 34:3 (June 1994): 393–398.

Cohen, G. "Journalistic Elder Abuse." *Gerontologist* 34:3 (June 1994): 399–401.

Drozdiak, W. "Elderly Dutch Reach for Political Power in 'Granny Revolution.'" *Washington Post* (3 May 1994): A16.

Fairlie, H. "Talkin' 'bout My Generation." *The New Republic* (28 March 1988): 19–23.

Gaines, J. "Aging Populace Alters Suburbs." *Boston Globe* (8 May 1994): A1.

Gelfand, D. *The Aging Network.* New York: Springer, 1993.

Hubbard, P., et al. "Seniors for Justice." *Gerontologist* 32:6 (December 1992): 856–858.

Hutton, William R. "Society Should Do More for the Elderly." In *The Elderly: Opposing Viewpoints,* edited by D. Bender and B. Leone, 104–111. San Diego, CA: Greenhave Press, 1990.

Jirovec, R., and J. Erich. "The Dynamics of Political Participation Among the Urban Elderly." Paper presented at the 43rd Annual Scientific Meeting of the Gerontological Society of America, Boston, MA, November 16–20, 1990.

Kerr-Layton, D. "Gray Panthers Discrimination Update." *Network Newsletter* (November 1993): 1.

Kiser, G. "Selecting Seniors for the Vice Presidency." *Aging and Society* (March 1992): 85.

Kingson, E. R., et al. *Ties That Bind: The Interdependence of Generations.* Washington, DC: Seven Locks Press, 1986.

Kleyman, Paul. *Senior Power: Growing Old Rebelliously.* San Francisco, CA: Glide Publications, 1974.

Kotlikoff, L. *Generational Accounting: Knowing Who Pays, and When, for What We Spend.* New York: The Free Press, 1992.

Lacayo, R. "The Generation Gap." *Time* (29 October 1990): 40.

Laslett, P., and J. Fishkin. *Justice Between Age Groups and Generations.* New Haven, CT: Yale University Press, 1992.

Meier, B. "A Friend of the Consumer Says She Will Keep Fighting." *New York Times* (26 October 1991): 16(N), 48(L).

Minkler, M. "Generational Equity and the Public Policy Debate: Quagmire or Opportunity." In *A Good Old Age?,* edited by P. Homer and M. Holstein, 222–239. New York: A Touchstone Book by Simon & Schuster, 1990.

Moody, Harry. "Book Review of *Ties That Bind,*" *Gerontologist* 27 (June 1987): 396–398.

Risen, J. "White House Backs Off Social Security Freeze." *Los Angeles Times* (9 February 1993): A1.

Rosenbaum, W., and J. Button. "The Unquiet Future of Intergenerational Politics." *Gerontologist* 33:4 (August 1993): 481–490.

Rosenblatt, R. "Eight Million Elderly May Be a Tough Sell for Clinton." *Los Angeles Times* (16 February 1993): A1.

Smith, Lee. "The Tyranny of America's Old." *Fortune* (13 January 1992): 68–72.

Torres-Gil, F. *The New Aging: Politics and Change in America.* Chicago, IL: Auburn House, a division of Greenwood Publishing, 1991.

Van Tassel, D., and J. Meyer, eds. *U.S. Aging Policy Interest Groups.* Westport, CT: Greenwood Press, 1992.

Wallace, S., and Williamson, R., *The Senior Movement: References and Resources.* New York: G.K. Hall, 1992.

Weisskopf, M. "Shaking Telephone Tree at the Grass Roots: Huge Senior Citizens Lobby." *Washington Post* (11 June 1993): A1.

Further Readings

Callahan, D. "Health Care Struggle Between Young and Old." *Society* 28:6 (September/October 1991): 29–31.

Cook, F., and S. Barrett. *Support for the American Welfare State.* New York: Columbia University Press, 1992.

Daniels, N. *Am I My Parents' Keeper?* New York: Oxford University Press, 1988.

Kingson, E., and J. Williamson. "Generational Equity or Privatization of Social Security." *Society* 28:6 (September/October 1991): 38–41.

Kuhn, M. *No Stone Unturned: The Life and Times of Maggie Kuhn.* New York: Ballantine Books, 1992.

Myles, J., and J. Quadagno, eds. *States, Labor Markets, and the Future of Old-Age Policy.* Philadelphia: Temple University Press, 1992.

Subject Index

cognitive functions, basic, 231–236
cognitive mechanics, 234
cognitive pragmatics, 234
cognitive processes, 231–243
cognitive process approach, 236
cohorts, 77–78
college students' attitudes about age, 30, 52–53
colonial days, 15
community centers, 380
compassionate stereotyping, 25
competency as an adult, 14
complex carbohydrates, 133
confidante, 110–111
confidence games, 299
Confucian Book of Rites, 370
congregate dining, 399
Congress, members of, 392
constrictive birth rates, 11
constrictive personality, 62
consumer education, 304
Consumer Education Council, 403
consumerism, 166
Continuing Care Retirement Community, 216–217
continuity theory, 58–59
convoy model, 111–112
coping mechanisms, 59–60
Coping with Death scale, 338
coronary artery disease, 124
cost of living adjustment (COLA), 183
couch potato, 371
Council on Aging, 218
couples, elderly, 96–97
credit card fraud, 297
Creutzfeld-Jacob disease, 249
crime, fighting, 289–290
crimes against persons, 287–288
criminals
    aging, 290–291
    older professional, 291–292
critical gerontology, 86–87
critical perspective, 5, 86, 199
cross sectional studies, 81–82, 238
cross-cultural approach, 363–370
crystallized intelligence, 237
Cuban elders, 324–325

D

dating, 103–105
day-care centers, 400
deadline decade, 53
death
    attitudes toward, 336–339
    causes of, 8–9
    facing and preparing for, 358
    on demand, 352
    rates, 7
death anxiety, 338
death competency, 338
Death Doctor, 335
death-denying society, 336
Death March, 387

death on demand, 352
Declaration of Independence, 17
delirium, 247
dementia, 247–249
demography, 268
Denmark, pensions in, 379
dependent lifestyle, 211
depressive disorders, 245
Detroit syndrome, 11
developing nations, 364–369
developmental biology, 3
developmental tasks of aging, 57
diabetes, 128, 134
Diagnostic and Statistical Manual for Mental Disorders (DSM-IV), 244, 246
diet, 132–134
    and pathology, 133–134
    Japanese, 132–133
dietary patterns, 133
digestive processes, 133
discrimination
    against older workers, 157–162
    on the job, 159–162
disengagement
    role of individual in, 71
    role of society in, 71
    satisfaction with, 71
disengagement theory, 69–72
disorders, 244–249
    affective, 246
    anxiety, 244–245
    functional, 244–246
    generalized, 244
    obsessive/compulsive, 244–245
    organic, 246–249
    personality, 245
displaced homemakers, 312
distribution of income, 179–181
distribution of wealth, 177–179
diverticulitis, 133–134
divorced, elderly, 102–103
divorcees, 313–314
DNA, 131
door-to-door sales, 297–298
double standard of aging, 314–315
double suicide, 285–286
dowager's hump, 127
downsizing, 208–209, 212–213
drivers, older, 121–122
driving difficulties, 235
drug abuse, 301–304
drugs, miracle, 300
drugs, prescription, 301–302
Duke longitudinal study, 142
dying
    at home, 346–347
    awareness contexts, 343
    care of in hospitals, 342–343
    euphemisms for, 336
    stages of, 340–341
Dying Person's Bill of Rights, 343–344

E

early retirement, 154–156
egalitarian societies, 368
ego development, 49
eight stages of man, 48–49
ejaculatory control, 140–141
elder abuse, 281, 292–296
    causes of, 293–95
elder abuse victim
    age of, 295
    profile of typical, 294
elder status, 366–369
Elder-Liker study, 59–60
Elderhostel, 401
elections, 391
emphysema, 128
employment discrimination, 158–159
employment programs, 400
employment resources, 158–159
energy, 135–136
environmental factors in aging, 137
environments, living, 204–224
EPIC movement, 389
Equal Employment Opportunity Commission, 159–160
equity theory, 110–111
error theories, 130–132
estate fraud, 8
ethics on aging, 355–356
ethnic elders, improving the status of, 330–331
ethnicity, 75–76
ethnography, 85
euphemisms for old age, 14
euthanasia, active and passive, 351
evolution, 131
evolutionary theory of aging, 3, 131
exchange theory, 82–83
exercise, 132–136
    regular, 135
    weight bearing, 128
exercising the mind, 242–243
extended family, 369–370
extramarital intercourse of aged, 143
extroversion, 47

F

falls, 126
family development in later life, 96–100
family support systems, 370
    weakened, 268–269
fast food diet, 133
fear of aging, 52–53
fear of attack, 288
fear of death, 337–339
Fear of Death Scale, 338
feeding tubes, 348
Feminine Mystique, 2
feminization of poverty, 312
fertility, 364–365
fiber, 133, 134

filial piety, 371
financial status
  diversity in, 177–179
  of aged, 177–181
  of older women, 314
flexible work hours, 169
Florida, retirement haven, 10
fluid intelligence, 237
formal age, 364
Foster Grandparent Program, 401–402
Fountain of Age, 2
four generation family, 79
Franklin Village, 84–85
fraud, 296–301
  credit card, 297
  estate, 298
  investment, 298
  land and home-equity, 296
  mail order, 296–297
  Medicare and Medicaid, 298–299
  telephone, 297
  television, 296–297
free radicals, 131–132
friendly visitor program, 400
friends, elders as, 110–111
fruit flies, 3
frustration-aggression hypothesis, 39
full time employment, 166–168
full-timing, 213
functional age, 364
functional limitations, 123
funeral industry, 357
funerals, 356–357

G

Gay liberation, 391
gender, 75–76
gene
  breast cancer, 130
  testing, 130
generation gap, 67–68, 80–81
generation, older, 52
Generation X, 14, 77–78
generational conflict, 404
generational equity, 404
generations, 77–79, 406–407
Generations United, 406
generativity, 49
genes, 130
genetic limit, 407
genetics, 129–130
Georgia Centenarians Study, 137
geriatric psychiatry, 223
gerontocracy, 394
gerontologist, 4
gerontology, 4
gerontophilia, 17
gerontophobia, 17
Good Times (television program), 23
grandparent, role of, 108
grandparenthood, 106–109
  impact of divorce, 109–110
  visitation rights, 109–110

granny dumping, 292
granny unit, 213–214
gray champions, 15
gray lobby, 397–398
Gray Panthers, 35, 218, 391, 396–397
graying of America, 6
graying of the planet, 364–366
Great Depression, 391
Green Thumb program, 400
greeting cards, 14
grief, stages of, 101
grief work, 100–101
guided imagery, 137

H

Habitat for Humanity, 93
Ham and Eggs movement, 389–390
happiness, 72
happy death movement, 347
health care expenses, out of pocket, 188–189
health problems, 123–128
health span, 138
health status, 122–128
health-care rationing, 404
heart disease, 123–124
Hemlock Society, 285, 351–352
high blood pressure, 8
high impact aerobics, 134
Hindus, older, 369
hip fracture, 126
Hispanic Americans, 321–325
  American experience, 323
  categories of, 322
  city-dwelling, 323
  demographics, 321–322
  ethnic variations of, 324–325
  extended family, 324
  migration patterns, 323
  minority status, 322–323
  utilization of services, 323–324
HMO, 213
Hmong refugees, 327
home ownership, 179–180, 204–245
home rental, 181
home-care crisis, 275–278
homeless elders, 193–194, 205–206
homeless men, 206
homeless women, 206
homeostasis, 121
homosexuals, aging, 140
hormone replacement therapy, 141
hospice movement, 345–347
Hospice of Connecticut, 345
hospital care, expensive, 189
hotels, single room only, 194–195
house, older, 207
housing
  age-integrated, 210
  age-segregated, 210
  dissatisfaction with, 206
  government programs, 207
  increasing maintenance, 206

low cost, 207–208
maintenance, 206
options, 210–217
shared, 213–214
shortage of, 207–208
humor, 137
Huntington's disease, 249–250
hypertension, 124
hypnotism, 137
hypochondria, 245

I

immune system, 121, 130–132
impotence, 144
income from various sources, 182
increased life expectancy, 7
Individual Retirement Accounts (IRA), 190
industrial revolution, 154
industrial societies, 367–369
inequality among elderly people, 179
inflation, 192
information highway, 15
information processing, 231–232
  slowing of, 235
informed consent to treatment, 354–355
instrumental activities of daily living, 258–260
integenerational norms, 267–267
integenerational relationships, changing, 269
Integration versus segregation, 210
integrity vs. despair, 49
intelligence, 236–238
  crystallized and fluid, 237
  quotient, 237–238
interdependence, 100–101
interest groups, 394
intergenerational contracts, 406
intergenerational relations, 14
intergenerational transfers, 406
internalized aging, 315
interventions, psychosocial, 274–275
intimacy, 95
introversion, 47
IQ tests, 236–237
issei, 326

J

Japan, 371–374
  centenarians in, 376
  community centers in, 377
  elder population in, 373–375
  family care of aged, 375–376
  Gold Plan for the Aged, 377
  government care of aged, 374–375
  health care programs, 374–375
  history of, 371–372
  life expectancy in, 373–374
  medical costs in, 376
  modernization in, 373

pensions in, 374
problems of modernization, 374–375
retirees, 374–376
retirement, 374
retirement homes in, 376–377
role of eldest son in, 372–374
Japanese American elders, 325–326
Japanese diet, 132–133
job sharing, 169
John Hopkins study, 144

K

kin relations, 106–108
kin structure, 105–107
Kinsey studies, 140–141
kissing, 104

L

labor force participation of aged, 375
late life, transitions, 57–58
late midlife astonishment, 315–316
later maturity, 56
learning, 239–240
leisure class of aged, 166
leisure climate, 207
leisure opportunities, 166–172
leisure time, loss of, 166
leisure values, 164, 166
Leisure World, 13, 209, 214
less-developed countries, 369
liberal views, 393
Life Care at Home, 213
life care communities, problems in, 216–217
life course, 50, 51
life cycle, 50
life event, 29
life expectancy, 19
life expectancy at birth, 10
life expectancy by age and race, 7
life narratives, 85
life periods, blurring, 51
life review, 341–342
life satisfaction, 71–72
life satisfaction index, 72–73
life span, 3, 8
average, 129
maximum, 129
life-care industry, 216
life-insurance companies, 213
lifestyle, 8, 137
of the poor, 192–198
lineage, 79–80
living alone, 204
living arrangements, diversity in, 204–205
living environments, 204–224
living will, 348–350
living with spouse, 204
locus of control, 62–63
longevity, 8, 129–138, 263–264
longevity of men vs. women, 8
longitudinal studies, 81–82, 338, 391

looking-glass self, 56
loss of bone mass, 127
lubricant, 143

M

Maas-Kuypers study, 59
mail-order fraud, 296–297
marital satisfaction, 97–98
levels of, 98
marital status of older people, 96–98
Marriott Corporation, 215
Masters and Johnson studies, 140–141
McDonald's, 168
McLain Movement, 389–390
Meals on Wheels, 399
meaning in everyday life, 83–85
media, 35–38
advertising, 36
stereotypes of age, 24
Media Watch Task Force, 35
median age of the population, 6
median family income, 178
Medicaid, 186–188
medical control of disease, 8
medical ethics, 347–349
medical expenses, 186–187
medical quackery, 299–301
Medicare, 186–188
fraud, 298–299
medicide, 352–353
medigap policies, 188–189
meditation, 137
memory, 240–242
primary, 241
sensory, 232
tertiary, 241–242
working, 241
menopause, 55
mental abilities, primary and secondary, 236
mental health, 132–137, 251
mentally ill, caring for, 250–251
Mexican Americans, 52
Michigan ruling on assisted suicide, 335
mid-life crisis, 53–54
mid-life transition, 54
middle age, 54–56
middle-aged women, 312
migration, 209–210
mind, exercising, 242–243
minority aged population, growth of, 310–311
minority status, 52
miracle drugs, 300
mobile home park, 212–213
mobile homes, 180–181, 212–213
models of aging, developmental, 63
Modern Maturity magazine, 395
modernization, 366–371
modernization theory, 366–374
moral obligations of adult children, 265–269
morale, 72

Mormons, 10
morphine, 345
mortality, 364–365
motor performance, 233–234
movies, 37
multiculturalism, 310
multipurpose senior centers, 398
muscles, 134
myths
about the older worker, 161
sexual 141–142

N

National Affordable Housing Act of 1990, 207
National Cancer Institute, 344
National Caucus and Center on Black Aged, 330, 396
National Committee to Preserve Social Security and Medicare, 395
National Council of Senior Citizens, 395
National Council on the Aging, 396
National Indian Council on Aging, 331
National Organization for Women, 391
National Pacific/Asian Resource Center on Aging, 331
National Safety Council, 126
Native American elders, 327–330
cultural uniformity and diversity, 328
education, 329
employment, 329–330
health characteristics, 330
income, 329–330
population data, 328–329
natural death legislation, 348–349
natural selection, 131
naturally occurring retirement community, 212
near-death experiences, 357–358
near-poor, 178–179, 196
needy people, 176
negative terms for aged, 17
Neighborhood Watch, 290
network analysis, 111–112
never-married elderly, 103
New Deal, 389
nisei, 326
nomadic society, 367
non-metropolitan, 195–196
nonindustrialized societies, 364–371, 366–370
norm of beneficence, 83
norm of reciprocity, 82–83
Norway, 378–381
nursing homes
expensive, 189–190
financial abuse, 221–222
finding one, 218
financing of, 221
gang visits, 221
making the decision, 217–218
mental health treatment, 223–224

wrinkles, 37

Y

yoga, 135
Young-Old, 5

youth cult, 17, 19
youth culture, 315
youth restorers, 300
youth-elder relationships, 16
yuppies, 19

Z

Zionism, 67–68

Name Index